D1522950

Handbook of
Spatial Cognition

Handbook of
Spatial Cognition

Edited by
David Waller and Lynn Nadel

American Psychological Association • Washington, DC

Published by
American Psychological Association
750 First Street, NE
Washington, DC 20002
www.apa.org

To order
APA Order Department
P.O. Box 92984
Washington, DC 20090-2984
Tel: (800) 374-2721; Direct: (202) 336-5510
Fax: (202) 336-5502; TDD/TTY: (202) 336-6123
Online: www.apa.org/pubs/books
E-mail: order@apa.org

In the U.K., Europe, Africa, and the Middle East, copies may be ordered from
American Psychological Association
3 Henrietta Street
Covent Garden, London
WC2E 8LU England

Typeset in Berkeley by Circle Graphics, Inc., Columbia, MD

Printer: United Book Press, Baltimore, MD
Cover Designer: Mercury Publishing Services, Rockville, MD

Library of Congress Cataloging-in-Publication Data

Handbook of spatial cognition / edited by David Waller and Lynn Nadel.
    p. cm.
 Includes bibliographical references and index.
 ISBN 978-1-4338-1204-0 — ISBN 1-4338-1204-5 1. Cognition. 2. Space perception. 3. Spatial behavior.
I. Waller, David. II. Nadel, Lynn.
 BF311.H3346 2013
 153.7'52—dc23
                    2012010309

British Library Cataloguing-in-Publication Data
A CIP record is available from the British Library.

Printed in the United States of America
First Edition

DOI: 10.1037/13936-000

Contents

Contributors

Tad T. Brunyé, PhD, U.S. Army NSRDEC; Department of Psychology, Tufts University, Medford, MA

Dr. Heinrich H. Bülthoff, Human Perception, Cognition, and Action Department, Max Planck Institute for Biological Cybernetics, Tübingen, Germany; Korea University, Seoul, Korea

Beth M. Casey, PhD, Lynch School of Education, Boston College, Boston, MA

Ken Cheng, PhD, Department of Biological Sciences, Macquarie University, Sydney, Australia

Sarah H. Creem-Regehr, PhD, Department of Psychology, University of Utah, Salt Lake City

Massimiliano Di Luca, PhD, School of Psychology, Max Planck Institute for Biological Cybernetics, Tübingen, Germany; University of Birmingham, Birmingham, England

Arne Ekstrom, PhD, Department of Psychology and Center for Neuroscience, University of California, Davis

Brett R. Fajen, PhD, Department of Cognitive Science, Rensselaer Polytechnic Institute, Troy, NY

Paul Graham, PhD, Centre for Computational Neuroscience and Robotics, School of Life Sciences, University of Sussex, Brighton, England

Harry Heft, PhD, Department of Psychology, Denison University, Granville, OH

Stephen C. Hirtle, PhD, School of Information Sciences, University of Pittsburgh, Pittsburgh, PA

Mark P. Holden, PhD, Department of Psychology, University of Western Ontario, London, Canada

Raymond P. Kesner, PhD, Department of Psychology, University of Utah, Salt Lake City

Timothy P. McNamara, PhD, Department of Psychology, Vanderbilt University, Nashville, TN

Betty J. Mohler, PhD, Human Perception, Cognition, and Action Department, Max Planck Institute for Biological Cybernetics, Tübingen, Germany

Daniel R. Montello, PhD, Geography Department, University of California, Santa Barbara

Lynn Nadel, PhD, Department of Psychology and Cognitive Science Program, University of Arizona, Tucson

Nora S. Newcombe, PhD, Department of Psychology, Temple University, Philadelphia, PA

John W. Philbeck, PhD, Department of Psychology, The George Washington University, Washington, DC

Flip Phillips, PhD, Department of Psychology and Neuroscience Program, Skidmore College, Sarasota Springs, NY

Martin Raubal, D.Tech, Institute of Cartography and Geoinformation, Swiss Federal Institute of Technology, Zurich, Switzerland

A. David Redish, PhD, Department of Neuroscience, University of Minnesota, Minneapolis

Jesse Sargent, PhD, Department of Psychology, Washington University in St. Louis, St. Louis, MO

Holly A. Taylor, PhD, Department of Psychology, Tufts University, Medford, MA

David Waller, PhD, Department of Psychology, Miami University, Oxford, OH

Preface

Knowing where one is, where resources are, and how to get to safety are some of the most fundamental and important challenges faced by all animals. When specified formally, these challenges seem to be exceedingly complex; yet they are routinely performed by even the simplest organisms and the most absent-minded people. Moreover, these basic abilities are typically prerequisites for—and may form a basis of—other more complex behaviors. As a result, understanding how people and other animals sense, interpret, behave in, create knowledge of, and communicate about space is central to a variety of disciplines and scholarly pursuits. Worldwide, thousands of researchers and scholars, including neuro-scientists, ethologists, psychologists, computer scientists, geographers, sociologists, architects, linguists, anthropologists, and philosophers, would describe *spatial cognition* as a critical component of their work. Because so many fields have a stake in understanding these basic abilities, spatial cognition is a field that serves to connect and to build understanding among people from a wide variety of scholarly pursuits. Yet, to date, there has not been a resource in the literature that has gathered and synthesized the diverse body of research into this funda-mental aspect of animal life.

This volume represents the culmination of a series of conversations with colleagues about the status of spatial cognition as an academic discipline and the need for a single, definitive volume that brings together and organizes its specialized content areas. Much as Neisser's *Cognitive Psychology*[1] helped to define the interdisciplinary work that psychologists had pursued in the decades prior to its publication, we hope that the present volume can be a first step toward bringing definition and structure to this increasingly diverse and multidisciplinary field. Collectively, the chapters of this book offer a far-ranging yet thorough discussion of how organisms interact with space—from the neurological underpinning of spatial thought to the perceptual, cognitive, interpersonal, sociological, and cultural influences on it.

Unlike many edited volumes in which contributors focus primarily on their own work, reiterate their own findings, or describe research in their lab that did not fit in their other published works, the current volume tasked its contributors with creating concise concep-tual overviews of their areas of expertise. One of the guiding principles in editing the volume was to encourage our contributors to maintain an approachable introductory tone. Thus, more than many scholarly professional works, these chapters offer an abundance of helpful examples for understanding complex concepts as well as brief introductions to the tools and

---

[1]Neisser, U. (1967). *Cognitive psychology*. Englewood Cliffs, NJ: Prentice Hall.

methods used to investigate spatial cognition. We are honored to have enlisted some of the most eminent scholars in the field of spatial cognition, and readers will be treated to lucid reviews of historically influential constructs and theories from some of the very researchers who have been formative in creating them.

We hope that this volume will encourage spatial cognition researchers in academic settings to offer advanced undergraduate courses in spatial cognition, and the book has been structured to facilitate this function. Each chapter presents a broad introductory overview of a topic area and ends with a handful of special references that the chapter authors have chosen for interested readers to pursue. The suggested articles at the end of each chapter often represent seminal papers in the field and provide an ideal supplement to the book in pedagogical settings by offering students the opportunity to delve more deeply into the topics that interest them.

The book should also be a resource for (a) scholars who are just getting into the field of spatial cognition (e.g., first-year graduate students); (b) researchers in disciplines such as architecture, geography, or computer science for which spatial cognition is a central element of competence; and (c) colleagues who collaborate with spatial cognition researchers. For established spatial researchers, the book will serve to organize their field, to update them on contemporary issues and controversies, and—we hope—to inspire fruitful directions for future research.

We would like to acknowledge the many colleagues and friends whose thoughts and conversations made this book possible. A complete list of these individuals would be inappropriately expansive, and it must suffice here to thank only a small fraction. We thank Mary Hegarty, Earl Hunt, Jack Loomis, and Dan Montello for foundational guidance and support. We also recognize and honor the influence of Reg Golledge, whose contributions to our field and to the development of our own thought were truly profound. Finally, we offer a special thanks to Yael and Noga Zerubavel: Yael for planting the original seed that began this effort and Noga for providing the daily support and understanding that enabled us to actualize it.

Handbook of
Spatial Cognition

INTRODUCTION: FRAMEWORKS FOR UNDERSTANDING SPATIAL THOUGHT (OR WRAPPING OUR HEADS AROUND SPACE)

David Waller and Lynn Nadel

Spatial cognition is a branch of cognitive science that seeks to understand how humans and other animals perceive, interpret, mentally represent, and interact with the spatial characteristics of their environment. These characteristics include object and scene properties, such as size, shape, and scale, as well as relations among objects, such as distance, direction, orientation, and location. Unlike many areas of cognitive science, spatial cognition is defined by these contents of thought—not the processes that underlie their manifestation. As such, the study of spatial cognition involves potentially all mental processes—from attention and perception to memory, categorization, problem solving, and language. Because it cuts across so many psychological processes, the study of spatial cognition brings together a diversity of interests, perspectives, and approaches and is relevant to a wide range of scholars and applied scientists. At the same time, its wide-ranging topics and diversity of interests may give the field an appearance of a fragmented or loosely connected discipline. The present volume represents an initial attempt to encapsulate this field—to familiarize readers with the critical concepts and distinctions that motivate the field and to introduce readers to the essential research that has helped to form it.

Nearly all behavior has spatial consequences, and many of the psychological processes that underlie behavior have spatial content. Finding one's car in a parking lot, getting home from work, and find-ing a subway stop in an unfamiliar city are clear instances of how people use spatial cognition to guide navigation. Yet, in each of these instances, the psychological structures and processes that underlie the behavior—for example, the relative use of perceptual and mnemonic processes—may be quite different. Of course, spatial cognition is also a fundamental aspect of behaviors that do not involve navigation. Recalling which arm is raised on the Statue of Liberty or determining whether a picture frame is aligned with the walls on which it is hung also involves spatial processing—not of one's own relationship with the world but of the relations among objects in the world. These and other examples make it clear that spatial cognition underlies a great deal of our behavior.

If spatial cognition is involved in so much of our behavior, it is a daunting task for scholars to bring structure and organization to the field. In this introductory chapter, we examine three ways that scholars have traditionally organized the diversity of phenomena the field of spatial cognition comprises. Each of these organizational schemata provides a handful of high-level distinctions that enable one to contextualize the diversity of spatial thought. The three schemata organize the field of spatial cognition in terms of differences in (a) the nature of the environment and the organism's fit to it, (b) the mental structures and processes that subserve spatial thought, and (c) the parameterization of spatial

DOI: 10.1037/13936-001
Handbook of Spatial Cognition, D. Waller and L. Nadel (Editors)

information itself. These three possibilities call for different foci of investigation and give rise to different sets of issues and different ways of contextualizing our understanding of spatial cognition. We hope that our brief discussion of these three frameworks introduces readers to many of the critical distinctions that motivate theory and research into spatial cognition.

ENVIRONMENTAL DIFFERENCES TO DISTINGUISH SPATIAL THOUGHT

One common and influential way of organizing spatial phenomena is to differentiate according to the psychologically relevant distinctions in an organism's environment. This approach is sensitive to the functional relevance of spatial behavior and views the diversity of phenomena in spatial cognition as reflecting the diversity of means by which organisms fit with or adapt to different environments. An extreme exemplar of this approach is the ecological framework introduced by James Gibson. Gibson's now-classic book on visual and spatial perception (Gibson, 1979) begins with a series of chapters that are devoted more to a description of the environment and the information that it provides than to the psychological structures and processes that an observer would bring to bear on their perception. This primacy of external over internal structure results from recognizing the importance of an organism's environment and conceptualizing spatial cognition with respect to the fit between an animal and its environment.

Within the literature of spatial cognition, *environmental scale* offers perhaps the most common means of functionally dividing the field. Indeed, the concept of scale lies at the heart of the discipline and has been a core theme, especially in the literature of behavioral geography. Most contemporary researchers do not regard scale as an independent property of the environment but rather as a relationship between the environment and an organism's ability to interact with it. Thus, for example, *small-scale spaces* are not necessarily small in physical extent but consist of those environments that require a

relatively small amount of action to apprehend—perhaps only eye and head movements. Montello (1993) labeled such spaces *figural* and noted as an example that a very large environment such as a forest or town could be psychologically regarded as a small-scale space when it is viewed from an airplane or depicted on a map. Typically, small-scale spaces consist of manipulable objects on which—not within which—one can act. We may also consider symbolic spatial information, such as a map or a figure, as a type of small-scale space. *Medium-scale spaces,* such as rooms or small forest clearings, are environments that surround an observer and within which one can move; however, medium-scale environments do not require significant locomotion to apprehend. These spaces enable organisms to interact with local features—to throw, kick, or move things within one's own sphere of immediately actionable space. Finally, *large-scale spaces,* such as towns, buildings, and forests are functionally defined as those that require significant locomotion to know. Knowledge of such spaces is typically thought to require an integration of the organism's separate experiences into a global representation, although the richness and the properties of this representation are matters of ongoing debate.

A tripartite division of spatial cognition on the basis of the functional scale of the environment has been proposed by several authors (e.g., Grüsser, 1983; Tversky, 2003) and serves to organize much of our literature.[1] For example, a great deal of psychological research has focused on people's ability to encode, store, and mentally manipulate spatial information from standardized paper and pencil tests (for overviews, see Carroll, 1993; Eliot & Smith, 1984; Hegarty & Waller, 2005). The stimuli in these tests are typically figures—for example, line drawings of shapes that are to be mentally rotated, folded, or flipped. Such figures are clearly small-scale stimuli inasmuch as they can typically be viewed by the test-taker in a single glance. The cognitive abilities and psychological processes that enable people to perform these tests were the topic of intense research in the first half of the 20th century, and as a result,

---

[1]Behavioral geographers (e.g., Montello, 1993) may introduce a fourth level of scale for truly large geographic regions, such as states or countries, that cannot realistically be fully apprehended by foot travel.

much is known about how people perceive, interpret, and mentally manipulate small symbolic media such as maps and images (see Chapter 6, this volume). Importantly, however, most of the research that has attempted to link these small-scale spatial abilities to people's behavior in large-scale spaces (e.g., navigation) has found relatively weak and tenuous relations between the domains. For example, it is rare for performance on small-scale spatial ability measures to account for more than 10% of the variance in people's large-scale navigation behavior (Hegarty & Waller, 2005; but see Kozhevnikov, Motes, Rasch, & Blajenkova, 2006). The separability of people's aptitudes with large- versus small-scale spaces may thus lend credence to the notion that scale can provide a meaningful dimension for organizing the diversity of spatial thought.

A significant body of research has also investigated spatial cognition at the medium scale of space. Such research examines, for example, how people remember the relative locations of objects in a room (e.g., Mou & McNamara, 2002; Shelton & McNamara, 2001), how they account for their changing relationships to other objects as they move (e.g., Simons & Wang, 1998), or what information they use to regain their orientation after disorientation (e.g., Cheng & Newcombe, 2005). Most of the basic experimental research in spatial cognition focuses on spatial behavior in medium-scale spaces, perhaps because much of our day-to-day behavior plays out at this scale. We move about familiar spaces, use the objects typically found in them, and react to changes in where things are or where we are in these types of spaces.

Research that is applied to spatial cognition in large-scale spaces typically examines *navigation,* a complex behavior that combines the physical act of locomotion with a suite of cognitive abilities such as place memory, imagery, and planning. The cognitive components of navigation are sometimes collectively referred to as *wayfinding.* As a complex and coordinated set of mental and physical factors, navigation itself has been the topic of a great deal of research. Fundamental psychological mechanisms underlying navigation minimally include (a) *piloting*—the ability to use sets of landmarks to determine or maintain a direction of travel; (b) *dead reckoning*—the ability to determine one's position on the basis of information about one's velocity and acceleration; and (c) *cognitive mapping*—the use of a global mental representation of one's environment.[2] Each of these elements of navigation (reviewed by Gallistel, 1990) has been the focus of a large literature, often involving nonhuman animals. In the present volume, each of these navigational mechanisms is reviewed and developed in separate chapters (piloting: Chapter 7; dead reckoning: Chapter 5; cognitive mapping: Chapter 8).

COGNITIVE DISTINCTIONS TO DISTINGUISH SPATIAL THOUGHT

A second basis for organizing the field of spatial cognition (and the basis that forms the broadest outline of the present volume) recognizes a primary distinction between cognition that is needed for interaction with one's immediate environment and cognition that is based on stored knowledge about space. This approach essentially organizes space temporally into (a) online structures and processes that handle dynamic transient spatial information and (b) offline structures and processes that encode, store, and retrieve spatial information over the long term. The distinction between online and offline treatment of spatial information parallels the distinction between perception and memory in the general cognitive literature.

Online spatial processes enable an organism to situate itself in the present moment and to interpret and use spatial relationships such as distances and directions to achieve immediate goals. In addition to abilities such as distance perception and object recognition (reviewed in Chapter 4), the phenomenon of *spatial updating* has also played a prominent role in the literature on online spatial abilities. Spatial updating is typically conceived as the ability to change one's representation of spatial relations as a result of one's movement through an environment. The ability is closely related to dead reckon-

---

[2]Note that the concept of navigation is not necessarily exhausted by discussion of these three underlying processes. Some investigators have noted that processes such as reorientation (Wang & Spelke, 2002) and beacon following (Waller & Lippa, 2007) also serve critical functions in navigation.

ing, although the term *updating* tends to connote a focus on the content of the mental representation (i.e., what is updated), whereas dead reckoning tends to focus more on the processes that account for self-motion[3] and on the ability to maintain a sense of where one is with respect to a known starting point. Although humans are known to use offline forms of spatial updating (see, e.g., Amorim, Glasauer, Carpinot, & Berthoz, 1997), the continuousness of our updating ability and its sensitivity to ongoing information about movement makes it a cornerstone of the literature on online spatial abilities.

Offline spatial processes involve the long-term encoding, storage, and retrieval of spatial information and enable complex behaviors such as navigation, route planning, and direction giving. The structure and organization of spatial memory has generated a substantial research literature, which is reviewed and synthesized in the present volume by Timothy P. McNamara (Chapter 9). Memorial processes become increasingly relevant when one considers spatial cognition for culturally mediated behaviors (see Chapters 12 and 14).

There is a perennial interplay between psychological theories that focus explanations of behavior on structure in the environment and those that focus on structure in the organism. This dynamic, which can be traced historically through philosophers such as Plato, Aristotle, Descartes, Kant, Husserl, and Heidegger, manifests in the contemporary field of spatial cognition as differing approaches with respect to the relative importance and use of online versus offline processes in spatial behavior. For example, as we described earlier, researchers from an ecological tradition focus on the ongoing interpretation of spatial information in relation to an organism's immediate goals and attempt to describe as much behavior as possible in terms of these relations. Such a tradition minimizes the view of cognitive psychology as information processing and instead focuses on the online, unmediated pickup of information by an organism. However, cognitivist

approaches tend to be more sympathetic to the idea of spatial information from the environment being internally processed by an organism in the service of achieving goals. These approaches place an increased focus on the idea of an organism creating enduring internal representations of the environment on which to base spatial behavior. For these scientists, the nature of the representation—what is included, what is lost, how it is organized, and how it interacts with other representations—forms the basis of much of their research.

Finally, it is worth briefly noting another perennial topic in psychology and philosophy of mind that is relevant to a cognitive approach toward understanding spatial thought: the issue of nature versus nurture. Characterizing the degree to which some spatial competencies are inborn and others depend critically on experience enables theorists to understand fundamental aspects of human nature and to address longstanding questions about the architecture of human cognitive systems (e.g., Fodor, 1983). Much of the developmental literature in spatial cognition is reviewed in the present volume by Holden and Newcombe (Chapter 10), and recent experiments relevant to the emergence of spatial competencies in animals is reviewed in the chapter by Nadel (Chapter 8).

ANALYTICAL DISTINCTIONS TO DISTINGUISH SPATIAL THOUGHT

The third type of framework for understanding the field of spatial cognition focuses on spatial information itself and organizes the varieties of spatial thought around the ways in which spatial relations can be formally specified. Probably the two most investigated spatial relations have been those specifying distance and direction. Both distance and direction information can be formally specified in different ways and with qualitatively different levels of specificity, and humans—and many other animals—appear to be flexible and adaptive in the use of these different types of spatial information.

---

[3]At the risk of complicating these concepts even more, it is worth noting that dead reckoning is also closely related to the concept of *path integration*. Like dead reckoning, path integration processes involve tracking one's changing position over self-movement. Some researchers, however, use the term *path integration* to connote a buildup of knowledge about the outbound path, as opposed merely to knowledge of one's current position.

The specification of distance and direction both require a reference system that minimally indicates an origin and a scale.[4] With respect to specifying an origin, one may choose either (a) oneself or (b) another object. In the former case, self-to-object distances (often referred to as *egocentric distances*) and directions are coded—for example, registering how far a tree is from oneself. In the latter case, object-to-object distances (often referred to as *exocentric*) or directions are coded—for example, knowing how far the tree is from a boulder. It is worth noting that the perception of egocentric distance is, in some ways, qualitatively different from the perception of exocentric distances. For example, estimates of egocentric distances are differentially sensitive to cue manipulations (Loomis, Da Silva, Philbeck, & Fukusima, 1996) and are differentially able to exhibit perception–action dissociations (Wraga, Creem, & Proffitt, 2000) than those of exocentric distances. The differences between these types of distance estimates lend support to the psychological relevance of the distinction between reference systems that facilitate coding of either egocentric or exocentric distances.

The scale applied by a reference system relates to the degree to which fine-grained, quantitative, or continuously graded information is available or necessary for the representation of a spatial relation. Gradations in the scaling of spatial information were delineated by Piaget and Inhelder (1967), who discussed these differences in the context of human development. According to their account, infants and children before the age of 5 or 6 are primarily sensitive to *topological* spatial relations, which include relatively imprecise and categorical relations such as proximity, separation, order, and enclosure. Knowledge and use of topological relations was thought to precede that of *projective* relations, which, unlike topological relations, are able to account for the role of specific, different, and changing viewpoints. As a final developmental stage, children around the age of eight or nine were thought to develop the use of *metric* relations, which express

fine-grained and continuous information. Although contemporary theorists may debate whether these classes of spatial scales represent an inevitable developmental sequence, most researchers find it helpful to distinguish between types of spatial knowledge that are more or less precise or fine-grained.

For example, in the contemporary literature on spatial imagery, there is a clear distinction between categorical and coordinate spatial information. The work of Kosslyn and his colleagues (e.g., Kosslyn, Thompson, Gitelman, & Alpert, 1998) has been formative in illustrating fundamental differences between these types of knowledge. For example, when estimating the location of a stimulus with respect to a horizontal bar, categorical judgments (e.g., is the stimulus above or below the bar) are associated with activation of the left cerebral hemisphere, whereas coordinate judgments (e.g., is the stimulus within 0.5 inches of the bar) are associated with activation of the right hemisphere. More generally, conceptualizing spatial cognition in terms of proximity (topological, categorical) and precision (metric, Euclidean) is a common means of bringing structure to the varieties of spatial thought (Allen & Haun, 2004).

The idea of mentally coding spatial information by means of qualitatively different kinds of metrics is naturally tied to the issue of how these types of information interact or combine to support a unified behavioral response and a phenomenologically coherent cognition. The ways that humans combine categorical and continuous information has been the focus of a burgeoning literature based on the pioneering work of Janellen Huttenlocher and her colleagues (e.g., Huttenlocher, Hedges, & Duncan, 1991). These researchers have put forth a precise mathematical model that attempts to capture how people combine nonmetric information about an object's category (e.g., knowledge that a location is in a particular quadrant of space) with precise metric information about it (e.g., knowledge about its specific location within the space). The model generally does quite well predicting patterns of bias that

---

[4]The term *scale* in this section should not be confused with the previous use of the term to indicate the psychological extent of an environment. Here, *scale* refers to the characteristics of a quantitative system of measurement, as it might be used in the phrase *Celsius scale*.

people make in estimating the locations of remembered objects. One of the more interesting claims that emerges from this literature is the idea that systematic biases in spatial responses (e.g., remembering that an object is located closer to its category center than it actually is) may have an adaptive function—by increasing precision, a systematic bias may be able to increase accuracy.

In addition to an origin and a scale, a reference system for directional knowledge must use a *reference direction,* which provides a relational basis for representing directions or orientations. Researchers have generally shown greater interest in understanding how humans represent *azimuthal* directions—those parallel to the ground—than elevations. Broadly speaking, reference directions can be classified as either *egocentric,* which specify directions with respect to one's own current or remembered orientation (e.g., the tree is 45 degrees to my left), or *allocentric,* which specify directions with respect to the spatial structure of an "other" aspect of the environment. Allocentric reference directions themselves can be subdivided on the basis of the relationship between the reference direction and the locations or objects that are coded. When directions are specified with respect to the global structure of the environment (e.g., "north" or "toward the mountains"), one can be said to use an *environmental* reference direction. Alternatively, when leveraging the spatial structure of the represented object or objects (e.g., "to the cat's left"), one can be said to use an *intrinsic* reference direction. Determining the situations in which one or the other reference direction is used has become an increasingly important topic in the psychological literature, and much of this literature is summarized in the current volume by McNamara (Chapter 9) and by Taylor and Brunyé (Chapter 12). Finally, it is worth noting that the use of spatial reference frames is also a prominent topic in cross-cultural research in spatial cognition. Indeed, the frames of reference that tend to be preferentially selected and used by people in Western cultures are not necessarily those that are used in other cultures (e.g., Levinson, 1996). Such findings help to inform us about universal aspects of human cognition, as well as raising important questions about the generalizability of many segments of our literature.

ENVIRONMENTAL, COGNITIVE, AND ANALYTICAL APPROACHES TO SPATIAL THOUGHT

Although we have presented in separate sections three different means of organizing and conceptualizing the field of spatial cognition, it is important to acknowledge that these frameworks do not represent competing theories and are not as distinct as their presentation here might suggest. In practice, these frameworks are complementary; they are frequently overlapping and nonorthogonal. Thus, a close reading of the literature will show, for example, that transient psychological processes tend to be associated with those that are egocentric. Similarly, because acquiring knowledge of large-scale spaces requires memory, this sort of knowledge tends to be associated with offline processes and, in many cases, allocentric representations. Whether one's principal organizational framework involves distinctions based on environmental, psychological, or analytical differences, it is important to realize that concepts from the other frameworks are likely necessary to develop a full understanding of a phenomenon.

As an example of the close mutually reinforcing ties among the three frameworks, consider the elegant paradigm introduced by Cheng (1986; see also Gallistel, 1990) to examine how animals reorient (see also Chapter 10, this volume). In these experiments, an animal learns to associate one corner of a small chamber with a reward. The animal is subsequently removed from the chamber, disoriented, and then returned to the chamber to find the reward. Cheng first used this paradigm with rats, manipulating the cues that were available to them to reorient and to find their reward. In these experiments, the available cues provided either (a) geometric information, available from the shape of the chamber (most commonly rectangular) and (b) featural information, available from either distinctive objects in the chamber or other various local cues such as a painted wall within the chamber. In general, Cheng found that rats were quite sensitive to the overall geometry of their environment and—somewhat surprisingly—that they were relatively insensitive to the featural information within it. Thus, for example, when featural information conflicted with geometric information (e.g., during learning, the target location was a corner next to a landmark, but during testing, the landmark had moved to a different corner), the rats generally relied on the geometric information to reorient. This paradigm was adapted for humans by Elizabeth Spelke and her colleagues, who observed children reorienting in a 1.9 m × 1.2 m rectangular chamber and drew similar conclusions about their use of spatial information to reorient: The shape of the chamber aided reorientation, whereas small distinctive landmarks placed near the targets did not (Hermer & Spelke, 1996).

Seen through the lens of a functional division of psychological space, one might question whether Hermer and Spelke's (1996) results and conclusions adequately accounted for the concept of environmental scale. Researchers so inclined might wonder whether a child's "navigation" within a small chamber can truly be generalized to the large, naturalistic environments in which we commonly navigate in everyday life. These questions were addressed by Learmonth, Nadel, and Newcombe (2002; see also Learmonth, Newcombe, & Huttenlocher, 2001), who demonstrated that children who are tested in relatively large navigable spaces are increasingly sensitive to featural information such as landmarks, especially when the landmarks are known to be stable, immovable parts of the larger environment.

An alternative reaction to the work of Hermer and Spelke (1996) might come from researchers who tend to cast spatial cognition in terms of the psychological structures and processes that enable it. For example, a researcher who is interested in online processes might focus on understanding how children become disoriented in this paradigm. Such a tack was taken by Wang and Spelke (2000), who examined the process of disorientation in adult humans, asking whether knowledge of one's immediate environment is better conceptualized as a set of relationships that are dynamically updated online or as an enduring knowledge structure. By examining the variability of participants' pointing errors before and after disorientation, Wang and Spelke concluded that (a) knowledge of one's immediate surroundings is primarily dependent on dynamically updated egocentric information and (b) enduring spatial knowledge in this situation may consist of

little more than a representation of the shape of the surrounding space.

Finally, a researcher interested in how human cognition organizes and parameterizes spatial information might respond to Hermer and Spelke's (1996) findings by setting out to examine more incisively how people mentally represent geometric information. Sturz, Gurley, and Bodily (2011) noted that there are two possible ways to describe this geometric knowledge. First, geometric knowledge of an enclosure could consist of a representation of the global shape of the space, coded, for example, with respect to an extracted principal axis of the space. For instance, participants in Hermer and Spelke's experiments may have relied on knowledge that the overall shape of the testing chamber was a rectangle. Alternatively, the geometric information that is coded in this paradigm may consist primarily of knowledge of the multiple local parts that compose the overall shape. For example, participants could remember the rectangular enclosure as a set of relatively long and relatively short walls connected at right angles. Recent work by Sturz et al. suggested that generally human knowledge of the geometry of their surrounding space is better described as global knowledge of the overall shape than as knowledge of local geometry (see also Lourenco & Huttenlocher, 2007).

As these examples show, any sufficiently rich and interesting finding in the field of spatial cognition can be approached from multiple mutually reinforcing directions. Thus, although most research (including the research described in this volume) is described principally in terms of only one of these frameworks, active and thoughtful readers will do well to relate and understand them in the context of the others.

SUMMARY OF THE PRESENT VOLUME

The chapters that follow are divided into three major sections and are roughly ordered to cover topics ranging from basic physical processes to more molar, holistic, and interpersonal influences on spatial thought. Despite this approximate ordering of the chapters, readers should not feel compelled to read them in order. Each chapter stands sufficiently on its own as a concise yet thorough review of a topic area.

The volume begins with two chapters that synthesize and review current neuroscientific research on brain structures and mechanisms that underlie spatial cognition. Brain areas that are particularly relevant for spatial processing include the hippocampus, covered by Redish and Ekstrom (Chapter 1), and the parietal lobe, reviewed by Kesner and Creem-Regehr (Chapter 2).

The next handful of chapters focus on online perceptual processes, including (a) information about the environment that enables organisms to interact with it (Fajen & Phillips, Chapter 3), (b) what sensory information informs us about space and how it is processed and combined in perception (Mohler et al., Chapter 4), and (c) how people maintain awareness of space during their own motion (Philbeck & Sargent, Chapter 5). This section ends with a chapter by Casey (Chapter 6) about the mental abilities that underlie performance on basic spatial tasks and the differences between men and women on some of these abilities.

The next section deals primarily with memory of space and includes chapters about (a) how animals use landmarks to navigate (Cheng & Graham, Chapter 7), (b) how and whether humans form mental representations of the global characteristics of environments (Nadel, Chapter 8), (c) how humans organize their spatial memory and the properties of memory that affect and result from this organization (McNamara, Chapter 9), and (d) how knowledge of space—particularly the ability to combine different sources of spatial information—develops in infancy and childhood into mature competence (Holden & Newcombe, Chapter 10). The section ends with a chapter by Hirtle (Chapter 11) that introduces readers to the formal models that researchers have used to represent our understanding of space.

The final section includes three chapters that examine broader interpersonal dimensions of spatial thought, as well as contextual factors that affect how we think about space. Taylor and Brunyé (Chapter 12) review an extensive body of literature on spatial language, focusing on human flexibility in spatial thought as well as the grounding of language processes in perception and action. Montello and Raubal (Chapter 13) then lay out the functions and applications of spatial cognition, addressing the question of why it is important to study and understand spatial cognition. Finally, Heft (Chapter 14) presents a framework for understanding environmental behavior in a way that focuses on description, context, and embeddedness (rather than detached intellectual analysis) and includes the influence of cultural forces on our understanding of space.

References

Allen, G. L., & Haun, D. B. M. (2004). Proximity and precision in spatial memory. In G. Allen (Ed.), *Human spatial memory: Remembering where* (pp. 41–63). Mahwah, NJ: Erlbaum.

Amorim, M.-A., Glasauer, S., Carpinot, K., & Berthoz, A. (1997). Updating an object's orientation and location during nonvisual navigation: A comparison between two processing modes. *Attention, Perception, & Psychophysics, 59,* 404–418. doi:10.3758/BF03211907

Carroll, J. B. (1993). *Human cognitive abilities: A survey of factor-analytical studies*. New York, NY: Cambridge University Press. doi:10.1017/CBO9780511571312

Cheng, K. (1986). A purely geometric module in the rat's spatial representation. *Cognition, 23,* 149–178. doi:10.1016/0010-0277(86)90041-7

Cheng, K., & Newcombe, N. S. (2005). Is there a geometric module for spatial orientation? Squaring theory and evidence. *Psychonomic Bulletin & Review, 12,* 1–23. doi:10.3758/BF03196346

Eliot, J. & Smith, M. (1984). *An international directory of spatial tests*. Windsor, England: NFER-Nelson.

Fodor, J. A. (1983). *The modularity of mind*. Cambridge, MA: MIT Press.

Gallistel, C. R. (1990). *The organization of learning*. Cambridge, MA: MIT Press.

Gibson, J. J. (1979). *The ecological approach to visual perception*. Hillsdale, NJ: Erlbaum.

Grüsser, O. J. (1983). Multimodal structure of the extrapersonal space. In A. Hein & M. Jeannerod (Eds.), *Spatially oriented behaviors* (pp. 327–352). New York, NY: Springer-Verlag. doi:10.1007/978-1-4612-5488-1_18

Hegarty, M., & Waller, D. (2005). Individual differences in spatial abilities. In P. Shah & A. Miyake (Eds.), *Handbook of higher-level visuospatial thinking* (pp. 121–169). New York, NY: Cambridge University Press.

Hermer, L., & Spelke, E. (1996). Modularity and development: The case of spatial reorientation. *Cognition, 61,* 195–232. doi:10.1016/S0010-0277(96)00714-7

Huttenlocher, J., Hedges, L., & Duncan, S. (1991). Categories and particulars: Prototype effects in estimating spatial location. *Psychological Review, 98,* 352–376. doi:10.1037/0033-295X.98.3.352

Kosslyn, S. M., Thompson, W. L., Gitelman, D. R., & Alpert, N. M. (1998). Neural systems that encode categorical vs. coordinate spatial relations: PET investigations. *Psychobiology, 26,* 333–347.

Kozhevnikov, M., Motes, M. A., Rasch, B., & Blajenkova, O. (2006). Perspective-taking vs. mental rotation transformations and how they predict spatial navigation performance. *Applied Cognitive Psychology, 20,* 397–417. doi:10.1002/acp.1192

Learmonth, A. E., Nadel, L., & Newcombe, N. S. (2002). Children's use of landmarks: Implications for modularity theory. *Psychological Science, 13,* 337–341. doi:10.1111/j.0956-7976.2002.00461.x

Learmonth, A. E., Newcombe, N. S., & Huttenlocher, J. (2001). Toddler's use of metric information and landmarks to reorient. *Journal of Experimental Child Psychology, 80,* 225–244. doi:10.1006/jecp.2001.2635

Levinson, S. C. (1996). Frames of reference and Molyneux's question: Cross-linguistic evidence. In P. Bloom, M. Peterson, L. Nadel, & M. Garrett (Eds.), *Language and space* (pp. 109–169). Cambridge, MA: MIT press.

Loomis, J. M., Da Silva, J. A., Philbeck, J. W., & Fukusima, S. S. (1996). Visual perception of location and distance. *Current Directions in Psychological Science, 5,* 72–77. doi:10.1111/1467-8721.ep10772783

Lourenco, S. F., & Huttenlocher, J. (2007). Using geometry to specify location: implications for spatial coding in children and nonhuman animals. *Psychological Research, 71,* 252–264. doi:10.1007/s00426-006-0081-3

Montello, D. R. (1993). Scale and multiple psychologies of space. In A. U. Frank & I. Campari (Eds.), *Spatial information theory: A theoretical basis for GIS*

(pp. 312–321). Berlin, Germany: Springer-Verlag. doi:10.1007/3-540-57207-4_21

Mou, W., & McNamara, T. P. (2002). Intrinsic frames of reference in spatial memory. *Journal of Experimental Psychology: Learning, Memory, and Cognition, 28,* 162–170. doi:10.1037/0278-7393.28.1.162

Piaget, J., & Inhelder, B. (1967). *The child's conception of space.* New York, NY: Norton.

Shelton, A. L., & McNamara, T. P. (2001). Systems of spatial reference in human memory. *Cognitive Psychology, 43,* 274–310. doi:10.1006/cogp.2001.0758

Simons, D. J., & Wang, R. F. (1998). Perceiving real-world viewpoint changes. *Psychological Science, 9,* 315–320. doi:10.1111/1467-9280.00062

Sturz, B. R., Gurley, T., & Bodily, K. D. (2011). Orientation in trapezoid-shaped enclosures: Implications for theoretical accounts of geometry learning. *Journal of Experimental Psychology: Animal Behavior Processes, 37,* 246–253. doi:10.1037/a0021215

Tversky, B. (2003). Structures of mental spaces: How people think about space. *Environment and Behavior, 35,* 66–80. doi:10.1177/0013916502238865

Waller, D., & Lippa, Y. (2007). Landmarks as beacons and associative cues: Their role in route learning. *Memory & Cognition, 35,* 910–924. doi:10.3758/BF03193465

Wang, R. F., & Spelke, E. (2000). Updating egocentric representations in human navigation. *Cognition, 77,* 215–250. doi:10.1016/S0010-0277(00)00105-0

Wang, R. F., & Spelke, E. S. (2002). Human spatial representation: Insights from animals. *Trends in Cognitive Sciences, 6,* 376–382. doi:10.1016/S1364-6613(02)01961-7

Wraga, M., Creem, S. H., & Proffitt, D. R. (2000). Perception–action dissociations of a walkable Müller-Lyer configuration. *Psychological Science, 11,* 239–243. doi:10.1111/1467-9280.00248

Part I

NEUROSCIENTIFIC DIMENSIONS OF SPATIAL COGNITION

CHAPTER 1

HIPPOCAMPUS AND RELATED AREAS: WHAT THE PLACE CELL LITERATURE TELLS US ABOUT COGNITIVE MAPS IN RATS AND HUMANS

A. David Redish and Arne Ekstrom

One of the most striking examples of how neurons code complex cognition is the activity of the *place cell* in the rodent hippocampus. Thus, any discussion of the hippocampal neurophysiology of spatial cognition needs to start from the fact that spatial location is a primary driver of neural firing patterns in the rodent hippocampus (O'Keefe & Dostrovsky, 1971), and spatial firing is clearly the best first-order description of rodent hippocampal representations (for a review, see Redish, 1999). Nonspatial information is also represented in the rodent hippocampus, reliably modulating neural firing there but arriving separately through distinct neuroanatomical pathways. Spatial information is also a key component of neural representations in the human hippocampus, as are nonspatial aspects.

In this chapter, we present an integrated framework of rodent and human hippocampal function on the basis of the idea that although space plays a primary role in hippocampal function, nonspatial variables overlap and share processing resources within the hippocampus as well. We start with a quick review of the anatomy, and then we turn to a review of the properties of place cells in the rodent hippocampus, identifying what is known about how spatial firing is achieved and how multiple maps are represented and examining the differences in representation across anatomical dimensions of

hippocampus. From there, we turn to properties of place cells, identifying three phenomena that we connect to questions of human spatial cognition: (a) *phase precession*, in which sequences representing potential trajectories are played out during behavior; (b) *replay*, in which sequences are played out during rest periods; and (c) *context sensitivity*, in which attention to task and environment plays an important role in determining which spatial representations are active at any time. Finally, we work backward to discuss what is known about hippocampal inputs, including the recently discovered *grid cells* and the differences between lateral and medial entorhinal cortex, as well as perirhinal and postrhinal inputs into these structures. In the second section, we turn to the human hippocampus, reviewing what is known about spatial representations in the human hippocampus and the adjacent medial temporal lobe cortical structures. Our discussion focuses on evidence from lesion, functional magnetic resonance imaging (fMRI), and invasive recording studies in humans, and we examine the role of the human hippocampus in representing multiple spatial routes and contexts, as well as the role of the human parahippocampal cortex in visual–spatial representation. We conclude with a discussion about a general role for the hippocampus in episodic memory and how this

A. David Redish was supported by National Institutes of Health grant R01 MH08031. Arne Ekstrom was supported by an Alfred P. Sloan Research Fellowship and by the University of California, Davis, Faculty Grants for Research.

DOI: 10.1037/13936-002
Handbook of Spatial Cognition, D. Waller and L. Nadel (Editors)

relates to both future thinking and consolidation of past episodic information into general knowledge about the world.

ANATOMY

Anatomically, both the rodent and primate (including human) hippocampus can be subdivided into three primary subregions (dentate gyrus [DG], CA3, and CA1). These structures differ in connectivity, component interneurons, and projection neurons (Amaral & Lavenex, 2007; van Strien, Cappaert, & Witter, 2009). In addition, the hippocampus is anatomically differentiable along the dorsal-to-ventral (sometimes called the septal-to-temporal) axis and along the proximal-to-distal axis (Amaral & Lavenex, 2007). In the primate (including humans), the dorsal–ventral axis is transformed through development into a posterior-to-anterior axis, with the primate posterior hippocampus corresponding to the rodent dorsal hippocampus and the primate anterior hippocampus corresponding to the rodent ventral hippocampus. A simplified anatomical diagram is shown in Color Plate 1.

PLACE CELLS IN THE RODENT HIPPOCAMPUS

The canonical place cell in the hippocampus is defined by a restricted firing field (or tuning curve) to a unimodal spatial area in an open environment. As a rat runs around the floor of a 1-m cylinder, foraging for food pellets thrown in at random intervals, a given place cell primarily fires its spikes in a single unimodal area, called a *place field*. Different place cells have different place fields (see Color Plate 2). The population activity encodes the location of the animal in the cylinder. However, this description belies a host of complexity now known to exist. Place cells can be found in all three components of the hippocampus (DG, CA3, CA1), but DG place fields tend to be sparser (Gothard, Hoffman, Battaglia, & McNaughton, 2001; Jung & McNaughton, 1993) and more sensitive to subtle changes in an environment (Leutgeb, Leutgeb, Moser, & Moser, 2007). Current theories suggest that the sparse activity in the DG plays a primary role

in *pattern separation,* a process of making similar representations more dissimilar, whereas recurrent connectivity in CA3 plays a role in *pattern completion,* a process of transitioning a partial instantiation into a stored complete representation (McClelland, McNaughton, & O'Reilly, 1995; McNaughton & Morris, 1987; Redish, 1999). Pattern separation allows for simpler storage because dissimilar patterns are less likely to interfere with each other (Hertz, Krogh, & Palmer, 1991; McNaughton & Morris, 1987); pattern completion allows for content-addressable memories, retrieving complete memories by their partial content (Hebb, 1949/2002; Hertz et al., 1991).

Supporting these hypotheses, manipulations of the DG affect the ability to recognize subtle spatial differences between tasks and environments (Gilbert, Kesner, & Lee, 2001). In contrast, CA3 provides pattern completion processes, such as the presence of place fields after landmark removal (Nakazawa et al., 2002; Pico, Gerbrandt, Pondel, & Ivy, 1985) and in the dark (Markus, Barnes, McNaughton, Gladden, & Skaggs, 1994). CA3 place fields depend on the DG for pattern separation (McHugh et al., 2007) but not for recall of place fields (McNaughton, Barnes, Meltzer, & Sutherland, 1989). CA1 place fields depend on CA3 for pattern completion (Nakazawa et al., 2002) but not for the existence of place fields (Mizumori, McNaughton, Barnes, & Fox, 1989).

Along the dorsal-to-ventral axis, place fields increase in size, with smaller place fields in the dorsal region and broader place fields in ventral regions (Jung, Wiener, & McNaughton, 1994; Kjelstrup et al., 2008; Royer, Sirota, Patel, & Buzsáki, 2010), suggesting a multiscale representation of space (Fiete, Burak, & Brookings, 2008; Maurer, Vanrhoads, Sutherland, Lipa, & McNaughton, 2005). Very broad place fields could provide large-scale contextual cues and may be why the ventral hippocampus is often associated with contextual and environmental–emotional associations (Bannerman et al., 2004), although the dorsal, intermediate, and ventral hippocampi each interact differently with other structures (van Strien et al., 2009). The spatial representations embodied in place fields are dependent on three factors: *sensory cues* (sometimes called the *local view,* even though those sensory cues are not necessarily visual), *dead reckoning* (sometimes called *path integration*[1]), and nonspatial (contextual) cues. As we will see, these nonspatial cues are fundamentally different from the spatial representations and are better understood as *map selection.*

Several theories in the 1990s (see Redish, 1999, for a review) suggested that the place fields in the hippocampus are dependent on dead-reckoning representations. Dead reckoning entails the maintenance of a position representation from self-motion information: If I know I am at location (x, y) and take a step $(\Delta x, \Delta y)$, then I know I am at location $(x + \Delta x, y + \Delta y)$. Of course, the updating calculation does not have to be done in Cartesian coordinates, but there are computational reasons to expect it not to be done in polar coordinates (Gallistel, 1990). A few models of successful dead-reckoning systems have been proposed (Burak & Fiete, 2009; Conklin & Eliasmith, 2005; Müller & Wehner, 1988; Samsonovich & McNaughton, 1997; Wittmann & Schwegler, 1995), but the actual mechanism underlying the dead-reckoning system remains unknown.

Although some early theories suggested that the hippocampus itself was the computational dead-reckoning component (Samsonovich & McNaughton, 1997), other theories suggested that the dead-reckoning component had to be an input to the system, because of computational limitations due to the nonspatial representations in the hippocampus (Redish, 1999). Lesion studies have been unable to resolve this controversy, with some studies reporting that animals can perform dead reckoning without a hippocampus (Alyan & McNaughton, 1999) and others reporting that they cannot (Maaswinkel, Jarrard, & Whishaw, 1999). Unfortunately, as with any lesion study, these results are complicated by the availability of other mechanisms capable of solving the tasks without dead-reckoning and behavioral components of the tasks that may require hippocampus but not dead reckoning. Nevertheless, the evidence that hippocampal representations are driven by dead-reckoning components is incontrovertible. The cleanest demonstrations of this are the continued firing of place cells in the dark and after cue removal (as long as the animal is able to localize itself beforehand; Markus et al., 1994; Nakazawa et al., 2002; O'Keefe & Conway, 1978) and after manipulations were done that decoupled the hippocampus from the sensory representations (Knierim, Kudrimoti, & McNaughton, 1998). Critically, the externally provided sensory cues are associated with internally driven dead-reckoning information, not the other way around. This means that (at least in rats) the internal coordinate system is primary and external cues are associated with it, not the other way around (Gallistel, 1990; Knierim, Kudrimoti, & McNaughton, 1995; Redish, 1999).

Computationally, this result makes sense if one examines how animals make novel environments familiar. When an animal enters a new environment, it can maintain a representation of position relative to its starting point through dead-reckoning systems, but dead-reckoning systems have the intrinsic problem that systematic errors build up over time unless they are corrected (Gallistel, 1990). Once the animal knows the sensory cues for each position in the environment, it can correct those errors with the remembered sensory cues. Of course, knowing the cues at each position depends on the animal being familiar with the environment. To break this cycle, animals explore outward from a home base (Birke, 1983), associating the sensory cues with the dead-reckoning coordinates. As the dead-reckoning system drifts, the animal will have to return to the home base to reset its dead-reckoning coordinate system (Redish, 1999). Consistent with this explanation, outbound journeys as animals explore environments are slow and meandering, whereas return journeys are fast and direct (Drai & Golani, 2001). What this means is that place cells fire initially on entry into an environment but that they take time to tune up (Wilson & McNaughton, 1993).

Familiarizing oneself with an environment entails learning the relationship between locations within the environment sufficiently to be able to predict the effect of taking a path through the environment. Spatial cognition thus often critically involves spatial

---

[1]It is important to distinguish *path integration* in the sense of maintaining a representation of a distance to a home-base from "path integration" meaning integration over a path variable (sometimes referred to as a *path integral*). To reduce confusion, we consistently use the term *dead reckoning* for maintenance of a position representation, updated from motion cues (Gallistel, 1990).

sequences, particularly in terms of navigating along those sequences. The dynamics of place cell firing show two important sequential representations when examined at fine time scales: (a) phase precession and (b) replay.

Phase Precession

In addition to the single cell data, recording electrodes provide access to a slower signal, measured in the lower frequencies (1–300 Hz) called *local field potentials* (LFPs), which primarily reflect synaptic effects (Buzsáki, 2006; Katzner et al., 2009). In the hippocampus, LFPs reflect the information processing state of the system, identified primarily by either a slow 7 Hz rhythm (*theta*) seen during navigation, attentive behavior, and REM sleep or a broader-spectrum (*large amplitude irregular activity* or LIA) signal punctuated by 100 ms 200 Hz *sharp-wave ripple complexes* seen during nonattentive behaviors and slow-wave sleep (Bragin et al., 1995; O'Keefe & Nadel, 1978; Vanderwolf, 1971; Ylinen et al., 1995). During theta, the hippocampal system primarily processes information entering from the entorhinal cortex, whereas sharp waves reflect information processing generated in the CA3 region (Bragin et al., 1995; Buzsáki, 2006; Hasselmo & Bower, 1993; Ylinen et al., 1995).

As animals run along a path, the phase relationship between the firing of a given place cell and the 7 Hz LFP theta changes such that spiking precesses from late in the theta cycle on entry into a place field to earlier in the cycle on exit from the field (O'Keefe & Recce, 1993; Skaggs, McNaughton, Wilson, & Barnes, 1996). This change in phase relationship as an animal passes through a place field is called *phase precession*. It is useful to think of the effect of phase precession on the neural ensemble: Because place cells fire late in the theta rhythm on entry into place fields but early on exit from the place field, within each theta cycle, there is a sequence of firing along the path of the rat (Skaggs et al., 1996; see Color Plate 3). In fact, it is possible that phase precession is an epiphenomenon of an internal sequence and motion: Within each theta cycle, some mechanism drives a sequence of activity along the path of the animal, and that sequence precesses as the animal moves forward (Lisman & Redish, 2009).

When first observed, it was suggested that phase precession could serve to improve the representation of location (O'Keefe & Recce, 1993; Skaggs et al., 1996) and that it does so on linear paths (Jensen & Lisman, 2000). However, on two-dimensional paths, place cells are omnidirectional (Markus et al., 1995; Muller, Bostock, Taube, & Kubie, 1994) and phase precess on the approach from any direction (Huxter, Senior, Allen, & Csicsvari, 2008; Skaggs et al., 1996). As originally noted by Skaggs et al. (1996), there are three possible relationships between phase precession and omnidirectionality: (a) The place fields in each direction can start from the same point and precess outward, suggesting that place fields receive a "kick" to start and reflect a memory of the recent past. This would imply identical locations of the entry into a place field in each direction but varied exits. (b) The place fields in the two directions can cross, such that phase precession measures travel through the place field. This would imply that the center of the place field would be identical from any direction. (c) The place fields in the two directions could end at the same point, precessing inward, suggesting that place fields predict distance from a future goal. This would imply that the entry of the place field would differ between directions, but exits from the place field would coincide. This question was definitively settled by a pair of recent papers carefully examining bidirectional place fields (on the cue-rich linear track, Battaglia, Sutherland, & McNaughton, 2004; and on the cylinder foraging task, Huxter et al., 2008). In both of these papers, place fields were found to shift between directions such that they ended at the same location, definitively confirming the third hypothesis: Place fields predict distance to a goal (Lisman & Redish, 2009).

This hypothesis also suggests that phase precession should depend on forward motion of the animal. Unfortunately, when rats stop moving, the hippocampus no longer shows place fields or the theta rhythm. However, a recent pair of experiments examined animals running on a fixed wheel, so that the animals were in motion (thus showing theta) but not moving in space. Hirase, Czurkó, Csicsvari, and Buzsáki (1999) found that place cells of animals simply placed in the running wheel within their place fields showed continuous firing at a single phase of theta. In contrast, Pastalkova, Itskov, Amarasingham, and Buzsáki (2008) found that animals who had to run in the wheel for a set time (thus with a goal) showed clear phase precession. These data strongly suggest that phase precession is related to the presence of a goal. As shown in Color Plate 3, thinking of phase precession at the ensemble level provides a clear explanation for the differences between these processes. In a recent study of spatial decision making, Johnson and Redish (2007) found that during deliberative pauses, spatial representations swept ahead of the animal, first down one potential path and then down the other. Although the animals were paused, the hippocampus remained in the theta state, likely due to the presence of attentive theta (O'Keefe & Nadel, 1978), and the observed sequential firing was aligned to the theta rhythm, much like phase precession.

Phase precession entails sequential representations of paths toward a goal, and is likely related to planning, spatial navigation abilities, and goal finding. It is possible to disrupt the sequential representations of phase precession without disrupting the place fields themselves (Robbe & Buzsáki, 2009). Disrupting these sequences has profound effects on an animal's ability to navigate, particularly on hippocampally dependent spatial memory tasks (Pastalkova et al., 2008; Robbe & Buzsáki, 2009).

Replay

Although hippocampal place cells fire the majority of spikes in their place fields, they also occasionally fire spikes outside the place field, most notably at locations where the animals pause and rest at reward-delivery sites (O'Keefe & Nadel, 1978; Redish, 1999). If one decodes the spatial position represented at a given time by a recorded hippocampal ensemble, the position decoded reflects the position of the animal (Wilson & McNaughton, 1993; Zhang, Ginzburg, McNaughton, & Sejnowski, 1998), particularly once the place fields have stabilized with experience (Frank, Stanley, & Brown, 2004; Kentros et al., 1998; Wilson & McNaughton, 1993). However, at reward sites, decoded positions do not reflect the current position of the animal; instead, they reflect other positions in the environment and in previously experienced environments (Jackson, Johnson, &

Redish, 2006; Jensen & Lisman, 2000; Karlsson & Frank, 2009; Kudrimoti, Barnes, & McNaughton, 1999; see Color Plate 4). During these pause times, the hippocampus switches modes such that the local field potential no longer shows the 7 Hz theta rhythm, but rather shows a more broad spectrum local field potential, LIA, punctuated by 200 Hz bursts termed *ripples* or *sharp waves* (Buzsáki, Leung, & Vanderwolf, 1983; O'Keefe & Nadel, 1978).

These representations entail not only the firing of a coordinated set of out-of-field place cells but also the lack of firing of in-field place cells. These phenomena were first discovered during sleep and were shown to entail a *reactivation* or *replay* of recently experienced spatial memories—the specific pattern of neural firing seen during behavior is repeated during the subsequent sleep (Kudrimoti et al., 1999; Wilson & McNaughton, 1994).

It is still unclear how much these replays and reactivations drive an improvement of representation within the hippocampus itself (Buzsáki, 1989), a coordination of memory across cortical structures (Alvarez & Squire, 1994; Teyler & DiScenna, 1985), or actual information transferred to cortical structures (Marr, 1971; McClelland et al., 1995). These issues are still unresolved (for reviews, see Nadel & Moscovitch, 1997; Sutherland & McNaughton, 2000). Nevertheless, there is clear evidence for a role of sharp waves in learning (Ego-Stengel & Wilson, 2010; Girardeau, Benchenane, Wiener, Buzsáki, & Zugaro, 2009), as well as an interaction between hippocampus and downstream structures. Several cortical areas, including visual cortex (Ji & Wilson, 2007) and prefrontal cortex (Euston, Tatsuno, & McNaughton, 2007), show reactivation of representations after behavior. Similarly, hippocampal sharp waves precede coordinated activity across cortical ensembles (Hoffman & McNaughton, 2002). However, it is not yet known whether cortical representations can reactivate without hippocampal input. Sharp-wave events in the hippocampus also have effects on noncortical structures: They trigger reactivation of reward-related activity in the portions of the nucleus accumbens known to receive hippocampal input (Lansink et al., 2008).

As noted previously, in addition to reactivating during subsequent sleep, hippocampal ensembles also reactivate during awake, rest behaviors when the hippocampus transitions from the theta to LIA states (Jackson et al., 2006; Karlsson & Frank, 2009). Just as reactivation is higher during sleep after behavior than before (Kudrimoti et al., 1999; Wilson & McNaughton, 1994), reactivation increases throughout experience on a task (Jackson et al., 2006; O'Neill, Senior, & Csicsvari, 2006) and preferentially represents other tasks after a behavior rather than before (Jackson et al., 2006; Karlsson & Frank, 2009).

Although replay during sleep has so far only been shown to be forward in order (i.e., to be a replay of the recent paths; Nádasdy, Hirase, Czurkó, Csicsvari, & Buzsáki, 1999; Skaggs & McNaughton, 1996), replay during awake, rest behaviors has now been shown to include both forward, backward, and even novel sequences (Davidson, Kloosterman, & Wilson, 2009; Foster & Wilson, 2006; Gupta, van der Meer, Touretzky, & Redish, 2010). The presence of novel sequences never experienced by the rat implies that there may be a second role for hippocampal replay: that of mental exploration, possibly linking together separate components of a cognitive map.

Context Sensitivity

Remapping of place fields seems to be primarily random between environments; that is, the probability of a cell having a place field in one environment, and the location of the field in that environment, is independent of whether the cell has a field in another environment and independent of the location of the field in the other environment (Barnes, Suster, Shen, & McNaughton, 1997; Guzowski, McNaughton, Barnes, & Worley, 1999; Muller & Kubie, 1987; Redish, 1999). Some studies have, however, also reported partial remapping, in which some cells show similar representations between two visually similar environments (e.g., Skaggs & McNaughton, 1998). These similarities, however, may be due to realignments of the dead-reckoning coordinate system in each box (Redish & Touretzky, 1998b); separating the dead-reckoning coordinate systems between the two boxes increases remapping (Colgin et al., 2010; Fuhs, Van Rhoads, Casale, McNaughton, & Touretzky, 2005).

Map selection occurs through a categorization process (likely involving pattern separation in the DG and pattern completion in CA3). Bistability in map recall ability should produce bimodality in water maze performance on a trial-by-trial basis—recall of the correct map would allow proper navigation to the goal, whereas recall of the incorrect map would leave the animals lost. This is exactly what was found (Barnes et al., 1997): Proper navigation requires not only locating oneself correctly but also locating oneself on the correct map.

If different tasks or subtasks within an environment were represented by different maps, place cells switching place fields would appear to be sensitive to nonspatial signals (Redish & Touretzky, 1997). If the animal divided its attention between two maps, repetitive map switching would appear as noise in the activity of place cells as the animal traverses the place field (Olypher, Lansky, & Fenton, 2002). Both of these phenomena occur.

As noted previously, under certain conditions, place cells are sensitive to other factors beyond the spatial location of the animal (see Redish, 1999, for a review of the primary literature on this topic). The multiple-map hypothesis suggests that these nonspatial sensitivities are due to changes in the underlying active map. Directional sensitivity depends on regularity of the traversals of the paths (Markus et al., 1995); sensitivity to subtask components depends on the different goal orientations rather than the cues provided (Eichenbaum, Kuperstein, Fagan, & Nagode, 1987); and sensitivity to episodic events develops with experience and depends on the salience of the event (Moita, Rosis, Zhou, LeDoux, & Blair, 2004). For example, place fields are remapped after being exposed to a fear-conditioning experiment (Moita et al., 2004).

In simple foraging tasks, place cells show unexpectedly high variability in spiking on different traverses through a place field (Fenton & Muller, 1998). On goal-directed tasks, the variability in spatial firing of place fields drops (Olypher et al., 2002), such that at times when animals are approaching a single goal, the variability closes in on the expected inherent variability due to other factors (Jackson & Redish, 2007; Kelemen &

Fenton, 2010). When forced to avoid shock in two different reference frames, hippocampal representations switch between those reference frames but tended to be in the relevant reference frame when the animal was close to the shock zone in a given reference frame (Kelemen & Fenton, 2010).

Analogously, in experiments that place dead reckoning in conflict with external cues (Gothard et al., 2001; Gothard, Skaggs, & McNaughton, 1996; Redish, Rosenzweig, Bohanick, McNaughton, & Barnes, 2000), animals were unable to find a reward unless the hippocampus had reset to the correct coordinate frame (Rosenzweig, Redish, McNaughton, & Barnes, 2003).

Inputs to the Hippocampus

The primary informational input into the hippocampus comes from entorhinal cortex, which is divided into the medial and lateral entorhinal cortex (MEC and LEC, respectively). Early studies of MEC found that MEC cells contained spatial information (Quirk, Muller, Kubie, & Ranck, 1992). However, our understanding of representations in medial entorhinal cortex took a quantum leap forward with the discovery of grid cells by Fyhn, Molden, Witter, Moser, and Moser (2004): These cells show multipeaked tuning curves to spatial location in a triangle tessellated pattern (see Color Plate 5). Grid cells cover the space and contain sufficient spatial information to decode position (Hafting, Fyhn, Molden, Moser, & Moser, 2005). The spacing of the triangular tessellation (the "grid") increases from dorsal to ventral MEC, paralleling the increased place field sizes seen in the hippocampus (Hafting et al., 2005; Kjelstrup et al., 2008).

As noted previously, the hippocampus seems to be an association between spatial coordinates (the dead-reckoning or "path integration" system) and external cues (the "local view"). This means that when the internal spatial coordinate system shifts, the external cues will be misaligned, suggesting to the animal that it is in a different environment, which should drive a remapping process (Redish, 1999; Redish &

Touretzky, 1998b). Fyhn, Hafting, Treves, Moser, and Moser (2007) explicitly tested this by examining the changes in grid cell firing under conditions in which place fields shifted or remained constant. In cases in which there was only limited remapping (*rate remapping*), the grid cell population remained constant, but in cases in which there was total remapping (*map shifting*), the grid cell population shifted and/or rotated its grid fields (Fyhn et al., 2007). It is notable that the grid cells themselves translated or rotated as a group, like head direction cells[2] but unlike the hippocampal place cells, which remapped.

The multiple-map theory of hippocampal spatial representations suggests that spatial and nonspatial information should enter the hippocampus through different pathways (Henriksen et al., 2010; Manns & Eichenbaum, 2006; Redish, 1999). Early studies found spatial representations in medial entorhinal cortex (Quirk et al., 1992), but there were no reports of spatial representations in lateral entorhinal cortex. This question was settled by Hargreaves, Rao, Lee, and Knierim (2005), who found that medial entorhinal cells showed more spatial information than lateral entorhinal cells. In a similar manner, recordings of postrhinal cells showed spatial firing, whereas perirhinal cells did not. In general, the postrhinal cortex tends to receive spatial input, predominantly from the cingulate, parietal, and occipital cortices, whereas the perirhinal cortex tends to receive polymodal, less spatial input, predominantly from piriform, frontal, and insular cortices (Furtak, Wei, Agster, & Burwell, 2007).

These data suggest that two pathways converge on the hippocampal formation: a spatial pathway (parietal, postrhinal cortex, and medial entorhinal) combined with a contextual, object-recognition, less spatial pathway (polymodal sensory, perirhinal cortex, and lateral entorhinal). However, current detailed anatomical studies of the entorhinal–hippocampal interaction suggest that the detailed connectivity may be both more complete and more segregated than these earlier studies imply (see van Strien et al., 2009).

---

[2]Head direction cells are the other primary spatial tuning curve seen in rat navigation tasks. They show generally unimodal tuning curves to the orientation of the rat in space (the direction in space that the head is facing). They are found in a network of structures, including postsubiculum, entorhinal cortex, the dorsal nucleus of the anterior thalamus, and the lateral mammilary bodies. In general, they have properties similar to place and grid cells: (a) they show landmark sensitivity, but those landmarks are associated with internal representations, not the other way around, and (b) they do not remap between environments (see Taube, 2007, and Redish, 1999, for reviews).

SPATIAL REPRESENTATIONS IN THE HUMAN MEDIAL TEMPORAL LOBE

Similar to work in rats, experimental lesion work suggests that damage to the human hippocampus impairs several forms of spatial cognition. These include memory for the spatial relations of multiple objects in an arena (Bohbot et al., 1998) and the spatial relations of objects within a scene (Hartley, Wei, Agster, & Burwell, 2007), as well as the ability to learn spatial information from a shifted viewpoint (King, Burgess, Hartley, Vargha-Khadem, & O'Keefe, 2002), draw maps of recently learned virtual environments (Spiers et al., 2001), and learn virtual analogues of the Morris Water Maze and the eight-arm maze (Goodrich-Hunsaker, Livingstone, Skelton, & Hopkins, 2010). Hippocampal contributions appear particularly pronounced when patients with hippocampal lesions have to remember multiple spatial routes to different locations or several different spatial environments with distinct routes Bohbot, Lerch, Thorndycraft, Iaria, & Zijdenbos, 2007; Corkin, 2002). For example, patients with hippocampal lesions did not show deficits when retrieving a single route to a hidden location but were impaired when retrieving the location of multiple hidden objects within a spatial environment (Bohbot et al., 1998, 2007). These findings suggest that the human spatial memory system may be similar to that of the rodent, with computations involving multiple routes and environments largely dependent on an intact hippocampus.

The neural basis of human spatial memory relies on more than hippocampus alone. In addition, the human hippocampus likely plays a role in more than just spatial cognition. As with rodents, there is reason to believe that some of this "extraspatial" hippocampal function may relate to a more general role in episodic memory (Cohen & Eichenbaum, 1993), which we discuss in more detail later in this chapter. It is clear that other brain systems, such as the parahippocampal cortex and retrosplenial cortex, also support spatial memory in humans. As we shall see, these include visual–spatial scene processing and survey representation.

Human Spatial Navigation: Role of the Parahippocampal Cortex in Spatial Processing

Several studies have suggested that some forms of spatial memory remain intact following hippocampal damage. This includes the ability of patients with hippocampus damage to find the location of a recently learned hidden object within a room (Bohbot et al., 1998) and to perform eye movements to the locations of recently learned spatial cues (Ploner et al., 2000). Along these lines, the classic patient H. M., one of the first studied patients with medial temporal lobe damage, did not show deficits in many aspects of spatial memory, including knowledge of the layout of his apartment (Bohbot & Corkin, 2007; Corkin, 2002). However, the posterior parts of H. M.'s hippocampus, which other studies have suggested might be important for spatial processing (Hartley, Maguire, Spiers, & Burgess, 2003), were largely intact (Corkin, Amaral, Gonzalez, Johnson, & Hyman, 1997). H. M., however, was deficient on learning new spatial routes, particularly storing and retrieving multiple new spatial routes, suggesting that the parts of his hippocampus that were damaged were at least relevant for some forms of spatial processing (Bohbot & Corkin, 2007).

Consistent with a role for extrahippocampal regions in spatial processing, several findings have suggested that the posterior parahippocampal cortex, an area in humans that receives strong input from visual areas (Witter, 2002), provides some "simple" allocentric processing of visual–spatial information (Bohbot & Corkin, 2007; Burgess, Maguire, & O'Keefe, 2002). Consistent with this argument, some of the same lesion studies cited earlier showed that patients with parahippocampal lesions[3] had profound deficits in the same spatial tasks on which patients with more exclusive hippocampal damage

---

[3]Because parahippocampal cortex is one of the major inputs into the hippocampus (via entorhinal cortex), these lesions may affect functionality in the hippocampus. It is also important to consider that lesions in humans are opportunistic—human lesions are produced for a reason other than the actual experiment being performed (usually due to stroke or surgical intervention, such as to treat seizures). Neither of these types of lesions can be expected to strictly obey anatomical boundaries. In most studies, though, including the ones cited earlier, authors typically demonstrate focal deficits on the basis of structural MRIs. These caveats about patient lesions studies are important to keep in mind; they argue for the importance of validating these findings using other testing modalities. In the case of parahippocampal cortex involvement in navigation, fMRI studies also argue for a role for this structure in spatial cognition.

did not show deficits (Bohbot et al., 1998; Habib & Sirigu, 1987; Ploner et al., 2000). Together, these data suggest a critical role for the parahippocampal cortex in spatial memory, particularly in visual–spatial processing.

Functional Magnetic Resonance Imaging Studies of Visual–Spatial Processing in the Medial Temporal Lobe

Although fMRI is based on an indirect measure of neural activity using the blood oxygen–level dependent (BOLD) signal (Ogawa & Lee, 1990), it remains one of the few techniques for observing neural activity in deep brain structures such as the hippocampus. However, fMRI is not a direct measure of neural activity, and its exact relation to underlying neural activity remains an area of active research (Logothetis, 2008). Several studies have suggested that the BOLD signal in the visual cortex and other neocortical areas, such as the parahippocampal cortex, reflect synaptic activity (Ekstrom, Suthana, Millett, Fried, & Bookheimer, 2009; Logothetis, 2008) similar to what might be observed with invasive electroencephalography (equivalent to the LFP in the rat). However, the exact relation between the BOLD signal and neural activity in the hippocampus remains unclear (Ekstrom, 2010). Even at the highest resolutions, it is unlikely that fMRI can provide a window into the activity of single neurons, particularly in areas such as the hippocampus that utilize sparse coding (Ekstrom et al., 2009; Logothetis, 2008). The fact that fMRI is unlikely to reflect the activity of single neurons in an area such as the hippocampus under most behavioral conditions puts obvious limitations on using fMRI as a means to measure things such as place cell activity. However, fMRI is also one of the few methods available that can be used with individuals free of any neurological impairment. Although invasive recordings and lesion studies provide direct information about a structure such as the hippocampus, they are limited to patients with clinical conditions such as epilepsy. Thus, although not a direct measure, assuming the appropriate caution, fMRI provides valuable evidence about the functions of areas such as the hippocampus and parahippocampal cortex during navigation. Because fMRI is a non-invasive tool and can thus be used routinely with healthy participants, its convergence with lesion and invasive studies is particularly informative to our current considerations.

Several fMRI studies have supported a role for the parahippocampal cortex in allocentric spatial scene processing. The parahippocampal cortex typically activates during scene processing and virtual navigation (Aguirre, Detre, Alsop, & D'Esposito, 1996; Ekstrom et al., 2009; Epstein, 2008; Epstein & Kanwisher, 1998) and shows less activation in participants who are blind who imagine navigating compared with sighted controls (Deutschländer et al., 2009). Committeri et al. (2004) further showed that when participants viewed two objects in a visual scene and made judgments about which of the two objects is closer to a third landmark, the parahippocampal cortex showed greater activation than when they made judgments about which object was located closer to them. Janzen and van Turennout (2004) demonstrated greater parahippocampal activation when participants viewed landmarks that they used to successfully locate targets, compared with viewing landmarks without navigational relevance to which they nonetheless attended. These findings then suggested that the parahippocampal cortex plays a role in simple scene processing, allocentric processing of visual–spatial information, and processing of landmarks during navigation.

Invasive Recordings in Humans Implicate the Hippocampus and Parahippocampal Cortex in Distinct Aspects of Spatial Navigation

Ekstrom et al. (2003) recorded directly from 317 neurons in the hippocampus, parahippocampal cortex, and other areas (frontal lobes and amygdala) of patients with epilepsy while they performed a virtual navigation experiment. In the task, patients freely explored a two-dimensional virtual environment, searching for passengers and delivering them to salient landmarks. Ekstrom et al. (2003) found cells in the hippocampus that responded robustly to spatial location (see Color Plate 6); these neurons did not show changes in firing rate for viewing landmarks. Many of these neurons also showed modulations according to the patient's goal, changing firing rate depending on the store that a patient searched for, reminiscent of findings in the rodent (Ainge, van der Meer, Langston, & Wood, 2007; Ferbinteanu & Shapiro, 2003). In addition to neurons responsive to spatial location, Ekstrom et al. (2003) also found cells that increased firing dependent on what landmark a participant viewed. These neurons were active from a variety of spatial positions, consistent with previous studies in the monkey that have also noted view-responsive neurons within the hippocampus and parahippocampal gyrus (Rolls & O'Mara, 1995). Together, these data support a possible division of labor within the hippocampus and parahippocampal cortex—whereas neurons in the human hippocampus increased firing rate at specific locations, neurons in the parahippocampal cortex increased firing rate during viewing landmarks.

A second study by Jacobs, Kahana, Ekstrom, Mollison, and Fried (2010) investigated patients with epilepsy undergoing seizure monitoring and found place responsive neurons in a virtual circular environment, replicating the findings of Ekstrom et al. (2003). Jacobs et al. found that these place-responsive neurons tended to be directionally tuned on the circular track such that they only fired when the patient navigated one way around the track and not the other, similar to findings in the rodent. Jacobs et al. also examined the firing rate of entorhinal neurons in the same task. They did not find evidence for grid-cell-like firing, instead reporting that entorhinal neurons increased firing nonspecifically for one direction around the circular track compared with another. One issue when considering whether this study provides evidence against grid cells in humans is that it is not currently clear where and whether the human homologue of medial entorhinal cortex exists (Doeller, Barry, & Burgess, 2010; Insausti, Tunon, Sobreviela, Insausti, & Gonzalo, 1995). Given the differences between lateral and medial entorhinal representations in rodents (reviewed earlier), the Jacobs et al. cells may have come from lateral entorhinal cortex. At this point, the only evidence for grid cells in humans comes from an fMRI study by Doeller et al. (2010), who found evidence for hexagonal spatial correlations in entorhinal BOLD activity.

BROADER ROLES FOR THE HIPPOCAMPUS

Our discussion of the possible role for the hippocampus in context-dependent spatial processing begs the question of a possible larger role for the hippocampus in episodic memory. Indeed, the first studies on the classic patient H. M. suggested that his greatest deficits were in learning and remembering new events (Scoville & Milner, 1957). This finding was confirmed by later studies showing that patients with hippocampal damage experience profound deficits in remembering locations and episodes compared with semantic memory abilities such as learning new facts about the world (Vargha-Khadem et al., 1997). In particular, hippocampal lesions appear to have the most significant effects when patients attempt to retrieve the associated context under which they learned specific items while leaving the ability to recognize a word intact (Diana, Yonelinas, & Ranganath, 2007; Holdstock, Mayes, Gong, Roberts, & Kapur, 2005; Yonelinas et al., 2002). Numerous fMRI studies have similarly supported a selective role for the hippocampus in episodic memory, particularly in storing and retrieving recently acquired information within specific spatial and/or temporal contexts (Ekstrom & Bookheimer, 2007; Eldridge, Engel, Zeineh, Bookheimer, & Knowlton, 2005; Rekkas et al., 2005; Staresina & Davachi, 2009). Invasive single neuron recording studies in patients with electrodes implanted in the hippocampus learning item–scene pairings demonstrate similar results (Viskontas, Knowlton, Steinmetz, & Fried, 2006). Together, these data argue for a more general hippocampal role in episodic memory, particularly in associating items with specific experimental contexts. Analogous data exist for the rat, in which hippocampal lesions have implications beyond simple spatial abilities, particularly in the association of stimuli with contextual representations and the ability to recall rather than simply recognize stimuli (Cohen & Eichenbaum, 1993; Eichenbaum, Yonelinas, & Ranganath, 2007; Redish, 1999).

Egocentric and Allocentric Representations as Forms of Episodic Memory

One possible way to integrate the findings on a general role for the human hippocampus in episodic memory with the place cell literature we have discussed so far is that spatial location represents a specialized case of episodic memory representation. As discussed earlier in the chapter, we can conceive of a sequence of place cells as a route or a list of items or objects. This idea would explain the involvement of the hippocampus in both route-based and context-dependent memory as a form of multiple maps. According to this conception, when the hippocampus integrates item or route information with contextual representations, slight changes in context will trigger different constellations of place cells based on different maps.

Successful navigation frequently involves computation of new routes and trajectories to a location on the basis of an interaction between the internally and externally driven navigation systems. This type of computation frequently involves a form of allocentric memory in which a participant must integrate internal coordinate systems with external landmarks to compute a new trajectory. An example of this type of computation would be something one might experience during driving. Having driven two different roads several times but never having explored a third road that connects the two, on the basis of the relative direction of the first two roads and locations of intersection of the third road, one can derive a means of connecting the two roads with the third road. We thus can assume, on the basis of our internal representation of the spatial layout and information provided by the intersection of the third road (visual updating), that it may provide a shortcut to our familiar road, although we have not driven it. This type of computation is, by its nature, flexible in that information must be utilized and computed in a novel fashion (Eichenbaum et al., 2007; Johnson, van der Meer, & Redish, 2007). A role for the hippocampus in flexible decision making can describe one possible way in which the hippocampus might be involved in egocentric and allocentric memory as well as episodic memory more generally.

Phase Precession, Future Thinking, and Episodic Memory

Armed with this theoretical framework for considering episodic memory, we can now begin to try to integrate ideas about rodent phase precession with human episodic memory. Although phase precession has yet to be demonstrated within the human hippocampus, intracranial field recordings from the human hippocampus demonstrate the presence of theta oscillations that increase with movement, much like what is seen in the rodent (Ekstrom et al., 2005). This finding suggests that at least two important components of phase precession, place cells and theta oscillations, are present in the human hippocampus, suggesting the strong possibility that phase precession is also present in the human hippocampus. A fascinating proposal relating to the function of phase precession generally in the rodent and human is the activation of specific sets of place cells to allow "sweeping" through possible sets of sequences of place cells for route planning (Jensen & Lisman, 1996; Johnson & Redish, 2007; Lisman & Redish, 2009). Thus, faced with an intersection, one could potentially envision several different routes on the basis of previous experience and choose the correct choice on the basis of one's navigational goal. Although the mechanisms in humans for this type of sequential place cell activation have yet to be explored and the evidence from rodents for the role of sequential place cell activation is as yet unknown, phase precession is an intriguing analogue that potentially relates to episodic future thinking. For example, just as one can imagine what one had for dinner last night, one can imagine what one might have for dinner tonight.

Intriguingly, constructing events in the future, referred to as *episodic future thinking,* may involve some of the same brain circuits as remembering past episodic memory (Buckner & Carroll, 2007). A superposition of the involved brain areas is practically indistinguishable. For example, similar areas (inferior parietal lobe, frontal cortex, hippocampus) frequently show activation during both retrieval of episodic events and prospective coding (Schacter & Addis, 2007). Furthermore, patients with hippocampal lesions show deficits in imagining and constructing future events (Hassabis, Kumaran, Vann, & Maguire, 2007). Thus, both humans and rats possess similar neural systems for past thinking and prospective coding. How networks of cells might participate in this process is an intriguing area of future research.

Well-Learned Routes and Semantic Memory

Although we have spent a significant amount of time discussing reactivation of sequences in rodents in this chapter, we have not devoted much time to this issue in humans. As yet, no single neuron recordings from humans have suggested that spiking patterns during sleep and quiet wakefulness may recapitulate those during wakefulness. The only significant hint so far in this direction comes from a study with patients with implanted depth electrodes who viewed videos of familiar, famous characters and then named the videos they saw during a subsequent retrieval task (Gelbard-Sagiv, Mukamel, Harel, Malach, & Fried, 2008). The pattern of neural firing rate showed significant correlations between encoding and retrieval that were specific to the video recollected. Several lines of behavioral and neuroimaging results also argue for the presence of mechanisms involved in consolidation of memories during sleep (Stickgold, Malia, Maguire, Roddenberry, & O'Connor, 2000; Takashima et al., 2006; Walker, 2009). Although evidence on these points is still developing, slow wave sleep likely provides one mechanism for consolidation of episodic memories, and rapid eye movement (REM) sleep likely provides a means for strengthening and consolidation of motor memories (Diekelmann & Born, 2010).

Although the details of reactivation and sleep-related consolidation remain to be fully worked out in humans, there is little doubt that episodic memories typically undergo a process of consolidation, possibly within hours and lasting years, into semantic memories (McClelland et al., 1995; Nadel & Moscovitch, 1997; Ribot, 1882/1977). Semantic memories refer to well-learned facts about the world that may have had an episodic component at some point but because of repetition, particularly across multiple contexts, have lost their unique episodic character. An interesting analogue exists between semantic memory and spatial navigation in that semantic memory may represent a form of well-learned routes that no longer require the hippocampus (Day, Weisend, Sutherland, & Schallert, 1999; Marr, 1971; Redish & Touretzky, 1998a; Tse et al., 2007). There is extensive evidence that when rats use schemas, they rely on cortical- rather than hippocampal-based mechanisms (Tse et al., 2007). Humans, similarly, likely utilize

multiple spatial forms of representation that do not require the hippocampus and may represent spatial layouts in some cases using a more rigid, schema-like form of navigation.

Human Extrahippocampal Representation: Survey Representation in Retrosplenial Cortex

In addition to the ability to represent first-person navigational information (a direct representation of visual information during navigation likely shared amongst most mammals including rodents), humans have the additional capacity to create pictorial maps of spatial environments (Thorndyke & Hayes-Roth, 1982). Humans typically create maps by picturing spatial information as if looking down on it (with a bird's eye view). Survey perspectives involve different cognitive strategies than first-person representations because they involve visualization of the relation between different objects and their relative locations directly rather than having to integrate this information across multiple viewpoints. One interesting proposal is that survey representation may be a special case of object representation. According to this conception, a spatial layout may be rendered as a single object with multiple textures that can be simultaneously viewed and manipulated through visual imagery (Shelton & Gabrieli, 2002; Thompson, Slotnick, Burrage, & Kosslyn, 2009). This idea also suggests that survey representation should share mechanisms in common with semantic memory because the operations occur on the basis of familiar layouts of objects and their axes (Shelton & Gabrieli, 2002). Survey representation likely derives largely from parietal and retrosplenial interactions, particularly those concerned with representation of objects within space (Galati, Pelle, Berthoz, & Committeri, 2010), rather than depending directly on the medial temporal lobes. It is an interesting question, whose answer is yet unknown, whether such survey-like representations also occur in rodents.

SUMMARY

In this chapter, we have explored spatial and non-spatial representations in the rodent and human hippocampus. Recordings from both rodents and humans show clear evidence of spatial representations in place cells, but both also include nonspatial representations as well. In the rodent, nonspatial information modulates the spatial—in particular, in the representation of maps and coordinate reference frames. It has been firmly established that the human hippocampus plays roles beyond navigation, particularly in remembering past episodes and planning future events. Experiments in rodents have suggested similar critical roles in episodic memory, and recent experiments analyzing representational sequences in the rodent hippocampus have suggested possible roles in planning future events as well.

SUGGESTED REFERENCES FOR FURTHER READING

Ekstrom, A. D., Kahana, M. J., Caplan, J. B., Fields, T. A., Isham, E. A., Newman, E. L. & Fried, I. (2003, September 11). Cellular networks underlying human spatial navigation. *Nature, 425,*184–188. doi:10.1038/nature01964

Direct evidence for spatial representations in human hippocampus taken from intrahippocampal recordings from epileptic patients.

Fenton, A. A., Lytton, W. W., Barry, J. M., Lenck-Santini, P.-P., Zinyuk, L. E., Kubík, . . . Olypher, A. V. (2010). Attention-like modulation of hippocampus place cell discharge. *The Journal of Neuroscience, 30,* 4613–4625. doi:10.1523/JNEUROSCI.5576-09.2010

Evidence that rats switch between multiple maps within single tasks, dependent on the attention paid to each map.

Hassabis, D., Kumaran, D., Vann, S. D., & Maguire, E. A. (2007). Patients with hippocampal amnesia cannot imagine new experiences. *Proceedings of the National Academy of Sciences of the United States of America, 104,* 1726–1731. doi:10.1073/pnas.0610561104

Patients with hippocampal damage are impaired at episodic future thinking.

O'Keefe, J., & Nadel, L. (1978). *The hippocampus as a cognitive map.* Oxford, England: Clarendon Press.

The initial argument that the hippocampus plays a central role in spatial navigation and the cognitive map.

Redish, A. D. (1999) *Beyond the cognitive map: From place cells to episodic memory.* Cambridge, MA: MIT Press.

An integration of the spatial and memory theories of hippocampal function.

References

Aguirre, G. K., Detre, J. A., Alsop, D. C., & D'Esposito, M. (1996). The parahippocampus subserves topographical learning in man. *Cerebral Cortex, 6,* 823–829. doi:10.1093/cercor/6.6.823

Ainge, J. A., van der Meer, M. A. A., Langston, R. F., & Wood, E. R. (2007). Exploring the role of context-dependent hippocampal activity in spatial alternation behavior. *Hippocampus, 17,* 988–1002. doi:10.1002/hipo.20301

Alvarez, P., & Squire, L. R. (1994). Memory consolidation and the medial temporal lobe: A simple network model. *Proceedings of the National Academy of Sciences of the United States of America, 91,* 7041–7045. doi:10.1073/pnas.91.15.7041

Alyan, S., & McNaughton, B. L. (1999). Hippocampectomized rats are capable of homing by path integration. *Behavioral Neuroscience, 113,* 19–31. doi:10.1037/0735-7044.113.1.19

Amaral, D., & Lavenex, P. (2007). Hippocampal neuroanatomy. In P. Andersen, R. Morris, D. Amaral, T. Bliss, & J. O'Keefe (Eds.), *The hippocampus book* (pp. 37–114). New York, NY: Oxford University Press.

Bannerman, D. M., Rawlins, J. N., McHugh, S. B., Deacon, R. M., Yee, B. K., Bast, T., . . . Feldon, J. (2004). Regional dissociations within the hippocampus—memory and anxiety. *Neuroscience and Biobehavioral Reviews, 28,* 273–283. doi:10.1016/j.neubiorev.2004.03.004

Barnes, C. A., Suster, M. S., Shen, J., & McNaughton, B. L. (1997, July 17). Multistability of cognitive maps in the hippocampus of old rats. *Nature, 388,* 272–275. doi:10.1038/40859

Battaglia, F. P., Sutherland, G. R., & McNaughton, B. L. (2004). Local sensory cues and place cell directionality: Additional evidence of prospective coding in the hippocampus. *The Journal of Neuroscience, 24,* 4541–4550. doi:10.1523/JNEUROSCI.4896-03.2004

Birke, L. I. A. (1983). Some issues and problems in the study of animal exploration. In J. Archer & L. I. A. Birke (Eds.), *Exploration in animals and humans* (pp. 1–21). Cambridge, England: Van Nostrand Reinhold.

Bohbot, V. D., & Corkin, S. (2007). Posterior parahippocampal place learning in H. M. *Hippocampus, 17,* 863–872. doi:10.1002/hipo.20313

Bohbot, V. D., Kalina, M., Stepankova, K., Spackova, N., Petrides, M., & Nadel, M. (1998). Spatial memory deficits in patients with lesions to the right hippocampus and to the right parahippocampal cortex. *Neuropsychologia, 36,* 1217–1238. doi:10.1016/S0028-3932(97)00161-9

Bohbot, V. D., Lerch, J., Thorndycraft, B., Iaria, G., & Zijdenbos, A. P. (2007). Gray matter differences correlate with spontaneous strategies in a human virtual navigation task. *The Journal of Neuroscience, 27*, 10078–10083. doi:10.1523/JNEUROSCI.1763-07.2007

Bragin, A., Jando, G., Nádasdy, Z., Hetke, J., Wise, K., & Buzsáki, G. (1995). Gamma (40–100 Hz) oscillation in the hippocampus of the behaving rat. *The Journal of Neuroscience, 15*, 47–60.

Buckner, R. L., & Carroll, D. C. (2007). Self-projection and the brain. *Trends in Cognitive Sciences, 11*, 49–57. doi:10.1016/j.tics.2006.11.004

Burak, Y., & Fiete, I. R. (2009). Accurate path integration in continuous attractor network models of grid cells. *PLoS Computational Biology, 5*(2). doi:10.1371/journal.pcbi.1000291

Burgess, N., Maguire, E. A., & O'Keefe, J. (2002). The human hippocampus and spatial and episodic memory. *Neuron, 35*, 625–641. doi:10.1016/S0896-6273(02)00830-9

Buzsáki, G. (1989). Two-stage model of memory trace formation: A role for "noisy" brain states. *Neuroscience, 31*, 551–570. doi:10.1016/0306-4522(89)90423-5

Buzsáki, G. (2006) *Rhythms of the brain*. New York, NY: Oxford University Press.

Buzsáki, G., Leung, L. W., & Vanderwolf, C. H. (1983). Cellular bases of hippocampal EEG in the behaving rat. *Brain Research, 287*, 139–171.

Cohen, N. J., & Eichenbaum, H. (1993). *Memory, amnesia, and the hippocampal system*. Cambridge, MA: MIT Press.

Colgin, L. L., Leutgeb, S., Jezek, K., Leutgeb, J. K., Moser, E. I., McNaughton, B. L., & Moser, M.-B. (2010). Attractor-map versus autoassociation based attractor dynamics in the hippocampal network. *Journal of Neurophysiology, 104*, 35–50. doi:10.1152/jn.00202.2010

Committeri, G., Galati, G., Paradis, A. L., Pizzamiglio, L., Berthoz, A., & LeBihan, D. (2004). Reference frames for spatial cognition: Different brain areas are involved in viewer-, object-, and landmark-centered judgments about object location. *Journal of Cognitive Neuroscience, 16*, 1517–1535. doi:10.1162/0898929042568550

Conklin, J., & Eliasmith, C. (2005). A controlled attractor network model of path integration in the rat. *Journal of Computational Neuroscience, 18*, 183–203. doi:10.1007/s10827-005-6558-z

Corkin, S. (2002). What's new with the amnesic patient H. M.? *Nature Reviews Neuroscience, 3*, 153–160. doi:10.1038/nrn726

Corkin, S., Amaral, D. G., Gonzalez, R. G., Johnson, K. A., & Hyman, B. T. (1997). H. M.'s medial temporal lobe lesion: Findings from magnetic resonance imaging. *The Journal of Neuroscience, 17*, 3964–3979.

Davidson, T. J., Kloosterman, F., & Wilson, M. A. (2009). Hippocampal replay of extended experience. *Neuron, 63*, 497–507. doi:10.1016/j.neuron.2009.07.027

Day, L. B., Weisend, M., Sutherland, R. J., & Schallert, T. (1999). The hippocampus is not necessary for a place response but may be necessary for pliancy. *Behavioral Neuroscience, 113*, 914–924. doi:10.1037/0735-7044.113.5.914

Deutschländer, A., Stephan, T., Hufner, K., Wagner, J., Wiesmann, M., Strupp, M., . . . Jahn, K. (2009). Imagined locomotion in the blind: An fMRI study. *NeuroImage, 45*, 122–128. doi:10.1016/j.neuroimage.2008.11.029

Diana, R. A., Yonelinas, A. P., & Ranganath, C. (2007). Imaging recollection and familiarity in the medial temporal lobe: A three-component model. *Trends in Cognitive Sciences, 11*, 379–386. doi:10.1016/j.tics.2007.08.001

Diekelmann, S., & Born, J. (2010). The memory function of sleep. *Nature Reviews Neuroscience, 11*, 114–126.

Doeller, C. F., Barry, C., & Burgess, N. (2010, February 4). Evidence for grid cells in a human memory network. *Nature, 463*, 657–661. doi:10.1038/nature08704

Drai, D., & Golani, I. (2001). SEE: A tool for the visualization and analysis of rodent exploratory behavior. *Neuroscience and Biobehavioral Reviews, 25*, 409–426. doi:10.1016/S0149-7634(01)00022-7

Ego-Stengel, V., & Wilson, M. A. (2010). Disruption of ripple-associated hippocampal activity during rest impairs spatial learning in the rat. *Hippocampus, 20*, 1–10.

Eichenbaum, H., Kuperstein, M., Fagan, A., & Nagode, J. (1987). Cue-sampling and goal- approach correlates of hippocampal unit activity in rats performing an odor-discrimination task. *The Journal of Neuroscience, 7*, 716–732.

Eichenbaum, H., Yonelinas, A. P., & Ranganath, C. (2007). The medial temporal lobe and recognition memory. *Annual Review of Neuroscience, 30*, 123–152. doi:10.1146/annurev.neuro.30.051606.094328

Ekstrom, A. (2010). How and when the fMRI BOLD signal relates to underlying neural activity: The danger in dissociation. *Brain Research Reviews, 62*, 233–244. doi:10.1016/j.brainresrev.2009.12.004

Ekstrom, A. D., & Bookheimer, S. Y. (2007). Spatial and temporal episodic memory retrieval recruit dissociable functional networks in the human brain. *Learning & Memory, 14*, 645–654. doi:10.1101/lm.575107

Ekstrom, A. D., Caplan, J. B., Ho, E., Shattuck, K., Fried, I., & Kahana, M. J. (2005). Human hippocampal theta activity during virtual navigation. *Hippocampus, 15,* 881–889. doi:10.1002/hipo.20109

Ekstrom, A. D., Kahana, M. J., Caplan, J. B., Fields, T. A., Isham, E. A., Newman, E. L., & Fried, I. (2003, September 11). Cellular networks underlying human spatial navigation. *Nature, 425,* 184–188. doi:10.1038/nature01964

Ekstrom, A., Suthana, N., Millett, D., Fried, I., & Bookheimer, S. (2009). Correlation between BOLD fMRI and theta-band local field potentials in the human hippocampal area. *Journal of Neurophysiology, 101,* 2668–2678. doi:10.1152/jn.91252.2008

Eldridge, L. L., Engel, S. A., Zeineh, M. M., Bookheimer, S. Y., & Knowlton, B. J. (2005). A dissociation of encoding and retrieval processes in the human hippocampus. *The Journal of Neuroscience, 25,* 3280–3286. doi:10.1523/JNEUROSCI.3420-04.2005

Epstein, R. A. (2008). Parahippocampal and retrosplenial contributions to human spatial navigation. *Trends in Cognitive Sciences, 12,* 388–396. doi:10.1016/j.tics.2008.07.004

Epstein, R., & Kanwisher, N. (1998, April 4). A cortical representation of the local visual environment. *Nature, 392,* 598–601. doi:10.1038/33402

Euston, D. R., Tatsuno, M., & McNaughton, B. L. (2007, November 16). Fast-forward playback of recent memory sequences in prefrontal cortex during sleep. *Science, 318,* 1147–1150. doi:10.1126/science.1148979

Fenton, A. A., & Muller, R. U. (1998). Place cell discharge is extremely variable during individual passes of the rat through the firing field. *Proceedings of the National Academy of Sciences of the United States of America, 95,* 3182–3187. doi:10.1073/pnas.95.6.3182

Ferbinteanu, J., & Shapiro, M. L. (2003). Prospective and retrospective memory coding in the hippocampus. *Neuron, 40,* 1227–1239. doi:10.1016/S0896-6273(03)00752-9

Fiete, I. R., Burak, Y., & Brookings, T. (2008). What grid cells convey about rat location. *The Journal of Neuroscience, 28,* 6858–6871. doi:10.1523/JNEUROSCI.5684-07.2008

Foster, D. J., & Wilson, M. A. (2006, March 30). Reverse replay of behavioural sequences in hippocampal place cells during the awake state. *Nature, 440,* 680–683. doi:10.1038/nature04587

Frank, L. M., Stanley, G. B., & Brown, E. N. (2004). Hippocampal plasticity across multiple days of exposure to novel environments. *The Journal of Neuroscience, 24,* 7681–7689. doi:10.1523/JNEUROSCI.1958-04.2004

Fuhs, M. C., VanRhoads, S. R., Casale, A. E., McNaughton, B., & Touretzky, D. S. (2005). Influence of path integration versus environmental orientation on place cell remapping between visually identical environments. *Journal of Neurophysiology, 94,* 2603–2616. doi:10.1152/jn.00132.2005

Furtak, S. C., Wei, S.-M., Agster, K. L., & Burwell, R. D. (2007). Functional neuroanatomy of the parahippocampal region in the rat: The perirhinal and postrhinal cortices. *Hippocampus, 17,* 709–722. doi:10.1002/hipo.20314

Fyhn, M., Hafting, T., Treves, A., Moser, M.-B., & Moser, E. I. (2007, March 8). Hippocampal remapping and grid realignment in entorhinal cortex. *Nature, 446,* 190–194. doi:10.1038/nature05601

Fyhn, M., Molden, S., Witter, M. P., Moser, E. I., & Moser, M.-B. (2004, August 27). Spatial representation in the entorhinal cortex. *Science, 305,* 1258–1264. doi:10.1126/science.1099901

Galati, G., Pelle, G., Berthoz, A., & Committeri, G. (2010). Multiple reference frames used by the human brain for spatial perception and memory. *Experimental Brain Research, 206,* 109–120.

Gallistel, C. R. (1990). *The organization of learning.* Cambridge, MA: MIT Press.

Gelbard-Sagiv, H., Mukamel, R., Harel, M., Malach, R., & Fried, I. (2008, October 3). Internally generated reactivation of single neurons in human hippocampus during free recall. *Science, 322,* 96–101. doi:10.1126/science.1164685

Gilbert, P. E., Kesner, R. P., & Lee, I. (2001). Dissociating hippocampal subregions: A double dissociation between dentate gyrus and CA1. *Hippocampus, 11,* 626–636. doi:10.1002/hipo.1077

Girardeau, G., Benchenane, K., Wiener, S. I., Buzsáki, G., & Zugaro, M. B. (2009). Selective suppression of hippocampal ripples impairs spatial memory. *Nature Neuroscience, 12,* 1222–1223. doi:10.1038/nn.2384

Goodrich-Hunsaker, N. J., Livingstone, S. A., Skelton, R. W., & Hopkins, R. O. (2010). Spatial deficits in a virtual water maze in amnesic participants with hippocampal damage. *Hippocampus, 20,* 481–491.

Gothard, K. M., Hoffman, K. L., Battaglia, F. P., & McNaughton, B. L. (2001). Dentate gyrus and CA1 ensemble activity during spatial reference frame shifts in the presence and absence of visual input. *The Journal of Neuroscience, 21,* 7284–7292.

Gothard, K. M., Skaggs, W. E., & McNaughton, B. L. (1996). Dynamics of mismatch correction in the hippocampal ensemble code for space: Interaction between path integration and environmental cues. *The Journal of Neuroscience, 16,* 8027–8040.

Gupta, A. S., van der Meer, M. A. A., Touretzky, D. S., & Redish, A. D. (2010). Hippocampal replay is not a simple function of experience. *Neuron, 65,* 695–705. doi:10.1016/j.neuron.2010.01.034

Guzowski, J. F., McNaughton, B. L., Barnes, C. A., & Worley, P. F. (1999). Environment-specific expression of the immediate-early gene ARC in hippocampal neuronal ensembles. *Nature Neuroscience, 2,* 1120–1124. doi:10.1038/16046

Habib, M., & Sirigu, A. (1987). Pure topographical disorientation: a definition and anatomical basis. *Cortex, 23,* 73–85.

Hafting, T., Fyhn, M., Molden, S., Moser, M.-B., & Moser, E. (2005, August 11). Microstructure of a spatial map in the entorhinal cortex. *Nature, 436,* 801–806. doi:10.1038/nature03721

Hargreaves, E. L., Rao, G., Lee, I., & Knierim, J. J. (2005, June 17). Major dissociation between medial and lateral entorhinal input to dorsal hippocampus. *Science, 308,* 1792–1794. doi:10.1126/science.1110449

Hartley, T., Bird, C. M., Chan, D., Cipolotti, L., Husain, M., Vargha-Khadem, F., & Burgess, N. (2007). The hippocampus is required for short-term topographical memory in humans. *Hippocampus, 17,* 34–48. doi:10.1002/hipo.20240

Hartley, T., Maguire, E. A., Spiers, H. J., & Burgess, N. (2003). The well-worn route and the path less traveled: Distinct neural bases of route following and wayfinding in humans. *Neuron, 37,* 877–888. doi:10.1016/S0896-6273(03)00095-3

Hassabis, D., Kumaran, D., Vann, S. D., & Maguire, E. A. (2007). Patients with hippocampal amnesia cannot imagine new experiences. *Proceedings of the National Academy of Sciences of the United States of America, 104,* 1726–1731. doi:10.1073/pnas.0610561104

Hasselmo, M. E., & Bower, J. M. (1993). Acetylcholine and memory. *Trends in Neurosciences, 16,* 218–222. doi:10.1016/0166-2236(93)90159-J

Hebb, D. O. (2002). *The organization of behavior.* New York, NY: Wiley. (Original work published 1949)

Henriksen, E. J., Colgin, L. L., Barnes, C. A., Witter, M. P., Moser, M.-B., & Moser, E. I. (2010). Spatial representation along the proximodistal axis of CA1. *Neuron, 68,* 127–137. doi:10.1016/j.neuron.2010.08.042

Hertz, J., Krogh, A., & Palmer, R. G. (1991). *Introduction to the theory of neural computation.* Reading, MA: Addison Wesley.

Hirase, H., Czurkó, A., Csicsvari, J., & Buzsáki, G. (1999). Firing rate and theta-phase coding by hippocampal pyramidal neurons during 'space clamping.' *European Journal of Neuroscience, 11,* 4373–4380. doi:10.1046/j.1460-9568.1999.00853.x

Hoffman, K. L., & McNaughton, B. L. (2002, September 20). Coordinated reactivation of distributed memory traces in primate neocortex. *Science, 297,* 2070–2073. doi:10.1126/science.1073538

Holdstock, J. S., Mayes, A. R., Gong, Q. Y., Roberts, N., & Kapur, N. (2005). Item recognition is less impaired than recall and associative recognition in a patient with selective hippocampal damage. *Hippocampus, 15,* 203–215. doi:10.1002/hipo.20046

Huxter, J. R., Senior, T. J., Allen, K., & Csicsvari, J. (2008). Theta phase-specific codes for two- dimensional position, trajectory and heading in the hippocampus. *Nature Neuroscience, 11,* 587–594. doi:10.1038/nn.2106

Insausti, R., Tunon, T., Sobreviela, T., Insausti, A. M., & Gonzalo, L. M. (1995). The human entorhinal cortex: A cytoarchitectonic analysis. *The Journal of Comparative Neurology, 355,* 171–198. doi:10.1002/cne.903550203

Jackson, J. C., Johnson, A., & Redish, A. D. (2006). Hippocampal sharp waves and reactivation during awake states depend on repeated sequential experience. *The Journal of Neuroscience, 26,* 12415–12426. doi:10.1523/JNEUROSCI.4118-06.2006

Jackson, J., & Redish, A. D. (2007). Network dynamics of hippocampal cell-assemblies resemble multiple spatial maps within single tasks. *Hippocampus, 17,* 1209–1229. doi:10.1002/hipo.20359

Jacobs, J., Kahana, M. J., Ekstrom, A. D., Mollison, M. V., & Fried, I. (2010). A sense of direction in human entorhinal cortex. *Proceedings of the National Academy of Sciences of the United States of America, 107,* 6487–6492. doi:10.1073/pnas.0911213107

Janzen, G., & van Turennout, M. (2004). Selective neural representation of objects relevant for navigation. *Nature Neuroscience, 7,* 673–677. doi:10.1038/nn1257

Jensen, O., & Lisman, E. (1996). Hippocampal CA3 region predicts memory sequences: Accounting for the phase precession of place cells. *Learning & Memory, 3,* 279–287. doi:10.1101/lm.3.2-3.279

Jensen, O., & Lisman, J. E. (2000). Position reconstruction from an ensemble of hippocampal place cells: Contribution of theta phase encoding. *Journal of Neurophysiology, 83,* 2602–2609.

Ji, D., & Wilson, M. A. (2007). Coordinated memory replay in the visual cortex and hippocampus during sleep. *Nature Neuroscience, 10,* 100–107. doi:10.1038/nn1825

Johnson, A., & Redish, A. D. (2007). Neural ensembles in CA3 transiently encode paths forward of the animal at a decision point. *The Journal of Neuroscience, 27,* 12176–12189. doi:10.1523/JNEUROSCI.3761-07.2007

Johnson, A., van der Meer, M. A. A., & Redish, A. D. (2007). Integrating hippocampus and striatum in decision-making. *Current Opinion in Neurobiology, 17,* 692–697. doi:10.1016/j.conb.2008.01.003

Jung, M. W., & McNaughton, B. L. (1993). Spatial selectivity of unit activity in the hippocampal granular layer. *Hippocampus, 3,* 165–182. doi:10.1002/hipo.450030209

Jung, M. W., Wiener, S. I., & McNaughton, B. L. (1994). Comparison of spatial firing characteristics of the dorsal and ventral hippocampus of the rat. *The Journal of Neuroscience, 14,* 7347–7356.

Karlsson, M. P., & Frank, L. M. (2009). Awake replay of remote experiences in the hippocampus. *Nature Neuroscience, 12,* 913–918. doi:10.1038/nn.2344

Katzner, S., Nauhaus, I., Benucci, A., Bonin, V., Ringach, D. L., & Carandini, M. (2009). Local origin of field potentials in visual cortex. *Neuron, 61,* 35–41. doi:10.1016/j.neuron.2008.11.016

Kelemen, E., & Fenton, A. A. (2010). Dynamic grouping of hippocampal neural activity during cognitive control of two spatial frames. *PLoS Biology, 8*(6). doi:10.1371/journal.pbio.1000403

Kentros, C., Hargreaves, E., Hawkins, R. D., Kandel, E. R., Shapiro, M., & Muller, R. V. (1998, June 26). Abolition of long-term stability of new hippocampal place cell maps by NMDA receptor blockade. *Science, 280,* 2121–2126. doi:10.1126/science.280.5372.2121

King, J. A., Burgess, N., Hartley, T., Vargha-Khadem, F., & O'Keefe, J. (2002). Human hippocampus and viewpoint dependence in spatial memory. *Hippocampus, 12,* 811–820. doi:10.1002/hipo.10070

Kjelstrup, K. B., Solstad, T., Brun, V. H., Hafting, T., Leutgeb, S., Witter, M. P., . . . Moser, M.-B. (2008, July). Finite scale of spatial representation in the hippocampus. *Science, 321,* 140–143. doi:10.1126/science.1157086

Knierim, J. J., Kudrimoti, H. S., & McNaughton, B. L. (1995). Place cells, head direction cells, and the learning of landmark stability. *The Journal of Neuroscience, 15,* 1648–1659.

Knierim, J. J., Kudrimoti, H. S., & McNaughton, B. L. (1998). Interactions between idiothetic cues and external landmarks in the control of place cells and head direction cells. *Journal of Neurophysiology, 80,* 425–446.

Kudrimoti, H. S., Barnes, C. A., & McNaughton, B. L. (1999). Reactivation of hippocampal cell assemblies: Effects of behavioral state, experience, and EEG dynamics. *The Journal of Neuroscience, 19,* 4090–4101.

Lansink, C. S., Goltstein, P. M., Lankelma, J. V., Joosten, R. N. J. M. A., McNaughton, B. L., & Pennartz, C. M. A. (2008). Preferential Reactivation of Motivationally Relevant Information in the Ventral Striatum.

The Journal of Neuroscience, 28, 6372–6382. doi:10.1523/JNEUROSCI.1054-08.2008

Leutgeb, J. K., Leutgeb, S., Moser, & M.-B., Moser, E. I. (2007, February 16). Pattern separation in the dentate gyrus and CA3 of the hippocampus. *Science, 315,* 961–966. doi:10.1126/science.1135801

Lisman, J., & Redish, A. D. (2009). Prediction, sequences and the hippocampus. *Philosophical Transactions of the Royal Society B: Biological Sciences, 364*(1521),1193–1201.

Logothetis, N. K. (2008, June 12). What we can do and what we cannot do with fMRI. *Nature, 453,* 869–878. doi:10.1038/nature06976

Maaswinkel, H., Jarrard, L. E., & Whishaw, I. Q. (1999). Hippocampectomized rats are impaired in homing by path integration. *Hippocampus, 9,* 553–561. doi:10.1002/(SICI)1098-1063(1999)9:5<553::AID-HIPO9>3.0.CO;2-G

Manns, J. R., & Eichenbaum, H. (2006). Evolution of declarative memory. *Hippocampus, 16,* 795–808. doi:10.1002/hipo.20205

Markus, E. J., Barnes, C. A., McNaughton, B. L., Gladden, V. L., & Skaggs, W. E. (1994). Spatial information content and reliability of hippocampal CA1 neurons: Effects of visual input. *Hippocampus, 4,* 410–421. doi:10.1002/hipo.450040404

Markus, E. J., Qin, Y., Leonard, B., Skaggs, W. E., McNaughton, B. L., & Barnes, C. A. (1995). Interactions between location and task affect the spatial and directional firing of hippocampal neurons. *The Journal of Neuroscience, 15,* 7079–7094.

Marr, D. (1971). Simple memory: A theory of archicortex. *Philosophical Transactions of the Royal Society B: Biological Sciences, 262*(841), 23–81. doi:10.1098/rstb.1971.0078

Maurer, A. P., Vanrhoads, S. R., Sutherland, G. R., Lipa, P., & McNaughton, B. L. (2005). Self-motion and the origin of differential spatial scaling along the septo-temporal axis of the hippocampus. *Hippocampus, 15,* 841–852. doi:10.1002/hipo.20114

McClelland, J. L., McNaughton, B. L., & O'Reilly, R. C. (1995). Why there are complementary learning systems in the hippocampus and neocortex: Insights from the successes and failures of connectionist models of learning and memory. *Psychological Review, 102,* 419–457. doi:10.1037/0033-295X.102.3.419

McHugh, T. J., Jones, M. W., Quinn, J. J., Balthasar, N., Coppari, R., Elmquist, J. K., . . . Tonegawa, S. (2007, July 6). Dentate gyrus nmda receptors mediate rapid pattern separation in the hippocampal network. *Science, 317,* 94–99. doi:10.1126/science.1140263

McNaughton, B. L., Barnes, C. A., Meltzer, J., & Sutherland, R. J. (1989). Hippocampal granule cells are necessary for normal spatial learning but not for spatially-selective pyramidal cell discharge. *Experimental Brain Research, 76,* 485–496. doi:10.1007/BF00248904

McNaughton, B. L., & Morris, R. G. M. (1987). Hippocampal synaptic enhancement and information storage within a distributed memory system. *Trends in Neurosciences, 10,* 408–415. doi:10.1016/0166-2236(87)90011-7

Mizumori, S. J. Y., McNaughton, B. L., Barnes, C. A., & Fox, K. B. (1989). Preserved spatial coding hippocampus CA1 pyramidal cells during reversible suppression in CA3c output: Evidence for pattern completion in hippocampus. *The Journal of Neuroscience, 9,* 3915–3928.

Moita, M. A., Rosis, S., Zhou, Y., LeDoux, J. E., & Blair, H. T. (2004). Putting fear in its place: Remapping of hippocampal place cells during fear conditioning. *The Journal of Neuroscience, 24,* 7015–7023. doi:10.1523/JNEUROSCI.5492-03.2004

Müller, M., & Wehner, R. (1988). Path integration in desert ants, cataglyphis fortis. *Proceedings of the National Academy of Sciences of the United States of America, 85,* 5287–5290. doi:10.1073/pnas.85.14.5287

Muller, R. U., Bostock, E., Taube, J. S., & Kubie, J. L. (1994). On the directional firing properties of hippocampal place cells. *The Journal of Neuroscience, 14,* 7235–7251.

Muller, R. U., & Kubie, J. L. (1987). The effects of changes in the environment on the spatial firing of hippocampal complex-spike cells. *The Journal of Neuroscience, 7,* 1951–1968.

Nádasdy, Z., Hirase, H., Czurkó, A., Csicsvari, J., & Buzsáki, G. (1999). Replay and time compression of recurring spike sequences in the hippocampus. *The Journal of Neuroscience, 19,* 9497–9507.

Nadel, L., & Moscovitch, M. (1997). Memory consolidation, retrograde amnesia and the hippocampal complex. *Current Opinion in Neurobiology, 7,* 217–227. doi:10.1016/S0959-4388(97)80010-4

Nakazawa, K., Quirk, M. C., Chitwood, R. A., Watanabe, M., Yeckel, M. F., Sun, L. D., . . . Tonegawa, S. (2002, May 30). Requirement for hippocampal CA3 NMDA receptors in associative memory recall. *Science, 297,* 211–218. doi:10.1126/science.1071795

Ogawa, S., & Lee, T. M. (1990). Magnetic resonance imaging of blood vessels at high fields: in vivo and in vitro measurements and image simulation. *Magnetic Resonance in Medicine, 16,* 9–18. doi:10.1002/mrm.1910160103

O'Keefe, J., & Conway, D. H. (1978). Hippocampal place units in the freely moving rat: Why they fire where they fire. *Experimental Brain Research, 31,* 573–590.

O'Keefe, J., & Dostrovsky, J. (1971). The hippocampus as a spatial map. Preliminary evidence from unit activity in the freely moving rat. *Brain Research, 34,* 171–175. doi:10.1016/0006-8993(71)90358-1

O'Keefe, J., & Nadel, L. (1978). *The hippocampus as a cognitive map.* Oxford, England: Clarendon Press.

O'Keefe, J., & Recce, M. (1993). Phase relationship between hippocampal place units and the EEG theta rhythm. *Hippocampus, 3,* 317–330. doi:10.1002/hipo.450030307

Olypher, A. V., Lansky, P., & Fenton, A. A. (2002). Properties of the extra-positional signal in hippocampal place cell discharge derived from the over-dispersion in location-specific firing. *Neuroscience, 111,* 553–566. doi:10.1016/S0306-4522(01)00586-3

O'Neill, J., Senior, T., & Csicsvari, J. (2006). Place-selective firing of ca1 pyramidal cells during sharp wave/ripple network patterns in exploratory behavior. *Neuron, 49,* 143–155. doi:10.1016/j.neuron.2005.10.037

Pastalkova, E., Itskov, V., Amarasingham, A., & Buzsáki, G. (2008, September 5). Internally generated cell assembly sequences in the rat hippocampus. *Science, 321,* 1322–1327. doi:10.1126/science.1159775

Pico, R. M., Gerbrandt, L. K., Pondel, M., & Ivy, G. (1985). During stepwise cue deletion, rat place behaviors correlate with place unit responses. *Brain Research, 330,* 369–372. doi:10.1016/0006-8993(85)90700-0

Ploner, C. J., Gaymard, B. M., Rivaud-Pechoux, S., Baulac, M., Clemenceau, S., Samson, S., & Pierrot-Deseilligny, C. (2000). Lesions affecting the para-hippocampal cortex yield spatial memory deficits in humans. *Cerebral Cortex, 10,* 1211–1216. doi:10.1093/cercor/10.12.1211

Quirk, G. J., Muller, R. U., Kubie, J. L., & Ranck, J. B., Jr. (1992). The positional firing properties of medial entorhinal neurons: Description and comparison with hippocampal place cells. *The Journal of Neuroscience, 12,* 1945–1963.

Redish, A. D. (1999). *Beyond the cognitive map: From place cells to episodic memory.* Cambridge, MA: MIT Press.

Redish, A. D., Rosenzweig, E. S., Bohanick, J. D., McNaughton, B. L., & Barnes, C. A. (2000). Dynamics of hippocampal ensemble realignment: Time vs. space. *The Journal of Neuroscience, 20,* 9289–9309.

Redish, A. D., & Touretzky, D. S. (1997). Cognitive maps beyond the hippocampus. *Hippocampus, 7,* 15–35. doi:10.1002/(SICI)1098-1063(1997)7:1<15::AID-HIPO3>3.0.CO;2-6

Redish, A. D., & Touretzky, D. S. (1998a). The role of the hippocampus in solving the Morris water maze. *Neural Computation, 10,* 73–111. doi:10.1162/089976698300017908

Redish, A. D., & Touretzky, D. S. (1998b). Separating hippocampal maps. In N. Burgess, K. Jeffery, & J. O'Keefe (Eds.), *Spatial functions of the hippocampal formation and the parietal cortex* (pp. 203–219). New York, NY: Oxford University Press.

Rekkas, P. V., Westerveld, M., Skudlarski, P., Zumer, J., Pugh, K., Spencer, D. D., & Constable, R. T. (2005). Neural correlates of temporal-order judgments versus those of spatial-location: Deactivation of hippocampus may facilitate spatial performance. *Brain and Cognition, 59,* 103–113. doi:10.1016/j.bandc.2005.05.013

Ribot, T. A. (1977). Diseases of memory. In D. N. Robinson (Ed.), *Significant contributions to the history of psychology, 1759–1920, Series C: Medical psychology* (Vol. 1). Washington, DC: University Publications of America. (Original work published 1882)

Robbe, D., & Buzsáki, G. (2009). Alteration of theta timescale dynamics of hippocampal place cells by a cannabinoid is associated with memory impairment. *The Journal of Neuroscience, 29,* 12597–12605. doi:10.1523/JNEUROSCI.2407-09.2009

Rolls, E. T., & O'Mara, S. M. (1995). View responsive neurons in the primate hippocampal complex. *Hippocampus, 5,* 409–424. doi:10.1002/hipo.450050504

Rosenzweig, E. S., Redish, A. D., McNaughton, B. L., & Barnes, C. A. (2003). Hippocampal map realignment and spatial learning. *Nature Neuroscience, 6,* 609–615. doi:10.1038/nn1053

Royer, S., Sirota, A., Patel, J., & Buzsáki, G. (2010). Distinct representations and theta dynamics in dorsal and ventral hippocampus. *The Journal of Neuroscience, 30,* 1777–1787. doi:10.1523/JNEUROSCI.4681-09.2010

Samsonovich, A. V., & McNaughton, B. L. (1997). Path integration and cognitive mapping in a continuous attractor neural network model. *The Journal of Neuroscience, 17,* 5900–5920.

Schacter, D. L., & Addis, D. R. (2007). The cognitive neuroscience of constructive memory: Remembering the past and imagining the future. *Philosophical Transactions of the Royal Society B: Biological Sciences, 362*(1481), 773–786. doi:10.1098/rstb.2007.2087

Scoville, W. B., & Milner, B. (1957). Loss of recent memory after bilateral hippocampal lesions. *Journal of Neurology, Neurosurgery & Psychiatry, 20,* 11–21. doi:10.1136/jnnp.20.1.11

Shelton, A. L., & Gabrieli, J. D. (2002). Neural correlates of encoding space from route and survey perspectives. *The Journal of Neuroscience, 22,* 2711–2717.

Skaggs, W. E., & McNaughton, B. L. (1996, March 29). Replay of neuronal firing sequences in rat hippocampus during sleep following spatial experience. *Science, 271,* 1870–1873. doi:10.1126/science.271.5257.1870

Skaggs, W. E., & McNaughton, B. L. (1998). Spatial firing properties of hippocampal CA1 populations in an environment containing two visually identical regions. *The Journal of Neuroscience, 18,* 8455–8466.

Skaggs, W. E., McNaughton, B. L., Wilson, M. A., & Barnes, C. A. (1996). Theta phase precession in hippocampal neuronal populations and the compression of temporal sequences. *Hippocampus, 6,* 149–172. doi:10.1002/(SICI)1098-1063(1996)6:2<149::AID-HIPO6>3.0.CO;2-K

Spiers, H. J., Burgess, N., Maguire, E. A., Baxendale, S. A., Hartley, T., Thompson, P. J., & O'Keefe, J. (2001). Unilateral temporal lobectomy patients show lateralized topographical and episodic memory deficits in a virtual town. *Brain: A Journal of Neurology, 124,* 2476–2489. doi:10.1093/brain/124.12.2476

Staresina, B. P., & Davachi, L. (2009). Mind the gap: Binding experiences across space and time in the human hippocampus. *Neuron, 63,* 267–276. doi:10.1016/j.neuron.2009.06.024

Stickgold, R., Malia, A., Maguire, D., Roddenberry, D., & O'Connor, M. (2000, October 13). Replaying the game: Hypnagogic images in normals and amnesics. *Science, 290,* 350–353. doi:10.1126/science.290.5490.350

Sutherland, G. R., & McNaughton, B. L. (2000). Memory trace reactivation in hippocampal and neocortical neuronal ensembles. *Current Opinion in Neurobiology, 10,* 180–186. doi:10.1016/S0959-4388(00)00079-9

Takashima, A., Petersson, K. M., Rutters, F., Tendolkar, I., Jensen, O., Zwarts, M. J., . . . Fernandez, G. (2006). Declarative memory consolidation in humans: A prospective functional magnetic resonance imaging study. *Proceedings of the National Academy of Sciences of the United States of America, 103,* 756–761. doi:10.1073/pnas.0507774103

Taube, J. S. (2007). The head direction signal: Origins and sensory-motor integration. *Annual Review of Neuroscience, 30,* 181–207. doi:10.1146/annurev.neuro.29.051605.112854

Teyler, T. J., & DiScenna, P. (1985). The role of hippocampus in memory: A hypothesis. *Neuroscience and Biobehavioral Reviews, 9,* 377–389. doi:10.1016/0149-7634(85)90016-8

Thompson, W. L., Slotnick, S. D., Burrage, M. S., & Kosslyn, S. M. (2009). Two forms of spatial imagery: Neuroimaging evidence. *Psychological Science, 20,* 1245–1253. doi:10.1111/j.1467-9280.2009.02440.x

Thorndyke, P. W., & Hayes-Roth, B. (1982). Differences in spatial knowledge acquired from maps and navigation. *Cognitive Psychology, 14,* 560–589. doi:10.1016/0010-0285(82)90019-6

Tse, D., Langston, R. F., Kakeyama, M., Bethus, I., Spooner, P. A., Wood, E. R., . . . Morris, R. G. M. (2007, April 6). Schemas and memory consolidation. *Science, 316,* 76–82. doi:10.1126/science.1135935

Vanderwolf, C. H. (1971). Limbic-diencephalic mechanisms of voluntary movement. *Psychological Review, 78,* 83–113. doi:10.1037/h0030672

van Strien, N. M., Cappaert, N. L. M., & Witter, M. P. (2009). The anatomy of memory: An interactive overview of the parahippocampal–hippocampal network. *Nature Reviews Neuroscience, 10,* 272–282. doi:10.1038/nrn2614

Vargha-Khadem, F., Gadian, D. G., Watkins, K. E., Connelly, A., Van Paesschen, W., & Mishkin, M. (1997, July 18). Differential effects of early hippocampal pathology on episodic and semantic memory. *Science, 277,* 376–380. doi:10.1126/science.277.5324.376

Viskontas, I., Knowlton, B., Steinmetz, P. N., & Fried, I. (2006). Differences in mnemonic procesing by neurons in the human hippocampus and parahippocampal region. *Journal of Cognitive Neuroscience, 18,* 1654–1662. doi:10.1162/jocn.2006.18.10.1654

Walker, M. P. (2009). The role of slow wave sleep in memory processing. *Journal of Clinical Sleep Medicine, 5,* S20–S26.

Wilson, M. A., & McNaughton, B. L. (1993, August 20). Dynamics of the hippocampal ensemble code for space. *Science, 261,* 1055–1058. doi:10.1126/science.8351520

Wilson, M. A., & McNaughton, B. L. (1994, July 29). Reactivation of hippocampal ensemble memories during sleep. *Science, 265,* 676–679. doi:10.1126/science.8036517

Witter, M. P. (2002). The parahippocampal region: Past, present, and future. In M. P. Witter & F. Wouterlood (Eds.), *The parahippocampal region: Organization and role in cognitive function* (pp. 3–19). Oxford, England: Oxford University Press.

Wittmann, T., & Schwegler, H. (1995). Path integration— A network model. *Biological Cybernetics, 73,* 569–575. doi:10.1007/BF00199549

Ylinen, A., Bragin, A., Nádasdy, Z., Jando, G., Szabo, I., Sik, A., & Buzsáki, G. (1995). Sharp wave-associated high-frequency oscillation (200 Hz) in the intact hippocampus: Network and intracellular mechanisms. *The Journal of Neuroscience, 15,* 30–46.

Yonelinas, A. P., Kroll, N. E., Quamme, J. R., Lazzara, M. M., Sauve, M. J., Widaman, K. F., & Knight, R. T. (2002). Effects of extensive temporal lobe damage or mild hypoxia on recollection and familiarity. *Nature Neuroscience, 5,* 1236–1241. doi:10.1038/nn961

Zhang, K., Ginzburg, I., McNaughton, B. L., & Sejnowski, T. J. (1998). Interpreting neuronal population activity by reconstruction: Unified framework with application to hippocampal place cells. *Journal of Neurophysiology, 79,* 1017–1044.

CHAPTER 2

PARIETAL CONTRIBUTIONS TO SPATIAL COGNITION

Raymond P. Kesner and Sarah H. Creem-Regehr

Parietal cortex subserves many functions extending across sensory, motor, and cognitive processes and has historically been discussed in terms of its associative functions. It is a significant task to define the parietal contributions to cognition because it is difficult to find a unified view of posterior parietal cortex (PPC) function (Cisek, 2008). However, it is well established that the PPC is critical for spatial cognition of the self, objects, and the environment, using numerous different spatial representations and reference frames (Colby & Goldberg, 1999). It is our hope that an understanding of the specificity of parietal functioning for different spatial information and task goals can help to define the processes underlying spatial cognition.

In this chapter, we initially review the role of the PPC in mediating different forms of spatial representations, which include egocentric versus allocentric frames of reference, regions of space near and far, egocentric spatial representations in visuomotor control, judgments of spatial relations, navigation, and categorical (topological) versus coordinate (metric) relations. Given the importance of a role for the PPC in subserving spatial attention, the next section reviews the contribution of the PPC in the mediation of neglect, covert attention, and spatial attention based on binding of spatial features. We next review the involvement of the PPC in dynamic spatial information processing including perceptual, working, and long-term memory.

Finally, we examine role of the PPC in mental imagery and spatial transformations. It is recognized that the PPC is also important for processing of nonspatial information, including, for example, processing of temporal and number information, but in this chapter we concentrate primarily on the contribution of the PPC to spatial cognition. Our goal is to present and integrate human and nonhuman animal (rat and monkey) approaches and findings to provide a more complete understanding of parietal contributions to spatial cognition.

ANATOMY

A description of the anatomical substrates of the parietal cortex provides a basis for understanding parietal function with respect to spatial cognition. This section presents anatomical descriptions of parietal cortex in humans, monkeys, and rats.

Humans

In humans, the PPC is located posterior to the postcentral sulcus and is divided by the intraparietal sulcus (IPS) into the superior parietal lobe (SPL) and the inferior parietal lobe (IPL; see Color Plate 7a). The IPL is further divided into an anterior region; the supramarginal gyrus; and a posterior region, the angular gyrus. The IPL borders the superior temporal gyrus (STG), extending along the superior border of the temporal lobe. The STG

DOI: 10.1037/13936-003
Handbook of Spatial Cognition, D. Waller and L. Nadel (Editors)

ends at the temporal-parietal junction (TPJ). The precuneus is the medial portion of PPC, anterior to the parieto-occipital sulcus, posterior to the paracentral lobule and superior to the subparietal sulcus (Culham, Cavina-Pratesi, & Singhal, 2006). Along the IPS, additional subdivisions have been identified on the basis of neuroanatomical properties and functional homologies with the monkey PPC (Culham & Kanwisher, 2001), as described next.

Monkeys

As in humans, the IPS divides the PPC into the SPL and IPL in monkeys. However, the area above the IPS in macaques supports somatosensory processing, and the area below the IPS supports visuomotor control, more functionally similar to the human SPL. Thus, in comparison, it has been proposed that the human IPL is unique (Glover, 2004; but see Rushworth, Behrens, & Johansen-Berg, 2006). The IPS has been well studied in monkeys, and neuroanatomical subdivisions have been identified that correspond to different sensorimotor functions and frames of reference. The lateral intraparietal area (LIP) is found on the posterior part of the lateral bank of the IPS, and the anterior intraparietal area (AIP) occupies the anterior part. The medial intraparietal area (MIP) and PE are located on the medial bank of the IPS and the SPL. The most ventral part of the IPS is labeled the ventral intraparietal area (VIP; see Color Plate 7b). The functions of these regions are described in a later section. Particularly important for the sections described next are the human homologs of the AIP, parietal eye fields (PEF) and macaque LIP, VIP, and the parietal reach regions (PRR, including MIP and V6a). Broadly, the monkey parietal areas have anatomical connections with areas of the prefrontal cortex, premotor cortex, and the frontal and supplementary eye fields (Colby & Goldberg, 1999) as well as the superior colliculus (MIP) and parahippocampal gyrus (posterior IPL; Rushworth et al., 2006).

Rats

Reep, Chandler, King, and Corwin (1994) delineated the boundaries of the rodent PPC. They defined the rodent PPC as cortical tissue that has pronounced connections with lateral posterior thalamus, lateral dorsal thalamus, and posterior nuclei but no input from ventrobasal complex or dorsal lateral geniculate (Reep et al., 1994; see Color Plate 7c). It should be noted that rats have no true pulvinar, but it is likely that the homologous structure is the lateral posterior thalamus. With these criteria, the PPC region of the rat is approximately 3.5 to 4.5 mm caudal to bregma, and 1.5 to 5 mm lateral to midline (Reep et al., 1994). This region of rodent cortex has connections with ventrolateral orbital and medial orbital cortex, medial agranular cortex, and retrosplenial cortex. These patterns of thalamocortical and cortico-cortical connections are similar to those in human and nonhuman primates, and there now seems to be general agreement among investigators of this anatomical definition of rat PPC. There are also a number of cortico-cortical connections, including somatosensory cortex, visual cortex, auditory cortex, orbital frontal and medial prefrontal cortices (Reep et al., 1994).

FORMS OF SPATIAL REPRESENTATIONS: FRAMES OF REFERENCE—EGOCENTRIC VERSUS ALLOCENTRIC

Spatial reference frames represent space with respect to specific referents. *Egocentric* spatial representations relate directly to the body axes, whereas *allocentric* representations are independent of the observer (O'Keefe & Nadel, 1978). Examples of egocentric spatial representations include those that use eye-centered, head-centered, and arm-centered frames of reference; in each case, aspects of the environment are represented with respect to a body part (eyes, arms, head). When an animal navigates through space, sensory inputs are registered initially according to such body-centered frames of reference. Similarly, overt behavior requires that motor outputs be coded in egocentric formats compatible with action (in terms of left, right, straight ahead, etc.). In contrast, allocentric spatial representations code the relationships between landmarks in the environment and between places, without reference to the observer or any part of its body. Because they include prominent and salient features of the environment (objects and places), they are useful for spatial orientation and spatial navigation. From a memory and navigational point of view, one needs to use multiple egocentric views from different spatial viewpoints to code the relationships between remote landmarks in the environment and between places in order to generate allocentric spatial representations. Thus, it is likely that there are important reciprocal relationships between egocentric and allocentric spatial frames of reference.

The PPC appears to create both egocentric and allocentric spatial representations, using various spatial features. Egocentric representations include ideothetic information based on vestibular inputs encoding translational and rotational accelerations, proprioceptive feedback from muscles tendons and joints, and visual cues such as linear and radial optic flow cues. Allocentric representations include information about environmental features primarily on the basis of visual and other sensory cues (auditory, somatosensory, olfactory). Information about locomotor commands (efference copies) may also contribute in the short term (Berthoz, 1999).

FORMS OF SPATIAL REPRESENTATIONS: REGIONS OF SPACE—NEAR VERSUS FAR

It is useful to divide the spatial environment into egocentrically defined regions that extend from a viewer's near to far space. These regions have been defined functionally in terms of what an actor might do within them (Grüsser, 1983), computationally for the information for space perception available in near versus far regions (Cutting & Vishton, 1995), and neurally with respect to the neuroanatomical, neuropsychological, and neurochemical mechanisms that contribute to processing space in these regions (Previc, 1998; Rizzolatti & Camarda, 1987). Although the labels for regions of space differ among theories, we may broadly conceptualize spaces of the body, around the body (within reach), and beyond the body (Tversky, 2003). Traditional usage in the neuropsychological and attention literature refers to these as *personal*, *peripersonal*, and *extrapersonal* spaces, respectively (Rizzolatti & Camarda, 1987).

Research suggests that perception and spatial cognition within these different regions of space may also be supported by different regions of the PPC. Patients with unilateral neglect, most commonly due to inferior parietal lesions, show failures in awareness of stimuli in their contralesional space (see the section on attention later in this chapter). This neglect of a space can be specific to personal, peripersonal, or extrapersonal space in different individuals. For example, an individual may neglect the left half of his or her face (in a mirror) while still responding accurately to external spaces, or one might show neglect for the peripersonal space within reach but not at farther distances (Danckert & Ferber, 2006). The boundaries of peripersonal and extrapersonal space have also been shown to be malleable and subject to remapping as a function of one's own dynamic representation of the body.

In macaque monkeys, bimodal neuronal activity in the intraparietal cortex (with both somatosensory and visual receptive fields) has been modulated by the monkey's experience with using a rake that extended the space reachable by the arm (Iriki, Tanaka, & Iwamura, 1996). Before the use of the rake, visual receptive fields covered the space reachable by the arm. After experience with the rake that extended the monkey's reach, the visual receptive fields expanded to include the space within reach of the rake. The expansion seen in these visual receptive fields suggested that the monkey's peripersonal space became extended as a function of their capability to act in the space. Similarly, in humans, patients with peripersonal neglect extended their neglect into extrapersonal space when using a hand-held wand to bisect a line beyond the patients' normal reaching distance (Berti & Frassinetti, 2000). Studies of both healthy and brain-damaged humans support these findings as well (Ackroyd, Riddoch, Humphreys, Nightingale, & Townsend, 2002; Longo & Lourenco, 2007). There is also evidence for the specialization of the dorsal parietal system for perception of objects in near versus far spaces (Quinlan & Culham, 2007).

EGOCENTRIC SPATIAL REPRESENTATIONS

There are several ways to describe the body-based coordinate systems used in spatial cognition. This section describes the contribution of the parietal cortex for the egocentric representations used by humans, monkeys, and rats.

Humans

This section describes examples of the role of the PPC in humans. These include visuomotor control, judgments about spatial relations with respect to the body, as well as navigation and path integration.

Eye and arm movements.   Evidence for the role of the PPC in egocentric spatial representation in humans comes in large part from neuropsychological studies in patients with lesions and, more recently, functional neuroimaging in healthy adults. The PPC plays a role in tasks requiring egocentric visuomotor control. The PPC is the endpoint of the dorsal stream of visual processing, historically defined as a system for spatial processing, named the *where system* by Ungerleider & Mishkin (1982), in contrast to a ventral *what system* for object processing, localized to the inferior temporal cortex. This "what versus where" dichotomy was revised by Goodale and Milner (1992; Milner & Goodale, 1995) to emphasize the dorsal stream as subserving visual–spatial functions for action. Double dissociations in patients with visual-form agnosia and optic ataxia provided initial evidence for the claim of separable visual systems. Visual agnosic patient DF, who had a lesion to her occipital–temporal cortex, showed deficits in making perceptual judgments about her surroundings, such as conscious judgments of shape or orientation. However, her actions directed at these same targets, such as placing a card in the correct orientation of a slot or grasping an object, were accurate to the spatial dimensions of the target. In contrast, it was argued that patients with optic ataxia resulting from damage to superior parietal cortex are able to recognize and discriminate objects but have difficulty performing precise actions directed toward targets.

More recently, several theories have been put forward that subdivide the dorsal stream into dorsal and ventral areas (Buxbaum & Kalenine, 2010; Creem-Regehr, 2009; Glover, 2004; Johnson & Grafton, 2003; Rizzolatti & Matelli, 2003), distinguishing between SPL and IPL function. In the framework of Rizzolatti and Matelli (2003), the dorso-dorsal stream (namely, the SPL) functions in online motor control as previously outlined by Milner and Goodale (1995). In contrast, the ventro–dorsal stream (namely, the IPL) more generally subserves

space perception and knowledge relating to actions (see Color Plate 8). Evidence for this framework comes partly from an examination of patients with ideomotor apraxia, typically due to left IPL cortex lesions. These patients show impairments in skilled object-related movements but are usually accurate with online reach and grasping, given sensory feedback. The left IPL is also critically involved in aspects of spatial processing and representation called into play in tasks requiring action planning, imagery, gestures, and action knowledge (Creem-Regehr, 2009).

There is considerable evidence for the processing of eye movements within the dorsal system, particularly the IPS and superior parietal lobule, revealed through monkey neurophysiology and human neuropsychological and neuroimaging research (Culham et al., 2006; Pierrot-Deseilligny, Milea, & Muri, 2004). Because our eyes are constantly moving, it is critical to have a mechanism that updates a spatial representation, maintaining a stable representation of the world. Parietal (LIP) neurons in the macaque respond during planning of a saccade to a spatial location and attention to that location. These neurons, which have been shown to have retinotopic receptive fields, perform this updating or remapping over eye movements (Duhamel, Colby, & Goldberg, 1992). In humans, PEFs have been identified medial to the IPS, notably more medial to the IPS in humans than in macaques (see Color Plates 7a and 7b). This area is active during saccadic and smooth pursuit eye movements as well as during saccades to remembered targets. There is evidence for the same type of eye-centered spatial updating with saccades in monkey and humans, with remapped responses corresponding to the goal of the saccade, showing a topographic representation in the human PEF (Medendorp, Goltz, & Vilis, 2005; Merriam, Genovese, & Colby, 2003).

The PPC has a well-established role in egocentric manual movements, including reaching and grasping. Optic ataxia is a neuropsychological disorder characterized by deficits in visually guided arm movements. Karnath and Perenin (2005) demonstrated recently in a group lesion analysis of 16 patients with optic ataxia that there were several loci of lesions including the SPL, the medial occipito–parietal junction and the junction between the SPL and the occipital cortex. Neuroimaging methods have identified activation in the medial IPS and the precuneus for reaching tasks (Connolly, Andersen, & Goodale, 2003; Prado et al., 2005). These regions are consistent with the monkey PRR (areas MIP and V6A) as well as the optic ataxia lesion analysis described previously (Culham et al., 2006). For grasping, extensive work has been conducted by Culham and colleagues using functional magnetic resonance imaging (fMRI) to identify anterior portions of the IPS (AIP; see Color Plate 7a) as the human grasping region (Culham, 2004; Culham et al., 2003). This is further supported by the method of transcranial magnetic stimulation (TMS), in which "virtual lesions" to the PPC have been applied and grip aperture size and orientation have been altered (Tunik, Frey, & Grafton, 2005).

Much of the work with overt grasping has been conducted with neutral shape objects. Recent investigations involving interactions with functionally meaningful objects such as tools suggest that the parietal mechanisms may differ (Buxbaum & Kalenine, 2010; Creem-Regehr, 2009; Johnson & Grafton, 2003). In contrast to the right or bilateral activation of the AIP and SPL for "neutral" grasping tasks, the representation of conceptual knowledge and tool use has been attributed to left IPL function. This is consistent with the identification of a left-hemisphere network of temporal, parietal, and frontal areas for manual praxis skills (for reviews see, Johnson-Frey, Newman-Norlund, & Grafton, 2005; Lewis, 2006), supported by both neuropsychological lesion analyses and neuroimaging results.

Egocentric spatial relations. Outside of the context of action, the neural mechanisms underlying the processing of egocentric and allocentric spatial representations have been studied with a few different paradigms in humans. In one paradigm, the egocentric task was a judgment of the position of a vertical bar with respect to the body midline, whereas the allocentric task was a judgment of the position of a vertical bar with respect to a horizontal bar presented behind the vertical one (Neggers, Scholvinck, van der Lubbe, & Potsma, 2005; Neggers, van der Lubbe, Ramsey, & Potsma, 2006). Using fMRI with healthy participants,

Neggers et al. (2006) found increased activation in the right SPL in the egocentric task compared with the allocentric task. It is notable that this task and related others such as the *Roelofs effect*—in which the perceived location of a target is influenced by its surrounding frame (Bridgeman, Peery, & Anand, 1997; Dassonville, Bridgeman, Kaur Bala, Thiem, & Sampanes, 2004)—show that there is some influence of allocentric representations on egocentric localization tasks. It has been debated whether these effects are limited to perceptual spatial judgments and do not occur with visually guided action. For example, Dassonville et al. (2004) proposed that the influence of an allocentric background in egocentric judgments could be attributed to a shift in perceived midline and need not indicate a dissociation between two visual systems for awareness and action. An investigation of the neural mechanisms using fMRI as in Neggers et al. (2006) helps to answer this question, because they found that the influence of allocentric information was associated with activation in occipital–temporal regions and not the parietal cortex, supporting the notion that the superior parietal representations of space are specific to egocentric frames of reference.

Iachini, Ruggiero, Conson, and Trojano (2009) went beyond the simple judgment tasks involving bars and dots to test parietal mechanisms in spatial frames of reference by using the *ego–allo task* (EAT; Iachini & Ruggiero, 2006) with right (RH) and left hemisphere (LH) parietal lesion participants. In this task, participants studied a triad of three-dimensional objects and answered an egocentric question ("Which was closer to or farther from you?") or allocentric question ("Which object was closer to or farther from another object?"). On the basis of the logic that the processing of coordinate spatial relationships is tightly linked to the egocentric frames of reference required for action and attributed to right parietal cortex specialization, Iachini et al. hypothesized that patients with RH parietal lesions would be impaired on the egocentric task (see the next section for more discussion of coordinate vs. categorical spatial processing). In contrast, they proposed that patients with LH parietal lesions would show impairment on the allocentric task, consistent with a proposed LH specialization in categorical spatial processing. Similarly, they also proposed that RH patients would show more impairment in tasks performed in near space consistent with execution of action, and LH patients would be more impaired in "far" space. Consistent with their prediction, right parietal patients were more impaired on the egocentric EAT in near space. There was a weaker association with LH deficits and allocentric space; the LH patients showed difficulty on both the egocentric and allocentric tasks.

Navigation and path integration. Virtual environment technology has been used in a number of studies with both human parietal lesion and fMRI approaches to test hypotheses about the neural mechanisms underlying spatial navigation and memory (Maguire, Frith, Burgess, Donnett, & O'Keefe, 1998; Rosenbaum, Ziegler, Winocur, Grady, & Moscovitch, 2004). One recent example is a large neuropsychological study in which 24 patients with unilateral parietal lesions were compared with 36 healthy participants (Weniger, Ruhleder, Wolf, Lange, & Irle, 2009). Two different virtual environment tasks were used, intended to tap different frames of reference. In the virtual park environment, participants navigated through an environment full of landmarks to find the shortest way to a pot with money, predicted to recruit an allocentric navigation strategy. In the virtual maze environment, participants were given the same task to solve in a maze of brick walls without any landmarks so that an egocentric navigation strategy was necessary. Parietal lesion participants were impaired on the virtual maze (egocentric without landmarks) but not on the virtual park (allocentric), supporting the claim that the parietal cortex is necessary for egocentric spatial navigation. Performance on the virtual maze also correlated with right precuneus volume, showing that increased volume was related to better performance. There was no difference in performance as a function of overall lesion laterality.

Consistent with the role of medial parietal cortex in egocentric spatial processing seen in neuropsychological studies, an fMRI study also identified particularly the precuneus in egocentric spatial updating during simulated self-motion (Wolbers, Hegarty, Buchel, & Loomis, 2008). The term *spatial updating* is used in navigation as the process

of keeping track of object locations in the environment with respect to one's own self-movement (see Chapter 5, this volume). It is similar to the notion of spatial updating during saccades as described earlier but involves changes as a result of full-body movement instead of just eye movements. This process is crucial for aspects of navigation in which objects may go out of view in both small- and large-scale spaces, such as path planning and, in general, acting on one's environment. In Wolbers et al. (2008), participants viewed and memorized objects at different distances in a virtual environment displayed in the MRI scanner. Activation in the precuneus and the dorsal precentral gyrus was found to be directly associated with the conjunction of two experimental manipulations: number of objects to remember and visual information for self-motion. Additional experiments ruled out that the precentral gyrus activation was simply due to eye movements and identified the precuneus activation as generalizable to both action- and nonaction-based responses. In contrast, the premotor cortex activity was specific to the corresponding motor component of spatial updating. Thus, there is good evidence from this work that the medial PPC supports the maintenance of an egocentric and transient spatial map.

The results of Wolbers et al. (2008) support a number of other functional neuroimaging studies that have implicated the medial and posterior PPC in related egocentric navigation tasks, including route encoding (Janzen & Weststeijn, 2007; Shelton & Gabrieli, 2002; van Asselen et al., 2006; Weniger et al., 2009; Wolbers, Weiller, & Buchel, 2004). Notably, recent research supports regions of the PPC, particularly the medial PPC/precuneus, as playing a more general role in representing the self and first-person perspective taking (Cavanna & Trimble, 2006; Pellijeff, Bonilha, Morgan, McKenzie, & Jackson, 2006; Vogeley & Fink, 2003). In the related context of self-processing, neuroimaging and neuropsychological results point to the TPJ as the neural basis of embodiment. The TPJ has been shown to underlie the integration of body-related information, processing of agency, and first-person imagery (Arzy, Thut, Mohr, Michel, & Blanke, 2006; Blanke & Arzy, 2005; Zacks, Vettel, & Michelon, 2003).

Animals

This section describes examples of egocentric representations in the parietal cortex of monkeys and rats. These include sensorimotor transformations, head direction, navigation and path integration, egocentric spatial relations, and binding across reference frames (egocentric–allocentric).

Sensorimotor transformations.   There is extensive support for the notion that sensory-to-motor coordinate transformations are subserved by different subregions of the IPS in monkeys (Colby, 1998; Colby & Goldberg, 1999). These anatomical and physiological data suggest several separate functional areas and multiple representations of space. These areas include the VIP area, which contains neurons that respond mostly to tactile stimulation of the head and face and vestibular stimulation encoding motion of the head. One function of the head-centered representation in area VIP could involve movements of the head, lips, and tongue to facilitate reaching with the mouth. In the MIP area, neurons respond to reach-related responses, including stimulus features of location and stimulus motion as well as selectivity for those stimuli within reaching distance. This suggests that area MIP contributes to a spatial representation involved in the control of arm movements. In the AIP cortex, there are neurons that respond to stimuli manipulable with the hand. The importance here is the shape of the hand rather than its position in egocentric space. Thus, AIP neurons subserve visual and motor representations involved in grasping. Finally, there is a LIP area, in which neurons respond to light flashes when a monkey looks at the stimulus. The function of LIP appears to be directly related to representing spatial locations that are attended to or locations that are salient, rather than to the planning of a specific movement. Neurons in area LIP also contribute to updating or remapping the representation of the stimulus during eye movements by encoding a memory trace of the initial fixation point. Thus, neurons in area LIP mediate a sensory-to-motor transformation and trigger an action-oriented spatial representation for the guidance of eye movements. As described previously, this process is impaired in patients with parietal cortex damage. The LIP area can construct an allocentric representation of space relative to the detection of objects. Thus, it appears that monkeys use multiple frames of reference to represent egocentric and allocentric space.

In a more recent study, Sato, Sakata, Tanaka, and Taira (2006) recorded the activity of neurons in the monkey's MIP region while the monkey was navigating through a virtual environment. They demonstrated that MIP neurons represent route knowledge based on the existence of location- and movement-selective neurons, implying that location and movement are independently represented in subsets of MIP neurons. This suggests that there may be unique combinations of specific movements and spatial locations to guide spatial navigation. Furthermore, temporary inactivation using muscimol in MIP areas totally disrupted the generation of routes.

In rats, like monkeys, the PPC may be involved in transforming spatial information provided by sensory cues into body-based coordinates necessary for implementation of a sequence of actions to reach a goal location. Based on single unit recording of neurons within the PPC, it was observed that PPC cells represent conjunctions of movements and locations. However, it should be noted that parietal cortex lesions did not interfere with learning a skilled paw-reaching test and there was no somatosensory neglect (Ward & Brown, 1997; but see Holm & Mogensen, 1993, who did report contralateral somatosensory neglect).

Head direction.   Does the PPC in rats play a role in mnemonic processing of egocentric spatial representations primarily on the basis of head-direction information? In the parietal cortex of rats, neurons have been found that encode spatial location and head-direction information; many of these cells are sensitive to multiple cues, including visual, proprioceptive, sensorimotor, and vestibular cue information (Chen, Lin, Barnes, & McNaughton, 1994; Chen, Lin, Green, Barnes, & McNaughton, 1994; McNaughton, Chen, & Markus, 1991). For example, as nicely summarized by Chen and Nakamura (1998), single-unit recording data suggest that rat parietal cortex may be involved in head-direction orientation representations and spatial memories. A small percentage of cells in PPC respond selectively to the rat's head orientation (Chen, Lin, Barnes, et al., 1994; Chen, Lin, Green, et al., 1994). These head-direction cells persist after the removal of visual cues (either by physically removing the cues or turning off the lights), and a subset of head-direction cells associate angular motion with head orientation (Chen, Lin, Barnes, et al., 1994; Chen, Lin, Green, et al., 1994). Therefore, it appears that PPC cells are responsive to an interaction between visual and sensorimotor inputs. Some of these PPC cells maintain short-term mnemonic information for head direction (Chen, Lin, Barnes, et al., 1994; Chen, Lin, Green, et al., 1994) and the spatial location of a tone (Nakamura & Takarajima, 1996). However, in recent studies PPC lesions did not markedly alter the firing characteristics of head-direction cells in the anterior thalamus (Calton, Turner, Cyrenne, Lee, & Taube, 2008). PPC lesion studies using a delayed matching-to-sample task for head direction in the dark have not yet been carried out, but hippocampal lesions or vestibular rotations between the study and test phase produce profound deficits (DeCoteau, Hoang, Huff, Stone, & Kesner, 2004). Thus, it appears that the PPC may play a role in mediating head-direction information, but more research will be needed.

Navigation and path integration.

Does the PPC play a role in mnemonic processing of path integration? Whishaw, McKenna, and Maaswinkel (1997) defined the process of *path integration* as the means by which an animal can determine its current environmental location as a function of keeping track of its own movements through space in relation to a known starting point or reference point and by integrating signals derived from its own locomotor movements over time. Path integration is assumed to be based on processing of egocentric information and appears to depend on vestibular signals generated by angular and linear acceleration during movements. This egocentric information can also be integrated with allocentric cues or landmarks visible in the environment. Support for the idea that egocentric information is sufficient comes from the finding that when visual cues are removed or otherwise unavailable (e.g., in darkness), there continues to be stable firing

of both place cells (Jeffery, Donnett, Burgess, & O'Keefe, 1997; Quirk, Muller, & Kubie, 1990) and head-direction cells (Golob & Taube, 1999), and furthermore, animals can still navigate effectively (Etienne & Jeffery, 2004).

One can measure the operation of path integration by allowing the animal to leave its home base, explore the platform to find a hidden food, and then carry the food back to the home base; path integration is measured in terms of the accuracy in finding the home base. Save, Guazzelli, and Poucet (2001) and Parron and Save (2004) have shown that PPC lesions resulted in inaccurate returns to home base. It should be noted that similar disruptive effects of path integration have been reported after lesions in hippocampus and entorhinal cortex (Parron & Save, 2004; Save et al., 2001; Whishaw & Jarrard, 1996). Thus, the data indicate that the PPC plays an important role in path integration, probably in cooperation with the hippocampus.

Egocentric spatial relations.

Does the PPC support the utilization of proximal rather than distal cues, further suggesting a role for the PPC in mediating egocentric information? Save and Poucet (2000) showed that in the Morris water maze, PPC lesioned rats were impaired in finding a hidden platform when three salient cues were located in the pool close to the correct location (proximal cues), but they were not impaired when only room cues (distal cues) were available to find the platform. Kolb and Walkey (1987) showed that PPC lesioned rats were impaired in finding a platform location in a landmark task in which the rats had to associate a visual cue with a site that was spatially discontiguous and where the relevant cue moved relative to the rest of the extra maze cues. This impairment manifested itself in the adoption of a looping strategy to locate a hidden platform. Foreman, Save, Thinus-Blanc, and Buhot (1992) found that the trajectories of rats turning and running between familiar visible targets at opposite ends of an area were less accurate in PPC lesioned rats than in controls. Furthermore, training PPC lesioned rats in the Morris water maze from a fixed start position in the dark resulted in inaccurate trajectories and subsequent difficulty in learning the task (Save & Moghaddam, 1996). In addition, PPC lesioned rats had difficulty in a route-learning task in a Hebb-Williams maze when distal cues were not available (Rogers & Kesner, 2007). In contrast, PPC lesioned rats were not impaired in learning an egocentric version of the radial arm maze (Kesner, Farnsworth, & DiMattia, 1989; King & Corwin, 1992). One possible interpretation for this result could be that in the eight-arm maze, trajectories are more constrained by the structure of the apparatus, so that difficulty in initiating accurate trajectories would not play a significant role in learning the task. Another interpretation of all these results is that PPC lesioned rats are impaired in the use of proximal cues because of a problem in processing topological information (see the next section on categorical [topological] vs. coordinate [metric] spatial representations).

Binding across reference frames (Egocentric–Allocentric). It has been suggested that learning to find a specific location in a water maze or a dry land version of the water maze may be a function of an interaction between egocentric and allocentric cues, and thus the PPC could play a role in the binding of egocentric and allocentric cues (Save, Poucet, Forman, & Thinus-Blanc, 1998). Support for this suggestion comes from the findings that PPC lesions disrupt both acquisition and retention of the Morris water maze and the dry land version of the water maze (DiMattia & Kesner, 1988; Hoh, Kolb, Eppel, Vanderwolf, & Cain, 2003; Kesner, Farnsworth, & Kametani, 1991; Kolb & Walkey, 1987), although the magnitude of this effect is small in some studies (see Kolb, Sutherland, & Whishaw, 1983; Save & Moghaddam, 1996).

Further support for the binding of egocentric and allocentric information in long-term memory comes from a study by Rogers and Kesner (2007). They trained rats in two versions of a modified Hebb-Williams maze to test the role of the PPC in processing egocentric and allocentric information during acquisition and retention. In the allocentric task version, the spatial arrangement allowed the rat to use extra maze cues present such as posters, a map, and a hanging doll. In the egocentric task version, there were raised opaque walls that allowed for few, if any, extra maze cues. Bilateral lesions were made to PPC before maze testing (acquisition) or after

maze testing (retention). The results indicated that lesions of the PPC impaired egocentric maze acquisition, but the animals had no difficulty in learning the allocentric version of the maze task. Similar deficits following PPC lesions were reported by Boyd and Thomas (1977) during acquisition of the standard Hebb-Williams maze, which did not give the rats an opportunity to use extra maze cues. During retention, lesions of the PPC produced a significant impairment on both maze versions, suggesting that the PPC may be combining both egocentric and allocentric information during normal learning of the maze, but after a PPC lesion the combined information may not be available to the animal. In contrast, it should be noted that during acquisition, lesions of the dorsal hippocampus impaired allocentric, but not egocentric, maze acquisition. During retention, lesions of the dorsal hippocampus produced short-lived, transient impairments on both maze versions. These results suggest that during acquisition, the hippocampus and PPC process spatial information in parallel; however, long-term retention of spatial information requires the PPC, with the dorsal hippocampus necessary for retrieval and/or access but not necessarily storage.

FORMS OF SPATIAL REPRESENTATIONS: CATEGORICAL (TOPOLOGICAL) VERSUS COORDINATE (METRIC)

In addition to the egocentric–allocentric distinction in spatial representation, it is also useful to consider the distinction between categorical and coordinate spatial relations (Kosslyn, 1987; Kosslyn et al., 1989). *Categorical relations* are defined as abstract, general properties of spatial structure such as relations of above/below or right/left. In contrast, *coordinate relations* are more precise metric relationships that can be described in absolute distances. In some circumstances, such as with visually guided actions, the metric properties specified in coordinate relations are necessary. In other contexts that do not rely on egocentric transformations, abstract descriptions of categorical relations may be more useful. The animal literature often refers to this distinction as *topological versus metric properties of space* (Gallistel, 1990).

Humans

In terms of parietal cortex function, research with humans makes a broad distinction between categorical representations as subserved by the left hemisphere and coordinate relations as subserved predominantly by the right hemisphere, specifically in the PPC. This claim has been made mostly on the basis of experimental studies with healthy participants using lateralized presentation paradigms in which a stimulus is presented to one hemifield for a short period of time, but some studies have also been carried out with neuropsychological patients with left and right parietal damage (Jager & Potsma, 2003; Laeng, 1994). An example of a task is a presentation of a dot and a line and a question of whether the dot is above or below the line (categorical) or whether it is within some precise distance of the line (coordinate) (Jager & Potsma, 2003). Other types of tasks include same/different judgments about stimuli that differ in categorical or coordinate relations (Laeng, 1994). The dissociation is generally supported by the data on lateralization, although there are still existing questions of how strong the lateralization evidence is (particularly the left hemisphere specialization for categorical processing) and whether there is a continuum that may be modulated by a factor other than the categorical/coordinate distinction, such as difficulty or spatial attention (Martin, Houssemand, Schiltz, Burnod, & Alexandre, 2008; van der Ham, Raemaekers, van Wezel, Oleksiak, & Potsma, 2009).

Functional neuroimaging has been used to test the neural distinction between coordinate and categorical processing in both perceptual and visual imagery/memory tasks (Baciu et al., 1999; Slotnick & Moo, 2006; Trojano, Conson, Maffei, & Grossi, 2006; Trojano et al., 2002), generally finding predicted lateralized differences in the angular gyrus, superior parietal lobule, and the prefrontal cortex. A recent fMRI study (van der Ham et al., 2009) used a spatial working memory paradigm to manipulate task difficulty and to test the alternate claim that coordinate and categorical processing are not fundamentally different but rather share underlying mechanisms that are influenced by task properties. In this task, participants made coordinate or categorical spatial decisions about the relationship between a dot and a cross after a varied retention interval, which served as a manipulation of task difficulty. Consistent with previous neuroimaging and neuropsychological results, support was found for differences in lateralization in the superior parietal cortex for the long retention interval, with the right hemisphere more active for coordinate processing and the left hemisphere more active for categorical processing. There was some evidence in support of lateralization differences as a function of task difficulty, but it was not consistent across spatial processing type. Right parietal activity correlated with difficulty in coordinate processing but not in categorical processing.

Animals

In humans, there is considerable emphasis on trying to demonstrate hemispheric differences, with categorical processing reflecting the left side of the brain and coordinate processing reflecting the right side of the brain. Clearly, some studies with humans have suggested that the right superior parietal cortex plays a role in coordinate processing of information. It appears that in monkeys no specific hemispheric specialization exists, and in rats specific hemispheric specialization has not been studied (for a review, see Vauclair, Yamazaki, & Güntürkün, 2006).

It is proposed that in rats the distinction between egocentric and allocentric space maps onto a distinction between metric relationships between stimuli, involving coordinate judgments and topological relationships between stimuli, which are often associated with categorical judgments. *Metric relationships* are defined as the relationship of angles and distances between objects as well as linear and angular distances, whereas topological relationships are represented by a connectedness relationship between objects that are not affected by metric modifications (Gallistel, 1990; Kuipers & Levitt, 1988; Poucet, 1993; Poucet & Hermann, 2001). Topological spatial information is based on associations between objects that involve relationships such as connectivity and containment (Gallistel, 1990; Poucet, 1993; Poucet & Hermann, 2001; Kuipers & Levitt, 1988). According to Poucet (1993), "Topology is a geometry originally based on the notions of continuity and limit, from which are derived the relations of compactedness, neighborhood, enclosure, and connectivity." Metric transformations are created by altering distances and angles between objects, whereas topological transformations involve either stretching or contracting the entire environment as a whole or disrupting particular relationships of enclosure or connectivity (Gallistel, 1990). On the basis of behavioral experiments, Poucet (1993) demonstrated that topological information, though crude in its representations of space, is essential to animals' spatial representations. In addition, because animals encode geometric relationships, they might extrapolate overall geometric structures as well, implying the use of topological information processing.

To test the hypothesis that the PPC processes topological spatial information (i.e., spatial configuration of objects) but not metric spatial information (i.e., spatial distances between objects), PPC and control lesioned rats were tested for novelty detection on both a metric and topological task. The PPC lesioned group displayed a marked disruption of novelty detection (assessed by object reexploration) relative to controls and dorsal hippocampal lesioned rats during the topological reorganizations, but had reexploration similar to controls for the metric changes, suggesting that the PPC is essential to processing of topological, but not metric, information (Goodrich-Hunsaker, Hunsaker, & Kesner, 2005). In contrast, rats with dorsal hippocampus lesions tested in the same task displayed a marked disruption of object reexploration relative to PPC lesioned and control rats in response to the distance changes but had reexploration similar to controls for the topological changes, suggesting that the dorsal hippocampus is essential for processing metric, but not topological, information (Goodrich-Hunsaker et al., 2005).

Further support for a PPC role in supporting topological spatial processing comes from a variety of sources. PPC involvement has been found when proximal cues are important, but it is less involved when distal cues are essential, supporting the idea that topological information is most likely based on connectedness or proximity between or among visual cues (Save & Poucet, 2000). Kolb and Walkey (1987) showed that PPC lesioned rats were impaired in finding a platform location in a landmark task in

which the rats had to associate a visual cue with a site that was spatially discontiguous and where the relevant cue moved relative to the rest of the extra maze cues. This impairment manifested itself in the adoption of a looping strategy to locate a hidden platform. In monkeys, PPC lesions disrupted spatial pattern discrimination only when the essential cue and site of reinforcement were separated (Mendoza & Thomas, 1975). Pohl (1973) obtained similar results when the landmark cue was discontiguous with the manipulandum. Additional evidence comes from the findings that PPC lesioned rats and inferior parietal cortex lesioned monkeys are impaired in learning a variety of mazes especially when the mazes employed do not provide access to many extra maze cues, thus promoting the use of egocentric as well local topological spatial cues (Barrow & Latto, 1996; Boyd & Thomas, 1977; Rogers & Kesner, 2007). Furthermore Nitz (2006) recorded from PPC cells in rats and found that many cells displayed sustained increases in neural activity as a function of distance between proximal points on the maze, providing cellular evidence of topological transformations that involve stretching or contracting entire routes through the maze.

In humans, patient RM, who had a bilateral parietal cortex lesion, displayed an impairment in learning topological relationships. RM was asked to determine whether a large dot was outside or inside a circle. RM was unable to learn this task, averaging 49% correct (18 out of 37 trials; Robertson, Treisman, Friedman-Hill, & Grabowecky, 1997). Similar observations show identical behavioral results with PPC lesioned rats (Goodrich-Hunsaker, Howard, Hunsaker, & Kesner, 2008). Initially, rats were trained to discriminate between a ball either inside or outside a ring. After reaching criterion, the rats received PPC lesions and when retested they were unable to make the discrimination. It should be noted that control rats and rats with dorsal hippocampal lesions had no serious difficulty in performing this topological task.

Thus, evidence supports the view that the PPC in rats represents topological, but not metric, information. In contrast, it appears that the hippocampus represents metric, but not topological, information. This lack of metric processing in the rat PPC stands in contrast to the research with humans that shows recruitment of the right PPC for both arm movements, such as reaching and pointing (as described in the earlier section), and coordinate spatial decisions that rely on metric properties. This discrepancy may reflect the different behavioral tasks used to assess human and monkey versus rat spatial cognition. It also may be that the PPC serves a more general spatial function of integrating proximal spatial information for spatial orientation with distal cues for route planning, an explanation that might bridge differences seen in parietal function across species in egocentric and allocentric frames of reference and metric versus topological processing (Calton & Taube, 2009).

ATTENTION TO SPATIAL INFORMATION

Although whole chapters in themselves could cover the large literature on the role of the parietal cortex in attention (e.g., Riddoch et al., 2010), we focus here on three targeted topics related to spatial cognition: the characteristic behavior and neural correlates of unilateral neglect, the related role of the PPC in covert spatial attention, and the binding of spatial features.

Unilateral Neglect and Covert Attention in Humans

Unilateral neglect is a disorder that is characterized by deficits in responding to, reporting, or orienting to stimuli in environmental space contralateral to the individual's brain lesion (Danckert & Ferber, 2006; Heilman, Watson, & Valenstein, 1993) and is most commonly attributed to right PPC damage. Commonly associated with functional impairments in spatial attention, neglect has more recently been considered as a syndrome involving multiple deficits of spatial cognition defined by spatial reference frames (egocentric and object-centered), structures of space (peripersonal and extrapersonal), local–global processing distinctions, and intention (Halligan, Fink, Marshall, & Vallar, 2003). Neglect is assessed with several standard tasks, including line cancellation, line bisection, and figure copying. In general, performance on the tasks indicates patterns of behavior in which failures to detect object

features are seen in contralesional space with respect to the individual's midline. In other words, lines are bisected with a bias toward the ipsilesional side, and lines or parts of figures in the contralesional side of space are omitted when participants are asked to cancel or copy them (see Danckert & Ferber, 2006, for a review). However, neglect may be more specific to peripersonal space versus extrapersonal space (or vice versa, as described earlier) or may also be defined with respect to an object's frame of reference, either consistent or inconsistent with an egocentric frame of reference.

Although it is difficult to identify a single critical brain lesion site for neglect, there are several commonly identified regions associated with a number of functional deficits seen in neglect. These include the IPL, the TPJ, and the superior temporal sulcus. Identification of these regions comes from analyses of lesion sites associated with identified behavioral deficits as described earlier (Karnath, Berger, Kuker, & Rorden, 2004; Mort et al., 2003) as well as the results from TMS studies in which a temporary functional lesion is applied to a normally functioning brain. Repetitive (r) TMS applied over the right parietal cortex has been shown to induce a rightward bias in line bisection similar to what is seen in patients with right hemisphere neglect (Fierro, Brighina, Piazza, Oliveri, & Bisiach, 2001). A related pattern of behavior, extinction, in which patients with parietal damage fail to report a contralesional stimulus when it is presented concurrently with an ipsilesional stimulus, has also been shown with rTMS applied to either the right or left parietal lobe (Hilgetag, Theoret, & Pascual-Leone, 2001).

Attentional biases are often put forth as an explanation of the nature of behavioral deficits in neglect. Specifically, the ability to perform covert attention shifting tasks was associated with processing in the PPC on the basis of data from patients with parietal lesions tested on the classic cueing task developed by Posner and colleagues (Posner, Nissen, & Ogden, 1978; Posner, Walker, Friedrich, & Rafal, 1984). This task requires a button-press response to a target presented in one of two locations surrounding a central fixation point. A cue appears before the target presentation either accurately (valid cue) or inaccurately (invalid cue) indicating the target location. Although all participants show slower performance with an invalid versus valid cue, patients with right parietal lesions showed a particular deficit on invalid cues to the ipsilesional side (when the target was presented on the contralesional side). Given that patients with parietal lesions showed normal orienting to valid cues in either side of space, these results suggested that the parietal cortex was specifically needed for disengaging attention from the ipsilesional side. TMS studies have supported this claim, showing that TMS applied over the posterior IPS and IPL impairs redirection of attention after an invalid cue (Chambers, Payne, Stokes, & Mattingley, 2004). Other neuroimaging results have suggested that the right TPJ subserves the direction of attention to novel and behaviorally relevant stimuli (Corbetta & Shulman, 2002; Mevorach, Humphreys, & Shalev, 2005), also consistent with the failure of patients with right TPJ lesions to respond to an unexpected stimulus on the contralesional side when invalidly cued.

Unilateral Neglect and Covert Attention in Animals

In monkeys, there is some evidence of hemispatial neglect of egocentric space following unilateral destruction of the PPC, especially area 7 (Deuel, 1987; Milner, 1987), but there is minimal evidence of an effect on spatial processing, such as visual search or discriminating moving patterns. Neglect in rats following PPC lesions has been most extensively studied by Corwin and Reep (1998) and King and Corwin (1992, 1993). They described effects similar to those observed in humans, including contralesional neglect of visual, auditory, and tactile stimuli; extinction; allesthesia; and disorders of spatial processing. Directed attention as measured for contralateral neglect involves overt orienting responses made by the head and neck to salient stimuli. Furthermore, the neglect can be observed following either right or left PPC lesions. Of interest is the observation that the same level of neglect was observed for proximal and distal stimuli. The circuitry that mediates this neglect involves the medial agranular cortex and thalamocortical basal ganglia networks (Reep & Corwin, 2009).

Using Posner's covert attention paradigm, described earlier, it has been shown that unilateral lesions of the parietal cortex in monkeys produce the same pattern of deficits observed in humans (Petersen & Robinson, 1986), though similarly lesioned rats do not display a deficit in covert attentional orienting (Rosner & Mittleman, 1996; Ward & Brown, 1997). In rhesus monkeys tested in the Posner paradigm, many cells in the IPS showed increased activity whenever the animal had to shift its attention, suggesting an important role for the parietal cortex in supporting covert orienting responses (Robinson, Bowman, & Kertzman, 1995).

SPATIAL ATTENTION BASED ON BINDING OF SPATIAL FEATURES

This section presents evidence for the role of the parietal cortex in the binding of features in both humans and animals. The studies presented involve binding within the visual modality and across modality (object–place).

Binding Within the Visual Modality—Humans

Treisman (1998) suggested that binding together different features of objects involves directing spatial attention to locations in which various features are currently active, while suppressing features from other locations to prevent erroneous binding. Furthermore, the parietal cortex may play an important role in ensuring that illusory conjunction errors do not appear in a variety of tasks, including search tasks. Thus, the PPC may be directly involved in perceptual binding between, for example, a shape and a color or a shape and a size, all of which require spatial attention. Support for this idea comes from the performance of patient RM, who had bilateral parietal cortex damage and who had difficulty in tasks requiring binding shape and color or shape and size. When shown two different colored letters, RM made many errors in the form of illusory conjunctions combining the shape of one letter with the color of the other (Friedman-Hill, Robertson, & Treisman, 1995). Similarly, in a visual search task requiring the detection of a target based on the conjunction of two features, RM made many errors, but RM had no difficulty in detecting a target based on one feature (Robertson et al., 1997). Using fMRI, Donner et al. (2002) reported greater activity in the right parietal cortex during conjunction search as compared with feature search, even when controlling for overall search difficulty. Shafritz, Gore, and Marois (2002) reported similar results with parietal cortex activation in conjunction search versus feature search for simultaneously presented information.

Binding Within the Visual Modality—Animals

To determine whether PPC lesions relative to sham lesions in rats result in the production of illusory-conjunction errors, a visual search paradigm was used with objects that varied either only on features of color or height (one feature) or the combination of color and height (two features; Kesner, 2009). In the one-feature condition, the subject was required to locate the targeted object among four other objects that differed in either color or height; that is, if the target object was a small black block, then four small white blocks for the color condition and four tall black blocks for the size condition would surround that object. In the two feature condition, the subject was required to locate the targeted object among four other objects that differed in both color and height; that is, if the target object was a small black block, then two small white blocks and two tall black blocks would randomly surround that object. The rule to be learned to obtain a food reward was to always discriminate between the different sized and colored objects to displace the targeted object. The results for color errors indicated that PPC lesioned rats relative to controls made only a few errors in detecting the one-feature component of the task, but they made many errors throughout all three blocks of trials for the two-feature condition, suggesting the appearance of illusory-conjunction errors. The results for size errors indicated that for the PPC lesioned rats relative to controls, there was an increase in errors for the two-feature condition, suggesting illusory-conjunction errors, but there were also some errors in the one-feature condition. Thus, it appears that the PPC supports the binding of visual features within a single object or landmark, a process that has been assumed to be mediated by spatial attention.

Binding Across Modality (Object–Place)—Humans

Even though there are many studies with humans that report on the role of PPC in the processing of objects or spatial locations, not many studies have dealt with the binding of objects and locations. One study (van Asselen et al., 2009) examined a population of patients who had had strokes resulting in varying degrees of parietal cortex damage. The results showed that in a combined object–place task, there was an impairment that was primarily due to damage in the left PPC. However, Berryhill, Drowos, and Olson (2009) found that retrieval of object–place associations did not result in impairment in patients with parietal cortex damage. On the basis of an fMRI analysis and a measure of memory confidence for the encoding and retrieval of object and spatial location associations, Sommer, Rose, Weiller, and Büchel (2005) reported bilateral SPL activations during encoding and retrieval. It is of interest to note that similar results were obtained for the parahippocampal area, which is directly connected to the superior parietal cortex. Sommer et al. (2005) interpreted the parietal cortex results as reflecting a role for the SPL in the allocation of attentional resources to the encoding and retrieval of object–place information. A related study showed that there is increased activation in the right lateral parietal cortex when one compares an object-in-a-context task with an object-only task (Suzuki, Tsukiura, Matsue, Yamadori, & Fujii, 2005). That many subareas of the parietal cortex appear to be involved in object–place binding probably reflects the use of different tasks in each of the experiments mentioned.

Binding Across Modality (Object–Place)—Animals

One possible role for the rodent parietal cortex could be to bind across modalities to maintain the association between landmark and spatial location information. In other words, the parietal cortex may not be involved in memory for a single landmark or a single spatial location but rather in the processing that assigns a specific landmark to a specific spatial location. To test this hypothesis, rats with small lesions of the parietal cortex were tested in an object and spatial location paired-associate task that required concurrent memory for both object and spatial location information. In addition, memory for landmark only or spatial location only information was also assessed. A deficit in the paired-associate task (which requires memory for both landmark and spatial location information), in the absence of deficits in either the landmark or the spatial location only memory, would support the idea that the PPC is involved in the memory for the combination of landmark and spatial location information. The results indicated that small lesions of the PPC as defined by Reep et al. (1994) and larger PPC lesions disrupted learning of the object–place paired-associate task but did not disrupt the learning of spatial or object discrimination (Long, Mellem, & Kesner, 1998). It should be noted that lesions of the hippocampus and especially the CA3 subregion of the hippocampus also disrupted object–place paired-associate learning (Gilbert & Kesner, 2002, 2003).

PERCEPTUAL AND IMPLICIT MEMORY FOR SPATIAL LOCATION

Research with both humans and rats shows a role for the parietal cortex in perceptual or implicit memory for spatial location. This evidence is presented in the sections that follow.

Humans

Perceptual and implicit memory based on spatial information could represent a process reflective of the operation of long-term memory or could reflect a dynamic temporal process that can be considered to be a component of a very short-term perceptual memory system. In patients with PPC damage, there is a deficit in spatial–perceptual repetition priming without a loss in working or explicit memory for spatial information (Ellis, Della Sala, & Logie, 1996). Krueger, Fischer, Heinecke, and Hagendorf (2007) used a location-based negative priming task with a prime-probe trial to determine, with fMRI, which cortical areas contribute to performance in the task. Participants were instructed to respond to the location of a prespecified target while ignoring a distractor at an irrelevant location. In this negative priming task they reported activation in the inferior parietal lobule associated with the priming compo-

nent of the task, suggesting a parietal contribution to perceptual priming for spatial location.

Animals

To examine whether results similar to that described for humans can be obtained in rats, two spatial continuous recognition training procedures were designed to query perceptual or episodic working memory and short-term or explicit memory in rats. A continuous recognition procedure was used to train rats on a 12-arm radial maze. The perceptual/implicit memory group received reinforcement at the end of each arm regardless of whether the arm was a novel arm or a repeated arm. This group showed decreased latencies when visiting repeated arms, displaying a repetition priming effect. The episodic/explicit memory group received reinforcement only when visiting an arm for the first time in a given sequence. This group showed increased latencies for repeated arms. After training, rats received PPC, hippocampus, or sham-operated and cortical control lesions. Retesting showed that relative to control and pretraining performance, the PPC lesioned rats were impaired in the perceptual/implicit memory condition but not in the episodic/explicit memory condition. In contrast, the hippocampal lesioned rats were impaired in the episodic/explicit episodic memory condition but not in the perceptual memory condition (Chiba, Kesner, & Jackson, 2002).

Thus, a double dissociation appears to exist between PPC and hippocampus for perceptual and implicit memory versus episodic and explicit memory operations, suggesting that the neural circuits centered on the hippocampus and PPC can operate independently of each other. This functional independence would require that spatial information could reach the hippocampus and PPC via separate neural pathways. Indeed, spatial information that reaches the dorsal lateral thalamus in the rat can be directed to the hippocampus via connections with the pre- and parasubiculum and medial entorhinal cortex and the PPC via direct connections. In the rat, there are no direct connections between the PPC and hippocampus. The parietal cortex and the hippocampus can interact via the entorhinal cortex or retrosplenial cortex and pre- and parasubiculum (Köhler, 1985; van Groen & Wyss, 1990; Witter et al., 2000).

To have an even better measure of perceptual and implicit memory, a new paradigm similar to paradigms used with humans was generated to measure positive as well as negative repetition priming for spatial locations in rats. In 48 repetition trials, all rats in the positive priming condition ran more quickly to the repeated spatial location. In the negative priming condition, it was assumed that rats not only actively attend to the positive stimulus but also actively inhibit responding to the negative stimulus (Neill &

Mathis, 1998). In 48 repetition trials, all rats in the negative priming condition ran more slowly to the repeated spatial location because the correct location had resulted in some inhibition on the previous trial. After training, rats received PPC lesions and then were retested. The results are shown in Figure 2.1 and indicate that PPC lesioned rats are impaired for both positive and negative priming (Kesner, 2000). In the positive priming paradigm, different rats received lesions of the hippocampus (Kesner,

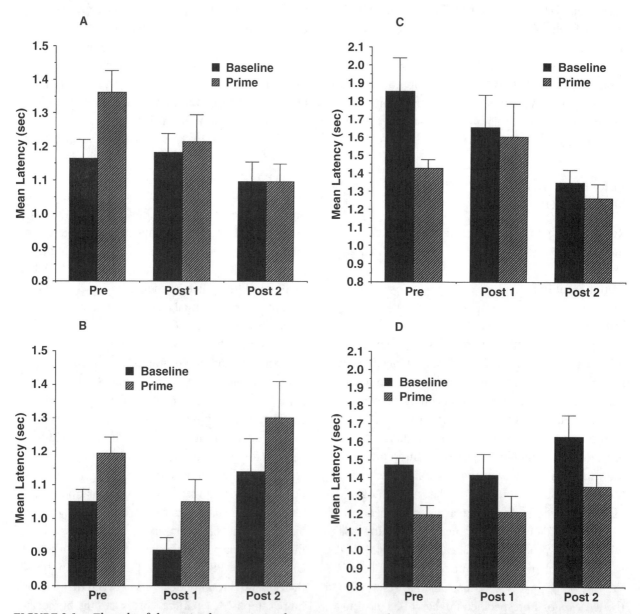

FIGURE 2.1.   The role of the parietal cortex in implicit memory. Mean latency (seconds) to respond in the baseline (base) condition and repetition (prime) condition for pre- and postsurgery within the negative priming condition for (a) parietal cortex lesioned group and (b) sham-operated control group as well as within the positive priming condition for (c) parietal cortex lesioned group and (d) sham-operated control group.

2000). The results indicate that rats with hippocampal lesions show normal positive priming. Thus, it appears that the PPC, but not the hippocampus, is directly involved in perceptual and implicit memory for spatial location information. The observation that the PPC does not mediate explicit memory is supported by the observation that PPC lesions do not disrupt performance in a five-choice serial reaction time task (Muir, Everitt, & Robbins, 1996).

WORKING MEMORY FOR SPATIAL INFORMATION

From a dynamic processing point of view, short-term or working memory operates on information that can be retained in memory briefly so that the information can potentially be used to modulate long-term memory processes and to guide behavior. In the context of spatial information processing, it can be shown that the parietal cortex plays an important role in spatial short-term or spatial working memory. Evidence from humans, monkeys, and rats is presented in this section.

Humans

In humans, it has been shown that lesions of the right PPC disrupt spatial working memory in a variety of tasks that involve spatial processing (for a recent review, see Olson & Berryhill, 2009). Furthermore, patients who display the neglect syndrome are impaired in spatial working memory (Malhotra, Mannan, Driver, & Husain, 2004). Additional research has shown that transient inactivation of the PPC using TMS disrupts spatial working memory (Kessels, d'Alfonso, Postma, & de Haan, 2000; Koch et al., 2005). Neuroimaging studies have shown that the PPC is activated in spatial working memory tasks (D'Esposito et al., 1998; Smith & Jonides, 1998) and appears to maintain spatial information throughout the delay period (Curtis, 2006; Linden, 2007). To be more specific, Curtis (2006) showed that in an oculomotor delayed-response task, fMRI results showed sustained maintenance of spatial information in the IPS. Furthermore, TMS applied to the PPC early in the delay period within the oculomotor delayed-response task disrupts performance, suggesting that the PPC may play a role in the retrospective coding of visual space. Thus, converging evidence from a variety of sources supports the idea that the PPC plays an important role in spatial short-term or working memory. It has been suggested that different modules may influence different domains or attributes of working memory, which in the case of spatial information could be based on the operation of a visual–spatial sketchpad associated with integration of visual and spatial information or episodic memory associated with the integration of spatial and temporal information (Baddeley, 2000).

Animals

In monkeys, sustained firing of cells in the PPC and LIP cortex was found during the delay associated with spatial working memory tasks (Constantinidis & Procyk, 2004; Constantinidis & Steinmetz, 1996). Of interest is the observation that neural firing during the delay period is disrupted by intervening, distracting stimuli, suggesting that the PPC neural activity is focused primarily on the most recent stimulus encountered (Constantinidis & Steinmetz, 1996), which supports the idea of retrospective coding of information, as reported in humans (Curtis, 2006). Furthermore, cooling of the PPC disrupts spatial working memory, and lesions of the PPC produce impairment in performance of the oculomotor delayed-response task (Curtis, 2006; Quintana & Fuster, 1993).

In contrast to findings from human and monkey studies, the PPC in rats does not appear to play a role in short-term or working memory for spatial information. For example, Kolb, Buhrmann, McDonald, and Sutherland (1994) reported that rats with PPC lesions were not impaired on a working memory spatial location task in an eight-arm maze. In addition, rats with PPC lesions were not impaired using a continuous recognition paradigm for spatial locations on a 12-arm radial maze, which requires the operation of working memory (Chiba et al., 2002).

LONG-TERM MEMORY

Humans

Because patients with PPC lesions do not show retrograde or anterograde amnesia, the acquisition of information to be stored in long-term memory has not been thoroughly investigated. Some data are available from studies using positron emission tomography (PET) scans in humans: It has been shown that the PPC is activated while participants memorized information observed in a film that depicted navigation in an urban area or while they explored and learned about a virtual reality environment (Maguire et al., 1998). In addition, in the same virtual reality environment, right PPC activity correlated highly with accuracy in performance (Maguire et al., 1998). In addition, a PET study showed that the PPC is activated in humans performing a memorized sequence of saccadic eye movements (Berthoz, 1999) and in taxi drivers generating a verbal description of routes through London (Maguire, Frackowiak, & Frith, 1997).

Some recent evidence points to a possible role of PPC in retrieval of autobiographical and episodic memory. For example, patients with ventral parietal cortex lesions were asked to remember a number of autobiographical memories that included spatial information. They were then asked to recall these events freely in as much detail as possible and were asked specific questions associated with the recalled memories. The results indicated that the recalled material was somewhat vague and did not contain much detail. However, when questioned for specific details related to their memories, they had no difficulty (Berryhill, Phuong, Picasso, Cabeza, & Olson, 2007).

In other tasks that require retrieval of episodic memory, lateral parietal cortex is activated in relation to contextual memory for spatial information. On the basis of the measurement of source memory, which involves retrieval of specific details of the encoding context of events and is reflective of the use of recollection rather than familiarity, a number of studies have indicated that source memory retrieval results in left superior and IPL activation, whereas estimates of recollection results in increased activation in the SPL (for reviews, see Ciaramelli, Grady, & Moscovitch, 2008; Uncapher & Wagner, 2009; Wagner, Shannon, Kahn, & Buckner, 2005). There are a number of explanations that have been offered to account for the role of the parietal cortex in mediating retrieval of episodic memory for all modalities, including space. One of the main ideas is based on the observation that the parietal cortex is

involved in working memory that can then interface with episodic retrieval through the use of an episodic buffer (Baddeley, 2000). An alternative model has suggested that the parietal cortex is activated by attentional processes that can then modulate episodic memory (Ciaramelli et al., 2008).

Animals

Because many of the studies with PPC lesioned rats that involve new learning were presented in an earlier section, we concentrate in this section on retention that presumably involves a role of storage and retrieval of spatial information in PPC. For example, it has been shown that in rats, lesions of the PPC disrupt retention of a spatial navigation task using either the water maze or dry land version of the water maze task (DiMattia & Kesner, 1988; Kesner et al., 1991; Save & Moghaddam, 1996). Furthermore, in a multiple-object scene task, PPC lesions disrupt retention of a previously learned discrimination in which a rat has to detect a change in the location of the object in a scene; however, they have no effect on a previously learned discrimination in which the rat has to detect a change in one of the objects (DeCoteau & Kesner, 1998). Finally, rats with PPC lesions do not react to a change consisting of removing a stimulus requiring a retrieval-dependent pattern-completion process (Save, Buhot, Foreman, & Thinus-Blanc, 1992).

Other examples of a role for PPC in storing spatial information in long-term memory that are also based on retention tests include a study by Kesner, DiMattia, and Crutcher (1987), who showed that in an eight-arm maze, PPC lesions placed in rats after training on four unbaited and four baited arms resulted in a deficit in retrieval from reference long-term memory but not short-term working or episodic memory. If one assumes that the presentation of unbaited arms reflects the operation of long-term memory and that the presentation of baited arms reflects the operation of short-term or working memory, then lesions of the PPC only disrupt long-term memory, not working memory. In a different study (the Hebb-Williams maze study described earlier), bilateral lesions were made to PPC before maze testing (acquisition) or after maze testing (retention; Rogers & Kesner, 2007). The results indicated that during acquisition, lesions of the PPC impaired egocentric maze acquisition but had no effect on the learning of an allocentric version of the maze task. During retention, lesions of the PPC produced a significant impairment on both maze versions, suggesting that the PPC may be combining both egocentric and allocentric information into long-term memory during normal learning of the maze and that after a PPC lesion, the combined information may not be available to the animal.

Finally, there is some support for the idea that the parietal cortex may be a site for long-term representation of complex spatial information. Cho and Kesner (1996; Cho, Kesner & Brodale, 1995) have shown that rats with parietal cortex lesions have a nongraded retrograde amnesia for four, but not two, previously learned spatial discriminations prior to surgery, suggesting that the deficit cannot be due to a performance or anterograde amnesia problem but rather appears to be a function of the amount or complexity of the spatial information to be stored and to be remembered.

To understand the role of the PPC in mediating perceptual, short-term or working memory, and long-term memory for spatial location information, it is important to recognize that there are not only regional differences within the PPC and its neural connections to other structures but there may also be some differences in terms of the PPC contribution to the processing of spatial mnemonic information. Regarding perceptual and implicit memory, findings from lesion and fMRI studies with humans and lesions in rats have shown that there is a contribution of the PPC to perceptual memory in both positive and negative priming paradigms in humans and rats. However, there has not been extensive research on the role of PPC on perceptual memory for spatial location. With respect to short-term or working memory, there is considerable evidence from lesion, neuroimaging, and TMS studies for the role of many subregions of the PPC in humans, and on the basis of lesions and single unit recording studies in monkeys, for a role of the PPC in processing of short-term or working memory. However, lesion data in rats do not support a role for the PPC in processing short-term or working memory, which could be due to the use of slightly different spatial

tasks than were used in humans and monkeys. With respect to long-term memory, the study of the role of PPC in long-term memory for spatial location has focused on its role during retrieval of previously learned information, with an emphasis on retrieval from long-term storage or access to newly stored information. According to neuroimaging and lesion data, there is clear involvement of the PPC during retrieval of spatial information, but the mechanisms associated with this PPC involvement are not clear. In rats, studies primarily on lesions or temporary inactivation of the PPC have provided good evidence for PPC involvement in long-term memory using a variety of different paradigms.

MENTAL IMAGERY AND SPATIAL TRANSFORMATIONS

Humans have the remarkable ability to imagine and transform spatial representations, a process that may be critical to many other spatial–cognitive tasks, such as navigation and action planning, and is largely supported by regions of the PPC as well as connected regions of the premotor cortex (Zacks, 2008). Much of the work on mental rotation has involved a classic task that requires a decision about the congruency of one rotated object with respect to another. Shepard and Metzler (1971) found that the time required to make the decision with respect to two- or three-dimensional figures was a function of the angular disparity between the two objects. This approach was extended to the study of images of other types of objects including body parts such as hands and feet (Cooper & Shepard, 1975; Parsons, 1987, 1994). Together, there is a body of work indicating that mental imagery and, specifically, mental rotation rely on analog spatial representations that match the spatial properties of the physical world, rather than propositional descriptions (Kosslyn, 1994; but see Pylyshyn, 2003). The emergence of functional neuroimaging techniques strengthened this hypothesis further, identifying neural substrates that correspond to visual, spatial, and motor processing. Both object and body-part rotation studies have shown activation in the PPC (primarily SPL and IPS), as well as in regions of the posterior temporal cortex (including MT), frontal cortex (supplementary motor area and lateral premotor cortex and some primary motor cortex), and cerebellum (Alivisatos & Petrides, 1996; Kosslyn, Digirolamo, Thompson, & Alpert, 1998; Podzebenko, Egan, & Watson, 2005; Seurinck, Vingerhoets, de Lange, & Achten, 2004; Wraga, Thompson, Alpert, & Kosslyn, 2003).

Despite significant overlap in patterns of activation for different mental transformation tasks, there are also distinctions identified in the neural mechanisms supporting these tasks that accompany behavioral differences as well. For example, in a task comparing two different egocentric rotations, Creem-Regehr, Neil, and Yeh (2007) found greater left PPC activation (and additional premotor cortex activation) for hand rotation and greater right PPC activation for perspective rotation, which is consistent with the notion that body-part and perspective transformations rely on different (intrinsic vs. extrinsic) egocentric spatial frames of reference for planning actions. As mentioned earlier, evidence from both neuropsychology and neuroimaging supports a left-lateralized parietal system for motor planning and intrinsic coordinate control (Buxbaum, Johnson-Frey, & Bartlett-Williams, 2005; Chaminade, Meltzoff, & Decety, 2005; Jax, Buxbaum, & Moll, 2006), as is seen in patients with ideomotor apraxia. A comparison of patients with right versus left parietal lesions also supports this distinction (Tomasino, Toraldo, & Rumiati, 2003).

SUMMARY

Parietal cortex is clearly important for spatial cognition. We have discussed the numerous functions of the PPC relating to spatial processing, from sensorimotor transformations to attention, to higher level navigation, memory, and imagery. Several themes emerge when considering spatial cognition across human and nonhuman animals. First, there is the importance of spatial reference frames and spatial frameworks. Although there is much evidence in support of egocentric processing in the PCC, there is also integration between egocentric and allocentric reference frames and clear distinctions in the parietal mechanisms underlying different forms of egocentric processing and spatial relations. This includes differences in eye-, head-, and hand-centered repre-

sentations, distinctions between near and far space, and the differential recruitment of parietal areas for coordinate/metric and categorical/topological information. A second emerging theme is the functional differences between superior, inferior, and medial PPC in humans with respect to their roles in egocentric processing. Third, there are the findings involving lateralization in parietal function. It is notable that although there are relatively clear distinctions between right and left hemisphere dominance for tasks such as reaching and grasping, neuropsychological deficits such as unilateral neglect and apraxia, and coordinate/categorical processing in humans, these distinctions do not emerge clearly in animal parietal function. Fourth, the PPC plays a critical role in attention. Even though our review focused on the role of spatial attention in neglect, covert attention, and binding of spatial features, the role of parietal mechanisms in attention is likely much more broad. Finally, there is evidence across all animals presented here that the parietal cortex is critical to memory processing, ranging from navigation and path integration to perceptual, working, and long-term memory, although again with some apparent differences between human and rodent parietal specialization. Although questions remain to be answered, this analysis of parietal function may begin to help to advance an understanding of how we perceive, act on, and remember the spaces around us.

SUGGESTED REFERENCES FOR FURTHER READING

Culham, J. C., Cavina-Pratesi, C., & Singhal, A. (2006). The role of parietal cortex in visuomotor control: What have we learned from neuroimaging? *Neuropsychologia, 44,* 2668–2684. doi:10.1016/j.neuropsychologia.2005.11.003

A comprehensive review of research from functional neuroimaging in humans supporting the roles of human parietal cortex in visuomotor function.

Halligan, P. W., Fink, G. R., Marshall, J. C., & Vallar, G. (2003). Spatial cognition: Evidence from visual neglect. *Trends in Cognitive Science, 7,* 125–133. doi:10.1016/S1364-6613(03)00032-9

An accessible review and analysis of research on visual neglect demonstrating the numerous complex systems of spatial cognition and their relation to posterior parietal cortex function.

Kesner, R. & Bucci, D. J. (2009). Attention, sensory-motor integration, and representation of spatial information functions of the parietal cortex: A comparative approach [Special issue]. *Neurobiology of Learning and Memory, 91*(2).

A special issue dedicated to parietal cortex function across rodents, nonhuman primates, and humans.

Sack, A. T. (2009). Parietal cortex and spatial cognition. *Behavioral Brain Research, 202,* 153–161. doi:10.1016/j.bbr.2009.03.012

A review article synthesizing evidence from neuropsychological, functional neuroimaging, and transcranial magnetic stimulation approaches to understanding the different functional contributions of the parietal cortex in spatial cognition.

References

Ackroyd, K., Riddoch, M. J., Humphreys, G. W., Nightingale, S., & Townsend, S. (2002). Widening the sphere of influence: Using a tool to extend extrapersonal visual space in a patient with severe neglect. *Neurocase, 8,* 1–12. doi:10.1093/neucas/8.1.1

Alivisatos, B., & Petrides, M. (1996). Functional activation of the human brain during mental rotation. *Neuropsychologia, 35,* 111–118. doi:10.1016/S0028-3932(96)00083-8

Arzy, S., Thut, G., Mohr, C., Michel, C. M., & Blanke, O. (2006). Neural basis of embodiment: Distinct contributions of temporoparietal junction and extrastriate body area. *The Journal of Neuroscience, 26,* 8074–8081. doi:10.1523/JNEUROSCI.0745-06.2006

Baciu, M., Koenig, O., Vernier, M., Bedoin, N., Rubin, C., & Segebarth, C. (1999). Categorical and coordinate spatial relations: fMRI evidence for hemispheric specialization. *Neuroreport, 10,* 1373–1378. doi:10.1097/00001756-199904260-00040

Baddeley, A. (2000). The episodic buffer: A new component of working memory? *Trends in Cognitive Sciences, 4,* 417–423. doi:10.1016/S1364-6613(00)01538-2

Barrow, C. J., & Latto, R. (1996). The role of inferior parietal cortex and fornix in route following and topographic orientation in cynomolgus monkeys. *Behavioural Brain Research, 75,* 99–112. doi:10.1016/0166-4328(96)00177-5

Berryhill, M. E., Drowos, D. B., & Olson, I. R. (2009). Bilateral parietal cortex damage does not impair associative memory for paired stimuli. *Cognitive Neuropsychology, 26,* 606–619. doi:10.1080/02643290903534150

Berryhill, M. E., Phuong, L., Picasso, L., Cabeza, R., & Olson, I. R. (2007). Parietal lobe and episodic memory: Bilateral damage causes impaired free recall of autobiographical memory. *The Journal of Neuroscience, 27,* 14415–14423. doi:10.1523/JNEUROSCI.4163-07.2007

Berthoz, A. (1999). Hippocampal and parietal contribution to topokinetic and topographic memory. In N. Burgess, K. J. Jeffery, & J. O'Keefe (Eds.), *The hippocampal and parietal foundations of spatial cognition* (pp. 381–403). New York, NY: Oxford University Press.

Berti, A., & Frassinetti, F. (2000). When far becomes near: Remapping of space by tool use. *Journal of Cognitive Neuroscience, 12,* 415–420. doi:10.1162/089892900562237

Blanke, O., & Arzy, S. (2005). The out-of-body experience: Disturbed self-processing at the temporo-parietal junction. *The Neuroscientist, 11,* 16–24. doi:10.1177/1073858404270885

Boyd, M. G., & Thomas, R. K. (1977). Posterior association cortex lesions in rats: Mazes, pattern discrimination and reversal learning. *Physiological Psychology, 5,* 455–461.

Bridgeman, B., Peery, S., & Anand, S. (1997). Interaction of cognitive and sensorimotor maps of visual space. *Perception & Psychophysics, 59,* 456–469. doi:10.3758/BF03211912

Buxbaum, L. J., Johnson-Frey, S. H., & Bartlett-Williams, M. (2005). Deficient internal models for planning hand–object interactions in apraxia. *Neuropsychologia, 43,* 917–929. doi:10.1016/j.neuropsychologia.2004.09.006

Buxbaum, L. J., & Kalenine, S. (2010). Action knowledge, visuomotor activation, and embodiment in the two action systems. *Annals of the New York Academy of Sciences, 1191,* 201–218. doi:10.1111/j.1749-6632.2010.05447.x

Calton, J. L., & Taube, J. S. (2009). Where am I and how will I get there from here? A role for posterior parietal cortex in the integration of spatial information and route planning. *Neurobiology of Learning and Memory, 91,* 186–196. doi:10.1016/j.nlm.2008.09.015

Calton, J. L., Turner, C. S., Cyrenne, D.-L. M., Lee, B. R., & Taube, J. S. (2008). Landmark control and updating of self-movement cues are largely maintained in head direction cells after lesions of the posterior parietal cortex. *Behavioral Neuroscience, 122,* 827–840. doi:10.1037/0735-7044.122.4.827

Cavanna, A. E., & Trimble, M. R. (2006). The precuneus: A review of its functional anatomy and behavioural correlates. *Brain: A Journal of Neurology, 129,* 564–583. doi:10.1093/brain/awl004

Chambers, C. D., Payne, J. M., Stokes, M. G., & Mattingley, J. B. (2004). Fast and slow parietal pathways mediate spatial attention. *Nature Neuroscience, 7,* 217–218. doi:10.1038/nn1203

Chaminade, T., Meltzoff, A. N., & Decety, J. (2005). An fMRI study of imitation: action representation and body schema. *Neuropsychologia, 43*, 115–127. doi:10.1016/j.neuropsychologia.2004.04.026

Chen, L. L., Lin, L.-H., Barnes, C. A., & McNaughton, B. L. (1994). Head-direction cells in the rat posterior cortex: II. Contributions of visual and ideothetic information to the directional firing. *Experimental Brain Research, 101*, 24–34. doi:10.1007/BF00243213

Chen, L. L., Lin, L.-H., Green, E. J., Barnes, C. A., & McNaughton, B. L. (1994). Head-direction cells in the rat posterior cortex: I. Anatomical distribution and behavioral modulation. *Experimental Brain Research, 101*, 8–23. doi:10.1007/BF00243212

Chen, L. L., & Nakamura, K. (1998). Head-centered representation and spatial memory in rat posterior parietal cortex. *Psychobiology, 26*, 119–127.

Chiba, A. A., Kesner, R. P., & Jackson, P. (2002). Two forms of spatial memory: A double dissociation between the parietal cortex and the hippocampus in the rat. *Behavioral Neuroscience, 116*, 874–883. doi:10.1037/0735-7044.116.5.874

Cho, Y. H., & Kesner, R. P. (1996). Involvement of entorhinal cortex or parietal cortex in long-term spatial discrimination memory in rats: Retrograde amnesia. *Behavioral Neuroscience, 110*, 436–442. doi:10.1037/0735-7044.110.3.436

Cho, Y. H., Kesner, R. P., & Brodale, S. (1995). Retrograde and anterograde amnesia for spatial discrimination in rats: Role of hippocampus, entorhinal cortex and parietal cortex. *Psychobiology, 23*, 185–194.

Ciaramelli, E., Grady, C. L., & Moscovitch, M. (2008). Top-down and bottom-up attention to memory: A hypothesis (AtoM) on the role of the posterior parietal cortex in memory retrieval. *Neuropsychologia, 46*, 1828–1851. doi:10.1016/j.neuropsychologia.2008.03.022

Cisek, P. (2008). A remarkable facilitating effect of parietal damage. *Neuron, 58*, 7–9. doi:10.1016/j.neuron.2008.03.025

Colby, C. L. (1998). Action-oriented spatial reference frames in cortex. *Neuron, 20*, 15–24. doi:10.1016/S0896-6273(00)80429-8

Colby, C. L., & Goldberg, M. E. (1999). Space and attention in parietal cortex. *Annual Review of Neuroscience, 22*, 319–349. doi:10.1146/annurev.neuro.22.1.319

Connolly, J. D., Andersen, R. A., & Goodale, M. A. (2003). FMRI evidence for a 'parietal reach region' in the human brain. *Experimental Brain Research, 153*, 140–145. doi:10.1007/s00221-003-1587-1

Constantinidis, C., & Procyk, E. (2004). The primate working memory networks. *Cognitive, Affective &*

Behavioral Neuroscience, 4, 444–465. doi:10.3758/CABN.4.4.444

Constantinidis, C., & Steinmetz, M. A. (1996). Neuronal activity in posterior parietal area 7a during the delay periods of a spatial memory task. *Journal of Neurophysiology, 76*, 1352–1355.

Cooper, L. A., & Shepard, R. N. (1975). Mental transformations in the identification of left and right hands. *Journal of Experimental Psychology: Human Perception and Performance, 1*, 48–56. doi:10.1037/0096-1523.1.1.48

Corbetta, M., & Shulman, G. L. (2002). Control of goal-directed and stimulus-driven attention in the brain. *Nature Reviews Neuroscience, 3*, 215–229. doi:10.1038/nrn755

Corwin, J. V., & Reep, R. L. (1998). Rodent posterior parietal cortex as a component of a cortical network mediating directed spatial attention. *Psychobiology, 26*, 87–102.

Creem-Regehr, S. H. (2009). Sensory–motor and cognitive functions of the human posterior parietal cortex involved in manual actions. *Neurobiology of Learning and Memory, 91*, 166–171. doi:10.1016/j.nlm.2008.10.004

Creem-Regehr, S. H., Neil, J. A., & Yeh, H. J. (2007). Neural correlates of two imagined egocentric transformations. *NeuroImage, 35*, 916–927. doi:10.1016/j.neuroimage.2006.11.057

Culham, J. C. (2004). Human brain imaging reveals a parietal area specialized for grasping. In N. Kanwisher & J. Duncan (Eds.), *Attention and performance XX: Functional brain imaging of visual cognition* (pp. 417–438). Oxford, England: Oxford University Press.

Culham, J. C., Cavina-Pratesi, C., & Singhal, A. (2006). The role of parietal cortex in visuomotor control: What have we learned from neuroimaging? *Neuropsychologia, 44*, 2668–2684. doi:10.1016/j.neuropsychologia.2005.11.003

Culham, J. C., Danckert, S. L., De Souza, J. F. X., Gati, J. S., Menon, R. S., & Goodale, M. A. (2003). Visually guided grasping produces fMRI activation in dorsal but not ventral stream brain areas. *Experimental Brain Research, 153*, 180–189. doi:10.1007/s00221-003-1591-5

Culham, J. C., & Kanwisher, N. G. (2001). Neuroimaging of cognitive functions in human parietal cortex. *Current Opinion in Neurobiology, 11*, 157–163. doi:10.1016/S0959-4388(00)00191-4

Curtis, C. E. (2006). Prefrontal and parietal contributions to spatial working memory. *Neuroscience, 139*, 173–180. doi:10.1016/j.neuroscience.2005.04.070

Cutting, J. E., & Vishton, P. M. (1995). Perceiving layout and knowing distances: The integration, relative potency, and contextual use of different information about depth. In W. Epstein & S. Rogers (Eds.), *Perception of space and motion* (pp. 69–117). New York, NY: Academic Press.

Danckert, J., & Ferber, S. (2006). Revisiting unilateral neglect. *Neuropsychologia, 44,* 987–1006. doi:10.1016/j.neuropsychologia.2005.09.004

Dassonville, P., Bridgeman, B., Kaur Bala, H., Thiem, P., & Sampanes, A. (2004). The induced Roelofs effect: Two visual systems or the shift of a single reference frame? *Vision Research, 44,* 603–611. doi:10.1016/j.visres.2003.10.017

DeCoteau, W. E., Hoang, L., Huff, L., Stone, A., & Kesner, R. P. (2004). Effects of hippocampus and medial caudate nucleus lesions on memory for direction information in rats. *Behavioral Neuroscience, 118,* 540–545. doi:10.1037/0735-7044.118.3.540

DeCoteau, W. E., & Kesner, R. P. (1998). Effects of hippocampal and parietal cortex lesions on the processing of multiple-object scenes. *Behavioral Neuroscience, 112,* 68–82. doi:10.1037/0735-7044.112.1.68

D'Esposito, M., Aguirre, G. K., Zarahn, E., Ballard, D., Shin, R. K., & Lease, J. (1998). Functional MRI studies of spatial and nonspatial working memory. *Cognitive Brain Research, 7,* 1–13. doi:10.1016/S0926-6410(98)00004-4

Deuel, R. K. (1987). Neural dysfunction during hemineglect after cortical damage in two monkey models. In M. Jeannerod (Ed.), *Neurophysiological and neuropsychological aspects of spatial neglect* (pp. 315–334). New York, NY: Elsevier. doi:10.1016/S0166-4115(08)61719-7

DiMattia, B. V., & Kesner, R. P. (1988). Spatial cognitive maps: Differential role of parietal cortex and hippocampal formation. *Behavioral Neuroscience, 102,* 471–480. doi:10.1037/0735-7044.102.4.471

Donner, T. H., Kettermann, A., Diesch, E., Ostendorf, F., Villringer, A., & Brandt, S. A. (2002). Visual feature and conjunction searches of equal difficulty engage only partially overlapping frontoparietal networks. *NeuroImage, 15,* 16–25. doi:10.1006/nimg.2001.0951

Duhamel, J. R., Colby, C. L., & Goldberg, M. E. (1992, January 3). The updating of the representation of visual space in parietal cortex by intended eye movements. *Science, 255,* 90–92. doi:10.1126/science.1553535

Ellis, A. X., Della Sala, S., & Logie, R. H. (1996). The bailiwick of visuo–spatial working memory: Evidence from unilateral spatial neglect. *Brain Research. Cognitive Brain Research, 3,* 71–78. doi:10.1016/0926-6410(95)00031-3

Etienne, A. S., & Jeffery, K. J. (2004). Path integration in mammals. *Hippocampus, 14,* 180–192. doi:10.1002/hipo.10173

Fierro, B., Brighina, F., Piazza, A., Oliveri, M., & Bisiach, E. (2001). Timing of right parietal and frontal cortex activity in visuo–spatial perception: A TMS study in normal individuals. *Neuroreport, 12,* 2605–2607. doi:10.1097/00001756-200108080-00062

Foreman, N., Save, E., Thinus-Blanc, C., & Buhot, M. C. (1992). Visually guided locomotion, distractibility, and the missing-stimulus effect in hooded rats with unilateral or bilateral lesions of parietal cortex. *Behavioral Neuroscience, 106,* 529–538. doi:10.1037/0735-7044.106.3.529

Friedman-Hill, S. R., Robertson, L., & Treisman, A. (1995, August 11). Parietal contributions to visual feature binding: Evidence from a patient with bilateral lesions. *Science, 269,* 853–855. doi:10.1126/science.7638604

Gallistel, C. R. (1990). *The organization of learning.* Cambridge, MA: MIT Press.

Gilbert, P. E., & Kesner, R. P. (2002). Role of the rodent hippocampus in paired-associate learning involving associations between a stimulus and a spatial location. *Behavioral Neuroscience, 116,* 63–71. doi:10.1037/0735-7044.116.1.63

Gilbert, P. E., & Kesner, R. P. (2003). Localization of function within the dorsal hippocampus: The role of the CA3 subregion in paired-associate learning. *Behavioral Neuroscience, 117,* 1385–1394. doi:10.1037/0735-7044.117.6.1385

Glover, S. (2004). Separate visual representations in the planning and control of action. *Behavioral and Brain Sciences, 27,* 3–24. doi:10.1017/S0140525X04000020

Golob, E. J., & Taube, J. S. (1999). Head direction cells in rats with hippocampal or overlying neocortical lesions: Evidence for impaired angular path integration. *The Journal of Neuroscience, 19,* 7198–7211.

Goodale, M. A., & Milner, A. D. (1992). Separate visual pathways for perception and action. *Trends in Neurosciences, 15,* 20–25. doi:10.1016/0166-2236(92)90344-8

Goodrich-Hunsaker, N. J., Howard, B. P., Hunsaker, M. R., & Kesner, R. P. (2008). Human topological task adapted for rats: Spatial information processes of the parietal cortex. *Neurobiology of Learning and Memory, 90,* 389–394. doi:10.1016/j.nlm.2008.05.002

Goodrich-Hunsaker, N. J., Hunsaker, M. R., & Kesner, R. P. (2005). Dissociating the role of the parietal cortex and dorsal hippocampus for spatial information processing. *Behavioral Neuroscience, 119,* 1307–1315. doi:10.1037/0735-7044.119.5.1307

Grüsser, O. J. (1983). Multimodal structure of the extrapersonal space. In A. Hein & M. Jeannerod (Eds.), *Spatially oriented behaviors* (pp. 327–352). New York, NY: Springer-Verlag. doi:10.1007/978-1-4612-5488-1_18

Halligan, P. W., Fink, G. R., Marshall, J. C., & Vallar, G. (2003). Spatial cognition: Evidence from visual neglect. *Trends in Cognitive Sciences, 7,* 125–133. doi:10.1016/S1364-6613(03)00032-9

Heilman, K. M., Watson, R. T., & Valenstein, E. (1993). Neglect and related disorders. In M. Heilman & E. Valenstein (Eds.), *Clinical neuropsychology* (4th ed., pp. 296–346). Oxford, England: Oxford University Press.

Hilgetag, C. C., Theoret, H., & Pascual-Leone, A. (2001). Enhanced visual spatial attention ipsilateral to rTMS-induced "virtual lesions" of human parietal cortex. *Nature Neuroscience, 4,* 953–957. doi:10.1038/nn0901-953

Hoh, T. E., Kolb, B., Eppel, A., Vanderwolf, C. H., & Cain, D. P. (2003). Role of the neocortex in the water maze task in the rat: A detailed behavioral and Golgi-Cox analysis. *Behavioural Brain Research, 138,* 81–94. doi:10.1016/S0166-4328(02)00237-1

Holm, S., & Mogensen, J. (1993). Contralateral somato-sensory neglect in unrestrained rats after lesion of the parietal cortex of the left hemisphere. *Acta Neurobiologiae Experimentalis, 53,* 569–576.

Iachini, T., & Ruggiero, G. (2006). Egocentric and allocentric spatial frames of reference. *Cognitive Processing, 7,* 126–127. doi:10.1007/s10339-006-0100-8

Iachini, T., Ruggiero, G., Conson, M., & Trojano, L. (2009). Lateralization of egocentric and allocentric spatial processing after parietal brain lesions. *Brain and Cognition, 69,* 514–520. doi:10.1016/j.bandc.2008.11.001

Iriki, A., Tanaka, M., & Iwamura, Y. (1996). Coding of modified body schema during tool use by macaque post-central neurons. *Neuroreport, 7,* 2325–2330. doi:10.1097/00001756-199610020-00010

Jager, G., & Potsma, A. (2003). On the hemispheric specialization for categorical and coordinate spatial relations: A review of the current evidence. *Neuropsychologia, 41,* 504–515. doi:10.1016/S0028-3932(02)00086-6

Janzen, G., & Weststeijn, C. G. (2007). Neural representation of object location and route direction: An event-related fMRI study. *Brain Research, 1165,* 116–125. doi:10.1016/j.brainres.2007.05.074

Jax, S. A., Buxbaum, L. J., & Moll, A. D. (2006). Deficits in movement planning and intrinsic coordinate control in ideomotor apraxia. *Journal of Cognitive Neuroscience, 18,* 2063–2076. doi:10.1162/jocn.2006.18.12.2063

Jeffery, K. J., Donnett, J. G., Burgess, N., & O'Keefe, J. M. (1997). Directional control of hippocampal place fields. *Experimental Brain Research, 117,* 131–142. doi:10.1007/s002210050206

Johnson, S. H., & Grafton, S. T. (2003). From "acting on" to "acting with": The functional anatomy of object-oriented action schemata. *Progress in Brain Research, 142,* 127–139. doi:10.1016/S0079-6123(03)42010-4

Johnson-Frey, S. H., Newman-Norlund, R., & Grafton, S. T. (2005). A distributed left hemisphere network active during planning of everyday tool use skills. *Cerebral Cortex, 15,* 681–695. doi:10.1093/cercor/bhh169

Karnath, H. O., Berger, M. F., Kuker, W., & Rorden, C. (2004). The anatomy of spatial neglect based on voxelwise statistical analysis: A study of 140 patients. *Cerebral Cortex, 14,* 1164–1172. doi:10.1093/cercor/bhh076

Karnath, H. O., & Perenin, M. T. (2005). Cortical control of visually guided reaching: Evidence from patients with optic ataxia. *Cerebral Cortex, 15,* 1561–1569. doi:10.1093/cercor/bhi034

Kesner, R. P. (2000). Behavioral analysis of the contribution of the hippocampus and parietal cortex to the processing of information: Interactions and dissociations. *Hippocampus, 10,* 483–490. doi:10.1002/1098-1063(2000)10:4<483::AID-HIPO15>3.0.CO;2-Z

Kesner, R. P. (2009). The posterior parietal cortex and long-term memory representation of spatial information. *Neurobiology of Learning and Memory, 91,* 197–206. doi:10.1016/j.nlm.2008.09.004

Kesner, R. P., DiMattia, B. V., & Crutcher, K. A. (1987). Evidence for neocortical involvement in reference memory. *Behavioral and Neural Biology, 47,* 40–53. doi:10.1016/S0163-1047(87)90145-2

Kesner, R. P., Farnsworth, G., & DiMattia, B. V. (1989). Double dissociation of egocentric and allocentric space following medial prefrontal and parietal cortex lesions in the rat. *Behavioral Neuroscience, 103,* 956–961. doi:10.1037/0735-7044.103.5.956

Kesner, R. P., Farnsworth, G., & Kametani, H. (1991). Role of parietal cortex and hippocampus in representing spatial information. *Cerebral Cortex, 1,* 367–373. doi:10.1093/cercor/1.5.367

Kessels, R. P., d'Alfonso, A. A., Postma, A., & de Haan, E. H. (2000). Spatial working memory performance after high-frequency repetitive transcranial magnetic stimulation of the left and right posterior parietal cortex in humans. *Neuroscience Letters, 287,* 68–70. doi:10.1016/S0304-3940(00)01146-0

King, V. R., & Corwin, J. V. (1992). Spatial deficits and hemispheric asymmetries in the rat following unilateral and bilateral lesions of posterior parietal or medial agranular cortex. *Behavioural Brain Research, 50,* 53–68. doi:10.1016/S0166-4328(05)80287-6

King, V. R., & Corwin, J. V. (1993). Comparison of hemi-inattention produced by unilateral lesions of the posterior parietal cortex or medial agranular prefrontal cortex in rats: Neglect, extinction, and the role of stimulus distance. *Behavioural Brain Research, 54,* 117–131. doi:10.1016/0166-4328(93)90070-7

Koch, G., Oliveri, M., Torriero, S., Carlesimo, G. A., Turriziani, P., & Caltagirone, C. (2005). rTMS evidence of different delay and decision processes in a fronto–parietal neuronal network activated during spatial working memory. *NeuroImage, 24,* 34–39. doi:10.1016/j.neuroimage.2004.09.042

Köhler, C. (1985). Intrinsic projections of the retrohippocampal region in the rat brain. I. The subicular complex. *The Journal of Comparative Neurology, 236,* 504–522. doi:10.1002/cne.902360407

Kolb, B., Buhrmann, K., McDonald, R., & Sutherland, R. J. (1994). Dissociation of the medial prefrontal, posterior parietal, and posterior temporal cortex for spatial navigation and recognition memory in the rat. *Cerebral Cortex, 4,* 664–680. doi:10.1093/cercor/4.6.664

Kolb, B., Sutherland, R. J., & Whishaw, I. Q. (1983). A comparison of the contributions of the frontal and parietal association cortex to spatial localization in rats. *Behavioral Neuroscience, 97,* 13–27. doi:10.1037/0735-7044.97.1.13

Kolb, B., & Walkey, J. (1987). Behavioural and anatomical studies of the posterior parietal cortex in the rat. *Behavioural Brain Research, 23,* 127–145. doi:10.1016/0166-4328(87)90050-7

Kosslyn, S. M. (1987). Seeing and imagining in the cerebral hemispheres: A computational approach. *Psychological Review, 94,* 148–175. doi:10.1037/0033-295X.94.2.148

Kosslyn, S. M. (1994). *Image and brain: The resolution of the imagery debate.* Cambridge, MA: MIT Press.

Kosslyn, S. M., Digirolamo, G. J., Thompson, W. L., & Alpert, N. M. (1998). Mental rotation of objects versus hands: Neural mechanisms revealed by positron emission tomography. *Psychophysiology, 35,* 151–161. doi:10.1111/1469-8986.3520151

Kosslyn, S. M., Koenig, O., Barrett, A., Cave, C. B., Tang, J., & Gabrieli, J. D. E. (1989). Evidence for two types of spatial representations: Hemispheric specialization for categorical and coordinate relations. *Journal of Experimental Psychology: Human Perception and Performance, 15,* 723–735. doi:10.1037/0096-1523.15.4.723

Krueger, F., Fischer, R., Heinecke, A., & Hagendorf, H. (2007). An fMRI investigation into the neural mechanisms of spatial attentional selection in a location-based negative priming task. *Brain Research, 1174,* 110–119. doi:10.1016/j.brainres.2007.08.016

Kuipers, B. J., & Levitt, T. S. (1988, Summer). Navigation and mapping in large-scale space. *AI Magazine, 9,* 25–42.

Laeng, B. (1994). Lateralization of categorical and coordinate spatial functions: A study of unilateral stroke patients. *Journal of Cognitive Neuroscience, 6,* 189–203. doi:10.1162/jocn.1994.6.3.189

Lewis, J. W. (2006). Cortical networks related to human tool use. *The Neuroscientist, 12,* 211–231. doi:10.1177/1073858406288327

Linden, D. E. (2007). The working memory networks of the human brain. *The Neuroscientist, 13,* 257–267. doi:10.1177/1073858406298480

Long, J. M., Mellem, J. E., & Kesner, R. P. (1998). The effects of parietal cortex lesions on an object/spatial location paired-associate task in rats. *Psychobiology, 26,* 128–133.

Longo, M. R., & Lourenco, S. F. (2007). Space perception and body morphology: Extent of near space scales with arm length. *Experimental Brain Research, 177,* 285–290. doi:10.1007/s00221-007-0855-x

Maguire, E. A., Frackowiak, R. S., & Frith, C. D. (1997). Recalling routes around London: Activation of the right hippocampus in taxi drivers. *Journal of Neuroscience, 17,* 7103–7110.

Maguire, E. A., Frith, C. D., Burgess, N., Donnett, J. G., & O'Keefe, J. (1998). Knowing where things are: Parahippocampal involvement in encoding object locations in virtual large-scale space. *Journal of Cognitive Neuroscience, 10,* 61–76. doi:10.1162/089892998563789

Malhotra, P., Mannan, S., Driver, J., & Husain, M. (2004). Impaired spatial working memory: One component of the visual neglect syndrome? *Cortex, 40,* 667–676. doi:10.1016/S0010-9452(08)70163-1

Martin, R., Houssemand, C., Schiltz, C., Burnod, Y., & Alexandre, F. (2008). Is there a continuity between categorical and coordinate spatial relations coding? Evidence from a grid/no-grid working memory paradigm. *Neuropsychologia, 46,* 576–594. doi:10.1016/j.neuropsychologia.2007.10.010

McNaughton, B. L., Chen, L. L., & Markus, E. J. (1991). "Dead reckoning," landmark learning, and the sense of direction: A neurophysiology and computational hypothesis. *Journal of Cognitive Neuroscience, 3,* 191–202. doi:10.1162/jocn.1991.3.2.190

Medendorp, W. P., Goltz, H. C., & Vilis, T. (2005). Remapping the remembered target location for anti-saccades in human posterior parietal cortex. *Journal of Neurophysiology, 94,* 734–740. doi:10.1152/jn.01331.2004

Mendoza, J. E., & Thomas, R. K., Jr. (1975). Effects of posterior parietal and frontal neocortical lesions in the squirrel monkey. *Journal of Comparative and*

Physiological Psychology, 89, 170–182. doi:10.1037/h0076657

Merriam, E. P., Genovese, C. R., & Colby, C. L. (2003). Spatial updating in human parietal cortex. *Neuron, 39,* 361–373. doi:10.1016/S0896-6273(03)00393-3

Mevorach, C., Humphreys, G. W., & Shalev, L. (2005). Attending to local form while ignoring global aspects depends on handedness: Evidence from TMS. *Nature Neuroscience, 8,* 276–277. doi:10.1038/nn1400

Milner, A. D. (1987). Animal models for the syndrome of spatial neglect. In M. Jeannerod (Ed.), *Neurophysiological and neuropsychological aspects of spatial neglect* (pp. 259–288). New York, NY: Elsevier.

Milner, A. D., & Goodale, M. A. (1995). *The visual brain in action.* Oxford, England: Oxford University Press.

Mort, D. J., Malhotra, P., Mannan, S. K., Rorden, C., Pambakian, A., Kennard, C., & Husain, M. (2003). The anatomy of visual neglect. *Brain: A Journal of Neurology, 126,* 1986–1997. doi:10.1093/brain/awg200

Muir, J. L., Everitt, B. J., & Robbins, T. W. (1996). The cerebral cortex of the rat and visual attentional function: Dissociable effects of mediofrontal, cingulate, anterior dorsolateral, and parietal cortex lesions on a five-choice serial reaction time ask. *Cerebral Cortex, 6,* 470–481. doi:10.1093/cercor/6.3.470

Nakamura, K., & Takarajima, A. (1996). Recognition of pattern position and shape by population vector in the spatial spreading associative neural network. *IEEE International Conference on Evolutionary Computation,* 780–785.

Neggers, S. F. W., Scholvinck, M. L., van der Lubbe, R. H., & Potsma, A. (2005). Quantifying the interactions between allo- and egocentric representations of space. *Acta Psychologica, 118,* 25–45. doi:10.1016/j.actpsy.2004.10.002

Neggers, S. F. W., van der Lubbe, R. H., Ramsey, N. F., & Potsma, A. (2006). Interactions between ego- and allocentric neuronal representations of space. *NeuroImage, 31,* 320–331. doi:10.1016/j.neuroimage.2005.12.028

Neill, W. T., & Mathis, K. M. (1998). Transfer-inappropriate processing: Negative priming and related phenomena. *Psychology of Learning and Motivation, 38,* 1–44. doi:10.1016/S0079-7421(08)60182-6

Nitz, D. A. (2006). Tracking route progression in the posterior parietal cortex. *Neuron, 49,* 747–756. doi:10.1016/j.neuron.2006.01.037

O'Keefe, J., & Nadel, L. (1978). *The hippocampus as a cognitive map.* Oxford, England: Oxford University Press.

Olson, I. R., & Berryhill, M. (2009). Some surprising findings on the involvement of the parietal lobe in human memory. *Neurobiology of Learning and Memory, 91,* 155–165. doi:10.1016/j.nlm.2008.09.006

Parron, C., & Save, E. (2004). Evidence for entorhinal and parietal cortices involvement in path integration in the rat. *Experimental Brain Research, 159,* 349–359. doi:10.1007/s00221-004-1960-8

Parsons, L. M. (1987). Imagined spatial transformations of one's hands and feet. *Cognitive Psychology, 19,* 178–241. doi:10.1016/0010-0285(87)90011-9

Parsons, L. M. (1994). Temporal and kinematic properties of motor behavior reflected in mentally simulated action. *Journal of Experimental Psychology: Human Perception and Performance, 20,* 709–730. doi:10.1037/0096-1523.20.4.709

Pellijeff, A., Bonilha, L., Morgan, P. S., McKenzie, K., & Jackson, S. R. (2006). Parietal updating of limb posture: An event-related fMRI study. *Neuropsychologia, 44,* 2685–2690. doi:10.1016/j.neuropsychologia.2006.01.009

Petersen, S. E., & Robinson, D. L. (1986). Damage to parietal cortex produces a similar deficit in man and monkey. *Investigative Ophthalmology & Visual Science, 27*(Supplement), 18.

Pierrot-Deseilligny, C., Milea, D., & Muri, R. M. (2004). Eye movement control by the cerebral cortex. *Current Opinion in Neurology, 17,* 17–25. doi:10.1097/00019052-200402000-00005

Podzebenko, K., Egan, G. F., & Watson, J. D. G. (2005). Real and imaginary rotary motion processing: Functional parcellation of the human parietal lobe revealed by fMRI. *Journal of Cognitive Neuroscience, 17,* 24–36. doi:10.1162/0898929052879996

Pohl, W. (1973). Dissociation of spatial discrimination deficits following frontal and parietal lesions in monkeys. *Journal of Comparative and Physiological Psychology, 82,* 227–239. doi:10.1037/h0033922

Posner, M. I., Nissen, M. J., & Ogden, O. C. (1978). Attended and unattended processing modes: The role of set for spatial location. In H. L. Pick & I. J. Saltzman (Eds.), *Modes of perceiving and processing information* (pp. 137–157). Hillsdale, NJ: Erlbaum.

Posner, M. I., Walker, J. A., Friedrich, F. A., & Rafal, R. D. (1984). Effects of parietal injury on covert orienting of attention. *The Journal of Neuroscience, 4,* 1863–1874.

Poucet, B. (1993). Spatial cognitive maps in animals: New hypotheses on their structure and neural mechanisms. *Psychological Review, 100,* 163–182. doi:10.1037/0033-295X.100.2.163

Poucet, B., & Hermann, T. (2001). Exploratory patterns of rats on a complex maze provide evidence for topological coding. *Behavioural Processes, 53,* 155–162.

Prado, J., Clavagnier, S., Otzenberger, H., Scheiber, C., Kennedy, H., & Perenin, M. T. (2005). Two cortical systems for reaching in central and peripheral vision. *Neuron, 48,* 849–858. doi:10.1016/j.neuron.2005.10.010

Previc, F. H. (1998). The neuropsychology of 3-D space. *Psychological Bulletin, 124,* 123–164. doi:10.1037/0033-2909.124.2.123

Pylyshyn, Z. (2003). Return of the mental image: Are there really pictures in the brain? *Trends in Cognitive Sciences, 7,* 113–118. doi:10.1016/S1364-6613(03)00003-2

Quinlan, D. J., & Culham, J. C. (2007). FMRI reveals a preference for near viewing in the human parieto-occipital cortex. *NeuroImage, 36,* 167–187. doi:10.1016/j.neuroimage.2007.02.029

Quintana, J., & Fuster, J. M. (1993). Spatial and temporal factors in the role of prefrontal and parietal cortex in visuomotor integration. *Cerebral Cortex, 3,* 122–132. doi:10.1093/cercor/3.2.122

Quirk, G. J., Muller, R. U., & Kubie, J. L. (1990). The firing of hippocampal place cells in the dark depends on the rats' recent experience. *The Journal of Neuroscience, 10,* 2008–2017.

Reep, R. L., Chandler, H. C., King, V., & Corwin, J. V. (1994). Rat posterior parietal cortex: Topography of cortico–cortical and thalamic connections. *Experimental Brain Research, 100,* 67–84. doi:10.1007/BF00227280

Reep, R. L., & Corwin, J. V. (2009). Posterior parietal cortex as part of a neural network for directed attention in rats. *Neurobiology of Learning and Memory, 91,* 104–113. doi:10.1016/j.nlm.2008.08.010

Riddoch, M. J., Chechlacz, M., Mevorach, C., Mavritsaki, E., Allen, H., & Humphreys, G. W. (2010). The neural mechanisms of visual selection: The view from neuropsychology. *Annals of the New York Academy of Sciences, 1191,* 156–181. doi:10.1111/j.1749-6632.2010.05448.x

Rizzolatti, G., & Camarda, R. (1987). Neural circuits for spatial attention and unilateral neglect. In M. Jeannerod (Ed.), *Neurophysiological and neuropsychological aspects of spatial atttention* (pp. 289–313). Amsterdam, The Netherlands: North-Holland. doi:10.1016/S0166-4115(08)61718-5

Rizzolatti, G., & Matelli, M. (2003). Two different streams from the dorsal visual system: Anatomy and functions. *Experimental Brain Research, 153,* 146–157. doi:10.1007/s00221-003-1588-0

Robertson, L., Treisman, A., Friedman-Hill, S., & Grabowecky, M. (1997). The interaction of spatial and object pathways: Evidence from Balint's syndrome. *Journal of Cognitive Neuroscience, 9,* 295–317. doi:10.1162/jocn.1997.9.3.295

Robinson, D. L., Bowman, E. M., & Kertzman, C. (1995). Covert orienting of attention in macaques. II. Contributions of parietal cortex. *Journal of Neurophysiology, 74,* 698–712.

Rogers, J. L., & Kesner, R. P. (2007). Hippocampal–parietal cortex interactions: Evidence from a disconnection study in the rat. *Behavioural Brain Research, 179,* 19–27. doi:10.1016/j.bbr.2007.01.019

Rosenbaum, R. S., Ziegler, M., Winocur, G., Grady, C. L., & Moscovitch, M. (2004). I have often walked down this street before: fMRI studies of the hippocampus and other structures during mental navigation of an old environment. *Hippocampus, 14,* 826–835. doi:10.1002/hipo.10218

Rosner, A. L., & Mittleman, G. (1996). Visuospatial attention in the rat and posterior parietal cortex lesions. *Behavioural Brain Research, 79,* 69–77. doi:10.1016/0166-4328(95)00263-4

Rushworth, M. F. S., Behrens, T. E. J., & Johansen-Berg, H. (2006). Connection patterns distinguish 3 regions of human parietal cortex. *Cerebral Cortex, 16,* 1418–1430. doi:10.1093/cercor/bhj079

Sato, N., Sakata, H., Tanaka, Y. L., & Taira, M. (2006). Navigation-associated medial parietal neurons in monkeys. *Proceedings of the National Academy of Sciences of the United States of America, 103,* 17001–17006. doi:10.1073/pnas.0604277103

Save, E., Buhot, M.-C., Foreman, N., & Thinus-Blanc, C. (1992). Exploratory activity and response to a spatial change in rats with hippocampal or posterior parietal cortical lesions. *Behavioural Brain Research, 47,* 113–127. doi:10.1016/S0166-4328(05)80118-4

Save, E., Guazzelli, A., & Poucet, B. (2001). Dissociation of the effects of bilateral lesions of the dorsal hippocampus and parietal cortex on path integration in the rat. *Behavioral Neuroscience, 115,* 1212–1223. doi:10.1037/0735-7044.115.6.1212

Save, E., & Moghaddam, M. (1996). Effects of lesions of the associative parietal cortex on the acquisition and use of spatial memory in egocentric and allocentric navigation tasks in the rat. *Behavioral Neuroscience, 110,* 74–85. doi:10.1037/0735-7044.110.1.74

Save, E., & Poucet, B. (2000). Involvement of the hippocampus and associative parietal cortex in the use of proximal and distal landmarks for navigation. *Behavioural Brain Research, 109,* 195–206. doi:10.1016/S0166-4328(99)00173-4

Save, E., Poucet, B., Forman, N., & Thinus-Blanc, C. (1998). The contribution of the associative parietal cortex and hippocampus to spatial processing in rodents. *Psychobiology, 26,* 153–161.

Seurinck, R., Vingerhoets, G., de Lange, F. P., & Achten, E. (2004). Does egocentric mental rotation elicit sex differences? *NeuroImage, 23,* 1440–1449. doi:10.1016/j.neuroimage.2004.08.010

Shafritz, K. M., Gore, J. C., & Marois, R. (2002). The role of the parietal cortex in visual feature binding. *Proceedings of the National Academy of Sciences of the United States of America, 99*, 10917–10922. doi:10.1073/pnas.152694799

Shelton, A. L., & Gabrieli, J. D. E. (2002). Neural correlates of encoding space from route and survey perspectives. *The Journal of Neuroscience, 22*, 2711–2717.

Shepard, R. N., & Metzler, J. (1971, February 19). Mental rotation of three-dimensional objects. *Science, 171*, 701–703. doi:10.1126/science.171.3972.701

Slotnick, S. D., & Moo, L. R. (2006). Prefrontal cortex hemispheric specialization for categorical and coordinate visual spatial memory. *Neuropsychologia, 44*, 1560–1568. doi:10.1016/j.neuropsychologia.2006.01.018

Smith, E. E., & Jonides, J. (1998). Neuroimaging analyses of human working memory. *Proceedings of the National Academy of Sciences of the United States of America, 95*, 12061–12068. doi:10.1073/pnas.95.20.12061

Sommer, T., Rose, M., Weiller, C., & Büchel, C. (2005). Contributions of occipital, parietal and parahippocampal cortex to encoding of object-location associations. *Neuropsychologia, 43*, 732–743. doi:10.1016/j.neuropsychologia.2004.08.002

Suzuki, M., Tsukiura, T., Matsue, Y., Yamadori, A., & Fujii, T. (2005). Dissociable brain activations during the retrieval of different kinds of spatial context memory. *NeuroImage, 25*, 993–1001. doi:10.1016/j.neuroimage.2004.12.021

Tomasino, B., Toraldo, A., & Rumiati, R. I. (2003). Dissociation between the mental rotation of visual images and motor images in unilateral brain-damaged patients. *Brain and Cognition, 51*, 368–371. doi:10.1016/S0278-2626(02)00570-5

Treisman, A. (1998). Feature binding, attention and object perception. *Philosophical Transactions of the Royal Society of London B: Biological Sciences, 353*, 1295–1306. doi:10.1098/rstb.1998.0284

Trojano, L., Conson, M., Maffei, R., & Grossi, D. (2006). Categorical and coordinate spatial processing in the imagery domain investigated by rTMS. *Neuropsychologia, 44*, 1569–1574. doi:10.1016/j.neuropsychologia.2006.01.017

Trojano, L., Grossi, D., Linden, D. E. J., Formisano, E., Goebel, R., Cirillo, S., . . . Di Salle, F. (2002). Coordinate and categorical judgements in spatial imagery: An fMRI study. *Neuropsychologia, 40*, 1666–1674. doi:10.1016/S0028-3932(02)00021-0

Tunik, E., Frey, S. H., & Grafton, S. T. (2005). Virtual lesions of the anterior intraparietal area disrupt goal-dependent on-line adjustments of grasp. *Nature Neuroscience, 8*, 505–511.

Tversky, B. (2003). Structures of mental spaces: How people think about space. *Environment and Behavior, 35*, 66–80. doi:10.1177/0013916502238865

Uncapher, M. R., & Wagner, A. D. (2009). Posterior parietal cortex and episodic encoding: Insights from fMRI subsequent memory effects and dual-attention theory. *Neurobiology of Learning and Memory, 91*, 139–154. doi:10.1016/j.nlm.2008.10.011

Ungerleider, L. G., & Mishkin, M. (1982). Two cortical visual systems. In D. J. Ingle, M. A. Goodale, & R. J. W. Mansfield (Eds.), *Analysis of visual behavior* (pp. 549–586). Cambridge, MA: MIT Press.

van Asselen, M., Kessels, R. P. C., Frijns, C. J. M., Kappelle, L. J., Neggers, S. F. W., & Postma, A. (2009). Object-location memory: A lesion-behavior mapping study in stroke patients. *Brain and Cognition, 71*, 287–294. doi:10.1016/j.bandc.2009.07.012

van Asselen, M., Kessels, R. P. C., Kappelle, L. J., Neggers, S. F. W., Frijns, C. J. M., & Postma, A. (2006). Neural correlates of human wayfinding in stroke patients. *Brain Research, 1067*, 229–238. doi:10.1016/j.brainres.2005.10.048

van der Ham, I. J. M., Raemaekers, M., van Wezel, R. J. A., Oleksiak, A., & Potsma, A. (2009). Categorical and coordinate spatial relations in working memory: An fMRI study. *Brain Research, 1297*, 70–79. doi:10.1016/j.brainres.2009.07.088

van Groen, T., & Wyss, J. M. (1990). The connections of presubiculum and parasubiculum in the rat. *Brain Research, 518*, 227–243. doi:10.1016/0006-8993(90)90976-I

Vauclair, J., Yamazaki, Y., & Güntürkün, O. (2006). The study of hemispheric specialization for categorical and coordinate spatial relations in animals. *Neuropsychologia, 44*, 1524–1534. doi:10.1016/j.neuropsychologia.2006.01.021

Vogeley, K., & Fink, G. R. (2003). Neural correlates of the first-person perspective. *Trends in Cognitive Sciences, 7*, 38–42. doi:10.1016/S1364-6613(02)00003-7

Wagner, A. D., Shannon, B. J., Kahn, I., & Buckner, R. L. (2005). Parietal lobe contributions to episodic memory retrieval. *Trends in Cognitive Sciences, 9*, 445–453. doi:10.1016/j.tics.2005.07.001

Ward, N. M., & Brown, V. J. (1997). Deficits in response initiation, but not attention, following excitotoxic lesions of posterior parietal cortex in the rat. *Brain Research, 775*, 81–90. doi:10.1016/S0006-8993(97)00915-3

Weniger, G., Ruhleder, M., Wolf, S., Lange, C., & Irle, E. (2009). Egocentric memory impaired and allocentric memory intact as assessed by virtual reality in subjects with unilateral parietal cortex lesions. *Neuropsychologia, 47*, 59–69. doi:10.1016/j.neuropsychologia.2008.08.018

Whishaw, I. Q., & Jarrard, L. E. (1996). Evidence for extrahippocampal involvement in place learning and hippocampal involvement in path integration. *Hippocampus, 6,* 513–524. doi:10.1002/(SICI)1098-1063(1996)6:5<513::AID-HIPO4>3.0.CO;2-J

Whishaw, I. Q., McKenna, J. E., & Maaswinkel, H. (1997). Hippocampal lesions and path integration. *Current Opinion in Neurobiology, 7,* 228–234. doi:10.1016/S0959-4388(97)80011-6

Witter, M. P., Naber, P., van Haeften, T., Machielsen, W., Rombouts, S., Barkhof, F., . . . Lopes da Silva, F. (2000). Cortico–hippocampal communication by way of parallel parahippocampal-subicular pathways. *Hippocampus, 10,* 398–410. doi:10.1002/1098-1063(2000)10:4<398::AID-HIPO6>3.0.CO;2-K

Wolbers, T., Hegarty, M., Buchel, C., & Loomis, J. M. (2008). Spatial updating: How the brain keeps track of changing object locations during observer motion. *Nature Neuroscience, 11,* 1223–1230. doi:10.1038/nn.2189

Wolbers, T., Weiller, C., & Buchel, C. (2004). Neural foundations of emerging route knowledge in complex spatial environments. *Cognitive Brain Research, 21,* 401–411. doi:10.1016/j.cogbrainres.2004.06.013

Wraga, M., Thompson, W. L., Alpert, N. M., & Kosslyn, S. M. (2003). Implicit transfer of motor strategies in mental rotation. *Brain and Cognition, 52,* 135–143. doi:10.1016/S0278-2626(03)00033-2

Zacks, J. M. (2008). Neuroimaging studies of mental rotation: A meta-analysis and review. *Journal of Cognitive Neuroscience, 20,* 1–19. doi:10.1162/jocn.2008.20013

Zacks, J. M., Vettel, J. M., & Michelon, P. (2003). Imagined viewer and object rotations dissociated with event-related fMRI. *Journal of Cognitive Neuroscience, 15,* 1002–1018. doi:10.1162/089892903770007399

Part II

ONLINE SYSTEMS: ACQUISITION AND MAINTENANCE OF SPATIAL INFORMATION

Chapter 3

SPATIAL PERCEPTION AND ACTION

Brett R. Fajen and Flip Phillips

Humans and other animals are remarkable in their ability to navigate through complex, dynamic environments. People effortlessly make their way along crowded sidewalks, squeezing through gaps between other pedestrians; circumventing obstacles; stepping over puddles, potholes, and sidewalk edges; and climbing stairs and ramps. Animals scurry over rough terrain, glide through dense forests, leap from branch to branch, and race after prey. How does spatial perception support these remarkable abilities? To what degree can the success of action be attributed to an accurate internal representation of the spatial layout of the environment? What properties of the environment must be perceived in order to control action? In this chapter, we address these and related questions by considering the role of spatial perception in the control of action.

Much of the study of spatial perception is focused on its role in more cognitive tasks, such as navigation with respect to distant landmarks. For reasons that we hope to make clear in this chapter, we believe that any general theory of spatial perception and cognition would not be complete without consideration of its role in the online, continuous guidance of action.

CONTRASTING VIEWS OF PERCEPTION AND ACTION

The theoretical approach that is arguably best suited to capture the tight coupling between information and action is the *ecological approach* introduced by James J. Gibson (1979). Because a comprehensive summary of the ecological approach is beyond the scope of this chapter, we direct the reader's attention to those principles that bear most directly on the issue of spatial perception. To set the stage, we first present a contrasting view of perception and action known as *model-based control*. The sharp contrast between the ecological and model-based approaches helps to explain some of the rather unorthodox views held by proponents of the ecological approach (cf. Warren, 1998).

The Model-Based Approach

Model-based control embraces the traditional view that the function of perception is to construct a metric three-dimensional model of the spatial layout of the environment (Loomis & Beall, 1998, 2004). This internal model is created by the perceptual system using both classic cues (e.g., binocular disparity, convergence, motion parallax—see Chapter 4, this volume) and internalized assumptions about the environment on the basis of past experience. In addition to an internal model of the spatial layout of the environment, models of the spatial envelope that encompasses the body and the dynamics of the body are also thought to play a critical role (Loomis & Beall, 1998). Thus, actions are planned on the basis of models of both the environment and the body. The success of action is largely attributed to the accuracy of these models.

Preparation of this chapter was supported by a grant from the National Institutes of Health (1R01EY019317) to Brett R. Fajen.

DOI: 10.1037/13936-004
Handbook of Spatial Cognition, D. Waller and L. Nadel (Editors)

In the case of internal models of the environment, the assumption of accuracy implies a close correspondence between perceptual space and physical space. Empirical support for this assumption comes from studies in which participants perform *visually directed actions*—that is, tasks in which participants view the environment prior to moving and then execute the movement without visual information, which is cut off at the instant that movement is initiated (see Loomis & Philbeck, 2006, for a review). For example, in blind walking studies, participants look at a target, close their eyes, and then blindly walk until they think they have reached the target. The accuracy with which people can perform this task under full cue conditions has been interpreted as evidence that internal models of the environment are sufficiently accurate to support the control of action (Philbeck & Loomis, 1997).

Although visually directed actions are often accurately performed, there is also an abundance of evidence suggesting an incommensurability between visual space and physical space (see Wagner, 2006, for a review). For example, physically straight lines in the environment can appear to be curved, and equally spaced depth intervals can appear to become increasingly compressed with viewing distance. In studies of 3-D shape perception, observers correctly judged concavities and convexities of irregular surfaces, but the magnitude of relief was consistently underestimated, suggesting that properties that remain invariant under affine transformation are reliably perceived but Euclidian metric properties are not (Todd, 2004).

Koenderink, van Doorn, and Lappin (2000) used a novel exocentric pointing task in which participants were instructed to align a pointer in one distant location with a target at another location. Although the task was performed in an open field under full-cue conditions, significant errors in pointing judgments were found. The direction and magnitude of errors across a range of distances allowed the authors to measure the curvature of visual space and led them to conclude that visual space is non-Euclidean—to be more specific, elliptical within a distance equal to one eyeheight and hyperbolic beyond that distance.

Distortions of visual space have been reported in many other studies (e.g., Phillips & Voshell,

2009; Todd & Norman, 2003; Todd, Tittle, & Norman, 1995). Although there is little consensus on the underlying geometry of visual space or even that there is a single geometry (Wagner, 2006), there is widespread agreement that visual space is not Euclidean. That is, the metric of visual space varies across location, distance, and a wide variety of task-specific factors.

How can we reconcile the idea that perceptual space is distorted with the fact that actions are generally successfully controlled? One answer is that actions are calibrated to correct for such distortions (Bingham, Zaal, Robin, & Shull, 2000; Vo, Ning, Bhattacharjee, Li, & Durgin, 2011). Another answer—one that we consider in detail in this chapter—is that many actions can be performed without an accurate metric representation of the spatial layout of the environment. In other words, metric properties are not accurately perceived because they do not need to be. From an ecological perspective, the apparent inconsistency between distorted visual space and successful action can be reconciled by reconsidering the assumption that actions are guided on the basis of internal models of the environment, as well as the assumption that the kinds of properties that must be perceived to control action are restricted to general-purpose properties of the spatial layout of the environment.

An Ecological Reformulation of the Problem of Spatial Perception

> The primary test field for theories of perception has, over the centuries, been overwhelmingly the general problem of space perception and, in particular, distance perception. The first step in addressing this problem is a question of the most fundamental kind: What is space? It is not difficult to appreciate that resolution of the scientific problem of how space is perceived depends ultimately on the correctness of the scientific presumption of what space is apropos perception and action. (Turvey, 2004, p. 25)

Recognizing that perception is first and foremost in the service of action, Gibson (1979) sought a reformulation of the problem of space perception more befitting a perceiving–acting system. The essence of Gibson's reformulation is illustrated in Color Plate 9, which helps to convey an important statement about the kinds of properties that an animal must perceive to successfully guide movement through its environment. Absent from this figure are labels of properties that are normally associated with spatial perception, such as the sizes, distances, and shapes of objects. From an ecological perspective, the important properties are those that are immediately relevant to the control of action, and the kind of spatial perception that is needed is that which allows for the perception of such properties. Thus, the hiker in Color Plate 9 who is intending to cross the stream need not perceive the width of the stream per se but rather whether the stream is leapable.

Gibson's (1979) insights into spatial perception and action inspired an enduring program of research aimed at identifying action-relevant properties, their specification by information (e.g., in *optic flow*, the streaming pattern of optical motion generated by self-motion), and their role in the control of action. This approach has been adopted in the study of a variety of tasks, including visually guided reaching (Anderson & Bingham, 2010), ball catching (Jacobs & Michaels, 2006), and steering a vehicle (Wann & Wilkie, 2004), to name a few, but has been most thoroughly developed in the context of visually controlled locomotion. In the next section of this chapter, we take a more in-depth look at the theoretical and empirical research on the perception of action-relevant properties and their role in the control of locomotion.

SPATIAL PERCEPTION AND THE CONTROL OF LOCOMOTION

How can locomotion be successfully controlled in complex, dynamic environments without a general-purpose metric representation of the spatial layout? In this section, we consider the kinds of action-relevant properties that must be perceived to select appropriate actions and guide movement, as well as the specification of these properties by information in optic flow.

Affordance Perception and the Selection of Action

Moving from one's current location to a goal is typically not simply a matter of walking a straight path over a flat ground surface. As in Color Plate 9, the environment contains obstacles that must be stepped over, avoided, or dodged and surfaces that vary in traction, slant, extent, and compliance and therefore in the degree to which they support legged locomotion. In such situations, the selection of safe and efficient routes requires that one take into account not only the layout of the environment but also one's body dimensions and movement capabilities. From an ecological perspective, the ability to consider such factors begins with the perception of affordances—that is, possibilities for action provided by the environment for an animal with particular dimensions and capabilities (see Fajen, Riley, & Turvey, 2009, for a recent review; Gibson, 1966, 1977, 1979; Warren, 1984).

Unlike other spatial properties, affordances are not properties of objects or environments themselves but rather *relational properties* in that they reflect the fit between the animal and its environment. The passability of an aperture, for example, depends not only on the size of the gap but also on the body dimensions of the actor. Thus, the gap between the tree and the boulder in Color Plate 9 may be passable for a person on foot but not for a person on a mountain bike. Because affordances are defined by the fit between the environment and the actor, the perception of affordances makes it possible to choose actions in a way that takes into account one's body dimensions and movement capabilities.

The term *fit* is used here in an extremely broad sense to capture not only relations that involve dimensions of the environment and the body but also their dynamic properties. Examples of the former include in Color Plate 9 the passability of the aperture between the tree and the rock, the sit-on-ability of the wall, and the reach-ability of the branch. Such affordances are sometimes referred to as *body-scaled affordances* because they reflect dimensions of the environment scaled to dimensions of the body. Affordances can also reflect relations between dynamic properties of the body and the environment, such as whether the Frisbee in Color Plate 9 is catchable for the dog or whether a fly ball in baseball is catchable for an outfielder (Fajen, Diaz, & Cramer, 2011; Oudejans, Michaels, Bakker, & Dolné, 1996). Such affordances depend on action capabilities rather than body dimensions and are therefore referred to as *action-scaled affordances*.

Some affordances reflect both the body dimensions and action capabilities of the actor. Consider, for example, the situation encountered by a cyclist waiting to cross a busy street. In such situations, the cyclist must perceive whether gaps between approaching vehicles afford safe passage, and he or she must do so in a way that takes into account both the dimensions of the bicycle and its acceleration capabilities. In fact, failure to consider one's movement capabilities has been implicated in bicycle accidents among children (Chihak et al., 2010; Plumert, Kearney, & Cremer, 2004).

Possibilities for action furnished by the environment are not fixed. Affordances can materialize, disappear, and vary because of changes in the material properties or the positions of objects in the environment. Such changes can occur over short time scales, such as when a gap between moving obstacles that affords safe passage at one moment collapses into a barrier at the next moment, and long time scales. The fluid nature of affordances is also a consequence of changes in the actor's body dimensions and movement capabilities. For a developing infant, whose body is undergoing rapid changes in size and strength, and for whom new modes of locomotion emerge suddenly, changes in affordances can be dramatic (Adolph, 2008). The ability of infants to adjust their motor decisions to their ever-changing body dimensions and movement capabilities attests to the flexibility and robustness with which affordances can be perceived.

Let us now return to the situation depicted in Color Plate 9. To choose a safe and efficient route, the hiker must take into account not only properties of the environment but also properties of the body. Because affordances are defined by the fit between the environment and the actor, to perceive affordances is to perceive the world in relation to one's body dimensions and movement capabilities. Thus, the theory of affordances offers a starting point for a seamless account of how actions are selected in a way that takes into account the fit between the environment and the body.

Optical Specification of Affordances

It is one thing to recognize the necessity of taking body dimensions and movement capabilities into account and another to claim that this can be achieved by perceiving affordances and without first perceiving spatial properties. After all, affordances depend on the relation between the environment and the actor. Thus, it is tempting to assume that the perception of affordances involves a cognitive process that combines knowledge of the environment acquired through spatial perception with knowledge of the body stored in memory (Loomis & Beall, 1998). From an ecological perspective, however, affordances are every bit as real as conventional spatial properties (Turvey, 1992)—they are not constructed by cognitive processes. Moreover, affordances are directly perceived, bypassing the need to first perceive spatial properties. Justifying the latter claim requires researchers to identify information in ambient energy arrays that specifies affordances.

A significant step in legitimizing the theory of affordances is the classic work of Warren and Whang (1987), who presented a solution to the affordance specification problem in the form of eyeheight-scaled information. Figure 3.1 depicts an observer viewing an aperture between a pair of stationary obstacles. If the width of the aperture is greater than the width of the observer's shoulders, the aperture is passable without rotating the shoulders. Thus, perceiving passability is a matter of perceiving the size of the aperture in relation to the width of the shoulders. The size of the aperture (G) is optically specified in units of eyeheight (E) in the following manner:

$$\frac{G}{E} = \frac{2\tan(\alpha/2)}{\tan\gamma} \qquad (1)$$

where α is the angle subtended by the inside edges of the obstacles and γ is the angle of declination of the base of the obstacles (Warren & Whang, 1987). Because shoulder width (W) is a constant proportion of standing eyeheight, Equation 1 means that aperture size is also specified in units of shoulder width. Thus, from an ecological perspective, perceiving passability is not a matter of first perceiving the size of the aperture in extrinsic units and then

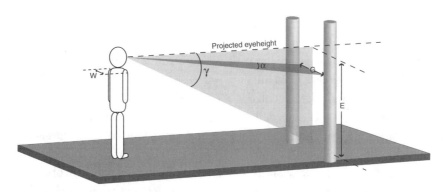

FIGURE 3.1.   Optical specification of aperture size by eyeheight-scaled information. G = the distance between the inside edges of the obstacles; E = eyeheight; W = shoulder width; α = the visual angle subtended by the inside edges of the obstacles; η = the angle of declination of the base of the obstacles.

comparing that estimate with knowledge of body width stored in memory.

The availability of eyeheight-scaled information bypasses the need to rely on knowledge of body dimensions and makes it possible for passability to be directly perceived. Compelling empirical evidence that people rely on eyeheight-scaled information to perceive aperture size and passability was provided by Warren and Whang (1987), who showed that subtle decreases in eyeheight make apertures appear more passable (see also Wraga, 1999).

The availability of eyeheight-scaled information provides an elegant solution to the problem of perceiving affordances that depend on dimensions of the body (i.e., body-scaled affordances). But what about action-scaled affordances, such as whether a moving target is interceptable or whether a busy street is crossable? Until recently, the few studies that considered action-scaled affordances focused on the reliability with which they are perceived (e.g., Oudejans, Michaels, Bakker, et al., 1996; Oudejans, Michaels, van Dort, & Frissen, 1996; Pepping & Li, 2000),

with little attention paid to the problem of how such affordances are perceived. Recently, however, Fajen and Matthis (2011) showed how the availability of eyeheight-scaled information also makes possible the specification of action-scaled affordances.

Consider the problem of perceiving whether it is possible to pass through a shrinking gap between a pair of converging obstacles before the gap closes (see Figure 3.2). Pedestrians routinely encounter such problems as they hurry through crowded environments. Passability is afforded if the minimum locomotor speed needed to safely pass through the gap (vmin) is less than the maximum speed that the actor is capable of moving (or willing to move). Fajen and Matthis (2011) showed that vmin is optically specified. The particular optical variable and its derivation are less relevant to the present discussion than the fact that vmin is optically specified by eyeheight-scaled information. The advantage of eyeheight-scaled information is that vmin is specified not in extrinsic units, which are meaningless to the visual–motor system, but rather in intrinsic

FIGURE 3.2.   The shrinking gap problem. Illustration of the shrinking gap problem, in which an observer must decide whether it is possible to pass through a shrinking gap between a pair of converging obstacles before the gap closes.

units. In particular, vmin is specified in units of the number of eyeheights that must be covered in the time remaining until the size of the gap is smaller than the shoulder width of the observer. Thus, just as the size of fixed-width gaps is optically specified in units of eyeheight, the minimum speed needed to safely pass through a shrinking gap is optically specified in units of eyeheights per remaining time. Further, vmin is specified in a way that takes into account the width of the observer's body. Thus, detecting such information is sufficient to allow for the perception of the passability of a shrinking gap, taking into account both the width of the observer's body and his or her locomotor capabilities.

To summarize, the claim that affordances can be directly perceived without internalized knowledge of body dimensions and movement capabilities is bolstered by the discovery of information that specifies affordances—both body-scaled affordances, such as the passability of fixed-width gaps, and action-scaled affordances, such as the passability of shrinking gaps. The perception of such affordances provides the basis for the ability to select actions in a way that takes into account one's body dimensions and movement capabilities.

Affordances and Conventional Spatial Properties

From an ecological perspective, conventional spatial properties take a back seat to affordances. In fact, affordances may be so fundamental to our perceptual experience that their perception may influence judgments of conventional spatial properties. The primacy of affordance perception is consistent with the substantial body of evidence demonstrating that judgments of spatial properties are influenced by the perceiver's morphology, physiology, and behavior (see Proffitt, 2006, 2008; Proffitt & Linkenauger, in press, for reviews). For example, objects that are slightly out of arm's reach are judged as closer when the perceiver's reaching capabilities are augmented by a hand-held tool (Witt & Proffitt, 2008; Witt, Proffitt, & Epstein, 2005). Hills are judged as steeper and egocentric distances along the ground are judged as farther when the energetic costs of walking increase (e.g., by wearing a heavy backpack) or when energy resources are depleted (e.g., when fatigued;

Bhalla & Proffitt, 1999; Proffitt, Bhalla, Grossweiler, & Midgett, 1995; Proffitt, Stefanucci, Banton, & Epstein, 2003). Golfers who have experienced recent success at putting judge the hole to be larger (Witt, Linkenauger, Bakdash, & Proffitt, 2008), and softball players who have experienced recent success at hitting judge the ball to be larger (Witt & Proffitt, 2005). To paraphrase Proffitt and Linkenauger (in press), dimensions of the world are scaled by action-relevant metrics that are derived from the perceiver's body dimensions and action capabilities.

Although such findings have generated a great deal of controversy (e.g., Durgin et al., 2009; Hutchison & Loomis, 2006; Proffitt, 2009; Proffitt, Stefanucci, Banton, & Epstein, 2006), one interpretation is that affordances are so fundamental to our perceptual experience that their perception influences verbal reports even when observers are instructed to judge conventional spatial properties (Witt & Riley, 2011). Thus, when people are instructed to judge the distance to a reachable object, their reports are influenced by the ability of the object to be reached. Because manipulations of reaching capabilities, such as using a tool, affect reach-ability, the object is judged to be closer when a tool is held.

These and similar findings are interesting because they suggest a reversal of the direction of influence between spatial properties and affordances that is promoted by model-based control. From a model-based perspective, the perception of conventional spatial properties comes first. To perceive possibilities for action, perception must be supplemented by knowledge of the spatial envelope and dynamics of the body that is stored in memory (Loomis & Beall, 1998). The findings of Proffitt, Witt, and colleagues suggest the opposite (e.g., Witt & Proffitt, 2008; Witt, Proffitt, & Epstein, 2005). Rather than spatial properties serving as the basis for the perception of affordances, affordance perception influences the estimation of spatial properties.

THE CONTROL PROBLEM

In the preceding section, we focused on the perception of affordances and its role in the selection of safe and efficient routes. Once an action or a route is selected, the actor must move to achieve the goal, which involves using perceptual information to more or less continuously regulate movements of the body. Warren (1988) referred to this as the *control problem*.

Information-Based Control

From an ecological perspective, the way in which visual information is used to continuously guide action is to a significant degree captured by a single general principle known as *information-based control* (Warren, 1998, 2006). This principle holds that for each of many locomotor tasks, there exists a means by which to achieve a successful outcome by moving so as to actively transform the optic array in a particular way. For example, walking to a stationary goal can be achieved by moving in a way that keeps the focus of expansion of the optic flow field on the goal (Gibson, 1958; Warren, Kay, Zosh, Duchon, & Sahuc, 2001). Thus, each task has associated with it a *law of control* that captures how a successful outcome can be brought about by moving so as to transform the optic array in a particular way.

These information-based solutions make use of the existence of *optical invariants*. In general, optical invariants are properties of the optic array or optic flow field that remain invariant across certain changes. For example, the focus of expansion is an optical invariant in that it specifies direction

of heading invariantly across changes in the structure of the environment. This makes it possible to perceive heading without first having to perceive the layout of the environment. In the context of the control problem, the kinds of optical invariants that are thought to play a role are those that remain invariant across conditions in which the actor is in a state that if maintained will bring about a successful outcome. We hope to give readers a better grasp of this elusive concept by showing how it has been put to work in information-based models of interception, fly-ball catching, and braking.

Intercepting a moving target. When people walk or run to intercept a moving target, such as a ball carrier in football, their behavior closely conforms to a simple heuristic known as the *constant bearing angle* (CBA) strategy (Chardenon, Montagne, Laurent, & Bootsma, 2004; Fajen & Warren, 2004, 2007; Lenoir, Musch, Thiery, & Savelsbergh, 2002). The bearing angle is the direction of the target relative to a fixed exocentric reference direction (see Figure 3.3a). Its rate of change serves an optical invariant because the value of the bearing angle remains the same whenever the actor is moving at a speed and in a direction that will eventually lead to a successful interception. Whenever the actor is moving too slowly such that the target will pass in

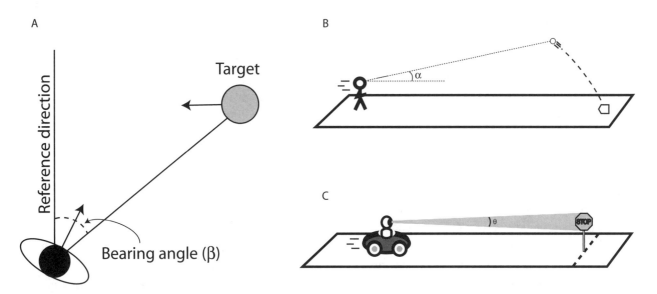

FIGURE 3.3. Optical information for interception, fly ball catching, and braking. Illustration of the relevant optical variables used in control strategies for intercepting a moving target (a), running to catch a fly ball (b), and braking to avoid a collision (c).

front, the bearing angle is decreasing, signifying that current speed is insufficient and that he or she needs to accelerate or turn farther ahead of the target. Likewise, whenever the actor is moving too quickly such that the target will pass behind, the bearing angle is increasing, signifying that current speed is excessive and he or she needs to decelerate or turn toward the target. Thus, the strategy of moving so as to leave the bearing angle invariant represents an information-based solution to the problem of intercepting moving targets.

Catching a fly ball. The *optical acceleration cancellation* (OAC) model of fly-ball catching is another example of an information-based solution (Chapman, 1968; McLeod, Reed, & Dienes, 2006; Michaels & Oudejans, 1992). In the OAC model, the optical invariant is the second temporal derivative of the elevation angle of the ball (see Figure 3.3b). When the fielder is running at a speed that will bring him or her to the landing location at the same time as the ball, the tangent of the angular acceleration of the elevation angle (α) will be zero. For a fly ball hit in front of the fielder, the tangent of the angular acceleration of α will be negative if the fielder is running too slowly and positive if the fielder is running too quickly. Thus, the information-based solution to the outfielder problem is to run so as to leave invariant the rate of change of $\tan(\alpha)$.

Braking to avoid a collision. The third example of an information-based model is the *tau-dot* model of braking introduced by David Lee (Bardy & Warren, 1997; Lee, 1976; Yilmaz & Warren, 1995). As a person approaches an object in the path of motion, the visual angle θ subtended by the object undergoes expansion (see Figure 3.3c). Lee (1976) demonstrated that the time remaining until the person collides with the object (i.e., the time-to-contact) is approximated by the ratio of θ to its rate of change $\dot{\theta}$, which Lee designated τ. Lee also showed that $\dot{\tau}$, which is the first temporal derivative of τ, could be used to control deceleration when braking to avoid a collision with the object in the path of motion. To be more specific, when the actor is decelerating at a rate that will eventually bring him or her to a

stop exactly at the object, $\dot{\tau}$ is equal to -0.5. When the rate of deceleration is insufficient, such that the person will collide with the object before speed reaches zero, $\dot{\tau}$ is less than -0.5, indicating that deceleration must be increased. Likewise, when the rate of deceleration is excessive, such that speed will reach zero before reaching the target, $\dot{\tau}$ is greater than -0.5, indicating that deceleration could be decreased. Thus, a strategy of decelerating so as to leave invariant the value of $\dot{\tau}$ at -0.5 offers an information-based strategy for the braking problem.

Although the CBA, OAC, and $\dot{\tau}$ models are designed for different tasks and rely on different optical information, a common thread ties these models together: that there exist optical variables whose values remain invariant whenever the actor is in a state that if maintained, will bring about a successful outcome. Much research has been devoted to identifying optical invariants for various tasks and testing hypotheses about the control strategies that capture how invariants are coupled to movement (see Fajen, 2005; Warren, 1998, for reviews).

Let us now return to the issue of spatial perception and its role in the continuous control of locomotion. Given the emphasis on tight perception–action coupling, it may appear that optical invariants make it possible to guide movement on the basis of the proximal stimulus alone without the perception of meaningful properties of the environment. After all, optical invariants such as $\dot{\tau}$ are complex functions of the actor's movement and the spatial layout of the environment. They do not map in any obvious way onto conventional properties that one normally associates with spatial perception and therefore do not provide the informational basis for what one would normally think of as spatial perception.

In fact, the optical invariants in the aforementioned models are not merely the proximal stimuli for guiding action. They also provide information about meaningful properties of the environment, or to be more specific, the observer's relation to its environment. For example, the first derivative of the bearing angle specifies the sufficiency of one's current velocity for intercepting a moving target. The second derivative of the elevation angle of a fly ball specifies the sufficiency of one's current running speed for arriving at the landing location at exactly the same time as the ball. The first derivative of the optical variable τ specifies the sufficiency of one's current rate of deceleration for stopping at an approached object. These optical variables provide information about what Bootsma (2009) called the *current future*—that is, what will eventually happen if one's current state (deceleration, running speed) remains constant. For the present purposes, the important and often overlooked point is that the guidance of action from an information-based perspective requires perception of one's current future. Although the current future is not what one normally thinks of as a spatial property, it is every bit as real as distance, size, shape, and so forth. Thus, from an information-based perspective, the kind of spatial perception that is needed to guide locomotion is that which makes transparent a particular action-relevant property of the world, one's current future.

Affordance Perception and Continuous Control

The information-based approach explains how the visual guidance of locomotion can be achieved without the perception of general-purpose spatial properties, thereby offering a compelling alternative to the more traditional model-based approach. A significant but often overlooked problem in the study of continuous control, however, is that movements must be guided in a way that takes into account one's movement capabilities. The importance of movement capabilities has been appreciated in the context of selecting appropriate actions (as discussed in the previous section Affordance Perception and the Selection of Action) but is often neglected in the context of continuous control.

To illustrate the relevance of movement capabilities in the guidance of locomotion, consider again the problem of running to intercept a moving target. If an actor is moving at a speed that is too slow, such that the target will pass in front if current speed and direction of locomotion are maintained, he or she can either accelerate, turn in

the direction that the target is moving, or do some combination of both. How should one's speed and direction be coordinated when running to intercept a target? A reasonable assumption is that the choice of when to change speeds and when to change directions should depend, at least in part, on the actor's locomotor capabilities. This point is illustrated in Figure 3.4, which shows how the speed needed to intercept the target depends on the direction in which the actor moves. Turning more than a few degrees to the right would allow the actor to intercept the target more quickly but would require moving at a speed that exceeds his or her maximum speed. Maintaining heading would allow the actor to intercept the target by running at less than 100% of maximum speed. Turning to the left would increase the time needed to intercept the target but would also allow the actor to run at an even slower speed. Clearly, the speed and direction of locomotion must be coordinated in a way that takes one's locomotor capabilities into account (Bastin, Fajen, & Montagne, 2010).

Interestingly, a variant of the visual information used in the shrinking gap problem (described in the earlier section Optical Specification of Affordances) specifies the locomotor speed needed to intercept a moving target by moving in any possible direction. In other words, actors who rely on such information can perceive how fast they would need to move to intercept the target as a function of the direction of locomotion, as illustrated in Figure 3.4. Furthermore, the locomotor speed needed to intercept the target is specified by eyeheight-scaled information. As such, the speed at which the actor needs to move is specified in intrinsic units equal to the number of eyeheights that must be covered in time remaining before the target reaches the locomotor axis (the black arrow in Figure 3.4). This means that required speed can be perceived in relation to maximum speed, which provides the basis for coordinating speed and direction in a way that takes into account one's locomotor capabilities.

Insofar as the relevant information specifies locomotor speed in relation to one's locomotor capabilities, the property that one perceives when

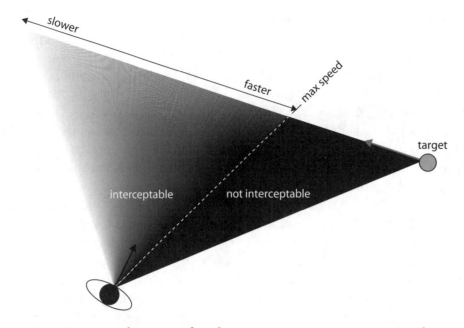

FIGURE 3.4.   Top-down view of an observer intercepting a moving target. The gradient illustrates how the locomotor speed needed to intercept the moving target (gray circle) varies as a function of the direction of locomotion. The dashed white line indicates the direction in which the observer would need to move to intercept the target at maximum speed. This line also partitions the space into directions in which the target is interceptable (left of dashed white line) and directions in which the target is not interceptable (right of dashed white line).

detecting such information is the intercept-ability of the target. In this regard, the aforementioned account represents an extension of the theory of affordances to the domain of continuous control. Thus, affordance perception plays a role not only in the selection of appropriate actions but also in the continuous guidance of locomotion (Fajen, 2005, 2007).

FROM LOCOMOTION TO NAVIGATION

Although the ecological approach has been most thoroughly developed in the context of locomotion, it is interesting to note that analogous views exist in the study of navigation, where it has been argued that spatial knowledge with weak geometric structure is sufficient to support navigation with respect to unseen objects and locations. For example, the ability to take shortcuts between previously learned locations appears to be based on landmarks rather than maplike survey knowledge that could be derived from path integration (Dyer, 1991; Foo, Warren, Duchon, & Tarr, 2005).

Similarly, when people navigate through a maze to find objects, they rely on landmarks rather than absolute distances and directions, suggesting that they acquire ordinal rather than metric knowledge of the environment (Harrison & Warren, 2011). Such findings align with the ecological approach in that behavior that appears to require metric knowledge of the environment may actually be achieved using knowledge of weaker nonmetric properties together with landmarks (see also, Chapter 14, this volume for an ecological perspective on navigation).

CONCLUSION

Most accounts of spatial perception implicitly assume that the most appropriate way to describe the environment is in those terms that are familiar to us from everyday language. People describe environments in terms of the distances, sizes, shapes, and orientations of objects and surfaces, and researchers therefore assume that the job of perception is to recover these properties. In this chapter, we have argued that there is an alternative, equally valid way of describing the environment—one that recognizes the importance of perception for the control of action. For a perceiving–acting agent, the relevant properties are not restricted to conventional spatial properties but also include possibilities for action—relational properties that reflect the fit between the environment and the actor. Such properties are every bit as real as conventional spatial properties and are specified by information in sensory arrays. The perception of such properties makes it possible for actors to select actions and guide movements in a way that takes into account both the environment and the dimensions and dynamics of the body. It is for these reasons that we believe that a general theory of spatial perception would not be complete without consideration of its role in the control of action.

SUGGESTED REFERENCES FOR FURTHER READING

Fajen, B. R. (2005). Perceiving possibilities for action: On the necessity of calibration and perceptual learning for the visual guidance of action. *Perception, 34*, 717–740. doi:10.1068/p5405

A critical review of research on visually guided action with a focus on the role of calibration, learning, and affordance perception.

Gibson, J. J. (1958). Visually controlled locomotion and visual orientation in animals. *British Journal of Psychology, 49*, 182–194. doi:10.1111/j.2044-8295.1958.tb00656.x

An influential paper that set the stage for the information-based approach to locomotion and provided formulae for basic locomotor tasks.

Loomis, J. M., & Beall, A. C. (2004). Model-based control of perception/action. In L. M. Vaina, S. A. Beardsley & S. K. Rushton (Eds.), *Optic flow and beyond* (p. 421–441). Boston, MA: Kluwer Academic.

An excellent overview of the model-based approach to visual control.

Turvey, M. T. (1992). Affordances and prospective control: An outline of the ontology. *Ecological Psychology, 4*, 173–187. doi:10.1207/s15326969eco0403_3

An outline of the ontological basis for understanding the prospective control of action.

Warren, W. H. (1998). Visually controlled locomotion: 40 years later. *Ecological Psychology, 10*, 177–219.

doi:10.1080/10407413.1998.9652682

A review of research on visually guided locomotion placed in the context of Gibson's (1958) paper.

Warren, W. H. (2006). The dynamics of perception and action. *Psychological Review, 113*, 358–389. doi:10.1037/0033-295X.113.2.358

An excellent review of theoretical approaches in perception and action with a focus on the integration of information-based and dynamical systems approaches.

References

Adolph, K. E. (2008). The growing body in action: What infant locomotion tells us about perceptually guided action. In M. B. R. Klatzky & B. MacWhinney (Eds.), *Embodiment, ego-space, and action* (pp. 275–321). Mahwah, NJ: Erlbaum.

Anderson, J., & Bingham, G. P. (2010). A solution to the online guidance problem for targeted reaches: Proportional rate control using relative disparity tau. *Experimental Brain Research, 205*, 291–306.

Bardy, B. G., & Warren, W. H. (1997). Visual control of braking in goal-directed action and sport. *Journal of Sports Sciences, 15*, 607–620. doi:10.1080/026404197367047

Bastin, J., Fajen, B. R., & Montagne, G. (2010). Controlling speed and direction during interception: An affordance-based approach. *Experimental Brain Research, 201*, 763–780. doi:10.1007/s00221-009-2092-y

Bhalla, M., & Proffitt, D. R. (1999). Visual–motor recalibration in geographical slant perception. *Journal of Experimental Psychology: Human Perception and Performance, 25*(4), 1076–1096. doi:10.1037/0096-1523.25.4.1076

Bingham, G. P., Zaal, F., Robin, D., & Shull, J. A. (2000). Distortions in definite distance and shape perception as measured by reaching without and with haptic feedback. *Journal of Experimental Psychology: Human Perception and Performance, 26*, 1436–1460. doi:10.1037/0096-1523.26.4.1436

Bootsma, R. J. (2009). Lee's 1976 paper. *Perception, 38*, 851.

Chapman, S. (1968). Catching a baseball. *American Journal of Physics, 36*, 868–870. doi:10.1119/1.1974297

Chardenon, A., Montagne, G., Laurent, M., & Bootsma, R. J. (2004). The perceptual control of goal-directed locomotion: A common control architecture for interception and navigation? *Experimental Brain Research, 158*, 100–108. doi:10.1007/s00221-004-1880-7

Chihak, B. J., Plumert, J. M., Ziemer, C. J., Babu, S., Grechkin, T., Cremer, J. F., & Kearney, J. K. (2010). Synchronizing self and object movement: How child and adult cyclists intercept moving gaps in a virtual environment. *Journal of Experimental Psychology: Human Perception and Performance, 36,* 1535–1552. doi:10.1037/a0020560

Durgin, F. H., Baird, J. A., Greenburg, M., Russell, R., Shaughnessy, K., & Waymouth, S. (2009). Who is being deceived? The experimental demands of wearing a backpack. *Psychonomic Bulletin & Review, 16,* 964–969. doi:10.3758/PBR.16.5.964

Dyer, F. C. (1991). Bees acquire route-based memories but not cognitive maps in a familiar landscape. *Animal Behaviour, 41,* 239–246. doi:10.1016/S0003-3472(05)80475-0

Fajen, B. R. (2005). Perceiving possibilities for action: On the necessity of calibration and perceptual learning for the visual guidance of action. *Perception, 34,* 717–740. doi:10.1068/p5405

Fajen, B. R. (2007). Affordance-based control of visually guided action. *Ecological Psychology, 19,* 383–410. doi:10.1080/10407410701557877

Fajen, B. R., Diaz, G., & Cramer, C. (2011). Reconsidering the role of movement in perceiving action-scaled affordances. *Human Movement Science, 30,* 504–533. doi:10.1016/j.humov.2010.07.016

Fajen, B. R., & Matthis, J. M. (2011). Direct perception of action-scaled affordances: The shrinking gap problem. *Journal of Experimental Psychology: Human Perception and Performance, 37,* 1442–1457. doi:10.1037/a0023510

Fajen, B. R., Riley, M. A., & Turvey, M. T. (2009). Information, affordances, and the control of action in sport. *International Journal of Sport Psychology, 40,* 79–107.

Fajen, B. R., & Warren, W. H. (2004). Visual guidance of intercepting a moving target on foot. *Perception, 33,* 689–715. doi:10.1068/p5236

Fajen, B. R., & Warren, W. H. (2007). Behavioral dynamics of intercepting a moving target. *Experimental Brain Research, 180,* 303–319. doi:10.1007/s00221-007-0859-6

Foo, P., Warren, W. H., Duchon, A., & Tarr, M. J. (2005). Do humans integrate routes into a cognitive map? Map- versus landmark-based navigation of novel shortcuts. *Journal of Experimental Psychology: Learning, Memory, and Cognition, 31,* 195–215. doi:10.1037/0278-7393.31.2.195

Gibson, J. J. (1958). Visually controlled locomotion and visual orientation in animals. *British Journal of Psychology, 49,* 182–194. doi:10.1111/j.2044-8295.1958.tb00656.x

Gibson, J. J. (1966). *The senses considered as perceptual systems.* Boston, MA: Houghton Mifflin.

Gibson, J. J. (1977). The theory of affordances. In R. S. J. Bransford (Ed.), *Perceiving, acting, and knowing: Toward an ecological psychology* (pp. 67–82). Hillsdale, NJ: Erlbaum.

Gibson, J. J. (1979). *The ecological approach to visual perception.* Boston, MA: Houghton Mifflin.

Harrison, M., & Warren, W. H. (2011). *The geometry of cognitive maps: Metric and ordinal strategies in human navigation.* Manuscript submitted for publication.

Hutchison, J. J., & Loomis, J. M. (2006). Does energy expenditure affect the perception of egocentric distance? A failure to replicate Experiment 1 of Proffitt, Stefanucci, Banton, and Epstein (2003). *Spanish Journal of Psychology, 9,* 332–338.

Jacobs, D. M., & Michaels, C. F. (2006). Lateral interception I: Operative optical variables, attunement, and calibration. *Journal of Experimental Psychology: Human Perception and Performance, 32,* 443–458. doi:10.1037/0096-1523.32.2.443

Koenderink, J. J., van Doorn, A. J., & Lappin, J. S. (2000). Direct measurement of the curvature of visual space. *Perception, 29,* 69–79. doi:10.1068/p2921

Lee, D. N. (1976). A theory of visual control of braking based on information about time-to-collision. *Perception, 5,* 437–459. doi:10.1068/p050437

Lenoir, M., Musch, E., Thiery, E., & Savelsbergh, G. J. (2002). Rate of change of angular bearing as the relevant property in a horizontal interception task during locomotion. *Journal of Motor Behavior, 34,* 385–401. doi:10.1080/00222890209601955

Loomis, J. M., & Beall, A. C. (1998). Visually controlled locomotion: Its dependence on optic flow, three-dimensional space perception, and cognition. *Ecological Psychology, 10,* 271–285. doi:10.1080/10407413.1998.9652685

Loomis, J. M., & Beall, A. C. (2004). Model-based control of perception/action. In L. M. Vaina, S. A. Beardsley, & S. K. Rushton (Eds.), *Optic flow and beyond* (pp. 421–441). Boston, MA: Kluwer Academic.

Loomis, J. M., & Philbeck, J. W. (2006). Measuring spatial perception with spatial updating and action. In M. B. R. Klatzky & B. MacWhinney (Eds.), *Embodiment, ego-space, and action* (pp. 1–43). New York, NY: Psychology Press.

McLeod, P., Reed, N., & Dienes, Z. (2006). The generalized optic acceleration cancellation theory of catching. *Journal of Experimental Psychology: Human Perception and Performance, 32,* 139–148. doi:10.1037/0096-1523.32.1.139

Michaels, C. F., & Oudejans, R. R. (1992). The optics and actions of catching fly balls: Zeroing out optical acceleration. *Ecological Psychology, 4,* 199–222. doi:10.1207/s15326969eco0404_1

Oudejans, R. R. D., Michaels, C. F., Bakker, F. C., & Dolné, M. A. (1996). The relevance of action in perceiving affordances: perception of catchableness of fly balls. *Journal of Experimental Psychology: Human Perception and Performance, 22,* 879–891. doi:10.1037/0096-1523.22.4.879

Oudejans, R. R., Michaels, C. F., van Dort, B., & Frissen, E. J. P. (1996). To cross or not to cross: The effect of locomotion on street-crossing behavior. *Ecological Psychology, 8,* 259–267. doi:10.1207/s15326969eco0803_4

Pepping, G., & Li, F. X. (2000). Changing action capabilities and the perception of affordances. *Journal of Human Movement Studies, 39,* 115–140.

Philbeck, J. W., & Loomis, J. M. (1997). Comparison of two indicators of perceived egocentric distance under full-cue and reduced-cue conditions. *Journal of Experimental Psychology: Human Perception and Performance, 23,* 72–85. doi:10.1037/0096-1523.23.1.72

Phillips, F., & Voshell, M. G. (2009). Distortions of posterior visual space. *Perception, 38,* 1045–1052. doi:10.1068/p6166

Plumert, J. M., Kearney, J. K., & Cremer, J. F. (2004). Children's perception of gap affordances: Bicycling across traffic-filled intersections in an immersive virtual environment. *Child Development, 75,* 1243–1253. doi:10.1111/j.1467-8624.2004.00736.x

Proffitt, D. R. (2006). Embodied perception and the economy of action. *Perspectives on Psychological Science, 1,* 110–122. doi:10.1111/j.1745-6916.2006.00008.x

Proffitt, D. R. (2008). The action-specific approach to spatial perception. In M. B. R. Klatzky & B. MacWhinney (Eds.), *Embodiment, ego-space, and action* (pp. 179–202). New York, NY: Psychology Press.

Proffitt, D. R. (2009). Affordances matter in geographical slant perception [Comment]. *Psychonomic Bulletin & Review, 16,* 970–972. doi:10.3758/PBR.16.5.970

Proffitt, D. R., Bhalla, M., Grossweiler, R., & Midgett, J. (1995). Perceiving geographical slant. *Psychonomic Bulletin & Review, 2,* 409–428. doi:10.3758/BF03210980

Proffitt, D. R., & Linkenauger, S. A. (in press). Perception viewed as phenotypic expression. In M. B. W. Prinz & A. Herwig (Eds.), *Tutorials in action science.* Cambridge, MA: MIT Press.

Proffitt, D. R., Stefanucci, J., Banton, T., & Epstein, W. (2003). The role of effort in perceiving distance. *Psychological Science, 14,* 106–112. doi:10.1111/1467-9280.t01-1-01427

Proffitt, D. R., Stefanucci, J., Banton, T., & Epstein, W. (2006). Reply to Hutchison and Loomis. *Spanish Journal of Psychology, 9,* 340–342.

Todd, J. T. (2004). The visual perception of 3D shape. *Trends in Cognitive Sciences, 8,* 115–121. doi:10.1016/j.tics.2004.01.006

Todd, J. T., & Norman, J. F. (2003). The visual perception of 3-D shape from multiple cues: Are observers capable of perceiving metric structure? *Perception & Psychophysics, 65,* 31–47. doi:10.3758/BF03194781

Todd, J. T., Tittle, J. S., & Norman, J. F. (1995). Distortions of three-dimensional space in the perceptual analysis of motion and stereo. *Perception, 24,* 75–86. doi:10.1068/p240075

Turvey, M. T. (1992). Affordances and prospective control: An outline of the ontology. *Ecological Psychology, 4,* 173–187. doi:10.1207/s15326969eco0403_3

Turvey, M. T. (2004). Space (and its perception): The first and final frontier. *Ecological Psychology, 16,* 25–29. doi:10.1207/s15326969eco1601_3

Vo, V., Ning, A., Bhattacharjee, A., Li, Z., & Durgin, F. (2011). Pointing accuracy at a target doesn't require perceiving its location accurately. *Journal of Vision, 11,* 944.

Wagner, M. (2006). *The geometries of visual space.* Mahwah, NJ: Erlbaum.

Wann, J. P., & Wilkie, R. M. (2004). How do we control high speed steering? In L. M. Vaina, S. A. Beardsley, & S. K. Rushton (Eds.), *Optic flow and beyond* (pp. 401–419). Dordrecht, Netherlands: Kluwer Academic.

Warren, W. H. (1984). Perceiving affordances: Visual guidance of stair climbing. *Journal of Experimental Psychology: Human Perception and Performance, 10,* 683–703. doi:10.1037/0096-1523.10.5.683

Warren, W. H. (1988). Action modes and laws of control for the visual guidance of action. In O. G. Meijer & K. Roth (Eds.), *Movement behavior: The motor–action controversy.* Amsterdam, Netherlands: North Holland. doi:10.1016/S0166-4115(08)62564-9

Warren, W. H. (1998). Visually controlled locomotion: 40 years later. *Ecological Psychology, 10,* 177–219. doi:10.1080/10407413.1998.9652682

Warren, W. H. (2006). The dynamics of perception and action. *Psychological Review, 113,* 358–389. doi:10.1037/0033-295X.113.2.358

Warren, W. H., Kay, B. A., Zosh, W. D., Duchon, A. P., & Sahuc, S. (2001). Optic flow is used to control human walking. *Nature Neuroscience, 4,* 213–216. doi:10.1038/84054

Warren, W. H., & Whang, S. (1987). Visual guidance of walking through apertures: Body-scaled information for affordances. *Journal of Experimental Psychology: Human Perception and Performance, 13,* 371–383. doi:10.1037/0096-1523.13.3.371

Witt, J. K., Linkenauger, S. A., Bakdash, J. Z., & Proffitt, D. R. (2008). Putting to a bigger hole: Golf performance relates to perceived size. *Psychonomic Bulletin & Review, 15,* 581–585. doi:10.3758/PBR.15.3.581

Witt, J. K., & Proffitt, D. R. (2005). See the ball, hit the ball. *Psychological Science, 16,* 937–938. doi:10.1111/j.1467-9280.2005.01640.x

Witt, J. K., & Proffitt, D. R. (2008). Action-specific influences on distance perception: A role for motor simulation. *Journal of Experimental Psychology: Human Perception and Performance, 34,* 1479–1492. doi:10.1037/a0010781

Witt, J. K., Proffitt, D. R., & Epstein, W. (2005). Tool use affects perceived distance, but only when you intend to use it. *Journal of Experimental Psychology: Human Perception and Performance, 31,* 880–888. doi:10.1037/0096-1523.31.5.880

Witt, J. K., & Riley, M. A. (2011). *Getting in touch with your inner Gibson: Reconciling action-specific and ecological approaches.* Manuscript submitted for publication.

Wraga, M. (1999). The role of eye height in perceiving affordances and object dimensions. *Perception & Psychophysics, 61,* 490–507. doi:10.3758/BF03211968

Yilmaz, E. H., & Warren, W. H., Jr. (1995). Visual control of braking: A test of the tau hypothesis. *Journal of Experimental Psychology: Human Perception and Performance, 21,* 996–1014. doi:10.1037/0096-1523.21.5.996

CHAPTER 4

MULTISENSORY CONTRIBUTIONS TO SPATIAL PERCEPTION

Betty J. Mohler, Massimiliano Di Luca, and Heinrich H. Bülthoff

How do we know where environmental objects are located with respect to our body? How are we are able to navigate, manipulate, and interact with the environment? In this chapter, we describe how capturing sensory signals from the environment and performing internal computations achieve such goals. The first step, called *early* or *low-level processing,* is based on the functioning of feature detectors that respond selectively to elementary patterns of stimulation. Separate organs capture sensory signals and then process them separately in what we normally refer to as senses: smell, taste, touch, audition, and vision. In the first section of this chapter, we present the sense modalities that provide sensory information for the perception of spatial properties such as distance, direction, and extent. Although it is hard to distinguish where early processing ends and high-level perception begins, the rest of the chapter focuses on the intermediate level of processing, which is implicitly assumed to be the a key component of several perceptual and computational theories (Gibson, 1979; Marr, 1982) and for the visual modality has been termed *mid-level vision* (see Nakayama, He, & Shimojo, 1995). In particular, we discuss the ability of the perceptual system to specify the position and orientation of environmental objects relative to other objects and especially relative to the observer's body. We present computational theories and relevant scientific results on individual sense modalities and on the integration of sensory information within and across the sensory modalities. Finally, in the last section of this chapter, we describe how the information processing approach has enabled a better understanding of the perceptual processes in relation to two specific high-level perceptual functions: self-orientation perception and object recognition.

SENSORY SYSTEMS IN SPATIAL PERCEPTION

To understand human spatial perception, one must first understand how sensory signals carry information about different spatial properties. This brief overview of the human senses highlights contributions to spatial perception and should not be considered an in-depth description of sensory physiology or anatomy. Interested readers can consult Moller (2002) or Wolfe et al. (2008) for more in-depth descriptions of the sensory systems and Boron and Boulpaep (2005) for physiology.

To perceive the spatial layout of the environment and produce successful actions (e.g., hitting a nail with a hammer, knocking on a door, manipulating an object, navigating through space), humans use several types of sensory information that are collected through different sense organs. Each sense is specialized to transduce and process information coming from one type of energy (kinetic for the body senses, air vibration for audition, photons for vision). Because of physical differences in stimuli and in the information that can be obtained, it is

DOI: 10.1037/13936-005
Handbook of Spatial Cognition, D. Waller and L. Nadel (Editors)

tempting and can be useful to consider the sensory systems as independent modules (Fodor, 1983) even though perception typically comes from processing multiple sources of sensory information at the same time. It is also tempting to regard sensation as a process in which information is passively received and no action is required, yet we recognize that organisms interact with the environment and purposefully seek information. To understand the information available through each of the sense organs, we will proceed with an overview of each sense relevant for spatial perception, though it should be kept in mind that the information available is not sensed passively and in isolation for each modality. The interactive and multisensory properties of the stimuli will become clear in the rest of the chapter.

Vestibular System

The vestibular system senses translational and rotational accelerations and thus allows us to perceive the direction of gravity relative to the body, self-motion, and changes in head orientation. This information is critical for navigation and for maintaining balance. Without a normally functioning vestibular system, humans have difficulty in stabilizing their posture and gait, as well in performing complex tasks. The vestibular portion of the inner ear contains two structures: the otolith organs, which are sensitive to linear acceleration; and the three semicircular canals, which are sensitive to rotational acceleration (Day & Fizpatrick, 2005). The three pairs of semicircular canals (anterior, posterior, and horizontal) are arranged symmetrically at the sides of the head and work in a push–pull fashion: When one is stimulated, its corresponding partner is inhibited. For example, whereas the right horizontal semicircular canal gets stimulated during head rotations to the right, the left horizontal semicircular canal gets stimulated by head rotations to the left (Day & Fizpatrick, 2005). This allows us to sense all directions of rotation. The otolithic organs (utricle and saccule) are orthogonally oriented at the sides of the head. They are sensitive to linear accelerations as they detect the displacement of small particles of calcium carbonate that sit above small hair cells. It is well known that signals from the otoliths are ambiguous indicators of self-orientation

and acceleration and that other sensory signals and previous experience are needed to resolve this ambiguity (e.g., MacNeilage, Banks, Berger, & Bülthoff, 2007).

The vestibular system clearly provides information relevant to spatial perception and to action. For example, it compensates for retinal image slip created by rotations of the head. In addition, with respect to distance or depth perception, the vestibular system provides information to the active viewer about relative angular orientation of the head when looking at different objects. The vestibular system may also indirectly provide information about the position of the body over time (as a derivative of linear and angular acceleration over time). For a recent review of the vestibular system, see Goldberg et al. (2011).

Body-Based Senses

The proprioceptive, kinesthetic, and haptic sensory systems all involve somatosensory information and combined are often referred to as *body-based senses. Proprioception* is the sense of the relative position of parts of the body with respect to each other. *Kinesthesia* is often used interchangeably with proprioception but with a greater emphasis on motion. Kinesthesia contributes to our proprioceptive sense by providing precise awareness of muscle movement and joint angles to coordinate our body movements when we are in motion in our environment. For example, proprioception and kinesthesia enable us to touch the tip of our nose with our eyes closed. Because proprioceptive signals provide sensory information about the position of the limbs, there needs to be a mapping to the external environment. The point-to-point mapping of the body surfaces in the brain, which was first referred to as a *sensory homunculus* (Penfield & Rasmussen, 1950), enables stimuli to be perceived as occurring at a specific location. It is now commonly accepted that there is a stored model of the body, or *body schema,* which contains representations of the shape and contours of the human body, a plan of the body surface, the location of body parts, the boundaries between body parts, and their relation to each other (de Vignemont, Tsakiris, & Haggard, 2005; Schwoebel & Coslett, 2005).

Recent research has investigated the role of this internal model of the body in the visual recognition of self (Costantini & Haggard, 2007; Tsakiris, Costantini, & Haggard, 2008) and the way that this internal model is updated as the body is in motion (Wolpert, Goodbody, & Husain, 1998). In addition, our body schema is what drives embodied or grounded cognition (Barsalou, 2008; Wilson, 2002), and it is increasingly considered a fundamental basis of offline cognition such as memory and language (Glenberg, 1997, 2010).

Haptics is the perception of objects through active tactile interaction. It requires two afferent subsystems, cutaneous and kinesthetic, and is generally used to refer to active manual exploration of the environment and manipulation of objects (Lederman & Klatzky, 2009b). Passive touch (cutaneous) alone is often used to refer to the sensory experience (or system in some cases), which involves passively experiencing contact on one's skin. The word *haptics,* on the other hand, refers to the ability to manipulate and experience the environment through active exploration. Therefore, haptics naturally also requires information from kinesthetic sources, because joints and muscles also move when actively touching an object. Many scientists have measured the sensitivity of humans in distinguishing a passive touch on their body, which depends on factors such as age, body location, and visual experience (see Lederman & Klatzky, 2009a, for a review). For example, humans demonstrate higher resolution of localization of a touch on their hand as compared with on their forearm (see Lederman & Klatzky, 2009a, Figure 2). It is known that the spatial resolution of the skin is not as fine as that of the visual system, but it is better than the resolution of the auditory system (see Sherrick & Cholewiak, 1986).

Audition

The collection of vibratory energies that leads to audition begins with the outer ear, which protrudes away from the head and is shaped like a cup to direct sounds toward the tympanic membrane. This structure transmits vibrations to the inner ear, which senses vibration through specialized hair cells (Boron & Boulpaep, 2005).

Spatial information can be recovered from auditory information. The brain can compare the signals transduced by hair cells from the two ears to determine the interaural time difference (ITD) and the interaural intensity difference (IID). Sounds produced to the right of the head's midline arrive at the right ear slightly earlier and stronger. The ITD and IID together provide localization information across the entire audible frequency range, where ITD is better at lower frequencies and IID is better for higher frequencies (see Blauert, 1997, for a review). However, the information does not uniquely specify the location of a sound in 3-D because sources placed along a cone around the interaural axis (the *cone of confusion*) have only small variations of ITD and ILD. Using only ITD and ILD leads to localization errors including elevation, front–back direction, and distance of the sound source. These types of confusion can be disambiguated by monoaural information, by the environmental effects (i.e., echoes) or by moving one's head. Monoaural information about location is created by modifying the original sounds through interactions with different anatomical parts of the head. If a sound has a wide spectrum, reflections from the outer structure of the ear (pinna), skull, and hair create characteristic modulations in magnitude and delay that can be used to locate the sound source and disambiguate ITD and ILD (see Blauert, 1997; Fay & Popper, 2005, for a review).

Auditory information about distance is relatively scarce compared with directional localization of sounds. Sound intensity and spectral content can be informative about absolute distance if the source is known but can also inform about changes in distance for unknown sources (Mershon, 1997). Room reflections are also used to estimate distance of a sound source if additional knowledge is available for this (Zahorik, Brungart, & Bronkhorst, 2005).

Scientists have investigated how informative auditory information is for spatial perception, focusing primarily on perception of sound-source direction (Wightman & Kistler, 1999) and distance (Zahorik et al., 2005). Furthermore, scientists have demonstrated that humans have the ability to update their own perception of location in space using only auditory targets (Ashmead, DeFord, & Northington, 1995; Loomis, Lippa, Klatzky, & Golledge, 2002).

Vision

The proportion of the human brain devoted to processing visual information far exceeds that of the other sensory systems. Therefore, it is not surprising that there has been a great deal of research on visual sensory information for spatial cognition. There are many properties of visual stimuli that carry information about space. The retinal projection contains information about radial (i.e., 2-D) space—the mapping on the retinal image corresponds with relative locations of objects in space. Although relative position of objects can be judged using only relative position on the retina (judgments for which we can achieve high precision), for absolute judgments of radial location we need to know the orientation of the eyes in space. Additional information from the muscles controlling the position and orientation of the body, neck, and eyes are necessary for such an absolute judgment (Klier & Angelaki, 2008).

For spatial information along the line of sight (distance or relative depth of objects), the situation is far more complex. The optical projection of the 3-D environment onto the 2-D sensitive surface of the eye does not preserve the depth dimension, and such information must be recovered from the visual signals. Several sources of optical information are simultaneously available to recover depth and distance (see, e.g., Boring, 1952; Cutting & Vishton, 1995). Such sources are not always sufficient to specify 3-D properties, and for this reason they were originally termed *cues* (Berkeley, 1709) from theater documents where the letter *Q* stood for the word *quando* (i.e., "when"), which in theater scripts indicated a trigger in response to information only hinted at. It is commonly believed that cues are processed in separate modules and the output of the computation is an estimate of the geometric properties of the environment (Bruno & Cutting, 1988; Bülthoff, 1991; Marr, 1982). There are many types of cues: Some are available in a single static image (*pictorial depth cues*), and others are defined by systematic transformations of the projection (*dynamic cues*). Still others are available through muscular

information such as convergence and accommodation (*oculomotor cues*). Finally, several cues depend on differences between the stimulation of the two eyes (*binocular cues*). Pictorial cues are optical patterns on one retinal image (without any information from kinesthetic or vestibular sense modalities) due to perspective effects (relative size, horizon ratio, relative height in the field of view, texture gradients, linear perspective, aerial perspective; see Gibson, 1979), contours, occlusion, optical distortions due to refraction, and illumination (e.g., shading, shadows, highlights, reflections). Dynamic cues are either due to the relative motion of objects or of their visible parts (which give rise to the kinetic depth effect; Wallach & O'Connell, 1953) or to the motion of the observer in the environment (motion parallax; Ives, 1929). Other cues are available because of *stereoscopic signals*—differences in the image projected on the two eyes—in the form of horizontal and vertical disparities (see Howard, 2002).

Several of the visual patterns in the retinal projections require prior knowledge or additional sensory information to be able to infer geometric properties. For example, with shading patterns, it is necessary to assume the reflectance properties of the object (Pentland, 1989), the local shape (Langer & Bülthoff, 2001), or the location of the light source (Mamassian & Goutcher, 2001) if they are not specified by other visual information (i.e., Erens, Kappers, & Koenderink, 1993). Using a single pattern to recover information about distance might not be always sufficient. Only by integrating several types of cues or information from other senses is the brain able to estimate spatial properties correctly.

MULTISENSORY INTEGRATION OF SPATIAL INFORMATION

The first section of this chapter provided an overview of the sensory systems that contribute to spatial perception. We have seen that each modality provides multiple sensory signals that are informative about the spatial properties of the environment, such as distances, angles, or shape. Here we describe how the brain processes these sensory signals to create a unique and coherent perception of the world.

The importance of this mechanism was captured by W. James (1890/1983), who wrote, "Space perception consists largely of two processes—reducing the various sense-feelings to a common measure and adding them together into the single all-including space of the real world" (pp. 268–269).

In our view, to obtain a perceptual estimate of an environmental property (e.g., the shape or size of an object, the location of an event), the brain uses sensory signals that do not determine uniquely their environmental causes (real shape, size, or location in physical space). The *perceptual estimate* represents the "best guess" about the world property, but it is not guaranteed to be veridical. To maximize the chance of making a good guess, the brain uses all information available, including stored knowledge about the situation. A growing number of scientists agree that the brain can solve the problem of obtaining a percept by combining sensory signals and prior knowledge in ways similar to Bayesian decision theory (Bülthoff, 1991; Bülthoff & Yuille, 1991; Kersten & Yuille, 2003; Knill & Richards, 1996; Körding, 2007; Mamassian, Landy, & Maloney, 2002). This way of framing the problem of perception has been referred to as *indirect perception* (Rock, 1997). In this framework, the process of integration assumes names such as *sensor fusion* or either *cue, multisensory,* or *multimodal integration,* depending on whether the information is integrated at the signal level or at the level of the estimate, and whether one or more sensory modalities are involved (Ernst & Bülthoff, 2004).

Fusion and Integration

Sensory signals can be more or less independent from each other when they are sensed, and it is critical for the perceptual system to be able to distinguish whether sensory signals are produced by one environmental event or many. Signals are *independent* when the sensory noise that affects the signals (i.e., due to the limited precision of the sensory organs and neural noise) has unrelated causes. Signals are independent, for example, when they are sensed through different sense modalities.

Consider the situation in which we knock on a door with our hand (Color Plate 10a). The haptic, auditory, and visual signals that specify the posi-

tion of where the hand hits the wood are captured by different sense organs. The neural information reaches separate brain areas, and processing is kept separate in relatively independent processing units called *modules* (Fodor, 1983). Nevertheless, we perceive the act of touching the wood, the sound of the knock, and the view of the hand hitting the door to be fused into a unified percept. If we were asked to judge the location of such a knock, we could do so by estimating both the radial position along the horizontal axis and the distance (Color Plate 10a). Sensory signals from all three modalities could be used to perform the task because each of them is informative about location. When such types of signals are available simultaneously, they are defined to be carrying redundant information about location (Ernst & Bülthoff, 2004).

There appears to be some difference in how the brain deals with redundant information coming from a single sense modality and when the signals are sensed cross-modally (Hillis, Ernst, Banks, & Landy, 2002). With unimodal signals, we do not have access to the individual estimates, and fusion is mandatory. For example, if texture and disparity information specify conflicting information about surface slant, we are unable to estimate the two slants independently. However, if the slant is specified by visual and haptic information, we can either judge the unified percept of slant, or we can judge each of the two composing slants. Note that there are many examples in which we would not want to fuse all sensory signals because they are not redundantly informative about the same environmental event. For example, if we are knocking and there is another sound in the room, it is important to keep the perception of these two events separate.

In what situations do people fuse multiple signals into one integrated percept? Multisensory integration is more likely when signals arise from approximately the same spatial location and are temporally coincident (Stein & Meredith, 1993). Radeau and Bertelson (1977, 1987) defined such factors as being structural, data driven, or bottom-up, although they also recognized that cognitive factors play an important role in the process. Several research lines have shown that such low-level factors are important, but they are used to make an inference about whether a common cause is responsible for the generation of all signals, a process called *identity decision* (Bedford, 2001; Helbig & Ernst, 2007). The extent of the integration is then a function of the probability that such a common cause exists (Körding et al., 2007; Roach, Heron, & McGraw, 2006; Shams & Beierholm, 2010). There are many cases in which the attribution of a common cause is purposefully used to lead to a false inference. A good example is the *ventriloquism effect*—the percept that speech utterances produced by the immobile lips of a puppeteer are attributed to a moving puppet. In this situation, the spatial discrepancy between visual and auditory signals is disregarded, leading to the percept of a single source through a process of *pairing* (Epstein, 1975; Radeau & Bertelson, 1977). The illusion is the misperception of the location of the auditory stimulus that is shifted toward the visual stimulus.

Strategies for Integration

Once the brain has assessed which sensory signals belong to the same distal event and has determined that the information about location is redundant, how is this information integrated? It has been argued that during normal interaction with the environment (e.g., knocking on a door), one strategy could be to rely entirely on one sense to determine the perceptual outcome. For example, we could rely on vision alone and disregard audition and proprioception (termed *vetoing* by Yuille & Bülthoff, 1996). The felt position of the hand would be "captured" by vision even when the hand is viewed through a prism that displaces it (Mon-Williams, Wann, Jenkinson, & Rushton, 1997). It might be the case that the visual modality normally leads to sufficiently precise estimates of position, and hence there is no reason to incorporate other information.

It has been proposed that, depending on the task, there is one sensory modality that is most appropriate, and the brain preferentially uses this modality (*modality appropriateness hypothesis;* Welch, DuttonHurt, & Warren, 1986). Accordingly, in conditions with reduced illumination, the sense of hand position dominates vision (Mon-Williams et al., 1997). However, the marked difference in precision of spatial judgments within one modality

argues against this hypothesis. As discussed in the previous section, visual judgments about angular position are much more precise than judgments in depth. Precision of proprioceptive judgments follows a different pattern because it is affected by the geometry of the arm (van Beers, Sittig, & Denier van der Gon, 1998). This means that by using only our vision we would be good at telling where the midline of the door is, but our estimate of the distance to the door using the same visual information would not be equally reliable. Instead, using proprioception alone we would be relatively more precise in judging distance. Thus, depending on the task and context, sensory signals are differently informative, and, as we discuss next, there are several advantages to considering how each signal should contribute to the final percept.

The Outcome of Integration

Integration fuses sensory information into a unique and coherent perception of the environment. But integration also mitigates several other types of errors that affect sensory information (see Clark & Yuille, 1990; Ernst & Banks, 2002; Ernst & Di Luca, 2011; Landy, Maloney, Johnston, & Young, 1995).

First, sensory signals are affected by noise due to the limited resolution of the sensors and by imperfect neural processing of information. When we make an estimate about the state of the world, the certainty with which we make such an estimate depends on this noise. This fact is illustrated by representing the probability (likelihood) that a state of the environment generated the sensory signal—when computed for all possible locations, this becomes the *likelihood function* (see Color Plate 10b). Likelihood functions are not equal for the three sensory signals because each signal is differently effective in specifying the location of the distal event. In certain cases, such functions are usually assumed to be Gaussian in shape, and their width is defined by the variance parameter (this assumption is not always valid, as in the case of visual information coming from some depth "cues"). The precision with which it is possible to estimate a property using a signal is defined as the *reliability* of the estimate, the inverse variance of a Gaussian likelihood function (Backus & Banks, 1999). Notice that signals can lead to estimates that differ widely in reliability.

Second, sensory signals might lead to estimates that are biased with respect to the true value of the property. This *bias* can be due to random noise (and thus vary at each measurement), or it might be constant. For example, if the rotation of the head around our neck is estimated inaccurately, we can still locate objects with a consistent precision across trials but always with a constant bias. Similarly, if there is a wall on one of the side of the door we are knocking on (Color Plate 10a), the wall will imbalance the intensity of the sound reaching the two ears, biasing perceived location to shift toward the wall. *Accuracy* is defined as the degree to which the estimate corresponds to the true physical value of the environmental property, but unlike reliability, accuracy cannot be quantified from the current signal or the current unisensory estimate.

It has been argued that integration of multiple sources of information creates a unified percept and can increase precision and accuracy of the estimate. The Bayesian approach says that with independent sensory signals and redundant estimates, the probability of the states of the environment considering all available estimates (referred to as the *posterior probability distribution*) is the point-by-point multiplication of the likelihood functions. The posterior probability has important properties for perception, such as stabilizing perception in case of ambiguous estimates (Color Plate 10d).

First, integration stabilizes perception in case of ambiguous estimates. For example, in some configuration of visual information (i.e., the Necker cube) or auditory cues (only ITD and ILD), sensory information is not sufficient to uniquely specify scene geometry. In this case, the likelihood function leading to an ambiguous estimate has two (or more) peaks. By integrating information within and across sensory modalities (i.e., Battaglia et al., 2010), the point-by-point multiplication that leads to the posterior distribution can disambiguate the percept by creating a function with a single, more prominent peak.

An evident difference between the shape of the posterior distribution and the likelihood function is their steepness. Through integration, the reliability of the posterior estimate obtained from Gaussian likelihood functions increases to become the sum of the reliabilities of the individual estimates. This is the maximum improvement that can be obtained in terms of precision (when integration is statistically optimal), and for this reason it is called *maximum likelihood estimation* (MLE). There have been several empirical demonstrations of the increase of reliability consistent with MLE (see Ernst & Di Luca, 2011). One of the first studies was conducted by measuring the precision of width judgments with a bar that could either be seen, touched, or seen and touched concurrently (Ernst & Banks, 2002).

Another effect of the integration is that the peak of the posterior distribution is closer to the peak of the likelihood function that leads to the most reliable estimates. If all likelihood distributions are Gaussian in shape and noise is independent, the position of the peak is simply the weighted average of the position of the peaks in the functions, and the weights are proportional to the reliabilities (Ernst, 2005). By recalling that the reliability of visual estimates changes for lateral and depth judgments, perception should follow either the visual or the haptic estimate depending on the task, and empirical results do demonstrate such a close-to-optimal weighting scheme (Gepshtein & Banks, 2003). Weighing of information according to reliability is also what drives the ventriloquism effect (Alais & Burr, 2004). Once an inference is made such that auditory and visual signals are generated by a common source, the perceived location of the auditory stimulus is shifted toward the visual stimulus, which is much more informative in terms of spatial location. This happens at the cost of creating the illusion of a speaking puppet.

Integration of Sensory Knowledge

At the beginning of this section we noted that sensory signals are not the only source of information that can be used to make a perceptual estimate. Knowledge accumulated from previous sensory experience can influence the processing of incoming information. In the estimate of spatial properties, prior knowledge can be integrated in the posterior distribution by simply representing this knowledge as a distribution of a priori probabilities of encountering a state of the environment, the *prior distribution*. In the knocking on the door scenario, the information represented in a prior distribution is composed of the experience of direction of knocking stimuli independent of actual sensory signals. Because we are usually the one knocking, the probability that the knock is located in front of our arm is higher than elsewhere (Color Plate 10c). Prior distributions are usually shallow and deviate from Gaussian shape, so they exert minor—but nevertheless important—influences on estimates when signals carry reliable information. If all sensory evidence is artificially reduced (e.g., with earplugs, blindfold, anesthesia), our best guess would be driven by the prior distribution. Psychophysical and sensorimotor learning experiments indicate that the perceptual outcome is consistent with independent encoding of prior information (i.e., Beierholm, Quartz, & Shams, 2009) and that the final result conforms with the predictions from the Bayesian framework (see Cheng, Shettleworth, Huttenlocher, & Rieser, 2007; Ernst & Di Luca, 2011).

Another type of prior knowledge that can be used for perception comes from the experience of multiple signals co-occurring, and as such is called a *coupling prior* (Ernst, 2005). It has been suggested that the acquisition of such a prior is what makes new signals effective in changing perception (Di Luca, Ernst, & Backus, 2010) and promotes multisensory integration (Ernst, 2007). Accordingly, research suggests that young children who have not had sufficient experience for a reliable coupling prior do not integrate multisensory information (Gori, Del Viva, Sandini, & Burr, 2008). The most frequent experience with co-occurring signals within each modality also explains why integration is stronger within than across modalities.

Such coupling priors are also important in maintaining perceptual calibration: Discrepancies between the estimates could be due to either noise or to bias, and the brain may continuously assess which one is the most likely cause (for a complete discussion, see Ernst & Di Luca, 2011). If in the past the estimates have always been correlated, the cause is most likely an effect of noise. Notice that as the discrepancy increases, it can become disadvantageous to integrate. For multimodal estimates (which are not subject to mandatory fusion; see earlier), breakdown of integration (Gepshtein, Burge, Ernst, & Banks, 2005) with

large discrepancies is a consequence of having a coupling prior whose shape deviates from Gaussian (e.g., Roach et al., 2006). On the other hand, a discrepancy may be more likely due to a miscalibration when either our knowledge of the mapping is scarce or the mapping between the estimates is weak compared with the evidence of a bias. For example, a short experience with audiovisual spatial discrepancy that induces the ventriloquist illusion also induces recalibration (Recanzone, 1998). In such cases, the brain might recalibrate one or both sensory estimates. To decide in which proportion the estimates need to be recalibrated, the brain should assess the probability of bias, which is only available through prior experience with the signals (see Di Luca, Machulla, & Ernst, 2009).

In the analysis of the information available for perception, we have made the assumption that sensory signals are passively gathered from the environment. Several researchers (e.g., Marr, 1982) have subscribed to this general approach, and it has led to a wealth of scientific findings. However, perception is also achieved from dynamic sensory information and through signals that are dependent on the movement of our body in the environment. In the example of knocking on a door, the tactile, auditory, and visual signals all depend on the extension of the arm. Because there is an inherent coupling of the signals in terms of their presence, magnitude, and reliability with the way in which we interact with the environment, integration should also be dependent on the way we move. For this reason, some researchers (Gibson, 1979) have criticized the assumption that perception is passively achieved, and it has been proposed that perception is better conceptualized as one of the components of the perception–action cycle (Neisser, 1976). In this view, our movements are a way of picking up relevant information about the environment or the task at hand (as it happens for gaze orienting, visual search, reading, etc.) and thus to change the way we process information. Such a way of framing the perception–action loop has been successfully applied to several cases, among which is the perception of the material properties of deformable objects. For example, squeezing a soft object with the hand requires the integration of compliance estimates from multiple fingers; the estimate obtained with the finger that moves more (and thus the one more likely to be reliable) is given more weight (Di Luca, 2011). Moreover, the brain treats haptic information obtained over different phases of exploratory movements differently, for example, by weighting more information obtained during squeezing motion than during object release in the final percept (Di Luca, Knörlein, Ernst, & Harders, 2011).

In sum, casting the issue of sensory information integration in terms of probabilistic inferences about the state of the stimulus that generated the sensory information allows scientists to explain several aspects of the perception of spatial properties, such as the disambiguation of estimates and the increase in precision and accuracy. Such a framework also helps us to understand the relation between processing of spatial information and previous knowledge. We examine this relationship in greater detail in the next section.

HIGH-LEVEL PERCEPTION

Thus far, we have primarily discussed low-level or mid-level perception as categorized by Nakayama et al. (1995). For *high-level* perception, we not only need to be able to move and understand our self-motion relative to the surrounding world, but we also typically refer to the surrounding world with respect to the objects themselves and not to the sensory signals that they produce and we experience. For example, we say that we heard a man knocking at the door, not that we received auditory stimulation to our ear, or that we saw a door rather than a pattern of edges. The perception of one's position and orientation in the world is often referred to as *self-motion perception* or *self-orientation perception* (this research often focuses on both body-based and visual–sensory information sources). The naming of objects falls under the research discipline of object and scene perception and, to be more specific, object recognition. (Most of the research in this field focuses on visual information, although research that is more recent has begun to investigate auditory and haptic sensory information sources.)

Humans have an impressive capability for recognizing objects, and it is not yet understood how exactly this is realized. With the rise of computer vision and the desire for machines to visually recognize objects for use in many applications, scientists from many disciplines have investigated how humans perform this function (Wallraven & Bülthoff, 2007). *Recognition* has often been used to refer to several high-level abilities (usually visual), including identification, categorization, and discrimination of objects. In this chapter, *recognition of an object* is used to refer to the successful classification of an object into a specific object class (Liter & Bülthoff, 1998).

We might first ask why the process of object recognition is so difficult to understand, given that it appears to be so easy for humans to perform. When performing visual object recognition, one determines whether the object currently being seen corresponds to an object that that has been seen in the past. One possibility (albeit a brute force approach) is that we somehow store all visual stimuli associated with an object and use these stored memories to recall that object in the future. This is likely an unrealistic model because even with the enormous memory capacity that it would require, one would still be unable to experience all possible visual images generated by an object. For example, objects vary in their distance and orientation to an observer. In addition, lighting, the context of the object (sometimes an object is alone or is surrounded by other objects), and finally, the shape of the object can vary over time. Yet, humans are able to recognize newly seen objects as objects that were previously seen despite these and other variations in the scene and object. Moreover, humans constantly vary their own physical orientation with respect to the world and yet still perceive the world as upright; they are able to recognize objects despite this change in physical viewing orientation. Therefore, before describing theories of object recognition in greater detail, we first discuss how humans determine their own orientation. These two areas of research are, of course, only two of the many high-level processes that have been examined from a multisensory integration perspective; we choose them here because of the wide interest and attention given to these topics.

Perception of Self-Orientation

When an observer moves, the sensory systems capture multiple signals: The retinal projections of the environment change, the vestibular organs sense acceleration, environmental sounds move with respect to the body, and so forth. As discussed earlier, because of the limitations of each of the sensory systems, information from multiple sense modalities is often necessary to navigate successfully. Vision, touch, and audition can provide contextual information to vestibular signals for a more robust and stable representation of perceived head orientation and movement. To illustrate this, try standing on one foot with your eyes open and then try again with your eyes closed; you will notice how much harder it becomes. If you then increase the amount of sensory information about changes in body orientation by lightly touching a surface with a finger or playing a localized sound, you should also notice that balance can be better maintained even when your eyes are closed (Jeka, 1997). Although information about head location and orientation comes from multiple modalities, such information may be somewhat incoherent or ambiguous. To study how multisensory integration forms a coherent perception of self-orientation, researchers introduce inconsistencies across the sensory modalities.

The earliest investigations about the influence of head orientation on perception showed that perceived subjective vertical of viewed objects was affected by body orientation; this is the so-called *Aubert illusion* (Asch & Witkin, 1948a; Aubert, 1861; see Color Plate 11). However, with more contextual visual information, it is the perceived orientation of self that is affected and not the object orientation (Asch & Witkin, 1948a, 1948b). Mittelstaedt (1986) proposed that subjective vertical is obtained through a vector sum of the visual and bodily estimates based on prior experience (Dyde, Jenkin, & Harris, 2006; Mittelstaedt, 1986). It was not until much later that this was shown to be equivalent to formulating the problem in terms of Bayesian MLE (De Vrijer, Medendorp, & Van Gisbergen, 2008; Laurens & Droulez, 2007; MacNeilage et al., 2007), where tilt estimates from the otoliths signals are combined with other sensory information (e.g. retinal line orientation). Because prior knowledge about head tilt indicates that small tilts are more likely than large tilts, this knowledge does not affect the estimates with normal postures, but it leads to errors with large deviations from vertical (De Vrijer et al., 2008).

The subjective visual vertical is thought to be distinct from another perception of "which way is up" or what is referred to as *perceptual upright* (Dyde et al., 2006) and is defined as the point at which objects are most easily recognized. It is notable that scientists have recently found that our own perception of self-motion (specifically self-orientation) influences the way we perceive object properties. Altering a person's sense of vertical upright and then having him or her estimate the stability of objects demonstrates the influence of self-orientation perspective on object properties. It was shown that subjective vertical (and not the actual orientation of the head) could be used to predict the reported stability of an object (Barnett-Cowan, Fleming, Singh, & Bülthoff, 2011). Further, it has been shown that alterations in physical (body) and visual (object) tilt changes both allocentric (gravity orientation) and egocentric (head orientation) representations of upright but that the vestibular system influences egocentric upright estimates more, and vision influences allocentric upright estimates more (Barnett-Cowan & Harris, 2008).

Theories of Object Recognition

As we pointed out earlier, one critical high-level perceptual function is the recognition of previously seen objects. When considering visual object perception (and not taking into consideration body-based senses), the problem could be simplified and conceived as a problem of 2-D retinal information that needs to be indexed or classified. For 2-D object recognition, two approaches have been suggested: an image-based model and a structural description model. *Image-based models* represent objects as a collection of viewpoint-dependent local features, whereas a *structural description* encodes objects in terms of their volumetric components and spatial relations. A review of behavioral studies concluded that although image-based models can explain many empirical findings, there appears to be a need for additional structural description of objects to explain human performance in object recognition tasks (Tarr & Bülthoff, 1998).

Although there have been many theories of object perception, Ullman (1996) divided three-dimensional object perception approaches into three categories: (a) invariant properties and feature space, (b) parts and structural descriptions, and (c) the alignment approach. Ullman suggested that all three approaches offer some insight into how humans perceive and recognize objects but that these approaches alone are insufficient to explain human object recognition and perception. We discuss each of these three approaches in turn.

First, *invariant properties and feature space theories* suggest that there is a method of recognizing geometric objects that is independent of the rotation, translation, and scale of the perceived object (as well as other variations such as lighting and some aspects of shape). Supporters of this approach have argued that certain properties such as area, elongation, perimeter length, and shape moments can be used to recognize objects (see Bolles & Cain, 1982, for examples and Gibson, 1979 for theory). Although this approach has worked in explaining the recognition of simple objects, for more complex objects, the use of such simple invariants has not proven to be useful without combining this approach with other approaches.

Parts and structural descriptions theories, as the name implies, suggest that objects are recognized not by global properties but by their parts (a widely cited theory is *recognition by components;* Biederman, 1987). This approach assumes that all objects can be broken down into a small set of "generic" components (which are shared by all objects). These generic components could be considered the basic building blocks of objects; therefore, this is an attractive approach because the number of generic components is limited and thus results in an obvious cost reduction for object recognition.

Although parts and structural description approaches are quite promising, they have a number of limitations. One obvious limitation is that many objects have the same parts and are yet recognized by humans as distinct objects. In addition, the question of which generic components should be used to distinguish objects from each other is critical to

the theory, and this varies on the basis of the group of objects that need to be recognized. Finally, it is not always trivial to determine which aspects of the object make up a part (Ullman, 1996).

Finally, the *alignment approach* develops the idea that recognition occurs by (a) transforming the viewed object in a way that reduces the differences between the viewed image and the corresponding stored model of the object and (b) comparing the transformed view with the stored model. This is to say that for all objects in the world, a set of known transformations is presumed possible (scaling, position, or orientation transformations). These transformations are made to enable a direct comparison between the viewed object and the possible object that it might be recognized as (Ullman, 1996; see Figure 4.1).

One aspect of object recognition that has received a great deal of attention is the dependence on viewing orientation. Through many psychophysical experiments, scientists have demonstrated that object recognition is viewpoint-dependent in humans (Bülthoff, Edelman, & Tarr, 1995) and in monkeys (Logothetis, Pauls, Bülthoff, & Poggio, 1994). This has been demonstrated in a number of studies that have shown that recognition performance decreases as the orientation is further from the trained orientation (Bülthoff & Edelman, 1992; Edelman & Bülthoff, 1992; Rock & Di Vita, 1987; Tarr & Pinker, 1989, 1991). This dependence on viewing direction has been shown even in the presence of stereo, shading, and motion cues (Bülthoff & Edelman, 1992). These findings go against theories that support a structural description because structural theories predict no dependence on viewing direction. The findings are also contrary to the alignment approach because although this approach should be sufficient to generalize over a wide range of viewing orientations, it is not view dependent. In addition, it has been shown that recognition for novel views improves after training with additional object views (Poggio & Edelman, 1990; Tarr & Pinker, 1989). For example, Bülthoff and Edelman (1992) showed that participants performed better on object recognition tasks when their orientation varied along a single axis (e.g., yaw, heading), which supports a two-dimensional image combination

FIGURE 4.1.   Demonstration of the view-dependency of object recognition. People are slower to recognize this shape when it is upside down, because they most often see it right side up. By turning the page upside down, it is easier to recognize that the figure is a map of the continental United States of America.

approach to three-dimensional object recognition (see Ullman, 1998). For a thorough and interesting review on the insights and progress on visual object perception in the past 20 years (psychophysical, neurological, and clinical), see Peissig and Tarr (2007).

Many scientists have also considered object recognition to be an active exploration process (Ernst, Lange, & Newell, 2007). The ability to generalize from a previously seen view of an object to new views of the same object involves some understanding of the spatial relations between the views. It has been shown that this process is facilitated when human observers experience walking or physically moving, thereby experiencing body-based sensory information (Christou & Bülthoff, 1999; Simons, Wang, & Roddenberry, 2002; Teramoto & Riecke, 2010) or object manipulations that are congruent to the changes in views (K. H. James et al., 2002; Meijer & van den Broek, 2010). It has been suggested that activity during view changes could facilitate the process of "mental rotation."

In addition, haptic object recognition is an active area of current research. Interestingly, it has been shown that although with visual object recognition best performance is observed from the front of a canonical view, people recognize an object best haptically when they explore the object from the opposite side of the canonical view (or the back; Newell, Ernst, Tjan, & Bülthoff, 2001). Moreover, auditory information can also be used for object categorization (Werner & Noppeney, 2010a, 2010b), and prior experience with auditory information has also been shown to influence categorization of objects (Adam & Noppeney, 2010).

CONCLUSION

In this chapter, we described how sensory information collected through multiple sense organs enables perception of spatial properties. We showed that humans possess several sensory systems, each attuned to one type of energy, limiting the quality of the perceptual estimate that can be obtained. Research suggests that integrating the information from the different sensory systems is a way of improving our perceptual abilities and of performing actions successfully. We described how multisensory integration is consistent with the view that the brain attempts to maximize the extraction of information according to Bayesian accounts of perception. We discussed the relevance of multisensory information to perception and action by describing interactive situations that require spatial information processing. Finally, we analyzed how the processing of sensory signals leads to the extraction of the information, which in turn leads to high-level perceptual processing that interacts with cognitive functions.

SUGGESTED REFERENCES FOR FURTHER READING

Bülthoff, I., & Bülthoff, H. H. (2003). Image-based recognition of biological motion, scenes and objects. In M. A. Peterson & G. Rhodes (Eds.), *Analytic and holistic processes in the perception of faces, objects, and scenes* (pp. 146–176). New York, NY: Oxford University Press.

This chapter is an excellent review of what is known about image-based recognition of objects as well as biological motion and scene recognition. The authors do an excellent job discussing the difficulties at all levels of scene recognition and leave the reader impressed with human's ability to recognize objects in the surrounding world.

Ernst, M. O., & Bülthoff, H. H. (2004). Merging the senses into a robust percept. *Trends in Cognitive Sciences, 8*, 162–169. doi:10.1016/j.tics.2004.02.002

This was one of the first articles to describe multisensory integration and is recommended for young scientists as well as those who have studied perception for some time and want to gain a greater understanding of the theory of multisensory integration.

Ernst, M. O., & Di Luca, M. (2011). Multisensory perception: From integration to remapping. In J. Trommershäuser, M. S. Landy, & K. Körding (Eds.), *Sensory cue integration* (pp. 224–250). Oxford, England: Oxford University Press.

This is a more advanced and in-depth description of the processes needed for multisensory integration, of how the brain maintains spatial calibration across the senses, as well as a review of recent research results on the topic.

Peissig, J., & Tarr, M. J. (2007). Visual object recognition: Do we know more now than we did 20 years ago? *Annual Review of Psychology, 58*, 75–96. doi:10.1146/annurev.psych.58.102904.190114

This review helps the reader to see what scientists have learned over the past 20 years about visual object recognition. This review discusses not only psychophysical and behavioral results but also the neural underpinnings of how humans recognize objects visually.

References

Adam, R., & Noppeney, U. (2010). Prior auditory information shapes visual category-selectivity in ventral occipito–temporal cortex. *NeuroImage, 52*, 1592–1602. doi:10.1016/j.neuroimage.2010.05.002

Alais, D., & Burr, D. C. (2004). The ventriloquist effect results from near-optimal bimodal integration. *Current Biology, 14*, 257–262.

Asch, S. E., & Witkin, H. A. (1948a). Studies in space orientation: I. Perception of the upright with displaced visual fields. *Journal of Experimental Psychology, 38*, 325–337. doi:10.1037/h0057855

Asch, S. E., & Witkin, H. A. (1948b). Studies in space orientation: II. Perception of the upright with displaced visual fields and with body tilted. *Journal of Experimental Psychology, 38*, 455–477. doi:10.1037/h0054121

Ashmead, D. H., DeFord, L. D., & Northington, A. (1995). Contribution of listeners' approaching motion to auditory distance perception. *Journal of Experimental Psychology: Human Perception and Performance, 21*, 239–256. doi:10.1037/0096-1523.21.2.239

Aubert, H. (1861). Eine scheinbare bedeutende Drehung von Objecten bei Neigung des Kopfes nach rechts oder links [Tilt of the head to the right or left causes a perceptual rotation of objects]. *Virchows Archiv, 20*, 381–393. doi:10.1007/BF02355256

Backus, B. T., & Banks, M. S. (1999). Estimator reliability and distance scaling in stereoscopic slant perception. *Perception, 28*, 217–242. doi:10.1068/p2753

Barnett-Cowan, M., Fleming, R. W., Singh, M., & Bülthoff, H. H. (2011). Perceived object stability depends on multisensory estimates of gravity. *PLoS ONE, 6*(4). doi:10.1371/journal.pone.0019289

Barnett-Cowan, M., & Harris, L. R. (2008). Perceived self-orientation in allocentric and egocentric space: Effects of visual and physical tilt on saccadic and tactile measures. *Brain Research, 1242*, 231–243. doi:10.1016/j.brainres.2008.07.075

Barsalou, L. W. (2008). Grounded cognition. *Annual Review of Psychology, 59*, 617–645. doi:10.1146/annurev.psych.59.103006.093639

Battaglia, P. W., Di Luca, M., Ernst, M. O., Schrater, P. R., Machulla, T., & Kersten, D. (2010). Within- and cross-modal distance information disambiguates visual size perception. *PLoS Computational Biology, 6*(3). doi:10.1371/journal.pcbi.1000697

Bedford, F. L. (2001). Towards a general law of numerical/object identity. *Current Psychology of Cognition, 20,* 113–175.

Beierholm, U. R., Quartz, S., & Shams, L. (2009). Bayesian priors are encoded independently from likelihoods in human multisensory perception. *Journal of Vision, 9*(5). doi:10.1167/9.5.23

Berkeley, G. (1709). *An essay towards a new theory of vision* (4th ed.). Dublin, Ireland: Jeremy Pepyat.

Biederman, I. (1987). Recognition-by-components: A theory of human image understanding. *Psychological Review, 94,* 115–147. doi:10.1037/0033-295X.94.2.115

Blauert, J. (1997). *Spatial hearing.* Cambridge, MA: MIT Press.

Bolles, R. C., & Cain, R. A. (1982). Recognizing and locating partially visible objects: The local feature-focus method. *The International Journal of Robotics Research, 1*(3), 57–82. doi:10.1177/027836498200100304

Boring, E. G. (1952). Visual perception as invariance. *Psychological Review, 59,* 141–148. doi:10.1037/h0060819

Boron, W., & Boulpaep, E. (2005). *Medical physiology.* Philadelphia, PA: Elsevier.

Bruno, N., & Cutting, J. E. (1988). Minimodularity and the perception of layout. *Journal of Experimental Psychology: General, 117,* 161–170. doi:10.1037/0096-3445.117.2.161

Bülthoff, H. H. (1991). Shape from X: Psychophysics and computation. In M. S. Landy (Ed.), *Computational models of visual processing* (pp. 305–330). Cambridge, MA: MIT Press.

Bülthoff, H. H., & Edelman, S. (1992). Psychophysical support for a 2-D view interpolation theory of object recognition. *Proceedings of the National Academy of Sciences of the United States of America, 89,* 60–64. doi:10.1073/pnas.89.1.60

Bülthoff, H. H., Edelman, S., & Tarr, M. J. (1995). How are three-dimensional objects represented in the brain? *Cerebral Cortex, 5,* 247–260. doi:10.1093/cercor/5.3.247

Bülthoff, H. H., & Yuille, A. L. (1991). Bayesian models for seeing shapes and depth. *Comments on Theoretical Biology, 2,* 283–314.

Cheng, K., Shettleworth, S. J., Huttenlocher, J., & Rieser, J. J. (2007). Bayesian integration of spatial information. *Psychological Bulletin, 133,* 625–637. doi:10.1037/0033-2909.133.4.625

Christou, C. G., & Bülthoff, H. H. (1999). View dependence in scene recognition after active learning.

Memory & Cognition, 27, 996–1007. doi:10.3758/BF03201230

Clark, J. J., & Yuille, A. L. (1990). *Data fusion for sensory information processing systems.* Norwell, MA: Kluwer Academic.

Costantini, M., & Haggard, P. (2007). The rubber hand illusion: Sensitivity and reference frame for body ownership. *Consciousness and Cognition, 16,* 229–240. doi:10.1016/j.concog.2007.01.001

Cutting, J. E., & Vishton, P. (1995). Perceiving layout and knowing distances: The integration, relative potency, and contextual use of different information about depth. In W. Epstein & S. Rogers (Eds.), *Perception of space and motion* (pp. 69–117). New York, NY: Academic Press.

Day, B. L., & Fizpatrick, R. C. (2005). The vestibular system. *Current Biology, 15*(15), R583–R586. doi:10.1016/j.cub.2005.07.053

de Vignemont, F. Tsakiris, M., & Haggard, P. (2005). Body mereology. In G. Knoblich, I. M. Thornton, M. Grosjean, & M. Shiffrar (Eds.), *Human body perception from the inside out* (pp. 147–170). New York, NY: Oxford University Press.

De Vrijer, M., Medendorp, W. P., & Van Gisbergen, J. A. M. (2008). Shared computational mechanism for tilt compensation accounts for biased verticality percepts in motion and pattern vision. *Journal of Neurophysiology, 99,* 915–930. doi:10.1152/jn.00921.2007

Di Luca, M. (2011). Perceived compliance in a pinch. *Vision Research, 51,* 961–967. doi:10.1016/j.visres.2011.02.021

Di Luca, M., Ernst, M. O., & Backus, B. (2010). Learning to use an invisible visual signal for perception. *Current Biology, 20,* 1860–1863. doi:10.1016/j.cub.2010.09.047

Di Luca, M., Knörlein, B., Ernst, M. O., & Harders, M. (2011). Effects of visual–haptic asynchronies and loading–unloading movements on compliance perception. *Brain Research Bulletin, 85,* 245–259. doi:10.1016/j.brainresbull.2010.02.009

Di Luca, M., Machulla, T., & Ernst, M. O. (2009). Recalibration of multisensory simultaneity: Cross-modal transfer coincides with a change in perceptual latency. *Journal of Vision, 9*(12). doi:10.1167/9.12.7

Dyde, R. T., Jenkin, M. R., & Harris, L. R. (2006). The subjective visual vertical and the perceptual upright. *Experimental brain research, 173,* 612–622.

Edelman, S., & Bülthoff, H. H. (1992). Orientation dependence in the recognition of familiar and novel views of three-dimensional objects. *Vision Research, 32,* 2385–2400. doi:10.1016/0042-6989(92)90102-O

Epstein, W. (1975). Recalibration by pairing: A process of perceptual learning. *Perception, 4,* 59–72. doi:10.1068/p040059

Erens, R. G., Kappers, A. M., & Koenderink, J. J. (1993). Perception of local shape from shading. *Perception & Psychophysics, 54,* 145–156. doi:10.3758/BF03211750

Ernst, M. O. (2005). A Bayesian view on multimodal cue integration. In G. Knoblich, *Human body perception from the inside out* (pp. 105–131). New York, NY: Oxford University Press.

Ernst, M. O. (2007). Learning to integrate arbitrary signals from vision and touch. *Journal of Vision, 7*(5). doi:10.1167/7.5.7

Ernst, M. O., & Banks, M. S. (2002, January 24). Humans integrate visual and haptic information in a statistically optimal fashion. *Nature, 415,* 429–433. doi:10.1038/415429a

Ernst, M. O., & Bülthoff, H. H. (2004). Merging the senses into a robust percept. *Trends in Cognitive Sciences, 8,* 162–169. doi:10.1016/j.tics.2004.02.002

Ernst, M. O., & Di Luca, M. (2011). Multisensory perception: from integration to remapping. In J. Trommershäuser, M. S. Landy, & K. Körding (Eds.), *Sensory cue integration* (pp. 224–250). Oxford, England: Oxford University Press.

Ernst, M. O., Lange, C., & Newell, F. N. (2007). Multisensory recognition of actively explored objects. *Canadian Journal of Experimental Psychology/Revue Canadienne de Psychologie Expérimentale, 61,* 242–253. doi:10.1037/cjep2007025

Fay, R., & Popper, A. (2005). Introduction to sound source localization. In A. N. Popper & R. R. Fay (Eds.), *Sound source localization* (Vol. 25, pp. 1–5). New York, NY: Springer. doi:10.1007/0-387-28863-5_1

Fodor, J. A. (1983). *Modularity of mind: An essay on faculty psychology.* Cambridge, MA: MIT Press.

Gepshtein, S., & Banks, M. S. (2003). Viewing geometry determines how vision and haptics combine in size perception. *Current Biology, 13,* 483–488. doi:10.1016/S0960-9822(03)00133-7

Gepshtein, S., Burge, J., Ernst, M. O., & Banks, M. S. (2005). The combination of vision and touch depends on spatial proximity. *Journal of Vision, 5*(11). doi:10.1167/5.11.7

Gibson, J. J. (1979). *The ecological approach to visual perception.* Boston, MA: Houghton Mifflin.

Glenberg, A. M. (1997). What memory is for. *Behavioral and Brain Sciences, 20,* 1–55.

Glenberg, A. M. (2010). Embodiment as a unifying perspective for psychology. *Cognitive Science, 1,* 586–596.

Goldberg, J. M., Wilson, V. J., Cullen, K. E., Angelaki, D. E., Broussard, D. M., Büttner-Ennever, J., . . . Minor, L. B. (2011). *The vestibular system: A sixth sense* (pp. 3–18). New York, NY: Oxford University Press.

Gori, M., Del Viva, M., Sandini, G., & Burr, D. C. (2008). Young children do not integrate visual and haptic form information. *Current Biology, 18,* 694–698. doi:10.1016/j.cub.2008.04.036

Helbig, H. B., & Ernst, M. O. (2007). Knowledge about a common source can promote visual–haptic integration. *Perception, 36,* 1523–1533. doi:10.1068/p5851

Hillis, J. M., Ernst, M. O., Banks, M. S., & Landy, M. S. (2002, November 22). Combining sensory information: Mandatory fusion within, but not between, senses. *Science, 298,* 1627–1630. doi:10.1126/science.1075396

Howard, I. P. (2002). *Seeing in depth.* Toronto, Canada: I Porteous.

Ives, H. E. (1929). Motion pictures in relief. *Journal of the Optical Society of America, 18,* 118–122. doi:10.1364/JOSA.18.000118

James, K. H., Humphrey, G. K., Vilis, T., Corrie, B., Baddour, B., & Goodale, M. A. (2002). "Active" and "passive" learning of three-dimensional object structure within an immersive virtual reality environment. *Behavior Research Methods, Instruments, & Computers, 34,* 383–390.

James, W. (1983). *The principles of psychology.* Cambridge, MA: Harvard University Press. (Original work published 1890)

Jeka, J. J. (1997). Light touch contact as a balance aid. *Physical Therapy, 77,* 476.

Kersten, D., & Yuille, A. L. (2003). Bayesian models of object perception. *Current Opinion in Neurobiology, 13,* 150–158. doi:10.1016/S0959-4388(03)00042-4

Klier, E. M., & Angelaki, D. E. (2008). Spatial Updating and the Maintenance of Visual Constancy. *Neuroscience, 156,* 801–818. doi:10.1016/j.neuroscience.2008.07.079

Knill, D. C., & Richards, W. (1996). *Perception as Bayesian inference.* Cambridge, England: Cambridge University Press.

Körding, K. (2007, October). Decision theory: What "should" the nervous system do? *Science, 318,* 606–610. doi:10.1126/science.1142998

Körding, K. P., Beierholm, U. R., Ma, W., Quartz, S., Tenenbaum, J. B., & Shams, L. (2007). Causal inference in multisensory perception. *PLoS ONE, 2*(9). doi:10.1371/journal.pone.0000943

Landy, M. S., Maloney, L. T., Johnston, E., & Young, M. (1995). Measurement and modeling of depth cue combination: In defense of weak fusion. *Vision Research, 35,* 389–412. doi:10.1016/0042-6989(94)00176-M

Langer, M. S., & Bülthoff, H. H. (2001). A prior for global convexity in local shape-from-shading. *Perception, 30,* 403–410. doi:10.1068/p3178

Laurens, J., & Droulez, J. (2007). Bayesian processing of vestibular information. *Biological Cybernetics, 96*, 389–404. doi:10.1007/s00422-006-0133-1

Lederman, S. J., & Klatzky, R. L. (2009a). Haptic perception: A tutorial. *Attention, Perception, & Psychophysics, 71*, 1439–1459. doi:10.3758/APP.71.7.1439

Lederman, S. J., & Klatzky, R. L. (2009b). Human haptics. In L. R. Squire (Ed.), *Encyclopedia of neuroscience* (Vol. 5, pp. 11–18). San Diego, CA: Academic Press. doi:10.1016/B978-008045046-9.01905-7

Liter, J. C., & Bülthoff, H. H. (1998). An introduction to object recognition. *Zeitschrift für Naturforschung, 53c*, 610–621.

Logothetis, N. K., Pauls, J., Bülthoff, H. H., & Poggio, T. (1994). View-dependent object recognition by monkeys. *Current Biology, 4*, 401–414. doi:10.1016/S0960-9822(00)00089-0

Loomis, J. M., Lippa, Y., Klatzky, R. L., & Golledge, R. G. (2002). Spatial updating of locations specified by 3-D sound and spatial language. *Journal of Experimental Psychology: Learning, Memory, and Cognition, 28*, 335–345. doi:10.1037/0278-7393.28.2.335

MacNeilage, P. B., Banks, M. S., Berger, D. R., & Bülthoff, H. H. (2007). A Bayesian model of the disambiguation of gravitoinertial force by visual cues. *Experimental Brain Research, 179*, 263–290. doi:10.1007/s00221-006-0792-0

Mamassian, P., & Goutcher, R. (2001). Prior knowledge on the illumination position. *Cognition, 81*, B1–B9. doi:10.1016/S0010-0277(01)00116-0

Mamassian, P., Landy, M. S., & Maloney, L. T. (2002). Bayesian modelling of visual perception. In R. P. Rao & B. A. Olshausen (Eds.), *Probabilistic models of the brain: Perception and neural function* (pp. 13–36). Cambridge, MA: MIT Press.

Marr, D. (1982). *Vision: A computational investigation into the human representation and processing of visual information*. San Francisco, CA: Freeman.

Meijer, F., & van den Broek, E. (2010). Representing 3D virtual objects: Interaction between visuo–spatial ability and type of exploration. *Vision Research, 50*, 630–635. doi:10.1016/j.visres.2010.01.016

Mershon, D. H. (1997). Phenomenal geometry and the measurement of perceived auditory distance. In R. Gilkey & T. Anderson (Eds.), *Binaural and spatial hearing in real and virtual environments* (pp. 257–274). New York, NY: Erlbaum.

Mittelstaedt, H. (1986). The subjective vertical as a function of visual and extraretinal cues. *Acta Psychologica, 63*, 63–85. doi:10.1016/0001-6918(86)90043-0

Moller, A. R. (2002). *Sensory systems: Anatomy and physiology* (1st ed.). San Diego, CA: Academic Press.

Mon-Williams, M., Wann, J. P., Jenkinson, M., & Rushton, K. (1997). Synaesthesia in the normal limb. *Proceedings of the Royal Society B: Biological Sciences, 264*, 1007–1010. doi:10.1098/rspb.1997.0139

Nakayama, K., He, Z. J., & Shimojo, S. (1995). Visual surface representation: A critical link between lower-level and higher level vision. In S. M. Kosslyn & D. N. Osherson (Eds.), *An invitation to cognitive science* (pp. 1–70). Cambridge, MA: MIT Press.

Neisser, U. (1976). *Cognition and reality*. San Francisco, CA: W. H. Freeman.

Newell, F. N., Ernst, M. O., Tjan, B. S., & Bülthoff, H. H. (2001). Viewpoint dependence in visual and haptic object recognition. *Psychological Science, 12*, 37–42. doi:10.1111/1467-9280.00307

Penfield, W., & Rasmussen, T. (1950). *The cerebral cortex of man. A clinical study of localization of function*. New York, NY: Macmillan.

Pentland, A. (1989). Shape information from shading: A theory about human perception. *Spatial Vision, 4*, 165–182. doi:10.1163/156856889X00103

Poggio, T., & Edelman, S. (1990, January). A network that learns to recognize three-dimensional objects. *Nature, 343*, 263–266. doi:10.1038/343263a0

Radeau, M., & Bertelson, P. (1977). Adaptation to auditory–visual discordance and ventriloquism in semirealistic situations. *Perception & Psychophysics, 22*, 137–146. doi:10.3758/BF03198746

Radeau, M., & Bertelson, P. (1987). Auditory–visual interaction and the timing of inputs: Thomas (1941) revisited. *Psychological Research, 49*, 17–22.

Recanzone, G. (1998). Rapidly induced auditory plasticity: The ventriloquism aftereffect. *Proceedings of the National Academy of Sciences, 95*, 869–875.

Roach, N., Heron, J., & McGraw, P. V. (2006). Resolving multisensory conflict: A strategy for balancing the costs and benefits of audio–visual integration. *Proceedings of the Royal Society B: Biological Sciences, 273*, 2159–2168. doi:10.1098/rspb.2006.3578

Rock, I. (1997). *Indirect perception*. Cambridge, MA: MIT Press.

Rock, I., & Di Vita, J. (1987). A case of viewer-centered object perception. *Cognitive Psychology, 19*, 280–293. doi:10.1016/0010-0285(87)90013-2

Schwoebel, J., & Coslett, H. B. (2005). Evidence for multiple, distinct representations of the human body. *Journal of Cognitive Neuroscience, 17*, 543–553. doi:10.1162/0898929053467587

Shams, L., & Beierholm, U. R. (2010). Causal inference in perception. *Trends in Cognitive Sciences, 14*, 425–432. doi:10.1016/j.tics.2010.07.001

Sherrick, C. E., & Cholewiak, R. W. (1986). Cutaneous sensitivity. In L. K. K. Boff & J. Thomas (Eds.), *Handbook of perception and human performance* (pp. 175–180). New York, NY: Wiley.

Simons, D. J., Wang, R. F., & Roddenberry, D. (2002). Object recognition is mediated by extraretinal information. *Perception & Psychophysics, 64,* 521–530. doi:10.3758/BF03194723

Stein, B. E., & Meredith, M. (1993). *The merging of the senses.* Cambridge, MA: MIT Press.

Tarr, M. J., & Bülthoff, H. H. (1998). Image-based object recognition in man, monkey and machine. *Cognition, 67,* 1–20. doi:10.1016/S0010-0277(98)00026-2

Tarr, M. J., & Pinker, S. (1989). Mental rotation and orientation dependence in shape recognition. *Cognitive Psychology, 21,* 233–282. doi:10.1016/0010-0285(89)90009-1

Tarr, M. J., & Pinker, S. (1991). Orientation-dependent mechanisms in shape recognition: Further issues. *Psychological Science, 2,* 207–209. doi:10.1111/j.1467-9280.1991.tb00135.x

Teramoto, W., & Riecke, B. E. (2010). Dynamic visual information facilitates object recognition from novel viewpoints. *Journal of Vision, 10*(13). doi:10.1167/10.13.11

Tsakiris, M., Costantini, M., & Haggard, P. (2008). The role of the right temporoparietal junction in maintaining a coherent sense of one's body. *Neuropsychologia, 46,* 3014–3018.

Ullman, S. (1996). *High-level vision: Object recognition and visual cognition.* Cambridge, MA: MIT Press.

Ullman, S. (1998). Three-dimensional object recognition based on the combination of views. *Cognition, 67,* 21–44. doi:10.1016/S0010-0277(98)00013-4

van Beers, R. J., Sittig, A. C., & Denier van der Gon, J. J. (1998). The precision of proprioceptive position sense. *Experimental Brain Research, 122,* 367–377. doi:10.1007/s002210050525

Wallach, H., & O'Connell, D. N. (1953). The kinetic depth effect. *Journal of Experimental Psychology, 45,* 205–217. doi:10.1037/h0056880

Wallraven, C., & Bülthoff, H. H. (2007). Object recognition in humans and machines. In N. Osaka, I. Rentschler, & I. Biederman (Eds.), *Object recognition, attention, and action* (pp. 89–104). Tokyo, Japan: Springer. doi:10.1007/978-4-431-73019-4_7

Welch, R. B., DuttonHurt, L., & Warren, D. (1986). Contributions of audition and vision to temporal rate perception. *Perception & Psychophysics, 39,* 294–300. doi:10.3758/BF03204939

Werner, S., & Noppeney, U. (2010a). Distinct functional contributions of primary sensory and association areas to audiovisual integration in object categorization. *The Journal of Neuroscience, 30,* 2662–2675. doi:10.1523/JNEUROSCI.5091-09.2010

Werner, S., & Noppeney, U. (2010b). Superadditive responses in superior temporal sulcus predict audiovisual benefits in object categorization. *Cerebral Cortex, 20,* 1829–1842. doi:10.1093/cercor/bhp248

Wightman, F. L., & Kistler, D. J. (1999). Resolution of front–back ambiguity in spatial hearing by listener and source movement. *Journal of the Acoustical Society of America, 105,* 2841–2853. doi:10.1121/1.426899

Wilson, M. (2002). Six views of embodied cognition. *Psychonomic Bulletin & Review, 9,* 625–636. doi:10.3758/BF03196322

Wolfe, J. M., Kluender, K. R., Levi, D. M., Bartoshuk, L. M., Herz, R. S., Klatzky, R. L., . . . Merfeld, D. M. (2008). *Sensation and perception* (2nd ed.). Sunderland, MA: Sinauer.

Wolpert, D. M., Goodbody, S. J., & Husain, M. (1998). Maintaining internal representations: The role of the human superior parietal lobe. *Nature Neuroscience, 1,* 529–533. doi:10.1038/2245

Yuille, A. L., & Bülthoff, H. H. (1996). Bayesian decision theory and psychophysics. In D. Knill & W. Richards (Eds.), *Perception as Bayesian inference* (pp. 123–161). Cambridge, MA: Cambridge University Press.

Zahorik, P., Brungart, D. S., & Bronkhorst, A. W. (2005). Auditory distance perception in humans: A summary of past and present research. *Acta Acustica United With Acustica, 91,* 409–420.

CHAPTER 5

PERCEPTION OF SPATIAL RELATIONS DURING SELF-MOTION

John W. Philbeck and Jesse Sargent

Humans are a highly mobile species, and our chief means of self-movement—locomotion—makes possible many of our uniquely human traits. Of course, the ability to move about would be of little use if we were unable to perceive and monitor our changing position in the environment. Thus, the ability to remain oriented when walking or traveling is crucial, and humans who lack this capacity are virtually helpless.

In this chapter, we discuss the means by which people *update*, or keep track of, their own location and orientation as they move, as well as the locations of objects in the environment. Navigation and locomotion take place across a wide range of spatial scales and time scales, and different instruments and methods are used at different scales. When navigating across country by car, one might follow a remembered series of highways and waypoints or use a dashboard-mounted satellite receiver that provides information about one's current location; when navigating at sea, one might use a similar device or a combination of sextants, clocks, compasses, and charts. By contrast, most people are able to navigate across their living room in the dark without reference to electronic devices and without performing explicit calculations. In this chapter, we focus on spatial updating at this relatively local spatial and temporal scale—that is, when moving among objects in the nearby environment.

The environmental representations that are maintained and updated online consist of more than what is currently perceivable. For example, while crossing one's living room in the dark, one is able to keep close track of where the pointy-cornered coffee table is throughout the journey. In this case, we may think of the object location as being maintained and updated in working memory (Sholl & Fraone, 2004). In the absence of direct, ongoing perceptual access to object location information during spatial updating, errors that accrue in the context of these working memory representations can provide insight into the nature of the updating system. Thus, although the subject of the current chapter is primarily online perception of spatial relations, we must also discuss updating of spatial memory.

A central problem in spatial updating while locomoting is to determine one's position and orientation relative to some *known location*. This is known as *fixing position*. The notion of there being a known location entails that the traveler has access to some kind of enduring representation of the environment—it might be a physical map or it might be the memory of a familiar location in a cognitive map. Importantly, this known location need not be an elaborate, high-fidelity representation of the surrounding environment. At a minimum, it could simply be a representation of the location of the starting point of one's current path. For example, if James Bond wakes up in the dark in an unfamiliar place, and then walks 5 m, he may not know where in the world he is, but spatial updating could tell him that he has walked 5 m from the place where he

DOI: 10.1037/13936-006
Handbook of Spatial Cognition, D. Waller and L. Nadel (Editors)

woke up. The way one fixes one's position depends on what kinds of sensory information are available. Two broad classes of methods have been identified: landmark-based navigation and path integration.

LANDMARK-BASED NAVIGATION

If vision is available, one can use *landmark-based navigation* (also known as *piloting* or *pilotage*) for position fixing (Gallistel, 1990; see also Chapter 7, this volume). Assuming that a landmark's location within the environment is known and that there are sufficient cues to determine its distance and direction, vision of the landmark allows individuals to fix their position within the environment without the need to update their location while moving. In a similar manner, touching a familiar landmark or hearing it make a characteristic sound can also provide information about one's location relative to the landmark. Vision of a distant landmark, such as the sun or a mountain, may provide poor information about one's location if cues to the landmark's distance are weak or imprecise. Nevertheless, such a landmark could still be useful as a *beacon,* allowing one to approach a destination by simply moving toward the landmark (i.e., *taxon navigation;* Gallistel, 1990; Redish, 1999; Waller & Lippa, 2007), or as an *azimuthal reference,* providing a cue to one's heading in the environment relative to some external reference frame (Loomis, Klatzky, Golledge, & Philbeck, 1999). In many of these cases, direct sensing of a familiar landmark can allow one to navigate effectively without requiring spatial updating. In general, updating may not be necessary in landmark-rich environments if one merely wants to fix one's position with respect to those landmarks.

PATH INTEGRATION

A second means of determining one's position while walking involves sensing self-motion signals and integrating these signals over time. This method is called *path integration* or *dead reckoning* (Gallistel, 1990; Mittelstaedt & Mittelstaedt, 1982; Séguinot, Maurer, & Etienne, 1993; Wehner & Wehner, 1986). Internally generated (or *idiothetic*) self-motion signals can come from sources such as the vestibular

apparatus, afferent and efferent signals associated with muscle activation (proprioception, kinesthesis, efference copy), and signals carrying information about changes in joint angles (Loomis et al., 1999; Mittelstaedt, 1985). Sensory signals carrying velocity information may be integrated over time to yield an estimate of displacement from the last known position; in a similar manner, acceleration information may be doubly integrated to estimate displacement. For example, if a person senses that he has been walking straight ahead at a rate of 1 m/s for 5 s, this would allow him to determine that he has moved 5 m from his starting point.

In theory, this kind of calculation could be done *explicitly* by estimating one's velocity, estimating the time elapsed since leaving the origin of travel, and then multiplying these two values. It is important, however, that path integration can also be performed *implicitly*. When we attempt to cross a room in the dark, we do not suddenly become disoriented when the lights are extinguished; we maintain a sense of our progress through the room without performing any explicit calculations. Presumably, this phenomenological sense of remaining oriented is based on implicit path integration processes. Indeed, Rieser (1999) argued that under these conditions, path integration is a one-stage process in which people directly perceive their changing location on the basis of sensory self-motion inputs. Both implicit and explicit path integration processes could be used in tandem, and as we discuss later, recent work has begun to investigate the factors that determine the relative weighting of these processes. There is also evidence that implicit path integration can occur automatically without consuming processing resources (e.g., Farrell & Robertson, 1998; Farrell & Thomson, 1998; May & Klatzky, 2000). We return to these issues shortly.

Vision provides a source of self-motion information by way of optic flow and thus could potentially be used for path integration. There is evidence that honeybees, for example, use optic flow for this purpose (Srinivasan, Zhang, & Bidwell, 1997). However, when vision is available in natural environments, optic flow is almost invariably confounded with information about objects. This means that information for both landmark-based navigation and path integration is available, and thus it is difficult to know how people use or weight these different sources of information. One way to remove this confound in experimental settings is to control the visual stimulus in a way that does not allow individual objects or visible features to be tracked—for example, by providing a flowing dot pattern in a virtual environment (e.g., Wolbers, Hegarty, Buchel, & Loomis, 2008). If the dot pattern is relatively dense, it is unlikely that individual dots could be tracked and used effectively for landmark-based navigation (Harris, Jenkin, & Zikovitz, 2000). When body-based self-motion information is available together with optic flow, the optical self-motion information tends to be weighted less during self-location updating (Campos, Byrne, & Sun, 2010; Harris et al., 2000; Kearns, Warren, Duchon, & Tarr, 2002; Klatzky, Loomis, Beall, Chance, & Golledge, 1998; Riecke, van Veen, & Bülthoff, 2000; Rushton, Harris, Lloyd, & Wann, 1998; Telford, Howard, & Ohmi, 1995; see also Mossio, Vidal, & Berthoz, 2008; Warren, Kay, Zosh, Duchon, & Sahuc, 2001). During real-world human navigation, in which both path integration and landmark-based position fixing are possible, there is unlikely to be a fixed ratio specifying the extent to which each method is used. Instead, this ratio likely changes dynamically, depending on the context. Nevertheless, when direct sensing of landmarks is possible, there is a strong tendency to rely preferentially on the landmarks (Foo, Warren, Duchon, & Tarr, 2005).

Another way to remove the confound of optic flow and information that could be used for landmark-based navigation is to exclude vision entirely. Occluding vision dramatically simplifies the question of how an individual might determine his or her location when moving. The complex changes in the visual world that typically transpire during walking are eliminated, and this greatly reduces or even eliminates the possibility of using landmark-based strategies. Simply restricting visual input does not necessarily guarantee that a task requires path integration, however. If audition is not restricted as well, one may be able to determine his or her location relative to a nearby sound source without having to update self-motion signals. Thus, many path integration tasks involve both a

blindfold and some means of minimizing auditory localization cues. If participants are able to count their paces, they may not need to sense or integrate their self-motion online—they merely have to count their paces to gain an approximate sense of their location. Thus, pace counting is often discouraged in studies of human path integration—for example, by requiring participants to recite nonsense syllables aloud (e.g., May & Klatzky, 2000).

Several tasks that have been used to study path integration in nonhuman animals include the water maze (e.g., Morris, Garrud, Rawlins, & O'Keefe, 1982), shortcutting (e.g., Alyan & McNaughton, 1999), and foraging tasks (e.g., Mittelstaedt & Mittelstaedt, 1982). There are several excellent reviews in the literature (Etienne & Jeffery, 2004; Gallistel, 1990; Maurer & Séguinot, 1995; McNaughton et al., 1996; Redish, 1999). Verifying that the animals in such situations are not relying on some other means than path integration is a challenge, however.

Perhaps the most impressive path integration of any species comes from the desert ant (Collett & Collett, 2000; Mittelstaedt & Mittelstaedt, 1982; Müller & Wehner, 1988; Wehner & Wehner, 1986). Desert ants travel along meandering trajectories while foraging for food in an environment that is virtually devoid of useful landmarks; after following paths that can measure hundreds of meters in length, they are able to return directly to the nest. Controlled testing has confirmed that the ants perform path integration throughout their trajectory. Honeybees and jumping spiders have also been shown to perform path integration (Dyer, Berry, & Richard, 1993; Mittelstaedt, 1985), as do geese (von Saint Paul, 1982), toads (Collett, 1982), and dogs (Séguinot, Cattet, & Benhamou, 1998). There has also been extensive investigation of path integration in rodents, including gerbils (Mittelstaedt & Glasauer, 1991) and rats (e.g., Alyan & McNaughton, 1999; Whishaw, Hines, & Wallace, 2001). Presumably, many other animal species that have yet to be tested are also capable of navigating by path integration.

In humans, pathway completion is a method that has been used frequently to study path integration (e.g., Allen, Kirasic, Rashotte, & Haun, 2004;

Klatzky et al., 1990; Loomis et al., 1993; Mittelstaedt & Glasauer, 1991; Philbeck, Klatzky, Behrmann, Loomis, & Goodridge, 2001; Worchel & Mauney, 1951; Worsley et al., 2001; for a review, see Loomis et al., 1999). In this method, the participant is blindfolded (thereby eliminating visual tracking of landmarks) and then guided along an outbound path consisting of multiple linear path segments separated by body rotations. The task is then to return to the origin by taking the shortest possible path. Performance generally deteriorates with the complexity of the path (Klatzky et al., 1990), but even when there are only two outbound path segments (i.e., *triangle completion*), participants tend to make systematic errors. In triangle completion tasks, when participants execute their final turn and straight path segment to return to the origin, they tend to generate turns and path lengths that are too large when small response values are required and too small when large response values are required (Klatzky, Loomis, & Golledge, 1997). We return to this issue in the next section, Models of Path Integration.

Another broad class of method for assessing human path integration ability involves perceptually directed action. In this method, observers are given perceptual information about a target location (e.g., by allowing them to see or hear the target). They then attempt to indicate the perceived (and subsequently remembered) target location by using some kind of motoric action. In one variant of this method—blindfolded (or visually directed) walking—observers view a target object and then cover their eyes and attempt to walk directly to the remembered target location without further assistance (e.g., Corlett, Patla, & Williams, 1985; Creem-Regehr, Willemsen, Gooch, & Thompson, 2005; Elliott, 1986; Loomis, Da Silva, Fujita, & Fukusima, 1992; Philbeck & Loomis, 1997; Rieser, Ashmead, Talor, & Youngquist, 1990; Steenhuis & Goodale, 1988; Sun, Campos, Young, & Chan, 2004; Thomson, 1980; Wu, Ooi, & He, 2004). There is little evidence of systematic error in stopping locations when the targets are initially viewed under well-lit viewing conditions at distances up to at least 24 m, although some undershooting tends to occur at longer target distances (Andre & Rogers, 2006).

In another example of perceptually directed action, observers view a target, then cover the eyes and walk on a path oblique to the target. At some unexpected location indicated by an experimenter, observers then turn and attempt to face the remembered target location (e.g., Fukusima, Loomis, & Da Silva, 1997; Sadalla & Montello, 1989; Sholl, 1987) or attempt to walk the rest of the way to the target (e.g., Philbeck, Loomis, & Beall, 1997). In yet another variant, observers view a target, then close the eyes and walk on a path passing alongside the remembered target location while attempting to continuously point to the target (Campos, Siegle, Mohler, Bülthoff, & Loomis, 2009; Loomis et al., 1992). The centroid of the locations where these continuous pointing angles intersect has been taken as a measure of the updated target location. In principle, accurate performance might be achieved despite inaccurate visual perception, either by explicitly "correcting" the initial visual perception and targeting a different location than the one perceived or through a more implicit perceptuomotor calibration that exactly offsets the perceptual error during response execution (Foley, Ribeiro, & Da Silva, 2004). These alternatives may be difficult to tease apart experimentally (Philbeck, Woods, Arthur, & Todd, 2008). Nevertheless, some researchers have argued that good performance on these tasks reflects not only accurate visual perception of the initial target location but also accurate self-motion updating (Creem-Regehr et al., 2005; Pham & Hicheur, 2009; Philbeck et al., 1997).

Angular spatial updating may be studied by exposing participants to a body and/or head rotation and then asking them to indicate the magnitude of the rotation in some way—for example, by making saccadic eye movements, by reproducing the rotation, or by manipulating a pointing device (Arthur, Philbeck, & Chichka, 2009; Bloomberg, Melvill Jones, Segal, McFarlane, & Soul, 1988; Blouin, Labrousse, Simoneau, Vercher, & Gauthier, 1998; Klatzky et al., 1990; Mergner, Nasios, Maurer, & Becker, 2001; Yardley, Gardner, Lavie, & Gresty, 1999). Performance in angular spatial updating tasks depends on a complex variety of factors. Factors associated with underperception of body rotations include very slow rotations (Bloomberg et al., 1988; Israël & Berthoz, 1989; Mergner, Nasios, & Anastasopoulos, 1998) and increased age of the perceiver (e.g., Guedry, 1974; Philbeck, Behrmann, & Loomis, 2001). Factors that tend to increase accuracy include the addition of proprioception and/or efference copy signals related to motion of the head around the neck (Blouin, Okada, Wolsley, & Bronstein, 1998; Nakamura & Bronstein, 1995) and active production of turns (Blouin, Okada, et al., 1998; Nakamura & Bronstein, 1995). There is some indication that body rotations are perceived more accurately if they are experienced relative to a reference point located straight ahead before the rotation as opposed to an eccentric reference point (Blouin, Labrousse, et al., 1998), but this is not always the case (Mergner et al., 2001). Idiosyncratic factors such as attention to egocentric versus allocentric reference frames can also influence angular self-motion updating (Mergner et al., 2001; Siegler, 2000).

MODELS OF PATH INTEGRATION

Excellent reviews of path integration models exist in the literature (e.g., Etienne & Jeffery, 2004; Gallistel, 1990; Klatzky et al., 1997; McNaughton et al., 1996; Redish, 1999), so here we only sketch the broad features of these models here and do not discuss them in detail. Some models of path integration in nonhuman animals assume that the animals perform operations analogous to trigonometry when integrating self-motion information to compute the current distance and direction relative to the last known location (e.g., Mittelstaedt & Mittelstaedt, 1982). These models often include a source of random variability, such that the current location estimate tends to become more variable as the traveled distance increases. Some models also incorporate processes that account for systematic biases in path integration that have been observed in some animals (Benhamou, Sauvé, & Bovet, 1990; Müller & Wehner, 1988). Other models are depicted as biologically plausible neural networks, describing how the known properties of head-direction cells, grid cells, and place cells (see Chapter 1, this volume) can collectively allow an animal to update its location over self-motion—for example, by operating as a continuous attractor network (Arleo & Gerstner,

2000; Guazzelli, Bota, & Arbib, 2001; Hartmann & Wehner, 1995; Maurer, 1998; McNaughton et al., 1996; Samsonovich & McNaughton, 1997; Stringer, Trappenberg, Rolls, & de Araujo, 2002; Wittmann & Schwegler, 1995).

The triangle completion task has been used in efforts to model path integration in humans. As we have seen, when the ideal length of the final path segment to the origin is relatively short, participants tend to produce a path segment that is too large; when the ideal response path length is relatively large, participants tend to produce a segment that is too small (Klatzky et al., 1990, 1997). In a similar manner, when the required response turn toward the origin is small, participants tend to produce a turn that is too large, and when the required turn is large, they tend to produce a turn that is too small. A model that captures this pattern is known as the *encoding error model* (Fujita, Klatzky, Loomis, & Golledge, 1993; Klatzky et al., 1990, 1997; Loomis et al., 1993). In accounting for the observed data, the model makes assumptions not only about when updating occurs during locomotion but also about what information is updated. To be more specific, information about path length and turn magnitudes is updated but only at particularly important time points, such as at the end of path segments. The model assumes that systematic error in the final stopping location (relative to the ideal stopping point at the origin) does not come from errors in computing or executing the final path. Instead, all systematic error is attributed to errors in encoding the passively guided portions of the path. The final response turn and path length are assumed to be executed on the basis of these encoded values without contributing any additional systematic error. In principle, individuals might update a representation of the distance and direction to the origin (the *homing vector*) continuously, on a moment-to-moment basis. In such a scheme, the homing vector is the only representation necessary to support a return to the origin—the total leg lengths and turn magnitudes would not need to be explicitly encoded. The encoding error model, however, assumes that the leg lengths and turn magnitudes are encoded but only at the end of each path or turn segment. Loomis et al. (1993) showed that humans can reproduce their recent trajectory quite accurately, thus demonstrating that they have encoded more information about the path than the homing vector. Path complexity effects, which we discuss shortly, also support this view.

The tendency to overshoot small required response parameters and undershoot large required parameters is not merely regression to the mean, a term implying that responses are influenced by accumulated exposure to the distribution of stimulus values. If such were the case, experiments consisting solely of large or solely of small required response parameters would yield responses that regress to very different values. Instead, participants tend to undershoot large required response values and overshoot small required values, even when they are exposed to only large or only small required response parameters (Klatzky, Beall, Loomis, Golledge, & Philbeck, 1999). This indicates that the pattern of over- and undershooting is not merely a response tendency made on the basis of accumulated exposure to the particular set of experimental paths. Presumably, it reflects systematic errors that accumulate on a trial-by-trial basis. The encoding error model suggests that these errors can be characterized in terms of a gain change and a constant offset (bias) introduced during self-motion encoding, but the sources of these types of errors remain poorly understood.

The encoding error model was designed to account for path integration along fairly simple paths involving discrete straight segments and body rotations. Clearly, some modification would be necessary to allow it to account for path integration along more complex, curving paths (Wiener & Mallot, 2006). Similarly, it does not provide an explicit mechanism for incorporating the effect of nonsensory factors on path integration, an issue we discuss in more detail shortly. Nevertheless, the model accounts for simple local-scale path integration performance surprisingly well.

PROCESSES UNDERLYING HUMAN PATH INTEGRATION

Now that we have covered some basic issues and methods used to study spatial updating, the previous discussion of whether path integration is an implicit or an explicit process may be extended to a consideration of automaticity, online versus offline processing, and global versus piecemeal updating. The idea that path integration occurs implicitly, as a unified process of perceiving self-motion and integrating this information to produce an updated self-position estimate, suggests that this process occurs automatically and online, at least to some extent.

Automaticity

A number of studies have suggested that the relationship between body-based (*egocentric*) and environment-based (*allocentric*) reference frames is updated automatically over self-motion (Farrell & Robertson, 1998; Farrell & Thomson, 1998; May & Klatzky, 2000). For example, Farrell and Robertson (1998) required participants to learn an array of object locations, don a blindfold, undergo varying degrees of actual or imagined whole body rotation, and then point to remembered object locations. In the control condition, participants rotated one way, then the other back to the learning heading. In the updating condition, participants simply rotated to a new heading. In the imagine condition, participants were instructed to imagine they were at a new heading (facing a particular object), and in the ignore condition, they were instructed, before rotation, to ignore the upcoming rotation and to subsequently point to objects as if they had not rotated. Results showed that error and response time (RT) were higher in the imagine and ignore conditions than in the control and updating conditions. Farrell and Robertson argued that if updating were an effortful process, participants in the ignore condition could have simply not engaged in that process. Rather, updating occurred automatically, and the misalignment of the actual physical heading and the pre-rotation test heading resulted in increased RT and pointing error. (The source of this well-documented misalignment effect has been the topic of some controversy, consideration of which is beyond the scope of the current chapter. For more on this issue, see Kessler & Thomson, 2010; May, 2004).

Waller, Montello, Richardson, and Hegarty (2002) showed that participants can be induced to ignore updating. Participants learned several paths from a single viewpoint, were blindfolded, and then pointed to remembered target locations as if they were standing at various locations or headings along the path. In general, pointing error and RT were greater for imagined headings that conflicted with the actual, physical heading, and this was true even when participants rotated between study and test so that actual heading at test was 180° opposed to the learning heading. However, if participants were instructed to imagine during this rotation that the path was fixed to their bodies and rotated with them, performance was worse for imagined headings aligned with actual physical heading than for imagined headings aligned with the learning heading. Other researchers have also shown that under certain conditions updated spatial perspectives may not be the most readily accessible (e.g., Mou, McNamara, Valiquette, & Rump, 2004). If a particular viewpoint is strongly indicated by intrinsic aspects of an object array and/or by instruction, this viewpoint can be easier to access than updated perspectives (Mou, Zhang, & McNamara, 2009). In general, however, humans tend to have trouble ignoring spatial changes caused by self-movement (Burgess, Spiers, & Paleologou, 2004; Simons & Wang, 1998).

Of course, humans do not automatically update the relationship between themselves and everything out in the world during self-motion. Wang and colleagues conducted several studies investigating the limits of automatic updating. In one study (Wang & Brockmole, 2003b), participants learned to point without vision to an array of five objects around them in a room and to five buildings on the surrounding campus. After learning the target locations, blindfolded participants turned to face either room or campus targets and made pointing responses. Results showed that RT and pointing error for campus targets were greater when participants had turned to face (and had recently pointed to) all the room targets. However, performance for room targets was unaffected when participants had turned to face (and had recently pointed to) all the campus targets. These data suggest the room target locations were updated automatically, but the campus targets were not. This group has also shown that automatic updating occurs for environments only if they are

real (not imagined) and experienced perceptually (not verbally described; Wang, 2004).

In summary, although spatial updating over self-motion appears to be automatic in some situations, it is not inevitable. In addition, there are data suggesting that any spatial information that is updated automatically is limited to the immediate environment and to information that has been learned by perceptual experience (*primary learning*) rather than described verbally or imagined (*secondary learning*; see Presson & Hazelrigg, 1984, for discussion of relevant primary and secondary learning).

Online Versus Offline Processing

As described earlier in the discussion of explicit and implicit path integration, *online updating* is thought to be a continuous one-stage process in which people directly perceive their changing location on the basis of sensory self-motion inputs. A different form of updating is *offline updating*, which is typically conceived of as a multistage process. That is, during self-motion, a record of self-displacement is created; afterward, this record is integrated with a preexisting representation of object locations in the local environment to produce an updated estimate of one's location within the environment. Amorim, Glasauer, Corpinot, and Berthoz (1997) provided evidence that the updating of spatial memory for objects and landmarks in the environment (other than the starting location) can occur either online or offline, depending on the focus of attention. Blindfolded participants updated the orientation of a target (a 3-D letter *F*) while walking along a simple nearby path, focusing attention either on the constantly changing location of the target relative to themselves (object-centered [OC] condition) or on their walking path (trajectory-centered [TC] condition). Indications of the target orientation after blind walking in the OC condition were faster because, it was argued, the target representations were already available in working memory (online). However, traversing the path was more error prone and took longer in the OC condition, presumably because online updating was more effortful. This study shows that there are two distinct modes of spatial updating (online and offline) and that participants may be induced to rely on one or the other by task instructions. Amorim et al. proposed that during locomotion, we actively update (online) only currently relevant parts of a particular layout or environment and then we reconstruct the rest later (offline) as needed.

Offline updating is likely to be especially important when updating multiple object locations. If environmental object locations are indeed updated offline as needed, path integration performance should be relatively insensitive to the number of potentially relevant locations in the environment. Alternatively, if updating of self-to-object relationships occurs online, there should be increasing load on spatial working memory as the number of updated objects increases, and this might be expected to have a negative impact on performance.

Following this logic, researchers have examined set size effects to study the relative primacy of online or offline updating in particular conditions. Wang et al. (2006) showed evidence that in a virtual environment, updating difficulty increases with target set size (one to three objects). Using functional magnetic resonance imaging, Wolbers, Hegarty, Buchel, and Loomis (2008) also showed evidence of online spatial updating in a virtual environment. Participants learned from one to four target object locations, the objects disappeared, and then during a delay period, participants saw either a stationary display or a forward translation as indicated by optic flow of a white dot pattern covering the floor plane. After the delay, participants indicated remembered (and sometimes updated) target locations. Results showed that during the delay period, blood oxygen–level dependent response in the precuneus increased with the number of target objects and was greater in the updating compared with the stationary conditions. This suggests that in this paradigm, processing during updating is sensitive to target set size. As indicated earlier, this would not be expected in the case of offline updating.

Hodgson and Waller (2006) conducted a theoretically similar study using a different paradigm. Participants learned the location of objects around them in a room and then indicated the updated object locations after blind whole body rotation. In this case, no set size effects (one to 15 objects) were observed in the error data, but RT increased

linearly with set size. These results are consistent with offline updating (see also Rieser & Rider, 1991). The difficulty of the offline updating, it was suggested, was reflected in the set size effect in the RT data. The discrepancy with the results of Wang et al. (2006) was attributed to the richer array of cues and landmarks available in real world environments relative to virtual environments; the richer cue context may have facilitated construction of reliable long-term memory for the layouts. In this view, participants had trouble forming enduring representations in the virtual environment and thus had to rely on online processing. These results suggest that when updating remembered object locations in the real world, at least during body rotations, we rely on offline updating of immediate environmental representations quite readily, that is, soon after direct perception (e.g., vision) of target locations becomes impossible, and even for very small set sizes.

Global Versus Piecemeal Updating

We have already discussed research showing that updating is not global in the strictest sense (Wang & Brockmole, 2003b). For example, as we walk through a building we do not update our location relative to all the rooms in the building but only with respect to the room we are in (Wang & Brockmole, 2003a). However, there is debate regarding the extent to which we update object locations in the immediate environment globally (as a unit, through a single updating process) or in piecemeal fashion (as distinct object locations, using at least partly independent processes for each object). Research by Wang and colleagues supports the idea that updating occurs primarily in piecemeal fashion (Wang, 1999; Wang & Brockmole, 2003b; Wang et al., 2006; Wang & Spelke, 2000; Wang & Spelke, 2002). Other work has shown evidence of global updating (Greenauer & Waller, 2008; Marchette & Shelton, 2010; Mou et al., 2004; Sargent, Dopkins, Philbeck, & Modarres, 2008). Central to this debate is the issue of whether the objects that are updated during locomotion are primarily represented within an egocentric reference frame (centered on the observer) versus an allocentric reference frame (centered on some aspect of the environment). In general, factors that favor egocentric encoding tend to result in piecemeal updating, whereas factors that favor allocentric encoding tend to result in global updating (Mou, McNamara, Rump, & Xiao, 2006; Xiao, Mou, & McNamara, 2009). To some extent, both global and piecemeal updating can occur simultaneously (Sargent, Dopkins, Philbeck, & Chichka, 2010).

NONSENSORY INFLUENCES ON PATH INTEGRATION

We have seen that people retain some memory of their recently traveled trajectory and that in some cases this configural trajectory memory can interfere with path integration (Klatzky et al., 1990). Although this configuration memory is based on sensory input and could even be stored in a format that mimics the original sensory input, it is a nonsensory input to path integration to the extent that it is available in memory rather than coming directly from the senses. This section considers evidence for other nonsensory factors that influence path integration. In particular, we discuss the role of memory of one's trajectory, memory of specific object locations, memory of the larger environmental structure, and active control of locomotion.

Path Complexity

At a minimum, when updating one's position through path integration, one could simply monitor the distance and direction to the last known position (i.e., homing vector). Because there is no accumulation of information about the overall trajectory under such a strategy, one would not expect there to be any performance cost associated with increasing path complexity. In practice, however, performance on pathway completion tasks often deteriorates as path complexity increases (Klatzky et al., 1990). In combination with other evidence (e.g., accurate performance in retracing recent trajectories and increasing latency to initiate the response path with increasing path complexity), Klatzky et al. (1990) interpreted this as evidence that participants were encoding metric properties of the path segments as they encountered them, rather than simply updating the homing vector. If this is true, path complexity effects are likely due, at least in part, to factors such as proactive interference

and limitations in working memory capacity (Allen, 1999). Indeed, in situations requiring updating along complex, multisegment paths (which presumably would discourage fine-grained encoding of the trajectory and thus also consumption of memory capacity), participants do not show negative effects of path complexity on updating performance (Wiener & Mallot, 2006).

Remembered Landmarks

In addition to remembering features of their recently traveled trajectory, people also encode and remember the location of objects in the environment. Updating the location of a remembered landmark or destination could potentially influence path integration by providing a salient focus for allocation of processing resources. Philbeck and O'Leary (2005) tested this idea. Their participants saw a target 6.2 m away and attempted to walk to it without vision. In one condition, a "landmark" was seen near the walking path before vision was obscured, located 4.2 m from the starting position. Participants in this condition walked near (but did not touch) the remembered landmark on the way to the target at 6.2 m. Within-subject response consistency in walking to the 6.2 m target nearly doubled in the landmark condition.

Remembered landmarks could exert influence on path integration by sharpening the precision of one's estimated location. When navigating by path integration, the precision of the current location estimate decreases as the individual moves progressively farther away from the last known location, because of the accumulation of noise in sensory self-motion signals (Etienne, Maurer, & Saucy, 1988). Directly sensing a landmark can remove any positional uncertainty that has accumulated: If a table is the only potential obstacle and you stub your toe on it, you suddenly know your location with certainty. Even if you do not touch the table, however, remembering and updating its location could enhance your certainty about your current location in a similar way. Remembered landmarks can potentially play an analogous role in navigation at larger scales (Rieser, 1999; Rieser, Frymire, & Berry, 1997). The maritime navigators in the Republic of Micronesia, who can travel great distances without reference to position sensing devices, cite the use of imaginary landmark islands (*etaks*) just over the horizon as important aids in monitoring their progress at sea (Gladwin, 1990; Hutchins, 1995).

Remembered Environmental Context

Memory of the spatial structure of the environment surrounding the observer (i.e., the *environmental context*) may play a distinct role in path integration, over and above the part played by memory of individual object locations. People can encode and remember more than a single feature of the environment (Hollingworth & Henderson, 2002). Indeed, when natural scenes containing multiple objects are glimpsed for only a few seconds, they can be recognized with surprising accuracy over long delays (Shepard, 1967). In many cases, at least some information about environmental context will be available in working memory because the traveler has recently seen the current surrounding environment. One could also call to mind a familiar environment through mental imagery or construct a novel mental image on the basis of a description using spatial language. Whatever the source, does remembered information about environmental context play a role in monitoring one's location during locomotion?

Rieser (1999; Rieser et al., 1997) studied this issue in a pathway completion task. The experimenters guided participants without vision along multi-segment paths and asked them to return to the origin of locomotion. When participants were allowed to see their actual surrounding environment before each trial, or imagined some other familiar environment, accuracy in reaching the origin was better than if participants had no knowledge of their actual location after undergoing a disorienting walk without vision prior to testing. Remembering an environmental context is thought to activate a spatially indexed framework (Kahneman, Treisman, & Gibbs, 1992) in which there are multiple opportunities to create associative links between elements in the remembered context and the incoming self-motion signals. Online associative structures that are more elaborate presumably provide more opportunities to facilitate path integration. For example, when walking among a constellation of remembered object locations, one might experience an analog of optic flow in

visual mental imagery, in which remembered object locations are imagined to approach and stream past during locomotion. This "imagined flow" could offer a kind of motion parallax information that is beneficial for updating one's changing location when walking (Rieser, 1999).

Several researchers have studied the influence of remembered environmental context on path integration specifically during whole-body rotations (Arthur, Philbeck & Chichka, 2007; Israël, Bronstein, Kanayama, Faldon, & Gresty, 1996; Siegler & Israël, 2002). For example, Arthur et al. (2009) showed that when participants are allowed to see the surrounding environment before undergoing a body rotation, their indications of the rotation magnitude are nearly twice as precise as when they undergo the same rotations without previewing the environment. It is notable that a similar preview advantage is obtained even when the "preview" consists of the instruction to imagine a sparse environment learned on the basis of spatial language. Thus, remembered environmental contexts need not possess a high level of detail to be effective for enhancing path integration (see also Siegler, 2000).

Active Versus Passive Control of Self-Motion

As we have seen, humans generally perform more poorly in pathway completion tasks than in tasks involving visually directed walking and indirect walking. These two types of studies differ along a number of dimensions, but one feature that may be relevant for explaining the performance differences concerns how much of the path is actively controlled. In one sense, control is active throughout the trajectory in both paradigms in that participants produce their own muscle activations to generate walking. However, the tasks differ in the extent to which participants are able to self-select their upcoming trajectory. In visually directed walking to a single previously viewed target, participants actively self-select the entire path. Performance typically remains good in indirect walking, in which the first segment of the path is "passive" (determined by the experimenters), and the response turn and length of the second segment are actively determined by the participant. In triangle completion, by contrast, a higher proportion of the path is passively guided: The first two segments and the intervening turn are passively guided, and the response turn and final segment are actively controlled.

Of course, triangle completion involves more complex paths than the typical visually directed walking studies, and as we have seen, this factor alone can affect performance (Klatzky et al., 1990). Philbeck, Klatzky, et al. (2001) tested the idea that active control is relevant for path integration by increasing the proportion of actively controlled path segments in a triangle completion task, thereby controlling for path complexity. In a typical triangle completion task, participants are passively guided along the first two legs of a triangle (L1 and L2) and the intervening turn (T1) and then actively generate a second turn (T2) and a third leg (L3) to return to the origin of the triangle. In Philbeck, Klatzky, et al. (2001), the proportion of actively controlled path segments was increased by placing a landmark at the location of T2 (i.e., on the walking path), between L2 and L3, and requiring participants to walk from T1 to the remembered landmark at T2 and from there back to the origin. Before each trial, participants saw the landmark and knew that they would be asked to walk there, but they did not know where the experimenter would take them on the first leg. Thus, the experimenter determined the length of the first leg, but after this "dropping off" point at the end of the first leg, the rest of the trajectory was determined by the participant. Performance in reaching the origin was significantly enhanced relative to performance in the standard triangle completion task. A control condition showed that there was no such enhancement when the landmark was previewed at a location displaced from the walking path. In sum, path integration performance was improved by a remembered landmark only when the landmark was informative about the upcoming trajectory. This is consistent with Philbeck and O'Leary's (2005) results in that the landmarks in that study also lay close to the walking path; thus, the visual preview again provided information that could be used to establish expectations about the upcoming trajectory. Establishing an expectation of the motor and/or spatial requirements of a trajectory before it is executed allows the traveler to compare incoming self-motion information against the expected values (Wolpert & Ghahramani, 2000); monitoring the resulting error signal may be a source of the facilitation in path integration.

SUMMARY

Humans update their position and orientation within the environment using two primary means: landmark-based navigation and path integration. Landmark-based navigation is typically used preferentially over path integration when vision is available. Nevertheless, people are able to use path integration to remain oriented and keep track of their motion even when vision is not available. Perceptually directed action and pathway completion tasks have been used extensively in studying path integration. Existing models of path integration, particularly the encoding error model, provide reasonably good fits to human data in simple updating tasks. The encoding error model is limited in several ways in that it is not designed to explain updating behavior along complex, curving trajectories and does not explicitly incorporate nonsensory factors (e.g., memory of environmental features) that are known to influence updating during self-motion. Much current research is focused on characterizing the factors that contribute to updating error. Other ongoing research themes include attempts to specify the mechanisms underlying updating, the types of information updated during locomotion, and when this information is updated. These efforts promise to yield more comprehensive and powerful models of human path integration and spatial updating more generally. This knowledge, in turn, will inform efforts to understand the brain mechanisms that are recruited during updating and aid in the diagnosis and treatment of navigation disorders.

SUGGESTED REFERENCES FOR FURTHER READING

Amorim, M., Glasauer, S., Corpinot, K., & Berthoz, A. (1997). Updating an object's orientation and location during nonvisual navigation: A comparison between two processing modes. *Perception & Psychophysics, 59*, 404–418. doi:10.3758/BF03211907

This article was the first to experimentally dissociate online from offline spatial updating. Illustrates the complexity of updating and establishes a source of individual differences in updating tasks.

Farrell, M. J., & Robertson, I. H. (1998). Mental rotation and automatic updating of body-centered spatial relationships. *Journal of Experimental Psychology: Learning, Memory, and Cognition, 24,* 227–233. doi:10.1037/0278-7393.24.1.227

One of the first papers to suggest that self-motion updating is automatic, this work spawned a number of subsequent studies that have elucidated the circumstances under which automatic updating occurs.

Klatzky, R. L., Loomis, J. M., & Golledge, R. G. (1997). Encoding spatial representations through nonvisually guided locomotion: Tests of human path integration. In D. Medin (Ed.), *The psychology of learning and motivation* (Vol. 37, pp. 41–84). San Diego, CA: Academic Press.

Reviews methods of measuring human path integration and outlines the encoding error model.

McNaughton, B. L., Battaglia, F. P., Jensen, O., Moser, E. I., & Moser, M. B. (2006). Path integration and the neural basis of the 'cognitive map.' *Nature Reviews Neuroscience, 7,* 663–678. doi:10.1038/nrn1932

Reviews recent advances in modeling path integration that use a computational neural network approach to account for the electrophysiological behavior of neurons in rats as they navigate.

Müller, M., & Wehner, R. (1988). Path integration in desert ants, Cataglyphis fortis. *Proceedings of the National Academy of Sciences, 85,* 5287–5290. doi:10.1073/pnas.85.14.5287

Describes the remarkable navigation ability of desert ants and illustrates the challenges of isolating path integration as the mechanism of self-motion updating in nonhuman animals.

Philbeck, J. W., Klatzky, R. K., Behrmann, M., Loomis, J. M., & Goodridge, J. (2001). Active control of locomotion facilitates nonvisual navigation. *Journal of Experimental Psychology: Human Perception and Performance, 27,* 141–153. doi:10.1037/0096-1523.27.1.141

Provides an analysis of several possible means by which active control of locomotion might act to facilitate path integration. Suggests that knowledge of upcoming pathway parameters plays an important role.

Wang, R., & Spelke, E. (2000). Updating egocentric representations in human navigation. *Cognition, 77,* 215–250. doi:10.1016/S0010-0277(00)00105-0

An influential and provocative work that sparked a vigorous series of subsequent spatial updating studies.

Although primarily focused on the frames of reference underlying spatial updating during self-motion, this work also highlights important issues concerning how environmental objects are updated (e.g., global vs. piecemeal updating).

References

Allen, G. (1999). Spatial abilities, cognitive maps, and wayfinding: Bases for individual differences in spatial cognition and behavior. In R. Golledge (Ed.), *Wayfinding behavior: Cognitive mapping and other spatial processes* (pp. 46–80). Baltimore, MD: Johns Hopkins University Press.

Allen, G. L., Kirasic, K. C., Rashotte, M. A., & Haun, D. B. (2004). Aging and path integration skill: Kinesthetic and vestibular contributions to wayfinding. *Perception & Psychophysics, 66,* 170–179. doi:10.3758/BF03194870

Alyan, S., & McNaughton, B. L. (1999). Hippocampectomized rats are capable of homing by path integration. *Behavioral Neuroscience, 113,* 19–31. doi:10.1037/0735-7044.113.1.19

Amorim, M.-A., Glasauer, S., Corpinot, K., & Berthoz, A. (1997). Updating an object's orientation and location during nonvisual navigation: A comparison between two processing modes. *Perception & Psychophysics, 59,* 404–418. doi:10.3758/BF03211907

Andre, J., & Rogers, S. (2006). Using verbal and blind-walking distance estimates to investigate the two visual systems hypothesis. *Perception & Psychophysics, 68,* 353–361. doi:10.3758/BF03193682

Arleo, A., & Gerstner, W. (2000). Spatial cognition and neuro-mimetic navigation: A model of hippocampal place cell activity. *Biological Cybernetics, 83,* 287–299. doi:10.1007/s004220000171

Arthur, J. C., Philbeck, J. W., & Chichka, D. (2007). Spatial memory enhances the precision of angular self-motion updating. *Experimental Brain Research, 183,* 557–568. doi:10.1007/s00221-007-1075-0

Arthur, J. C., Philbeck, J. W., & Chichka, D. (2009). Non-sensory inputs to angular path integration. *Journal of Vestibular Research, 19*(3–4), 111–125.

Benhamou, S., Sauvé, J. P., & Bovet, P. (1990). Spatial memory in large scale movements: Efficiency and limitation of the egocentric coding process. *Journal of Theoretical Biology, 145,* 1–12. doi:10.1016/S0022-5193(05)80531-4

Bloomberg, J., Melvill Jones, G., Segal, B., McFarlane, S., & Soul, J. (1988). Vestibular-contingent voluntary saccades based on cognitive estimates of remembered vestibular information. *Advances in Oto-Rhino-Laryngology, 41,* 71–75.

Blouin, J., Labrousse, L., Simoneau, M., Vercher, J. L., & Gauthier, G. M. (1998). Updating visual space during passive and voluntary head-in-space movements. *Experimental Brain Research, 122*, 93–100. doi:10.1007/s002210050495

Blouin, J., Okada, T., Wolsley, C. J., & Bronstein, A. (1998). Encoding target-trunk relative position: Cervical versus vestibular contribution. *Experimental Brain Research, 122*, 101–107. doi:10.1007/s002210050496

Burgess, N., Spiers, H. J., & Paleologou, E. (2004). Orientational manoeuvres in the dark: Dissociating allocentric and egocentric influences on spatial memory. *Cognition, 94*, 149–166. doi:10.1016/j.cognition.2004.01.001

Campos, J. L., Byrne, P., & Sun, H. J. (2010). The brain weights body-based cues higher than vision when estimating walked distances. *European Journal of Neuroscience, 31*, 1889–1898. doi:10.1111/j.1460-9568.2010.07212.x

Campos, J. L., Siegle, J. H., Mohler, B. J., Bülthoff, H. H., & Loomis, J. M. (2009). Imagined self-motion differs from perceived self-motion: Evidence from a novel continuous pointing method. *PLoS ONE, 4*(11). doi:10.1371/journal.pone.0007793

Collett, M., & Collett, T. S. (2000). How do insects use path integration for their navigation? *Biological Cybernetics, 83*, 245–259. doi:10.1007/s004220000168

Collett, T. S. (1982). Do toads plan routes? A study of the detour behavior of *Bufo viridis. Journal of Comparative Physiology, 146*, 261–271. doi:10.1007/BF00610246

Corlett, J. T., Patla, A. E., & Williams, J. G. (1985). Locomotor estimation of distance after visual scanning by children and adults. *Perception, 1*, 257–263. doi:10.1068/p140257

Creem-Regehr, S. H., Willemsen, P., Gooch, A. A., & Thompson, W. B. (2005). The influence of restricted viewing conditions on egocentric distance perception: Implications for real and virtual indoor environments. *Perception, 34*, 191–204. doi:10.1068/p5144

Dyer, F. C., Berry, N. A., & Richard, A. S. (1993). Honey-bee spatial memory: Use of route-based memories after displacement. *Animal Behaviour, 45*, 1028–1030. doi:10.1006/anbe.1993.1121

Elliott, D. (1986). Continuous visual information may be important after all: A failure to replicate Thomson (1983). *Journal of Experimental Psychology: Human Perception and Performance, 12*, 388–391. doi:10.1037/0096-1523.12.3.388

Etienne, A. S., & Jeffery, K. J. (2004). Path integration in mammals. *Hippocampus, 14*, 180–192. doi:10.1002/hipo.10173

Etienne, A. S., Maurer, R., & Saucy, F. (1988). Limitations in the assessment of path dependent information. *Behaviour, 106*, 81–110. doi:10.1163/156853988X00106

Farrell, M. J., & Robertson, I. H. (1998). Mental rotation and automatic updating of body-centered spatial relationships. *Journal of Experimental Psychology: Learning, Memory, and Cognition, 24*, 227–233. doi:10.1037/0278-7393.24.1.227

Farrell, M. J., & Thomson, J. (1998). Automatic spatial updating during locomotion without vision. *The Quarterly Journal of Experimental Psychology Section A: Human Experimental Psychology, 51*, 637–654. doi:10.1080/713755776

Foley, J. M., Ribeiro, N. P., & Da Silva, J. A. (2004). Visual perception of extent and the geometry of visual space. *Vision Research, 44*, 147–156. doi:10.1016/j.visres.2003.09.004

Foo, P., Warren, W. H., Duchon, A., & Tarr, M. J. (2005). Do humans integrate routes into a cognitive map? Map- versus landmark-based navigation of novel shortcuts. *Journal of Experimental Psychology: Learning, Memory, and Cognition, 31*, 195–215. doi:10.1037/0278-7393.31.2.195

Fujita, N., Klatzky, R. L., Loomis, J. M., & Golledge, R. G. (1993). The encoding-error model of pathway completion without vision. *Geographical Analysis, 25*, 295–314. doi:10.1111/j.1538-4632.1993.tb00300.x

Fukusima, S. S., Loomis, J. M., & Da Silva, J. A. (1997). Visual perception of egocentric distance as assessed by triangulation. *Journal of Experimental Psychology: Human Perception and Performance, 23*, 86–100. doi:10.1037/0096-1523.23.1.86

Gallistel, C. R. (1990). *The organization of learning.* Cambridge, MA: MIT Press.

Gladwin, T. (1990). *East is a big bird: Navigation and logic on Puluwat Atoll.* Cambridge, MA: Harvard University Press.

Greenauer, N., & Waller, D. (2008). Intrinsic array structure is neither necessary nor sufficient for non-egocentric coding of spatial layouts. *Psychonomic Bulletin & Review, 15*, 1015–1021. doi:10.3758/PBR.15.5.1015

Guazzelli, A., Bota, M., & Arbib, M. A. (2001). Competitive Hebbian learning and the hippocampal place cell system: Modeling the interaction of visual and path integration cues. *Hippocampus, 11*, 216–239. doi:10.1002/hipo.1039

Guedry, F. E. (1974). Psychophysics of vestibular sensation. In H. H. Kornhuber (Ed.), *Handbook of sensory physiology* (pp. 3–154). Berlin, Germany: Springer-Verlag.

Harris, L. R., Jenkin, M., & Zikovitz, D. C. (2000). Visual and non-visual cues in the perception of linear self-motion. *Experimental Brain Research, 135*, 12–21. doi:10.1007/s002210000504

Hartmann, G., & Wehner, R. (1995). The ant's path integration system: A neural architecture. *Biological Cybernetics, 73,* 483–493.

Hodgson, E., & Waller, D. (2006). Lack of set size effects in spatial updating: Evidence for offline updating. *Journal of Experimental Psychology: Learning, Memory, and Cognition, 32,* 854–866. doi:10.1037/0278-7393.32.4.854

Hollingworth, A., & Henderson, J. M. (2002). Accurate visual memory for previously attended objects in natural scenes. *Journal of Experimental Psychology: Human Perception and Performance, 28,* 113–136. doi:10.1037/0096-1523.28.1.113

Hutchins, E. (1995). *Cognition in the wild.* Cambridge, MA: MIT Press.

Israël, I., & Berthoz, A. (1989). Contribution of the otoliths to the calculation of linear displacement. *Journal of Neurophysiology, 62,* 247–263.

Israël, I., Bronstein, A. M., Kanayama, R., Faldon, M., & Gresty, M. A. (1996). Visual and vestibular factors influencing vestibular "navigation." *Experimental Brain Research, 112,* 411–419. doi:10.1007/BF00227947

Kahneman, D., Treisman, A., & Gibbs, B. J. (1992). The reviewing of object files: Object-specific integration of information. *Cognitive Psychology, 24,* 175–219. doi:10.1016/0010-0285(92)90007-O

Kearns, M. J., Warren, W. H., Duchon, A. P., & Tarr, M. J. (2002). Path integration from optic flow and body senses in a homing task. *Perception, 31,* 349–374. doi:10.1068/p3311

Kessler, K., & Thomson, L. A. (2010). The embodied nature of spatial perspective taking: Embodied transformation versus sensorimotor interference. *Cognition, 114,* 72–88. doi:10.1016/j.cognition.2009.08.015

Klatzky, R. L., Beall, A. C., Loomis, J. M., Golledge, R. G., & Philbeck, J. W. (1999). Human navigation ability: Tests of the encoding-error model of path integration. *Spatial Cognition and Computation, 1,* 31–65. doi:10.1023/A:1010061313300

Klatzky, R. L., Loomis, J. M., Beall, A. C., Chance, S. S., & Golledge, R. G. (1998). Spatial updating of self-position and orientation during real, imagined, and virtual locomotion. *Psychological Science, 9,* 293–298. doi:10.1111/1467-9280.00058

Klatzky, R. L., Loomis, J. M., & Golledge, R. G. (1997). Encoding spatial representations through nonvisually guided locomotion: Tests of human path integration. In D. Medin (Ed.), *The psychology of learning and motivation* (Vol. 37, pp. 41–84). San Diego, CA: Academic Press.

Klatzky, R. L., Loomis, J. M., Golledge, R. G., Cicinelli, J. G., Doherty, S., & Pellegrino, J. W. (1990). Acquisition of route and survey knowledge in the absence of vision. *Journal of Motor Behavior, 22,* 19–43.

Loomis, J. M., Da Silva, J. A., Fujita, N., & Fukusima, S. S. (1992). Visual space perception and visually directed action. *Journal of Experimental Psychology: Human Perception and Performance, 18,* 906–921. doi:10.1037/0096-1523.18.4.906

Loomis, J. M., Klatzky, R. L., Golledge, R. G., Cicinelli, J. G., Pellegrino, J. W., & Fry, P. A. (1993). Nonvisual navigation by blind and sighted: Assessment of path integration ability. *Journal of Experimental Psychology: General, 122,* 73–91. doi:10.1037/0096-3445.122.1.73

Loomis, J. M., Klatzky, R. L., Golledge, R. G., & Philbeck, J. W. (1999). Human navigation by path integration. In R. G. Golledge (Ed.), *Wayfinding behavior: Cognitive mapping and other spatial processes* (pp. 125–151). Baltimore, MD: Johns Hopkins Press.

Marchette, S., & Shelton, A. (2010). Object properties and frame of reference in spatial memory representations. *Spatial Cognition and Computation, 10,* 1–27. doi:10.1080/13875860903509406

Maurer, R. (1998). A connectionist model of path integration with and without a representation of distance to the starting point. *Psychobiology, 26,* 21–35.

Maurer, R., & Séguinot, V. (1995). What is modelling for? A critical review of the models of path integration. *Journal of Theoretical Biology, 175,* 457–475. doi:10.1006/jtbi.1995.0154

May, M. (2004). Imaginal perspective switches in remembered environments: Transformation versus interference accounts. *Cognitive Psychology, 48,* 163–206. doi:10.1016/S0010-0285(03)00127-0

May, M., & Klatzky, R. L. (2000). Path integration while ignoring irrelevant movement. *Journal of Experimental Psychology: Learning, Memory, and Cognition, 26,* 169–186. doi:10.1037/0278-7393.26.1.169

McNaughton, B. L., Barnes, C. A., Gerrard, J. L., Gothard, K., Jung, M. W., Knierim, J. J., . . . Weaver, K. L. (1996). Deciphering the hippocampal polyglot: The hippocampus as a path integration system. *The Journal of Experimental Biology, 199,* 173–185.

McNaughton, B. L., Battaglia, F. P., Jensen, O., Moser, E. I., & Moser, M. B. (2006). Path integration and the neural basis of the 'cognitive map. *Nature Reviews Neuroscience, 7,* 663–678. doi:10.1038/nrn1932

Mergner, T., Nasios, G., & Anastasopoulos, D. (1998). Vestibular memory-contingent saccades involve somatosensory input from the body support. *Neuroreport, 9,* 1469–1473. doi:10.1097/00001756-199805110-00041

Mergner, T., Nasios, G., Maurer, C., & Becker, W. (2001). Visual object localisation in space: Interaction of retinal, eye position, vestibular and neck proprioceptive information. *Experimental Brain Research, 141,* 33–51. doi:10.1007/s002210100826

Mittelstaedt, H. (1985). Analytical cybernetics of spider navigation. In F. G. Barth (Ed.), *Neurobiology of arachnids* (pp. 298–316). Berlin, Germany: Springer-Verlag. doi:10.1007/978-3-642-70348-5_15

Mittelstaedt, H., & Mittelstaedt, M. L. (1982). Homing by path integration. In F. Papi & H. G. Wallraff (Eds.), *Avian navigation* (pp. 290–297). New York, NY: Springer-Verlag. doi:10.1007/978-3-642-68616-0_29

Mittelstaedt, M. L., & Glasauer, S. (1991). Idiothetic navigation in gerbils and humans. *Zoologische Jahrbucher. Abteilung fur Allgemeine Zoologie und Physiologie der Tiere, 95,* 427–435.

Morris, R. G. M., Garrud, P., Rawlins, J. N. P., & O'Keefe, J. (1982, June 24). Place navigation impaired in rats with hippocampal lesions. *Nature, 297,* 681–683. doi:10.1038/297681a0

Mossio, M., Vidal, M., & Berthoz, A. (2008). Traveled distances: New insights into the role of optic flow. *Vision Research, 48,* 289–303. doi:10.1016/j.visres.2007.11.015

Mou, W., McNamara, T. P., Rump, B., & Xiao, C. (2006). Roles of egocentric and allocentric spatial representations in locomotion and reorientation. *Journal of Experimental Psychology: Learning, Memory, and Cognition, 32,* 1274–1290. doi:10.1037/0278-7393.32.6.1274

Mou, W., McNamara, T. P., Valiquette, C. M., & Rump, B. (2004). Allocentric and egocentric updating of spatial memories. *Journal of Experimental Psychology: Learning, Memory, and Cognition, 30,* 142–157. doi:10.1037/0278-7393.30.1.142

Mou, W., Zhang, H., & McNamara, T. P. (2009). Novel view scene recognition relies on identifying spatial reference directions. *Cognition, 111,* 175–186. doi:10.1016/j.cognition.2009.01.007

Müller, M., & Wehner, R. (1988). Path integration in desert ants, *Cataglyphis fortis. Proceedings of the National Academy of Sciences of the United States of America, 85,* 5287–5290. doi:10.1073/pnas.85.14.5287

Nakamura, T., & Bronstein, A. (1995). The perception of head and neck angular displacement in normal and labyrinthine-defective subjects: A quantitative study using a 'remembered saccade' technique. *Brain: A Journal of Neurology, 118,* 1157–1168. doi:10.1093/brain/118.5.1157

Pham, Q.-C., & Hicheur, H. (2009). On the open-loop and feedback processes that underlie the formation of trajectories during visual and nonvisual loco-

motion in humans. *Journal of Neurophysiology, 102,* 2800–2815. doi:10.1152/jn.00284.2009

Philbeck, J. W., Behrmann, M., & Loomis, J. M. (2001). Updating of locations during whole-body rotations in patients with hemispatial neglect. *Cognitive, Affective & Behavioral Neuroscience, 1,* 330–343. doi:10.3758/CABN.1.4.330

Philbeck, J. W., Klatzky, R. K., Behrmann, M., Loomis, J. M., & Goodridge, J. (2001). Active control of locomotion facilitates nonvisual navigation. *Journal of Experimental Psychology: Human Perception and Performance, 27,* 141–153. doi:10.1037/0096-1523.27.1.141

Philbeck, J. W., & Loomis, J. M. (1997). Comparison of two indicators of perceived egocentric distance under full-cue and reduced-cue conditions. *Journal of Experimental Psychology: Human Perception and Performance, 23,* 72–85. doi:10.1037/0096-1523.23.1.72

Philbeck, J. W., Loomis, J. M., & Beall, A. C. (1997). Visually perceived location is an invariant in the control of action. *Perception & Psychophysics, 59,* 601–612. doi:10.3758/BF03211868

Philbeck, J. W., & O'Leary, S. O. (2005). Remembered landmarks enhance the precision of path integration. *Psicológica, 26,* 7–24.

Philbeck, J. W., Woods, A. J., Arthur, J., & Todd, J. (2008). Progressive locomotor recalibration during blind walking. *Attention, Perception, & Psychophysics, 70,* 1459–1470. doi:10.3758/PP.70.8.1459

Presson, C. C., & Hazelrigg, M. D. (1984). Building spatial representations through primary and secondary learning. *Journal of Experimental Psychology: Learning, Memory, and Cognition, 10,* 716–722. doi:10.1037/0278-7393.10.4.716

Redish, A. D. (1999). *Beyond the cognitive map: From place cells to episodic memory.* Cambridge, MA: MIT Press.

Riecke, B. E., van Veen, H. A. H. C., & Bülthoff, H. H. (2000). Visual homing is possible without landmarks. In M. P. Institute (Ed.), *Tech. Rep. No. 82* (pp. 1–28). Max Planck Institut für biologische Kybernetik, Tübingen, Germany.

Rieser, J. J. (1999). Dynamic spatial orientation and the coupling of representation and action. In R. G. Golledge (Ed.), *Wayfinding behavior: Cognitive mapping and other spatial processes* (pp. 168–190). Baltimore, MD: Johns Hopkins University Press.

Rieser, J. J., Ashmead, D. H., Talor, C. R., & Youngquist, G. A. (1990). Visual perception and the guidance of locomotion without vision to previously seen targets. *Perception, 19,* 675–689. doi:10.1068/p190675

Rieser, J. J., Frymire, M., & Berry, D. (1997). *Geometrical constraints on imagery and action when walking without vision.* Paper presented at the meeting of the Psychonomic Society, Philadelphia, PA.

Rieser, J. J., & Rider, E. A. (1991). Young children's spatial orientation with respect to multiple targets when walking without vision. *Developmental Psychology, 27,* 97–107. doi:10.1037/0012-1649.27.1.97

Rushton, S. K., Harris, J. M., Lloyd, M. R., & Wann, J. P. (1998). Guidance of locomotion on foot uses perceived target location rather than optic flow. *Current Biology, 8,* 1191–1194. doi:10.1016/S0960-9822(07)00492-7

Sadalla, E. K., & Montello, D. R. (1989). Remembering changes in direction. *Environment and Behavior, 21,* 346–363. doi:10.1177/0013916589213006

Samsonovich, A., & McNaughton, B. L. (1997). Path integration and cognitive mapping in a continuous attractor neural network model. *The Journal of Neuroscience, 17,* 5900–5920.

Sargent, J., Dopkins, S., Philbeck, J., & Chichka, D. (2010). Chunking in spatial memory. *Journal of Experimental Psychology: Learning, Memory, and Cognition, 36,* 576–589. doi:10.1037/a0017528

Sargent, J., Dopkins, S., Philbeck, J., & Modarres, R. (2008). Spatial memory during progressive disorientation. *Journal of Experimental Psychology: Learning, Memory, and Cognition, 34,* 602–615. doi:10.1037/0278-7393.34.3.602

Séguinot, V., Cattet, J., & Benhamou, S. (1998). Path integration in dogs. *Animal Behaviour, 55,* 787–797. doi:10.1006/anbe.1997.0662

Séguinot, V., Maurer, R., & Etienne, A. S. (1993). Dead reckoning in a small mammal: The evaluation of distance. *Journal of Comparative Physiology A: Neuroethology, Sensory, Neural, and Behavioral Physiology, 173,* 103–113. doi:10.1007/BF00209622

Shepard, R. N. (1967). Recognition memory for words, sentences, and pictures. *Journal of Verbal Learning and Verbal Behavior, 6,* 156–163. doi:10.1016/S0022-5371(67)80067-7

Sholl, M. J. (1987). Cognitive maps as orienting schemata. *Journal of Experimental Psychology: Learning, Memory, and Cognition, 13,* 615–628. doi:10.1037/0278-7393.13.4.615

Sholl, M. J., & Fraone, S. (2004). Spatial working memory systems. In G. Allen (Ed.), *Remembering where: Advances in understanding spatial memory* (pp. 67–100). Mahwah, NJ: Erlbaum.

Siegler, I. (2000). Idiosyncratic orientation strategies influence self-controlled whole-body rotations in the dark. *Cognitive Brain Research, 9,* 205–207. doi:10.1016/S0926-6410(00)00007-0

Siegler, I., & Israël, I. (2002). The importance of head-free gaze control in humans performing a spatial orientation task. *Neuroscience Letters, 333,* 99–102. doi:10.1016/S0304-3940(02)01028-5

Simons, D. J., & Wang, R. F. (1998). Perceiving real-world viewpoint changes. *Psychological Science, 9,* 315–320. doi:10.1111/1467-9280.00062

Srinivasan, M., Zhang, S., & Bidwell, N. (1997). Visually mediated odometry in honeybees. *The Journal of Experimental Biology, 200,* 2513–2522.

Steenhuis, R. E., & Goodale, M. A. (1988). The effects of time and distance on accuracy of target-directed locomotion: Does an accurate short-term memory for spatial location exist? *Journal of Motor Behavior, 20,* 399–415.

Stringer, S. M., Trappenberg, T. P., Rolls, E. T., & de Araujo, I. E. T. (2002). Self-organizing continuous attractor networks and path integration: One-dimensional models of head direction cells. *Network: Computation in Neural Systems, 13,* 217–242.

Sun, H.-J., Campos, J. L., Young, M., & Chan, G. S. W. (2004). The contributions of static visual cues, non-visual cues, and optic flow in distance estimation. *Perception, 33,* 49–65. doi:10.1068/p5145

Telford, L., Howard, I. P., & Ohmi, M. (1995). Heading judgments during active and passive self-motion. *Experimental Brain Research, 104,* 502–510. doi:10.1007/BF00231984

Thomson, J. A. (1980). How do we use visual information to control locomotion? *Trends in Neurosciences, 3,* 247–250.

von Saint Paul, U. (1982). Do geese use path integration for walking home? In F. Papi & H. G. Wallraff (Eds.), *Avian navigation* (pp. 296–307). New York, NY: Springer-Verlag. doi:10.1007/978-3-642-68616-0_30

Waller, D., & Lippa, Y. (2007). Landmarks as beacons and associative cues: Their role in route learning. *Memory & Cognition, 35,* 910–924. doi:10.3758/BF03193465

Waller, D., Montello, D. R., Richardson, A. E., & Hegarty, M. (2002). Orientation specificity and spatial updating of memories for layouts. *Journal of Experimental Psychology: Learning, Memory, and Cognition, 28,* 1051–1063. doi:10.1037/0278-7393.28.6.1051

Wang, R. F. (1999). Representing a stable environment by egocentric updating and invariant representations. *Spatial Cognition and Computation, 1,* 431–445. doi:10.1023/A:1010043814328

Wang, R. F. (2004). Between reality and imagination: When is spatial updating automatic? *Perception & Psychophysics, 66,* 68–76. doi:10.3758/BF03194862

Wang, R. F., & Brockmole, J. (2003a). Human navigation in nested environments. *Journal of Experimental Psychology: Learning, Memory, and Cognition, 29,* 398–404. doi:10.1037/0278-7393.29.3.398

Wang, R. F., & Brockmole, J. (2003b). Simultaneous spatial updating in nested environments. *Psychonomic*

Bulletin & Review, 10, 981–986. doi:10.3758/BF03196562

Wang, R. F., Crowell, J. A., Simons, D. J., Irwin, D. E., Kramer, A. F., Ambinder, M. S., . . . Hsieh, B. B. (2006). Spatial updating relies on an egocentric representation of space: Effects of the number of objects. *Psychonomic Bulletin & Review, 13,* 281–286. doi:10.3758/BF03193844

Wang, R. F., & Spelke, E. (2000). Updating egocentric representations in human navigation. *Cognition, 77,* 215–250. doi:10.1016/S0010-0277(00)00105-0

Wang, R. F., & Spelke, E. (2002). Human spatial representation: Insights from animals. *Trends in Cognitive Sciences, 6,* 376–382. doi:10.1016/S1364-6613(02)01961-7

Warren, W. H., Jr., Kay, B. A., Zosh, W. D., Duchon, A. P., & Sahuc, S. (2001). Optic flow is used to control human walking. *Nature Neuroscience, 4,* 213–216. doi:10.1038/84054

Wehner, R., & Wehner, S. (1986). Path integration in desert ants. Approaching a long-standing puzzle in insect navigation. *Monitore Zoologico Italiano, 20,* 309–331.

Whishaw, I. Q., Hines, D. J., & Wallace, D. G. (2001). Dead reckoning (path integration) requires the hippocampal formation: Evidence from spontaneous exploration and spatial learning tasks in light (allothetic) and dark (idiothetic) tests. *Behavioural Brain Research, 127,* 49–69. doi:10.1016/S0166-4328(01)00359-X

Wiener, J. M., & Mallot, H. A. (2006). Path complexity does not impair visual path integration. *Spatial Cognition and Computation, 6,* 333–346. doi:10.1207/s15427633scc0604_3

Wittmann, T., & Schwegler, H. (1995). Path integration—a network model. *Biological Cybernetics, 73,* 569–575. doi:10.1007/BF00199549

Wolbers, T., Hegarty, M., Buchel, C., & Loomis, J. (2008). Spatial updating: How the brain keeps track of changing object locations during observer motion. *Nature Neuroscience, 11,* 1223–1230. doi:10.1038/nn.2189

Wolpert, D. M., & Ghahramani, Z. (2000). Computational principles of movement neuroscience. *Nature Neuroscience, 3,* 1212–1217. doi:10.1038/81497

Worchel, P., & Mauney, J. (1951). The effect of practice on the perception of obstacles by the blind. *Journal of Experimental Psychology, 41,* 170–176. doi:10.1037/h0055653

Worsley, C. L., Recce, M., Spiers, H. J., Marley, J., Polkey, C. E., & Morris, R. G. (2001). Path integration following temporal lobectomy in humans. *Neuropsychologia, 39,* 452–464. doi:10.1016/S0028-3932(00)00140-8

Wu, B., Ooi, T. L., & He, Z. J. (2004, March 4). Perceiving distance accurately by a directional process of integrating ground information. *Nature, 428,* 73–77. doi:10.1038/nature02350

Xiao, C., Mou, W., & McNamara, T. P. (2009). Use of self-to-object and object-to-object spatial relations in locomotion. *Journal of Experimental Psychology: Learning, Memory, and Cognition, 35,* 1137–1147. doi:10.1037/a0016273

Yardley, L., Gardner, M., Lavie, N., & Gresty, M. (1999). Attentional demands of perception of passive self-motion in darkness. *Neuropsychologia, 37,* 1293–1301. doi:10.1016/S0028-3932(99)00024-X

CHAPTER 6

INDIVIDUAL AND GROUP DIFFERENCES IN SPATIAL ABILITY

Beth M. Casey

Individual differences in spatial abilities have been a relatively neglected topic compared with the extensive research conducted on variations within other types of human intelligence (Lohman, 1996). Yet, collectively, the literature on spatial ability makes it clear that spatial skills are a critical component of general intelligence (W. Johnson & Bouchard, 2005). We use spatial reasoning on a wide range of tasks in our everyday life, from navigating in space, to estimating how much we can fit into a car trunk, to assembling a piece of furniture from instructions. Spatial skills are an important component of success in many professions; the National Science Board (2010) recently concluded that "a talent highly valuable for developing STEM [science, technology, engineering, math] excellence—spatial ability—is not measured and hence missed" (p. 9). These conclusions were influenced by new research showing spatial reasoning skills in high school to be strongly associated with educational and vocational outcomes, predicting choice of STEM majors and careers, above and beyond the effects of verbal and math abilities (Wai, Lubinski, & Benbow, 2009). Given our increasingly technological world, people of all professions may require progressively more sophisticated skill at interpreting information presented in spatial abstractions, such as graphs and diagrams (Terlecki, Newcombe, & Little, 2008). Within this context, it critical to understand the factors contributing to the strong and consistent gender differences found on key types of

spatial skills, with females performing more poorly than males starting as young as 4 years of age (Levine, Huttenlocher, Taylor, & Langrock, 1999; Voyer, Voyer, & Bryden, 1995).

In this chapter, I review research and provide a synthesis of critical issues relating to research on individual and group differences in spatial skills. Spatial skills encompass a wide range of abilities, but the key connection among them is that they involve reasoning about spatial elements of the world and often involve mentally visualizing the properties of space. I first provide a brief overview of different types of spatial skills and the psychometric approach used to identify these abilities. Although there are spatial skills for both environments and objects, I focus on object-based spatial skills because they are most influential in a range of fields that require the ability to visualize and mentally manipulate images to solve problems; they also show the largest group differences. I review the research on how these different types of object-based spatial skills are measured and discuss the methodologies that have been used to investigate them, including psychometric and experimental cognitive approaches. I then review recent research on underlying cognitive processes contributing to individual differences in these skills, such as spatial working memory capacity and strategy differences in solving spatial problems.

The second half of the chapter addresses group differences in object-based spatial skills, focusing on

DOI: 10.1037/13936-007
Handbook of Spatial Cognition, D. Waller and L. Nadel (Editors)

gender differences. Methodological factors influential in modifying the strength of these gender differences are discussed, as are explanations for why these factors might affect gender differences. Next, the literature on the neural mechanisms underlying these gender difference is reviewed, as is evidence for gender differences in underlying cognitive processes, such as working memory capacity and strategy differences. This is followed by a review and analysis of the effects of temporary activational and transitory influences on the spatial skills of males and females; these influences include fluctuations in hormone levels or momentary shifts in beliefs and emotions. The effects of training on gender differences are discussed as well as the educational implications of this gender research. In the concluding section, the literature on individual differences in spatial skills is considered within the context of theoretical frameworks that consider the influences of biopsychosocial factors on individual differences in how individuals learn to process spatial information.

DIFFERENT TYPES OF SPATIAL THINKING

The first step in understanding individual differences in spatial thinking is to address the range of spatial skills and the best ways of categorizing them. Much of the evidence investigating the differentiation among types of spatial abilities was conducted within the field of psychometrics. The psychometric approach typically studies individual differences through a correlational methodology, administering a battery of tests and analyzing the pattern and structure of relationships among the different measures using factor analytic techniques and, more recently, multidimensional scaling. The initial goal of the early work using this approach was to establish whether spatial skills are separate from general intelligence and whether spatial reasoning is a unitary concept or whether it is composed of separate abilities (Hegarty & Waller, 2004). Around the middle of the 20th century, pioneers such as Guilford (Guilford & Lacey, 1947) and Thurstone (1958) successfully established that spatial ability is not a homogeneous (unidimensional) concept but instead consists of clearly

distinguishable subcomponents each reflecting a separate underlying cognitive process (Hegarty & Waller, 2005; Quaiser-Pohl, Lehmann, & Eid, 2004; Vasilyeva & Lourenco, 2010).

It has been proposed by a number of researchers (Hegarty & Waller, 2004; Zacks, Vettel, & Michelon, 2003) that there are two primary types of constructs relating to individual differences in spatial ability. First, there are spatial skills involving object-based mental representations and manipulations of two- and three-dimensional objects in space. Such abilities are useful in a variety of everyday tasks, such as designing or interpreting a two-dimensional drawing or plan of a bookcase before constructing it or generating and manipulating mental images of the best way of rotating a table through a doorway. These skills are often manifested in tasks that involve the ability to translate 2-D pictures of objects into 3-D images to transform and manipulate them. The second category of spatial skills involves environment-based mental abilities, including those associated with the representation of large- and small-scale environments, way finding, mapping, and spatial orientation and perspective-taking (imagining what a scene looks like from different perspectives). Such abilities require observers to physically move and thus involve accounting for an egocentric frame of reference in relation to features of the object or the environment; in contrast, for object-based spatial tasks, the object is manipulated mentally in relation to the observer and/or the environment (Hegarty & Waller, 2004).

There is disagreement within the field as to whether object-based spatial skills (e.g., spatial visualization) and environment-based skills (e.g., perspective taking) reflect separate spatial factors (Allen, Kirasic, Dobson, Long, & Beck, 1996; Quaiser-Pohl et al., 2004). Several investigators have pointed to the limitations of inferring underlying cognitive processes based on the basis of factor analytic techniques (Hegarty & Waller, 2005). Depending on the type of tasks that are included in the exploratory factor analysis, one can arrive at different patterns of individual differences and, as a result, different conceptualizations of the underlying structure of spatial cognition (Carroll, 1993; McGee, 1979; Vasilyeva & Lourenco, 2010).

Another problem involved in trying to accurately identify the separate factors is that the tasks used in the factor analysis may not adequately measure the underlying concepts. For example, Hegarty and Waller (2004) proposed that tests of perspective-taking employed in past psychometric studies did not always measure participants' use of strategies based on egocentric transformations. Using a new measure of spatial perspective-taking, Kozhevnikov and Hegarty (2001) found a dissociation between object-based tasks and environment-based spatial tasks, a finding that has been confirmed in subsequent research (Hegarty & Waller, 2004).

It should be pointed out that the preponderance of research relating to individual and group differences in spatial skills has addressed object-based spatial skills (Linn & Petersen, 1985; Voyer et al., 1995). Consequently, the remainder of this chapter focuses on tasks that involve the manipulation of two- and three-dimensional objects in space rather than environment-based mental representations. For reviews of the literature and key findings on spatial representations of large- and small-scale environments, see articles and reviews by Acredolo (1981), Hegarty and Waller (2005), Shelton and Gabrieli (2004), and Vasilyeva and Lourenco (2010).

INDIVIDUAL DIFFERENCES IN OBJECT-BASED SPATIAL SKILLS

From an applied perspective, a focus on object-based spatial abilities may be particularly useful because these skills have been shown to relate most strongly to success in STEM fields when compared with other disciplines such as social sciences, humanities, and education (Kozhevnikov, Motes, & Hegarty, 2007; Vasilyeva & Lourenco, 2010; Wai et al., 2009). Object-based spatial skills, such as mental rotation ability, have been found to predict math performance in middle school, high school, and college students, especially for females (Burnett, Lane, & Dratt, 1979; Gallagher et al., 2000; Nuttall, Casey, & Pezaris, 2005). When a pool of talented youth was followed longitudinally, Lubinski and Benbow (2006) found that, in general, participants choosing math–science careers were those who had excelled in object-based skills. The importance of these types of skills for choosing math–science majors and careers was also found with a more diverse sample of students with a wider range of abilities (Wai et al., 2009).

Different Types of Object-Based Spatial Skills

Several major and influential meta-analyses have established there are three key types of object-based spatial skills: mental rotation, spatial visualization, and spatial perception (Carroll, 1993; Linn & Petersen, 1985; Lohman, 1979; Voyer et al., 1995). These abilities are briefly summarized next.

Mental rotation. Perhaps the most investigated of the object-based skills, mental rotation consists of the ability to look at an object or a picture of an object and to visualize what it might look like when rotated in 3-D space. The most commonly used measure of mental rotation is the Vandenberg and Kuse (1978) paper-and-pencil test, the Mental Rotations Test (MRT), which uses stimuli from the Shepard and Metzler stimulus series (1971). (See Figure 6.1 for an example of a recent adaptation

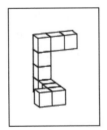 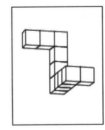 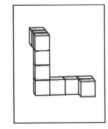 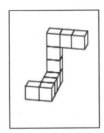 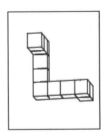

FIGURE 6.1.   An example of a test item on the more recent adaptation of the *Vandenberg Mental Rotations Test*. From "A Redrawn Vandenberg and Kuse Mental Rotations Test: Different Versions and Factors That Affect Performance," by M. Peters, B. Laeng, K. Latham, M. Jackson, R. Zaiyona, and C. Richardson, 1995, *Brain and Cognition, 28*, p. 6. Copyright 1995 by Elsevier. Reprinted with permission.

of the Vandenberg MRT by Peters, Laeng, et al., 1995.) In the Vandenberg test, each item shows a picture of a 3-D object on the left called the *standard*. On the right, there are pictures of four 3-D objects. Two correct pictures are identical to the standard but rotated to a different orientation; the two incorrect items are either mirror images of the standard (also rotated to different orientations) or figures that have feature differences from the standard. In addition to the Vandenberg MRT, there are a variety of tasks that use the Shepard and Metzler objects (Voyer et al., 1995); these are usually presented as simple mirror-image two-choice tasks and are often presented on a computer screen. Other less frequently used measures of mental rotation consist of 2-D mental rotation tasks in which a 2-D figure is rotated in 2-D rather than 3-D space— for example, the Cards Rotation Test (Ekstrom, French, & Harman, 1976) and the Spatial Relations subtest of the Primary Mental Abilities Test (Thurstone, 1958).

The Vandenberg MRT has been studied in depth in part because it has shown striking gender differences (favoring males) when compared with all other cognitive measures and has been found to be related to the ability to mentally transform and manipulate images, which is useful in a wide variety of fields, such as architecture, carpentry, mathematics, and engineering (e.g., Wai et al., 2009). Furthermore, the computer-based two-choice 3-D mental rotation tasks have been used extensively in information processing and neuroscience research on spatial skills (Voyer et al., 1995). In recent psychometric research, W. Johnson and Bouchard (2005) considered these types of mental rotation abilities to be an important component of general intelligence. They argued that the structure of human intelligence reflects distinctions among verbal, perceptual, and image rotation factors rather than fluid versus crystallized intelligence (Cattell, 1963). Furthermore, they argued that the processes involved in mental image rotation tasks have not been given the attention they deserve as important and relatively independent contributors to the manifestation of human intelligence.

Spatial visualization. The second type of object-based spatial skill involves spatial visualization, which consists of the multistep processing of spatial information. Examples of spatial visualization includes the ability to hold a shape in working memory and then search for the same shape hidden within a more complex figure (e.g., embedded figures) or the ability to examine a group of shapes and then mentally combine them together to create a new design (e.g., puzzles, pattern blocks, and tangrams). Related to these tasks are versions of the Block Design Subtest of the Wechsler Intelligence Scales (e.g., Wechsler, 2003), in which a 2-D red-and-white design pattern must be replicated by assembling 3-D blocks so that when combined together, the topside of the combined blocks shows the same pattern as the 2-D picture. (See Voyer et al., 1995, for a description of other spatial visualization tests.)

Spatial perception. The third type of object-based spatial tasks consists of spatial perception tasks in which individuals are required to determine spatial relationships with respect to their own bodies despite distracting information (Linn & Petersen, 1985). For example, in the Rod-and-Frame Test, participants must adjust (tilt) a rod to the upright, even when the rectangular frame surrounding the rod is tilted at a different orientation from the upright (Witkin & Asch, 1948). In the Water Levels Test, originally designed by Piaget and Inhelder (1956), when containers are tilted at various angles, individuals must predict the orientation of a water surface in the tilted bottle by drawing a line representing the water level. Both of these spatial perception tasks involve identifying the gravitational upright while ignoring distracting cues. There is some disagreement in the literature as to whether these types of spatial perception tasks should be classified within object-based spatial relations tasks (e.g., Linn & Petersen, 1985) or spatial orientation tasks involving small-scale environments (e.g., Ozer, 1987). For the present review, we consider them as part of object-based spatial tasks.

Experimental Cognitive Approaches to Individual Differences in Object-Based Skills

In the latter decades of the 20th century, the focus in the study of individual differences in spatial skills shifted from a psychometric approach to an experimental approach in which researchers examined the underlying cognitive processes that mediate individual differences in spatial skills. This research included an examination of working memory processes and the types of strategies used to solve these types of problems. Even more recently, a wealth of information has been provided by the exploration of brain activity occurring when solving spatial tasks. The use of functional magnetic resonance imaging (fMRI) techniques, for example, has made it possible to investigate individual differences in brain activity directly during the spatial problem-solving process (see, however, a general critique of fMRI procedures: Sanders, 2009). In what follows, I examine recent findings in how working memory resources and strategies affect individual differences. In addition, I discuss what contemporary research from the neurosciences tells us about these phenomena.

The role of working memory in understanding individual differences in spatial skills. Many tasks require the ability to hold information in memory while other information is being processed and utilized (Shah & Miyake, 1996). The mental system that enables this ability is typically conceptualized as *working memory*. In 1986, Baddeley proposed two subcomponents of working memory, with separate resources dedicated to processing verbal and spatial information. He identified the *visual–spatial sketchpad* as the mechanism for processing spatial working memory in which images are generated, maintained, and manipulated. Likewise, a *phonological loop* is the mechanism for processing verbal working memory. Interference paradigms have been used to assess these two separate subsystems. In general, this work has shown that, consistent with Baddeley's distinctions, concurrent spatial tasks disrupt the ability to retain spatial information in memory more than do verbal tasks;

the opposite pattern occurs with verbal interference tasks.

Shah and Miyake (1996) went further to assess whether these two types of working memory systems have differential impacts on higher level verbal and spatial problem-solving tasks. They found that a spatial span working memory task correlated with a spatial visualization task but not with a task of verbal ability. In contrast, a reading span working memory task correlated with the verbal ability measure but not with the spatial measure. Furthermore, active spatial working memory tasks predicted performance on a variety of spatial measures when compared with more passive short-term spatial memory tasks. (These short-term memory tasks primarily assess storage ability but do not include the processing components involved in working memory tasks.) Miyake, Friedman, Rettinger, Shah, and Hegarty (2001) found that the working memory constructs were sufficient to explain the intercorrelations among three types of object-based spatial ability measures (spatial visualization, spatial relations, and perceptual speed). Such research has been formative in establishing bridges between the psychometric literature on spatial ability and the experimental literature on working memory.

Individual differences in strategy use on mental rotation tasks. Another area of intensive research has involved the strategies that individuals use to solve spatial problems. There is a large literature showing individual differences in how people solve mental rotation tasks (Geiser, Lehmann, & Eid, 2006; Peters, Cloud, & Laeng, 1995). Examining data from participants' eye movements and verbal reports, Just and Carpenter (1985) provided compelling evidence that not everyone uses the same strategy when approaching mental rotation tasks. For example, some individuals tend to use a holistic strategy, consisting of the mental rotation of the whole stimulus, whereas others may use a part-by-part sequential rotation of the figure (Jordan, Wüstenberg, Heinze, Peters, & Jäncke, 2002). Still others may predominantly use an analytical strategy approach that involves reasoning rather than using mental rotation (Pezaris & Casey, 1991). Another strategy involves the use of spatial perspective-taking by finding the same vantage point on each of the figures provided and using critical features on the left or right side of the figure from that position to determine whether the figure is the same or a mirror image of the standard (Just & Carpenter, 1985). This latter strategy appears to allow the viewer to bypass mental rotation of images by making a left–right discrimination of features of the object using the same vantage point when comparing the choice figures with the standard. Further, even within those who use a holistic rotation approach, there are individual differences, with high spatial individuals showing the ability to mentally rotate faster than those with low spatial ability (Just & Carpenter, 1985).

Although this variation in strategy use can inform us about high-level cognition, it can also be frustrating from the experimenters' perspective because one cannot assume that when a group of people solve the same spatial problem that the same underlying cognitive processes are being used. Making the situation even more complicated, individuals do not always use the same strategy consistently even when solving different items within the same task; strategy choice within individuals varies as a function of practice and complexity of the task (Kyllonen, Lohman, & Woltz, 1984). Although the problem of variability in strategy use adds to the complexity of the research on spatial skills, it also has provided a research opportunity using an aptitude-treatment interaction approach by studying groups of individuals with high and low spatial and verbal abilities and examining the changes in their preferred use of either spatial or verbal strategies on spatial tasks as a function of varying conditions, such as item complexity and type of training (Kyllonen, Lohman, & Snow, 1984).

Neural correlates of individual differences in object-based spatial cognitions. This study of individual differences in strategy preferences has also been investigated thorough the lens of how neural processes relate to these different approaches to solving spatial problems. Kosslyn, Thompson, Gitelman, and Alpert (1998) proposed that there are

two ways of processing mental images, each subserved by a different area of the brain. They hypothesized that the right hemisphere predominantly processes images in terms of a metric, coordinate-like system in which parts are precisely located in space; the left hemisphere processes mental images using a categorical language-like system in which parts of the image are coded in spatial relations terms, such as "next to" or "on top of." Research in cognitive neuroscience has supported this dichotomy in hemispheric processing of spatial information (Hugdahl, Thomsen, & Ersland, 2006; Kosslyn et al., 1998).

With respect to the spatial abilities that have been identified by psychometric and experimental research, Kosslyn's model would predict three-dimensional mental rotation tasks, which depend heavily on positioning parts in precise locations in space, to be processed most successfully in the right hemisphere. This prediction has been supported in blood flow studies (Deutsch, Bourbon, Papanicolaou, & Eisenberg, 1988). It is notable that Wendt and Risberg (1994) found that for participants who had poorer skills at mental rotation, there was no distinct hemispheric asymmetry on a mental rotation task. Finally, it appears that problem-solving strategies are related to cerebral laterality effects. Those preferring an imagery mode tend to show stronger right-hemisphere involvement, whereas those who are more inefficient incorporate left-hemisphere involvement as well (Kosslyn et al., 1998).

Recently, Zacks (2008) conducted a meta-analysis of the neuroimaging research in relation to mental rotation performance. He concluded:

> The posterior parietal cortex (as well as regions extending down into the superior posterior occipital cortex) is consistently activated during mental rotation across a range of tasks, imaging modalities, and statistical analysis strategies. This region is therefore a good candidate for implementing the transformation-specific computations required to carry out mental rotation tasks. (p. 5)

Zacks et al. (2003) found that mental rotation and perspective taking are spatial tasks that activate the brain differently, and their research supports dissociation between mental rotation and perspective taking.

GROUP-LEVEL DIFFERENCES IN OBJECT-BASED SPATIAL SKILLS: A FOCUS ON GENDER

Another approach to the study of individual differences starts by dividing people into subgroups on the basis of individual characteristics and then investigates differences in how these subgroups solve spatial problems and the strategies that they use. This approach can be useful because it enables us to understand how and why group differences exist in cognitive performance, and it may suggest ways to intervene and improve performance within the lower performing groups. By far the greatest amount of research examining group differences in spatial skills has addressed gender differences. This intense focus on gender is due in part to the controversy over innate differences between males and females. Typically, hypotheses about the origin of gender differences are developed from either a genetic or an environmental perspective (Geary, 1996; Hyde, 2005), with researchers tending to take positions on only one side of this argument. The possibility of an interaction between heredity and environmental effects is acknowledged, but until recently, little theory or research has been able to develop this interactionist position. Following a review of this literature, I address the issue in greater depth.

Gender Differences on Types of Spatial Skills

Gender differences favoring males on some spatial skills can be substantial, particularly on mental rotation and spatial perception tasks. In large-scale environments, evidence of gender differences has been found in navigation and way finding. Vasilyeva and Lourenco (2010) summarized this research and concluded that it has been well documented that when asked to provide directions, males are more likely to indicate distance and cardinal information whereas females are more likely to use landmark information (Brown, Lahar,

& Mosley, 1998; Galea & Kimura, 1993; Ward, Newcombe, & Overton, 1986). It should be noted, however, that when participants are explicitly asked to use distance information or when cardinal direction is made more salient, the difference between females and males in strategy use virtually disappears (Ward et al., 1986).

Furthermore, there are other spatial tasks that show few or no gender differences (e.g., spatial visualization; Linn & Petersen, 1985; Voyer et al., 1995). There is also evidence of a female advantage (e.g., location memory; Silverman & Eals, 1992; Voyer, Postma, Brake, & Imperato-McGinley, 2007). Yet, typically, males have an advantage on a number of spatial tasks. Of course, there is wide variability in these spatial skills, with overlapping gender distributions; in addition, many females perform at the level of high performing males on these tests (Nuttall et al., 2005).

In terms of mental rotation ability, a meta-analysis by Linn and Petersen (1985) documented that skill at mental rotation shows both strong and consistent gender differences with a large effect size, corresponding to a Cohen's d statistic of 0.94. This indicates that men score 0.94 standard deviations higher on average than women on the mental rotation task. (Note that $d = .80$ or greater are often considered to be "large" effect sizes). Spatial perception measures also show gender differences, with males scoring 0.44 standard deviations higher on average than women (a moderate effect size; Voyer et al., 1995).

On some types of spatial tasks, there is evidence for a decrease in gender differences over time (Voyer et al., 1995), and this change is similar to that of a number of other cognitive abilities (e.g., mathematics; Feingold, 1988; Hyde, 2005). However, Voyer and his associates (1995) also found that the Vandenberg MRT showed a significant increase in gender differences over time (between 1902 and 1983). Thus, gender differences in mental rotation skills stand out in comparison to other types of gender differences. This type of skill also has practical importance in terms of academic performance, and was found to be a strong mediator of gender differences on the Mathematics Scholastic Aptitude Test (SAT-M) for high-ability college samples (Nuttall et al., 2005).

Furthermore, a recent international study examined mental rotation skills across 53 countries (Lippa, Collaer, & Peters, 2010). The researchers found that individuals in more economically developed countries (as assessed by per capita income and life expectancy) had higher mental rotation skills than those in less developed countries. It is surprising that they also found that greater gender equality (as assessed by United Nations indices) and higher levels of economic development were significantly and positively associated with larger gender differences. Why would greater gender equality and development in a country produce wider gender differences? It may be that spatial skills develop more in countries that are more technologically advanced and that males may be more involved in these technological activities than females.

Developmental findings. Gender differences in spatial skills have been found across a wide range of ages, with boys typically outperforming girls (E. S. Johnson & Meade, 1987). Although the largest effect sizes are found at middle school and higher (Linn & Petersen, 1985; Voyer et al., 1995), evidence for gender differences in spatial skills has been found in young children as well (Levine et al., 1999). Levine and her associates found evidence for a gender difference in children as young as 4 on 2-D mental rotation tasks, as well as other types of 2-D mental transformations using abstract shapes, with young boys scoring 0.25 standard deviations higher than girls; they found no gender differences on vocabulary tests (Levine et al., 1999). Thus, the differences were specific to spatial skills. There is also evidence for gender differences favoring males in young children in map reading, mazes, and block design (see review by Levine et al., 1999). In addition, there is some evidence for a male advantage in 5-year-olds on a 3-D mental rotation task (Casey, Erkut, Ceder, & Young, 2008). In this task, 3-D spatial skill was assessed using real objects made out of multilink cubes (similar to the Shepard and Metzler stimuli).

A series of experiments conducted by Vasilyeva and Bowers (2006) may shed some light on pos-

sible mechanisms underlying gender differences in mental rotation in young children. These researchers used a task in which children ages 3 to 6 were first presented with a large wooden layout shaped like an isosceles triangle with a target (red dot) located in one of the corners. They were then given a picture representing that triangular layout; but in the picture, the triangle was rotated either 90 or 180 degrees from the orientation of the original layout of the large triangle. The child was required to locate the place in the drawing where the target had previously been located. No gender differences were found under conditions in which the shape of the triangle was made explicit; for example, when the triangle was constructed out of wood boards (straight lines in the drawing) or dowels (dotted lines in the drawings). However, gender differences were found when the shape was represented only by three points; for example, three wooden dowels (and three dots for the drawing) at each of the vertices of the triangle. Thus, gender differences favoring boys emerged only when children had to generate an image of the triangle from limited information (three points) and then mentally rotate it in 2-D space, thus suggesting that early gender differences may arise when there is increased spatial processing load.

In recent research, evidence of gender differences in spatial skills has been found as early as 3 to 5 months of age using habituation tasks. Both Quinn and Liben (2008) and Moore and Johnson (2008) found evidence that male infants displayed a novelty preference for the mirror-image stimulus over the novel rotation of the familiar stimulus, whereas female infants divided attention equally between the two test stimuli. These findings indicate that attention to changes in stimuli on the basis of shifts in spatial orientation is stronger in male infants than female infants, suggesting that spatial gender differences emerge very early.

Methodological issues relating to gender differences in spatial skills. There has been an extensive literature investigating whether procedural factors associated with assessments can modify the spatial performance of females and males. A second related question is whether manipulation of these factors eliminates significant gender differences in spatial skills. There are a number of procedural manipulations that have been shown to affect the magnitude of gender differences on spatial tasks. Because of the large gender differences in mental rotation, the main body of this research has examined procedural effects specifically for this type of task. In an excellent recent overview of this literature, Voyer (2010) examined the effect of scoring procedures, type of task, stimulus type, instructions, and time pressure on gender differences in mental rotation. He found that methodological manipulations do in fact moderate gender differences but do not generally result in elimination of these differences.

One of the key methodological factors seems to be the amount of processing load placed on the participant when using different procedures. For example, in their meta-analysis, Voyer et al. (1995) showed that the four-choice MRT task produced greater gender differences than the two-choice task, although both types of tasks showed significant gender differences. One key difference is that the complexity of the stimulus array in the four-choice task is much greater than in the two-choice task, and this may substantially increase the amount of mental processing needed to solve the task. The simpler array may reduce the complexity, allowing some females to be more effective in applying different types of strategies. Stimulus factors relating to processing load also affect gender differences. It has been shown that gender differences are affected when any of the features in the rotated figures in the Vandenberg MRT are occluded, either partly or completely; Voyer and Hou (2006) found that occluded items showed larger gender differences than nonoccluded items, though the gender differences still remained for both types of stimuli. These results again suggest that gender differences may be increased by characteristics of the task that put increasing processing demands on the generation, encoding, and rotation of images.

A similar gender effect related to processing load was obtained in the study of 3- to 6-year-olds cited

earlier (Vasilyeva & Bowers, 2006) in which a male advantage emerged only when the stimulus to be rotated consisted of three points at the vertices of the triangle, thereby requiring the children to generate an image of the triangular structure as well as rotating it. An additional finding from this area of research is that the gender effect size is larger when abstract polygons such as the Shepard and Metzler figures are used ($d = 1.08$) rather than when concrete, easily remembered, verbally codable shapes are used, such as human-like figures rotated to the same orientations as the Shepard and Metzler figures ($d = .54$; Alexander & Evardone, 2008).

A final procedural factor that affects the degree of gender differences in mental rotation tasks involves differences in the approach to problem-solving tasks in general. For example, females may simply complete fewer items than males. To address this issue, an alternative ratio scoring procedure has been used that takes the ratio of the correct responses divided by the total number of items attempted. When using this scoring system, gender differences are generally reduced; however, they are still significant. A similar explanation has been that males outperform females because they are more willing to guess. However, findings show that when scores are adjusted for guessing, the gender differences remain (Voyer, 2010). Finally, it has been argued that gender differences should be greatly reduced or eliminated when the time pressure is removed because women may tend to be more anxious in response to time pressured situations (Goldstein, Haldane, & Mitchell, 1990). Further, time limits on the test may provide an advantage for using the holistic rotation strategy, which is preferred by males, and a disadvantage for using the analytical strategies preferred by females. In his meta-analysis, Voyer (2010) concluded that introducing time limits (whether short or long) does tend to increase the size of the gender differences. However, even with unlimited time, the effects sizes are still moderate.

In sum, procedural factors such as complexity of the stimulus array, time limits, and scoring procedures, appear to moderate gender differences but cannot account for all of them. Indeed, procedural differences that make the use of a holistic mental rotation strategy more necessary also tend to exacerbate gender differences.

Cognitive Processes and Strategy Differences as Mediators of Spatial Gender Differences

In this section, I address the question of how cognitive processes and strategy differences might serve as mediators of gender differences in spatial skills underlying cognitive processes that affect individual differences in spatial abilities. These include factors such as strategies and working memory.

Gender differences in strategy use. As mentioned earlier, for mental rotation problems, there is evidence that males tend to use the generally more efficient holistic strategies in which the object is pictured in the mind and then rotated as a whole. Women are more likely to prefer less effective strategies involving more analytical, sequential approaches, some of which involve part-by-part rotations (Jordan et al., 2002; Pezaris & Casey, 1991). Peters and his associates found that women reported using verbal strategies more than men (Peters, Cloud, et al., 1995). In fact, one of the reasons that mental rotation tasks may show much larger gender differences than other object-based spatial measures is that with mental rotation problems, alternative strategies (e.g., part-by-part, verbal or analytic approaches) are much less effective than holistic, image rotation approaches. In contrast, for spatial visualization tasks, step-by-step feature analyses can often be quite an effective alternative way of solving these problems.

Spatial working memory as a mediator of gender differences in spatial skills. In recent years, spatial working memory has been identified as another important component of gender differences. Kaufman (2007) showed that spatial working memory is a critical mediator of gender differences in mental rotation and spatial visualization skills. For the spatial short-term memory task, he asked participants to remember the location of blocks in an array. For the working memory tasks, he asked them to simultaneously memorize the location of blocks while processing either verbal or spatial information. He found a gender difference in the spatial working memory task but not in either the spatial short-term memory or verbal working memory. In addition, statistical analyses showed that spatial working memory completely mediated the relationship between gender and spatial ability. Thus, the key factor accounting for these gender differences in spatial skills seems to be the ability to maintain spatial representations in working memory within the context of other distracting spatial stimuli. These findings suggest that spatial working memory training may be a useful way to improve spatial skills in females, especially given the effectiveness of general working memory training on other groups of individuals (Klingberg, Forssberg, & Westerberg, 2002).

Is There Evidence for Underlying Neural Mechanisms Relating to Gender Differences in Spatial Skills?

There is evidence from fMRI research that males and females tend to process spatial information on mental rotation tasks with different patterns of brain activation. Males show predominantly parietal activation, whereas females show relatively more inferior frontal activation of the prefrontal cortex (Hugdahl et al., 2006; Jordan et al., 2002). Hugdahl et al.'s (2006) research suggests that males may be biased toward a coordinate processing approach and females biased toward a serial, categorical processing approach. One research team (Jordan et al., 2002) found that when participants were selected so that performance levels were equalized between males and females, their brains still exhibited different activation patterns during mental rotation tasks. This indicates that male and female differences in strategy choice on mental rotation even occur when the two groups are matched for spatial skill. Hahn, Jansen, and Heil (2010) found differences in pattern of neural activity measured using electroencephalogram recordings are also found between young boys and girls when they are completing 2-D mental rotation tasks. In this study, boys showed bilateral parietal activity while solving mental rotation tasks, whereas the girls' brain activity was lateralized toward the left hemisphere, again suggesting a more categorical way of processing the items.

When examining gray and white matter volume in the parietal lobes, recent research has shown proportionally greater gray matter volume in women compared with men (Hänggi et al., 2010; Koscik, O'Leary, Moser, Andreasen, & Nopoulos, 2009). Koscik and colleagues (2009) found that this morphologic difference was disadvantageous for women in terms of performance on the MRT. In contrast, males had proportionately greater parietal lobe surface area compared with females, and men who had this morphological pattern performed higher on the MRT. In summary, recent brain research suggests both functional and morphological differences between males and females are related to spatial processing.

Individual Differences Within and Between Genders: Transitory Effects on Spatial Skills

In this section, I address transitory effects on spatial skills. These have the potential to affect both individual differences within genders and between genders.

Activational effects of hormones. Hormones have been found to have activational effects on brain activity and on spatial functioning in many mammals. *Activational effects* are those that manifest in a transient fashion with changes in hormone levels. The extensive literature on this topic suggests that within females, spatial skills vary as a function of the menstrual cycle (Hausmann, Slabbekoorn, Van Goozen, Cohen-Kettenis, & Güntürkün, 2000; Kimura, 1999). For example, Hausmann et al. (2000) found a significant cycle difference in MRT performance, with high scores during the menstrual phase and low scores during the midluteal phase. Testosterone levels during the menstrual cycle had a strong and positive association with mental rotation performance, whereas estradiol had a negative one. Thus, testosterone and estradiol appear to be able to modulate spatial cognition during the menstrual cycle.

Some provocative findings have been obtained when examining the activating effects of hormones on spatial skills in both males and females through the direct administration of hormones to subgroups

of individuals. Some of this research was conducted through pre- and post-spatial assessments of male-to-female and female-to-male transsexuals. Researchers in Holland (Slabbekoorn, van Goozen, Megens, Gooren, & Cohen-Kettenis, 1999) found a pronounced effect of androgen treatment on spatial ability in female-to-male transsexuals over a period of 1.5 years. Untreated male-to-female transsexuals originally had higher scores on spatial tasks than untreated female-to-male transsexuals, as would be expected. However, after 3 months of cross-sex hormone treatment, the group difference had disappeared, whereas after about 10 months of hormone treatment, the sex difference was reversed (Slabbekoorn et al., 1999). Finally, one study examined the effects of direct administration of testosterone to normal female participants. Aleman, Bronk, Kessels, Koppeschaar, and van Honk (2004) found that a single administration of testosterone improved the females' MRT performance when compared with their pretest performance and with a control group given a placebo. In sum, the literature has documented the activating effects of hormones on spatial performance, especially when examining MRT.

Transitory effects of beliefs and emotions. When considering the transitory effects of beliefs and emotions on gender-based spatial skills, it is important to separate two questions that are often conflated in the literature. The first question is whether the transient effects of beliefs and emotions (usually manipulated empirically) can modify performance within females and males. In other words, is it possible to raise or lower spatial skills within a group of individuals through instructional manipulation of beliefs and emotions about spatial skills (e.g., stereotype threat or stereotype facilitation)? The second question is whether these instruction-induced changes in spatial skills are sufficient to eliminate the differences typically found between genders (favoring males) in spatial ability.

A recent set of studies has successfully documented researchers' ability to raise and lower spatial skills through specific instructions (Hausmann, Schoofs, Rosenthal, & Jordan, 2009; Moè, 2009; Wraga, Helt, Jacobs, & Sullivan, 2007). For example, Moè and Pazzaglia (2006) first tested participants' mental rotation skills and then repeated the test following three different sets of instructions to separate groups of participants: that males were better spatially, that females were better spatially, or that there was no difference between males and females spatially. Women who received instructions that females were more able, showed the greatest pre and post improvement in performance after instructions (showing a small effect size) and so did the men who were told that men were more able (showing a large effect size). In contrast, spatial performance showed the greatest decrement following instructions to those expecting to be less able (with the decrement in performance for females showing a moderate effect size and the decrement in males showing a large effect size). Other research has confirmed that when females are put in a stereotype threat instruction condition they tend to do worse than control groups on mental rotation and that stereotype facilitation and self-affirmation improve performance (Hausmann et al., 2009; Moè, 2009; Wraga et al., 2007). Thus, instructions appear to have a significant effect within genders.

However, in most of these studies, the researchers did not address the second question of whether instructions eliminate or vastly ameliorate gender differences in spatial ability. In the Moè and Pazzaglia (2006) study, although no direct statistical comparisons were made, the stereotype facilitation group for males scored an average of 15.67 on the MRT, whereas the stereotype facilitation group for females scored 11.63. In addition, Moè (2009) found that males and females did not differ when both groups were told that females did better on this test (the female facilitation group). However, although not directly tested, other average scores in this study suggest that males in the control and male stereotype facilitation groups may have outperformed the females in the female stereotype facilitation group. In sum, although females' and males' spatial skill levels can be effectively manipulated through instructions, further research is needed to determine whether this type of manipulation can eliminate the gender differences when compared with males' performance either in control conditions or in other conditions more optimal for males.

Some recent findings have suggested possible mechanisms for the transitory effect of hormone levels, beliefs, and emotions on level of spatial functioning. One possible mediating mechanism between stereotype beliefs and spatial skills is the type of strategy used to solve spatial problems. Moè, Meneghetti, and Cadinu (2009) studied individual differences within females, classifying their self-rated strategy use on the MRT and categorizing them as using either a holistic rotation strategy (e.g., I rotated the target stimulus to match the test stimulus) or an analytical strategy (e.g., I counted the cubes, or I rotated the stimulus piece by piece). The holistic group scored higher on the MRT than the analytical group. Furthermore, the tendency to use a holistic strategy mediated the relation between a woman's belief that it is possible to improve on masculine stereotyped tasks and level of performance on the MRT. Strategy research has shown that males are more likely to use a holistic strategy than females on MRT tasks (Jordan et al., 2002). These findings are consistent with the possibility that women who use a holistic strategy are in fact more capable of applying it, which in turn leads to their sense of self-confidence in being able to perform effectively on masculine stereotyped tasks.

Both the attitudinal research and the research on hormonal activation support a biopsychosocial view of gender differences in spatial skills. Through their transient effects on spatial skills, it appears that both social manipulation of attitudes and hormonal variations (through normal variations and direct administration) can affect the level of spatial functioning.

The Effects of Experience and Training on Increasing Spatial Skills in Females and Males

In previous sections, we have seen that, to some extent, performance on spatial tests represents a transitory ability that is influenced by internal and external circumstances. This suggests that spatial abilities might be trainable. As before, however, it is important to distinguish between two questions relating to the trainability of spatial ability. First, can spatial experience and training modify performance within females and males? Second, does spatial experience and training eliminate gender differences in spatial skills? A recent meta-analysis of over 217 studies has addressed both of these questions (Uttal, 2009). Uttal (2009) estimated the mean effect size difference between pre- and posttraining to be 0.60. Thus, training effects are substantial. It is notable, however, that pre–post changes in performance in groups without spatial training also showed an effect size of 0.45, indicating a significant improvement in performance as well. Thus, the repeated testing alone provided a moderate learning experience, though the effect size for the training group was significantly greater. These findings indicate that spatial abilities are somewhat malleable and can be substantially improved through interventions. In addition, Uttal documented that these training effects are relatively stable, remain effective over time, and are transferable to other related spatial skills. This meta-analysis also showed that training reduces the gender gap, but does not eliminate it.

Newcombe and her colleagues (Terlecki et al., 2008) asked whether long-term training efforts might lead to continued change in mental rotation skills and whether this pattern of change varied for males versus females. Participants were given 1 hour of training on a video game per day over a 12-week period. Males showed the greatest improvement at the beginning of training, whereas females showed the largest gains later in training (although the gender differences were not eliminated). These growth pattern differences between males and females have clear implications for the majority of training studies, which primarily have involved short-term training (Uttal, 2009). Thus, before we can conclude that it is not possible to eliminate gender differences with training, more studies are needed using extended training with a variety of different types of interventions.

Educational Implications

It may not be necessary to close the gender gap completely for training to be useful in reducing gender disparities, especially in STEM fields. Instead, what may be necessary is for both males and females to reach a certain level of competency at using their spatial reasoning when solving problems within a particular discipline. What is clear from the research is that boys and men have many more experiences with spatial information than girls and women, and these differences are present even before children come to school (Connor & Serbin, 1977). Such spatial experiences include: block play, action toys, video games, carpentry, car repair, technology, and so forth. As documented throughout this chapter, research now shows that over time, spatial skills are highly malleable. Our own research has shown that young girls especially benefit from early spatial interventions (Casey et al., 2008). Nevertheless, within educational settings from preschool through high school, spatial reasoning is rarely explicitly taught, putting girls at a particular disadvantage. On the basis of the present review, it is clear that to eliminate inequities in skill, spatial content should be systematically incorporated into our educational system at all levels.

THE BIOPSYCHOSOCIAL APPROACH AS A FRAMEWORK FOR UNDERSTANDING INDIVIDUAL DIFFERENCES

It is useful to consider these findings within a theoretical context in which genetic and environmental explanations are not considered as mutually exclusive alternatives for explaining individual differences in spatial ability. Furthermore, it is important to consider interactive models that are more complex. Such an interactive model may begin by considering the reciprocal effects that socialization, biology, and psychology have on the development of spatial cognition. For example, there are passive heredity–environment correlations that may arise when, for example, parents with certain genetic predispositions contribute to the spatial environment of their child. In addition, there are active heredity–environment correlations, in which, for example, children select their own spatial environment. In addition, individuals with different genetic predispositions react differently to the same spatial environmental input (Casey, 1996). Even within the neurobiology of the developing brain, heredity and internal environmental processes are inseparable (see Stiles, 2008, for a review of this perspective on developmental neurobiology).

As should be clear from this review, biological, social, psychological, and environmental factors interact at every level to affect individual differences in spatial skills. Emotional, hormonal, and methodological factors affect variations in spatial performance across individuals and between genders. There is evidence that cognitive structures and processes, such as working memory and strategy choices, influences spatial performance. Further, strategy choices have been found to connect to underlying neural activity and to spatial performance. Recently, investigators have begun to explore research designs that contribute to our understanding of the complex interrelationships between biology and environment. For example, it has been shown that broad socio–cultural factors such as poverty contribute to chronic stress, which in turn affects spatial processing in adulthood (Evans & Schamberg, 2009).

This biopsychosocial interactive approach has also been used to study gender differences. Using an environmental–biological interaction framework, Wraga et al. (2007) found that transient beliefs induced in social situations have a measurable effect on brain activity and on cognition. They presented instructions that elicited sex stereotypes in females and, through fMRI, assessed their participants' brain activity and mental rotation performance. Relatively poor MRT performance, found in females given negative female stereotypes, corresponded to increased activation in brain regions associated with increased emotional load. Higher MRT performance, found in females given positive female stereotypes, corresponded to increased activation in visual processing areas and complex working memory areas.

In conclusion, to understand individual differences in spatial skills more effectively, future research should continue to study biopsychosocial interactions relating to spatial skills. In reviewing the historical progression of this area of research, one is inevitably impressed with the qualitative change in the research that is conducted in the field of spatial skills; there is a recent shift toward addressing these complex questions in ways that are more creative. To continue to unravel the multifaceted interactions between biology, psychology, and society, additional methodologies and statistical approaches will be needed.

SUGGESTED REFERENCES FOR FURTHER READING

Johnson, W., & Bouchard, T. J. (2005). The structure of human intelligence: It is verbal, perceptual, and image rotation (VPR), not fluid and crystallized. *Intelligence, 33,* 393–416. doi:10.1016/j.intell.2004.12.002

A discussion of the role of mental rotation as a key component of general intelligence. The authors used psychometric techniques to show the importance of an image rotation factor as an aspect of general intelligence.

Vasilyeva, M., & Lourenco, S. F. (2010). Spatial development. In R. M. Lerner & W. F. Overton (Eds.), *The handbook of life-span development: Vol. 1. Cognition, biology, and methods across the life-span* (pp. 720–753). Hoboken, NJ: Wiley.

An overview of spatial development. The review of the literature is excellent because it provides a detailed analysis of research across the life span.

Voyer, D., Voyer, S., & Bryden, M. P. (1995). Magnitude of sex differences in spatial abilities: A meta-analysis and consideration of critical variables. *Psychological Bulletin, 117,* 250–270. doi:10.1037/0033-2909.117.2.250

A meta-analytic review of the literature on gender differences in spatial skills that documents gender differences in mental rotation and spatial perception but not spatial visualization.

Wai, J., Lubinski, D., & Benbow, C. P. (2009). Spatial ability for STEM domains: Aligning over 50 years of cumulative psychological knowledge solidifies its importance. *Journal of Educational Psychology, 101,* 817–835. doi:10.1037/a0016127

This longitudinal analysis of the impact of spatial skills on STEM career choices of individual with a wide range of abilities is a useful way of understanding the long-term influences of spatial skills in high school on later life choices.

Zacks, J. M. (2008). Neuroimaging studies of mental rotation: A meta-analysis and review. *Journal of Cognitive Neuroscience, 20,* 1–19. doi:10.1162/jocn.2008.20013

A meta-analysis of neuroimaging studies of mental rotation, identifying the areas of the brain that are activated during mental rotation.

References

Acredolo, L. P. (1981). Small- and large-scale spatial concepts in infancy and childhood. In L. S. Liben, A. H. Patterson, & N. Newcombe (Eds.), *Spatial representation and behavior across the life span* (pp. 63–81). New York, NY: Academic Press.

Aleman, A., Bronk, E., Kessels, R. P. C., Koppeschaar, H. P. F., & van Honk, J. (2004). A single administration of testosterone improves visuospatial ability in young women. *Psychoneuroendocrinology, 29,* 612–617. doi:10.1016/S0306-4530(03)00089-1

Alexander, G. M., & Evardone, M. (2008). Blocks and bodies: Sex differences in a novel version of the mental rotations test. *Hormones and Behavior, 53,* 177–184. doi:10.1016/j.yhbeh.2007.09.014

Allen, G. L., Kirasic, K. C., Dobson, S. H., Long, R. G., & Beck, S. (1996). Predicting environmental learning from spatial abilities: An indirect route. *Intelligence, 22,* 327–355. doi:10.1016/S0160-2896(96)90026-4

Baddeley, A. D. (1986). *Working memory.* Oxford, England: Clarendon Press.

Brown, L. N., Lahar, C. J., & Mosley, J. L. (1998). Age- and gender-related differences in strategy use for route information. *Environment and Behavior, 30,* 123–143.

Burnett, S. A., Lane, D. M., & Dratt, L. M. (1979). Spatial visualization and sex differences in quantitative ability. *Intelligence, 3,* 345–354.

Carroll, J. B. (1993). *Human cognitive abilities: A survey of factor-analytic studies.* Cambridge, England: Cambridge University Press. doi:10.1017/CBO9780511571312

Casey, M. B. (1996). Understanding individual differences in spatial ability within females: A nature/nurture interactionist framework. *Developmental Review, 16,* 241–260. doi:10.1006/drev.1996.0009

Casey, M. B., Erkut, S., Ceder, I., & Young, J. M. (2008). Use of a storytelling context to improve girls' and boys' geometry skills in kindergarten. *Journal of Applied Developmental Psychology, 29,* 29–48. doi:10.1016/j.appdev.2007.10.005

Cattell, R. B. (1963). Theory of fluid and crystallized intelligence: A critical experiment. *Journal of Educational Psychology, 54,* 1–22. doi:10.1037/h0046743

Connor, J. M., & Serbin, L. A. (1977). Behaviorally based masculine- and feminine-activity-preference scales for preschoolers: Correlations with other classroom behaviors and cognitive tests. *Child Development, 48,* 1411–1416. doi:10.2307/1128500

Deutsch, G., Bourbon, W. T., Papanicolaou, A. C., & Eisenberg, H. M. (1988). Visuospatial tasks compared via activation of regional cerebral blood flow. *Neuropsychologia, 26,* 445–452. doi:10.1016/0028-3932(88)90097-8

Ekstrom, R. B., French, J. W., & Harman, H. H. (1976). *Manual for kit of factor-referenced cognitive tests.* Princeton, NJ: Educational Testing Service.

Evans, G. W., & Schamberg, M. A. (2009). Childhood poverty, chronic stress, and adult working memory. *Proceedings of the National Academy of Sciences of the United States of America, 106,* 6545–6549. doi:10.1073/pnas.0811910106

Feingold, A. (1988). Cognitive gender differences are disappearing. *American Psychologist, 43,* 95–103. doi:10.1037/0003-066X.43.2.95

Galea, L. A. M., & Kimura, D. (1993). Sex differences in route learning. *Personality and Individual Differences, 14,* 53–65. doi:10.1016/0191-8869(93)90174-2

Gallagher, A. M., De Lisi, R., Holst, P. C., McGillicuddy-De Lisi, A. V., Morely, M., & Calahan, C. (2000). Gender differences in advanced mathematical problem solving. *Journal of Experimental Child Psychology, 75,* 165–190. doi:10.1006/jecp.1999.2532

Geary, D. C. (1996). Sexual selection and sex differences in mathematical abilities. *Behavioral and Brain Sciences, 19,* 229–284. doi:10.1017/S0140525X00042400

Geiser, C., Lehmann, W., & Eid, M. (2006). Separating "rotators" from "nonrotators" in the mental rotations test: A multigroup latent class analysis. *Multivariate Behavioral Research, 41,* 261–293. doi:10.1207/s15327906mbr4103_2

Goldstein, D., Haldane, D., & Mitchell, C. (1990). Sex differences in visual-spatial ability: The role of performance factors. *Memory & Cognition, 18,* 546–550. doi:10.3758/BF03198487

Guilford, J. P., & Lacey, J. I. (1947). *Printed classification tests: Army Air Forces Aviation Psychology Research Program Report No. 5.* Washington, DC: Government Printing Office.

Hahn, N., Jansen, P., & Heil, M. (2010). Preschoolers' mental rotation: Sex differences in hemispheric asymmetry. *Journal of Cognitive Neuroscience, 22,* 1244–1250. doi:10.1162/jocn.2009.21236

Hänggi, J., Büchmann, A., Mondadori, C. R. A., Henke, K., Jancke, L., & Hock, C. (2010). Sexual dimorphism in the parietal substrate associated with visuospatial cognition independent of general intelligence. *Journal of Cognitive Neuroscience, 22,* 139–155. doi:10.1162/jocn.2008.21175

Hausmann, M., Schoofs, D., Rosenthal, H. E. S., & Jordan, K. (2009). Interactive effects of sex hormones and gender stereotypes on cognitive sex differences—A psychobiosocial approach. *Psychoneuroendocrinology, 34,* 389–401. doi:10.1016/j.psyneuen.2008.09.019

Hausmann, M., Slabbekoorn, D., Van Goozen, S. H., Cohen-Kettenis, P. T., & Güntürkün, O. (2000). Sex hormones affect spatial abilities during the menstrual cycle. *Behavioral Neuroscience, 114,* 1245–1250. doi:10.1037/0735-7044.114.6.1245

Hegarty, M., & Waller, D. (2004). A dissociation between mental rotation and perspective-taking spatial abilities. *Intelligence, 32,* 175–191. doi:10.1016/j.intell.2003.12.001

Hegarty, M., & Waller, D. (2005). Individual differences in spatial abilities. In P. Shan & A. Miyake (Eds.), *The Cambridge handbook of visuospatial thinking*, (pp. 121–169). New York: NY: Cambridge University Press.

Hugdahl, K., Thomsen, T., & Ersland, L. (2006). Sex differences in visuo–spatial processing: An fMRI study of mental rotation. *Neuropsychologia, 44*, 1575–1583. doi:10.1016/j.neuropsychologia.2006.01.026

Hyde, J. S. (2005). The gender similarities hypothesis. *American Psychologist, 60*, 581–592. doi:10.1037/0003-066X.60.6.581

Johnson, E. S., & Meade, A. C. (1987). Developmental patterns of spatial ability: An early sex difference. *Child Development, 58*, 725–740. doi:10.2307/1130210

Johnson, W., & Bouchard, T. J. (2005). The structure of human intelligence: It is verbal, perceptual, and image rotation (VPR), not fluid and crystallized. *Intelligence, 33*, 393–416. doi:10.1016/j.intell.2004.12.002

Jordan, K., Wüstenberg, T., Heinze, H., Peters, M., & Jäncke, L. (2002). Women and men exhibit different cortical activation patterns during mental rotation tasks. *Neuropsychologia, 40*, 2397–2408. doi:10.1016/S0028-3932(02)00076-3

Just, M. A., & Carpenter, P. A. (1985). Cognitive coordinate systems: Accounts of mental rotation and individual differences in spatial ability. *Psychological Review, 92*, 137–172. doi:10.1037/0033-295X.92.2.137

Kaufman, S. B. (2007). Sex differences in mental rotation and spatial visualization ability: Can they be accounted for by differences in working memory capacity? *Intelligence, 35*, 211–223. doi:10.1016/j.intell.2006.07.009

Kimura, D. (1999). *Sex and cognition*. Cambridge, MA: MIT Press.

Klingberg, T., Forssberg, H., & Westerberg, H. (2002). Increased brain activity in frontal and parietal cortex underlies the development of visuospatial working memory capacity during childhood. *Journal of Cognitive Neuroscience, 14*, 1–10. doi:10.1162/089892902317205276

Koscik, T., O'Leary, D., Moser, D. J., Andreasen, N. C., & Nopoulos, P. (2009). Sex differences in parietal lobe morphology: Relationship to mental rotation performance. *Brain and Cognition, 69*, 451–459. doi:10.1016/j.bandc.2008.09.004

Kosslyn, S. M., Thompson, W. T., Gitelman, D. R., & Alpert, N. M. (1998). Neural systems that encode categorical versus coordinate spatial relations: PET investigations. *Psychobiology, 26*, 333–347.

Kozhevnikov, M., & Hegarty, M. (2001). A dissociation between object-manipulation spatial ability and spatial orientation ability. *Memory & Cognition, 29*, 745–756. doi:10.3758/BF03200477

Kozhevnikov, M., Motes, M. A., & Hegarty, M. (2007). Spatial visualization in physics problem solving. *Cognitive Science, 31*, 549–579. doi:10.1080/15326900701399897

Kyllonen, P. C., Lohman, D. F., & Snow, R. E. (1984). Effects of aptitudes, strategy training and task facets on spatial task performance. *Journal of Educational Psychology, 76*, 130–145. doi:10.1037/0022-0663.76.1.130

Kyllonen, P. C., Lohman, D. F., & Woltz, D. J. (1984). Componential modeling of alternative strategies for performing spatial tasks. *Journal of Educational Psychology, 76*, 1325–1345. doi:10.1037/0022-0663.76.6.1325

Levine, S. C., Huttenlocher, J., Taylor, A., & Langrock, A. (1999). Early sex differences in spatial skills. *Developmental Psychology, 35*, 940–949. doi:10.1037/0012-1649.35.4.940

Linn, M. C., & Petersen, A. C. (1985). Emergence and characterization of gender differences in spatial abilities: A meta-analysis. *Child Development, 56*, 1479–1498. doi:10.2307/1130467

Lippa, R. A., Collaer, M. L., & Peters, M. (2010). Sex differences in mental rotation and line angle judgments are positively associated with gender equality and economic development across 53 nations. *Archives of Sexual Behavior, 39*, 990–997. doi:10.1007/s10508-008-9460-8

Lohman, D. F. (1979). *Spatial ability: A review and reanalysis of the correlational literature* (Technical Report No. 8). Retrieved from http://faculty.education.uiowa.edu/dlohman/

Lohman, D. F. (1996). Spatial ability and g. In I. Dennis & P. Tapsfield (Eds.), *Human abilities: Their nature and assessment* (pp. 97–116). Hillsdale, NJ: Erlbaum.

Lubinski, D., & Benbow, C. P. (2006). Study of mathematically precocious youth after 35 years: Uncovering antecedents for the development of math–science expertise. *Perspectives on Psychological Science, 1*, 316–345. doi:10.1111/j.1745-6916.2006.00019.x

McGee, M. G. (1979). Human spatial abilities: Psychometric studies and environmental, genetic, hormonal, and neurological influences. *Psychological Bulletin, 86*, 889–918. doi:10.1037/0033-2909.86.5.889

Miyake, A., Friedman, N. P., Rettinger, D. A., Shah, P., & Hegarty, M. (2001). How are visuospatial working memory, executive functioning, and spatial abilities related? A latent-variable analysis. *Journal of Experimental Psychology: General, 130*, 621–640. doi:10.1037/0096-3445.130.4.621

Moè, A. (2009). Are males always better than females in mental rotation? Exploring a gender belief explanation. *Learning and Individual Differences, 19,* 21–27. doi:10.1016/j.lindif.2008.02.002

Moè, A., Meneghetti, C., & Cadinu, M. (2009). Women and mental rotation: Incremental theory and spatial strategy use enhance performance. *Personality and Individual Differences, 46,* 187–191. doi:10.1016/j.paid.2008.09.030

Moè, A., & Pazzaglia, F. (2006). Following the instructions! Effects of gender beliefs in mental rotation. *Learning and Individual Differences, 16,* 369–377.

Moore, D. S., & Johnson, S. P. (2008). Mental rotation in human infants: A sex difference. *Psychological Science, 19,* 1063–1066. doi:10.1111/j.1467-9280.2008.02200.x

National Science Foundation, National Science Board (2010). *Preparing the next generation of STEM innovators: Identifying and developing our nation's human capital* (Report No. NSB-10-33). Retrieved from http://www.nsf.gov/nsb/stem/innovators.jsp

Nuttall, R., Casey, M. B., & Pezaris, E. (2005). Spatial ability as a mediator of gender differences on mathematics tests: A biological–environmental framework. In A. M. Gallagher & J. C. Kaufman (Eds.), *Gender differences in mathematics* (pp. 121–142). New York, NY: Guilford Press.

Ozer, D. J. (1987). Personality, intelligence, and spatial visualization: Correlates of mental rotations test performance. *Journal of Personality and Social Psychology, 53,* 129–134. doi:10.1037/0022-3514.53.1.129

Peters, M., Cloud, B., & Laeng, B. (1995). Spatial ability, student gender, and academic performance. *Journal of Engineering Education, 84,* 69–73.

Peters, M., Laeng, B., Latham, K., Jackson, M., Zaiyona, R., & Richardson, C. (1995). A redrawn Vandenberg and Kuse mental rotations test: Different versions and factors that affect performance. *Brain and Cognition, 28,* 39–58. doi:10.1006/brcg.1995.1032

Pezaris, E., & Casey, M. B. (1991). Girls who use "masculine" problem-solving strategies on spatial tasks: Proposed genetics and environmental factors. *Brain and Cognition, 17,* 1–22. doi:10.1016/0278-2626(91)90062-D

Piaget, J., & Inhelder, B. (1956). *The child's conception of space.* London, England: Routledge & Kegan Paul.

Quaiser-Pohl, C., Lehmann, W., & Eid, M. (2004). The relationship between spatial abilities and representations of large-scale space in children—A structural equation modeling analysis. *Personality and Individual Differences, 36,* 95–107. doi:10.1016/S0191-8869(03)00071-0

Quinn, P. C., & Liben, L. S. (2008). A sex difference in mental rotation in young infants. *Psychological Science, 19,* 1067–1070. doi:10.1111/j.1467-9280.2008.02201.x

Sanders, L. (2009). Trawling the brain: New findings raise questions about reliability of fMRI as gauge of neural activity. *Science News, 176,* 16–20. doi:10.1002/scin.5591761320

Shah, P., & Miyake, A. (1996). The separability of working memory resources for spatial thinking and language processing: An individual differences approach. *Journal of Experimental Psychology: General, 125,* 4–27. doi:10.1037/0096-3445.125.1.4

Shelton, A. L., & Gabrieli, J. D. E. (2004). Neural correlates of individual differences in spatial learning strategies. *Neuropsychology, 18,* 442–449. doi:10.1037/0894-4105.18.3.442

Shepard, R. N., & Metzler, J. (1971, February 19). Mental rotation of three-dimensional objects. *Science, 171,* 701–703. doi:10.1126/science.171.3972.701

Silverman, I., & Eals, M. (1992). Sex differences in spatial abilities: Evolutionary theory and data. In J. Barkow, I. Cosmides, & J. Tooby (Eds.), *The adapted mind: Evolutionary psychology and the generation of culture* (pp. 533–549). New York, NY: Oxford University Press.

Slabbekoorn, D., van Goozen, S. H. M., Megens, J., Gooren, L. J. G., & Cohen-Kettenis, P. T. (1999). Activating effects of cross-sex hormones on cognitive functioning: A study of short-term and long-term hormone effects in transsexuals. *Psychoneuroendocrinology, 24,* 423–447. doi:10.1016/S0306-4530(98)00091-2

Stiles, J. (2008). *The fundamentals of brain development: Integrating nature and nurture.* Cambridge, MA: Harvard University Press.

Terlecki, M. S., Newcombe, N. S., & Little, M. (2008). Durable and generalized effects of spatial experience on mental rotation: Gender differences in growth patterns. *Applied Cognitive Psychology, 22,* 996–1013. doi:10.1002/acp.1420

Thurstone, T. G. (1958). *Manual for the SRA primary mental abilities.* Chicago, IL: Science Research Associates.

Uttal, D. H. (2009, April). *Training spatial skills: What works, for whom, and for how long?* Paper presented at the meeting of the Society for Research in Child Development, Denver, CO.

Vandenberg, S. G., & Kuse, A. R. (1978). Mental rotation, a group test of three-dimensional spatial visualization. *Perceptual and Motor Skills, 47,* 599–604. doi:10.2466/pms.1978.47.2.599

Beth M. Casey

Vasilyeva, M., & Bowers, E. (2006). Children's use of geometric information in mapping tasks. *Journal of Experimental Child Psychology, 95,* 255–277. doi:10.1016/j.jecp.2006.05.001

Vasilyeva, M., & Lourenco, S. F. (2010). Spatial development. In R. M. Lerner & W. F. Overton (Eds.), *The handbook of life-span development: Vol. 1. Cognition, biology, and methods across the life-span* (pp. 720–753). Hoboken, NJ: Wiley.

Voyer, D. (2010, May). *The impact of procedural factors on evidence for gender differences in spatial tasks.* Paper presented at the Spatial Intelligence and Learning Center Spatial Learning Conference, Cambridge, MA.

Voyer, D., & Hou, J. (2006). Types of items and the magnitude of gender differences on the mental rotations test. *Canadian Journal of Experimental Psychology/ Revue canadienne de psychologie expérimentale, 60,* 91–100. doi:10.1037/cjep2006010

Voyer, D., Postma, A., Brake, B., & Imperato-McGinley, J. (2007). Gender differences in object memory location: A meta-analysis. *Psychonomic Bulletin & Review, 14,* 23–38. doi:10.3758/BF03194024

Voyer, D., Voyer, S., & Bryden, M. P. (1995). Magnitude of sex differences in spatial abilities: A meta-analysis and consideration of critical variables. *Psychological Bulletin, 117,* 250–270. doi:10.1037/0033-2909. 117.2.250

Wai, J., Lubinski, D., & Benbow, C. P. (2009). Spatial ability for STEM domains: Aligning over 50 years of cumulative psychological knowledge solidifies its importance. *Journal of Educational Psychology, 101,* 817–835. doi:10.1037/a0016127

Ward, S. L., Newcombe, N., & Overton, W. F. (1986). Turn left at the church or three miles north: A study of direction giving and sex differences. *Environment and Behavior, 18,* 192–213. doi:10.1177/0013916586182003

Wechsler, D. (2003). *Technical and interpretive manual of the Wechsler Intelligence Scale for Children-IV.* New York, NY: Psychological Corporation.

Wendt, P. E., & Risberg, J. (1994). Cortical activation during visual-spatial processing: Relation between hemispheric asymmetry of blood flow and performance. *Brain and Cognition, 24,* 87–103. doi:10.1006/ brcg.1994.1005

Witkin, H. A., & Asch, S. E. (1948). Studies in space orientation. IV. Further experiments on perception of the upright with displaced visual fields. *Journal of Experimental Psychology, 38,* 762–782. doi:10.1037/ h0053671

Wraga, M., Helt, M., Jacobs, E., & Sullivan, K. (2007). Neural basis of stereotype-induced shifts in women's mental rotation performance. *Social Cognitive and Affective Neuroscience, 2,* 12–19. doi:10.1093/scan/ nsl041

Zacks, J. M. (2008). Neuroimaging studies of mental rotation: A meta-analysis and review. *Journal of Cognitive Neuroscience, 20,* 1–19. doi:10.1162/ jocn.2008.20013

Zacks, J. M., Vettel, J. M., & Michelon, P. (2003). Imagined viewer and object rotations dissociated with event-related fMRI. *Journal of Cognitive Neuroscience, 15,* 1002–1018. doi:10.1162/089892903770007399

Part III

OFFLINE SYSTEMS: ENCODING, STORAGE, AND RETRIEVAL OF SPATIAL INFORMATION

CHAPTER 7

SPATIAL MEMORY: PLACE LEARNING, PILOTING, AND ROUTE KNOWLEDGE

Ken Cheng and Paul Graham

Most of the natural world is dotted with sizeable objects that are stable over a substantial portion of animals' lives. Exceptions are bare deserts and open seas. Many terrestrial animals can use these stable objects—*landmarks*—for navigation. Landmarks are used in diverse ways: to define a place, to chart a direction to a goal (piloting), or to form and execute stereotypical routes. In this chapter, we approach these phenomena taxonomically, focusing on bees and ants among invertebrate animals and rats and pigeons among vertebrate animals, although a number of other species are mentioned. For the most part, we leave out humans, in part because humans are so well represented in other chapters in this volume.

INVERTEBRATES' USE OF LANDMARKS

The largest repertoire of navigational research on invertebrates concerns insects, primarily ants and bees. Like larger brained, longer lived animals, individual insects also take advantage of landmarks to aid navigation back to important locations. Intrigue regarding the mechanisms of insect navigation is ancient, but the scientific study of insect navigation has prospered since the pioneering work of Nobel Laureates Niko Tinbergen (Tinbergen, 1951) and Karl von Frisch (von Frisch, 1967). Tinbergen (1951) famously demonstrated the importance of visual landmarks for ground nesting digger wasps as they tried to locate their inconspicuous nest entrances. He placed rings of pinecones around individual wasps' nest entrances. On returning from foraging journeys, wasps would search for their nest at the center of a ring of pinecones even when the ring had been displaced by Tinbergen. He showed that insects learned something about the landmarks surrounding an important location, a finding that set the stage for decades of experimentation using landmark displacements and manipulations, which are still used in modern studies of insect navigation.

Using Landmarks to Define a Place

For small insects that may be easily perturbed by air currents or ground undulations, visual input provides accurate feedback about any unintended movements. Hoverflies (T. S. Collett & Land, 1975) and *Tetragonisca* guard bees (Kelber & Zeil, 1997) use vision to maintain a stable position in space. Similarly, Junger (1991) showed in a beautiful experiment how water striders maintain a desirable position on a flowing stream by keeping the retinotopic view of the world fixed. Individual water striders were allowed to establish a station on an artificial stream that had a single elevated lamp as a landmark. The water striders tried to keep the elevation of the lamp constant. If the lamp was lowered, the water striders increased their rowing frequency to compensate for the perceived slip downstream. Likewise, if the lamp was elevated, water striders allowed their rowing frequency to decrease and let

DOI: 10.1037/13936-008
Handbook of Spatial Cognition, D. Waller and L. Nadel (Editors)

themselves slip downstream to restore the lamp's elevation to its original value.

Memory of a visual scene can also be used to return to a fixed location in three-dimensional space after a prolonged excursion. For instance, male hoverflies often leave their station to chase potential mates. After each chase, however, they return to their original hover location. In their seminal work, T. S. Collett and Land (1975) showed that a fly's return to its original hover location was driven by the memory of the visual scene as seen from the original hover point. Remembering how the world appeared from a target place is a neat way of confirming that one has reached that location. More important, one can use the discrepancy between one's current view of the world and the view stored at the goal to drive the search for that goal. This use of a remembered view of the world to guide the search for a goal has come to be known as *snapshot matching,* following the work of Cartwright and Collett (1982, 1983, 1987).

The Snapshot Model

Cartwright and Collett (1983) trained honeybees to find a sucrose feeder at a point defined by a triangular landmark array. To ensure that the bees learned the landmarks, the array of landmarks and feeder was shifted in the experimental room from trial to trial. On tests with the feeder removed, trained bees searched accurately at the fictive feeder position defined by the array. After the bees had learned the task, the array was transformed to probe how landmarks were encoded and used. When the array was expanded, bees searched at a location that provided the best match to the directions of landmarks as seen from the goal.

Similarly, walking ants searching for their nest entrance or a feeder guide their search by stored views of the world as seen previously from the goal (e.g., Durier, Graham, & Collett, 2003; Narendra, Si, Sulikowski, & Cheng, 2007; Wehner & Räber, 1979). Color Plate 12 shows a typical experimental demonstration of how a stored view guides an ant's search. Wehner, Michel, and Antonsen (1996) placed a trio of landmarks around the nest entrance of a *Cataglyphis fortis* colony. When the ants were displaced to a similar landmark array on a distant

test ground they searched accurately at the fictive nest position. In contrast to bees, if the array was expanded by a factor of two, the search distribution became scattered. The sharp search peak at the center returned if the landmarks in the expanded array were doubled in size. Although distances to landmarks did not match, in this array the retinotopic view at the center matched the view from the goal location of the training array. Similar results were found in the Australian desert ant *Melophorus bagoti* (Narendra et al., 2007; for a review, see Cheng, Narendra, Sommer, & Wehner, 2009). The term *snapshot* now refers to any behavioral model that describes an organism's 2-D memory of visual landmarks and scenes. We next look at the details of what components constitute an insect's snapshot.

What is in a snapshot?   Insects have very different visual systems from vertebrates (Land & Nilsson, 2002), and it is important for us to imagine what the world looks like to an insect. Three primary factors make an insect's eye view of the world different from the way we see the world: (a) the palette of visual features available to an insect is different, (b) insects have much lower visual resolution than we do, and (c) most insects have a nearly 360° panoramic field of view. With respect to the available features, we know from extensive pattern recognition experiments with honeybees and *Drosophila* flies that insects encode scenes using apparent size (Cartwright & Collett, 1983; Ernst & Heisenberg, 1999), edge orientation (Srinivasan, Zhang, & Witney, 1994), color (Hempel de Ibarra, Giurfa, & Vorobyev, 2002; Lehrer, 1999; Tang, Wolf, Xu, & Heisenberg, 2004), and vertical center of gravity (Ernst & Heisenberg, 1999). When we consider this limited palette of available features and the low resolution, we can make sense of the cues that insects seem to use as landmarks in the natural world. Because efficient navigation requires information that can be used over a reasonable distance, this is likely to come from large environmental features. Classic and modern studies have demonstrated navigational control by such large features (e.g., mountains: Menzel, Geiger, Jeorges, Müller, & Chittka, 1998; Southwick & Buchmann, 1995; forest edges: von Frisch & Lindauer, 1954). A long-held idea has been that these large objects may gain their salience by contrasting against the sky and being part of the skyline (Fourcassié, 1991; Fukushi, 2001; Towne & Moscrip, 2008; van Iersal & van den Assem, 1964; Wehner et al., 1996; Wehner & Räber, 1979). Recent evidence from ants has demonstrated that skylines can be sufficient for charting a direction of travel. P. Graham and Cheng (2009a) used an artificial arena to generate a skyline profile that mimicked the skyline profile of a natural panoramic scene. The crude skyline was enough for the ants to chart an initial direction of travel even though color cues, the distance distribution of objects, and orientation relative to a celestial compass were all radically different from the ants' familiar foraging locations (Color Plate 12b).

Having an extensive field of view (Point c) seems to be useful for snapshot matching, and consequently, studies show that snapshots incorporate a large part of a visual scene. The studies described previously (Cartwright & Collett, 1983; Wehner et al., 1996; Color Plate 12) indirectly suggested that snapshots are extensive. A more explicit test of the range of a single snapshot, however, comes from experiments with wood ants (Durier et al., 2003). Wood ants were trained to search for food in the center of an equilateral array of three cylinders, and in control tests with no feeder, the search peak was focused on the fictive feeder position. Then, in probe tests, the triangular array was distorted so as to give two possible matching solutions, in which either the apparent sizes of the cylinders matched those in the snapshot or the angles between landmarks were correct. If ants used restricted snapshots of each cylinder, they would search where the apparent size of each cylinder is correct. In fact, the ants showed a broader search pattern, suggesting that they had learned both apparent sizes of the cylinders and the angles between them. The snapshot in this case must have extended at least 120° from the midline.

As well as being extensive, snapshots are also inclusive, including both the distant panorama and landmarks close to a route or a place. Close landmarks can be used to pinpoint a location precisely because the landmarks' appearance on the retina changes appreciably with movement. Thus, with an array of experimentally provided landmarks defining a feeder position, honeybees rely more heav-

ily on landmarks that are closer than more distant (Cheng, Collett, Pickhard, & Wehner, 1987). The more distant panorama, however, is more stable in appearance, providing useful contextual information. Laboratory experiments controlling distant cues show their usefulness. P. Graham, Durier, and Collett (2004) trained a group of wood ants within a white curtained arena to find food midway between a small and a large cylinder, so that the two landmarks subtended different retinal angles at the goal. They were then tested with the small and large cylinders replaced by two cylinders of the same intermediate size. This test array allows ants to make a perfect retinotopic match with the snapshot of the world from the feeder location in training. The ants, however, searched midway between the cylinders, rather than in the predicted position closer to the cylinder that replaced the large training cylinder. They behaved as if they were unable to identify which of the two cylinders was a replacement for the large cylinder and which for the small. A second group of ants was trained with one wall of the white arena covered with large black shapes. The randomly patterned curtain could not be used to pinpoint the feeder because the array of feeder plus landmarks was moved relative to the pattern throughout training. When tested with the intermediate cylinders, however, these ants searched correctly at the point where the sizes of landmarks matched those found at the feeder location during training. The ants' snapshots thus seem to bind together features of the patterned curtain and the cylinder, with the contextual information provided by the patterned wall serving to disambiguate the landmarks. For example, when an ant close to the goal is facing one cylinder, the contextual pattern falls mostly on one eye and not the other. When facing the other cylinder, the patterned wall would fall mostly on the other eye.

Experiments outdoors with natural panoramas provide more evidence for the functional role of contextual information provided by the panorama. Strong panoramic cues can make up for weak local cues in landmark-based search. Thus, honeybees navigate by a landmark set in its usual context, even if the appearance of the landmark is significantly changed (T. S. Collett & Kelber, 1988). Conversely, wood ants may ignore a familiar landmark seen in the wrong context (P. Graham, Fauria, & Collett, 2003). Honeybees required to search at two different locations with respect to two different landmarks in the same context encounter response competition between the two tasks, whereas response competition can be avoided if those tasks are undertaken in different panoramic contexts (Cheng, 2005).

How is a snapshot used? Snapshot matching is a matter of iteratively reducing the discrepancy between one's current view of the world and one's stored snapshot. This can be thought of as a two-step process: (a) align the current view of the world with that of the stored snapshot and (b) move to make current image more similar to the snapshot. For flying insects, the ability to translate in all directions without changing their body orientation simplifies the job of snapshot alignment. Experiments with wasps and bees (e.g., T. S. Collett, 1995; for a review, see Cheng, 2000) have shown how individuals adopt a preferred body orientation both when departing and when returning to their nest. Maintaining a preferred orientation reduces the size of the search space greatly because when close to the goal, landmarks will already be close to the positions they occupy in the goal snapshot stored when facing in the same preferred direction. In other words, this strategy eliminates the need to mentally rotate images in search of the best orientation. Bees can control their body orientation with the aid of a celestial or magnetic compass (Frier, Edwards, Smith, Neale, & Collett, 1996; Lindauer, 1960), or they may use aspects of the landmark configuration, such as flying parallel to a wall (Cheng, 1999).

Compass cues are also available to ants, but they can only walk in the direction of their longitudinal body axis, making the alignment of a current view with a stored snapshot more difficult. Åkesson and Wehner (2002) showed how ants can use compass information and approach direction when locating a goal within an ambiguous array of landmarks. Ants were trained to return directly from a food site to their nest, which was located close to one cylinder (SE cylinder) within a square array of four similar cylinders. Foragers were then tested with the array placed on unfamiliar terrain. When ants approached

the array from their usual compass direction, they searched principally in the correct position. Approaches from an unusual direction, however, resulted in search distributions with two peaks. One peak was in the correct position relative to the ant's sky compass (near the SE cylinder), and the other was correct relative to the approach direction. Both compass cues and approach direction can help resolve the ambiguity inherent in the array. This study did not report the fine-grained behaviors used to align current and stored views during snapshot use. One mechanism used by wood ants indoors is to face conspicuous landmarks, both when acquiring and using snapshots (Durier et al., 2003; Nicholson, Judd, Cartwright, & Collett, 1999). Central Australian desert ants have been observed to walk the expected distance from one landmark toward another in searching for their nest (Narendra et al., 2007). This process deserves far more study.

Once images are aligned, the insect needs to move to reduce the mismatch. It could do this in two ways. First, if it can identify features or landmarks that are common to both the current view and the stored snapshot, then it can calculate the movement direction that will bring the views into agreement. This would require the insect to recognize visual features at retinal locations away from their location in the stored snapshot. This kind of position invariant feature recognition is computationally nontrivial, although some evidence suggests that insects are capable of this (*Drosophila*: Tang et al., 2004; cockroaches: Kwon, Lent, & Strausfeld, 2004; wood ants: Lent, Graham, & Collett, 2010). A second possible mechanism is that insects could perform gradient descent on an error score measuring the discrepancy between the current view and the stored snapshot. This possibility is computationally more parsimonious and has consequently been popular in the robotics community (Mangan & Webb, 2009; Zampoglou, Szenher, & Webb, 2006; Zeil, Hofmann, & Chahl, 2003). For example, one algorithm is to keep going in the same direction if the error score is reducing but change direction if the error increases. Such a strategy uses behavior to substitute for the neural hardware and software required for solving difficult perceptual problems. A parallel is found in the behavior of saccades used to direct a limited high-resolution fovea, visual or tactile, onto relevant stimuli (Catania & Remple, 2004).

Using Landmarks Over Large Scales

Landmarks are used to guide routes and perhaps, in honeybees, to guide maplike behaviors. The idea of map-based navigation in honeybees, however, remains contentious.

Routes. We have seen how landmarks can be used to guide a return to a discrete location. World knowledge, however, is not limited just to important locations. Many insect species learn and remain faithful to habitual routes (Kohler & Wehner, 2005; Rosengren & Fortelius, 1986; Santschi, 1913), primarily for foraging. Therefore, some of their spatial knowledge is expressed in the information required to guide those routes, which can be extraordinarily long. Orchid bees, for example, have been reported to use routes of over 10 km to visit sparsely distributed orchids in a fixed order (Janzen, 1971).

The precision required to guide a route is less than that required to get to a single important location, because to successfully follow a route, one does not need to visit a sequence of precise goals in a rigid order. The animal only has to produce a sensible direction for a particular point on the route and make sure that they stay within a route corridor. We thus see landmarks used differently for route guidance than for snapshot matching. For example, T. S. Collett, Dillmann, Giger, and Wehner (1992) allowed desert ants to develop routes with one landmark (a triangular shape) placed to the left of the direct homeward path and a second landmark (a cylinder) to the right. Once familiar with this arrangement, ants were taken to a test field and placed in front of one of the landmarks. They detoured around the test landmark so as to place it on the same side of the retina as they would have experienced in the training. They did not, however, match the retinal size of the landmark in the way that would be expected if they were using a snapshot to control their path. Other heuristic uses of landmarks that keep insects safely within a familiar route include associating compass headings with visually recognized places (M. Collett, Collett, Bisch, & Wehner,

1998), beacon aiming (Chittka, Kunze, Shipman, & Buchmann, 1995; P. Graham et al., 2003), and visual centering (Heusser & Wehner, 2002).

Maplike behavior. An important and commonly addressed question is whether views and landmarks inform insects about where they are in the world, in addition to what they should do. That is, can insects organize their large set of spatial memories into a single representation of the world, a so-called cognitive map? In ants, numerous attempts have failed to demonstrate that navigational information is combined in any way that might be described as a cognitive map (Andel & Wehner, 2004; M. Collett, Collett, Chameron, & Wehner, 2003; Knaden & Wehner, 2006). In fact, insect spatial memories seem to be largely insulated from each other. An elegant experiment by Wehner, Boyer, Loertscher, Sommer, and Menzi (2006) showed how the information for guiding outbound and inbound routes is independent. Using barriers, Australian desert ants (*M. bagoti*) were forced to spatially separate outbound and inbound routes so that the ants took a looped route from nest to feeder and back. On key tests, experienced ants on their inbound journey were captured from the feeder along the inbound route or near the nest and then displaced to a point on their habitual outbound route. Despite this being a familiar location, the ants behaved as if they were lost and only managed to return home if their systematic search led them by chance to discover their familiar inbound route.

A long controversy surrounds the notion of cognitive mapping in honeybees (Dyer, 1991; Gould, 1986; Menzel et al., 2005; Wehner & Menzel, 1990). Evidence comes from displacement experiments in which honeybees on their way to a goal (feeder or hive) were displaced. Gould (1986) first reported that the bees headed to the goal they were en route to, but this pattern of results has failed to be replicated, with several studies indicating that the bees flew in the compass direction they were originally flying in, exhibiting route-based behavior rather than maplike behavior (Dyer, 1991; Wehner & Menzel, 1990). Menzel et al. (2005) tracked honeybees in displacement experiments using harmonic radar and found that displaced bees indeed first flew off the route (compass direction) they were executing. After the route behavior, however, many bees then headed to a goal, either the feeder or the hive. This was interpreted as map-based behavior but can also be explained as route vectors associated with views (Cheng, 2006).

Summary.   It is fair to conclude from the literature that, for the most part, views and landmarks simply inform insects on what to do and not where they are in the world (Cheng, 2006; T. S. Collett & Collett, 2002; Wehner, 2003, 2009). Landmark information is associated with instructions that piece routes together, in the fashion of visual signposts (T. S. Collett & Collett, 2002) or visually based servomechanisms (Cheng, 2006).

VERTEBRATES' USE OF LANDMARKS

The bulk of research advancing our understanding of landmark use in vertebrates has featured domestic rats and domestic pigeons. However, a number of other species, including wild or wild-caught animals, have also been examined. Far more research has been devoted to how animals pinpoint a goal than to route navigation, the topic with which we begin this section.

Routes

Routes are much studied in insect models but little studied in vertebrate animals. Perhaps the larger sizes of vertebrate animals and their correspondingly larger distances of movements make the study of routes difficult. One classic study on wild rats documented the development of routes in a new territory. Calhoun's (1963) book was more famous for documenting social interactions in wild rats confined to a sizeable (approximately 1,000 m²) but delimited plot (Ramsden & Adams, 2009). However, he also documented thoroughly the historical development of trails over the nearly 2 years that the rats spent in the enclosure. An elaborate system of trails flourished, and the rats reportedly followed the trails much of the time. In one remarkable observation, the rats even tunneled under approximately 25 cm of snow over frozen ground, retracing some of the trails between

their homes and the food boxes in the middle of the enclosure (Figure 7.1). This original study on trail blazing has not been followed up systematically to our knowledge. In recent times, a video has been made of lab rats let loose in a field (Berdoy & Stewart, 2002). These lab rats established trails as well, but details are not provided.

The advent of global positioning devices has led to studies detailing the paths that homing pigeons take over the natural landscape. The pigeons often use landmarks to guide their often stereotypical and idiosyncratic routes home, following well marked routes such as roads (Biro, Meade, & Guilford, 2004; Lipp et al., 2004). Such stereotypical routes may add significant travel distance but presumably lessen the cognitive processing required for navigation. The stereotypy is reminiscent of insect navigation, such as the routes of the Australian desert ant *M. bagoti* (Kohler & Wehner, 2005). It is unclear how the landmarks on the route guide navigation, and manipulation of large-scale geographic features is of course difficult.

Landmark Use in Rodents

The confined space of a laboratory does not allow routes of any substantial distance, but lab studies have demonstrated amply the use of landmarks by domesticated rats. Convincing evidence had already emerged from Edward Tolman's laboratory in the first half of the 20th century. In one example from Tolman's lab, Ritchie (1947) trained rats to go to one of the arms of a T maze in the center of a rectangular room. The stem was flipped from side to side, so that the starting point varied. Ritchie found that a sizeable cage rack played a large role in defining places. Moving it from one corner of the room to the diagonally opposite corner induced the majority of rats (24/32) to go to the opposite arm, the unrewarded arm during training.

Later in the 20th century, and up to the present, the radial maze developed by Olton and Samuelson (1976) and the swimming pool developed by Morris (1981) were much used to study landmark use in rats, with variants extending to other lab animals as well. The radial maze consists of a central platform with multiple—typically eight—arms radiating from it. Food is placed at the ends of each arm, and the

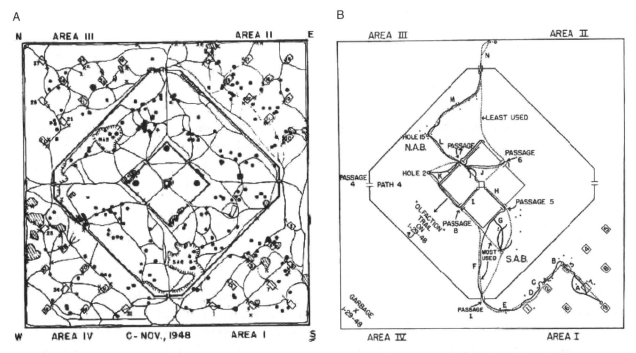

FIGURE 7.1.   Route following behavior in wild rats. (a) Wild rats were left alone in an enclosed outdoor space (approximately 30 m square) to live and breed. Nest boxes were provided in the enclosure, and food was available in food boxes in the middle. The figure shows the network of crisscrossing routes blazed and used by the rats in their first year in the enclosure. (b) Following routes under approximately 25 cm of snow. Snow had fallen earlier in the first winter and froze on the ground. On the night before these observations, approximately 25 cm of snow had fallen. Some rats, however, managed to get to the food boxes in the center. They did so by attempting to chart routes under the snow. Dotted lines show normal routes used by the rats. Solid lines show routes under snow. From *The Ecology and Sociology of the Norway Rat* ([a] p. 17, [b] p. 76) by J. B. Calhoun, 1963, Bethesda, MD: U.S. Department of Health, Education, and Welfare, Public Health Service. In the public domain.

rat is typically in the central platform to start a trial. Rats learn quickly to visit the arms without repeat visits, maximizing foraging efficiency. Manipulations of cues give evidence that rats rely primarily on spatial memory instead of following a completely stereotypical order, such as always choosing the next arm to the right or left, or choosing at random (Brown, 1992; Olton & Samuelson, 1976; Roberts, 1984). Brown also found that the rats typically survey a prospective arm before choosing or rejecting it, making "microchoices" that have little relation to whether the arm had been visited. Nonetheless, their final or "macrochoices" are far from random and are correct at a high rate. Systematic rotation of landmarks showed the control of landmarks on radial-maze performance (Suzuki, Augerinos, & Black, 1980). For example, when an array of landmarks hung on curtains around the maze was rotated 180° in the middle of a trial, the rats subsequently behaved as if the world had rotated. They went

to the arms they had not visited according to the rotated array of landmarks.

The swimming pool apparatus, variously called the Morris pool, water maze, or Morris maze (although nothing is mazelike about an expanse of open water in a pool), is typically filled with water that is rendered opaque, with a hidden platform for the rats to find to escape the water (to which they are averse). As such, no local or "beacon" cues at the target location are available. With the animals typically placed in different start locations, they are forced to use landmarks in or around the pool. Indeed, manipulations show that rats rely on landmarks for finding the platform. For example, some studies feature a circular pool surrounded by a circular enclosure of tall curtains (Chamizo, Mantiega, Rodrigo, & Mackintosh, 2006; Rodrigo, Chamizo, McLaren, & Mackintosh, 1997). Landmarks hung on the curtain could then be rotated from trial to trial, requiring the rats to localize the platform with respect to the experimental landmarks.

What is it about landmarks that rats use for localization? Classic cognitivist thinking is that rats (in contrast to insects) encode the configuration of landmarks in a maplike fashion, including the metric relations between them (O'Keefe & Nadel, 1978; Tolman, 1948). The term *cognitive map* appeared in the title of both these cited works. Evidence suggests that for rodents, places are not defined by isolated objects at or around the site but rather by some larger array of surrounding landmarks. For example, with chipmunks and golden-mantled ground squirrels, a feeder on a pole that was moved a small distance away from its habitual location was not sought out initially; the squirrels instead searched at the original location where the feeder had been (Devenport & Devenport, 1994). In a radial maze in the lab, single objects could be placed at the end of each arm, on a curtain surrounding the maze. When these landmarks were rearranged at random in the middle of a trial, the rats searched at random after the transformation (Suzuki et al., 1980). They did not seek out the objects associated with arms they had not yet visited. Thus, a configural change seems to mean a new space to them, in which "all bets are off."

One kind of configural property that rats and many other vertebrate animals might use is the geometry of surfaces and objects (Cheng, 1986; Cheng & Newcombe, 2005; Twyman & Newcombe, 2010; Vallortigara, 2009). *Geometric properties* refer to the arrangement of points in space, irrespective of the featural properties of the points, such as what color they reflect, whether they form a rough or smooth surface, and so forth (Gallistel, 1990). Thus, the rectangular shape of a rectangular arena constitutes a geometric property, that of shape, but the fact that one wall is white constitutes a featural property. The idea of a geometric module first arose following the observation that rats make systematic confusions between diagonally opposite locations, which are geometrically equivalent (Cheng, 1986). Since then, much research and various theories on the topic have followed. The topic is discussed in other chapters in this volume (see Chapters 8 and 10), so we focus instead on use of landmarks as individual objects.

Another line of research on female gerbils, testing their use of individual landmarks in an arena, suggested an elemental view of the use of landmarks (T. S. Collett, Cartwright, & Smith, 1986). This much-cited study, reviewed earlier, was based on earlier work on honeybees (Cartwright & Collett, 1982, 1983). For the gerbils as well as for the bees, the landmarks in the middle part of the arena were typically moved from trial to trial so that they alone defined the goal position where a seed could be found. The gerbils could learn to locate the target using a single landmark or multiple landmarks, either identical-looking or distinct ones. Evidence indicated that they encoded the direction and distance to landmarks, or a vector. Multiple vectors are encoded so that with a multiple-landmark array, the removal of a single landmark did not disrupt performance. As with honeybees (Cheng et al., 1987), the shortest vector, associated with the nearest landmark, was weighted the most. In case of conflict with more distant landmarks on transformation tests, the gerbils searched at the target location associated with the nearest landmark to the goal. Trajectory planning was also implicated, because when lights were turned out while a gerbil was en route, it continued to the goal in the dark.

An influential *vector-sum model* was proposed from the study. According to this model, the animal encodes goal-to-landmark vectors for individual landmarks. This component made the model elemental in nature. In the case of an array of identical landmarks, however, configural information enables the animal to distinguish which landmark is which. Configural information was not proposed for trajectory planning. Here, individual landmarks drive behavior separately and independently. For each encoded landmark, the animal added to the self-to-landmark vector, estimated from incoming perceptual information, the inverse of the remembered landmark-to-goal vector. The use of multiple landmarks, rather than a single landmark, would add accuracy to navigation (Kamil & Cheng, 2001).

Elemental Use of Landmarks: The Case of Pigeons

T. S. Collett et al.'s (1986) study on gerbils influenced a body of lab-based research on domesticated pigeons that further developed the vector-sum model (for a review, see Cheng, Spetch, Kelly, & Bingman, 2006). The vector-sum model was proposed for pigeons and examined by Cheng (1988, 1989) in experiments in a square arena inside a cluttered lab providing plenty of landmarks. Unlike T. S. Collett et al.'s gerbil study, the goal for the pigeon was typically located at a single spot in the arena, making many cues usable for pinpointing the target. A key finding supporting the vector-sum model, better called the *vector-averaging model*, is that with landmark shifts, birds searched somewhere on a line connecting the goal location according to the shifted landmark and the goal according to unshifted landmarks. This is best illustrated by an example (Color Plate 13). Pigeons were trained to find hidden food 20 cm in front of a tall, narrow blue cardboard. The goal was near one corner of the arena and constant from trial to trial, making the entire arena, and what lay beyond, usable landmarks. On one test, the blue board on the wall was shifted 30 cm to the left. Now the target location according to the cardboard was 30 cm to the left of the Earth-based target location, which is also the location specified by whichever of the unshifted landmarks that the birds encoded. Averaging the dictates of these landmark-to-goal vectors means searching somewhere on the straight line connecting the two theoretical goal locations, a prediction derivable mathematically from vector algebra. That was precisely what the pigeons did in this transformation test (Cheng, 1988) and others like it (Cheng, 1988, 1989).

A 2-D snapshot is unlikely to account for the pigeon's behavior. Transformations that do not change the positions of landmarks, although modifying the appearance of landmarks, had no systematic effect on search behavior (Cheng, 1988). Thus, doubling the width of a stripe on the wall or the height of a nearby wooden block did not drive the pigeons to search further from the landmark. From the standpoint of matching a 2-D image, they should have. Distance to landmarks seems to be a key component of what is encoded.

Complications soon arose with the vector-sum model that required modifying some of its details while retaining its spirit. The pigeons, along with black-capped chickadees and three species of cor-

vids, were strongly predisposed to maintain a fixed distance from a surface, such as a wall (Cheng & Sherry, 1992; Gould-Beierle & Kamil, 1998; Spetch, Cheng, & Mondloch, 1992). Thus, when a landmark near a wall was moved in a direction diagonal to the wall, the peak density of searching shifted more in the direction parallel to the wall than in the direction perpendicular to the wall (Cheng & Sherry, 1992). According to the original vector-sum model, the peak density of searching should have shifted in a diagonal direction, the direction of landmark shift. Adding a component of perpendicular distance to the model, however, allows the modified elemental model to work again, albeit with added assumptions (Cheng et al., 2006).

Even though the vector-sum model suggests the averaging of multiple cues, pigeons often use just a single landmark in conflict situations. In some studies, pigeons were trained to search in the middle of an array of four identical landmarks. When the array was expanded, they typically matched the vector to just a single landmark, both on a touch-screen task (Spetch, Cheng, & MacDonald, 1996) and in an arena (Spetch et al., 1997). Other experiments with pigeons, however, showed that they can and do encode the vectors to multiple individual landmarks. Sutton (2002) trained pigeons with irregular arrays of landmarks. In manipulations reminiscent of T. S. Collett et al.'s (1986) study on gerbils, the shifting of any individual landmark had no effect on shifting the peak density of searching. The pigeons ignored the shifted landmark and "went with" the rest of the unshifted array.

Cue Competition in Using Landmarks

Cue competition is often found in learning to use individual landmarks to locate a target (Chamizo, 2003; Cheng & Spetch, 1998). Prior learning on the basis of one set of landmarks may interfere with the learning of a new landmark later added to the set, the phenomenon of *blocking* (Kamin, 1969). Thus, when rats had already learned to use a set of three landmarks around a circular pool to locate the hidden platform, they failed to learn the relation of the platform to an added fourth landmark (Rodrigo et al., 1997). Simultaneous presentation of multiple landmarks may also interfere with learning landmark-goal relations, the phenomenon of *over-shadowing* (Pavlov, 1927). In one example, pigeons and humans learned to locate a target on a touch-screen monitor using multiple landmarks (Spetch, 1995). For a landmark at a fixed distance from the target, subjects learned its relation to the target best if it was the nearest landmark to the target, rather than the second nearest. Thus, a very near landmark overshadowed the learning of a landmark at an intermediate distance.

Cue competition is not always found. In particular, individual landmarks typically do not interfere with learning to locate the target according to the shape of the environment (Hayward, McGregor, Good, & Pearce, 2003; Pearce, Ward-Robinson, Good, Fussell, & Aydin, 2001; Wall, Botly, Black, & Shettleworth, 2004; for a review, see Cheng & Newcombe, 2005). But data that are more recent indicate cue competition from larger featural cues, such as an entire wall with a distinctive color, can be found in some circumstances. Yet in other circumstances, facilitation can also be found, in which competing featural information helps the learning of geometry (M. Graham, Good, McGregor, & Pearce, 2006; Pearce, Graham, Good, Jones, & McGregor, 2006; for a review, see Cheng, 2008).

View-Based Navigation in Vertebrate Animals

View-based matching, which we have already reviewed in the case of insect navigation, has been proposed recently as an account of rat navigation. Two studies tested the possibility that rats might confuse diagonally opposite corners because the two locations share similarities in visual appearance even if features at the corners or on the walls differ at the two locations (Cheung, Stürzl, Zeil, & Cheng, 2008; Stürzl, Cheung, Cheng, & Zeil, 2008). Thus, the pattern of edges formed by walls, ground, and "sky" (ceiling) are similar at the two locations, as are the shapes and brightnesses of the ground and the sky. The modeling used mostly a pixel-by-pixel matching process, which means comparing only the brightness level of corresponding points between currently perceived image and target image (snapshot). With no or minimal image processing, rotational errors were readily produced.

An elaborate model derived from edge-based views has recently been proposed to explain rat navigation in lab situations (Sheynikhovich, Chavarriaga, Strösslin, Arleo, & Gerstner, 2009). *Edge-based* means that the view is based primarily on parsing the orientation of contour edges in the visual world. Elaborating on O'Keefe and Nadel's (1978) distinction, such views then drive two different navigational systems, the *taxon* and *locale* systems. The taxon system uses views to drive behavior directly, similar in spirit to the insect models. The locale system uses views to construct an allocentric representation of space through head-direction cells, grid cells, and place cells (see Chapters 1 and 2, this volume). The taxon system can only operate when the agent starts repeatedly from the same point in space. When the start point varies from trial to trial, the locale system must be relied on. The model accounts for a host of data from rats in swimming pools and rectangular arenas.

Modeling search behavior on the basis of view-based matching deserves to be examined in other experimental situations. For example, room cues defining the absolute position in space often fail to control behavior when the apparatus on which the animal is tested is shifted (Hamilton, Akers, et al., 2009; Hamilton et al., 2008; Hamilton, Akers, Weisend, & Sutherland, 2007; Skinner et al., 2003; Skinner, Horne, Murphy, & Martin, 2010). Hamilton and colleagues (2007, 2008) trained rats to find a target in a round pool in a room full of cues above the pool wall. After training, rats were tested with the pool translated so that target position relative to the pool conflicted with target position relative to the room. In many conditions, rats typically preferred to search at the target position relative to the pool. In the one condition in which rats preferred the target position relative to the room, the pool walls were made very low (by filling the pool full; Hamilton et al., 2008). This preference, however, was transient, and with further training, the rats again preferred the target relative to the pool (Hamilton, Akers, et al., 2009). Hamilton and colleagues suggested that a two-stage process might account for such results. The distal room cues might have set a directional frame, and then the pool was used to pinpoint the target location, perhaps as a vector from a point on the wall or a distance from the wall. It is also possible that view-based matching accounts for some of the results (Hamilton, Johnson, Redhead, & Verney, 2009). When the pool walls are prominent, they dominate the target view and end up driving behavior to the target relative to the pool. When the pool walls are low, matching the view with respect to room cues becomes more important. How view matching may or may not account for various patterns of data deserves to be rigorously modeled to test such loose intuitions.

Whereas Hamilton and colleagues (2007, 2008) started rats in various locations, Skinner and colleagues started rats with just two starting points in two setups, on a T maze or square arena (Skinner et al., 2003, 2010). With two starting points, this made taxon learning a distinct likelihood. The arena was at different positions in the two setups. Learning to go in the same direction to reach a target proved to be generally easy. *Place learning*—that is, going to the same place in the room—often proved difficult. This was the case when the rat faced the same direction at the two start points, that is, when the maze was translated between the two setups so that the starting arms of the T maze were parallel. However, place learning was relatively easy when the starting views differed. This was the case whether the starting point was identical (but the maze rotated) or different. The authors suggested that the view at the start may have been associated with a particular route to take to get to the target (Skinner et al., 2010), a theme echoed in insect navigation.

CONCLUSION

We have focused in this review on invertebrate and vertebrate species that have been most studied: ants, bees, pigeons, and rats. Space limitations prevent us from reviewing a host of other species whose landmark-based behaviors have been studied in the burgeoning field of comparative cognition (Shettleworth, 2009, 2010). In closing, we draw out two common themes: route following and view-based navigation.

Route following is ubiquitous, found in insects, birds, and mammals (Biro et al., 2004; Calhoun, 1963; Kohler & Wehner, 2005; Lipp et al., 2004).

In some cases, we have detailed characterization of routes, sometimes based on technological innovations such as global positioning systems (Biro et al., 2004; Kohler & Wehner, 2005; Lipp et al., 2004). The research agenda now needs to focus on how routes are learned and established and what decisional and other cognitive processes take place in the performance of routes. Adding a neurophysiological dimension would also be highly interesting, when the technology is available for recording from the brains of animals freely moving over substantial distances in natural scales of travel.

View-based navigation is another strong theme throughout both the invertebrate and vertebrate literatures on landmark use. Exploring what is common and what is different about the use of views in diverse animals is emerging as an important research theme. The role of panoramic views, in addition to a collection of individual landmarks, in navigation has taken on recent interest. Thus, the skyline, only a component of the panorama, has been shown to be important for insects (P. Graham & Cheng, 2009a, 2009b; Towne & Moscrip, 2008). View-based navigation plays a major part in Sheynikhovich et al.'s recent (2009) model of rat navigation. At least two major roles for the panorama may be distinguished, and these roles are not mutually exclusive. The panorama may serve as a contextual cue (among others) for identifying and using individual landmarks. The panorama may also be used directly for navigation. These roles could form major research agendas in different taxa. Landmark use highlights the evolution of intelligent behavior in many animals, and taking a comparative approach should prove fruitful in the years to come.

SUGGESTED REFERENCES FOR FURTHER READING

Cartwright, B. A., & Collett, T. S. (1983). Landmark learning in bees. *Journal of Comparative Physiology A: Neuroethology, Sensory, Neural, and Behavioral Physiology, 151,* 521–543. doi:10.1007/BF00605469

This paper demonstrated that bees search for a goal using a 2-D snapshot of the view from that place. The authors proposed an algorithmic model of this behavior, which is a seminal model in the field of robotic navigation.

Cheng, K., Narendra, A., Sommer, S., & Wehner, R. (2009). Traveling in clutter: Navigation in the Central Australian desert ant *Melophorus bagoti*. *Behavioural Processes, 80,* 261–268. doi:10.1016/j.beproc.2008.10.015

In recent times, the Australian desert ant has proved a powerful study species because of its impressive navigation in complex environments. This paper reviews the first 5 years of experiments with this ant.

Cheng, K., & Spetch, M. L. (1998). Mechanisms of landmark use in mammals and birds. In S. Healy (Ed.), *Spatial representation in animals* (pp. 1–17). Oxford, New York: Oxford University Press.

A review of landmark use in birds and mammals that is still widely cited. Themes such as the use of multiple cues and cue competition are described.

Gallistel, C. R. (1990). *The organization of learning.* Cambridge, MA: MIT Press.

Even today, the chapters on spatial cognition (and others) continue to be influential. Thorough reviews of classic work and thought-provoking theories characterize the book.

Sheynikhovich, D., Chavarriaga, R., Strösslin, T., Arleo, A., & Gerstner, W. (2009). Is there a geometric module for spatial orientation? Insights from a rodent navigational model. *Psychological Review, 116,* 540–566. doi:10.1037/a0016170

A recent model of rodent navigation incorporating both behavioral and neurophysiological data. Data from single cells (place cells, grid cells, head direction cells) and behavior in swimming pools and arenas are modeled.

Zeil, J., Hofmann, M. I., & Chahl, J. S. (2003). Catchment areas of panoramic snapshots in outdoor scenes. *Journal of the Optical Society of America, 20,* 450–469. doi:10.1364/JOSAA.20.000450

By analyzing the statistics of natural complex images, the authors showed that panoramic views can guide a search for a goal without complex visual processing or extracting or labeling objects.

References

Åkesson, S., & Wehner, R. (2002). Visual navigation in desert ants *Cataglyphis fortis*: Are snapshots coupled to a celestial system of reference? *The Journal of Experimental Biology, 205,* 1971–1978.

Andel, D., & Wehner, R. (2004). Path integration in desert ants, *Cataglyphis fortis*: How to make a homing ant run away from home. *Proceedings of the Royal Society B: Biological Sciences, 271,* 1485–1489. doi:10.1098/rspb.2004.2749

Berdoy, M., (Producer & Director) & Stewart, P. (Director). (2002). *The natural history of the rat* [Video recording]. England: Ratlife.

Biro, D., Meade, J., & Guilford, T. (2004). Familiar route loyalty implies visual pilotage in the homing pigeon. *Proceedings of the National Academy of Sciences of the United States of America, 101,* 17440–17443. doi:10.1073/pnas.0406984101

Brown, M. F. (1992). Does a cognitive map guide choices in the radian-arm maze? *Journal of Experimental Psychology: Animal Behavior Processes, 18,* 56–66. doi:10.1037/0097-7403.18.1.56

Calhoun, J. B. (1963). *The ecology and sociology of the Norway rat.* Bethesda, MD: U.S. Department of Health, Education, and Welfare.

Cartwright, B. A., & Collett, T. S. (1982, February). How honey bees use landmarks to guide their return to a food source. *Nature, 295,* 560–564. doi:10.1038/295560a0

Cartwright, B. A., & Collett, T. S. (1983). Landmark learning in bees. *Journal of Comparative Physiology A: Neuroethology, Sensory, Neural, and Behavioral Physiology, 151,* 521–543. doi:10.1007/BF00605469

Cartwright, B. A., & Collett, T. S. (1987). Landmark maps for honeybees. *Biological Cybernetics, 57,* 85–93. doi:10.1007/BF00318718

Catania, K. C., & Remple, F. E. (2004). Tactile foveation in the star-nosed mole. *Brain, Behavior and Evolution, 63,* 1–12. doi:10.1159/000073755

Chamizo, V. D. (2003). Acquisition of knowledge about spatial location: Assessing the generality of the mechanism of learning. *Quarterly Journal of Experimental Psychology B: Comparative and Physiological Psychology, 56,* 102–113.

Chamizo, V. D., Mantiega, R. D., Rodrigo, T., & Mackintosh, N. J. (2006). Competition between landmarks in spatial learning: The role of proximity to the goal. *Behavioural Processes, 71,* 59–65. doi:10.1016/j.beproc.2005.11.003

Cheng, K. (1986). A purely geometric module in the rat's spatial representation. *Cognition, 23,* 149–178. doi:10.1016/0010-0277(86)90041-7

Cheng, K. (1988). Some psychophysics of the pigeon's use of landmarks. *Journal of Comparative Physiology A: Neuroethology, Sensory, Neural, and Behavioral Physiology, 162,* 815–826. doi:10.1007/BF00610970

Cheng, K. (1989). The vector sum model of pigeon landmark use. *Journal of Experimental Psychology: Animal Behavior Processes, 15,* 366–375. doi:10.1037/0097-7403.15.4.366

Cheng, K. (1999). Landmark-based spatial search in honeybees. II. Using gaps and blocks. *Animal Cognition, 2,* 79–90. doi:10.1007/s100710050027

Cheng, K. (2000). How honeybees find a place: Lessons from a simple mind. *Animal Learning & Behavior, 28,* 1–15. doi:10.3758/BF03199768

Cheng, K. (2005). Context cues eliminate retroactive interference effects in honeybees (*Apis mellifera*). *The Journal of Experimental Biology, 208,* 1019–1024. doi:10.1242/jeb.01499

Cheng, K. (2006). Arthropod navigation: Ants, bees, crabs, spiders finding their way. In E. A. Wasserman & T. R. Zentall (Eds.), *Comparative cognition: Experimental explorations of animal intelligence* (pp. 189–209). Oxford, England: Oxford University Press.

Cheng, K. (2008). Whither geometry? Troubles of the geometric module. *Trends in Cognitive Sciences, 12,* 355–361. doi:10.1016/j.tics.2008.06.004

Cheng, K., Collett, T. S., Pickhard, A., & Wehner, R. (1987). The use of visual landmarks by honeybees: Bees weight landmarks according to their distance from the goal. *Journal of Comparative Physiology A: Neuroethology, Sensory, Neural, and Behavioral Physiology, 161,* 469–475. doi:10.1007/BF00603972

Cheng, K., Narendra, A., Sommer, S., & Wehner, R. (2009). Traveling in clutter: Navigation in the Central Australian desert ant *Melophorus bagoti. Behavioural Processes, 80,* 261–268. doi:10.1016/j.beproc.2008.10.015

Cheng, K., & Newcombe, N. S. (2005). Is there a geometric module for spatial orientation? Squaring theory and evidence. *Psychonomic Bulletin & Review, 12,* 1–23. doi:10.3758/BF03196346

Cheng, K., & Sherry, D. F. (1992). Landmark-based spatial memory in birds (*Parus atricapillus* and *Columba livia*): The use of edges and distances to represent spatial positions. *Journal of Comparative Psychology, 106,* 331–341. doi:10.1037/0735-7036.106.4.331

Cheng, K., & Spetch, M. L. (1998). Mechanisms of landmark use in mammals and birds. In S. Healy (Ed.), *Spatial representation in animals* (pp. 1–17). Oxford, New York: Oxford University Press.

Cheng, K., Spetch, M. L., Kelly, D. M., & Bingman, V. P. (2006). Small-scale spatial cognition in pigeons. *Behavioural Processes, 72,* 115–127. doi:10.1016/j.beproc.2005.11.018

Cheung, A., Stürzl, W., Zeil, J., & Cheng, K. (2008). Information content of panoramic images: II. View-based navigation in nonrectangular experimental arenas. *Journal of Experimental Psychology: Animal Behavior Processes, 34,* 15–30. doi:10.1037/0097-7403.34.1.15

Chittka, L., Kunze, J., Shipman, C., & Buchmann, S. L. (1995). The significance of landmarks for path integration in homing honeybee foragers. *Naturwissenschaften, 82,* 341–343. doi:10.1007/BF01131533

Collett, M., Collett, T. S., Bisch, S., & Wehner, R. (1998, July). Local and global vectors in desert ant navigation. *Nature, 394,* 269–272. doi:10.1038/28378

Collett, M., Collett, T. S., Chameron, S., & Wehner, R. (2003). Do familiar landmarks reset the global path integration system of desert ants? *The Journal of Experimental Biology, 206,* 877–882. doi:10.1242/jeb.00176

Collett, T. S. (1995). Making learning easy: The acquisition of visual information during the orientation flights of social wasps. *Journal of Comparative Physiology A: Neuroethology, Sensory, Neural, and Behavioral Physiology, 177,* 737–747. doi:10.1007/BF00187632

Collett, T. S., Cartwright, B. A., & Smith, B. A. (1986). Landmark learning and visuo–spatial memories in gerbils. *Journal of Comparative Physiology A: Neuroethology, Sensory, Neural, and Behavioral Physiology, 158,* 835–851. doi:10.1007/BF01324825

Collett, T. S., & Collett, M. (2002). Memory use in insect visual navigation. *Nature Reviews Neuroscience, 3,* 542–552. doi:10.1038/nrn872

Collett, T. S., Dillmann, E., Giger, A., & Wehner, R. (1992). Visual landmarks and route following in desert ants. *Journal of Comparative Physiology A: Neuroethology, Sensory, Neural, and Behavioral Physiology, 170,* 435–442. doi:10.1007/BF00191460

Collett, T. S., & Kelber, A. (1988). The retrieval of visuo–spatial memories by honeybees. *Journal of Comparative Physiology A: Neuroethology, Sensory, Neural, and Behavioral Physiology, 163,* 145–150. doi:10.1007/BF00612004

Collett, T. S., & Land, M. F. (1975). Visual spatial memory in a hoverfly. *Journal of Comparative Physiology, 100,* 59–84. doi:10.1007/BF00623930

Devenport, J. A., & Devenport, L. D. (1994). Spatial navigation in natural habitats by ground-dwelling sciurids. *Animal Behaviour, 47,* 727–729. doi:10.1006/anbe.1994.1099

Durier, V., Graham, P., & Collett, T. S. (2003). Snapshot memories and landmark guidance in wood ants. *Current Biology, 13,* 1614–1618. doi:10.1016/j.cub.2003.08.024

Dyer, F. C. (1991). Bees acquire route-based memories but not cognitive maps in a familiar landscape. *Animal Behaviour, 41,* 239–246. doi:10.1016/S0003-3472(05)80475-0

Ernst, R., & Heisenberg, M. (1999). The memory template in *Drosophila* pattern vision at the flight simulator. *Vision Research, 39,* 3920–3933. doi:10.1016/S0042-6989(99)00114-5

Fourcassié, V. (1991). Landmark orientation in natural situations in the red wood ant *Formica lugubris* Zett. (Hymenoptera Formicidae). *Ethology Ecology and Evolution, 3,* 89–99. doi:10.1080/08927014.1991.9525376

Frier, H. J., Edwards, E., Smith, C., Neale, S., & Collett, T. S. (1996). Magnetic compass cues and visual pattern learning in honeybees. *The Journal of Experimental Biology, 199,* 1353–1361.

Fukushi, T. (2001). Homing in wood ants, *Formica japonica*: Use of the skyline panorama. *The Journal of Experimental Biology, 204,* 2063–2072.

Gallistel, C. R. (1990). *The organization of learning.* Cambridge, MA: MIT Press.

Gould, J. L. (1986, May). The locale map of honeybees: Do insects have cognitive maps? *Science, 232,* 861–863. doi:10.1126/science.232.4752.861

Gould-Beierle, K., & Kamil, A. C. (1998). Use of landmarks in three species of food-storing corvids. *Ethology, 104,* 361–377. doi:10.1111/j.1439-0310.1998.tb00075.x

Graham, M., Good, M. A., McGregor, A., & Pearce, J. M. (2006). Spatial learning based on the shape of the environment is influenced by properties of the objects forming the shape. *Journal of Experimental Psychology: Animal Behavior Processes, 32,* 44–59. doi:10.1037/0097-7403.32.1.44

Graham, P., & Cheng, K. (2009a). Ants use the panoramic skyline as a visual cue during navigation. *Current Biology, 19,* R935–R937. doi:10.1016/j.cub.2009.08.015

Graham, P., & Cheng, K. (2009b). Which portion of the natural panorama is used for view-based navigation in the Australian desert ant? *Journal of Comparative Physiology A: Neuroethology, Sensory, Neural, and Behavioral Physiology, 195,* 681–689. doi:10.1007/s00359-009-0443-6

Graham, P., Durier, V., & Collett, T. S. (2004). The binding and recall of snapshot memories in wood ants (*Formica rufa* L.). *The Journal of Experimental Biology, 207,* 393–398. doi:10.1242/jeb.00771

Graham, P., Fauria, K., & Collett, T. S. (2003). The influence of beacon-aiming on the routes of wood ants. *The Journal of Experimental Biology, 206,* 535–541. doi:10.1242/jeb.00115

Hamilton, D. A., Akers, K. G., Johnson, T. E., Rice, J. P., Candelaria, F. T., & Redhead, E. S. (2009). Evidence for a shift from place navigation to directional responding in one variant of the Morris water maze. *Journal of Experimental Psychology: Animal Behavior Processes, 35,* 271–278. doi:10.1037/a0013260

Hamilton, D. A., Akers, K. G., Johnson, T. E., Rice, J. P., Candelaria, F. T., Sutherland, R. J., & Redhead, E. S. (2008). The relative influence of place and direction in the Morris water task. *Journal of Experimental Psychology: Animal Behavior Processes, 34,* 31–53. doi:10.1037/0097-7403.34.1.31

Hamilton, D. A., Akers, K. G., Weisend, M. P., & Sutherland, R. J. (2007). How do room and apparatus cues control navigation in the Morris water task? Evidence for distinct contributions to a movement vector. *Journal of Experimental Psychology: Animal Behavior Processes, 33,* 100–114. doi:10.1037/0097-7403.33.2.100

Hamilton, D. A., Johnson, T. E., Redhead, E. S., & Verney, S. P. (2009). Control of rodent and human spatial navigation by room and apparatus cues. *Behavioural Processes, 81,* 154–169. doi:10.1016/j.beproc.2008.12.003

Hayward, A., McGregor, A., Good, M. A., & Pearce, J. M. (2003). Absence of overshadowing and blocking between landmarks and the geometric cues provided by the shape of a test arena. *Quarterly Journal of Experimental Psychology B: Comparative and Physiological Psychology, 56,* 114–126.

Hempel de Ibarra, N., Giurfa, M., & Vorobyev, M. (2002). Discimination of coloured patterns by honeybees through chromatic and achromatic cues. *Journal of Comparative Physiology A: Neuroethology, Sensory, Neural, and Behavioral Physiology, 188,* 503–512. doi:10.1007/s00359-002-0322-x

Heusser, D., & Wehner, R. (2002). The visual centring response in desert ants, *Cataglyphis fortis. The Journal of Experimental Biology, 205,* 585–590.

Janzen, D. H. (1971, January). Euglossine bees as long-distance pollinators of tropical plants. *Science, 171,* 203–205. doi:10.1126/science.171.3967.203

Junger, W. (1991). Waterstriders (*Gerris paludum* F.) compensate for drift with a discontinuously working visual position servo. *Journal of Comparative Physiology A: Neuroethology, Sensory, Neural, and Behavioral Physiology, 169,* 633–639. doi:10.1007/BF00193553

Kamil, A. C., & Cheng, K. (2001). Way-finding and landmarks: The multiple-bearings hypothesis. *The Journal of Experimental Biology, 204,* 103–113.

Kamin, L. J. (1969). Predictability, surprise, attention, and conditioning. In B. J. Campbell & R. M. Church (Eds.), *Punishment and aversive behavior* (pp. 279–296). New York, NY: Appleton-Century-Crofts.

Kelber, A., & Zeil, J. (1997). *Tetragonisca* guard bees interpret expanding and contracting patterns as unintended displacement in space. *Journal of*

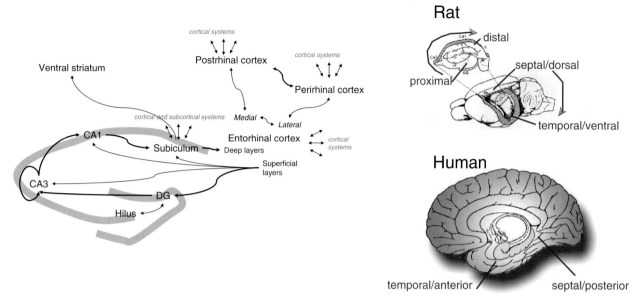

COLOR PLATE 1.   Hippocampal anatomy in the rat and human. Wiring diagram based on the details known from rat anatomy. The actual anatomy is much more complex, including differences in connectivity along transverse and septal–temporal axes. The right figures show the location of the hippocampi, making clear the proximal–distal and septal–temporal axes. The septal–temporal axis proceeds from dorsal to ventral in the rat brain, whereas it proceeds from posterior to anterior in the human. Image of rodent hippocampus from *The Hippocampus Book* (p. 46), by P. Andersen, R. Morris, D. Amaral, T. Bliss, and J. O'Keefe (Eds.), 2007, Oxford, England: Oxford University Press. Copyright 2007 by Oxford University Press. Adapted with permission. Image of human hippocampus from *Overview: Space, Memory, and the Hippocampus*, by J. O'Keefe, 2010, retrieved from http://www.ucl.ac.uk/cdb/research/okeefe/research. Copyright 2010 by University College London. Adapted with permission. See Amaral & Lavenex (2007), Furtak et al. (2007), and van Strien et al. (2009) for more detail.

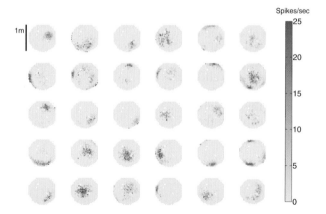

COLOR PLATE 2.   Place cells. Thirty place cells simultaneously recorded from a cylinder foraging task. Data courtesy Jadin Jackson, Redish Lab.

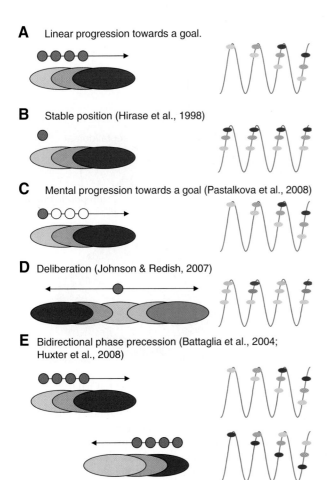

A Linear progression towards a goal.

B Stable position (Hirase et al., 1998)

C Mental progression towards a goal (Pastalkova et al., 2008)

D Deliberation (Johnson & Redish, 2007)

E Bidirectional phase precession (Battaglia et al., 2004; Huxter et al., 2008)

COLOR PLATE 3.   Phase precession as sequences. (a) When rats run along a linear path to a goal (left, sequential positions shown as gray circles, place fields shown as colored ovals), place cells precess along the 7 Hz theta local field potential rhythm. Notice that the phase of the red cell precesses earlier each cycle. This has the effect of producing a sweep along the path of the animal each cycle. (b) When the animal is running in place, place cells fire at a given theta phase, and the sweep remains constant in each theta cycle. (c) If the animal is running in place, but has a goal, place cells phase precess. (d) During deliberation, sweeps alternate directions. (e) In tasks with bidirectional cells, place cells phase precess in both directions. The exits of the place fields in each direction coincide, implying that phase precession represents travel toward a goal.

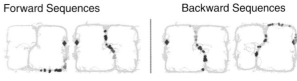

Forward Sequences   Backward Sequences

Shortcut/Untravelled but Conjoined Paths

start ▭ end

COLOR PLATE 4.   "Replay" of sequences. Each panel shows an example sequence played out during a sharp wave. The location of the rat is shown by the black diamond. Place fields that fire during the sharp wave are plotted at the centers of their place fields. Top left: forward sequences. Top right: backward sequences. Bottom: Conjoined pairs of backward and forward sequences producing paths untraveled by the rat. Rats ran in left-circle, right-circle, and alternating (figure-8) paths. From "Hippocampal Replay Is Not a Simple Function of Experience," by A. S. Gupta, M. A. A. van der Meer, D. S. Touretzky, and A. D. Redish, 2010, *Neuron*, 65, p. 697. Copyright by 2010 Elsevier. Adapted with permission.

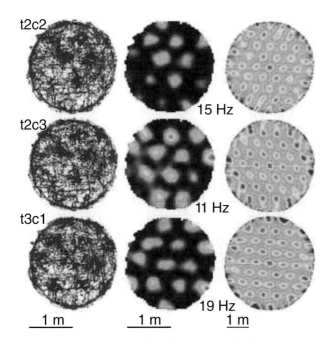

COLOR PLATE 5.   Grid Cells. Left panels show gray dots for every location sampled by the rat. Red dots indicate positions when the cell in question fired a spike. Tuning curves are shown in the middle panels. The right panels show spatial correlations, demonstrating the regularity of the grid. Three cells are shown. Labels indicate tetrode and cell ID. Frequencies in middle panels report maximum firing rate for that cell. From "Microstructure of a Spatial Map in the Entorhinal Cortex," by T. Hafting, M. Fyhn, S. Molden, M.-B. Moser, and E. Moser, 2005, *Nature, 436,* p. 802. Copyright 2005 by Nature Publishing Group. Adapted with permission.

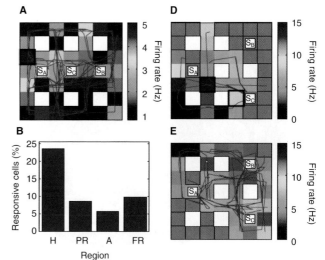

COLOR PLATE 6.   Place cells from the human medial temporal lobe. (a) Place field of a hippocampal cell. SA, SB, SC indicate landmarks ("shops"). (b) Place fields were much more common in hippocampal recordings than from other structures (parahippocampal regions, amygdala, frontal regions). (d, e) Place field showing significant spatial tuning only while searching for shop SC (panel d) but not other shops (panel e). (Panel *c* not included here.) From "Cellular Networks Underlying Human Spatial Navigation," by A. D. Ekstrom, M. J. Kahana, J. B. Caplan, T. A. Fields, E. A. Isham, E. L. Newman, and I. Fried, 2003, *Nature, 425,* p. 185. Copyright 2003 by Nature Publishing Group. Adapted with permission.

A

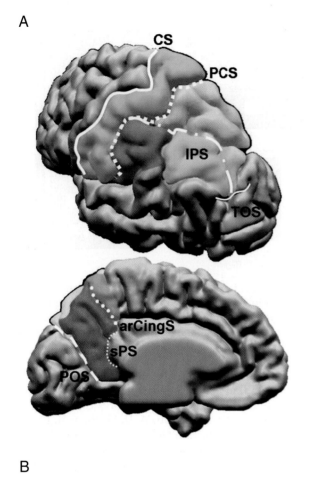

CS

PCS

IPS

TOS

arCingS

sPS

POS

COLOR PLATE 7. Parietal cortex in human, monkey, and rat. (a) Lateral (top) and medial (bottom) views of the human parietal regions. In the top image, blue = postcentral gyrus (BA 3, 2, 1), tan = superior parietal lobule (SPL, BA 5), yellow = SPL (BA 7), dark green = inferior parietal lobule (IPL, supramarginal gyrus, BA 40), light green = IPL (angular gyrus, BA 39), CS = central sulcus, IPS = intraparietal sulcus, PCS = postcentral sulcus, TOS = transverse occipital sulcus. In the bottom image, gold = precuneus (BA 5), orange = precuneus (BA 7), arCingS = ascending ramus of the cingulate sulcus, POS = parieto–occipital sulcus, sPS = subparietal sulcus. From "The Role of Parietal Cortex in Visuomotor Control: What Have We Learned From Neuroimaging?" by J. C. Culham, C. Cavina-Pratesi, and A. Singhal, 2006, *Neuropsychologia, 44,* p. 2669. Copyright 2006 by Elsevier. Reprinted with permission. (b) Monkey parietal cortex (left) and unfolded intraparietal sulcus (right). From "Connection Patterns Distinguish 3 Regions of Human Parietal Cortex," by M. F. S. Rushworth, T. E. J. Behrens, and H. Johansen-Berg, 2006, *Cerebral Cortex, 16,* p. 1419. Copyright 2006 by Oxford University Press. Reprinted with permission. (c) Rat brain and parietal cortex (black). AGm = medial agranular cortex, Fr1 = frontal cortex, Fr2 = frontal cortex 2, Oc1 = occipital cortex 1, and Oc2L = lateral occipital cortex 2, Par1 = parietal cortex 1, Par 2 = parietal cortex 2, PPC = posterior parietal cortex, Te1 = temporal cortex 1, Te2 = temporal cortex 2, Te 3 = temporal cortex 3, VLO = ventrolateral–orbital cortex. From "Posterior Parietal Cortex As Part of a Neural Network for Directed Attention in Rats," by R. L. Reep, and J. V. Corwin, 2009, *Neurobiology of Learning and Memory, 91,* p. 106. Copyright 2009 by Elsevier. Reprinted with permission.

B

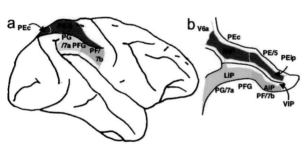

a PEc

PG
/7a PFG
PF/
7b

b V6a

PEc

PE/5 PEip

LIP

PG/7a PFG AIP
PF/7b
VIP

C

AGm
(Fr2)

PPC

Oc1

Fr1

Par 1

Oc2L

Te1

VLO

Par 2

Te3 Te2

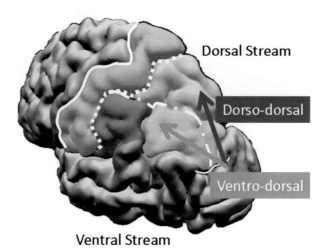

Dorsal Stream

Dorso-dorsal

Ventro-dorsal

Ventral Stream

COLOR PLATE 8.   Schematic pathways of dorso–dorsal and ventro–dorsal pathways of the posterior parietal cortex. Dorso–dorsal and ventro–dorsal pathways from "The Role of Parietal Cortex in Visuomotor Control: What Have We Learned From Neuroimaging?" J. C. Culham, C. Cavina-Pratesi, and A. Singhal, 2006, *Neuropsychologia, 44,* p. 2669. Copyright 2006 by Elsevier. Reprinted with permission.

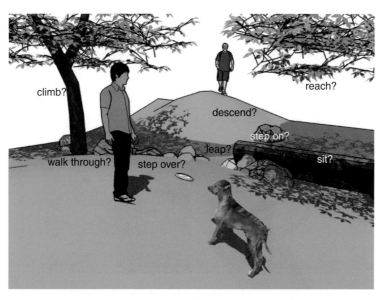

COLOR PLATE 9.   Action-relevant properties for a hiker walking through a cluttered environment.

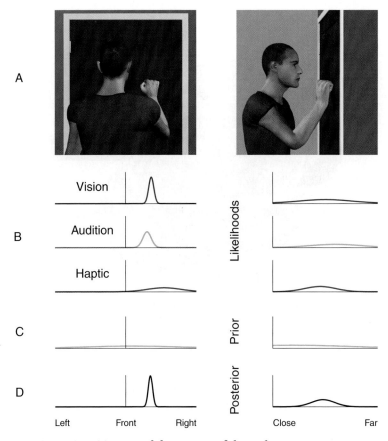

COLOR PLATE 10.   Visual description of the multisensory integration process for estimates of the location (both in terms of azimuth and distance) of one's hand knocking on a door. Visual, haptic, and auditory information and prior experience with these senses all contribute to the estimate of the location of one's hand when knocking on a door, as is described in detail in the text.

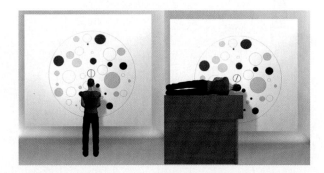

COLOR PLATE 11.   The subjective visual vertical experimental paradigm. (Left) subjective vertical of the line in the center while standing; (right) subjective vertical while a person is lying on their side is no longer a vertical line, but rather slanted in the direction of the body rotation.

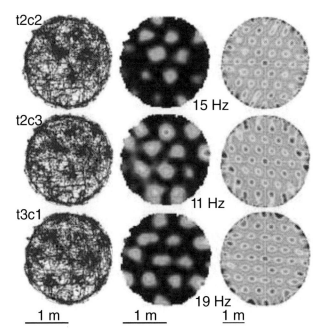

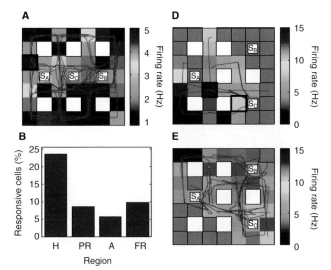

COLOR PLATE 5.   Grid Cells. Left panels show gray dots for every location sampled by the rat. Red dots indicate positions when the cell in question fired a spike. Tuning curves are shown in the middle panels. The right panels show spatial correlations, demonstrating the regularity of the grid. Three cells are shown. Labels indicate tetrode and cell ID. Frequencies in middle panels report maximum firing rate for that cell. From "Microstructure of a Spatial Map in the Entorhinal Cortex," by T. Hafting, M. Fyhn, S. Molden, M.-B. Moser, and E. Moser, 2005, *Nature, 436,* p. 802. Copyright 2005 by Nature Publishing Group. Adapted with permission.

COLOR PLATE 6.   Place cells from the human medial temporal lobe. (a) Place field of a hippocampal cell. SA, SB, SC indicate landmarks ("shops"). (b) Place fields were much more common in hippocampal recordings than from other structures (parahippocampal regions, amygdala, frontal regions). (d, e) Place field showing significant spatial tuning only while searching for shop SC (panel d) but not other shops (panel e). (Panel *c* not included here.) From "Cellular Networks Underlying Human Spatial Navigation," by A. D. Ekstrom, M. J. Kahana, J. B. Caplan, T. A. Fields, E. A. Isham, E. L. Newman, and I. Fried, 2003, *Nature, 425,* p. 185. Copyright 2003 by Nature Publishing Group. Adapted with permission.

A

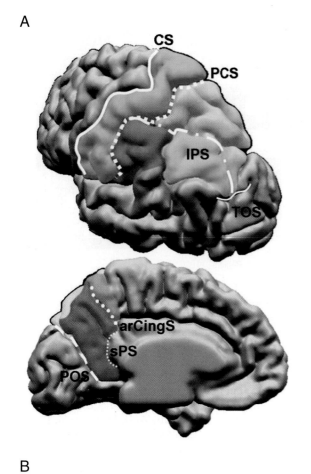

CS

PCS

IPS

TOS

arCingS

sPS

POS

B

a PEc

PG
/7a PFG
PF/
7b

b V6a

PEc

PE/5 PEip

LIP

PG/7a PFG AIP
PF/7b

VIP

C

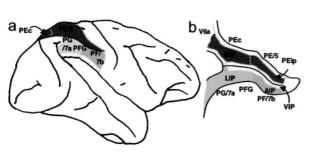

AGm
(Fr2)

PPC

Fr1

Par 1

Oc1

Oc2L

VLO

Par 2

Te1

Te3 Te2

COLOR PLATE 7.   Parietal cortex in human, monkey, and rat. (a) Lateral (top) and medial (bottom) views of the human parietal regions. In the top image, blue = postcentral gyrus (BA 3, 2, 1), tan = superior parietal lobule (SPL, BA 5), yellow = SPL (BA 7), dark green = inferior parietal lobule (IPL, supramarginal gyrus, BA 40), light green = IPL (angular gyrus, BA 39), CS = central sulcus, IPS = intraparietal sulcus, PCS = postcentral sulcus, TOS = transverse occipital sulcus. In the bottom image, gold = precuneus (BA 5), orange = precuneus (BA 7), arCingS = ascending ramus of the cingulate sulcus, POS = parieto–occipital sulcus, sPS = subparietal sulcus. From "The Role of Parietal Cortex in Visuomotor Control: What Have We Learned From Neuroimaging?" by J. C. Culham, C. Cavina-Pratesi, and A. Singhal, 2006, *Neuropsychologia, 44,* p. 2669. Copyright 2006 by Elsevier. Reprinted with permission. (b) Monkey parietal cortex (left) and unfolded intraparietal sulcus (right). From "Connection Patterns Distinguish 3 Regions of Human Parietal Cortex," by M. F. S. Rushworth, T. E. J. Behrens, and H. Johansen-Berg, 2006, *Cerebral Cortex, 16,* p. 1419. Copyright 2006 by Oxford University Press. Reprinted with permission. (c) Rat brain and parietal cortex (black). AGm = medial agranular cortex, Fr1 = frontal cortex, Fr2 = frontal cortex 2, Oc1 = occipital cortex 1, and Oc2L = lateral occipital cortex 2, Par1 = parietal cortex 1, Par 2 = parietal cortex 2, PPC = posterior parietal cortex, Te1 = temporal cortex 1, Te2 = temporal cortex 2, Te 3 = temporal cortex 3, VLO = ventrolateral–orbital cortex. From "Posterior Parietal Cortex As Part of a Neural Network for Directed Attention in Rats," by R. L. Reep, and J. V. Corwin, 2009, *Neurobiology of Learning and Memory, 91,* p. 106. Copyright 2009 by Elsevier. Reprinted with permission.

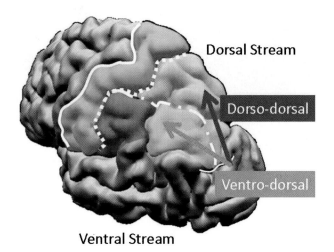

Dorsal Stream

Dorso-dorsal

Ventro-dorsal

Ventral Stream

COLOR PLATE 8.   Schematic pathways of dorso–dorsal and ventro–dorsal pathways of the posterior parietal cortex. Dorso–dorsal and ventro–dorsal pathways from "The Role of Parietal Cortex in Visuomotor Control: What Have We Learned From Neuroimaging?" J. C. Culham, C. Cavina-Pratesi, and A. Singhal, 2006, *Neuropsychologia, 44,* p. 2669. Copyright 2006 by Elsevier. Reprinted with permission.

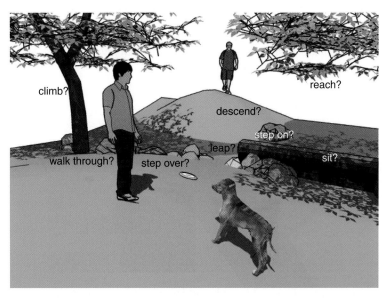

COLOR PLATE 9.   Action-relevant properties for a hiker walking through a cluttered environment.

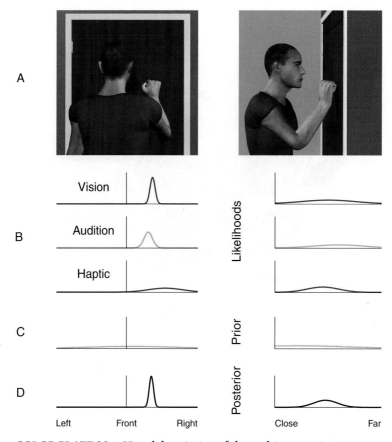

A

B Vision Audition Haptic Likelihoods

C Prior

D Posterior

Left Front Right Close Far

COLOR PLATE 10. Visual description of the multisensory integration process for estimates of the location (both in terms of azimuth and distance) of one's hand knocking on a door. Visual, haptic, and auditory information and prior experience with these senses all contribute to the estimate of the location of one's hand when knocking on a door, as is described in detail in the text.

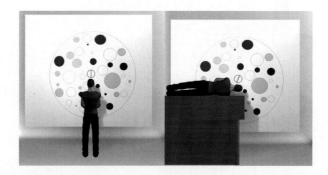

COLOR PLATE 11. The subjective visual vertical experimental paradigm. (Left) subjective vertical of the line in the center while standing; (right) subjective vertical while a person is lying on their side is no longer a vertical line, but rather slanted in the direction of the body rotation.

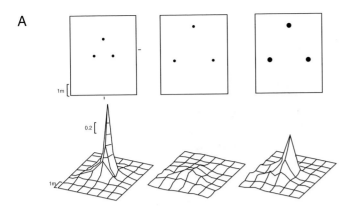

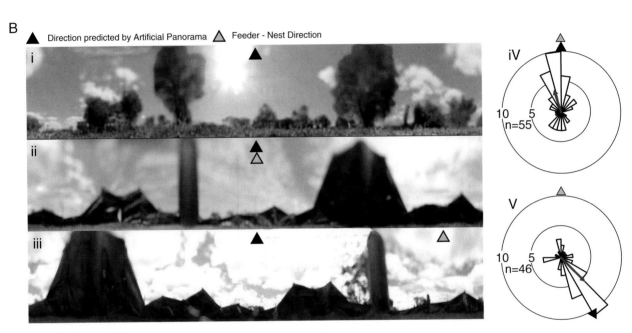

COLOR PLATE 12.   Landmark-based search behavior in insects. (a) Landmark-based searching in desert ants. Search distributions in desert ants, *Cataglyphis fortis*, trained with a triangular landmark array around their nest. Tests were done on a distant test field with the training array (left) and with two transformations of the array. In the middle, the array had been expanded to double the interlandmark distances. On the right, the array had been expanded to double the interlandmark distances, and the cylinders forming the array had been doubled in size so that from the fictive target, the array looked as it would at the target location in training. From "Visual Navigation in Insects: Coupling of Egocentric and Geocentric Information," by R. Wehner, B. Michel, and P. Antonsen, 1996, *The Journal of Experimental Biology, 199*, p. 133. Copyright 1996 by The Company of Biologists. Reprinted with permission. (b) Navigating by skyline. Australian desert ants, *Melophorus bagoti*, were trained to forage from a feeder at a constant direction and distance from the nest. (i) The panoramic view from the feeder, obtained from a photo taken using a panoramic lens attached to a digital camera and then unwarped using image processing software. The view is cylindrical and wraps around, with the right edge meeting the left edge. (ii) The panorama was reconstructed in a test arena made of black cloth to match the skyline (elevation of the tops of terrestrial objects) at the feeder. The elevation was matched every 15°, and the artificial skyline was aligned in the same compass direction as the skyline encountered at the feeder. (iii) The same panorama made of black cloth rotated by 150°. (iv) Behavior of desert ants in the artificial skyline panorama in ii. Bars show the number of ants heading off initially in each sector of 15°. Ants were significantly oriented in the direction to the nest according to both the compass heading and the skyline. (v) Behavior of desert ants in the rotated skyline panorama in (iii), with the same conventions as in (iv). The test disentangled the predictions of a heading based on the compass direction from the feeder to the nest (gray triangle) and a heading based on the skyline seen at the feeder (black triangle). The ants clearly followed the artificial skyline in their initial heading. From "Ants Use the Panoramic Skyline as a Visual Cue During Navigation," by K. Cheng and P. Graham, 2009, *Current Biology, 19*, p. 936. Copyright 2009 by Elsevier. Reprinted with permission.

A

B

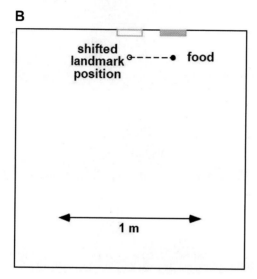

COLOR PLATE 13.   Experimental set-up for testing how pigeons search for a precise location containing *food*. (a) A photograph of the setup. A 1.6 m square arena was surrounded on three sides by black walls. One side remained open to allow entry by the birds. A blue stripe on one wall provided a distinct cue near the target, with the food located 20 cm in front of the center of the stripe. In training, the food was buried in a small indentation on the floor and was covered with sawdust. (b) An overhead view of the arena showing the blue stripe in its normal position (solid color) and on a test in a shifted position (hatched color), in which the blue stripe was shifted 30 cm to the left of its location in training. On control and shift tests, the food and the indentation were both absent. On a shifted test, the vector-averaging model predicts that the peak of searching should be located on the line segment connecting two theoretical targets (dotted line segment), the goal according to the unshifted landmarks (filled dot, training location of food) and the goal according to the shifted landmark (open dot, 30 cm to the left). Results from this series of tests supported the vector-averaging model.

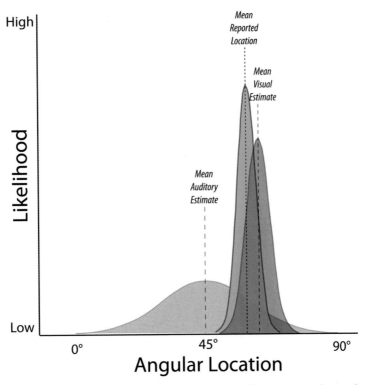

COLOR PLATE 14.   Bayesian combination of auditory and visual estimates of angular location. In this example, each modality provides a different estimate of location, each associated with a specific reliability (the inverse of variance). Linear combination of the two distributions results in a cross-modal response distribution that is biased away from the mean visual estimate, yet has a lower variance than either of the unimodal estimates. Thus, even though bias is introduced, the average error is minimized.

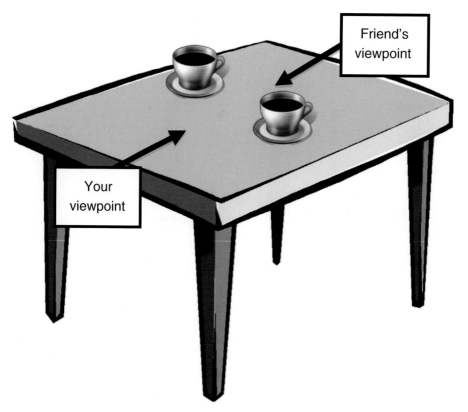

COLOR PLATE 15. Ambiguous spatial reference. With two possible reference frames, yours and your friend's, identifying a specific spatial location can be ambiguous.

COLOR PLATE 16. Reference frame availability. The term *above* could refer to key location A, B, or C, depending on the reference frame invoked—absolute (A), relative (B), or intrinsic (C).

COLOR PLATE 17.   WikEar. On selection of a destination, *WikEar* creates an educational audio tour. From "WikEar: Automatically Generated Location-Based Audio Stories Between Public City Maps," by J. Schöning, B. Hecht, M. Rohs, and N. Starosielski, 2007, *Adjunct Proceedings of the 9th International Conference on Ubiquitous Computing.* Copyright 2007 by Johannes Schöning. Reprinted with permission.

Comparative Physiology A: Neuroethology, Sensory, Neural, and Behavioral Physiology, 181, 257–265. doi:10.1007/s003590050112

Knaden, M., & Wehner, R. (2006). Ant navigation: Resetting the path integrator. *The Journal of Experimental Biology, 209,* 26–31. doi:10.1242/jeb.01976

Kohler, M., & Wehner, R. (2005). Idiosyncratic route memories in desert ants, *Melophorus bagoti:* How do they interact with path integration vectors? *Neurobiology of Learning and Memory, 83,* 1–12. doi:10.1016/j.nlm.2004.05.011

Kwon, H. W., Lent, D. D., & Strausfeld, N. J. (2004). Spatial learning in the restrained American cockroach *Periplaneta americana. The Journal of Experimental Biology, 207,* 377–383. doi:10.1242/jeb.00737

Land, M. F., & Nilsson, D. E. (2002). *Animal eyes.* New York, NY: Oxford University Press.

Lehrer, M. (1999). Dorsoventral asymmetry of colour discrimination in bees. *Journal of Comparative Physiology A: Neuroethology, Sensory, Neural, and Behavioral Physiology, 184,* 195–206. doi:10.1007/s003590050318

Lent, D., Graham, P., & Collett, T. S. (2010). Insect navigation: Saccade-like turns to learnt visualfeatures as a mechanism of image matching. *Proceedings of the National Academy of Sciences of the United States of America, 107,* 16348–16353. doi:10.1073/pnas.1006021107

Lindauer, M. (1960). Time-compensated sun orientation in bees. *Cold Spring Harbor Symposia on Quantitative Biology, 25,* 371–377. doi:10.1101/SQB.1960.025.01.039

Lipp, H.-P., Vyssotski, A. L., Wolfer, D. P., Renaudineau, S., Savini, M., Tröster, G., & Dell'Omo, G. (2004). Pigeon homing along highways and exits. *Current Biology, 14,* 1239–1249. doi:10.1016/j.cub.2004.07.024

Mangan, M., & Webb, B. (2009). Modelling place memory in crickets. *Biological Cybernetics, 101,* 307–323. doi:10.1007/s00422-009-0338-1

Menzel, R., Geiger, K., Jeorges, J., Müller, U., & Chittka, L. (1998). Bees travel novel homeward routes by integrating separately acquired vector memories. *Animal Behaviour, 55,* 139–152. doi:10.1006/anbe.1997.0574

Menzel, R., Greggers, U., Smith, A., Berger, S., Brandt, R., Brunke, S., . . . Watzl, S. (2005). Honeybees navigate according to a map-like spatial memory. *Proceedings of the National Academy of Sciences of the United States of America, 102,* 3040–3045. doi:10.1073/pnas.0408550102

Morris, R. G. M. (1981). Spatial localization does not require the presence of local cues. *Learning and Motivation, 12,* 239–260. doi:10.1016/0023-9690(81)90020-5

Narendra, A., Si, A., Sulikowski, D., & Cheng, K. (2007). Learning, retention and coding of nest-associated visual cues by the Australian desert ant, *Melophorus bagoti. Behavioral Ecology and Sociobiology, 61,* 1543–1553. doi:10.1007/s00265-007-0386-2

Nicholson, D. J., Judd, P. D., Cartwright, B. A., & Collett, T. S. (1999). Learning walks and landmark guidance in wood ants (*Formica rufa*). *The Journal of Experimental Biology, 202,* 1831–1838.

O'Keefe, J., & Nadel, L. (1978). *The hippocampus as a cognitive map.* Oxford, England: Clarendon Press.

Olton, D. S., & Samuelson, R. J. (1976). Remembrance of places passed: Spatial memory in rats. *Journal of Experimental Psychology: Animal Behavior Processes, 2,* 97–116. doi:10.1037/0097-7403.2.2.97

Pavlov, I. P. (1927). *Conditioned reflexes.* Oxford, England: Oxford University Press.

Pearce, J. M., Graham, M., Good, M. A., Jones, P. M., & McGregor, A. (2006). Potentiation, overshadowing, and blocking of spatial learning based on the shape of the environment. *Journal of Experimental Psychology: Animal Behavior Processes, 32,* 201–214. doi:10.1037/0097-7403.32.3.201

Pearce, J. M., Ward-Robinson, J., Good, M., Fussell, C., & Aydin, A. (2001). Influence of a beacon on the spatial learning based on the shape of the test environment. *Journal of Experimental Psychology: Animal Behavior Processes, 27,* 329–344. doi:10.1037/0097-7403.27.4.329

Ramsden, E., & Adams, J. (2009). Escaping the laboratory: The rodent experiments of John B. Calhoun & their cultural influence. *Journal of Social History, 42,* 761–797. doi:10.1353/jsh/42.3.761

Ritchie, B. F. (1947). Studies in spatial learning. III. Two paths to the same location and two paths to two different locations. *Journal of Experimental Psychology, 37,* 25–38. doi:10.1037/h0056717

Roberts, W. A. (1984). Some issues in animal spatial memory. In H. L. Roitblat, T. G. Bever, & H. S. Terrace (Eds.), *Animal cognition* (pp. 425–443). Hillsdale, NJ: Erlbaum.

Rodrigo, T., Chamizo, V. D., McLaren, I. P. L., & Mackintosh, N. J. (1997). Blocking in the spatial domain. *Journal of Experimental Psychology: Animal Behavior Processes, 23,* 110–118. doi:10.1037/0097-7403.23.1.110

Rosengren, R., & Fortelius, W. (1986). Ortstreue in foraging ants of the *Formica rufa* group—Hierarchy of orienting cues and long-term memory. *Insectes Sociaux, 33,* 306–337. doi:10.1007/BF02224248

Santschi, F. (1913). Comment s'orientent les fourmis [How do ants orient?]. *Revue Suisse de Zoologie, 21,* 347–426.

Shettleworth, S. J. (2009). The evolution of comparative cognition: Is the snark still a boojum? *Behavioural Processes, 80,* 210–217. doi:10.1016/j.beproc. 2008.09.001

Shettleworth, S. J. (2010). *Cognition, evolution, and behavior* (2nd ed.). New York, NY: Oxford University Press.

Sheynikhovich, D., Chavarriaga, R., Strösslin, T., Arleo, A., & Gerstner, W. (2009). Is there a geometric module for spatial orientation? Insights from a rodent navigational model. *Psychological Review, 116,* 540–566. doi:10.1037/a0016170

Skinner, D. M., Etchegary, C. M., Ekert-Maret, E. C., Baker, C. J., Harley, C. W., Evans, J. H., & Martin, G. M. (2003). An analysis of response, direction, and place learning in an open field and T maze. *Journal of Experimental Psychology: Animal Behavior Processes, 29,* 3–13. doi:10.1037/0097-7403.29.1.3

Skinner, D. M., Horne, M. R., Murphy, K. E. A., & Martin, G. M. (2010). Rats' orientation is more important than start point location for successful place learning. *Journal of Experimental Psychology: Animal Behavior Processes, 36,* 110–116. doi:10.1037/ a0015773

Southwick, E. E., & Buchmann, S. L. (1995). Effects of horizon landmarks on homing success in honey bees. *American Naturalist, 146,* 748–764. doi:10.1086/285823

Spetch, M. L. (1995). Overshadowing in landmark learning: Touch-screen studies with pigeons and humans. *Journal of Experimental Psychology: Animal Behavior Processes, 21,* 166–181. doi:10.1037/0097-7403.21.2.166

Spetch, M. L., Cheng, K., & MacDonald, S. E. (1996). Learning the configuration of a landmark array: I. Touch-screen studies with pigeons and humans. *Journal of Comparative Psychology, 110,* 55–68. doi:10.1037/0735-7036.110.1.55

Spetch, M. L., Cheng, K., MacDonald, S. E., Linkenhoker, B. A., Kelly, D. M., & Doerkson, S. R. (1997). Use of landmark configuration in pigeons and humans: II. Generality across search tasks. *Journal of Comparative Psychology, 111,* 14–24. doi:10.1037/0735-7036.111.1.14

Spetch, M. L., Cheng, K., & Mondloch, M. V. (1992). Landmark use by pigeons in a touch-screen spatial search task. *Animal Learning & Behavior, 20,* 281–292. doi:10.3758/BF03213382

Srinivasan, M. V., Zhang, S. W., & Witney, K. (1994). Visual discrimination of pattern orientation by honeybees: Performance and implications for corti-

cal processing. *Philosophical Transactions of the Royal Society B: Biological Sciences, 343,* 199–210. doi:10.1098/rstb.1994.0021

Stürzl, W., Cheung, A., Cheng, K., & Zeil, J. (2008). Information content of panoramic images: I. Rotational errors and the similarity of views in rectangular arenas. *Journal of Experimental Psychology: Animal Behavior Processes, 34,* 1–14. doi:10.1037/0097-7403.34.1.1

Sutton, J. E. (2002). Multiple-landmark piloting in pigeons (*Columbia livia*): Landmark configuration as a discriminative cue. *Journal of Comparative Psychology, 116,* 391–403. doi:10.1037/0735-7036.116.4.391

Suzuki, S., Augerinos, G., & Black, A. H. (1980). Stimulus control of spatial behavior on the eight-arm radial maze. *Learning and Motivation, 11,* 1–18. doi:10.1016/0023-9690(80)90018-1

Tang, S., Wolf, R., Xu, S., & Heisenberg, M. (2004, August). Visual pattern recognition in Drosophila is invariant for retinal position. *Science, 305,* 1020–1022. doi:10.1126/science.1099839

Tinbergen, N. (1951). *The study of instinct.* Oxford, England: Oxford University Press.

Tolman, E. C. (1948). Cognitive maps in rats and men. *Psychological Review, 55,* 189–208. doi:10.1037/ h0061626

Towne, W. F., & Moscrip, H. (2008). The connection between landscapes and the solar ephemeris in honeybees. *The Journal of Experimental Biology, 211,* 3729–3736. doi:10.1242/jeb.022970

Twyman, A. D., & Newcombe, N. S. (2010). Five reasons to doubt the existence of a geometric module. *Cognitive Science, 34,* 1315–1356.

Vallortigara, G. (2009). Animals as natural geometers. In L. Tommasi, M. A. Peterson, & L. Nadel (Eds.), *Cognitive biology* (pp. 83–104). Cambridge, MA: MIT Press.

van Iersal, J. J. A., & van den Assem, J. (1964). Aspects of orientation in the digger wasp *Bembix rostrata*. *Animal Behaviour, 1,* 145–162.

von Frisch, K. (1967). *The dance language and orientation of bees.* Cambridge, MA: Belknap Press.

von Frisch, K., & Lindauer, M. (1954). Himmel und Erde in Konkurrenz bei der Orientierung der Bienen [Sky and Earth in competition in the orientation of bees]. *Naturwissenschaften, 41,* 245–253. doi:10.1007/ BF00634944

Wall, P. L., Botly, L. C. P., Black, C. K., & Shettleworth, S. J. (2004). The geometric module in the rat: Independence of shape and feature learning. *Learning & Behavior, 32,* 289–298. doi:10.3758/ BF03196028

Wehner, R. (2003). Desert ant navigation: How miniature brains solve complex tasks. *Journal of Comparative Physiology A: Neuroethology, Sensory, Neural, and Behavioral Physiology, 189,* 579–588. doi:10.1007/s00359-003-0431-1

Wehner, R. (2009). The architecture of the desert ant's navigational toolkit (Hymenoptera: Formicidae). *Myrmecological News, 12,* 85–96.

Wehner, R., Boyer, M., Loertscher, F., Sommer, S., & Menzi, U. (2006). Ant navigation: One-way routes rather than maps. *Current Biology, 16,* 75–79. doi:10.1016/j.cub.2005.11.035

Wehner, R., & Menzel, R. (1990). Do insect have cognitive maps? *Annual Review of Neuroscience, 13,* 403–414. doi:10.1146/annurev.ne.13.030190.002155

Wehner, R., Michel, B., & Antonsen, P. (1996). Visual navigation in insects: Coupling of egocentric and geocentric information. *The Journal of Experimental Biology, 199,* 129–140.

Wehner, R., & Räber, F. (1979). Visual spatial memory in desert ants, genus *Cataglyphis* (Formicidae, Hymenoptera). *Experientia, 35,* 1569–1571. doi:10.1007/BF01953197

Zampoglou, M., Szenher, M., & Webb, B. (2006). Adaptation of controllers for image-based homing. *Adaptive Behavior, 14,* 381–399. doi:10.1177/1059712306072338

Zeil, J., Hofmann, M. I., & Chahl, J. S. (2003). Catchment areas of panoramic snapshots in outdoor scenes. *Journal of the Optical Society of America, 20,* 450–469. doi:10.1364/JOSAA.20.000450

CHAPTER 8

COGNITIVE MAPS

Lynn Nadel

In his seminal 1948 paper, Tolman introduced the notion of cognitive maps in the following way: "In the course of learning something like a field map of the environment gets established in the rat's brain" (p. 192). He went on to distinguish between "narrow and strip-like maps" and "relatively broad and comprehensive maps" (p. 193), pointing out that only the latter kinds of maps would support flexible behavior in a variable environment.

Although the notion of cognitive maps has been used in many different ways in the years since this seminal paper, the present chapter retains a focus on cognitive maps as "relatively broad and comprehensive" spatial representations. Tolman (1948) discussed spatial cognitive maps in the context of a broader discussion of forms of learning, making the important claim that the kind of learning that involves cognitive maps might be qualitatively different from other kinds of learning. Although this chapter does not stress this issue, I return at the end with support for the idea that learning about and using cognitive maps conveys unique features—such as flexibility—of the ways in which this knowledge can be expressed in behavior.

Tolman (1948) provided support for his idea of cognitive maps by discussing data from a variety of experiments. These studies explored several concepts that remain important to any discussion of cognitive maps today.

1. *Latent learning.* This is the idea that learning can occur independently of reward, as demonstrated when a rat that is not motivated by hunger, thirst or a need to escape nonetheless moves in, and seems to learn about, the features of a novel environment (e.g., Tolman & Honzik, 1930).

2. *Vicarious trial and error* (VTE). This is the idea, first introduced by Muenzinger (1938), that rats at a choice point in a maze engage in a looking-back-and-forth behavior that seems to reflect their analysis of the situation and their subsequent choice of which way to turn. We see later that an apparent neurophysiological correlate of this phenomenon has recently been discovered.

3. *Hypotheses.* This is the idea, introduced by Krechevsky (1932), that a rat learning how to navigate successfully in a maze engages in systematic choices rather than random behavior, as if the animal has a hypothesis about what to do. In this context, Tolman (1948) compared the *place hypotheses* subserved by cognitive maps with *response hypotheses* subserved by other forms of learning. The notion of place learning has become critical to any discussion of the function of the hippocampus, which appears to be central to cognitive mapping (O'Keefe & Nadel, 1978).

These concepts, so central to Tolman's (1948) treatment, reappear at various points in the chapter.

DOI: 10.1037/13936-009
Handbook of Spatial Cognition, D. Waller and L. Nadel (Editors)

From the perspective of psychologists now studying spatial cognition, the key questions about cognitive maps concern such things as how we acquire the knowledge indicative of such maps, what properties they have, how we use them, how they change over the life span, and how they might vary from individual to individual or between groups (e.g., genders). Before turning to these questions, though, it is important to define what we mean by the term *cognitive map*.

WHAT IS A COGNITIVE MAP?

A cognitive map is best defined as a mental representation of the environment that captures, in some specifiable way, the spatial relations among things in the world. Such a mental representation can be used to recognize places, to compute distances and directions, and in practical terms, to help an organism find its way from where it is to where it wants to be. As Downs and Stea (1973) pointed out some time ago, there is no need to assume that an internal cognitive map actually looks like a map in the head, and current evidence suggests this is not the case. That is, unlike the representations one can find in various regions of visual cortex, there is no topological mapping between entities in the external world and ensembles of neurons in the brain structures involved in forming cognitive maps. Rather, the mental representation and neurobiological substrates that underlie a cognitive map act like, rather than literally look like, a map. It is an open question whether the brain creates and maintains such maplike representations in the long term or whether it generates the behavior indicative of a map on the fly, so to speak. I defer discussion of this issue until later, because it is not critical to our consideration of what it means to behave as though one had a map in one's head.

A key feature of cognitive maps is that they represent information in a viewpoint-independent fashion; that is, as if from a survey or bird's eye perspective. Another key feature of cognitive maps is that they represent configurations, rather than simple associations, between features of the environment. Finally, in contrast to spatial representations that depend on egocentric reference frames, cognitive maps depend on an allocentric frame (see Introduction, Chapters 9, and 12, this volume). There has been considerable debate about the relative importance and roles of egocentric versus allocentric representations, and it is beyond the scope of this chapter to join that debate (see Burgess et al., 2006, for a comprehensive review). I take it as a given that, functionally speaking, allocentric spatial representations—and hence cognitive maps—exist and play an important role in behavior.

HOW DOES ONE ACQUIRE A COGNITIVE MAP?

Given that cognitive maps represent environmental realities, they are necessarily acquired through interactions with the external world—as pointed out by Tolman (1948), one acquires cognitive maps by exploring the environment. Nonetheless, some of the properties of our cognitive maps may come not from individual experiences in the world but rather from specific features of the machinery—the cells, circuits and networks in the brain—within which they are realized. This possibility suggests that any discussion of cognitive maps and their properties will benefit from analysis of how they are built out of neurons. Chapter 1 of this volume provides some of the required information, and in what follows, I provide additional background meant to complement their discussion.

Building on Tolman's (1948) suggestion and the discovery of *place cells* (O'Keefe & Dostrovsky, 1971), O'Keefe and Nadel (1978) argued that the hippocampal formation provided the basis for both building and storing cognitive maps. In their view, such maps required the combination of several kinds of information—both sensory and motor—that allowed an organism to represent places, distances, and directions. Several more recent discoveries, in addition to the discovery of place cells, have helped understand how the hippocampus might combine these various inputs to create maps. James Ranck first reported in the 1980s the discovery of neurons in the rat postsubiculum that seem to encode the direction in which an animal is facing—the so-called *head-direction cells*. These were more fully described in two papers published some years later (Taube, Muller, & Ranck, 1990a,1990b). Work since then has uncovered a set of structures containing these head-direction cells, including the lateral dorsal nucleus of the thalamus (Mizumori & Williams, 1993), the anterior thalamic nuclei (Taube, 1995), the posterior parietal cortex (Chen, Lin, Green, Barnes, & McNaughton, 1994), and the lateral mammillary nucleus (Blair, Cho, & Sharp, 1998). A third critical cell type has been uncovered in the medial entorhinal cortex, the so-called *grid cells,* whose activity profiles differ from place cells in that each grid cell is active at multiple locations in the environment (Hafting, Fyhn, Molden, Moser, & Moser, 2005). What is more, these locations are not random but rather highly regular in that collectively they comprise what literally looks (to the scientist recording the cells' activity) like a grid. This property is independent of the features of the environment the animal explores, hence the gridlike activity patterns must result from the brain's own construction.

The medial entorhinal cortex (MEC) contains not only these grid cells but also some head-direction cells, some cells that appear to combine both of these properties together, and yet another type of cell that is particularly responsive to vertical surfaces, the so-called *border cell* (Solstad, Boccara, Kropff, Moser, & Moser, 2008) or *boundary vector cell* (Lever, Burton, Jeewajee, O'Keefe, & Burgess, 2009). Given that the MEC is one of the major inputs to the hippocampus and its place cells, these various findings are highly supportive of the notion that the hippocampus constructs, from its inputs, an internal map of the spatial properties of the environment— a cognitive map. Of course, the foundational results leading to this notion came from work with rodents, and it is important to ask whether similar findings obtain in humans. Obtaining recordings from individual neurons in humans is nontrivial, but several studies of patients with epilepsy with in-dwelling microelectrodes have made this possible, and they have confirmed the presence of neurons responsive to spatial location in the human hippocampus and entorhinal cortex (Ekstrom et al., 2003; J. Jacobs, Kahana, Ekstrom, Mollison, & Fried, 2010) and hence the likelihood that these structures are important for cognitive maps in both rats and humans.

In addition, evidence for grid cells in the human in a network centered on the entorhinal cortex was provided in a recent functional magnetic resonance imaging study (Doeller, Barry, & Burgess, 2010).

In addition to evidence for the various kinds of spatially tuned neurons in humans, there is abundant support from studies of patients with damage in the hippocampal system, or from neuroimaging studies in spatial tasks, to confirm that in humans as well as in rats the hippocampus is critically involved in forming and using cognitive maps. This literature is already too extensive to review here (see Spiers & Maguire, 2007, for a recent review, and Howard et al., 2011; Morgan, MacEvoy, Aguirre, & Epstein, 2011; Suthana, Ekstrom, Moshirvaziri, Knowlton, & Bookheimer, 2009; Xu, Evensmoen, Lehn, Pintzka, & Haberg, 2010, for recent examples).

Several recent studies have addressed the question of where these maps come from. In constructing an internal representation of an environment, one needs information not only about what is in that environment but also how the various components of the environment—objects in it and surfaces that compose it—relate to one another spatially. It is clear that information about the features of the environment and about the movement of the animal through the environment (literally or figuratively) contribute to the construction of cognitive maps. Before considering these contributions in more detail, it is worth exploring the question of how the various neurons that compose the mapping system emerge during early development. One possibility is that they are present more or less from birth and that the ability to map external space is part of our nature, more or less, as suggested by the nativist philosopher Kant in the 1700s. A second possibility is that these cells, and their spatial properties, emerge as a function of early experiences moving around in the world, a position more in line with the views of empiricist philosophers such as Poincare, who argued at the beginning of the 20th century that spatial knowledge must result from our earliest interactions with the world.

The results of two recent studies, from separate labs, support the first of these two positions (Langston et al., 2010; Wills et al., 2010). Both studies recorded from place cells, head-direction

157

cells, and grid cells in rat pups starting from 16 days of postnatal life, during their first exposure to any environment outside of their home cage. In both studies, head-direction cells were present at the outset, place cells showed up next, and grid cells emerged last. That cells of all these types were evident the first time an animal was exposed to the external environment is most consistent with the idea that the framework required to create internal cognitive maps is prefigured in the nervous system prior to specific experiences moving around in space. Recent cross-cultural work (Izard, Pica, Spelke, & Dehaene, 2011) supports the view that, independent of specific training, children spontaneously develop geometrical intuitions consistent with the principles of Euclidean geometry.

Thus, the neural machinery for the construction of cognitive maps, and hence some aspects of the spatial knowledge these maps ultimately contain, seems to be built into our wiring from the outset and emerges during brain maturation independent of specific experiences in space. Of course, this wiring only provides the spatial scaffold for creating maps and cannot provide the actual content of these maps because the content depends on the specific, and unpredictable, combinations of things we experience in our own lives. Nonetheless, the fact that this scaffold is apparently built-in means that some of the properties of our cognitive maps come not from experience but from inheritance.

With the involvement of this scaffolding system, specific cognitive maps are acquired through the exploration of environments an organism is exposed to. This exploration allows an organism to learn about where things are located and how they relate to one another and to the surfaces of the environment. This contingent knowledge is what must be used in figuring out first which environment we are in and then how to get around it in service of specific needs such as finding food, a mate, safety, or our way home.

Active exploration of an environment is the most direct way in which one can acquire a cognitive map and the way that most animals other than humans normally acquire such maps in the wild. This exploration typically involves moving one's entire body within the environment, but it can also reflect

merely moving one's eyes. Humans have developed a number of secondary means by which map knowledge can be acquired, from pictures drawn in sand or on paper, to words used to describe spatial attributes of the environment, to GPS systems that substitute for all or most of the aforementioned. Much of what was known about cognitive maps until recently came from studies of active exploration, but more recent work has focused either on secondary acquisition or on the use of virtual environments. It remains unclear whether the maps acquired by exploring an environment in virtual space are equivalent in all important respects to those we acquire through direct experience, although there is some indication that GPS users acquire less accurate spatial representations (Ishikawa, Fujiwara, Imai, & Okabe, 2008). In all cases, the acquisition of a cognitive map seems to involve the weaving together of information gained in multiple instants; that is, one typically cannot acquire a map in a single moment but only over some period of time. Thus, acquiring a cognitive map is unlike learning to recognize a face or a fact about the world, which can be done in one go. Acquiring maps necessarily involves sequences and the knitting together of information gained at separate times.

The studies of rat pups alluded to earlier showed one more thing of interest here: Although various spatial cells were present at the outset, these cells and the broader system of which they were a part were refined over time and became more precise. This finding matches what we know about the emergence of cognitive mapping abilities in children: Although rudimentary abilities exist at a relatively early age, adultlike cognitive mapping capacity continues to develop for many years. We discuss this developmental story next, after we describe some of the properties of cognitive maps and how they are used.

PROPERTIES OF COGNITIVE MAPS

As already suggested, cognitive maps represent spaces, what is contained within them, and the relations among these contents. Thus, my cognitive map of the house I live in represents the rooms in the house and their relation to each other, along with the contents of each room and the relations among these contents. My cognitive map of the city I live in (Tucson) represents the mountains in all directions, the few large buildings, the university campus at which I work, the various neighborhoods I visit with any frequency, the roads on which I drive and bike, and so on.

I focus here on several questions about these representations: How detailed and accurate are they? Are there certain features of the environment that are more (or less) likely to be captured by them? Chapter 9 in this volume also discusses the properties of spatial representations at some length.

Details, Accuracy, and Features

Tolman (1948) raised this issue in his seminal paper: Are cognitive maps mere "sketch maps"? We now understand what seems intuitively obvious: Our cognitive map of a given region becomes progressively more detailed as we gain increasing exposure to that region (e.g., Golledge, 1999). What starts out as a sketchy map with few details becomes increasingly fleshed out over time and with experience. Without further experience, details can "fade," and maps become sketchy again over time. Cognitive maps are not only sketchy on occasion but also routinely contain systematic distortions (e.g., Tversky, 1992), though these do not render them unusable.

Cognitive maps capture information about various details of the environment, including landmarks, paths and routes, and metric features. Early notions of cognitive mapping assumed that these kinds of details about an environment were acquired in sequence: First one learned about landmarks, then about routes, and only then did one have metric information about the environment (e.g., Siegel & White, 1975). There was little empirical support for this idea, which was rooted in Piagetian assumptions about the sequence with which knowledge about space emerged in development. Ishikawa and Montello (2006) explored the issue of the microgenesis of cognitive map knowledge in a systematic way, showing that for many individuals information about all three aspects of environmental knowledge can accrue right from the first exposure. The quantitative knowledge about the environment these individuals quickly acquire

tends to be approximate rather than precise. Other individuals, who incidentally tended to report having a poor "sense of direction," did not acquire maplike knowledge early on, and indeed there is reason to suspect they never did so. As a result of this and other research, there is generally little support for the idea that some kinds of details (e.g., landmarks, routes) are necessarily acquired before others (e.g., quantitative relations, maplike structures).

In the construction of a cognitive map, certain aspects of the environment seem to play a more important role than others. To start, large stable objects and features are the focus of map creation. Chakraborty, Anderson, Chaudhry, Mumford, and Jeffery (2004) showed that a cue capable of helping to define the place field of a neuron in the hippocampus loses that ability if its stability is undermined in full view of the animal. Thus, stable landmarks are necessary to anchor a space and form the scaffolding to which all subsequent details can be added. In addition, the general shape of the environment, as conveyed by the mostly distal surfaces forming it, is also a crucial part of one's cognitive map. This combination of geometry and landmarks defines a given space, and in this sense, such information has a privileged status in the creation of cognitive maps. Although most of the work on cognitive maps has been focused on visual information, it is clear from work with both rats and humans that information from multiple sensory modalities can be integrated into a single map (e.g., Kelly & Avraamides, 2011).

HOW COGNITIVE MAPS ARE USED

Given that one has acquired a cognitive map of an environment, what can one do with it? Roughly speaking, one can use a map to locate oneself, to orient or reorient oneself, and to find one's way using familiar routes or even novel paths if necessary.

Location
Imagine that you are transported to a location while blindfolded and that on arrival and removal of the blindfold, you have to figure out where you are. How would you do this? The answer appears to be that you would search the environment for familiar

landmarks or features that would allow you to "call up" the relevant cognitive map, thereby identifying the environment in which you now find yourself. Without such familiar features, you would be forced to conclude that you are in a new environment for which you do not possess any map. For many people this can be a quite disorienting experience; for most, it is an invitation to start building a new map.

Orientation and Reorientation

Connected to locating oneself in a particular environment is the problem of determining one's orientation within that environment. Knowing that I am in Times Square in New York City when I emerge from a subway station is not enough to set me off in the right direction—I also need to know my orientation, or heading direction. How one accomplishes this feat has been the focus of an extensive series of studies on the process of *reorientation*— the ability to reestablish one's bearings after one has lost them. As discussed at length in a number of other chapters in this volume (Introduction, Chapters 9, 10, and 14), these studies began with the striking finding by Cheng (1986) that animals fail to use featural information in combination with geometric information to find a reward in an enclosed box.

The conclusion that rats had a "geometric module," subsequently extended to humans by Hermer and Spelke (1994, 1996), was clearly somewhat overstated, because there are conditions under which even young children clearly combine geometric and featural information; for instance, Learmonth, Nadel, and Newcombe (2002) showed that the same children either did or did not combine information from these two sources, depending on the size of the test apparatus (a result consistent with recent work in reorienting rats; Maes, Fontanari, & Regolin, 2009), whereas Hupbach and Nadel (2005) showed that such combining occurred readily in a rhombus-shaped environment as soon as the children were able to perform in the situation.

The broader question of the relative importance of geometric and featural information in spatial cognition has been much debated in recent years. The emerging consensus appears to be that both kinds of information are important, that there are individual differences in their deployment, and that even within an individual there are times when one or the other, or both, are preferentially deployed (see Lew, 2011, for an excellent recent review). That these two are fundamentally distinct, however, is supported by the recent finding that individuals with Williams syndrome are incapable of using geometric information to reorient in the standard task, but can nonetheless use landmarks (a blue wall) to do so (Lakusta, Dessalegn, & Landau, 2010).

Not all features of the environment are equally useful in establishing one's orientation. O'Keefe and Nadel (1978) argued that distal cues were more useful than proximal cues because the relations among distal cues did not change much as an organism moved about in the world, once again demonstrating the importance of featural stability in cognitive mapping. Support for the priority of distal features comes from the work of Cressant, Muller, and Poucet (1997) on place cells and that of Zugaro et al. (2004) and Zugaro, Berthoz, and Wiener (2001) on head-direction cells. In both cases, distal but not proximal cues controlled the activity patterns of the relevant neurons. The fact that distal, but not proximal, cues are critical for calibrating the head-direction system might help us understand the conflicting results from the reorientation studies. Nadel and Hupbach (2006) argued that features can be combined with geometrical information when the test room is sufficiently large that those features are taken as "distal," not "proximal," by the head-direction system.

Wayfinding

Given knowledge of one's location and bearing, how does one use a cognitive map to get to some other location? The short answer is that cognitive maps provide relevant information about where a goal is located, the routes one can take to get there from the current location, and the landmarks one will observe along the way. This information, collectively, allows one to get to and from places in the environment. Problems arise when the commonly used path is, for some reason, unavailable. It is in such cases that cognitive maps prove their merit, by providing the organism with the possibility of taking a new path. Indeed, this possibility has since Tolman

(1948) been taken as one of the defining features of cognitive maps. More recently, Etienne, Maurer, Georgakopoulos, and Griffin (1999) suggested that an organism can be said to have a cognitive map only if it can "perform adequate new routes, that is, choose the most economical alternative path (such as a shortcut or a detour) under new conditions" (p. 197–198).

In contrast to being totally dependent on the habitual use of specific routes, cognitive maps are inherently flexible and thus enable organisms to take a detour or use a shortcut. The ability to do this depends on the existence of a system that keeps the animal oriented appropriately in space, such that it always knows in which direction the goal lies, even when the need to take a detour might actually involve moving away from the goal momentarily. A recent study of detour behavior in rats, using a maze quite similar to one first introduced in Tolman's lab, showed both that they are quite efficient in rapidly finding detours around a barrier and that there are localized changes in hippocampal place cell firing associated with the region around the barrier (Alvernhe, Save, & Poucet, 2011).

Simulation of Future States

Tolman described a critical aspect of the behavior one can observe when a rat is moving through a maze and reaches a choice point. As noted earlier, rats will sometimes pause at the choice point and look from side to side, as if they are thinking about the consequences of taking one path or the other. We now know that this VTE behavior is accompanied by quite specific patterns of behavior in the rat's hippocampus, typically referred to as *preplay*. Briefly, as has been shown in several labs (Davidson, Kloosterman, & Wilson, 2009; Foster & Wilson, 2006; Gupta, van der Meer, Touretzky, & Redish, 2010), one can observe in a rat sitting at the choice point, sequences of activity in hippocampal place cells that would be seen were the rat to actually traverse a particular path. This preplay appears to be the neurobiological basis of Tolman's VTE behavior—a rat at a choice point can activate the neurons that predict which places an animal will move through and, presumably, what will be encountered in those places. This simulation could

allow the animal to decide at the choice point which path is most likely to lead to the goal.

Such data suggest that one of the major functions of cognitive maps is to allow individuals to generate expectations of the future. In the limited case described here, the future is merely what is likely to be around the corner. But we now know that the hippocampal system critical for cognitive mapping is also critical for remembering the past and imagining the future. Individuals with damage in the hippocampal system are not only lost in space at the moment but also have a devastating syndrome involving the loss of both detailed episodic memories and the ability to imagine their future in any coherent detail (Hassabis, Kumaran, Vann, & Maguire, 2007). This linkage between cognitive maps and episodic experience helps us understand why the same brain system is central to both spatial cognition and memory.

Place Learning

Tolman (1948) noted that cognitive maps allow rats to use *place* hypotheses. What this means, as we have just seen, is that rats can use their cognitive maps to tell them where they are, where they want to go, and how to get there. Tolman also noted that rats can use various hypotheses to solve tasks and that place hypotheses are but one type. A distinction between place and response hypotheses was critical to debates about animal learning in the 1940s, leading to the conclusion that animals can indeed use multiple behavioral strategies, depending on the situation and available cues (e.g., Restle, 1957; see Chapter 14, this volume, for further discussion of these studies and their implications).

What is entailed in using a place hypothesis, and how can we tell when an animal or human is using one? In the classic rat studies, animals initially learned to choose one arm of a T maze, typically for food or water reward. After learning, the start arm of the apparatus was rotated 180° and the rat given a choice between returning to the same place or making the same response (body turn to left or right). In general, when the rats can see the environment, about 75% choose the same place rather than the same response. In other words, they were using a place hypothesis. When the external environment is cut off by using quite high walls or by entirely covering the maze or enclosing it in a curtained environment with few distinguishing features, the use of response hypotheses increases, and the use of place hypotheses decreases.

In addition to place and response hypotheses, O'Keefe and Nadel (1978) argued that rats could use *cue hypotheses*, involving the approach to, or avoidance of, a specific landmark or cue. They argued, and showed in a study with rats (O'Keefe, Nadel, Keightley, & Kill, 1975), that the hippocampal system, and its cognitive map function, was essential for the use of place hypotheses. Rats with lesions in this system learned to approach a cue that signaled the availability of reward, but were incapable of learning to approach a place for the same reward. Much the same thing has now been shown for humans in studies with neurological patients and also in studies using neuroimaging in healthy adults. Iaria, Petrides, Dagjer, Pike, and Bohbot, (2003), for example, showed that humans using place hypotheses (in a virtual environment) activate their hippocampus, whereas those using a response hypothesis activate their caudate nucleus.

HOW COGNITIVE MAPPING EMERGES IN DEVELOPMENT

Insofar as cognitive mapping depends on the hippocampal system, the status of this system should determine cognitive mapping capacity across development. It has long been known that the hippocampus is a relatively late-developing brain structure. Although most hippocampal neurons are born before birth, effective connectivity throughout the structure is only established sometime later. Synapse formation continues well after birth, as does myelination (Ábrahám et al., 2010; Seress, Ábrahám, Tornóczky, & Kosztolányi, 2001). This delayed maturation has important behavioral consequences.

The development of the ability to use a place strategy in rats has been studied in several labs. Generally, place strategy utilization emerges about 21 days postnatal, well after the ability to use other strategies in the same behavioral situation. For example, work in my lab (Nadel & Willner, 1989) explored the use of various strategies in both the

T maze and the water maze. We showed that the ability to use a place strategy emerges some days after cue strategies can be deployed, a result that has been seen in other labs as well (e.g., Rudy, Stadker-Morris, & Albert, 1987). Much the same picture has been observed in studies with toddlers. The ability to use place strategies and engage in map-based (allocentric) spatial behavior seems to emerge only after 21 months (Newcombe, Huttenlocher, Drimmey, & Wiley, 1998). Response learning appears relatively mature early in life, whereas place learning does not (Leplow et al., 2003).

Not only does hippocampal function emerge late in humans but it also continues to develop for some time. A recent study by Nardini, Thomas, Knowland, Braddick, and Atkinson (2009) looked at the emergence of viewpoint-independent spatial reorientation in a task that required understanding of how the overall space was structured. Children younger than 6 years of age were not capable of flexible behavior from arbitrary viewpoints, suggesting that adultlike performance on allocentric spatial tasks continues to improve through the first decade of life. Using a virtual reality task based on the ubiquitous Morris water maze, Piper, Acevedo, Craytor, Murray, and Raber (2010) showed that dramatic improvements in performance could still be observed between 9 and 10 years of age.

Children not only perform less well in navigation tasks, they also appear to place different emphasis on the various kinds of information available in the task. Bullens et al. (2010) tested children (5 and 7 years of age) and adults on a task that provided landmarks, boundary information, and distal cues useful for coding direction. Adults relied mainly on stable boundary cues, but children used both landmarks and boundary cues to the same extent. Further, adults coded angular information using distal cues, whereas children coded distance more accurately than angle, suggesting difficulties in using the distal cues (see also Leplow et al., 2003). Overall, the data supported the view that children can use the same kinds of information as adults, but less well, and as a consequence, they weight various information sources differently than adults (see Learmonth, Newcombe, Sheridan, & Jones, 2008; Newcombe & Huttenlocher, 2006).

VARIATIONS IN COGNITIVE MAPPING

Considerable attention has been paid to the ways in which cognitive mapping varies across individuals. In what follows, I briefly review such individual variation, including some discussion of gender and age effects.

Gender Differences

The question of whether males and females differ in their cognitive mapping ability is a vexing one. Considerable work has been done in both animals and humans to explore this question, with as yet inconclusive results. What does appear to be well established is that the different genders prefer to use different forms of information as they move about the world. Roughly speaking, one can say that using maps invokes several kinds of information. That is, maps involve explicitly spatial information such as distances and directions, along with other information, such as landmarks, that is not in itself spatial. Landmark information becomes spatial when it is incorporated into a map and stands in relation to other landmarks whose distance and direction are coded. A map combines these features.

It appears that males prefer to use explicitly spatial and geometric information as they move about the world, whereas females prefer to use landmarks. Because these different forms of information play more or less important roles in various aspects of cognitive mapping, it is possible to assert that males and females differ in quite obvious ways when behavior depends more critically on one form of information or the other. A recent demonstration of this difference between the genders comes from the work of Chai and Jacobs (2010), who tested the effects of removing directional (slant) and positional (landmark) cues from a human spatial virtual reality task. Males were most affected by removal of the directional cues, whereas females were most affected by removal of the positional cues.

Work in rats first suggested that strategy use in females can vary as a function of where the animals are in their estrus cycle. Female rats in proestrus, or those injected with estradiol, are much more likely to use place strategies than are those in estrus (Korol, Malin, Borden, Busby, & Couper-Leo, 2004).

Whether these hormonally mediated variations in spatial strategy use are also seen in humans is unclear. There is some evidence that testosterone levels influence performance in a spatial navigation task; women with low levels of testosterone perform more poorly than men or than women with high levels (Burkitt, Widman, & Saucier, 2007). Independent of these hormonal effects, Rummel, Epp, and Galea (2010) suggested that female rats overall are less likely to use place strategies than male rats, which they postulated may reflect differences in the relative efficacy of striatal and hippocampal systems in the two genders, those responsible for response and place learning respectively. In accord with this idea, Schoenfeld, Lehmann, and Leplow (2010) showed that human males perform better on a virtual reality navigation task that typically depends on hippocampal place learning but that no difference existed on a task involving only path integration. Finally, the male advantage in place learning seems to be most obvious in certain phases of the standard navigational task in a virtual reality setting. Woolley et al. (2010) showed that the largest gender difference was observed in the initial phase of the task, when participants were plotting a direction in which to head. This phase is critically dependent on the processing of distal features of the environment that indicate directions, as we have seen earlier.

Overall, the data support the view that males and females differ largely in the way they deploy the various types of spatial information. Because many types of information can be integral to using cognitive maps, it seems incorrect to say that one gender is better than another at cognitive mapping. Interested readers should consult the work of Lawton and her colleagues, and Postma and his colleagues (De Goede & Postma, 2008; Lawton, 1994, 2001; Lawton & Kallai, 2002; Postma, Izendoorn, & De Haan, 1998).

Individual Differences

Because the use of cognitive maps depends on specific brain systems, and because such systems can vary in efficacy from one individual to another, it is highly likely that there will be substantial variations in cognitive mapping behavior across individuals. I briefly discuss two kinds of evidence that enable us to describe and understand such individual differences: data from various animals as they learn about and behave in space and data from a unique population of humans.

In the animal world, the mastery of space is essential: Mobile organisms must know how to navigate effectively and how to find what they need when they need it. It is hardly surprising, therefore, that evidence of a spatial mapping function for the hippocampus and its analogues extends back in evolution for over 350 million years. Some species, however, put extra demands on knowledge about space. Some species engage in seasonal migrations that demand impressive spatial abilities; others use space more locally, such as the various animals that cache food in a large number of places and retrieve it some time later with great accuracy. Still others show important differences in space use between males and females. What is intriguing about each of these examples is that variations in space utilization are matched by variations in the relative size of the hippocampus (e.g., Clayton, 1995; Sherry, Jacobs, & Gaulin, 1992).

Gender differences across animal species are equally interesting. An important difference emerges between species that are monogamous and those that are polygynous. In the former, males and females generally share most behaviors, and there is little difference in the extent to which they utilize space. In the latter, males and females differ considerably in their spatial behavior, with males frequently moving across great expanses of space, whereas females tend to stay put. In these species, it is generally the case that males have considerably larger hippocampi than females (see L. F. Jacobs, 1995).

These comparative data are matched by the fascinating results reported for a special population of humans, taxi drivers. In London, taxi drivers must undergo extensive learning about the spatial layout of the city, so that they can readily figure out how to get from one place to another in a city known for its one-way streets and frequent street-name changes. In a series of studies, Maguire and her colleagues (e.g., Maguire et al., 2000) have shown that this learning apparently increases the size of the posterior hippocampus, whose volume correlated with how long the person had been a taxi driver.

Differences With Age

We have already observed that cognitive mapping changes during early development. What happens at the other end of life? The short answer is that, in many individuals, development is played out in reverse: What slowly improves over the first decade of life, slowly deteriorates over the last. This has been observed in both rats and humans. Barnes, Nadel, and Honig (1980) looked at the effect of aging on the use of spatial strategies in rats in a T maze. As was noted earlier, in this situation, rats can use any of several strategies; place strategies are dependent on the hippocampal cognitive mapping system, whereas response and cue strategies are not. Barnes et al. showed that aged rats are less likely to use place strategies than young rats. Barnes has shown in a host of studies (e.g., Rosenzweig & Barnes, 2003) that hippocampal function declines in aged rats; one such effect involves the loss of stability in place cell firing patterns and the consequent loss of stable mapping functions. Old rats frequently fail to retrieve the correct map when put back into a familiar environment, as indicated by their place cells firing in the "wrong" places (Barnes, Suster, Shen, & McNaughton 1997). Such instability would render the use of place strategies quite risky, and it is not surprising that old rats prefer to use other, presumably more reliable, strategies to solve the T maze task.

Much the same thing is seen in humans. Newman and Kaszniak (2000) created a real-world task for humans that could also be solved with multiple strategies, and showed that healthy older adults used fewer place strategies than younger humans, a result that was confirmed in a subsequent study from this group using virtual reality (Laurance et al., 2002). These findings have been replicated recently, again in a virtual environment (Jansen, Schmelter, & Heil, 2010). Participants were tested for route knowledge, landmark knowledge, and configurational knowledge; only the latter showed significant decline with age. Similarly, Schoenfeld et al. (2010) showed that older adults performed more poorly than young adults on two types of virtual reality tasks, one involving pointing to a start point after passive displacement, the other resembling the water maze task.

CONCLUSION

We have learned a lot about cognitive maps since Tolman (1948) first introduced the idea over 60 years ago. Their implementation in the brain is well on its way to being understood, providing an excellent example of how a complex cognitive function can be instantiated in neural circuits. The fact that cognitive maps can be carefully studied in rats as well as humans has made this possible. We also know a great deal about how organisms acquire these maps, how these maps can be used in behavior, and how mapping abilities change across the life span. We are beginning to learn about differences across individuals as well.

In what remains of this chapter, I address two issues raised earlier, the first by Tolman (1948) and the second by a number of investigators over the years. As discussed at the outset, Tolman framed his discussion of cognitive maps in the learning theory debates of his day. Cognitive maps were presumed by him to underlie an organism's capacity to do place learning, which he took to be qualitatively different from response learning. O'Keefe and Nadel (1978) adopted the same position in their discussion of cognitive maps. The first issue, then, concerns what our current understanding of cognitive maps says about the assertion that the learning based on such maps might follow different rules than other kinds of learning. The second issue concerns the existence of maps themselves. Do we really have maplike representations in our heads? Or do we merely behave in ways suggestive of such maps, all the while depending on non-maplike representations?

Learning Principles

As noted at the outset, Tolman's (1948) discussion of cognitive maps took place within a learning theory framework. He stressed the idea that there were multiple forms of learning and the notion that the kind of learning that involved cognitive maps— place learning—was different from other kinds of learning. This idea was adopted and expanded on by O'Keefe and Nadel (1978), who assumed that the cognitive mapping system had special properties. For present purposes, we can focus on their idea that cognitive maps were acquired during exploration and

that, as a consequence, learning could take place within this system during exploration and without the need for rewards. Thus, as with Tolman, much of the learning involving cognitive maps falls into the category of *latent learning*—that is, it simply happens whether or not the organism has a reason to learn about the environment. (This is not to say that motivation plays no role in the acquisition of cognitive maps. One cannot learn about something one pays no attention to, so at a minimum, motivation can influence how much detail one acquires when mapping a new environment.)

One direct consequence of the idea that learning within the cognitive mapping system transpires during exploration of novelty is a prediction that contradicts traditional views about associative learning. A fundamental premise of these views, starting with Rescorla and Wagner (1972), is that learning about something new in the environment occurs if, and only if, that novel stimulus predicts something that was not already predicted by already familiar stimuli. In contrast, the cognitive map perspective does not require this assumption; learning about novel stimuli occurs whether or not these stimuli predict something new about the world. These contrasting perspectives lead to different assumptions about what should happen in the *blocking paradigm* first described by Kamin (1968). In this paradigm, an organism is first trained that a stimulus, say A, leads to an outcome, say X (A → X). On completion of this training, a novel stimulus, say B, is now introduced along with A, so that now A + B → X. What Kamin and many others have shown, using tones and flashing lights as the stimuli and such things as shock or food or water as the outcome, is that the novel stimulus (B) does not seem to become paired with X. That is, the organism fails to learn that B → X, presumably because the occurrence of X was already fully predicted by the stimulus A.

According to cognitive map theory, this paradigm should yield a different result in a spatial situation. Consider the case in which an organism explores an environment and becomes familiar with all of the stimuli in it. What happens when a novel stimulus is introduced into this familiar space? Rather than predicting blocking, cognitive map theory predicts that the organism will acquire knowledge about the novel stimulus, incorporating it into its map of that space. This prediction has been subject to extensive testing in recent years, with initially confusing but now quite conclusive results: Under some conditions, and with respect to certain aspects of the spatial environment, blocking is not observed (e.g., Doeller & Burgess, 2008; Hardt, Hupbach, & Nadel, 2009; but see Horne, Iordanova, & Pearce, 2010). A recent study of hippocampal place cells demonstrates the same thing at the level of individual neurons (Barry & Muller, 2011). Thus, it currently appears that the acquisition of cognitive maps does not strictly follow the same principles of learning more generally.

Do Cognitive Maps Exist?

As already noted, the hippocampal coding of cognitive maps does not resemble an actual map in the head. That is, there is no topological relation between the objects and spatial relations being mapped and their representation in the hippocampus. Put most succinctly, nearby neurons in the hippocampus do not represent nearby places in the world. In what sense, then, is it appropriate to state that this brain structure and its neighbors construct cognitive maps? Some have argued that there is no need to postulate the existence of cognitive maps at all, that the behaviors (and physiology) suggesting such maps can be readily understood without assuming actual maps in the head (e.g., Bennett, 1996; Mackintosh, 2002; see also Chapter 14, this volume). This assertion rests on the view that there is no actual evidence from either behavior or physiology that demands the postulation of maps and that Occam's razor then requires that we eschew this more complicated notion in favor of simpler forms of explanation.

One way to maintain such a view is to hold that the principles of behavior based on cognitive maps are no different from those based on other forms of mental representations. We have just seen in our discussing of blocking that there are some situations in which the learning presumed to be subserved by cognitive maps cannot be understood within traditional learning theory frameworks. Thus, there appears to be behavioral evidence favoring the existence of real maps.

What about the physiology? It is, in principle, hard to argue for or against specific forms of neural representation on the basis of the kinds of data one can generate in electrophysiological studies. The activity one observes in the brain (of rats or humans) can be the result of many things, including the results of both encoding and retrieval operations. Place cells, grid cells, and head-direction cells all show quite stable activity profiles with repeated exposures to the same environment, but this by itself does not prove that they are part of a permanently created cognitive map in the head. However, recent studies exploring hippocampal replay, discussed earlier, do shed more light on this question.

To reiterate, a rat in a familiar environment at a choice point will show activity in its hippocampus indicative of preplaying the sequence of places it would visit if it moved in one direction through the maze or another. As we noted, what Tolman (1948) referred to as VTE behavior at the choice point likely is reflected in this hippocampal preplay as the animal looks back and forth while deciding which way to turn.

Neither replay nor preplay (as described previously) provides conclusive evidence for the existence of cognitive maps. However, the recent study by Gupta et al. (2010) comes a lot closer to this goal. In this case, rats preplayed sequences of places cells (and hence places) that they had never traversed before. The authors concluded that these preplays are evidence for the construction of cognitive maps. Although the physiological data are hardly conclusive at present, they are quite consistent with behavioral evidence favoring the view that cognitive maps are real, that they are constructed in the brains of animals of all kinds, and that they play an important role in many aspects of their behavior.

In my view, perhaps the strongest argument in favor of the existence of cognitive maps as real entities in the brain comes from a consideration of the computational advantages of having such mental representations. Maps are enormously powerful informational tools, because every point on a map is related to every other point within the reference frame of the map. The alternative to such a model of the world would be an extremely large number of pairwise links, an endless list of routes from every point to every other point. Much the same can be said about maplike representations in the brain. One maplike representation, in all its configurational glory, can represent an immense amount of information in a compact form, using far fewer connections to do so. Such efficiency represents quite a payoff, because connections are expensive in neural terms; it takes a lot of energy to build and maintain them, and any arrangement that can minimize the sheer amount of wiring in the brain is highly adaptive. Mobile organisms that need to master space to survive can do so most efficiently by creating mental maps. Does this prove they do so? Of course not. But it makes a compelling case.

SUGGESTED REFERENCES FOR FURTHER READING

Burgess, N. (2006). Spatial memory: How egocentric and allocentric combine. *Trends in Cognitive Sciences* 10, 551–557. doi:10.1016/j.tics.2006.10.005

An excellent review of the issue of frames of reference and how they interact in the service of spatial behavior.

Golledge, R. G. (1999). Human wayfinding and cognitive maps. In R. G. Golledge (Ed.), *Wayfinding behavior. Cognitive mapping and other spatial processes* (pp. 5–45). Baltimore, MD: Johns Hopkins University Press.

An overview of all the issues relating to cognitive maps from one of the field's most important contributors.

Jacobs, L. F. (1995). The ecology of spatial cognition. In E. Alleva, H.-P. Lipp, L. Nadel, A. Fasolo, & L. Ricceri (Eds.), *Behavioural brain research in naturalistic and semi-naturalistic settings: Possibilities and perspectives* (pp. 301–322). Boston, MA: Kluwer Academic. doi:10.1007/978-94-011-0091-5_16

A thorough look at the issue of spatial cognition in comparative perspective.

Lew, A. R. (2011) Looking beyond the boundaries: Time to put landmarks back on the cognitive map? *Psychological Bulletin, 137,* 484–507. doi:10.1037/a0022315

A superb recent review of the literature on spatial reorientation and the roles played in it by landmarks and geometric knowledge.

O'Keefe, J., & Nadel, L. (1978). *The hippocampus as a cognitive map.* Oxford, England: Clarendon Press.

The argument for cognitive maps, and their neurobiological instantiation in the hippocampus, from philosophical, psychological, physiological and neuroscientific perspectives.

References

Ábrahám, H., Vincze, A., Jewgenow, I., Veszprémi, B., Kravják, A., Gömöri, E., & Seress, L. (2010). Myelination in the human hippocampal formation from midgestation to adulthood. *International Journal of Developmental Neuroscience, 28,* 401–410. doi:10.1016/j.ijdevneu.2010.03.004

Alvernhe, A., Save, E., & Poucet, B. (2011). Local remapping of place cell firing in the Tolman detour task. *European Journal of Neuroscience, 33,* 1696–1705. doi:10.1111/j.1460-9568.2011.07653.x

Barnes, C. A., Nadel, L., & Honig, W. K. (1980). Spatial memory deficits in senescent rats. *Canadian Journal of Psychology/Revue canadienne de psychologie, 34,* 29–39. doi:10.1037/h0081022

Barnes, C. A., Suster, M. S., Shen, J., & McNaughton, B. L. (1997, July 17). Multistability of cognitive maps in the hippocampus of old rats. *Nature, 388,* 272–275. doi:10.1038/40859

Barry, J., & Muller, R. (2011). Updating the hippocampal representation of space: Place cell firing fields are controlled by a novel spatial stimulus. *Hippocampus, 21,* 481–494. doi:10.1002/hipo.20764

Bennett, A. T. D. (1996). Do animals have cognitive maps? *The Journal of Experimental Biology, 199,* 219–224.

Blair, H. T., Cho, J., & Sharp, P. E. (1998). Role of the lateral mammillary nucleus in the rat head direction circuit: A combined single unit recording and lesion study. *Neuron, 21,* 1387–1397. doi:10.1016/S0896-6273(00)80657-1

Bullens, J., Nardini, M., Doeller, C. F., Braddick, O., Postma, A., & Burgess, N. (2010). The role of landmarks and boundaries in the development of spatial memory. *Developmental Science, 13,* 170–180. doi:10.1111/j.1467-7687.2009.00870.x

Burgess, N. (2006). Spatial memory: How egocentric and allocentric combine. *Trends in Cognitive Sciences, 10,* 551–557. doi:10.1016/j.tics.2006.10.005

Burkitt, J., Widman, D., & Saucier, D. M. (2007). Evidence for the influence of testosterone in the performance of spatial navigation in a virtual water maze in women but not in men. *Hormones and Behavior, 51,* 649–654. doi:10.1016/j.yhbeh.2007.03.007

Chai, X. J., & Jacobs, L. F. (2010). Effects of cue types on sex differences in human spatial memory. *Behavioural Brain Research, 208,* 336–342. doi:10.1016/j.bbr.2009.11.039

Chakraborty, S., Anderson, M. I., Chaudhry, A. M., Mumford, J. C., & Jeffery, K. J. (2004). Context-independent directional cue learning by hippocampal place cells. *European Journal of Neuroscience, 20,* 281–292. doi:10.1111/j.1460-9568.2004.03464.x

Chen, L. L., Lin, L. H., Green, E. J., Barnes, C. A., & McNaughton, B. L. (1994). Head-direction cells in the rat posterior cortex. I. Anatomical distribution and behavioral modulation. *Experimental Brain Research, 101,* 8–23. doi:10.1007/BF00243212

Cheng, K. (1986). A purely geometric module in the rat's spatial representation. *Cognition, 23,* 149–178. doi:10.1016/0010-0277(86)90041-7

Clayton, N. S. (1995). Comparative studies of food-storing, memory and the hippocampus in Parids. *Hippocampus, 5,* 499–510. doi:10.1002/hipo.450050603

Cressant, A., Muller, R. U., & Poucet, B. (1997). Failure of centrally placed objects to control the firing fields of hippocampal place cells. *The Journal of Neuroscience, 17,* 2531–2542.

Davidson, T. J., Kloosterman, F., & Wilson, M. A. (2009). Hippocampal replay of extended experience. *Neuron, 63,* 497–507. doi:10.1016/j.neuron.2009.07.027

De Goede, M., & Postma, A. (2008). Gender differences in memory for objects and their locations: A study on automatic versus controlled encoding and retrieval contexts. *Brain and Cognition, 66,* 232–242. doi:10.1016/j.bandc.2007.08.004

Doeller, C. F., Barry, C., & Burgess, N. (2010, February 4). Evidence for grid cells in a human memory network. *Nature, 463,* 657–661. doi:10.1038/nature08704

Doeller, C. F., & Burgess, N. (2008). Distinct error-correcting and incidental learning of location relative to landmarks and boundaries. *Proceedings of the National Academy of Sciences of the United States of America, 105,* 5909–5914. doi:10.1073/pnas.0711433105

Downs, R. M., & Stea, D. (1973). Cognitive maps and spatial behavior: Process and products. In R. M. Downs & D. Stea (Eds.), *Image and environment* (pp. 8–26). Chicago, IL: Aldine.

Ekstrom, A. D., Kahana, M. J., Caplan, J. B., Fields, T. A., Isham, E. A., Newman, E. L., & Fried, I. (2003, September 11). Cellular networks underlying human spatial navigation. *Nature, 425,* 184–188. doi:10.1038/nature01964

Etienne, A. S., Maurer, R., Georgakopoulos, J., & Griffin, A. (1999). Dead reckoning (path integration), landmarks, and representation of space in a comparative perspective. In R. G. Golledge (Ed.), *Wayfinding behavior. Cognitive mapping and other spatial processes* (pp. 197–228). Baltimore, MD: Johns Hopkins University Press.

Foster, D. J., & Wilson, M. A. (2006, March 30). Reverse replay of behavioural sequences in hippocampal place cells during the awake state. *Nature, 440,* 680–683. doi:10.1038/nature04587

Golledge, R. G. (1999). Human wayfinding and cognitive maps. In R. G. Golledge (Ed.), *Wayfinding behavior. Cognitive mapping and other spatial processes* (pp. 5–45). Baltimore, MD: Johns Hopkins University Press.

Gupta, A. S., van der Meer, A. A., Touretzky, D. S., & Redish, A. D. (2010). Hippocampal replay is not a simple function of experience. *Neuron, 65,* 695–705. doi:10.1016/j.neuron.2010.01.034

Hafting, T., Fyhn, M., Molden, S., Moser, M.-B., & Moser, E. I. (2005, August 11). Microstructure of a spatial map in the entorhinal cortex. *Nature, 436,* 801–806. doi:10.1038/nature03721

Hardt, O., Hupbach, A., & Nadel, L. (2009). Factors moderating blocking in human place learning: The role of task instructions. *Learning & Behavior, 37,* 42–59. doi:10.3758/LB.37.1.42

Hassabis, D., Kumaran, D., Vann, S. D., & Maguire, E. A. (2007). Patients with hippocampal amnesia cannot imagine new experiences. *Proceedings of the National Academy of Sciences of the United States of America, 104,* 1726–1731. doi:10.1073/pnas.0610561104

Hermer, L., & Spelke, E. S. (1994, July 7). A geometric process for spatial reorientation in young children. *Nature, 370,* 57–59. doi:10.1038/370057a0

Hermer, L., & Spelke, E. S. (1996). Modularity and development: The case of spatial reorientation. *Cognition, 61,* 195–232. doi:10.1016/S0010-0277(96)00714-7

Horne, M. R., Iordanova, M. D., & Pearce, J. M. (2010). Spatial learning based on boundaries in rats is hippocampus-dependent and prone to over-shadowing. *Behavioral Neuroscience, 124,* 623–632. doi:10.1037/a0020824

Howard, L. R., Yu, Y., Mill, R. D., Morrison, L. C., Knight, R., Loftus, M. M., . . . Spiers, H. J. (2011, November). *Human hippocampus encodes Euclidean distance and future path to goals during real-world navigation.* Poster presented at the meeting of the Society for Neuroscience, Washington, DC.

Hupbach, A., & Nadel, L. (2005). Reorientation in a rhombic-shaped environment: No evidence for an encapsulated geometric module. *Cognitive Development, 20,* 279–302. doi:10.1016/j.cogdev.2005.04.003

Iaria, G., Petrides, M., Dagjer, A., Pike, B., & Bohbot, V. D. (2003). Cognitive strategies dependent on the hippocampus and caudate nucleus in human navigation: Variability and change with practice. *The Journal of Neuroscience, 23,* 5945–5952.

Ishikawa, T., Fujiwara, H., Imai, O., & Okabe, A. (2008). Wayfinding with a GPS-based mobile navigation system: A comparison with maps and direct experience.

Journal of Environmental Psychology, 28, 74–82. doi:10.1016/j.jenvp.2007.09.002

Ishikawa, T., & Montello, D. R. (2006). Spatial knowledge acquisition from direct experience in the environment: Individual differences in the development of metric knowledge and the integration of separately learned places. *Cognitive Psychology, 52,* 93–129. doi:10.1016/j.cogpsych.2005.08.003

Izard, V., Pica, P., Spelke, E. S., & Dehaene, S. (2011). Flexible intuitions of Euclidean geometry in an Amazonian indigene group. *Proceedings of the National Academy of Sciences of the United States of America, 108,* 9782–9787. doi:10.1073/pnas.1016686108

Jacobs, J., Kahana, M. J., Ekstrom, A. D., Mollison, M. V., & Fried, I. (2010). A sense of direction in human entorhinal cortex. *Proceedings of the National Academy of Sciences of the United States of America, 107,* 6487–6492. doi:10.1073/pnas.0911213107

Jacobs, L. F. (1995). The ecology of spatial cognition. In E. Alleva, H.-P. Lipp, L. Nadel, A. Fasolo, & L. Ricceri (Eds.), *Behavioural brain research in naturalistic and semi-naturalistic settings: Possibilities and perspectives* (pp. 301–322). Boston, MA: Kluwer Academic. doi:10.1007/978-94-011-0091-5_16

Jansen, P., Schmelter, A., & Heil, M. (2010). Spatial knowledge acquisition in younger and elderly adults: A study in a virtual environment. *Experimental Psychology, 57,* 54–60. doi:10.1027/1618-3169/a000007

Kamin, L. (1968). Attention-like processes in classical conditioning. In M. R. Jones (Ed.), *Miami symposium on the prediction of behavior: Aversive stimulation* (pp. 9–32). Miami, FL: University of Miami Press.

Kelly, J. W., & Avraamides, M. N. (2011). Cross-sensory transfer of reference frames in spatial memory. *Cognition, 118,* 444–450. doi:10.1016/j.cognition.2010.12.006

Korol, D. L., Malin, E. L., Borden, K. A., Busby, R. A., & Couper-Leo, J. (2004). Shifts in preferred learning strategy across the estrous cycle in female rats. *Hormones and Behavior, 45,* 330–338. doi:10.1016/j.yhbeh.2004.01.005

Krechevsky, I. (1932). "Hypotheses" in rats. *Psychological Review, 39,* 516–532. doi:10.1037/h0073500

Lakusta, L., Dessalegn, B., & Landau, B. (2010). Impaired geometric reorientation caused by genetic defect. *Proceedings of the National Academy of Sciences of the United States of America, 107,* 2813–2817. doi:10.1073/pnas.0909155107

Langston, R. F., Ainge, J. A., Couey, J. J., Canto, C. B., Bjerknes, T. L., Witter, M. P., . . . Moser, M.-B. (2010, June 18). Development of the spatial representation system in the rat. *Science, 328,* 1576–1580. doi:10.1126/science.1188210

Laurance, H. E., Thomas, K. G., Newman, M. C., Kaszniak, A. W., Nadel, L., & Jacobs, W. J. (2002). Older adults map novel environments but do not place learn: Findings from computerized spatial task. *Aging, Neuropsychology, and Cognition, 9,* 85–97. doi:10.1076/anec.9.2.85.9547

Lawton, C. A. (1994). Gender differences in way-finding strategies—Relationship to spatial ability and spatial anxiety. *Sex Roles, 30,* 765–779. doi:10.1007/BF01544230

Lawton. C. A. (2001). Gender and regional differences in spatial referents used in direction giving. *Sex Roles, 44,* 321–337. doi:10.1023/A:1010981616842

Lawton, C. A., & Kallai, J. (2002). Gender differences in wayfinding strategies and anxiety about wayfinding: A cross-cultural comparison. *Sex Roles, 47,* 389–401. doi:10.1023/A:1021668724970

Learmonth, A. E., Nadel, L., & Newcombe, N. S. (2002). Children's use of landmarks: Implications for modularity theory. *Psychological Science, 13,* 337–341. doi:10.1111/j.0956-7976.2002.00461.x

Learmonth, A. E., Newcombe, N. S., Sheridan, N., & Jones, M. (2008). Why size counts: Children's spatial reorientation in large and small enclosures. *Developmental Science, 11,* 414–426. doi:10.1111/j.1467-7687.2008.00686.x

Leplow, B., Lehnung, M., Pohl, J., Herzog, A., Ferstl, R., & Mehdorn, M. (2003). Navigational place learning in children and young adults as assessed with a standardized locomotor search task. *British Journal of Psychology, 94,* 299–317. doi:10.1348/000712603767876244

Lever, C., Burton, S., Jeewajee, A., O'Keefe, J., & Burgess, N. (2009). Boundary vector cells in the subiculum of the hippocampal formation. *The Journal of Neuroscience, 29,* 9771–9777. doi:10.1523/JNEUROSCI.1319-09.2009

Lew, A. R. (2011). Looking beyond the boundaries: Time to put landmarks back on the cognitive map? *Psychological Bulletin, 137,* 484–507. doi:10.1037/a0022315

Mackintosh, N. J. (2002). Do not ask whether they have a cognitive map, but how they find their way about. *Psicológica, 23,* 165–185.

Maes, J. H. R., Fontanari, L., & Regolin, L. (2009). Spatial reorientation in rats (*Rattus norvegicus*): Use of geometric and featural information as a function of arena size and feature location. *Behavioural Brain Research, 201,* 285–291. doi:10.1016/j.bbr.2009.02.026

Maguire, E. A., Gadian, D. G., Johnsrude, I. S., Good, C. D., Ashburner, J., Frackowiak, R. S. J., & Frith, C. D. (2000). Navigation-related structural change in the hippocampi of taxi drivers. *Proceedings of* the National Academy of Sciences of the United States of America, 97, 4398–4403. doi:10.1073/pnas.070039597

Mizumori, S. J., & Williams, J. D. (1993). Directionally selective mnemonic properties of neurons in the lateral dorsal nucleus of the thalamus of rats. The Journal of Neuroscience, 13, 4015–4028.

Morgan, L. K., MacEvoy, S. P., Aguirre, G. K., & Epstein, R. A. (2011). Distances between real-world locations are represented in the human hippocampus. The Journal of Neuroscience, 31, 1238–1245. doi:10.1523/JNEUROSCI.4667-10.2011

Muenzinger, K. F. (1938). Vicarious trial and error at a point of choice: I. A general survey of its relation to learning efficiency. The Journal of Genetic Psychology, 53, 75–86.

Nadel, L., & Hupbach, A. (2006). Cross-species comparisons in development: The case of the spatial "module." In M. H. Johnson & Y. Munakata (Eds.), Attention and performance (Vol. XXI, pp. 499–511). Oxford, England: Oxford University Press.

Nadel, L., & Willner, J. (1989). Some implications of post-natal maturation in the hippocampal formation. In V. Chan-Palay & C. Kohler (Eds.), The hippocampus: New vistas (pp. 17–31). New York, NY: A. R. Liss.

Nardini, M., Thomas, R. L., Knowland, V. C. P., Braddick, O. J., & Atkinson, J. (2009). A viewpoint-independent process for spatial reorientation. Cognition, 112, 241–248. doi:10.1016/j.cognition.2009.05.003

Newcombe, N. S., & Huttenlocher, J. (2006). Development of spatial cognition. In D. Kuhn & R. S. Siegler (Eds.), Handbook of child psychology: Vol. 2. Cognition, perception, and language (6th ed., pp. 734–776). New York, NY: Wiley.

Newcombe, N., Huttenlocher, J., Drimmey, A. B., & Wiley, J. G. (1998). The development of spatial location coding: Place learning and dead reckoning in the second and third years. Cognitive Development, 13, 185–200. doi:10.1016/S0885-2014(98)90038-7

Newman, M. C., & Kaszniak, A. W. (2000). Spatial memory and aging: Performance on a human analog of the Morris water maze. Aging, Neuropsychology, and Cognition, 7, 86–93. doi:10.1076/1382-5585(200006)7:2;1-U;FT086

O'Keefe, J., & Dostrovsky, J. (1971). The hippocampus as a spatial map: Preliminary evidence from unit activity in the freely-moving rat. Brain Research, 34, 171–175. doi:10.1016/0006-8993(71)90358-1

O'Keefe, J., & Nadel, L. (1978). The hippocampus as a cognitive map. Oxford, England: Clarendon Press.

O'Keefe, J., Nadel, L., Keightley, S., & Kill, D. (1975). Fornix lesions selectively abolish place learning in the rat. Experimental Neurology, 48, 152–166. doi:10.1016/0014-4886(75)90230-7

Piper, B. J., Acevedo, S. F., Craytor, M. J., Murray, P. W., & Raber, J. (2010). The use and validation of the spatial navigation Memory Island test in primary school children. Behavioural Brain Research, 210, 257–262. doi:10.1016/j.bbr.2010.02.040

Postma, A., Izendoorn, R., & De Haan, E. H. F. (1998). Sex differences in object location memory. Brain and Cognition, 36, 334–345. doi:10.1006/brcg.1997.0974

Rescorla, R. A., & Wagner, A. R. (1972). A theory of Pavlovian conditioning: Variations in the effectiveness of reinforcement and nonreinforcement. In A. H. Black & W. F. Prokasy (Eds.), Classical conditioning II: Current research and theory (pp. 64–99). New York, NY: Appleton-Century-Crofts.

Restle, F. (1957). Discrimination of cues in mazes: A resolution of the 'place-vs-response' question. Psychological Review, 64, 217–228. doi:10.1037/h0040678

Rosenzweig, E. S., & Barnes, C. A. (2003). Impact of aging on hippocampal function: Plasticity, network dynamics, and cognition. Progress in Neurobiology, 69, 143–179. doi:10.1016/S0301-0082(02)00126-0

Rudy, J. W., Stadker-Morris, S., & Albert, P. (1987). Ontogeny of spatial navigation behaviors in the rat: dissociation of "proximal"-and "distal"-cue-based behaviors. Behavioral Neuroscience, 101, 62–73. doi:10.1037/0735-7044.101.1.62

Rummel, J., Epp, J. R., & Galea, L. A. M. (2010). Estradiol does not in?uence strategy choice but place strategy choice is associated with increased cell proliferation in the hippocampus of female rats. Hormones and Behavior, 58, 582–590. doi:10.1016/j.yhbeh.2010.07.009

Schoenfeld, R., Lehmann, W., & Leplow, B. (2010). Effects of age and sex in mental rotation and spatial learning from virtual environments. Journal of Individual Differences, 31, 78–82. doi:10.1027/1614-0001/a000014

Seress, L., Ábrahám, H., Tornóczky, T., & Kosztolányi, Gy. (2001). Cell formation in the human hippocampal formation from mid-gestation to the late postnatal period. Neuroscience 105, 831–843. doi:10.1016/S0306-4522(01)00156-7

Sherry, D. F., Jacobs, L. F., & Gaulin, S. J. C. (1992). Adaptive specialization of the hippocampus. Trends in Neurosciences, 15, 298–303. doi:10.1016/0166-2236(92)90080-R

Siegel, A. W., & White, S. H. (1975). The development of spatial representations of large-scale environments. In H. W. Reese (Ed.), Advances in child development and behavior (Vol. 10, pp. 9–55). New York, NY: Academic Press.

Solstad, T., Boccara, C. N., Kropff, E., Moser, M.-B., & Moser, E. I. (2008, December 19). Representation of geometric borders in the entorhinal cortex. *Science, 322,* 1865–1868. doi:10.1126/science.1166466

Spiers, H. J., & Maguire, E. A. (2007). The neuroscience of remote spatial memory: A tale of two cities. *Neuroscience, 149,* 7–27. doi:10.1016/j.neuroscience. 2007.06.056

Suthana, N. A., Ekstrom, A. D., Moshirvaziri, S., Knowlton, B., & Bookheimer, S. Y. (2009). Human hippocampal CA1 involvement durimg allocentric encoding of spatial information. *The Journal of Neuroscience, 29,* 10512–10519. doi:10.1523/JNEUROSCI.0621-09.2009

Taube, J. S. (1995). Head direction cells recorded in the anterior thalamic nuclei of freely moving rats. *The Journal of Neuroscience, 15,* 70–86.

Taube, J. S., Muller, R. U., & Ranck, J. B., Jr. (1990a). Head-direction cells recorded from the postsubiculum in freely moving rats. I. Description and quantitative analysis. *The Journal of Neuroscience, 10,* 420–435.

Taube, J. S., Muller, R. U., & Ranck, J. B., Jr. (1990b). Head-direction cells recorded from the postsubiculum in freely moving rats. II. Effects of environmental manipulations. *The Journal of Neuroscience, 10,* 436–447.

Tolman, E. C. (1948). Cognitive maps in rats and men. *Psychological Review, 55,* 189–208. doi:10.1037/h0061626

Tolman, E. C., & Honzik, C. H. (1930). Introduction and removal of reward, and maze performance in rats. *University of California Publications in Psychology, 4,* 257–275.

Tversky, B. (1992). Distortions in cognitive maps. *Geoforum, 23,* 131–138. doi:10.1016/0016-7185 (92)90011-R

Wills, T. J., Cacucci, F., Burgess, N., & O'Keefe, J. (2010, June 18). Development of the hippocampal cognitive map in preweanling rats. *Science, 328,* 1573–1576. doi:10.1126/science.1188224

Woolley, D. G., Vermaercke, B., Op de Beeck, H., Wagemans, J., Gantois, I., D'Hooge, R., . . . Wenderoth, N. (2010). Sex differences in human virtual water maze performance: Novel measures reveal the relative contribution of directional responding and spatial knowledge. *Behavioural Brain Research, 208,* 408–414. doi:10.1016/j.bbr.2009.12.019

Xu, J., Evensmoen, H. R., Lehn, H., Pintzka, C. W. S., & Haberg, A. K. (2010). Persistent posterior and transient anterior medial temporal lobe activity during navigation. *NeuroImage, 52,* 1654–1666. doi:10.1016/j.neuroimage.2010.05.074

Zugaro, M. B., Arleo, A., Dejean, C., Burguiere, E., Khamassi, M., & Wiener, S. I. (2004). Rat antero-dorsal thalamic head direction neurons depend upon dynamic visual signals to select anchoring landmark cues. *European Journal of Neuroscience, 20,* 530–536. doi:10.1111/j.1460-9568.2004.03512.x

Zugaro, M. B., Berthoz, A., & Wiener, S. I. (2001). Background, but not foreground, spatial cues are taken as references for head direction responses by rat anterodorsal thalamus neurons. *The Journal of Neuroscience, 21,* RC154–RC155.

CHAPTER 9

SPATIAL MEMORY: PROPERTIES AND ORGANIZATION

Timothy P. McNamara

Many human activities, ranging from retrieving a cell phone from a purse to making one's way to work and back home, depend on the ability to remember the locations of objects in the environment. Our reliance on such spatial memories is so ubiquitous in daily life, and our use of them is so effortless in most situations, that we may not appreciate their fundamental importance. For prehistoric humans, survival depended on the ability to use spatial memories effectively to guide actions in space. They were essential, for instance, for finding the way back to a previously discovered source of food or water, for safely returning home after a sudden change of weather, and for not getting lost while foraging and hunting.

The goal of this chapter is to review empirical and theoretical advancements in the scientific understanding of human spatial memory. I attend primarily to spatial memories acquired from direct experience, such as vision and locomotion, and on spaces sufficiently large to afford movement, such as translation and rotation, although I take the liberty of referring to a few studies that investigated memories of table-top-sized "environments." My decision to focus on these topics should not be interpreted as a comment on the importance of other kinds of spatial memories, such as those obtained from language or indirect sources (e.g., maps). Indeed, for modern humans, external representations of space, such as guidebooks and vehicle navigation systems, and the

knowledge acquired from them, may be at least as important for effective navigation as mental representations of an environment acquired from direct experience. Because these topics are investigated in other chapters of this volume (see Chapters 13 and 14), as well as in other reviews (see Golledge, 1999; Montello, 2005), I elected not to cover them in this chapter.

This chapter is divided into six principal sections. I begin by discussing the elemental types of spatial knowledge: object–place knowledge, route knowledge, environmental shape knowledge, and survey knowledge. In the second section, I investigate classical and current theories of the acquisition of spatial knowledge. The third section discusses properties of spatial knowledge, such as its hierarchical structure and orientation dependence. In the fourth section, I examine the concept of spatial reference systems and the nature of the reference systems used in spatial memory. I then review contemporary cognitive models of spatial memory, with an eye for identifying similarities among them. I close the chapter with a summary and prospectus for future research on human spatial memory.

TYPES OF SPATIAL KNOWLEDGE

Spatial memories are composed of several types of spatial knowledge. In this section, I review four types of spatial knowledge: knowledge of objects

DOI: 10.1037/13936-010
Handbook of Spatial Cognition, D. Waller and L. Nadel (Editors)

and places, knowledge of routes, knowledge of environmental shape, and knowledge of spatial layout (i.e., survey knowledge).

Object–Place Knowledge

Spatial memories, as the term is used in this chapter, are memories of the locations of objects, places, and environmental features. Such memories are constructed from knowledge of the identities and appearances of entities in the environment. I use the term *object–place* to refer to this type of knowledge, with the aim of capturing the notion that whereas some of these environmental entities naturally would be considered objects (e.g., coffee table, stop sign), others correspond to significant locations of greater extent and less well-defined boundaries (e.g., small city park, path intersection, saddle between two hills). *Landmark knowledge* (e.g., Siegel & White, 1975) is a special case of object–place knowledge. People know the identities of many objects and places in their environments that may not serve as landmarks. *Landmarks* are entities of special significance to spatial memory and navigation (e.g., Couclelis, Golledge, Gale, & Tobler, 1987): They are used to indicate the locations of other objects and places (e.g., the restaurant is at the top of the Sheraton Hotel), they may be the goals of navigation (e.g., I am going to the state capitol), they mark the locations of changes of direction (e.g., turn left at the Convention Center), and they are used to maintain course (e.g., you will pass the Ryman on your right). In Siegel and White's (1975) classical theory of the acquisition of spatial knowledge (discussed subsequently), landmark knowledge is the first to be acquired and is the building block of other types of spatial knowledge.

Route Knowledge

Route knowledge consists of knowledge of sequences of landmarks and associated decisions and actions (e.g., Siegel & White, 1975). Actions specify the steps needed to get to the next landmark on the route (e.g., turn left at the laundromat and drive one block to 20th Ave.). Landmarks functioning in this way correspond to associative cues.

Landmarks can also serve as beacons or as goals of navigation (e.g., Waller & Lippa, 2007). A naviga-

tor uses a beacon by guiding locomotion toward it, and as long as each successive landmark is perceptible from its predecessor on a route, route knowledge need not contain a great deal of information about actions to be taken at each landmark. Waller and Lippa (2007) investigated these two functions of landmarks in route learning in desktop virtual environments. They found that routes containing beacon landmarks were learned more efficiently than routes containing associative cue landmarks and that beacon-based route learning was less enduring and produced poorer knowledge of environmental directions than did associative-cue-based route learning. Knowledge of routes in all but the simplest of environments almost certainly includes landmarks that function as associative cues, as beacons, and even as both.

In Siegel and White's (1975) theory, early in acquisition, route knowledge does not represent metric information such as distance, temporal duration, or turning angles. According to this theory, such metric properties are only acquired gradually with experience in an environment. However, as discussed subsequently, there is growing evidence that route knowledge contains metric properties from early in the acquisition of spatial knowledge.

Environmental Shape Knowledge

Many, if not most, humans now live in largely carpentered worlds. In such environments, the shapes of rooms, corridors, streetscapes, and even bounded green spaces can be salient. There is emerging evidence that knowledge of environmental shape is a fundamental type of spatial knowledge and that it is used in navigation.

Cheng (1986) first discovered the importance of environmental shape in reorientation. He found that when rats searched for the known location of food in rectangular enclosures under certain conditions, they often committed *rotational errors* in which they searched equally in both the correct location and the incorrect location differing from the correct one by 180° of rotation. For instance, if the correct location were in one of the corners, the rotational error would be the corner diagonally opposite to the correct corner. These errors occurred even when proximal, nongeometric featural cues, such as visual patterns or olfactory cues, were available to allow the rat to distinguish the correct location from the rotational error. Similar findings have been observed in many species, including humans (for a review, see Cheng & Newcombe, 2005).

Although there have been many demonstrations of the limitations of such findings (e.g., Cheng, 2008; Hupbach & Nadel, 2005; Huttenlocher, 2008; Learmonth, Nadel, & Newcombe, 2002), there is ample evidence that adults are sensitive to environmental geometry when they learn a new environment (e.g., Schmidt & Lee, 2006; Shelton & McNamara, 2001) and when they reorient and navigate (e.g., Hartley, Trinkler, & Burgess, 2004; Kelly, McNamara, Bodenheimer, Carr, & Rieser, 2008, 2009; Nardi, Newcombe, & Shipley, 2010). It is unknown whether these findings generalize to natural environments. Perhaps the best evidence that they may comes from studies showing that people are sensitive to geographical slant when learning and navigating in large-scale virtual environments (e.g., Restat, Steck, Mochnatzki, & Mallot, 2004; Steck, Mochnatzki, & Mallot, 2003).

Survey Knowledge

Survey knowledge is knowledge of the overall spatial layout of an environment. This knowledge includes Euclidean ("straight-line") distances and interpoint directions defined in a common reference system. A key characteristic of survey knowledge is that the spatial relations between locations can be retrieved or inferred even if travel has never occurred between the locations. Survey knowledge of an environment is often referred to as a *cognitive map* (a term coined by Tolman, 1948). Survey knowledge is typically considered the most advanced type of knowledge obtained about an environment (e.g., Siegel & White, 1975). Behaviors taken to be the signature of survey knowledge include the abilities to create efficient routes (e.g., taking shortcuts), to point directly to unseen locations, and to estimate Euclidean distances. Experimental investigations of survey knowledge have usually examined the conditions that lead to its acquisition. Such studies are reviewed in the next section.

ACQUISITION OF SPATIAL KNOWLEDGE

The classical theory of the acquisition of spatial knowledge was proposed by Siegel and White (1975) to explain the stagewise development of spatial ability in children. This developmental theory was founded on Siegel and White's analysis of the sequence of representations acquired by adults when they learned a new environment. According to this theory, the identities and appearances of landmarks are learned first, followed by routes between landmarks. Route knowledge is assumed to be nonmetric early in acquisition, consisting of the order of landmarks and the appropriate actions to be taken at each one in the sequence. Through experience, route knowledge can acquire metric properties and specify distances, temporal durations, and turning angles. The most sophisticated form of spatial knowledge is survey knowledge, which is assumed to be derived from accumulated route knowledge (e.g., Thorndyke & Hayes-Roth, 1982).

Although this theoretical framework has been enormously influential, there is empirical evidence that questions its generality (for reviews, see Ishikawa & Montello, 2006; Montello, 1998). The limitations of the classical theory are apparent in the findings of Ishikawa and Montello's (2006) study. Participants in this experiment were passively transported by automobile along two routes in a private residential area. The routes passed around and over many hills, and afforded few views of distant landmarks. Learning took place over 10 days (one session per week for 10 weeks); on the fourth and subsequent days, participants were transported along a connecting route between the two routes and encouraged to learn the spatial relation between them. Participants' knowledge of the routes and their interrelations was tested using landmark recall, direction estimates, route and Euclidean distance estimates, and map drawing.

Performance was above chance on all tasks after the first session and near perfect on some, such as landmark sequence recall and route distance estimation. Direction estimates and more difficult distance estimates (e.g., Euclidean estimates within the more complex route) were only moderately accurate and improved minimally over the course of learning. Substantial individual differences were observed.

Some participants performed well after only one or two sessions and maintained high performance levels on all tasks across all sessions. Another subgroup of participants performed poorly throughout the experiment and showed little learning on the more challenging tasks, even after 12 to 14 hours of exposure to the routes. Only about half of the participants improved monotonically over the course of learning, and those gains were not large.

These findings largely validate the theoretical distinction between route and survey knowledge, because tasks sensitive to route information, such as landmark sequence recall and route distance estimation, produced similar patterns of results, and tasks sensitive to the layout of the routes, such as Euclidean distance estimation, direction estimates, and map drawing, produced results similar to each other but different from the route tasks. These results, however, contradict several key predictions of the classical theory. Landmark knowledge and route knowledge were acquired almost simultaneously. Route knowledge seemed to contain some quantitative information from the beginning (see also Buchner & Jansen-Osmann, 2008). Even at the earliest stages of learning, participants had some knowledge of the spatial layout of the routes. Finally, although some participants gained more accurate knowledge of the layouts of the routes over the course of learning, few of them could be characterized as having gained accurate survey knowledge of the environments (see also Gärling, Böök, Lindberg, & Nilsson, 1981; Golledge, Ruggles, Pellegrino, & Gale, 1993).

Overall, the evidence on spatial knowledge acquisition is most consistent with Montello's theoretical framework (Ishikawa & Montello, 2006; Montello, 1998). According to this theory, the process of acquiring knowledge of the spatial structure of large-scale environments consists of incremental accumulation of metric knowledge instead of stagewise transitions between qualitatively distinct types of spatial knowledge. Spatial knowledge is never limited solely to nonmetric information. This theory emphasizes the importance of *knowledge integration*—combining knowledge about separately learned places into more complex hierarchically organized representations—in spatial knowledge

acquisition (e.g., Greenauer & Waller, 2010; Kelly & McNamara, 2010). However, even this theoretical framework does not predict or explain the large individual differences observed by Ishikawa and Montello (2006).

PROPERTIES OF SPATIAL KNOWLEDGE

Spatial knowledge has several key properties. In this section, I review four aspects of spatial knowledge that have proven to be especially important in understanding human spatial behavior.

Fragmented

Spatial knowledge is typically fragmented, in the sense that it consists of a patchwork of detailed knowledge of some areas and only sparse knowledge of other, possibly neighboring, areas (e.g., Appleyard, 1970; Lynch, 1960). Survey knowledge never has the property of being of uniformly high fidelity for all familiar areas.

Distorted

A second key property of spatial knowledge is that memories of spatial relations, such as distances, angles, and orientation, often differ from the physical values in systematic and predictable ways (e.g., Tversky, 1992, 2000). As discussed subsequently, such distortions have played a prominent role in the development of theories of spatial memory.

Estimates of Euclidean distances are greater when locations are separated by a barrier or boundary (e.g., Kosslyn, Pick, & Fariello, 1974; McNamara, 1986; Newcombe & Liben, 1982) and tend to increase with the "clutter" between the locations (e.g., Thorndyke, 1981). Boundary effects occur even when the boundaries are subjective (e.g., Carbon & Leder, 2005; McNamara, Hardy, & Hirtle, 1989). Estimates of route distance increase with the number of turns (e.g., R. W. Byrne, 1979; Sadalla & Magel, 1980) and the number of intersections (e.g., Sadalla & Staplin, 1980). Distance estimates are also asymmetric under certain circumstances (e.g., McNamara & Diwadkar, 1997; Newcombe, Huttenlocher, Sandberg, & Lie, 1999; Sadalla, Burroughs, & Staplin, 1980). In particular, distances from less salient places or objects to more salient places or objects (i.e., landmarks or reference points) are underestimated relative to the reverse. Angles of intersection between roads are remembered as being closer to 90° than they are in reality (e.g., R. W. Byrne, 1979; Moar & Bower, 1983; Sadalla & Montello, 1989; Tversky, 1981). Disparate regions of space, such as states or continents, are remembered as being aligned with each other, and individual regions of space are remembered as being oriented with canonical reference axes (e.g., Stevens & Coupe, 1978; Tversky, 1981). For instance, people believe that North America and South America are vertically aligned, even though the east coast of the United States is roughly aligned with the west coast of South America. These biases produce systematic errors in judgments of the relative directions between objects and cities.

Hierarchical

There is strong evidence that memories of the locations of objects in the environment are organized categorically and hierarchically, such that a region of space may be represented as a whole, containing other regions and locations and, as a part, contained in larger regions. One indication that spatial memories are hierarchical is that judgments of the spatial relations between cities or objects are affected by the spatial relations between superordinate regions (e.g., McNamara, 1986; Stevens & Coupe, 1978; Tversky, 1981). For instance, in Stevens and Coupe's (1978) experiments, Reno was judged to be northeast of San Diego, even though it is actually northwest. According to hierarchical models of spatial memory, this error occurs, at least in part, because people represent Reno in Nevada, San Diego in California, and Nevada east of California. These spatial relations imply that Reno should be east of San Diego. Other evidence consistent with the hierarchical representation of space includes the effects of boundaries on distance estimations (cited previously), the effects of region membership on judgments of orientation (e.g., Maki, 1981; Wilton, 1979) and proximity (e.g., Allen, 1981), and errors in estimates of latitude, bearing, and distance at global scales (e.g., Friedman & Brown, 2000; Friedman, Brown, & McGaffey, 2002; Friedman & Montello, 2006).

Even stronger evidence for hierarchical representations can be found in studies in which task performance is shown to depend on the structure of explicit hierarchical models of spatial memory (e.g., Hirtle & Jonides, 1985; Huttenlocher, Hedges, & Duncan, 1991; McNamara, 1986; McNamara et al., 1989). For instance, McNamara et al. (1989, Experiment 1) required subjects to learn the locations of objects in a large room; the objects were unrelated and there were no physical or perceptual boundaries in the space. After learning, subjects were asked to recall all of the objects multiple times, to estimate distances between pairs of objects, and to take part in an item recognition test in which the measure of interest was spatial priming (e.g., McNamara, Ratcliff, & McKoon, 1984). The latent hierarchical structure in each subject's recall protocols was modeled with the ordered-tree algorithm (e.g., Reitman & Rueter, 1980). Distance estimations and spatial priming were conditionalized on whether pairs of objects were in the same or different subtrees, controlling for Euclidean distance. Different subtrees were assumed to correspond to different subjective regions of space. Participants underestimated distances between pairs of objects in the same subjective region relative to pairs of objects in different subjective regions, and spatial priming was greater between pairs in the same subjective region than between pairs in different subjective regions. Additional analyses showed that spatial priming increased with the depth at which object pairs were categorized in the hierarchical trees. These findings provide strong evidence that spatial memories are organized hierarchically, even when the layout lacks explicit perceptual organization.

Huttenlocher et al. (1991; see also Lansdale, 1998) developed an elegant mathematical hierarchical model of positional uncertainty and bias in memory for the location of single object—the *category adjustment model* (CAM). According to this model, location is encoded at a fine-grained level and at a categorical level. Encoding at both levels varies in precision but is unbiased. Even though both representations are unbiased, bias can occur in the recall of location for two reasons. One source of bias arises from the manner in which fine-grained and categorical information are combined. Recall of location is a weighted average of the fine-grain value and the *prototype,* or average value, of the category. The relative magnitudes of the weights depend on the relative precisions of the two sources of information: As the precision of the fine-grain value decreases relative to the precision of the prototype, the fine-grain value is weighted less relative to the prototype. Hence, greater bias toward the prototype occurs as the fine-grain values become less precise relative to the prototype. These concepts are illustrated in Figure 9.1. The second source of bias arises because reports of the locations of objects are constrained to lie within a category, and consequently, the distribution of memory reports will be truncated at category boundaries. This fact implies that the retrieved loca-

tion of an object near a category boundary will be biased toward the center of the category. These two sources of bias are referred to as *prototype effects* and *boundary effects,* respectively.

Huttenlocher et al. (1991) tested the model with a task requiring participants to remember the location of a single dot in a circle. The categories corresponded to the quadrants of the circle created by implicit vertical and horizontal axes centered on the circle. Huttenlocher et al. showed that the model provided an excellent account of quantitative properties of bias in this task. The CAM is important because it shows that bias in the remembered location of an object is not necessary for there to be bias in the report of an object's location from memory, and it demonstrates how general principles of

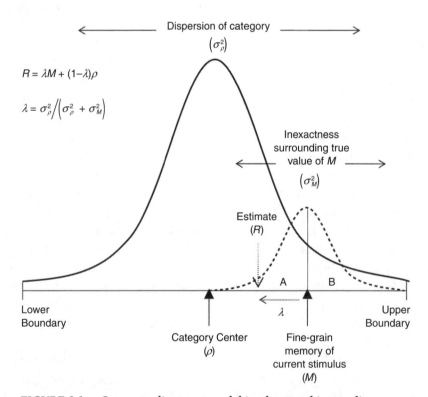

FIGURE 9.1.   Category-adjustment model implemented in one dimension. R = reported location of the object; M = mean of the distribution of fine-grain memory (M corresponds to the object's true location); ρ = prototype; λ = weight on fine-grain memory. As σ_M^2 decreases (i.e., precision of fine-grain memory increases), the weight on the fine-grain memory approaches 1; as σ_M^2 increases (i.e., precision of fine-grain memory decreases), the weight on the fine-grain memory approaches 0. From "Category Effects on Stimulus Estimation: Shifting and Skewed Frequency Distributions," by S. Duffy, J. Huttenlocher, L. V. Hedges, and E. L. Crawford, 2010, *Psychonomic Bulletin & Review, 17,* p. 225. Copyright 2010 by Springer. Reprinted with permission.

spatial memory (e.g., categorical representation, exact and inexact encoding) can be implemented formally.

Subsequent research has shown that the model can be extended in several important ways. Fitting and colleagues (Fitting, Wedell, & Allen, 2007, 2008a, 2008b) have shown that the model can be generalized to account for multiple environmental cues (e.g., letters on the outer edge of the circle) and that such cues aid fine-grain memory and, when memory demands are high, the nature of the categories. The CAM also may apply to memory of real-world geography (Friedman, 2009). A fundamental assumption of the CAM is that memory for location is unbiased. Sampaio and Wang (2009) tested this assumption by having participants choose between their own biased reproduction of the target location and the correct target location after reporting the target location. The majority of participants chose the correct target location in preference to their own biased reproduction on most trials, showing that they retained and were able to access a representation of the original target location (cf. Werner & Diedrichsen, 2002). Challenges to the model may exist in its ability to account for effects of the distributions of targets on location estimates (e.g., Lipinski, Simmering, Johnson, & Spencer, 2010; Spencer & Hund, 2002; Spetch, Friedman, Bialowas, & Verbeek, 2010).

The hierarchical structure of spatial memory has been shown to affect navigation behavior in virtual environments. Wiener and Mallot (2003) found that people minimized the number of region boundaries crossed when navigating to a goal location and that they tended to choose paths that permitted the quickest access to the region containing the goal location. Wiener, Schnee, and Mallot (2004) showed further that subjects learned environments faster and searched more efficiently when environments were divided into regions than when they were not. Their results also revealed that navigation strategies seemed to depend on the alignment of the dominant reference directions between different levels of the hierarchical mental representation (see also Werner

& Long, 2003; Werner & Schindler, 2004). (The concept of spatial reference directions and axes will be explored in detail subsequently.)

Orientation Dependent

People recall and recognize spatial relations between objects more efficiently from some perspectives than from others (see McNamara, 2003, for a review). This pattern of results is referred to as *orientation dependence*. These privileged perspectives are usually aligned with (i.e., they are parallel or orthogonal to) experienced points of view (e.g., Shelton & McNamara, 2001) but also may be aligned with salient intrinsic axes of the array of objects (e.g., Mou, Liu, & McNamara, 2009; Mou & McNamara, 2002). Typical results are illustrated in Figure 9.2. There is evidence that spatial memories also may be viewpoint dependent (e.g., Easton & Sholl, 1995; Waller, 2006). Behaviorally, this means that performance is better when the test perspective matches the location of the observer, in addition to his or her orientation, at the time of learning.[1]

SPATIAL REFERENCE SYSTEMS

Spatial reference systems are necessary for the specification of location and orientation in space. The location of my home, for instance, can be specified by describing its position with respect to the boundaries of the state (e.g., my home is in the central portion of Tennessee), by providing its street address and zip code, or by describing its position relative to an observer (e.g., my home is 1.2 miles distant and 60° left of my facing direction as I write this paragraph). People represent in memory the spatial properties of a multitude of environments. Just as spatial reference systems are required to specify the locations of objects in physical space, so too spatial reference systems must be used by human memory systems to represent the locations of objects in the environment.

Spatial reference systems are relational systems consisting of reference objects, located objects, and the spatial relations that exist among them (e.g., Rock, 1973, 1992; Talmy, 1983). The reference objects

---

[1]Orientation-independent performance has been observed in several published investigations of spatial memory (e.g., Evans & Pezdek, 1980; Presson, DeLange, & Hazelrigg, 1989; Presson & Hazelrigg, 1984; Richardson, Montello, & Hegarty, 1999, real-walk condition; Sholl & Nolin, 1997, Experiments 3 and 4). McNamara (2003) discussed possible explanations of these findings in detail.

A

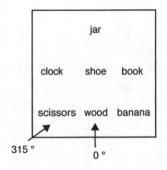

B

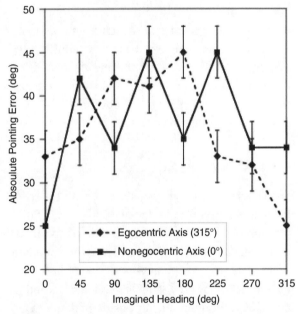

FIGURE 9.2.   Method and results of Mou and McNamara (2002). (a) Bilaterally symmetric layout used by Mou and McNamara (2002). All participants viewed the layout of objects from the viewpoint of 315°; half were instructed to learn the layout in columns parallel to 315° (clock, jar, scissors, shoe, etc.), and half were instructed to learn the layout in columns parallel to 0° (scissors, clock, wood, shoe, jar, etc.). Arrows were not displayed. (b) Absolute pointing error in judgments of relative direction. For participants who learned the layout along the 315° axis (egocentric intrinsic axis), performance was better on 315° than on 0°; the pattern was reversed for those who learned the layout along the 0° axis (nonegocentric intrinsic axis). Results for both groups demonstrate orientation dependence of spatial memory. Adapted from "Intrinsic Frames of Reference in Spatial Memory" by W. Mou and T. P. McNamara, 2002, *Journal of Experimental Psychology: Learning, Memory, and Cognition, 28,* p. 166–167. Copyright 2002 by the American Psychological Association.

may be any objects whose positions are known or established as a standard and may include other objects in the environment, abstract coordinate axes, the observer, and so forth. Many schemes for classifying spatial reference systems have been proposed over the years (e.g., Hart & Moore, 1973; Levinson, 1996; Paillard, 1991; Pani & Dupree, 1994; Tversky, Lee, & Mainwaring, 1999). For the purposes of understanding the use of spatial memories in navigation and other actions in space, it is useful to distinguish egocentric and allocentric (or environmental) reference systems (e.g., Klatzky, 1998).

Egocentric reference systems specify location and orientation with respect to the organism, and include eye-, head-, and body-based coordinate systems. Returning to the previous example, the description of my home's location relative to my position uses an egocentric reference system. Viewpoint dependence in human scene recognition, as discussed previously, implies that visual memories of scenes are coded in egocentric reference systems. Neurophysiological studies have shown that the primate brain uses a variety of egocentric reference systems to represent locations of objects in space (e.g., Andersen, Snyder, Bradley, & Xing, 1997; Snyder, Grieve, Brotchie, & Andersen, 1998).

Allocentric reference systems define spatial relations with respect to elements of the environment, such as the perceived direction of gravity, the sun's azimuth, landmarks, or the walls of a room (e.g., Wehner, Michel, & Antonsen, 1996). Abstract reference systems, such as coordinates of latitude and longitude, also qualify as allocentric reference systems. Returning again to the descriptions of my home's location, identifying the state and giving a street address both qualify as uses of allocentric reference systems. Human behavioral research indicates that egocentric and allocentric reference systems are used to represent the spatial structure of the environment (e.g., Burgess, 2008; Mou, McNamara, Valiquette, & Rump, 2004; Sholl, 2001; Wang & Spelke, 2002; Xiao, Mou, & McNamara, 2009). Neurophysiological research converges on the same conclusion (e.g., Andersen et al., 1997; Matsumura et al., 1999; Snyder et al., 1998).

An important subcategory of allocentric reference systems is *intrinsic reference systems*. These reference systems were introduced as a means to specify the spatial structure of objects or forms (e.g., Marr, 1982; Rock, 1973). In such cases, the objects or forms usually have inherent facets, such as natural fronts, backs, tops, or bottoms that can be used to define reference axes. The human body is a paradigmatic example (e.g., Franklin & Tversky, 1990). Intrinsic reference systems can also be defined by features of a collection of objects (e.g., Mou & McNamara, 2002; Tversky, 1981). The rows and columns formed by chairs in a classroom constitute an intrinsic reference system. Intrinsic reference systems also may be defined by less explicit perceptual organization, such as an axis of bilateral symmetry or the mutual alignment of several objects, or even by the arbitrary configuration of a set of objects as seen from a particular view (e.g., Greenauer & Waller, 2008; Mou et al., 2009; Mou, Zhao, & McNamara, 2007; Shelton & McNamara, 2001). An example is illustrated in Figure 9.2.

The concept of spatial reference systems proves useful for accounting for two key properties of spatial knowledge. First, the orientation dependence of spatial memories is typically interpreted as indicating that the spatial layout of an environment is mentally represented using a dominant reference direction (e.g., Shelton & McNamara, 2001). Interobject spatial relations that are specified with respect to this reference direction can be retrieved, whereas other spatial relations must be inferred (e.g., Klatzky, 1998), introducing costs in latency and errors. The preferred directions in judgments of relative direction, for example, correspond to intrinsic directions in the layout that are experienced or are highlighted by instructions or layout geometry (e.g., Mou & McNamara, 2002; Mou et al., 2007; Shelton & McNamara, 2001). These preferred directions correspond to the dominant reference directions. A simple model of this form that accounts for orientation dependence in judgments of relative direction is illustrated in Figure 9.3.

The second key property explained by spatial reference systems is the hierarchical structure of spatial knowledge. This property may result from

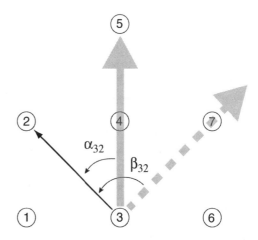

FIGURE 9.3. Schematic depiction of an orientation dependent model of enduring spatial memory. Circles symbolize the represented objects. Interobject spatial relations are symbolized by vectors; for simplicity only the spatial relation between Objects 3 and 2 is represented. Dashed and solid gray arrows symbolize reference directions in memory of 315° and 0° (e.g., egocentric and nonegocentric axis groups in Figure 9.2, respectively). Consider the 0° reference direction: The direction from 3 to 2 is represented in memory with respect to 0° (α_{32}). Because the direction from Object 3 to Object 2 relative to 0° is explicitly represented in memory, a task such as "Imagine you are standing at 3 and facing 4. Point to 2" is relatively easy, because that direction can be retrieved from memory. By contrast, a task such as "Imagine you are standing at 3 and facing 7. Point to 2" is relatively difficult, because the spatial relation between Objects 3 and 2 is not represented relative to 315° and therefore must be inferred, which produces measurable performance costs. The reverse is true for memories using the reference direction of 315°. An important feature of the model is that it uses an allocentric reference system, yet produces orientation dependent performance.

the use of spatial reference systems at multiple scales (e.g., Meilinger & Vosgerau, 2010; Poucet, 1993). A region of space that can be viewed in its entirety from a single vantage point with minimal locomotion (*vista scale*, as defined by Montello & Golledge, 1999) may be represented in a locally defined spatial reference system. Spatial reference systems used in neighboring regions of space may be interrelated in higher order reference systems in which the local reference systems serve as elements. For instance, the spatial layout of each of the rooms in a house may be specified in spatial reference systems unique to the room. These spatial reference systems may serve as elements in a higher order reference system defining the spatial relations among the rooms.

Reference systems within the same level and between levels of the hierarchy need not use common reference directions; that is, conceptual "north" in one region may or may not correspond to conceptual "north" in a neighboring region. The acquisition of skills attributed to the possession of survey knowledge, such as pointing accurately to unseen targets, may occur when the reference directions in such locally defined reference systems become integrated in such a way that all are aligned (Meilinger, 2008; Montello & Pick, 1993). Werner and colleagues (Werner & Long, 2003; Werner & Schindler, 2004) have shown that misalignment of reference directions in such a reference system hierarchy impairs wayfinding performance and produces less accurate knowledge of interobject directions. Experiments reported by Wang and Brockmole (2003a) provided evidence that people maintain orientation with respect to a single reference system as they navigate. These researchers had participants walk from a room in a building on a college campus to the outdoors and then back inside to the room. When oriented with respect to the room, participants lost track of their orientation with respect to the campus, and when oriented with respect to the campus, they lost track of their orientation with respect to the room (see also Wang & Brockmole, 2003b).

COGNITIVE MODELS OF SPATIAL MEMORY

Cognitive models of spatial memory attempt to explain how the spatial structure of an environment is represented in memory and how memories of familiar environments are used to guide actions in space. Contemporary models employ both egocentric and allocentric representations of space, and although there are important differences between models in the nature of those representations and in the ways they are used, the models are fundamentally quite similar.

Nature of the Models

Contemporary models of spatial memory include an egocentric system that computes and represents self-to-object spatial relations needed for spatially directed motor activity, such as walking, reaching, and grasping. In the models proposed by Burgess and colleagues (e.g., Burgess, 2008; P. Byrne, Becker, & Burgess, 2007) and by Mou, McNamara, and colleagues (e.g., Mou et al., 2004; Xiao et al., 2009), spatial relations represented in this system are relatively transient and decay in the absence of perceptual support or deliberate rehearsal (see also Waller & Hodgson, 2006).[2] In Sholl's model (Holmes & Sholl, 2005; Sholl, 2001; Sholl & Nolin, 1997) and in Wang and Spelke's model (2002), this system is dynamic but can represent more enduring egocentric self-to-object spatial relations. Recent evidence implicates the role of a transient egocentric system in spatial updating but this evidence is far from definitive (Kelly, Avraamides, & Loomis, 2007; Waller & Hodgson, 2006; Xiao et al., 2009).

The second major system in all of the models is an allocentric system. Wang and Spelke's (2002) model is perhaps the most unusual, in that the allocentric system in this model only represents environmental shape. In all of the remaining models, the allocentric system represents object-to-object spatial relations in an enduring manner. These spatial relations could include body-to-object spatial relations in which the body is treated like another object in the environment. The other major difference among models, at least among those that specify the nature of the reference systems used in the allocentric system (Burgess's model does not), is whether the spatial reference system is orientation dependent or independent. Mou and McNamara claim that the allocentric system uses an orientation-dependent, intrinsic reference system (as discussed in the section, Spatial Reference Systems). Sholl, in contrast, claims that an orientation independent reference system is used, at least in well-learned environments.

Finally, Wang and Spelke's (2002) model includes a third system in which the appearances of familiar landmarks and scenes are represented.

---

[2]Waller and Hodgson (2006) distinguished between transient and enduring systems but are agnostic on the nature of the spatial reference systems used by each system.

These representations are viewpoint dependent and can be conceived of as visual–spatial "snapshots" of the environment (e.g., Burgess, Spiers, & Paleologou, 2004; Diwadkar & McNamara, 1997; Wang & Simons, 1999). Valiquette and McNamara (2007) attempted to find evidence for such a system and to determine whether it could be distinguished from an environmental system. They asked participants to learn the locations of objects in a room from two points of view, one of which was aligned with salient environmental frames of reference (the mat on which the objects were placed and the walls of the room), and the other of which was misaligned with those same frames of reference (viz, a view from the corner of the room). Participants then took part in judgments of relative direction (e.g., "Imagine you are standing at the shoe, facing the lamp; point to the banana") and old–new scene recognition. Performance in judgments of relative direction was best for the imagined heading parallel to the aligned learning view and no better for the imagined heading parallel to the misaligned learning view than for unfamiliar headings. This pattern of orientation-dependent performance replicates previous findings (Shelton & McNamara, 2001; Valiquette, McNamara, & Labrecque, 2007). Performance in scene recognition, however, was equally good for the two familiar views and better for familiar than for novel views (see also Waller, 2006). These findings are consistent with a model in which interobject spatial relations are represented in an allocentric system using intrinsic reference systems, as specified in Mou and McNamara's model, and visual memories of landmarks and scenes are stored in a viewpoint-dependent system, as specified in Wang and Spelke's model.

This viewpoint-dependent system may account for the effectiveness of the *look-back strategy* in wilderness navigation (e.g., Cornell, Heth, & Rowat, 1992). Routes often look quite different coming and going, leading to navigational errors on the return trip. The look-back strategy involves occasionally stopping and turning around to view one's route in the opposite direction while navigating in unfamiliar wilderness environments. These look-back views

may be stored in the viewpoint dependent system and support place recognition when returning.

Spatial Updating in the Models

To navigate effectively in familiar environments, people must keep track of their position and orientation in space as they move. This ability is referred to as *spatial updating*.[3] Spatial updating in cognitive models of spatial memory takes place at two levels. Self-to-object spatial relations are continuously and efficiently updated in the egocentric system as a navigator locomotes through an environment. This updating process allows the navigator to pass through apertures (e.g., doorways), follow paths, avoid obstacles and hazards, and so forth. At the same time, the navigator must update a representation of his or her position in the environment, to remain oriented and to locate distant goals. This updating process takes place in the allocentric system. According to Mou and McNamara (Mou et al., 2004; Xiao et al., 2009), navigators update their position with respect to the intrinsic reference system used to represent the spatial structure of the local environment. Sholl's model is the most explicit about the allocentric updating process. In this model, the egocentric system is referred to as the *self-reference system,* and it codes self-to-object spatial relations in body-centered coordinates using the body axes of front–back, right–left, and up–down (e.g., Bryant & Tversky, 1999; Franklin & Tversky, 1990). The engagement of the self-reference system with the physical environment determines the position of a representation of the self-reference system in the allocentric system. As a person moves in the environment, the axes of the representational self-reference system are moved to the corresponding new position in the allocentric system representation.

SUMMARY AND PROSPECTUS

Learning a new environment typically begins by learning routes from place to place; even in large-scale outdoor environments, navigation usually takes advantage of trails of some kind. People

[3]Spatial updating processes are explored more fully in Chapter 5 of this volume.

quickly acquire knowledge of the identities of important objects and places, or landmarks, and the sequential order of landmarks on routes. Route knowledge has at least quasi-metric properties early during acquisition. Humans and many other organisms seem to be sensitive to the shape of the immediate environment and to depend on environmental shape to reorient. With extensive experience in an environment, people sometimes acquire knowledge of its overall layout, or survey knowledge. The acquisition of spatial knowledge is best characterized as the incremental accumulation of quantitative spatial relations. Spatial knowledge does not seem to be limited to qualitative, nonmetric information at any point during acquisition.

Humans represent the locations of objects in space using egocentric and allocentric reference systems, and actions in space almost certainly depend on both egocentric and allocentric representations of the environment. There is evidence that the process of learning a new environment involves interpreting the spatial structure of that environment in terms of an allocentric spatial reference system. Interobject spatial relations seem to be specified with respect to a small number of reference directions. This aspect of the mental representation produces one of its key properties, orientation dependence: Interobject spatial relations can be utilized more efficiently from perspectives aligned with the dominant reference directions in memory. These reference directions are typically parallel to points of view experienced during learning but also may be determined by instructions and by properties of the environment, such as the mutual alignment of several objects or geographical slant. The use of spatial reference systems at multiple scales may explain why spatial knowledge is hierarchically organized.

Cognitive models of spatial memory specify roles for three types of spatial memories: Egocentric self-to-object spatial relations, which are used to guide locomotion in the nearby environment; viewpoint-dependent representations of landmarks and scenes, which are used for place recognition; and allocentric representations of object-to-object spatial relations, which are used primarily for wayfinding. There are differences among the models in the properties of each of these representation systems and in the

manner in which they are used in navigation. For instance, in some models, the egocentric system computes and represents transient representations, whereas in other models, these representations are more enduring. In one model, the environmental system only represents the shape of the environment and is used for reorientation, whereas in the others, it represents object-to-object spatial relations and is used for virtually all locomotion in familiar environments. Despite these differences, however, the models are quite similar in terms of their overall architecture.

The scientific understanding of human spatial memory has advanced enormously since Tolman (1948) presaged the distinction between route and survey knowledge with his categorization of spatial memories into "strip maps" and "comprehensive maps." Significant progress has been made in understanding the nature and acquisition of spatial memories, how remembered spatial relations are used to guide actions, and properties of spatial updating processes. But much remains to be discovered. Many important avenues of future research are indicated by the findings reviewed in this chapter. A few especially promising ones might include the following.

There is abundant evidence of the hierarchical organization of enduring spatial memories, but the processes involved in the formation of such representations are not well understood. Of special interest are the mechanisms used to establish correspondences between representations that use different reference directions and the spatial updating processes used to switch from one hierarchical level to another. The relative importance of egocentric and allocentric representations in various spatial tasks, their dynamical properties, and the processes by which egocentric representations in sensorimotor systems are transformed into allocentric representations, and vice versa, are largely unknown.

To a significant degree, cognitive models of spatial memory primarily describe the perceptual–cognitive architecture of the human spatial memory system. For this reason, they have varying amounts to say about the various topics covered previously in this chapter. All are intimately concerned with object–place knowledge, survey knowledge, spatial reference systems, and spatial updating. However, none of these models has much to say about route knowledge, the acquisition of spatial knowledge, or the nature of spatial knowledge (e.g., distortions). An important direction for future research will be to extend these models to account for a broader array of findings in the spatial memory literature. I look forward, with optimism, to seeing the empirical and theoretical fruits of these efforts to understand how people remember where they have been and how they find their way home.

SUGGESTED REFERENCES FOR FURTHER READING

Cheng, K., & Newcombe, N. S. (2005). Is there a geometric module for spatial orientation? Squaring theory and evidence. *Psychonomic Bulletin & Review, 12,* 1–23. doi:10.3758/BF03196346

An excellent critical review of research on the role of geometry in reorientation.

Huttenlocher, J., Hedges, L. V., & Duncan, S. (1991). Categories and particulars: Prototype effects in estimating spatial location. *Psychological Review, 98,* 352–376. doi:10.1037/0033-295X.98.3.352

This article presents the category adjustment model and experimental results in support of it.

Ishikawa, T., & Montello, D. R. (2006). Spatial knowledge acquisition from direct experience in the environment: Individual differences in the development of metric knowledge and the integration of separately learned places. *Cognitive Psychology, 52,* 93–129. doi:10.1016/j.cogpsych.2005.08.003

This article reviews classical and contemporary theories of spatial knowledge acquisition and presents experimental findings favoring the latter.

Klatzky, R. L. (1998). Allocentric and egocentric spatial representations: Definitions, distinctions, and interconnections. In C. Freksa, C. Habel & K. F. Wender (Eds.), *Spatial cognition: An interdisciplinary approach to representing and processing spatial knowledge* (pp. 1–17). Berlin, Germany: Springer-Verlag.

This chapter provides a lucid and concise analysis of spatial reference systems as employed in spatial memory and navigation.

Shelton, A. L., & McNamara, T. P. (2001). Systems of spatial reference in human memory. *Cognitive Psychology, 43,* 274–310. doi:10.1006/cogp.2001.0758

This article presents novel findings on interactions between egocentric viewpoint and environmental

frames of reference in the selection of reference directions in memory and advances an explanation of orientation dependence in terms of reference directions selected at the time of learning.

References

Allen, G. L. (1981). A developmental perspective on the effects of "subdividing" macrospatial experience. *Journal of Experimental Psychology: Human Learning and Memory, 7,* 120–132. doi:10.1037/0278-7393.7.2.120

Andersen, R. A., Snyder, L. H., Bradley, D. C., & Xing, J. (1997). Multimodal representation of space in the posterior parietal cortex and its use in planning movements. *Annual Review of Neuroscience, 20,* 303–330. doi:10.1146/annurev.neuro.20.1.303

Appleyard, D. (1970). Styles and methods of structuring a city. *Environment and Behavior, 2,* 100–117. doi:10.1177/001391657000200106

Bryant, D. J., & Tversky, B. (1999). Mental representations of perspective and spatial relations from diagrams and models. *Journal of Experimental Psychology: Learning, Memory, and Cognition, 25,* 137–156. doi:10.1037/0278-7393.25.1.137

Buchner, A., & Jansen-Osmann, P. (2008). Is route learning more than serial learning? *Spatial Cognition and Computation, 8,* 289–305. doi:10.1080/13875860802047201

Burgess, N. (2008). Spatial cognition and the brain. *Annals of the New York Academy of Sciences, 1124,* 77–97. doi:10.1196/annals.1440.002

Burgess, N., Spiers, H. J., & Paleologou, E. (2004). Orientational manoeuvres in the dark: Dissociating allocentric and egocentric influences on spatial memory. *Cognition, 94,* 149–166. doi:10.1016/j.cognition.2004.01.001

Byrne, P., Becker, S., & Burgess, N. (2007). Remembering the past and imagining the future: A neural model of spatial memory and imagery. *Psychological Review, 114,* 340–375. doi:10.1037/0033-295X.114.2.340

Byrne, R. W. (1979). Memory for urban geography. *The Quarterly Journal of Experimental Psychology, 31,* 147–154. doi:10.1080/14640747908400714

Carbon, C.-C., & Leder, H. (2005). The wall inside the brain: Overestimation of distances crossing the former Iron Curtain. *Psychonomic Bulletin & Review, 12,* 746–750. doi:10.3758/BF03196767

Cheng, K. (1986). A purely geometric module in the rat's spatial representation. *Cognition, 23,* 149–178. doi:10.1016/0010-0277(86)90041-7

Cheng, K. (2008). Whither geometry? Troubles of the geometric module. *Trends in Cognitive Sciences, 12,* 355–361. doi:10.1016/j.tics.2008.06.004

Cheng, K., & Newcombe, N. S. (2005). Is there a geometric module for spatial orientation? Squaring theory and evidence. *Psychonomic Bulletin & Review, 12,* 1–23. doi:10.3758/BF03196346

Cornell, E. H., Heth, C. D., & Rowat, W. L. (1992). Wayfinding by children and adults: Response to instructions to use look-back and retrace strategies. *Developmental Psychology, 28,* 328–336. doi:10.1037/0012-1649.28.2.328

Couclelis, H., Golledge, R. G., Gale, N., & Tobler, W. (1987). Exploring the anchor-point hypothesis of spatial cognition. *Journal of Environmental Psychology, 7,* 99–122. doi:10.1016/S0272-4944(87)80020-8

Diwadkar, V., & McNamara, T. P. (1997). Viewpoint dependence in scene recognition. *Psychological Science, 8,* 302–307. doi:10.1111/j.1467-9280.1997.tb00442.x

Duffy, S., Huttenlocher, J., Hedges, L. V., & Crawford, E. L. (2010). Category effects on stimulus estimation: Shifting and skewed frequency distributions. *Psychonomic Bulletin & Review, 17,* 224–230. doi:10.3758/PBR.17.2.224

Easton, R. D., & Sholl, M. J. (1995). Object array structure, frames of reference, and retrieval of spatial knowledge. *Journal of Experimental Psychology: Learning, Memory, and Cognition, 21,* 483–500. doi:10.1037/0278-7393.21.2.483

Evans, G. W., & Pezdek, K. (1980). Cognitive mapping: Knowledge of real-world distance and location information. *Journal of Experimental Psychology: Human Learning and Memory, 6,* 13–24. doi:10.1037/0278-7393.6.1.13

Fitting, S., Wedell, D. H., & Allen, G. L. (2007). Memory for spatial location: Cue effects as a function of field rotation. *Memory & Cognition, 35,* 1641–1658. doi:10.3758/BF03193498

Fitting, S., Wedell, D. H., & Allen, G. L. (2008a). Cue usage in memory for location when orientation is fixed. *Memory & Cognition, 36,* 1196–1216. doi:10.3758/MC.36.6.1196

Fitting, S., Wedell, D. H., & Allen, G. L. (2008b). External cue effects on memory for spatial location within a rotated task field. *Spatial Cognition and Computation, 8,* 219–251. doi:10.1080/13875860802039216

Franklin, N., & Tversky, B. (1990). Searching imagined environments. *Journal of Experimental Psychology: General, 119,* 63–76. doi:10.1037/0096-3445.119.1.63

Friedman, A. (2009). The role of categories and spatial cuing in global-scale location estimates. *Journal of Experimental Psychology: Learning, Memory, and Cognition, 35,* 94–112. doi:10.1037/a0013590

Friedman, A., & Brown, N. R. (2000). Reasoning about geography. *Journal of Experimental Psychology: General, 129,* 193–219. doi:10.1037/0096-3445.129.2.193

Friedman, A., Brown, N. R., & McGaffey, A. P. (2002). A basis for bias in geographical judgments. *Psychonomic Bulletin & Review, 9,* 151–159. doi:10.3758/BF03196272

Friedman, A., & Montello, D. R. (2006). Global-scale location and distance estimates: Common representations and strategies in absolute and relative judgments. *Journal of Experimental Psychology: Learning, Memory, and Cognition, 32,* 333–346. doi:10.1037/0278-7393.32.3.333

Gärling, T., Böök, A., Lindberg, E., & Nilsson, T. (1981). Memory for the spatial layout of the everyday physical environment: Factors affecting rate of acquisition. *Journal of Environmental Psychology, 1,* 263–277. doi:10.1016/S0272-4944(81)80025-4

Golledge, R. G. (1999). Human wayfinding and cognitive maps. In R. G. Golledge (Ed.), *Wayfinding behavior: Cognitive mapping and other spatial processes* (pp. 5–45). Baltimore, MD: Johns Hopkins University Press.

Golledge, R. G., Ruggles, A. J., Pellegrino, J. W., & Gale, N. D. (1993). Integrating route knowledge in an unfamiliar neighborhood: Along and across route experiments. *Journal of Environmental Psychology, 13,* 293–307. doi:10.1016/S0272-4944(05)80252-X

Greenauer, N., & Waller, D. (2008). Intrinsic array structure is neither necessary nor sufficient for non-egocentric coding of spatial layouts. *Psychonomic Bulletin & Review, 15,* 1015–1021. doi:10.3758/PBR.15.5.1015

Greenauer, N., & Waller, D. (2010). Micro- and macroreference frames: Specifying the relations beween spatial categories in memory. *Journal of Experimental Psychology: Learning, Memory, and Cognition, 36,* 938–957. doi:10.1037/a0019647

Hart, R. A., & Moore, G. T. (1973). The development of spatial cognition: A review. In R. M. Downs & D. Stea (Eds.), *Image and environment* (pp. 246–288). Chicago, IL: Aldine.

Hartley, T., Trinkler, I., & Burgess, N. (2004). Geometric determinants of human spatial memory. *Cognition, 94,* 39–75. doi:10.1016/j.cognition.2003.12.001

Hirtle, S. C., & Jonides, J. (1985). Evidence of hierarchies in cognitive maps. *Memory & Cognition, 13,* 208–217. doi:10.3758/BF03197683

Holmes, M. C., & Sholl, M. J. (2005). Allocentric coding of object-to-object relations in overlearned and novel environments. *Journal of Experimental Psychology: Learning, Memory, and Cognition, 31,* 1069–1087. doi:10.1037/0278-7393.31.5.1069

Hupbach, A., & Nadel, L. (2005). Reorientation in a rhombic environment: No evidence for an encapsulated geometric module. *Cognitive Development, 20,* 279–302. doi:10.1016/j.cogdev.2005.04.003

Huttenlocher, J. (2008). Coding location: The view from toddler studies. *American Psychologist, 63,* 641–648. doi:10.1037/0003-066X.63.8.641

Huttenlocher, J., Hedges, L. V., & Duncan, S. (1991). Categories and particulars: Prototype effects in estimating spatial location. *Psychological Review, 98,* 352–376. doi:10.1037/0033-295X.98.3.352

Ishikawa, T., & Montello, D. R. (2006). Spatial knowledge acquisition from direct experience in the environment: Individual differences in the development of metric knowledge and the integration of separately learned places. *Cognitive Psychology, 52,* 93–129. doi:10.1016/j.cogpsych.2005.08.003

Kelly, J. W., Avraamides, M. N., & Loomis, J. M. (2007). Sensorimotor alignment effects in the learning environment and in novel environments. *Journal of Experimental Psychology: Learning, Memory, and Cognition, 33,* 1092–1107. doi:10.1037/0278-7393.33.6.1092

Kelly, J. W., & McNamara, T. P. (2010). Reference frames during the acquisition and development of spatial memories. *Cognition, 116,* 409–420. doi:10.1016/j.cognition.2010.06.002

Kelly, J. W., McNamara, T. P., Bodenheimer, B., Carr, T. H., & Rieser, J. J. (2008). The shape of human navigation: How environmental geometry is used in the maintenance of spatial orientation. *Cognition, 109,* 281–286. doi:10.1016/j.cognition.2008.09.001

Kelly, J. W., McNamara, T. P., Bodenheimer, B., Carr, T. H., & Rieser, J. J. (2009). Individual differences in using geometric and featural cues to maintain spatial orientation: Cue quantity and cue ambiguity are more important than cue type. *Psychonomic Bulletin & Review, 16,* 176–181. doi:10.3758/PBR.16.1.176

Klatzky, R. L. (1998). Allocentric and egocentric spatial representations: Definitions, distinctions, and interconnections. In C. Freksa, C. Habel, & K. F. Wender (Eds.), *Spatial cognition: An interdisciplinary approach to representing and processing spatial knowledge* (pp. 1–17). Berlin, Germany: Springer-Verlag.

Kosslyn, S. M., Pick, H. L., Jr., & Fariello, G. R. (1974). Cognitive maps in children and men. *Child Development, 45,* 707–716. doi:10.2307/1127837

Lansdale, M. W. (1998). Modeling memory for absolute location. *Psychological Review, 105,* 351–378. doi:10.1037/0033-295X.105.2.351

Learmonth, A. E., Nadel, L., & Newcombe, N. S. (2002). Children's use of landmarks: Implications for modularity theory. *Psychological Science, 13,* 337–341. doi:10.1111/j.0956-7976.2002.00461.x

Levinson, S. C. (1996). Frames of reference and Molyneux's question: Crosslinguistic evidence. In P. Bloom, M. A. Peterson, L. Nadel, & M. F. Garrett (Eds.), *Language and space* (pp. 109–169). Cambridge, MA: MIT Press.

Lipinski, J., Simmering, V. R., Johnson, J. S., & Spencer, J. P. (2010). The role of experience in location estimation: Target distributions shift location memory biases. *Cognition, 115,* 147–153. doi:10.1016/j.cognition.2009.12.008

Lynch, K. (1960). *The image of the city.* Cambridge, MA: MIT Press.

Maki, R. H. (1981). Categorization and distance effects with spatial linear orders. *Journal of Experimental Psychology. Human Learning and Memory, 7,* 15–32. doi:10.1037/0278-7393.7.1.15

Marr, D. (1982). *Vision.* San Francisco, CA: Freeman.

Matsumura, N., Nishijo, H., Tamura, R., Eifuku, S., Endo, S., & Ono, T. (1999). Spatial- and task-dependent neuronal responses during real and virtual translocation in the monkey hippocampal formation. *The Journal of Neuroscience, 19,* 2381–2393.

McNamara, T. P. (1986). Mental representations of spatial relations. *Cognitive Psychology, 18,* 87–121. doi:10.1016/0010-0285(86)90016-2

McNamara, T. P. (2003). How are the locations of objects in the environment represented in memory? In C. Freksa, W. Brauer, C. Habel, & K. F. Wender (Eds.), *Spatial cognition III: Routes and navigation, human memory and learning, spatial representation and spatial learning* (pp. 174–191). Berlin, Germany: Springer-Verlag.

McNamara, T. P., & Diwadkar, V. (1997). Symmetry and asymmetry of human spatial memory. *Cognitive Psychology, 34,* 160–190. doi:10.1006/cogp.1997.0669

McNamara, T. P., Hardy, J. K., & Hirtle, S. C. (1989). Subjective hierarchies in spatial memory. *Journal of Experimental Psychology: Learning, Memory, and Cognition, 15,* 211–227. doi:10.1037/0278-7393.15.2.211

McNamara, T. P., Ratcliff, R., & McKoon, G. (1984). The mental representation of knowledge acquired from maps. *Journal of Experimental Psychology: Learning, Memory, and Cognition, 10,* 723–732. doi:10.1037/0278-7393.10.4.723

Meilinger, T. (2008). The network of reference frames theory: A synthesis of graphs and cognitive maps. In C. Freksa, N. S. Newcombe, P. Gärdenfors & S. Wölfl (Eds.), *Spatial cognition VI* (pp. 344–360). Berlin, Germany: Springer-Verlag.

Meilinger, T., & Vosgerau, G. (2010). Putting egocentric and allocentric into perspective. In C. Hölscher, T. F. Shipley, M. O. Belardinelli, J. A. Bateman,

& N. S. Newcombe (Eds.), *Spatial cognition VII* (pp. 207–221). Berlin, Germany: Springer-Verlag. doi:10.1007/978-3-642-14749-4_19

Moar, I., & Bower, G. H. (1983). Inconsistency in spatial knowledge. *Memory & Cognition, 11,* 107–113. doi:10.3758/BF03213464

Montello, D. R. (1998). A new framework for understanding the acquisition of spatial knowledge in large-scale environments. In M. J. Egenhofer & R. G. Golledge (Eds.), *Spatial and temporal reasoning in geographic information systems* (pp. 143–154). New York, NY: Oxford University Press.

Montello, D. R. (2005). Navigation. In P. Shah & A. Miyake (Eds.), *The Cambridge handbook of visuospatial thinking* (pp. 257–294). New York, NY: Cambridge University Press.

Montello, D. R., & Golledge, R. G. (1999). Scale and detail in the cognition of geographic information. *Report of Specialist Meeting of Project Varenious.* Santa Barbara, CA: University of California–Santa Barbara.

Montello, D. R., & Pick, H. L., Jr. (1993). Integrating knowledge of vertically aligned large-scale spaces. *Environment and Behavior, 25,* 457–484. doi:10.1177/0013916593253002

Mou, W., Liu, X., & McNamara, T. P. (2009). Layout geometry in encoding and retrieval of spatial memory. *Journal of Experimental Psychology: Human Perception and Performance, 35,* 83–93. doi:10.1037/0096-1523.35.1.83

Mou, W., & McNamara, T. P. (2002). Intrinsic frames of reference in spatial memory. *Journal of Experimental Psychology: Learning, Memory, and Cognition, 28,* 162–170. doi:10.1037/0278-7393.28.1.162

Mou, W., McNamara, T. P., Valiquette, C. M., & Rump, B. (2004). Allocentric and egocentric updating of spatial memories. *Journal of Experimental Psychology: Learning, Memory, and Cognition, 30,* 142–157. doi:10.1037/0278-7393.30.1.142

Mou, W., Zhao, M., & McNamara, T. P. (2007). Layout geometry in the selection of intrinsic frames of reference from multiple viewpoints. *Journal of Experimental Psychology: Learning, Memory, and Cognition, 33,* 145–154. doi:10.1037/0278-7393.33.1.145

Nardi, D., Newcombe, N. S., & Shipley, T. F. (2010). The role of slope in human reorientation. In C. Hölscher, T. F. Shipley, M. O. Belardinelli, J. A. Bateman, & N. S. Newcombe (Eds.), *Spatial cognition VII* (pp. 32–40). Berlin, Germany: Springer-Verlag. doi:10.1007/978-3-642-14749-4_6

Newcombe, N., Huttenlocher, J., Sandberg, E., & Lie, E. (1999). What do misestimations and asymmetries in spatial judgment indicate about spatial representation? *Journal of Experimental Psychology: Learning, Memory, and Cognition, 25,* 986–996. doi:10.1037/0278-7393.25.4.986

Newcombe, N., & Liben, L. S. (1982). Barrier effects in the cognitive maps of children and adults. *Journal of Experimental Child Psychology, 34,* 46–58. doi:10.1016/0022-0965(82)90030-3

Paillard, J. (Ed.). (1991). *Brain and space.* New York, NY: Oxford University Press.

Pani, J. R., & Dupree, D. (1994). Spatial reference systems in the comprehension of rotational motion. *Perception, 23,* 929–946. doi:10.1068/p230929

Poucet, B. (1993). Spatial cognitive maps in animals: New hypotheses on their structure and neural mechanisms. *Psychological Review, 100,* 163–182. doi:10.1037/0033-295X.100.2.163

Presson, C. C., DeLange, N., & Hazelrigg, M. D. (1989). Orientation specificity in spatial memory: What makes a path different from a map of the path? *Journal of Experimental Psychology: Learning, Memory, and Cognition, 15,* 887–897. doi:10.1037/0278-7393.15.5.887

Presson, C. C., & Hazelrigg, M. D. (1984). Building spatial representations through primary and secondary learning. *Journal of Experimental Psychology: Learning, Memory, and Cognition, 10,* 716–722. doi:10.1037/0278-7393.10.4.716

Reitman, J. S., & Rueter, H. H. (1980). Organization revealed by recall orders and confirmed by pauses. *Cognitive Psychology, 12,* 554–581. doi:10.1016/0010-0285(80)90020-1

Restat, J. D., Steck, S. D., Mochnatzki, H. F., & Mallot, H. A. (2004). Geographial slant facilitates navigation and orientation in virtual environments. *Perception, 33,* 667–687. doi:10.1068/p5030

Richardson, A. E., Montello, D. R., & Hegarty, M. (1999). Spatial knowledge acquisition from maps and from navigation in real and virtual environments. *Memory & Cognition, 27,* 741–750. doi:10.3758/BF03211566

Rock, I. (1973). *Orientation and form.* New York, NY: Academic Press.

Rock, I. (1992). Comment on Asch and Witkin's "Studies in space orientation: II." *Journal of Experimental Psychology: General, 121,* 404–406. doi:10.1037/0096-3445.121.4.404

Sadalla, E. K., Burroughs, W. J., & Staplin, L. J. (1980). Reference points in spatial cognition. *Journal of Experimental Psychology: Human Learning and Memory, 6,* 516–528. doi:10.1037/0278-7393.6.5.516

Sadalla, E. K., & Magel, S. G. (1980). The perception of traversed distance. *Environment and Behavior, 12,* 65–79. doi:10.1177/0013916580121005

Sadalla, E. K., & Montello, D. R. (1989). Remembering changes in direction. *Environment and Behavior, 21,* 346–363. doi:10.1177/0013916589213006

Sadalla, E. K., & Staplin, L. J. (1980). The perception of traversed distance: Intersections. *Environment and Behavior, 12,* 167–182. doi:10.1177/0013916580122003

Sampaio, C., & Wang, R. F. (2009). Category-based errors and the accessibility of unbiased spatial memories: A retrieval model. *Journal of Experimental Psychology: Learning, Memory, and Cognition, 35,* 1331–1337. doi:10.1037/a0016377

Schmidt, T., & Lee, E. Y. (2006). Spatial memory organized by environmental geometry. *Spatial Cognition and Computation, 6,* 347–369. doi:10.1207/s15427633scc0604_4

Shelton, A. L., & McNamara, T. P. (2001). Systems of spatial reference in human memory. *Cognitive Psychology, 43,* 274–310. doi:10.1006/cogp.2001.0758

Sholl, M. J. (2001). The role of a self-reference system in spatial navigation. In D. R. Montello (Ed.), *Spatial information theory: Foundations of geographical information science* (pp. 217–232). Berlin, Germany: Springer-Verlag.

Sholl, M. J., & Nolin, T. L. (1997). Orientation specificity in representations of place. *Journal of Experimental Psychology: Learning, Memory, and Cognition, 23,* 1494–1507. doi:10.1037/0278-7393.23.6.1494

Siegel, A. W., & White, S. H. (1975). The development of spatial representations of large-scale environments. In H. W. Reese (Ed.), *Advances in child development and behavior* (Vol. 10, pp. 9–55). New York, NY: Academic Press.

Snyder, L. H., Grieve, K. L., Brotchie, P., & Andersen, R. A. (1998, August 27). Separate body- and world-referenced representations of visual space in parietal cortex. *Nature, 394,* 887–891. doi:10.1038/29777

Spencer, J. P., & Hund, A. M. (2002). Prototypes and particulars: Geometric and experience-dependent spatial categories. *Journal of Experimental Psychology: General, 131,* 16–37. doi:10.1037/0096-3445.131.1.16

Spetch, M. L., Friedman, A., Bialowas, J., & Verbeek, E. (2010). Contributions of category and fine-grained information to location memory: When categories don't weigh in. *Memory & Cognition, 38,* 154–162. doi:10.3758/MC.38.2.154

Steck, S. D., Mochnatzki, H. F., & Mallot, H. A. (2003). The role of geographical slant in virtual environment navigation. In C. Freksa, W. Brauer, C. Habel, & K. F. Wender (Eds.), *Spatial cognition III: Routes and navigation, human memory and learning, spatial representation and spatial learning* (pp. 62–76). Berlin, Germany: Springer-Verlag.

Stevens, A., & Coupe, P. (1978). Distortions in judged spatial relations. *Cognitive Psychology, 10,* 422–437. doi:10.1016/0010-0285(78)90006-3

Talmy, L. (1983). How language structures space. In H. L. Pick, Jr., & L. P. Acredolo (Eds.), *Spatial orientation: Theory, research, and application* (pp. 225–282). New York, NY: Plenum Press.

Thorndyke, P. W. (1981). Distance estimation from cognitive maps. *Cognitive Psychology, 13,* 526–550. doi:10.1016/0010-0285(81)90019-0

Thorndyke, P. W., & Hayes-Roth, B. (1982). Differences in spatial knowledge acquired from maps and navigation. *Cognitive Psychology, 14,* 560–589. doi:10.1016/0010-0285(82)90019-6

Tolman, E. C. (1948). Cognitive maps in rats and men. *Psychological Review, 55,* 189–208. doi:10.1037/h0061626

Tversky, B. (1981). Distortions in memory for maps. *Cognitive Psychology, 13,* 407–433. doi:10.1016/0010-0285(81)90016-5

Tversky, B. (1992). Distortions in cognitive maps. *Geoforum, 23,* 131–138. doi:10.1016/0016-7185(92)90011-R

Tversky, B. (2000). Remembering spaces. In E. Tulving & F. I. M. Craik (Eds.), *The Oxford handbook of memory* (pp. 363–378). New York, NY: Oxford University Press.

Tversky, B., Lee, P., & Mainwaring, S. (1999). Why do speakers mix perspectives? *Spatial Cognition and Computation, 1,* 399–412. doi:10.1023/A:1010091730257

Valiquette, C. M., & McNamara, T. P. (2007). Different mental representations for place recognition and goal localization. *Psychonomic Bulletin & Review, 14,* 676–680. doi:10.3758/BF03196820

Valiquette, C. M., McNamara, T. P., & Labrecque, J. S. (2007). Biased representations of the spatial structure of navigable environments. *Psychological Research, 71,* 288–297. doi:10.1007/s00426-006-0084-0

Waller, D. (2006). Egocentric and nonegocentric coding in memory for spatial layout: Evidence from scene recognition. *Memory & Cognition, 34,* 491–504. doi:10.3758/BF03193573

Waller, D., & Hodgson, E. (2006). Transient and enduring spatial representations under disorientation and self-rotation. *Journal of Experimental Psychology. Learning, Memory, and Cognition, 32,* 867–882. doi:10.1037/0278-7393.32.4.867

Waller, D., & Lippa, Y. (2007). Landmarks as beacons and associate cues: Their role in route learning. *Memory & Cognition, 35,* 910–924. doi:10.3758/BF03193465

Wang, R. F., & Brockmole, J. R. (2003a). Human navigation in nested environments. *Journal of Experimental*

Psychology: Learning, Memory, and Cognition, 29, 398–404. doi:10.1037/0278-7393.29.3.398

Wang, R. F., & Brockmole, J. R. (2003b). Simultaneous spatial updating in nested environments. *Psychonomic Bulletin & Review, 10*, 981–986. doi:10.3758/BF03196562

Wang, R. F., & Simons, D. J. (1999). Active and passive scene recognition across views. *Cognition, 70*, 191–210. doi:10.1016/S0010-0277(99)00012-8

Wang, R. F., & Spelke, E. S. (2002). Human spatial representation: Insights from animals. *Trends in Cognitive Sciences, 6*, 376–382. doi:10.1016/S1364-6613(02)01961-7

Wehner, R., Michel, B., & Antonsen, P. (1996). Visual navigation in insects: Coupling of egocentric and geocentric information. *The Journal of Experimental Biology, 199*, 129–140.

Werner, S., & Diedrichsen, J. (2002). The time course of spatial memory distortions. *Memory & Cognition, 30*, 718–730. doi:10.3758/BF03196428

Werner, S., & Long, P. (2003). Cognition meets Le Corbusier: Cognitive principles of architectural design. In C. Freksa, W. Brauer, C. Habel, & K. F. Wender (Eds.), *Spatial cognition III: Routes and navigation, human memory and learning, spatial*

representations and spatial learning (pp. 112–126). Berlin, Germany: Springer-Verlag.

Werner, S., & Schindler, L. E. (2004). The role of spatial reference frames in architecture: Misalignment impairs way-finding performance. *Environment and Behavior, 36*, 461–482. doi:10.1177/0013916503254829

Wiener, J. M., & Mallot, H. A. (2003). 'Fine-to-Coarse' route planning and navigation in regionalized environments. *Spatial Cognition and Computation, 3*, 331–358. doi:10.1207/s15427633scc0304_5

Wiener, J. M., Schnee, A., & Mallot, H. A. (2004). Use and interaction of navigation strategies in regionalized environments. *Journal of Environmental Psychology, 24*, 475–493. doi:10.1016/j.jenvp.2004.09.006

Wilton, R. N. (1979). Knowledge of spatial relations: The specification of the information used in making inferences. *The Quarterly Journal of Experimental Psychology, 31*, 133–146. doi:10.1080/14640747908400713

Xiao, C., Mou, W., & McNamara, T. P. (2009). Use of self-to-object and object-to-object spatial relations in locomotion. *Journal of Experimental Psychology: Learning, Memory, and Cognition, 35*, 1137–1147. doi:10.1037/a0016273

CHAPTER 10

THE DEVELOPMENT OF LOCATION CODING: AN ADAPTIVE COMBINATION ACCOUNT

Mark P. Holden and Nora S. Newcombe

The study of spatial development is the study of how children acquire mature spatial competence. This definition seems simple, but it actually poses a major problem: What is *mature spatial competence?* Specifying the standard to which developing capabilities are compared is prerequisite to thinking about the nature of the road to adult capabilities, to evaluating how far children have advanced, and to answering the ultimate developmental question of what accounts for observed developmental sequences. Yet, the study of adult cognition is an ongoing enterprise, views of adult spatial cognition are quite varied, and models have changed over time (Landau, 2003; Newcombe, 2002; Tversky, 2000). So, what standard do we use? To address this problem, we start this chapter with a brief overview of four approaches to characterizing how people represent location of objects in their spatial environment, arguing for an adaptive and Bayesian position over three other options. We then use the adaptive framework to organize our discussion of spatial development.

FOUR APPROACHES TO MATURE SPATIAL REPRESENTATION

The *Euclidean position* regarding adult spatial cognition is the oldest approach. In this view, adults' spatial representations preserve metric relations among elements within an objective frame of refer-

ence, resulting in a maplike representation of space (e.g., Piaget & Inhelder, 1948/1967; Siegel & White, 1975). These Euclidean (or survey) representations allow the accurate solution of spatial problems, such as perspective taking (Piaget & Inhelder, 1948/1967) and navigation of novel routes, as when taking shortcuts or travelling around detours (Siegel & White, 1975). However, criticisms of Piagetian theory in general and of aspects of Piaget's approach to spatial development in particular have led to a waning in the use of this framework, strictly construed, to study spatial development (see the overview in Newcombe & Huttenlocher, 2000).

The *nonmetric position* was inspired by findings that challenged the Euclidean position. Adults frequently misplace locations in ways that show systematic bias, they regularize irregular spaces, and they make startling errors that violate geometric axioms. For example, the majority of adults erroneously believe that Philadelphia is north of Rome (Tversky, 1981), that the California coastline runs north–south (Tversky 1981), and that street intersections are closer to right angles than they truly are (Byrne, 1979). These errors can lead to surprising results, such as Lynch's (1960) finding that many Boston residents believe its park to be a square with five right-angled corners. Most challenging to the Euclidean position is that human spatial judgments often do not treat the distance from A to B as equal to that from B to A (McNamara, 1991; McNamara & Diwadkar,

DOI: 10.1037/13936-011
Handbook of Spatial Cognition, D. Waller and L. Nadel (Editors)

191

1997; Sadalla, Burroughs, & Staplin, 1980). These errors have been taken to imply that "spatial knowledge is not Euclidean like actual space" (Tversky, 1999, p. 39) and even that "spatial representations may be purely nonmetric" (McNamara, 1991, p. 147). From this point of view, there is little impetus for developmental research because there are few hypotheses about ways in which earlier spatial representations could be worse than so-called mature ones. Indeed, with a few possible exceptions (Acredolo & Boulter, 1984), developmentalists have not used this position to guide their research.

The *modularity position* approaches spatial thinking in a different way from either the Euclidean or the nonmetric positions, postulating that separate modules with different characteristics govern spatial functioning. Following Fodor's (1983) discussion, each module is thought to be domain-specific, unable to accept information of any other type (*encapsulated*), neurally specialized, and processing its unique information automatically. A geometric module has been postulated for the spatial domain (Cheng, 1986; Gallistel, 1990; Hermer & Spelke, 1994, 1996). Cheng (1986) proposed that when individuals (humans and animals alike) are disoriented, they gain their bearings using geometric cues (e.g., long wall to the left, short wall to the right); other relevant information (e.g., scent cues) can then be fit into this geometric frame. Study of human development using the reorientation paradigm has shown that children 18 to 24 months of age do not spontaneously use feature information (a bright blue wall) for reorientation in small rectangular spaces but readily use geometric information (Hermer & Spelke, 1994, 1996). Human adults and children older than 6 years are able to combine geometric and feature information flexibly. It has been proposed that spatial language allows penetration of the encapsulated geometric module (e.g., Shusterman & Spelke, 2005). However, despite its early promise, a number of recent findings have called into question the validity of the geometric module and the associated modular approach to spatial development (see Cheng, 2008; Twyman & Newcombe, 2010).

The *adaptive combination position* integrates the Euclidean and nonmetric positions, suggesting that spatial representations are built from a variety of sources that are combined based on evidence concerning their validity. In many cases, sources of information are *hierarchical,* that is, structured so that they nest metric information within nonmetric (or categorical) information. In this model, errors arise through the use of heuristics. For example, according to Stevens and Coupe (1978), most people erroneously judge that Reno is east of San Diego because they know that Nevada (the category in which they place Reno) is mostly east of California (the category in which they place San Diego). The influence of categories and boundaries on spatial judgments has been shown repeatedly (Hirtle & Jonides, 1985; Maki, 1981; McNamara, 1986; Newcombe, Huttenlocher, Sandberg, Lie, & Johnson, 1999; Wilton, 1979).

One explanation for such results is that spatial information is stored hierarchically, at varying levels of specificity (Wilton, 1979). When making spatial judgments, adults first access stored information at the coarsest level, using more fine-grained information only if it seems needed to make the given judgment. That is, they may use good enough heuristics rather than more effortful processes. In this view, systematic errors are not necessarily due to distorted representations, but are the result of using cognitive shortcuts.

A more specific kind of hierarchical model is a *Bayesian* one, which suggests that human adults combine multiple sources of information by weighting each piece according to its reliability (Huttenlocher, Hedges, & Duncan, 1991; see also Chapter 4, this volume). This process is optimal in that it minimizes error across multiple estimates. For example, imagine estimating the location of a bird, about which you have both visual and auditory information (i.e., you can both see it and hear its song). Let us also assume that the two modalities lead to slightly different estimates of the bird's location and that the reliability of the visual estimate is greater than that of the auditory one. The two estimates can be imagined as overlapping probability distributions—one wider and one thinner—each centered about its mean (see Color Plate 14). Under a Bayesian framework, the cross-modal estimate of location is a linear combination of the two unimodal estimates weighted by their respective reliabilities. This combination would yield a final estimate of position that is closer to the visual mean estimate than to the auditory one, but not the same. Note that although the integrated estimate is biased away from the visual estimate, the distribution of integrated estimates has a lower variance than either of the two unimodal estimates. Because variance is the inverse of reliability, the reliability of this integrated estimate is greater than that of either unimodal estimate alone. Indeed, by weighting each cue in this manner, the reliability of the integrated estimate is maximized, thus minimizing error across multiple estimates, even though bias may be introduced on a trial-by-trial basis (for reviews, see Deneve & Pouget, 2004; and Ernst & Bülthoff, 2004).

In Huttenlocher et al.'s (1991) *category adjustment model* (CAM) of spatial memory, two specific kinds of information—categorical and metric—are optimally combined. For example, one might recall that one's keys are located "on the table" (categorical) and that they are about 4 inches from the upper and left edges (metric). The CAM assumes that the category is represented by a prototypical (central) value, and that this value is combined with the metric estimate to yield an optimal integrated estimate of location. This combination of categorical and metric values predicts that individual estimates will be biased toward central (prototypical) values but that overall error across multiple estimates is minimized. Such bias has been found in many studies of spatial cognition, including location reproduction in simple shapes (Huttenlocher et al., 1991), natural scenes (Holden, Curby, Newcombe, & Shipley, 2010), location recognition (Sampaio & Wang, 2009), and directional pointing tasks (Spencer & Hund, 2002, 2003; see Cheng, Shettleworth, Huttenlocher, & Rieser, 2007, for a more extensive overview). Bias toward category prototypes has also been shown in value estimates in several other continuous dimensions, such as size, time, and shade of gray (Duffy, Huttenlocher, & Crawford, 2006; Huttenlocher, Hedges, & Bradburn, 1990; Huttenlocher, Hedges, & Prohaska, 1988; Huttenlocher, Hedges, & Vevea, 2000; Lee & Brown, 2003).

Other kinds of spatial information may also be combined in an optimal manner. Newcombe and Huttenlocher (2006) argued for an adaptive combination model: People make active and adaptive use of relevant information to support spatial estimates, including information from different sensory modalities and from both geometry and features (thus addressing the data generated by research out of the modularity position surveyed earlier). Within the reorientation paradigm, rearing and training effects lend support to aspects of this model, showing that experience with feature cues increases the likelihood of their use (Brown, Spetch, & Hurd, 2007; Kelly, Spetch, & Heth, 1998; Ratliff & Newcombe, 2008b; Twyman, Friedman, & Spetch, 2007; Twyman, Newcombe, & Gould, 2012). Most modular accounts would predict no changes with experience (see Twyman & Newcombe, 2010). Along similar lines, Cheng et al. (2007) discussed how egocentric coding and inertial navigation may be integrated with allocentric information. Importantly, Cheng et al. also pointed out that we should not always expect integration. When two different cues specify widely disparate locations for the same object, the conflict may lead to one or the other cue being selected and relied on. However, the influence of experience may still be seen in the selection process (e.g., Ratliff & Newcombe, 2008b).

In the remainder of this chapter, we organize our discussion of spatial development by exploring the development of the three capabilities necessary for the hierarchically organized adaptive combination of information specifying spatial location as considered in the CAM model: categorical coding, metric coding, and the process of combining these cues. We then turn to a separate examination of what we have learned about development using the reorientation paradigm, in which optimal performance requires the combination of a variety of categorical and metric cues. Due to length limitations, we do not discuss egocentric coding and inertial navigation, nor do we discuss the use of nonvisual cues (e.g., auditory cues, olfactory or slope gradients). In addition, we do not discuss wayfinding, perspective taking, or navigation. All these functions depend on location coding but involve much more besides.

DEVELOPMENT OF CATEGORICAL CODING

Space is inherently continuous. *Spatial categories*, as we define them, are any regions that constrain the number of possible locations (e.g., in a search task) by using coarse, relational information and by grouping points in continuous space and treating them as equivalent. Thus, it may seem that metric (or at least fine-grained) coding is basic to spatial cognition and that *categorical spatial coding,* or the parsing of space into constituent components, would be imposed on continuous space. One might even speculate that fine-grained coding comes first developmentally. Yet, Piaget and Inhelder (1948/1967) suggested exactly the opposite, hypothesizing that infants first consider the world as divided into topological categories such as touching versus not touching or continuous versus broken. Along similar lines, recent work on infant spatial categorization has asked about the origin of spatial categories that are relevant to learning verbs, prepositions, and other relational language (e.g., containment vs. support or the path vs. manner of actions; see Göksun, Hirsh-Pasek, & Golinkoff, 2010). Surprising evidence has been found that spatial categorization appears even before 3 months of age. However, the data also show that spatial categorization develops. In this section, we review the relevant studies on starting points and change, noting three clear developmental trends: Children become increasingly able to use multiple referents to define spatial categories, they become increasingly able to abstract spatial relations across different exemplars, and they become increasingly less reliant on perceptual support to define category boundaries.

Spatial Categorization Using a Single Referent: Above–Below and Left–Right

To make inferences about infants' categorization of spatial relations, researchers often use measures of looking time. In such a paradigm, the infant is familiarized with a certain relation between an object and a referent, such as a small square shown above a line (Quinn, 1994). In familiarization, the relation is viewed multiple times, with the object (square) shown at various locations, each retaining the spatial relation (above the line). The infant is then shown the object in two novel absolute locations; in one case, the relation is familiar (above), and in the other, it is unfamiliar (below). A disparity in looking time between the two conditions (often with increased gaze time toward the

novel relation) indicates that the infant has formed a relational category.

Studies of infant spatial categorization have suggested that categories defined by a single perceptually available referent (e.g., above or below a line, left or right of a line) are identified earlier than those defined by multiple referents (e.g., between two lines). Even 3-month-olds can discriminate between positions above and below a horizontal line referent (Quinn, 1994; Quinn, Cummins, Kase, Martin, & Weissman, 1996) or between positions to the left or right of a vertical line referent (Quinn, 2004). It is notable that because the novel locations are equidistant from the familiarized locations, the difference in looking time is not due to a discrepancy in the distance moved (i.e., to use of fine-grained information). Furthermore, control trials reveal that infants are able to discriminate a novel within-category position from familiar positions, ruling out the possibility that infants are simply not sensitive to within-category changes in position. Finally, categorization of spatial relations does not rely on a simple boundary-crossing rule (i.e., on one side of the referent versus the other side), because 3-month-olds did not dishabituate to novel locations on the opposite side of a diagonal line referent (Quinn, 2004). Taken together, these findings suggest that by 3 months, infants can categorize according to the spatial relations of above–below and left–right relative to a referent.

Amazingly, there is evidence that the ability to form simple spatial categories may even be present within days of birth. Newborns can differentiate open and closed geometric shapes (Turati, Simion, & Zanon, 2003) and an above–below relationship between two shapes (Antell & Caron, 1985; Gava, Valenza, & Turati, 2009). Thus, it appears that simple spatial categorization arises early and is present within days of birth.

Despite these striking demonstrations of early categorization, it is important to note also that there are clear limitations to these early spatial categories. First, early spatial relations do not generalize across different objects. That is, the spatial categories only apply to the object(s) that the infants are familiarized with (e.g., squares, circles); testing with novel objects (e.g., triangles) in familiar and unfamiliar spatial positions yields no difference in looking time (Quinn et al., 1996; Quinn, Polly, Furer, Dobson, & Narter, 2002). An abstract category of *above* or *below,* irrespective of objects, is not formed until approximately 6 months of age. Second, early spatial categories require perceptual support; without a visible referent, 3-month-olds do not impose boundaries (e.g., based on body axes, gravitation, or a spatial midline) to form categories until 6 months of age (Quinn, 1994). Finally, early spatial categories only make use of a single referent. More mature spatial representations make use of multiple sources of information, as described in the next section.

Spatial Categorization Using Multiple Referents: Between

In work analogous to the above–below studies described earlier, Quinn, Norris, Pasko, Schmader, and Mash (1999) examined infants' categorization of locations between two reference bars. Regardless of whether the bars were horizontal or vertical, the infants did not distinguish the novel spatial relation (i.e., outside the bars). It is notable that this null result was upheld even after doubling the number of training trials, ruling out the possibility that two referents might require twice the exposure for infants to derive a spatial category. Only by 6 months of age did infants categorize locations as between two referents (Quinn, Adams, Kennedy, Shettler, & Wasnik, 2003; Quinn et al., 1999).

From the preceding section, we know that 6-month-olds are capable of forming abstract categories of *above* and *below* (i.e., categories that extend to novel objects). This raises an interesting question: When do infants form an abstract spatial category of *between?* Does the ability to form abstract categories appear at approximately 6 months of age, or is there a common specific-to-abstract developmental trend across all spatial categorizations, such that abstract categories develop months later than concrete ones (Casasola & Cohen, 2002; Quinn et al., 2003)? Quinn et al. (2003) explored this issue and found that 6- to 7-month-olds did not form an abstract version of the category *between* but that 9- to 10-month-olds did. Taken together with the findings that 3-month-olds form concrete—but not abstract—categories of *above* and *below,* this pattern

strongly suggests that the different spatial categories each undergo a concrete-to-abstract progression. It remains to be seen, however, whether this trend is specific to each individual relation or to classes of relations (e.g., those defined by a single versus multiple referents).

That infants can discriminate spatial relations is clearly a precursor to the ability to use categorical information to encode object locations. However, although we know that adults code locations hierarchically, using both categorical and metric information (e.g., Huttenlocher et al., 1991), we cannot say for certain, on the basis of the evidence presented here, that infants code locations categorically, because the infants did not need to remember any specific location. Nevertheless, that infants can distinguish spatial categories is a critical step toward categorical coding of locations.

Spatial Categories Without Perceptual Support: Imposing Categorical Boundaries

One limitation of the categories discussed thus far is that all depend heavily on visually available reference frames (e.g., a line referent for left–right discriminations). However, adult spatial cognition often involves nonperceptual factors, such as imposing mental boundaries on spaces (e.g., "The keys are on the left side of the table" or "The dot is in the upper, right quadrant of the circle"; Huttenlocher et al., 1991; Huttenlocher, Newcombe, & Sandberg, 1994) or using conceptual information to define spatial categories (Holden et al., 2010). In experimental situations, we can identify categories based on subdivision by examining error patterns. Briefly, the CAM suggests that location memory errors are biased toward the center of the category (we will return to this topic in discussing cue combination and the CAM). Thus, given a space such as a long, narrow sandbox, systematic errors biased toward the midline would indicate that the sandbox is the category, whereas errors showing bias toward the one-quarter and three-quarter points would suggest that a boundary was mentally imposed at the midline, defining two categories, each with its own center.

Huttenlocher et al. (1994) showed that adults make these latter location memory errors, dividing the sandbox into *left* and *right* categories using the midline. In contrast, children 6 years and under are biased toward the midline, indicating no subdivision (Huttenlocher et al., 1994; Schutte, Spencer, & Schöner, 2001). Only by about age 7 do children show the adult pattern of bias away from the midline, across multiple tasks (e.g., Huttenlocher et al., 1994; see also Hund & Spencer, 2003; Sandberg, 1999; Sandberg, Huttenlocher, & Newcombe, 1996; Spencer & Hund, 2002, 2003). This implies that category boundaries are not mentally imposed until relatively late in development. However, it appears that these results also depend on the demands of the task, and it may not mean that children under 7 are unable to use nonperceptual cues to form spatial categories. When Huttenlocher et al.'s (1994) sandbox task was modified to become a paper-and-pencil version, even 4-year-olds showed evidence of subdivision. What remains unclear is whether the difference in results between the sandbox and drawing tasks is due to differences in spatial scale or to the fact that a sandbox and hidden toy are objects whereas the drawn rectangle and dot are not. What is clear is the developmental progression such that mental subdivision of space becomes increasingly common and differentiated (Newcombe & Huttenlocher, 2000).

Are Spatial Categories Flexible?

With the ability to impose boundaries on spaces comes the question of how one determines where to place the boundaries. In many instances, these follow fairly obvious rules (e.g., divide at the midpoint of a sandbox or rectangle, or use the vertical and horizontal axes to divide a circle into quadrants; Huttenlocher et al., 1991, 1994). However, a major question regarding these imposed boundaries is whether they are rigidly or flexibly defined—a question that is important to the evaluation of a Bayesian approach. Initial work by Huttenlocher, Hedges, Corrigan, and Crawford (2004) suggested that geometrically defined categories were immutable, at least in estimating location of dots in a circle. However, several studies have recently found evidence that the default categorization scheme can be altered in certain instances (Crawford & Jones, 2011; Hund & Plumert, 2005; Sampaio & Wang, 2010; Simmering & Spencer, 2007; Verbeek & Spetch, 2008). Using nongeometric feature cate-

gories generally requires support: perceptual support, with boundaries available throughout the trial (e.g., Simmering & Spencer, 2007), or categorical support, with category membership directly given (Sampaio & Wang, 2010, Experiment 2), with unique objects found exclusively within a single category (Sampaio & Wang, 2010, Experiment 3) or with the number of objects per category high (Crawford & Jones, 2011). Under these conditions, spatial categorization seems to be used in a somewhat flexible manner by adults and by older children (Hund & Plumert, 2005). It remains an open and interesting question whether younger children show flexibility or rigidity in their spatial categorization in the traditional tasks.

Section Summary

We have outlined evidence that suggests that spatial categorization is present within the first months (Quinn, 1994), and perhaps even days, of life (Gava et al., 2009). However, as we have seen, this categorization also undergoes several developmental trends. First, young children become increasingly able to use multiple referents to help define categories; they progress from using a single referent (Quinn, 1994) to multiple referents (Quinn et al., 1999). The second trend is a clear sequence of concrete-to-abstract; abstract spatial categories (those that are irrespective of the training objects) seem to not be formed until several months after the corresponding concrete categories (e.g., Quinn et al., 1996, 2003). Finally, children also progress from using visible cues to define category boundaries to imposing their own boundaries (Huttenlocher et al., 1994). It is unknown, however, whether these boundaries become more or less flexible with age.

DEVELOPMENT OF METRIC CODING

The second major class of information that we consider is *metric coding* of location. Relating this topic to the previous section, we can say that whereas categorical coding coarsely restricts the possible search locations (e.g., the keys are on the table), metric coding either specifies a precise absolute location (e.g., 4 inches from the upper and left edges) or a location defined metrically in a relative way (e.g., a shorter distance than the width of the table). Precise metric coding may rely on a Cartesian system of coordinates (distances along *x* and *y* axes) or a vector system (distance and angle from a referent).

Clearly, precisely (or even relatively) coding locations requires more fine-grained information than categorical coding can typically provide alone. Piaget believed that this type of distance coding did not develop until about 6 years of age (Piaget & Inhelder, 1948/1967). More recent evidence suggests that the origins of metric coding may appear as early as 5 months, but also shows that there is age-related change: Early origins do not imply mature competence. We can again identify several developmental trends, discussed here in approximate order of their appearance in development. First, during infancy, children become increasingly able to bind a specific object to its precise spatial location. Second, between 18 and 24 months, children become able to use distance from distal landmarks to identify specific locations, in a process called *place learning*. Refinement of this ability continues into elementary school. Third, over the preschool years, children begin to distinguish absolute and relative coding of distances, with increasing flexibility regarding which kind of coding to use in which situation.

Infant Starting Points

Early efforts to look at the origins of metric coding used fairly complex paradigms that required search for hidden objects, as in the well-known A-not-B error (which also often constrains search to discrete locations and involves the buildup of reaching habits). Studies of these kinds suggested that location memory in infants is undeveloped. Yet, as with the studies reviewed in the previous section, research using looking-time measures has provided evidence for much earlier competence. For example, 3-month-old infants can distinguish between locations even within a category (Quinn et al., 1996). In another study that directly tested infants' ability to code metric location, Newcombe, Huttenlocher, and Learmonth (1999) used a violation-of-expectation paradigm. In their study, 5-month-olds were familiarized with a hiding event, in which an object was hidden and then "discovered" at a given location within a 3-foot-long sandbox. In the critical trials,

though, the object was removed from a different location (12 inches away) from where it had been hidden. The infants looked longer when the object emerged from the unexpected location than when it emerged from the expected one. However, this could be due to a categorical kind of distinction, because some locations may have been seen as "in the box" versus "near the end." Thus, in a second experiment, infants were tested with location violations of only 8 inches; these were judged by adult observers as being "in the box," rather than "at the end." Five-month-olds still gazed for a longer time at the object emerging from a novel location, suggesting that they could differentiate between the specific locations. Finally, data showed that this was not because of a relatively simple discrimination between a location where an event occurred versus one where nothing occurred; infants dishabituate even when the "unexpected" locations had previously been used as hiding locations, indicating that 5-month-olds can discriminate between hiding locations used recently and those used previously. Newcombe, Sluzenski, and Huttenlocher (2005) followed up on these findings, showing that infants brought these abilities with them to the laboratory rather than forming them during the familiarization trials (which could be regarded as "teaching" trials).

Development of Object-Location Binding in Infancy

One important caveat to the findings of Newcombe, Huttenlocher, and Learmonth (1999) is that although the children could detect a location violation, they did not detect an object violation. If a specific object was hidden at a given location and a different object was removed from that same location, then the infants did not show any reaction in looking time. This suggests that, although 5-month-olds have the rudiments of coding metric locations, they do not remember specific objects as having particular locations. This ability to bind objects to their locations also requires a developmental process.

There is ample evidence that, from a young age, featural information is used to individuate objects. For example, 4.5-month-olds can use featural information to help identify objects (Wilcox, 1999; Wilcox & Baillargeon, 1998). And, as outlined in the preceding section, locations can be discriminated by at least 5 months of age (Newcombe, Huttenlocher, & Learmonth, 1999). Yet, young infants may neglect one kind of information while remembering the other, suggesting that the binding of features defining object identity to cues specifying location is not achieved automatically (e.g., Leslie, Xu, Tremolet, & Scholl, 1998; Mareschal & Johnson, 2003).

On the basis of computational modeling, Mareschal, Plunkett, and Harris (1999) predicted that object-location binding would develop between 7.5 and 9.5 months of age. More recent evidence has supported this prediction, demonstrating that the object identities (as identified by shape) and spatial locations of two different objects are integrated by approximately 9 months of age (Káldy & Leslie, 2003). In these studies, 9-month-olds dishabituated when either or both of two objects swapped spatial locations; in contrast, 6.5-month-olds were only partially successful, remembering only the location of the most recently hidden object or even failing to dishabituate if they were momentarily distracted during the retention interval. These results are in line with previous conclusions regarding the development of the capacity to assign specific objects to specific locations (Baillargeon, DeVos, & Graber, 1989; Baillargeon & Graber, 1988).

It is interesting to note that the developmental trend toward being able to bind specific objects with their metric locations is effectively the opposite of the concrete-to-abstract trend seen in categorical coding. That is, as we outlined in the previous section, infants form categories on the basis of spatial relations that initially only apply to the exemplar objects; for fine-grained coding, however, infants initially discriminate metric locations irrespective of object identity.

Development of Place Learning in the Toddler Years and Beyond

The ability to code metric locations in the studies of infants need not imply the existence of place learning, because distance and direction information were likely defined with respect to the local frame of reference. That is, the boundaries of the container were continually visible and surrounded the search space. Place learning, by contrast, requires coding distances from distal landmarks and often involves integrating across multiple views not supported by an immediate perceptual frame (Newcombe & Huttenlocher, 2000). Place learning, in which distances and directions from different landmarks are used to fix locations, is known to develop relatively late in nonhuman animals (see Nadel, 1990). It therefore seems likely that this ability would also develop late in human children.

Newcombe, Huttenlocher, Drummey, and Wiley (1998) devised a task to examine place learning in a continuous space. Children were asked to search for toys hidden in a long, rectangular sandbox after they had moved to the other side of the box. Critically, one group of children performed this task with visual access to distal landmarks, whereas a second group performed the task in an environment in which these landmarks were not available. Children 21 months old and younger did not show any difference in their search patterns in the two environments (i.e., regardless of the availability of distal cues). In contrast, 22-month-olds and older children did refine their searches when distal cues were available. These results therefore support the conclusion that place learning develops relatively late in the second year of life (as also implied by the data of DeLoache & Brown, 1983). Further support comes from Balcomb, Newcombe, and Ferrara (2011), who found a sharp transition at the end of the second year of life, using a paradigm analogous to the Morris water maze, traditionally used to assess place learning in rodents, in which children searched for a puzzle located under one of many carpet tiles in a circular enclosure.

The fact that 22-month-olds begin to demonstrate place learning does not mean that they exhibit mature levels of competence. There is clear evidence that children continue to develop in this regard over the next several years of life. For example, 5-year-olds do not perform as well as older children and adults in keeping track of where they have been in a radial arm maze task (Aadland, Beatty, & Maki, 1985). Even children as old as 7 years do not perform as well as older participants in modifications of the Morris water maze task, which involves finding a hidden object in either a circular enclosure or on a large open field by using distal landmarks (Overman, Pate, Moore, & Peuster, 1996). There is also change between 5 and 7 years and adulthood in the use of intramaze cues, boundary information, and distance and direction from distal cues (Bullens, Nardini, et al., 2010).

One possible explanation for the relatively abrupt transition between 21 and 22 months of age in the use of distal cues is that the ability depends on hippocampal maturation, which is thought to appear at approximately that age (e.g., Diamond, 1990, 1995). However, the fact that place learning continues to develop over the course of the next several years may also argue for an experiential component; specifically, as children begin to gain experience with skilled locomotion, they may become more able to devote attentional resources to distal objects than to maintaining an upright posture (Newcombe & Huttenlocher, 2000). Furthermore, the evidence that 16-month-olds can use more proximal cues (e.g., the geometric frame of a sandbox), but not distal cues, suggests that development may partially involve the use of increasingly distant landmarks to fix spatial locations. In addition, there is evidence of experience-dependent change in the use of indirect cues during the early elementary school years (Bullens, Szekely, Vedder, & Postma, 2010).

Development of Relational and Absolute Coding of Extent

In the research considered so far, the emphasis has been on absolute metric coding of an exact distance. However, in many situations, coding relative distance is equally or more important. For example, when we describe an object as near another object (e.g., the teddy bear was near the bed), the absolute distance between the target object (bear) and the referent object (bed) is not the only consideration. The bear's distance to the bed relative to that of other objects to the bed seems to be important in judging nearness; for example, the teddy bear could be judged as far from the bed if many other toys were closer to the bed.

The presence or absence of other intervening objects is critical to adults' judgments of *near*, as well as to 3- and 4-year-olds' judgments of the

nearness of objects (or whether one object was nearby another; Hund & Naroleski, 2008; Hund & Plumert, 2007). Thus, the category of *near* relies on the ability to judge distance, but in a relative, not an absolute, way. In a placement task, the relational coding of *nearby* influenced memory for specific locations across all age groups (albeit in different ways; Hund & Naroleski, 2008). In fact, in experiments examining memory for the length of a line or dowel, relational coding of distance is evident in infancy (Duffy, Huttenlocher, Levine, & Duffy, 2005; Huttenlocher, Duffy, & Levine, 2002) and seems to predominate over absolute coding of distance through the age of 4 years (Huttenlocher et al., 2002) and even beyond, with mature performance not evident until 8 years (Duffy, Huttenlocher, & Levine, 2005; Vasilyeva, Duffy, & Huttenlocher, 2007).

What about coding of location in large real-world spaces? To explore this issue, Uttal, Sandstrom, and Newcombe (2006) studied children's use of the relation *middle*. Adapting a method from nonhuman animal studies (e.g., Collett, Cartwright, & Smith, 1986; see also Chapter 7, this volume), Uttal et al. trained adults and 4- and 5-year-olds to search for an object in the middle of two landmarks. At test, the distance between the landmarks was doubled. If children encode absolute distance, they would have searched for the toy at the trained distance from either of the landmarks; if, however, they encode the location relationally (i.e., that the hiding location is equidistant from the two landmarks), they would then have searched in the middle. Both the 4- and 5-year-olds did search according to the relation *middle*. Similarly, Spetch and Parent (2006) found that 3-, 4-, and 5-year-olds all searched according to the relation *middle*. Interestingly, Uttal et al. also included trials in which one of the landmarks was removed, to determine whether children also retained a vector coding of absolute distance to guide search. The results showed that children can use either type of coding and that they flexibly switch strategies depending on task demands.[1]

Spatial scaling involves mapping corresponding proportions or distances from a model environment

[1]One possible caveat to these studies, however, is that there might be something special about the relation *middle*. Would expansion tests requiring other relations (e.g., the three-quarter point between two landmarks) yield similar results? To our knowledge, no studies have performed this test with children. However, we do have clues to the answer from research on spatial scaling.

(or map) to the reference environment. The use of maps and models is often considered separately from the type of relational information discussed here, because using them requires not only scaling but also the ability to recognize the correspondence between the symbolic representation and the true space (DeLoache, 1989, 1995; DeLoache, Kolstad, & Anderson, 1991). Children generally understand symbolic correspondence by about age 3, which allows us to ask whether relative distance is used to constrain search. When hiding locations vary along a single dimension of an enclosed space (i.e., in a long, narrow sandbox), all 4-year-olds, and about half of 3-year-olds, can use relational information from simple maps to constrain their search (Huttenlocher, Newcombe, & Vasilyeva, 1999; Huttenlocher, Vasilyeva, Newcombe, & Duffy, 2008).

In sum, research on using relative or proportional distance information to encode location in continuous spaces versus using absolute distance converges on similar conclusions. The capacity to use relational information to recall locations is evident in infancy. It coexists with a capacity to code absolute location at least by 4 years but often dominates over it. Mature and flexible use of both relational and absolute metric coding is consolidated in the elementary school years.

Section Summary

As with categorical coding, the rudiments of metric coding seem to appear early. However, we can again identify several developmental trends. Although metric coding may appear by 5 months of age (Newcombe, Huttenlocher, & Learmonth, 1999), infants become progressively more able to bind specific objects to their specific spatial locations (e.g. Káldy & Leslie, 2003). In the second year of life, children become able to use distance from distal landmarks to identify specific locations (i.e., they show place learning; Balcomb et al., 2011; Newcombe et al., 1998), with continuing development into the early elementary school years that is at least partially experience dependent. Over the preschool and elementary school years, children begin to use both absolute and relative distance information to recall specific locations, with relative information predominating at first.

DEVELOPMENT OF CUE COMBINATION

Thus far we have shown that both categorical and metric coding of location undergo substantial development over the first months and years of life. In this light, we now turn to discussion of the development of cue combination. Recall that in our discussion of adult spatial processing, we described Bayesian models of optimal cue combination; several studies have examined this process in adults (e.g. Alais & Burr, 2004; Ernst & Banks, 2002; Gepshtein & Banks, 2003; Hillis, Watt, Landy, & Banks, 2004; Huttenlocher et al., 1991). According to these models, when different pieces of information—about location, for example—are combined, each piece is weighted according to its reliability; this weighted averaging of multiple sources of information minimizes average error, even though bias may be introduced on a trial-by-trial basis. Using the framework of this chapter thus far, we first consider the combination of cues that we have labeled *categorical* and *metric*. From there, we turn to other cue types and their combination.

Category Adjustment Effects: Combining Metric and Categorical Estimates of Location

We previously described the basic formulation of Huttenlocher et al.'s (1991) CAM when we discussed adult spatial processing. We have shown that spatial categories are formed within the first few months of life and that metric information is also coded early. When can the two kinds of information be combined? To the best of our knowledge, the youngest age that has been explicitly tested for hierarchical spatial cue combination is 16 months. Huttenlocher et al. (1994) asked 16-month-olds to search for hidden objects in a long, narrow sandbox. Analysis of the toddlers' errors showed that their responses were systematically biased toward the center of the sandbox. This pattern of bias remained even when the sandbox was surrounded by a white curtain, when children moved laterally along the side of the box between hiding and search, and when children viewed hiding and then initiated search from different ends of the sandbox. These conditions respectively rule out explanations that appeal to the use of distal cues to guide search, to laziness (in searching from the end, children actually must walk past the correct location to show the bias pattern), or to the effects of perceptual foreshortening (because hiding and search vantage points differ). It is therefore clear that by 16 months at the latest, children combine categorical information (the frame of the sandbox) and metric information (the precise location within the sandbox) about object location.

However, even though young children can combine these pieces of information, one would still predict developmental changes in error (bias) patterns. For example, we have already discussed the fact that categories become less dependent on physical boundaries; as these categories become subdivided, the direction of bias changes, reflecting the new categorization structure. We have also reviewed evidence that the accuracy of fine-grained coding increases over the course of development; this suggests that later estimates may be relatively less reliant on categorical information. Finally, spatial tasks involving a single dimension are solved at an earlier age than those involving two dimensions, suggesting that combination in 2-D space would likely develop later. These latter two predicted trends are considered, in turn, next.

First, we consider changes in the accuracy and durability of metric coding and how this affects the optimal combination of metric and categorical information. When metric coding becomes less reliable (whether due to encoding circumstances, interference, or decay), the CAM predicts that its weight will decrease relative to that of categorical information. For example, if metric information decays relatively more quickly than categorical information, the CAM predicts that increased delays between study and test would result in increasingly biased estimates of location toward category centers. This is precisely what Huttenlocher et al. (1991) reported when adults were required to recall locations after longer delays.

Relating this to development, one might expect that the durability of metric coding increases with age. This would suggest that when comparing location memory errors on trials with long and short retention intervals, the difference in error magnitude

will be greater for younger children; that is, because their metric information is quicker to decay, they would become increasingly reliant on categorical information to estimate location. Hund and Plumert (2002) explored this issue by asking 7-, 9-, and 11-year-olds, as well as adults, to learn the locations of several objects in an open square box divided into quadrants by walls. Participants then attempted to replace the objects into their exact locations either immediately after learning or after a 12-minute delay. The results showed an interesting U-shaped developmental trend in bias, such that younger children and adults tended to exhibit greater bias. This appears to be due to two different developmental changes. First, the authors convincingly argued that metric and categorical information are assigned their weights independently of one another. That said, one trend across development appears to be increased attention to (and weighting of) categorical information during learning (e.g., Plumert, 1994), leading to increased bias. The second trend is that, as predicted, younger children's fine-grained estimates of location are subject to greater decay (see also Hund & Plumert, 2002, 2003, 2005; Recker, Plumert, Hund, & Reimer, 2007). The U-shaped bias pattern across ages, then, is due to changes in how categorical and metric information are independently weighted, which, in turn, affects their optimal combination.

Second, as we reviewed previously, tasks in which locations vary along a single dimension, versus along multiple dimensions, are solved by children at an earlier age. One might therefore suspect that the early competence in hierarchical cue combination shown by 16-month-olds would have been unlikely had locations varied along two dimensions. Furthermore, one would expect that competence would continue to grow through development. Sandberg et al. (1996) asked children (ages 5–10) to recall locations within a blank circle. Like adults, children of all ages coded metric (fine-grained) location along both the radial and angular dimensions. However, categorical coding for 5- to 8-year-olds was found only along the radial dimension. Only by age 9 or 10 did children show the adult patterns of categorical bias in both dimensions. This suggests that adult-like levels of hierarchical cue combination in two-dimensional spaces are not reached until approximately 10 years of age.

It is notable that the lack of categorical coding for angular information found by Sandberg et al. (1996) is not due to an intrinsic difficulty with coding angular information. When the task was modified so that only angular information was to be remembered, even the youngest children showed categorical coding of angle information. Furthermore, the difficulty with two dimensions is also not due to difficulty in imposing boundaries. Recall that even 4- and 5-year-olds did so in paper-and-pencil tasks when locations varied along a single dimension (Huttenlocher et al., 1994). In fact, 7-year-olds still fail to show radial and angular categorization even when horizontal and vertical lines are present to delineate the typical adult category structure (Sandberg, 1999). This suggests that the relatively late development of the capacity to combine hierarchical spatial cues in 2-D spaces is not due to underdeveloped spatial abilities but rather to limitations in encoding and/or processing capacity, which prevents children from noticing the central tendency of two dimensions simultaneously (Sandberg, 1999).

The overall story of the development of hierarchical cue combination therefore follows directly from the trends we have discussed with respect to both categorical and metric coding. There is evidence of hierarchical cue combination at a relatively young age (16 months) but only for the most simple of tasks. As development progresses, metric information becomes more reliable, changing the weights associated with optimal combination. However, with development, categories also undergo significant change. As categories become less rigidly defined by physical boundaries, error patterns shift to reflect the new categorization scheme; furthermore, children also develop the ability to process multiple dimensions of spatial categories simultaneously. The story of development is therefore one of shifting weights as both metric and categorical systems become increasingly refined. Whatever the current state of development of each cue, it will determine its relative weight in forming an integrated estimate. In the next section, we begin to examine adaptive combination of other sorts of cues.

Other Kinds of Combination

As outlined earlier, some of the clearest evidence in favor of adult Bayesian combination has come from studies of intermodal cue combination. For example, Ernst and Banks (2002) showed that adults optimally combine haptic and visual information. Participants were asked to make judgments about the height of objects, or their orientation, on the basis of visual information alone, haptic information alone, or a combination of the two. When both cues were available, they were surreptitiously made to conflict with one another (i.e., each provided a slightly different estimate). Because each modality was tested initially in isolation, one can predict a priori their relative weightings and how this will affect the combined estimate. Given that intermodal combination requires estimates from different sensory systems to be integrated, one might expect that such a combinatory process would develop later than within-sensory combination; however, Bayesian combination of cues appears to be performed automatically and with little to no effort.

To examine the development of Bayesian cross-modal cue integration directly, Gori, Del Viva, Sandini, and Burr (2008) adapted Ernst and Banks's (2002) technique for use with 5- to 10-year-olds. Their results clearly show that the 8- to 10-year olds, like adults, did combine the sources of information in a statistically ideal manner. However, in all children younger than 8, the information was not combined at all—one sensory modality dominated the other (which modality dominated depends on the task used).

Using an entirely different task, and one in the spatial domain, Nardini, Jones, Bedford, and Braddick (2008) found similar results. Nardini et al. used a simple, short-range navigation task in which participants were asked to return an item to its initial location in a small arena. Visual cues from landmarks as well as self-generated motion (proprioceptive and vestibular) cues were available either singly or jointly. Unlike adults, children in the task (spanning ages 4–8) did not combine cues in an optimal manner. Instead, as in Gori et al.'s (2008) study, one modality dominated estimates of spatial location. In another spatial investigation, Bullens, Klugkist, and Postma (2011) found shifting reliance on visual and nonvisual cues to locate objects following self-movement in comparing 5-, 7- and 9-year-olds. The data suggested that even 9-year-olds may not be combining information optimally in their paradigm.

Taken together, these results make a compelling case that optimal multisensory integration does not develop until at least 8 years of age, and perhaps later. Nardini et al. (2008) suggested that protracted development might result from the need to accumulate data establishing correspondence between signals; they suggested that combining information across modalities into a common reference frame may require that each individual spatial representation system be fully developed. Whatever the reason, multisensory cues or spatial cues of different kinds appear to be relatively difficult to combine adaptively. This area of research needs much more exploration.

DEVELOPMENT IN THE REORIENTATION PARADIGM

The reorientation task has been the primary focus for the debate regarding the virtues of a modular approach to spatial development. The participant enters an enclosure and is shown the hiding location of some object in one of its corners, is disoriented, and is then asked to locate the hidden object. Geometric information in a rectangular space (e.g., long wall to the left, short wall to the right) will narrow the potential choices to two (though in spaces of other shapes—e.g., trapezoid—geometry can narrow the choices to one). Often, in studies using rectangular arenas, the space also contains a feature that can disambiguate the two choices (e.g., one blue wall, three white walls). If children split their choices between the corners identified by geometry, one can conclude that they used geometric cues to recall the location but did not integrate the feature information that would have yielded the unambiguous solution.

In the analytic terms developed so far, the task involves the coding of relative distance information, the sense relation between the two relative distances, and the pasting of a categorical cue onto the relative distance-plus-sense information.

Developmental work has shown that in the absence of feature information, 18- to 24-month-olds readily use relational distance information (geometry) to constrain their searches to the two geometrically correct corners (Hermer & Spelke, 1994, 1996). However, even 3-, 4-, and 5-year-olds did not appear to combine this geometric coding with feature information to disambiguate between the geometrically correct corners in a small rectangular arena (Hermer & Spelke, 1994, 1996). But more recent work has shown that this delay is largely due to the task demands. Children as young as 18 months were able to use both feature and geometric information to search correctly in an enclosure that was larger than that of Hermer and Spelke (1994, 1996) but retained the proportional lengths of the walls (Learmonth, Nadel, & Newcombe, 2002; Learmonth, Newcombe, & Huttenlocher, 2001). Further work has suggested that several factors were critical, such as the ability to move about the environment (Learmonth, Newcombe, Sheridan, & Jones, 2008; see also Twyman & Newcombe, 2010). In addition, Twyman et al. (2007) showed that even a few trials of training children to use feature cues (in the absence of unique geometry) was enough to catalyze their combined use of feature and geometric information, even in a small arena, when both types of information were present.

Taken together, this evidence suggests that children are able to use both sources of information as early as 18 months and that findings in which children do not integrate features and geometry are due more to task demands than to true developmental constraints. However, there is an important caveat to this conclusion. The locations of hidden toys are discrete (i.e., there are only four choices, each located at the junction of two walls). The use of discrete hiding locations means that it is impossible to know for certain whether children are integrating cues in an optimal manner (in the sense of weighting each cue by its reliability or certainty) or whether they are using some other weighting system. That is, without evidence of systematic bias reducing overall error variance, we cannot conclude that these toddlers are combining information in a Bayesian manner; such a demonstration would require both a continuous search space and variation in the reliability of scalar and/or feature cues. To the best of our knowledge, no one has varied the reliability of these cues, although the work outlined in the preceding section did show bias in children's error patterns in continuous spaces.

CONCLUSION

This chapter has summarized spatial development as viewed through the lens of a hierarchical and combinatory approach to mature spatial coding. We have summarized evidence that infants begin with surprising abilities to code spatial extent and to group the spatial world into categories, and yet we have not endorsed a nativist point of view. Rather, we see these abilities as strong starting points for a rich series of developmental transitions, many of which have been charted but many of which remain to be delineated. A particular need is for more research that examines how children combine different kinds of spatial information, whether their combination processes are truly Bayesian, and what experiences change their combinatorial processes (assuming experience has a role). Future research along these lines will need to become increasingly mathematical and test quite specific models. Such research can also benefit from a comparative approach—especially because manipulating rearing experiences of human infants is quite difficult—and from interchange with neuroscience work that delineates with increasing precision what kinds of spatial information are taken up and suggests how combinatorial processes might operate. Last, new research can integrate types of information this chapter touched on only lightly or not at all, notably the role of egocentric coding and inertial navigation, the role of nonvisual modalities, and the role of gradients.

SUGGESTED REFERENCES FOR FURTHER READING

Cheng, K., Shettleworth, S. J., Huttenlocher, J., & Rieser, J. J. (2007). Bayesian integration of spatial information. *Psychological Bulletin, 133,* 625–637. doi:10.1037/0033-2909.133.4.625

A broad overview of how a Bayesian approach applies to spatial memory.

Ernst, M. O., & Banks, M. S. (2002, January). Humans integrate visual and haptic information in a statistically optimal fashion. *Nature, 415,* 429–433. doi:10.1038/415429a

An already classic experiment exemplifying precise and elegant work on Bayesian combination.

Huttenlocher, J., Hedges, L. V., & Duncan, S. (1991). Categories and particulars: Prototype effects in estimating spatial location. *Psychological Review, 98,* 352–376. doi:10.1037/0033-295X.98.3.352

The original specification of a hierarchical and Bayesian approach to spatial location coding.

Nardini, M., Jones, P., Bedford, R., & Braddick, O. (2008). Development of cue integration in human navigation. *Current Biology, 18,* 689–693. doi:10.1016/j.cub.2008.04.02

A pioneering investigation of the development of Bayesian cue integration—the starting point, we hope, for much more investigation.

Newcombe, N. S., & Huttenlocher, J. (2000). *Making space: The development of spatial representation and spatial reasoning.* Cambridge, MA: MIT Press.

An overview of many more phenomena in spatial development than could be covered in this chapter.

Twyman, A. D., & Newcombe, N. S. (2010). Five reasons to doubt the existence of a geometric module. *Cognitive Science, 34,* 1315–1356. doi:10.1111/j.1551-6709.2009.01081.x

A review and critique of a modular approach to spatial processing and development.

References

Aadland, J., Beatty, W. W., & Maki, R. H. (1985). Spatial memory of children and adults assessed in the radial maze. *Developmental Psychobiology, 18,* 163–172. doi:10.1002/dev.420180208

Acredolo, L. P., & Boulter, L. T. (1984). Effects of hierarchical organization on children's judgments of distance and direction. *Journal of Experimental Child Psychology, 37,* 409–425. doi:10.1016/0022-0965(84)90068-7

Alais, D., & Burr, D. (2004). The ventriloquist effect results from near-optimal bimodal integration. *Current Biology, 14,* 257–262.

Antell, S. E. G., & Caron, A. J. (1985). Neonatal perception of spatial relationships. *Infant Behavior and Development, 8,* 15–23. doi:10.1016/S0163-6383(85)80013-8

Baillargeon, R., DeVos, J., & Graber, M. (1989). Location memory in 8-month-old infants in a non-search AB task: Further evidence. *Cognitive Development, 4,* 345–367. doi:10.1016/S0885-2014(89)90040-3

Baillargeon, R., & Graber, M. (1988). Evidence of location memory in 8-month-old infants in a nonsearch AB task. *Developmental Psychology, 24*, 502–511. doi:10.1037/0012-1649.24.4.502

Balcomb, F., Newcombe, N. S., & Ferrara, K. (2011). Finding where and saying where: Developmental relationships between place learning and language in the second year. *Journal of Cognition and Development, 12*, 315–331. doi:10.1080/15248372.2010.544692

Brown, A. A., Spetch, M. L., & Hurd, P. L. (2007). Growing in circles: Rearing environment alters spatial navigation in fish. *Psychological Science, 18*, 569–573. doi:10.1111/j.1467-9280.2007.01941.x

Bullens, J., Klugkist, I., & Postma, A. (2011). The role of local and distal landmarks in the development of object location memory. *Developmental Psychology, 47*, 1515–1524. doi:10.1037/a0025273

Bullens, J., Nardini, M., Doeller, C., Braddick, O., Postma, A., & Burgess, N. (2010). The role of landmarks and boundaries in the development of spatial memory. *Developmental Science, 13*, 170–180. doi:10.1111/j.1467-7687.2009.00870.x

Bullens, J., Szekely, E., Vedder, A., & Postma, A. (2010). The effect of experience on children's ability to show response and place learning. *British Journal of Developmental Psychology, 28*, 909–920. doi:10.1348/026151010X487285

Byrne, R. W. (1979). Memory for urban geography. *The Quarterly Journal of Experimental Psychology, 31*, 147–154. doi:10.1080/14640747908400714

Casasola, M., & Cohen, L. B. (2002). Infant categorization of containment, support and tight-fit spatial relationships. *Developmental Science, 5*, 247–264. doi:10.1111/1467-7687.00226

Cheng, K. (1986). A purely geometric module in the rat's spatial representation. *Cognition, 23*, 149–178. doi:10.1016/0010-0277(86)90041-7

Cheng, K. (2008). Whither geometry: Troubles with the geometric module. *Trends in Cognitive Sciences, 12*, 355–361. doi:10.1016/j.tics.2008.06.004

Cheng, K., Shettleworth, S. J., Huttenlocher, J., & Rieser, J. J. (2007). Bayesian integration of spatial information. *Psychological Bulletin, 133*, 625–637. doi:10.1037/0033-2909.133.4.625

Collett, T. S., Cartwright, B. A., & Smith, B. A. (1986). Landmark learning and visuo-spatial memories in gerbils. *Journal of Comparative Physiology A: Neuroethology, Sensory, Neural, and Behavioral Physiology, 158*, 835–851. doi:10.1007/BF01324825

Crawford, L. E., & Jones, E. L. (2011). The flexible use of inductive and spatial categories. *Memory & Cognition, 39*, 1055–1067. doi:10.3758/s13421-011-0089-9

DeLoache, J. S. (1989). Young children's understanding of the correspondence between a scale model and a larger space. *Cognitive Development, 4*, 121–139. doi:10.1016/0885-2014(89)90012-9

DeLoache, J. S. (1995). Early understanding and use of symbols: The model model. *Current Directions in Psychological Science, 4*, 109–113. doi:10.1111/1467-8721.ep10772408

DeLoache, J. S., & Brown, A. L. (1983). Very young children's memory for the location of objects in a large-scale environment. *Child Development, 54*, 888–897. doi:10.2307/1129893

DeLoache, J. S., Kolstad, D. V., & Anderson, K. N. (1991). Physical similarity and young children's understanding of scale models. *Child Development, 62*, 111–126. doi:10.2307/1130708

Deneve, S., & Pouget, A. (2004). Bayesian multisensory integration and cross-modal spatial links. *Journal of Physiology, Paris, 98*, 249–258. doi:10.1016/j.jphysparis.2004.03.011

Diamond, A. (1990). Rate of maturation of the hippocampus and the developmental progression of children's performance on the delayed non-matching to sample and visual paired comparison tasks. In A. Diamond (Ed.), *The development and neural bases of higher cognitive functions* (pp. 394–426). New York, NY: Annals of the New York Academy of Sciences.

Diamond, A. (1995). Evidence of robust recognition memory early in life when assessed by reaching behavior. *Journal of Experimental Child Psychology, 59*, 419–456. doi:10.1006/jecp.1995.1020

Duffy, S., Huttenlocher, J., & Crawford, L. E. (2006). Children use categories to maximize accuracy in estimation. *Developmental Science, 9*, 597–603. doi:10.1111/j.1467-7687.2006.00538.x

Duffy, S., Huttenlocher, J., & Levine, S. (2005). It is all relative: How young children code extent. *Journal of Cognition and Development, 6*, 51–63. doi:10.1207/s15327647jcd0601_4

Duffy, S., Huttenlocher, J., Levine, S., & Duffy, R. (2005). How infants code spatial extent. *Infancy, 8*, 81–90. doi:10.1207/s15327078in0801_5

Ernst, M. O., & Banks, M. S. (2002, January). Humans integrate visual and haptic information in a statistically optimal fashion. *Nature, 415*, 429–433. doi:10.1038/415429a

Ernst, M. O., & Bülthoff, H. H. (2004). Merging the senses into a robust percept. *Trends in Cognitive Sciences, 8*, 162–169. doi:10.1016/j.tics.2004.02.002

Fodor, J. A. (1983). *Modularity of mind: An essay on faculty psychology.* Cambridge, MA: MIT Press.

Gallistel, C. R. (1990). *The organization of learning.* Cambridge, MA: MIT Press.

Gava, L., Valenza, E., & Turati, C. (2009). Newborns' perception of left-right spatial relations. *Child Development, 80,* 1797–1810. doi:10.1111/j.1467-8624.2009.01368.x

Gepshtein, S., & Banks, M. S. (2003). Viewing geometry determines how vision and haptics combine in size perception. *Current Biology, 13,* 483–488. doi:10.1016/S0960-9822(03)00133-7

Göksun, T., Hirsh-Pasek, K., & Golinkoff, R. M. (2010). Trading spaces: Carving up events for learning language. *Perspectives on Psychological Science, 5,* 33–42. doi:10.1177/1745691609356783

Gori, M., Del Viva, M., Sandini, G., & Burr, D. C. (2008). Young children do not integrate visual and haptic form information. *Current Biology, 18,* 694–698. doi:10.1016/j.cub.2008.04.036

Hermer, L., & Spelke, E. S. (1994, July). A geometric process for spatial reorientation in young children. *Nature, 370,* 57–59. doi:10.1038/370057a0

Hermer, L., & Spelke, E. S. (1996). Modularity and development: The case of spatial reorientation. *Cognition, 61,* 195–232. doi:10.1016/S0010-0277(96)00714-7

Hillis, J. M., Watt, S. J., Landy, M. S., & Banks, M. S. (2004). Slant from texture and disparity cues: Optimal cue combination. *Journal of Vision, 4,* 967–992. doi:10.1167/4.12.1

Hirtle, S. C., & Jonides, J. (1985). Evidence of hierarchies in cognitive maps. *Memory & Cognition, 13,* 208–217. doi:10.3758/BF03197683

Hofstadter, M., & Reznick, J. S. (1996). Response modality affects human infant delayed-response performance. *Child Development, 67,* 646–658. doi:10.2307/1131838

Holden, M. P., Curby, K. M., Newcombe, N. S., & Shipley, T. F. (2010). A category adjustment approach to memory for spatial location in natural scenes. *Journal of Experimental Psychology: Learning, Memory, and Cognition, 36,* 590–604. doi:10.1037/a0019293

Hund, A. M., & Naroleski, A. R. (2008). Developmental changes in young children's spatial memory and language in relation to landmarks. *Journal of Cognition and Development, 9,* 310–339. doi:10.1080/15248370802247988

Hund, A. M., & Plumert, J. M. (2002). Delay-induced bias in children's memory for location. *Child Development, 73,* 829–840. doi:10.1111/1467-8624.00441

Hund, A. M., & Plumert, J. M. (2003). Does information about what things are influence children's memory for where things are? *Developmental Psychology, 39,* 939–948. doi:10.1037/0012-1649.39.6.939

Hund, A. M., & Plumert, J. M. (2005). The stability and flexibility of spatial categories. *Cognitive Psychology, 50,* 1–44. doi:10.1016/j.cogpsych.2004.05.002

Hund, A. M., & Plumert, J. M. (2007). What counts as *by?* Young children's use of absolute and relative distance to judge nearbyness. *Developmental Psychology, 43,* 121–133. doi:10.1037/0012-1649.43.1.121

Hund, A. M., & Spencer, J. P. (2003). Developmental changes in the relative weighting of geometric and experience-dependent location cues. *Journal of Cognition and Development, 4,* 3–38.

Huttenlocher, J., Duffy, S., & Levine, S. (2002). Infants and toddlers discriminate amount: Are they measuring? *Psychological Science, 13,* 244–249. doi:10.1111/1467-9280.00445

Huttenlocher, J., Hedges, L. V., & Bradburn, N. M. (1990). Reports of elapsed time: Bounding and rounding processes in estimation. *Journal of Experimental Psychology: Learning, Memory, and Cognition, 16,* 196–213. doi:10.1037/0278-7393.16.2.196

Huttenlocher, J., Hedges, L. V., Corrigan, B., & Crawford, L. E. (2004). Spatial categories and the estimation of location. *Cognition, 93,* 75–97. doi:10.1016/j.cognition.2003.10.006

Huttenlocher, J., Hedges, L. V., & Duncan, S. (1991). Categories and particulars: Prototype effects in estimating spatial location. *Psychological Review, 98,* 352–376. doi:10.1037/0033-295X.98.3.352

Huttenlocher, J., Hedges, L. V., & Prohaska, V. (1988). Hierarchical organization in ordered domains: Estimating the dates of events. *Psychological Review, 95,* 471–484. doi:10.1037/0033-295X.95.4.471

Huttenlocher, J., Hedges, L. V., & Vevea, J. L. (2000). Why do categories affect stimulus judgment? *Journal of Experimental Psychology: General, 129,* 220–241. doi:10.1037/0096-3445.129.2.220

Huttenlocher, J., Newcombe, N., & Sandberg, E. (1994). The coding of spatial location in young children. *Cognitive Psychology, 27,* 115–147. doi:10.1006/cogp.1994.1014

Huttenlocher, J., Newcombe, N. S., & Vasilyeva, M. (1999). Spatial scaling in young children. *Psychological Science, 10,* 393–398. doi:10.1111/1467-9280.00175

Huttenlocher, J., Vasilyeva, M., Newcombe, N. S., & Duffy, S. (2008). Developing symbolic capacity one step at a time. *Cognition, 106,* 1–12. doi:10.1016/j.cognition.2006.12.006

Káldy, Z., & Leslie, A. M. (2003). Identification of objects in 9-month-old infants: Integrating 'what' and 'where' information. *Developmental Science, 6,* 360–373. doi:10.1111/1467-7687.00290

Kelly, D. M., Spetch, M. L., & Heth, C. D. (1998). Pigeons' encoding of geometric and featural properties of a spatial environment. *Journal of Comparative*

Psychology, 112, 259–269. doi:10.1037/0735-7036.112.3.259

Kosslyn, S. M., Murphy, G. L., Bemesderfer, M. E., & Feinstine, K. J. (1977). Category and continuum in mental comparisons. *Journal of Experimental Psychology: General, 106,* 341–375. doi:10.1037/0096-3445.106.4.341

Landau, B. (2003). Spatial cognition. In V. Ramachandran (Ed.), *Encyclopedia of the human brain* (Vol. 4, pp. 394–418). San Diego, CA: Academic Press.

Learmonth, A. E., Nadel, L., & Newcombe, N. S. (2002). Children's use of landmarks: Implications for modularity theory. *Psychological Science, 13,* 337–341. doi:10.1111/j.0956-7976.2002.00461.x

Learmonth, A. E., Newcombe, N. S., & Huttenlocher, J. (2001). Toddler's use of metric information and landmarks to reorient. *Journal of Experimental Child Psychology, 80,* 225–244. doi:10.1006/jecp.2001.2635

Learmonth, A. E., Newcombe, N. S., Sheridan, N., & Jones, M. (2008). Why size counts: Children's spatial reorientation in large and small enclosures. *Developmental Science, 11,* 414–426. doi:10.1111/j.1467-7687.2008.00686.x

Lee, P. J., & Brown, N. R. (2003). Delay related changes in personal memories for September 11, 2001. *Applied Cognitive Psychology, 17,* 1007–1015. doi:10.1002/acp.982

Leslie, A. M., Xu, F., Tremolet, P. D., & Scholl, B. J. (1998). Indexing and the object concept: Developing 'what' and 'where' systems. *Trends in Cognitive Sciences, 2,* 10–18. doi:10.1016/S1364-6613(97)01113-3

Lynch, K. (1960). *The image of the city.* Cambridge, MA: MIT Press.

Maki, R. H. (1981). Categorization and distance effects with spatial linear orders. *Journal of Experimental Psychology: Human Learning and Memory, 7,* 15–32. doi:10.1037/0278-7393.7.1.15

Mareschal, D., & Johnson, M. H. (2003). The "what" and "where" of object representations in infancy. *Cognition, 88,* 259–276. doi:10.1016/S0010-0277(03)00039-8

Mareschal, D., Plunkett, K., & Harris, P. (1999). A computational and neuropsychological account of object-oriented behaviors in infancy. *Developmental Science, 2,* 306–317. doi:10.1111/1467-7687.00076

McNamara, T. P. (1986). Mental representations of spatial relations. *Cognitive Psychology, 18,* 87–121. doi:10.1016/0010-0285(86)90016-2

McNamara, T. P. (1991). Memory's view of space. In G. H. Bower (Ed.), *Advances in research and theory: The psychology of learning and motivation* (Vol. 27, pp. 147–186). San Diego, CA: Academic Press.

McNamara, T. P., & Diwadkar, V. (1997). Symmetry and asymmetry in human spatial memory. *Cognitive Psychology, 34,* 160–190. doi:10.1006/cogp.1997.0669

Nadel, L. (1990). Varieties of spatial cognition: Psychological considerations. In A. Diamond (Ed.), *The development and neural bases of higher cognitive functions* (pp. 613–636). New York, NY: Annals of the New York Academy of Sciences.

Nardini, M., Jones, P., Bedford, R., & Braddick, O. (2008). Development of cue integration in human navigation. *Current Biology, 18,* 689–693. doi:10.1016/j.cub.2008.04.021

Newcombe, N. S. (2002). Spatial cognition. In D. Medin (Ed.), *Stevens' handbook of experimental psychology* (3rd ed., pp. 113–163). New York, NY: Wiley. doi:10.1002/0471214426.pas0204

Newcombe, N. S., & Huttenlocher, J. (2000). *Making space: The development of spatial representation and spatial reasoning.* Cambridge, MA: MIT Press.

Newcombe, N. S., & Huttenlocher, J. (2006). Development of spatial cognition. In D. Kuhn & R. S. Seigler (Eds.), *Handbook of child psychology* (6th ed., pp. 734–776). New York, NY: Wiley.

Newcombe, N. S., Huttenlocher, J., Drummey, A. B., & Wiley, J. G. (1998). The development of spatial location coding: Place learning and dead reckoning in the second and third years. *Cognitive Development, 13,* 185–200. doi:10.1016/S0885-2014(98)90038-7

Newcombe, N. S., Huttenlocher, J., & Learmonth, A. E. (1999). Infants' coding of location in continuous space. *Infant Behavior and Development, 22,* 483–510. doi:10.1016/S0163-6383(00)00011-4

Newcombe, N., Huttenlocher, J., Sandberg, E., Lie, E., & Johnson, S. (1999). What do misestimations and asymmetries in spatial judgment indicate about spatial representation? *Journal of Experimental Psychology: Learning, Memory, and Cognition, 25,* 986–996. doi:10.1037/0278-7393.25.4.986

Newcombe, N. S., Sluzenski, J., & Huttenlocher, J. (2005). Pre-existing knowledge versus on-line learning: What do young infants really know about spatial location? *Psychological Science, 16,* 222–227. doi:10.1111/j.0956-7976.2005.00807.x

Overman, W. H., Pate, B. J., Moore, K., & Peuster, A. (1996). Ontogeny of place learning in children as measured in the radial arm maze, Morris search task, and open field task. *Behavioral Neuroscience, 110,* 1205–1228. doi:10.1037/0735-7044.110.6.1205

Piaget, J., & Inhelder, B. (1967). *The child's conception of space* (F. J. Langdon & J. L. Lunzer, Trans.). New York, NY: Norton. (Original work published 1948)

Plumert, J. M. (1994). Flexibility in children's use of spatial and categorical organizational strategies in recall. *Developmental Psychology, 30,* 738–747. doi:10.1037/0012-1649.30.5.738

Quinn, P. C. (1994). The categorization of above and below spatial relations by young infants. *Child Development, 65,* 58–69. doi:10.2307/1131365

Quinn, P. C. (2004). Spatial representation by young infants: Categorization of spatial relations or sensitivity to a crossing primitive? *Memory & Cognition, 32,* 852–861. doi:10.3758/BF03195874

Quinn, P. C., Adams, A., Kennedy, E., Shettler, L., & Wasnik, A. (2003). A development of an abstract category representation for the spatial relation between by 6- to 10-month-old infants. *Developmental Psychology, 39,* 151–163. doi:10.1037/0012-1649.39.1.151

Quinn, P. C., Cummins, M., Kase, J., Martin, E., & Weissman, S. (1996). Development of categorical representations for above and below spatial relations in 3- to 7-month-old infants. *Developmental Psychology, 32,* 942–950. doi:10.1037/0012-1649.32.5.942

Quinn, P. C., Norris, C. M., Pasko, R. N., Schmader, T. M., & Mash, C. (1999). Formation of a categorical representation for the spatial relation between by 6- to 7-month-old infants. *Visual Cognition, 6,* 569–585. doi:10.1080/135062899394948

Quinn, P. C., Polly, J. L., Furer, M. J., Dobson, V., & Narter, D. B. (2002). Young infants' performance in the object-variation version of the above-below categorization task: A result of perceptual distraction or conceptual limitation? *Infancy, 3,* 323–347. doi:10.1207/S15327078IN0303_3

Ratliff, K. R., & Newcombe, N. S. (2008). Reorienting when cues conflict: Evidence for an adaptive combination view. *Psychological Science, 19,* 1301–1307. doi:10.1111/j.1467-9280.2008.02239.x

Recker, K. M., Plumert, J. M., Hund, A. M., & Reimer, R. (2007). How do biases in spatial memory change as children and adults are learning locations? *Journal of Experimental Child Psychology, 98,* 217–232. doi:10.1016/j.jecp.2007.05.005

Sadalla, E. K., Burroughs, W. J., & Staplin, L. J. (1980). Reference points in spatial cognition. *Journal of Experimental Psychology. Human Learning and Memory, 6,* 516–528. doi:10.1037/0278-7393.6.5.516

Sampaio, C., & Wang, R. F. (2009). Category-based errors and the accessibility of unbiased spatial memories: A retrieval model. *Journal of Experimental Psychology: Learning, Memory, and Cognition, 35,* 1331–1337. doi:10.1037/a0016377

Sampaio, C., & Wang, R. F. (2010). Overcoming default categorical bias in spatial memory. *Memory & Cognition, 38,* 1041–1048. doi:10.3758/MC.38.8.1041

Sandberg, E. H. (1999). Cognitive constraints on the development of hierarchical organization skills. *Cognitive Development, 14,* 597–619. doi:10.1016/S0885-2014(99)00021-0

Sandberg, E. H., Huttenlocher, J., & Newcombe, N. S. (1996). The development of hierarchical representation of two-dimensional space. *Child Development, 67,* 721–739. doi:10.2307/1131858

Schutte, A. R., Spencer, J. P., & Schöner, G. (2003). Testing the dynamic field theory: Working memory for locations becomes more spatially precise over development. *Child Development, 74,* 1393–1417. doi:10.1111/1467-8624.00614

Shusterman, A., & Spelke, E. S. (2005). Language and the development of spatial reasoning. In P. Carruthers, S. Laurence, & S. Stitch (Eds.), *The innate mind: Structure and content* (pp. 89–106). New York, NY: Oxford University Press.

Siegel, A. W., & White, S. H. (1975). The development of spatial representations of large-scale environments. In H. W. Reese (Ed.), *Advances in child development and behavior* (Vol. 10, pp. 9–55). New York, NY: Academic Press.

Simmering, V. R., & Spencer, J. P. (2007). Carving up space at imaginary joints: Can people mentally impose arbitrary spatial category boundaries? *Journal of Experimental Psychology: Human Perception and Performance, 33,* 871–894. doi:10.1037/0096-1523.33.4.871

Spencer, J. P., & Hund, A. M. (2002). Prototypes and particulars: Geometric and experience-dependent spatial categories. *Journal of Experimental Psychology: General, 131,* 16–37. doi:10.1037/0096-3445.131.1.16

Spencer, J. P., & Hund, A. M. (2003). Developmental continuity in the processes that underlie spatial recall. *Cognitive Psychology, 47,* 432–480. doi:10.1016/S0010-0285(03)00099-9

Spetch, M. L., & Parent, M. B. (2006). Age and sex differences in children's spatial search strategies. *Psychonomic Bulletin & Review, 13,* 807–812. doi:10.3758/BF03194001

Stevens, A., & Coupe, P. (1978). Distortions in judged spatial relations. *Cognitive Psychology, 10,* 422–437. doi:10.1016/0010-0285(78)90006-3

Turati, C., Simion, F., & Zanon, L. (2003). Newborns' perceptual categorization for closed and open geometric forms. *Infancy, 4,* 309–325. doi:10.1207/S15327078IN0403_01

Tversky, B. (1981). Distortions in memory for maps. *Cognitive Psychology, 13,* 407–433. doi:10.1016/0010-0285(81)90016-5

Tversky, B. (1999). Talking about space. *PsycCRITIQUES, 44,* 39–40. doi:10.1037/001927

Tversky, B. (2000). Remembering space. In E. Tulving & F. I. M. Craik (Eds.), *Handbook of memory* (pp. 363–378). New York, NY: Oxford University Press.

Twyman, A., Friedman, A. D., & Spetch, M. L. (2007). Penetrating the geometric module: Catalyzing children's use of landmarks. *Developmental Psychology, 43,* 1523–1530. doi:10.1037/0012-1649.43.6.1523

Twyman, A. D., & Newcombe, N. S. (2010). Five reasons to doubt the existence of a geometric module. *Cognitive Science: A Multidisciplinary Journal, 34,* 1315–1356. doi:10.1111/j.1551-6709.2009.01081.x

Twyman, A. D., Newcombe, N. S., & Gould, T. G. (2012). Malleability in the development of spatial reorientation. *Developmental Psychobiology.* Advance online publication. doi:10.1002/dev.

Uttal, D. H., Sandstrom, L. B., & Newcombe, N. S. (2006). One hidden object, two spatial codes: Young children's use of relational and vector coding. *Journal of Cognition and Development, 7,* 503–525. doi:10.1207/s15327647jcd0704_4

Vasilyeva, M., Duffy, S., & Huttenlocher, J. (2007). Developmental changes in the use of absolute and relative information: The case of spatial extent. *Journal of Cognition and Development, 8,* 455–471. doi:10.1080/15248370701612985

Verbeek, E., & Spetch, M. (2008). Distortions in location memory. *Psychonomic Bulletin & Review, 15,* 328–336. doi:10.3758/PBR.15.2.328

Wilcox, T. (1999). Object individuation: Infants' use of shape, size, pattern, and color. *Cognition, 72,* 125–166. doi:10.1016/S0010-0277(99)00035-9

Wilcox, T., & Baillargeon, R. (1998). Object individuation in infancy: The use of featural information in reasoning about occlusion events. *Cognitive Psychology, 37,* 97–155. doi:10.1006/cogp.1998.0690

Wilton, R. N. (1979). Knowledge of spatial relations: The specification of the information used in making inferences. *The Quarterly Journal of Experimental Psychology, 31,* 133–146. doi:10.1080/14640747908400713

tag: modeling space

MODELS OF SPATIAL COGNITION

Stephen C. Hirtle

- looks @ approaches to modeling space table 11.1 provides a summary

There is a long history of building computational models in the field of spatial cognition for the purpose of positing underlying cognitive mechanisms, defining appropriate parameters, and testing empirical results. Such models include, but are not limited to, computer simulation models, process models, symbolic models, connectionist models, topological models, and mental models, which draw on the modeling practices in fields of cognitive psychology, geography, computer science, neuroscience, linguistics, and others. This chapter builds on an earlier paper by Mark, Freksa, Hirtle, Lloyd, and Tversky (1999) that focused on the contributions in Geographical Information Science (GIScience) of building cognitive models of geographical space by reviewing a number of modeling approaches that are specifically focused on issues of spatial cognition. That said, less space is given to neuroscience and linguistic models in this chapter, as they are covered in other chapters in this volume.

The chapter begins with a short overview of the development of models of spatial cognition, including the nature of modeling. This is followed by a detailed look at exemplar models in seven different areas, which highlights the diversity of approaches to modeling spatial cognition. Finally, the chapter ends with an annotated list of primary readings that should form the foundation of any future research in this area.

OVERVIEW

Worboys and Duckham (2004) defined a *model* to be

> an artificial construction in which parts of the one domain, termed the *source domain*, are represented by another domain, the *target domain*. The constituents of the source domain may, for example, be entities, relationships, processes, or any other phenomena of interest. (p. 135)

definition of a model

In the case of spatial cognition, the elements of the source domains are typically spatial entities, such as locations, whereas the elements of the target domain represent corresponding representations of those locations that are found in the model. This modeling process can be represented graphically as a *morphism* (Coombs, 1986; Worboys & Duckham, 2004), as indicated in Figure 11.1. In general, the source domain is quite large, whereas the target domain is a subset of locations of immediate interest. Figure 11.1 indicates that there is both a process of generating judgments in the source domain, indicated by t, and a process of generating judgments in the target domain, indicated by $m(t)$. The fit of the model can be measured by comparing the direct judgment t with the corresponding conjunction of $inv(m) \circ m(t) \circ m$, where $\circ$ indicates function composition.

DOI: 10.1037/13936-012
Handbook of Spatial Cognition, D. Waller and L. Nadel (Editors)

the modeling process

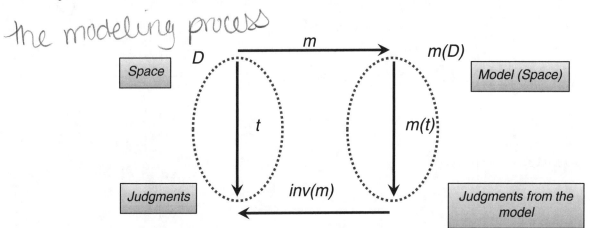

FIGURE 11.1. The modeling process. The relationship between the source domain *D* and model of the source domain *m(D)*, in which *t* is the process that generates judgments in the space and *m(t)* is the corresponding process that generates judgments from the model.

Reno vs. San Diego

As a simple example, consider the question, What is the direction from Reno, Nevada, to San Diego, California? The left side of Figure 11.1 represents what happens when this question is asked of participants in the lab. In the example, *D* is the set of city pairs and *t* is the process of generating orientations by the participants. The result of this process, still on the left side of the diagram, is a set of judgments, such as *t(Reno, San Diego) = southwest*. Note that actual direction from Reno to San Diego is southeast, but as Stevens and Coupe (1978) noted, people from the United States most often respond with the incorrect response of southwest.

A model of this cognitive process, shown on the right side of Figure 11.1, takes the entities and relationships in the source domain, *D*, and replaces them with new entities and relationships in the target domain, *m(D)*. The model suggested by Stevens and Coupe (1978) represented the spatial knowledge of spatial locations as nested propositions, such as *Nevada is east of California* and *Reno is in the western part of Nevada*. Another process, *m(t)*, takes propositional statements and uses the rules of the model to generate a conclusion, so that *m(t) (m(Reno), m(San Diego)) = m (southwest)*. In this straightforward example, we see that

$$inv(m) \circ m(t) \circ m = t,$$

where $\circ$ represents the function composition. Equality indicates that the model captures the empirical data in question, and therefore the model might reflect the underlying cognitive processes, at least at this one level of granularity. A strictly geographical model that would assign Reno and San Diego to their latitude and longitude and calculate the true bearing would not predict the judged direction and thus would fail as a model of the cognitive process. The power of building models is that the model can make new predictions that one could then test empirically in the lab. If the model fails on the new predictions, the model will need to be modified, if possible, or rejected, if not possible.

Modeling in both environmental geography and cognitive psychology became a topic of research in the later part of the 20th century. For example, Board (1967) argued that a map is a conceptual model of the physical entities that exist in space and that different maps reflect different conceptualizations (Montello, 2002). Within 10 years, models became much more formal and cognitively oriented, as researchers drew on inspiration from artificial intelligence. In one of the most influential projects, Benjamin Kuipers (1978) developed a multilevel approach to represent spatial knowledge and to account for various empirical findings in the literature. Kuipers's model is described in detail in the section, Robotic Models.

The building of models of spatial cognition was also influenced by the emergence of GIScience through a number of innovative conferences, such as the NATO Las Navas meeting in 1991 (Mark & Frank, 1991) and the Conference on Spatial Information Theory (COSIT) series, and by several journals, including *Spatial Cognition and Computation,* which began publication in 1999. GIScience is an emerging discipline that uses computer science, cognitive psychology, geography, and cartography, among other disciplines, to build a theoretical foundation for geographic information (Goodchild, 1992). In a sense, it is the science behind the geographic information systems (GIS), with a strong emphasis on the importance of the cognition of geographic space (Hirtle, 2011).

By way of surveying the vast literature, the next seven sections of this chapter look at a number of approaches to modeling, including qualitative models, synergistic models, robotic models, symbolic models, topological models, space syntax models, and geographical models. In each case, prominent examples of each type of modeling, along with the potential benefits to that approach, are given. To assist the reader in better understanding the relationship between the types of models, Table 11.1 summarizes each class of model, some of their formative proponents, their general approaches, and some application areas. Thus, when choosing a model to apply to a problem, one can compare potential approaches, either by the underlying structure or by the application area.

QUALITATIVE MODELS

One of the most productive areas in modeling for spatial cognition has been in the area of qualitative modeling. *Qualitative models,* in general, draw from a long history in artificial intelligence that examines how inferences are made on a collection of qualitative statements, such as *x* is next to *y* or *r* is older than *s*. *Qualitative spatial models* examine the kinds of inferences that can be drawn from qualitative spatial statements. These models are particularly useful for building natural language interfaces, as well as for determining the kinds of knowledge that must underlie common understanding of natural language spatial descriptions use for navigation or other purposes. It is worth noting that such models have been used in numerous applications, from robotics to architectural design (Freksa, Vrachliotis, & Bertel, 2004). For example, qualitative models can be used to encode textual descriptions that are of a qualitative nature, such as, "The plant specimens were found next to the river bed just past the large red oak" (Futch, Chin, McGranaghan, & Lay, 1992). Conversely, qualitative models can be used to create meaningful navigational instructions, such as, "Turn left just past the large red church at the end of the park," rather than quantitative instructions, such as, "Turn left in 600 feet," which were common in many of the first generation navigation systems. From the psychological point of view, such models are also useful in understanding spatial knowledge

---

TABLE 11.1

Distinctive Features, Proponents, and Application Areas for the Various Classes of Spatial Models Discussed in This Chapter

Class of models	Early proponents	Approach	Application areas
Qualitative	Cohn & Gotts (1996); Freksa (1991)	Qualitative reasoning	Qualitative reasoning, spatial linguistics
Synergistic	Portugali & Haken (1992)	Connectionist	Environmental psychology, urban design
Space syntax	Hillier & Hanson (1994)	Graph theory	Spatial cognition, pedestrian movement
Robotic	Kuipers (1978)	Symbolic	Spatial cognition, wayfinding, human–robot communications
Symbolic	Anderson (2005)	Cognitive architecture	Spatial judgments
Topological	Egenhofer (1989)	Set theory	Qualitative reasoning
Geographical	Freundschuh & Egenhofer (1997)	Conceptual framework	Spatial cognition, mental representations

and how individuals create complex spatial relationships from qualitative knowledge.

This section begins with one of the earliest cognitively driven examples of qualitative spatial models by Freksa (1991). Related approaches are by Cohn and his colleagues (Cohn, Bennett, Gooday, & Gotts, 1997; Cohn & Gotts, 1996). Freksa (1991) explored the notion of qualitative spatial reasoning as a platform for exploring the mechanisms behind spatial inferences, and developed a concrete approach to representing qualitative spatial knowledge. The approach focused on what Freksa termed a *conceptual neighborhood* of relations, which posits that the physical properties of space constrain the possible relations between objects. In one example, Freksa envisioned two speakers communicating about fish swimming in an aquarium. The conceptual neighborhood of relations would indicate that if one fish was below another at one instant in time and then later above it, then one can safely assume that the fish crossed each other at some point in the aquarium. This kind of coarse spatial knowledge is best modeled through qualitative statements that correspond to various knowledge states of the speakers.

Freksa (1992) outlined a formal specification of the qualitative reasoning algebra. For example, Figure 11.2 shows top-down schematic maps of the 15 possible qualitative arrangements of three objects, A, B, and C, where the locations of A and B are fixed, but C is allowed to move. A is always fixed at the lower intersection in the circle and B is fixed at the upper intersection. The location of C is coarsely coded by the arrow as being left, right, in front of, or behind the two referents. For example, the top row represents the three qualitative statements: C is in front and to the left of B, C is directly in front of B, and C is in front and to the right of B. Note the segment A–B is needed to define the primary axis. This work has been extended to include additional relations and constraints and has been applied to a number of geographic and spatial reasoning problems. Frank (1998) developed a related approach shown in Figure 11.3.

More recently, the notion of qualitative models has been extended to relatively complex behavior, such as wayfinding. One key insight with such models is that schematic representations, such

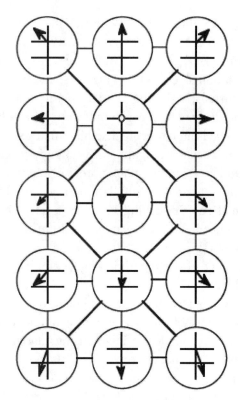

FIGURE 11.2.   Fifteen possible states for inferring the direction of C, given A and B. Within each possible state, the A is at the lower intersection and B is at the upper intersection. The arrow shows the direction from B to C along with the qualitative distance with regard to A. That is, C could be ahead of B, in line with B, between B and A, in line with A, or behind A, while at the same time to the left of the AB line, on the AB line, or to the right of the AB line. Links between the states represent possible transitions with slight movement of line BC. From *Theories and Methods of Spatio–Temporal Reasoning in Geographic Space* (p. 170), by A. U. Frank, I. Campari, and U. Formentini (Eds.), 1992, Berlin, Germany: Springer. Copyright 1992 by Springer. Reprinted with permission.

as one might find with the map of the London Underground, reflect the same kind of qualitative knowledge that was discussed by Freksa (1992) and Frank (1998). Klippel (2003) described the basic units as *wayfinding choremes*, defined as "mental conceptualizations of primitive functional wayfinding and route direction elements" (p. 1). Simply put, wayfinding choremes are the basic building

Front

FL   FR

Left   Right

BL   BR

Back

● Here
● Near
○ Far
○ Very far

FIGURE 11.3. Qualitative distances and directions. The qualitative distances and directions for two objects, colocated (here), near, far, or very far apart, while at the same time either front, back, left, right, front–right (FR), back–right (BR), back–left (BL), or front–left (FL) of the referent. From *Spatial Cognition—An Interdisciplinary Approach to Representation and Processing Spatial Knowledge* (p. 301), by C. Freksa, C. Habel, and K. F. Wender (Eds.), 1998, Berlin, Germany: Springer. Copyright 1998 by Springer. Reprinted with permission.

blocks of turns and angles that one might encounter at intersections along a path. Thus, a traveler might be asked to turn right, bear right, turn sharp right, and so on. The coarse granularity of wayfinding choremes offers only seven alternatives. These alternatives can be incorporated in chorematic focus maps (Klippel & Richter, 2004), where decision points are model as simplified intersections, as shown in Figure 11.4.

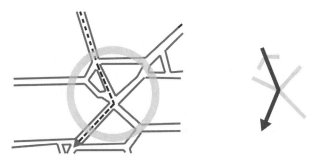

FIGURE 11.4. Construction of a chorematic focus map. The real world intersection is abstracted into the component angles along the navigational route. *Location Based Services & Telecartography* (p. 42), by G. Gartner (Ed.), 2004, Vienna, Germany: Copyright 2004 by Technical University of Vienna. Reprinted with permission.

SYNERGISTIC MODELS

Some of the most innovative models of spatial cognition have emerged out of the work of Juval Portugali and his colleagues at the Environmental Simulation Laboratory at Tel Aviv University. *Synergetic modeling* is an agent-based approach that describes how a series of interactions over time will lead to particular outcomes. The approach is useful for describing how complex environments develop over time as a result of simple interactions. In particular, Portugali and Haken (1992) proposed the notion of *synergetic interrepresentation networks* (SIRNs), which mediate internal (cognitive) representations of space with external (physical) artifacts. The approach shares much in common with neural network or connectionist models (Ghiselli-Crippa, Hirtle, & Munro, 1996) and has been applied to the self-organization of cities (Portugali, 2000) as well as to the dynamics of population shifts (Portugali, 1993).

SIRNs combine the notion of *synergetics*, which describes complex, self-organizing systems, and interrepresentational networks, which use a connectionistlike approach to modeling cognitive geography. The focus is thus on the dynamics of cognitive processing that occurs between internal and external representations of space. Haken and Portugali (1996) outlined how this model could be applied to various settings, including environmental learning. Internal and external inputs and outputs are mediated through a kind of collective variable, called *order parameters,* as shown in Figure 11.5. The movement through the space leads to new experiences, which update the model in small steps. Meaningful information, such as a Hebrew sign seen by an Israeli tourist in London, might be incorporated into their SIRN as a local landmark, whereas the same information to non-Hebrew-speaking tourist might be ignored. The model has accounted for a large number of other self-organizing principles.

As a clever demonstration of the SIRN process in operation, Portugali (1996b) pointed to a public, collective, serial reproduction game in which 60 participants took turns placing small buildings on a large floor space. There were only two rules: (a) Once placed, a building could not be moved, and (b) any new building could not block the entrance of an existing building. The resulting configurations

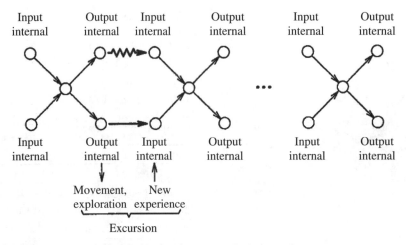

FIGURE 11.5.   SIRN for a cognitive map showing order parameters mediating internal and external representations. Order parameters are shown in the middle row. From *The Construction of Cognitive Maps* (p. 57), by J. Portugali (Ed.), 1996, Dordrecht, The Netherlands: Kluwer Academic. Copyright 1996 by Kluwer Academic. Reprinted with permission.

often reflected the structure of organic cities. Tall buildings were placed near other tall buildings, and small buildings were lined up in what looked like a street. Each response was influenced by the previous responses, similar to Bartlett's (1932) classic work on the stepwise transformations that occur in the reproductions of drawings.

The SIRN is also related to work on urban dynamic models that model cities through space syntax (Hillier & Hanson, 1994; Penn, 2003), which is described in the next section. Other connectionist approaches have been applied to the study of cognitive maps (Ghiselli-Crippa et al., 1996; Gopal, 1996; Kaplan, Weaver, & French, 1990; Sas, Reilly, & O'Hare, 2003).

SPACE SYNTAX MODELS

Space syntax is a rich framework for quantitatively measuring the layout of built spaces, both indoor and outdoor (Hillier & Hanson, 1994; Penn, 2003). Space syntax models physical space in terms of line of sight connectivity, which in turn can describe movement through the space. The approach draws on early work in environmental psychology by Lynch (1960), as well as on the importance of vistas in visual perception put forward by Gibson (1979). Space syntax has been used to account for both the

understanding of space (Penn, 2003) and the biases for certain nonoptimal paths that occur in navigation (Hölscher, Brösamle, & Vrachliotis, 2009).

Space syntax provides a set of quantitative tools for measuring the visibility and connectivity of space. The focus is on the topological connections between streets and sidewalks for outdoor spaces and halls and stairways for indoor spaces. At the same time, metric information is downplayed in the model (Montello, 2007). The connectivity of the space is represented by various graph theoretic measures, such as the topological connectivity graph. As Montello (2007) pointed out, "Any graph-theory index that can be calculated, such as the average number of nodes between subspaces, can be applied to these graph structures and related to psychological variables such as memorability" (p. iv-4). Space syntax also provides a natural way of measuring neighborhoods, where a neighborhood is well connected to other points within the neighborhood but not well connected to points in other neighborhoods.

In terms of the benefits of this approach, Penn (2003) outlined a number of areas in which space syntax has supported or expanded the understanding of spatial cognition. Most basic is the idea of movement patterns that occur from, for example, pedestrians or driving cars. Studies have consistently shown a strong correlation between the observed movement (number of people or number of cars passing through a given intersection) and the graphical measures of connectivity. Where there is variability in the correlations, more refined measures can be developed. In addition, Penn (2003) noted that the neighborhoods, which often are named local areas, and route hierarchies, which form the basis of route names and route instructions, can be predicted from the graphical structure of space.

Despite the power of the approach, there have been notable criticisms of it. Ratti (2004) argued that the lack of metric information or the failure to include any semantics of land use can lead to anomalies. Furthermore, a completely gridded environment, such as found in parts of Manhattan, would not vary on syntax measures and thus predict equal movement along all streets. Montello (2007) went on to argue that individual differences are important determiners of land use but are absent from space syntax theories. The roles of colors, textures, and landmarks are known to be useful in learning about the environment, maintaining orientation, and communicating about a physical environment (Tom & Denis, 2003). That said, perhaps the greatest benefit of space syntax has been the increased connections between geographers, environmental psychologists, and cognitive scientists over the past 10 years with regard questions about spatial understanding and environmental use.

ROBOTIC MODELS

Although not a single modeling approach, the area of robotics has provided a rich background for the development of models of spatial cognition, wayfinding strategies, and human–robot communications (Jefferies & Yeap, 2008). Two of the earliest and most influential approaches can be seen in the research of Kuipers (1978) and Yeap (1988), as described next. As reviewed here, *robotic models* are developed, in part, to provide a better understanding of human spatial cognition by examining what components are needed to build a useful and complete system.

Benjamin Kuipers (2008) began thinking about how to model spatial cognition while studying at MIT. The challenge of connecting various kinds of

knowledge, be it procedural, topological or metric, with the complexities of the spatial environment, led to an early model called TOUR (Kuipers, 1978), which was the first computational model to incorporate multiple types of spatial knowledge, most notably procedural, topological, and metrical. Procedural knowledge took the form of TURN and GO-TO commands, which was enough to generate basic directions. Connectivity of paths was provided by the topological level, whereas distance and direction were provided by the metrical level. Unfortunately, the model was not rich enough to account for interesting behavior; in particular, it was inadequate in its treatment of analog metrical representations (Kuipers, 2008). That is, there was no overall representation of locations, so the 2-D layout of places was inferred from relative distance and direction measurements from the current location.

To address some of the limitations of TOUR, Kuipers and his colleagues (Kuipers, 2000; Kuipers & Byun, 1991; Kuipers & Levitt, 1988) developed a richer framework based on a *spatial semantic hierarchy* (SSH). The SSH consisted of four distinct levels: control, causal, topological, and metrical, as shown in Figure 11.6. These levels are not independent but interlock through a variety of logical dependencies. Depending on the amount of knowledge and the nature of the incoming information, the agent may use one or more of the levels in concert to explore and move about the environment. As Kuipers (2008) pointed out in a personal and informative essay on the development of the SSH,

> The agent's cognitive map may have a global metrical map of one portion of the environment, a topological map of another, simply causal knowledge of the sequence of actions to take in a third, and then use the control level to explore unknown territory. Or, when pressed for time or preoccupied with other concerns, the agent may access only causal knowledge to follow a familiar route even though topological and metrical knowledge may be available. (p. 254)

Yeap (1988) developed a related approach on the basis of the notion that coarse sensors, such

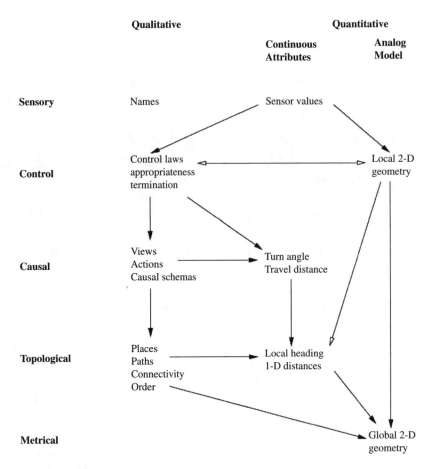

	Qualitative	**Quantitative**
		Continuous Attributes

FIGURE 11.6.   Spatial semantic hierarchy. The rows represent the five levels of the semantic hierarchy, whereas the columns represent the kinds of knowledge that are combined in building a global 2-D geometry of the space. Closed-headed arrows represent dependencies; open-headed arrows represent other potential information flows. From "The Spatial Semantic Hierarchy," by B. Kuipers, 2000, *Artificial Intelligence, 119*, p. 194. Copyright 2000 by Elsevier. Reprinted with permission.

range-finding sonar systems, can be used to create an *absolute space representation* (ASR). ASRs represent local space and are metric in nature. Adjacent ASRs can be linked through their entrances and exits using a topological graph. Recent work has extended the original approach to show how linked ASRs can be merged into a single *memory of immediate surroundings,* which is metric in nature with a single a frame of reference (Jefferies, Baker, & Weng, 2008).

In addition to metric and topological relations, research on human–robot interaction has been focused on modeling the reference frames that are used in spatial communication. As Levinson (1996) described, the three most commonly used reference frames are intrinsic reference systems, relative

reference systems, and absolute reference systems. *Intrinsic reference systems* use intrinsic properties of objects (e.g., "The ball is in front of a house") to locate other objects. *Relative reference systems* use a third object to locate one object in regard to another (e.g., "From the lake, the road is to the left of the cabin"). In *absolute reference systems,* global directions such as north or south are used in place of either intrinsic properties of objects or the relation between three objects. Moratz and his colleagues (Moratz, Fischer, & Tenbrink, 2001; Moratz, Tenbrink, Bateman, & Fischer, 2003) have built computational models that account for the varying reference frames used in giving verbal instructions about navigation. In a series of experiments

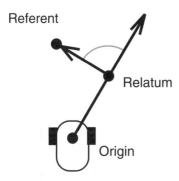

FIGURE 11.7.   Relative reference model. Complex relation indicating a referent that is left relative to the relatum, rather than the self-reference of being in front and slight left of the robot. From "Cognitive Modeling of Spatial Reference for Human–Robot Interaction," by R. Moratz, K. Fischer, and T. Tenbrink, 2001, *International Journal of Artificial Intelligence Tools*, 10, p. 597. Copyright 2001 by World Scientific. Reprinted with permission.

in which they asked individuals to use natural language to direct a robot, they examined the instructional strategies, the perspective used, and the types of reference systems that were used. It is interesting to note that in addition to standard commands (e.g., "Drive to cube on the right of the box"), participants used the robot's intrinsic properties about 20% of the time to produce commands (e.g., "Drive to the cube to your right"). Thus, the experimental results indicated that all three reference scales were used, even if the relative references are computationally more complex to model, as shown in Figure 11.7.

SYMBOLIC MODELS

ACT-R (revised)

As with other areas within cognitive psychology, *symbolic models* have provided a common way to account for empirical findings in spatial cognition. Adaptive control of thought-rational (ACT-R) models from Anderson and his colleagues (e.g., Anderson, 2005) are one of the most common frameworks. ACT-R is a cognitive–computer architecture for modeling cognitive processes (Anderson, 2005). The model is formalized as a computer simulation

in LISP, which contains both perceptual–motor modules, for interacting with the real world, and memory modules. The memory modules are further subdivided into declarative and procedural memory stores, where *declarative memory modules* consist of facts (e.g., "Three plus four equals seven"), whereas *procedural memory modules* consist of how to change one state into another, such as how to tie your shoe.

The use of ACT-R to model spatial knowledge is less common. However, several researchers have used this architecture to model spatial reasoning and spatial performance (Gugerty & Rodes, 2007; Gunzelmann, Anderson, & Douglass, 2004) by building on the distinction between coordinate and categorical spatial representations (Kosslyn, 2006). Gugerty and Rodes (2007), for example, extended the ACT-R framework by building a simple visual short-term memory (VSTM) buffer to represent coarsely coded, egocentrically referenced locations. Examples of the VSTM locations are shown in Figure 11.8; these are akin to the coarse codings used by Freksa and Klippel (see the Qualitative Models section). The model that was based on coarse codings of positions along with a mental rotation and the storage of categorical spatial information was able to account for the participants' performance with regard to a map-matching task, in which a participant had to determine the cardinal direction in an egocentric 3-D model, as if they were a pilot flying toward a specified location indicated on a north-up map.

In related work, Lyon, Gunzelmann, and Gluck (2008) developed a computational model of spatial visualization capacity. Participants were asked to mentally follow a 15-step path through at $5 \times 5 \times 5$ space. The results were modeled using the ACT-R architecture, which included an explicit mechanism for spatial interference. That is, accuracy in retracing a path dropped substantially as the number of near visits increased. Subjects would often mistake familiar nearby locations for the locations on the actual route. Only by including a parameter to measure this kind of spatial interference could the model account for the performance of subjects. The correspondence between the human data and the revised model with the spatial interference parameter included was

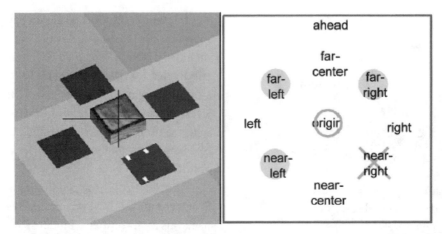

FIGURE 11.8. Egocentric spatial locations. A 3-D forward-looking view of a building surrounded by four parking lots is on the left. The coarse coding of the locations is on the right, where the filled circles correspond to empty parking lots, the X corresponds to the parking lot with the cars, and the circle corresponds to the center building. From "A Cognitive Model of Strategies for Cardinal Direction Judgments," by L. Gugerty and W. Rodes, 2007, *Spatial Cognition and Computation, 7*, p. 186. Copyright 2007 by Taylor & Francis. Reprinted with permission.

high, indicating that ACT-R may be able to provide insights into why visualizing new complex spatial material can be so difficult.

TOPOLOGICAL MODELS

Topological reasoning has been another cornerstone of modeling efforts in spatial cognition, particularly in the field of GIScience. Similar to the models discussed in earlier in theQualitative Models section of this chapter, *topological models* focus on topological aspects of space, in contrast to Euclidean aspects. This is not unlike the distinction between the topological and metrical layers (Kuipers, 2008) outlined in Robotic Models or the coordinate and categorical spatial representations (Kosslyn, 2006) discussed in the Symbolic Models section. Topological models typically begin with a series of postulates regarding basic topological properties, such as the connectivity of regions and boundaries. With these models, the focus is directed toward the issues of proximity, adjacency, coverage, and overlap. For example, topological models have been used to describe the extent of a California forest fire and how it reaches the edge of a populated neighborhood. The over-

lay of toxic plume with a residential neighborhood would be another common example of spatial problems of topology and overlap. There are also close ties with linguistic constructions of spatial concepts. For example, Mark et al. (1995) used topological models to account for how individuals interpret simple English sentences (e.g., "The road crosses the park") as described later.

In general, topological models tend to focus on people's knowledge of nonmetric relations, such as connectivity and overlap between regions (Egenhofer, 1989; Egenhofer & Herring, 1991). Consider simple regions that have no holes and consist of an interior ($^\circ$) and a boundary (∂). If objects X and Y share neither boundaries nor interiors, they are disjointed, such as Canada and Mexico. If they only share boundaries, then they meet, such as the United States and Canada. By examining all possible combinations of four intersections between boundaries and interiors, Figure 11.9 gives the eight possible relationships[1] that can occur. For example, r_1 indicates that the boundaries have nonempty intersections; that is, they share at least one point in common along their boundaries. However, the other relations are all

---

[1] Even though nine relations are listed, r_7 and r_{11} represent the same kind of relationship, namely one object covers the other.

	$\partial \cap \partial$	$° \cap °$	$\partial \cap °$	$° \cap \partial$	
r_0	($\emptyset$,	$\emptyset$,	$\emptyset$,	$\emptyset$)	A and B are disjoint
r_1	($\neg\emptyset$,	$\emptyset$,	$\emptyset$,	$\emptyset$)	A and B touch
r_3	($\neg\emptyset$,	$\neg\emptyset$,	$\emptyset$,	$\emptyset$)	A equals B
r_6	($\emptyset$,	$\neg\emptyset$,	$\neg\emptyset$,	$\emptyset$)	A is inside B
r_7	($\neg\emptyset$,	$\neg\emptyset$,	$\neg\emptyset$,	$\emptyset$)	A is covered by B
r_{10}	($\emptyset$,	$\neg\emptyset$,	$\emptyset$,	$\neg\emptyset$)	A contains B
r_{11}	($\neg\emptyset$,	$\neg\emptyset$,	$\emptyset$,	$\neg\emptyset$)	A covers B
r_{14}	($\emptyset$,	$\neg\emptyset$,	$\neg\emptyset$,	$\neg\emptyset$)	A and B overlap with distinct boundaries
r_{15}	($\neg\emptyset$,	$\neg\emptyset$,	$\neg\emptyset$,	$\neg\emptyset$)	A and B overlap with intersecting boundaries

FIGURE 11.9.   Four-intersection model of Egenhofer (1989). The table lists the nine possible combinations of interior (°) and a boundary (∂) intersections, where $\emptyset$ indicates intersection is empty and $\neg\emptyset$ indicates the intersection is not empty. For example, the second row says boundaries of A and B share at least one point, but the interior of each object does not share points with either the boundary or interior of the other object. Such an arrangement would only occur if the object touched but did not overlap. From "Point-Set Topological Spatial Relations," by M. J. Egenhofer and R. D. Franzosa, 1991, *International Journal of Geographical Information Systems, 5,* p. 170. Reprinted with permission.

empty, indicating that the interiors do not overlap nor do the interiors overlap with boundaries of the other object. This can only happen if the two regions meet with the boundaries touching. The nine-intersection model (not shown) is more complex than the four-intersection model and considers the possible intersections of the interior, boundary, and exterior of each point.

Egenhofer and his colleagues (Egenhofer, 1989; Egenhofer & Herring, 1991) have developed the four-intersection and nine-intersection models to account for the overlap of regions. A typical application has been to infer the kinds of possible transformations from one time slice to another. These transformations can be a result of various kinds of qualitative space–time inferences, for example, given a process and a state, what is the next most likely state, or given an ordered pair of states, what processes may have occurred?

Knauf, Rauh, and Renz (1997) provided evidence that people use the nine-intersection relationships when classifying spatial distributions in equivalent groups. In particular, they wrote, "In general, the results indicated that . . . Egenhofer's definition of topological relations are actually the most promising starting point for further psychological investigations on human conceptual topological knowledge" (p. 204).

More recently, Klippel (2009) explored the relationship between overlap and classification of geographical events, such as hurricanes crossing lands, and found a similar correspondence between the elements of Egenhofer's model and human conceptualization of space.

GEOGRAPHICAL MODELS

Geographic models of space have led to another rich area of study in spatial cognition. Although these models are not computational in the sense of the previous approaches, they are instrumental in providing a general framework of the variables that are critical to include in any formalization of spatial concepts. For example, it is often assumed in cognitive science that the mental representation of object space (small objects in the immediate surround) is fundamentally different from that of vista space (large objects viewed from a distance; Bell, 2002, 2006). However, the number of different kinds of spatial knowledge and how this knowledge relates to the size and manipulability of objects has been under dispute.

The range of possible models was neatly summarized in an influential paper by Freundschuh and Egenhofer (1997; see also Mark & Freundschuh, 1995). In this work, Freundschuh and Egenhofer summarized 15 different approaches that have been used to model the human conception of geographic space. Eleven of these models are of particular interest to psychologists and are shown in the columns of Figure 11.10. Central to these approaches are the properties of manipulability, locomotion, and size

of space. Each of these properties affords different operations for moving through the space and interacting with objects.

Both psychologists, such as Ittelson (1973), and geographers, such as Downs and Stea (1977), have made a basic distinction between large-scale spaces

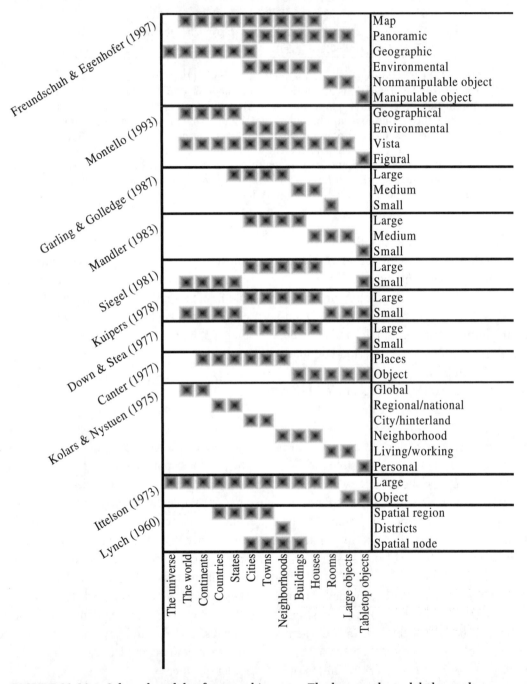

FIGURE 11.10. Selected models of geographic space. The lower column labels are the names assigned to the kind of space. Rows are labeled to increase in size from bottom to top. From "Human Conceptions of Spaces: Implications for Geographic Information Systems," by S. Freundschuh and M. J. Egenhofer, 1997, *Transactions in GIS*, 2, p. 369. Copyright 1997 by Blackwell. Reprinted with permission.

(room- or house-size spaces) and small-scale spaces that can be perceived in a single view, such as tabletop space of objects. The type of framework was extended by others, including psychologists, such as Mandler (1983), who added medium-scale spaces into the discussion, because there appears to be distinctions in the cognitive representations between objects one can manipulate (e.g., objects on a desktop) versus those that can be observed in a single view (e.g., objects in a room) versus those that can only be experienced through navigation (e.g., buildings in a neighborhood). Siegel (1981) argued that if navigation is an important criterion for establishing cognitive representations, large-scale objects, such as countries and continents, should be treated as small-scale spaces because they are learned through viewing a representation (typically a map), rather than by navigation. Montello (1993), although agreeing with the premise of Siegel (1981), named the largest spaces as geographical, implying that the role of scale is implicit in the representation. According to Montello (1993), tabletop objects were deemed to be figural, whereas spaces in between could be either environmental, if learned primarily through navigation, or vista, if able to be viewed from a single vantage point.

OTHER MODELS

The models reviewed in this chapter are but a small collection of a growing literature on models in spatial cognition. Those interested in expanding their scope beyond formal mathematical and computational models are encouraged to look at number of related areas. Tversky (1993; Tversky, Lee, & Mainwaring, 1999) has examined the mental models that individuals use both in memorizing the larger surrounding geographical environment and memorizing locations in an immediate personal space. Hegarty (2004) has been conducting a number of interesting applied studies on the mental models used in spatial reasoning with diagrams. Finally, scientific conferences, such as the Cognitive Science, Spatial Cognition, COSIT, GIScience, and Diagrammatic Reasoning meetings and many others, have regular papers and sessions on the models of spatial cognition as the area continues to grow in interest.

SUGGESTED REFERENCES FOR FURTHER READING

Allen, G. L. (2007). *Applied spatial cognition: From research to cognitive technology*. Mahwah, NJ: Erlbaum.

This book examines spatial cognition from an applied perspective.

Freundschuh, S., & Egenhofer, M. J. (1997). Human conceptions of spaces: Implications for geographic information systems. *Transactions in GIS, 2,* 361–375.

The geographical approach to modeling is well described in this paper. From it, one can gather a sense of how geographers and psychologists differ with regard to their models of space.

Golledge, R. G. (1999). *Wayfinding behavior: Cognitive mapping and other spatial processes*. Baltimore, MD: Johns Hopkins Press.

This book is one of the most comprehensive reference works in the spatial cognition literature and includes numerous chapters on modeling.

Jefferies, M. E., & Yeap, W. K. (Eds.). (2008). *Robot and cognitive approaches to spatial mapping*. Berlin, Germany: Springer-Verlag. doi:10.1007/978-3-540-75388-9

Both robotic and cognitive approaches to building spatial models are described in the chapters in this edited book.

Kuipers, B. (1978). Modeling spatial knowledge. *Cognitive Science, 2,* 129–153. doi:10.1207/s15516709cog0202_3

This article, which is one of the earliest papers to develop a formal model, introduces the TOUR model and discusses the benefits of modeling spatial knowledge.

Kuipers, B. (2000). The spatial semantic hierarchy. *Artificial Intelligence, 119,* 191–233. doi:10.1016/S0004-3702(00)00017-5

This article describes the updated SSH model in detail, with a clear discussion of how it models multiple interacting representations, both qualitative and quantitative.

Kuipers, B. (2008). An intellectual history of the spatial semantic hierarchy. In M. E. Jefferies & W. K. Yeap (Eds.), *Robotics and cognitive approaches to spatial mapping* (pp. 243–264). Berlin, Germany: Springer-Verlag. doi:10.1007/978-3-540-75388-9_15

This chapter presents an interesting personal history on the development of spatial models and how the author's understanding of commonsense knowledge of space has evolved.

Portugali, J. (Ed.). (1996a). *The construction of cognitive maps*. Dordrecht, Netherlands: Kluwer Academic. doi:10.1007/978-0-585-33485-1

This book presents a rich variety of spatial models for the construction of cognitive maps.

Portugali, J. (1996b). Inter-representation networks and cognitive maps. In J. Portugali (Ed.), *The construction of cognitive maps* (pp. 11–43). Dordrecht, Netherlands: Kluwer Academic. doi:10.1007/978-0-585-33485-1_2

A general overview of the synergistic interrepresentational networks is described in this important chapter.

References

Allen, G. L. (2007). *Applied spatial cognition: From research to cognitive technology.* Mahwah, NJ: Erlbaum.

Anderson, J. R. (2005). Human symbol manipulation within an integrated cognitive architecture. *Cognitive Science, 29,* 313–341. doi:10.1207/s15516709cog0000_22

Bartlett, F. C. (1932). *Remembering: A study in experimental and social psychology.* Cambridge, England: Cambridge University Press.

Bell, S. (2002). Spatial cognition and scale: A child's perspective. *Journal of Environmental Psychology, 22,* 9–27. doi:10.1006/jevp.2002.0250

Bell, S. (2006). Scale in children's experience with the environment. In C. Spencer & M. Blades (Eds.), *Children and their environments: Learning, using and designing spaces* (pp. 13–25). Cambridge, England: Cambridge University Press. doi:10.1017/CBO9780511521232.002

Board, C. (1967). Maps and models. In R. Chorley & P. Haggett (Eds.), *Models in geography* (pp. 671–725). London, England: Methuen.

Cohn, A. G., Bennett, B., Gooday, J., & Gotts, N. M. (1997). Qualitative spatial representation and reasoning with the region connection calculus. *GeoInformatica, 1,* 275–316. doi:10.1023/A:1009712514511

Cohn, A. G., & Gotts, N. M. (1996). The "egg-yolk" representation of regions with indeterminate boundaries. In P. A. Burrough & A. U. Frank (Eds.), *Geographic objects with indeterminate boundaries* (pp. 171–187). London, England: Taylor & Francis.

Coombs, C. H. (1986). *Psychology and mathematics. An essay on theory.* Ann Arbor, MI: University of Michigan Press.

Downs, R. M., & Stea, D. (1977). *Maps in minds: Reflections on cognitive mapping.* New York, NY: Harper & Row.

Egenhofer, M. J. (1989). *Spatial query languages.* Orono, ME: University of Maine.

Egenhofer, M. J., & Herring, J. (1991). *Categorizing binary topological relations between regions, lines,* and points in geographic databases (Technical Report). Orono, ME: Department of Surveying Engineering, University of Maine.

Frank, A. U. (1998). Formal models for cognition—Taxonomy of spatial location description and frames of reference. In C. Freksa, C. Habel, & K. F. Wender (Eds.), *Spatial cognition—An interdisciplinary approach to representation and processing spatial knowledge* (pp. 293–312). Berlin, Germany: Springer-Verlag.

Freksa, C. (1991). Qualitative spatial reasoning. In D. M. Mark & A. U. Frank (Eds.), *Cognitive and linguistic aspects of geographic space* (pp. 361–372). Dordrecht, Netherlands: Kluwer Academic.

Freksa, C. (1992). Using orientation information for qualitative spatial reasoning. In A. U. Frank, I. Campari, & U. Formentini (Eds.), *Theories and methods of spatio–temporal reasoning in geographic space* (pp. 162–178). Berlin, Germany: Springer. doi:10.1007/3-540-55966-3_10

Freksa, C., Vrachliotis, G., & Bertel, S. (Eds.). (2004). *Mental conceptions of emergent spaces in architectural design.* Bremen, Germany: Universät Bremen.

Freundschuh, S., & Egenhofer, M. J. (1997). Human conceptions of spaces: Implications for geographic information systems. *Transactions in GIS, 2,* 361–375.

Futch, S., Chin, D., McGranaghan, M., & Lay, J.-G. (1992). Spatial–linguistic reasoning in LEI (locality and elevation interpreter). In A. Frank, I. Campari, & U. Formentini (Eds.), *Theories and methods of spatio–temporal reasoning in geographic space* (pp. 318–327). New York, NY: Springer-Verlag. doi:10.1007/3-540-55966-3_19

Ghiselli-Crippa, T., Hirtle, S. C., & Munro, P. (1996). Connectionist models in spatial cognition. In J. Portugali (Ed.), *The construction of cognitive maps* (pp. 87–104). Dordrecht, Netherlands: Kluwer Academic. doi:10.1007/978-0-585-33485-1_5

Gibson, J. J. (1979). *The ecological approach to visual perception.* Boston, MA: Houghton Mifflin.

Golledge, R. G. (1999). *Wayfinding behavior: Cognitive mapping and other spatial processes.* Baltimore, MD: Johns Hopkins Press.

Goodchild, M. F. (1992). Geographical information science. *International Journal of Geographical Information Systems, 6,* 31–45. doi:10.1080/02693799208901893

Gopal, S. (1996). Connectionism and neural networks. In J. Portugali (Ed.), *The construction of cognitive maps* (pp. 69–85). Dordrecht, Netherlands: Kluwer Academic. doi:10.1007/978-0-585-33485-1_4

Gugerty, L., & Rodes, W. (2007). A cognitive model of strategies for cardinal direction judgments. *Spatial Cognition and Computation, 7,* 179–212. doi:10.1080/13875860701418230

Gunzelmann, G., Anderson, J., & Douglass, S. (2004). Orientation tasks with multiple views of space: Strategies and performance. *Spatial Cognition and Computation, 4,* 207–253. doi:10.1207/s15427633scc0403_2

Haken, H., & Portugali, J. (1996). Synergetics, inter-representation networks and cognitive maps. In J. Portugali (Ed.), *The construction of cognitive maps* (pp. 45–67). Dordrecht, Netherlands: Kluwer Academic. doi:10.1007/978-0-585-33485-1_3

Hegarty, M. (2004). Diagrams in the mind and in the world: Relations between internal and external visualizations. In A. Blackwell, K. Marriot, & A. Shimojima (Eds.), *Diagrams 2004, LNAI 2980* (pp. 1–13). Berlin, Germany: Springer.

Hillier, B., & Hanson, J. (1994). *The social logic of space.* Cambridge, England: Cambridge University Press.

Hirtle, S. C. (2011). Geographical design: Spatial cognition and geographical information science. *Synthesis Lectures on Human-Centered Informatics, 4,* 1–67. doi:10.2200/S00342ED1V01Y201103HCI011

Hölscher, C., Brösamle, M., & Vrachliotis, G. (2009). Challenges in multilevel wayfinding: A case study with the space syntax technique. *Environment and Planning B: Planning and Design, 39,* 63–82.

Ittelson, W. H. (1973). Environment perception and contemporary perceptual theory. In W. H. Ittelson (Ed.), *Environment and cognition* (pp. 1–19). New York, NY: Seminar.

Jefferies, M. E., Baker, J., & Weng, W. (2008). Robot cognitive mapping—A role for a global metric map in a cognitive mapping process. In M. E. Jefferies & W. K. Yeap (Eds.), *Robotics and cognitive approaches to spatial mapping* (pp. 265–279). Berlin, Germany: Springer-Verlag. doi:10.1007/978-3-540-75388-9_16

Jefferies, M. E., & Yeap, W. K. (Eds.). (2008). *Robotics and cognitive approaches to spatial mapping.* Berlin, Germany: Springer Verlag. doi:10.1007/978-3-540-75388-9

Kaplan, S., Weaver, M., & French, R. (1990). Active symbols and internal models: Towards a cognitive connectionism. *AI & Society, 4,* 51–71. doi:10.1007/BF01889764

Klippel, A. (2003). *Wayfinding choremes: Conceptualizing wayfinding and route direction elements.* Unpublished doctoral dissertation, Universät Bremen, Germany.

Klippel, A. (2009). Topologically characterized movement patterns: A cognitive assessment. *Spatial Cognition and Computation, 9,* 233–261. doi:10.1080/13875860903039172

Klippel, A., & Richter, K.-F. (2004). Chorematic focus maps. In G. Gartner (Ed.), *Location based services & telecartography* (pp. 39–45). Vienna, Austria: Geowissenschaftliche Mitteilungen.

Knauff, M., Rauh, R., & Renz, J. (1997). A cognitive assessment of topological spatial relations: Results from an empirical investigation. In S. C. Hirtle & A. U. Frank (Eds.), *Spatial information theory: A theoretical basis for GIS* (pp. 193–206). Berlin, Germany: Springer.

Kosslyn, S. M. (2006). You can play 20 questions with nature and win: Categorical versus coordinate spatial relations as a case study. *Neuropsychologia, 44,* 1519–1523. doi:10.1016/j.neuropsychologia.2006.01.022

Kuipers, B. (1978). Modeling spatial knowledge. *Cognitive Science, 2,* 129–153. doi:10.1207/s15516709cog0202_3

Kuipers, B. (2000). The spatial semantic hierarchy. *Artificial Intelligence, 119,* 191–233. doi:10.1016/S0004-3702(00)00017-5

Kuipers, B. (2008). An intellectual history of the spatial semantic hierarchy. In M. E. Jefferies & W. K. Yeap (Eds.), *Robotics and cognitive approaches to spatial mapping* (pp. 243–264). Berlin, Germany: Springer-Verlag. doi:10.1007/978-3-540-75388-9_15

Kuipers, B., & Byun, Y.-T. (1991). A robot exploration and mapping strategy based on a semantic hierarchy of spatial representations. *Robotics and Autonomous Systems, 8,* 47–63. doi:10.1016/0921-8890(91)90014-C

Kuipers, B., & Levitt, T. (1988). Navigation and mapping in large scale space. *AI Magazine, 9*(2), 25–43.

Levinson, S. (1996). Frames of reference and Molyneux's question: Crosslinguistic evidence. In P. Bloom & M. Peterson (Eds.), *Language and space* (pp. 109–169). Cambridge, MA: MIT Press.

Lynch, K. (1960). *The image of the city.* Cambridge, MA: MIT Press.

Lyon, D. R., Gunzelmann, G., & Gluck, K. A. (2008). A computational model of spatial visualization capacity. *Cognitive Psychology, 57,* 122–152. doi:10.1016/j.cogpsych.2007.12.003

Mandler, J. M. (1983). Representation. In P. Mussen (Ed.), *Handbook of child psychology* (4th ed., Vol. III, pp. 420–494). New York, NY: Wiley.

Mark, D. M., Comas, D., Egenhofer, M. J., Freundschuh, S., Gould, M., & Nunes, J. (1995). Evaluating and refining computational models of spatial relations through cross-linguistic human-subjects testing. In A. U. Frank & W. Kuhn (Eds.), *Spatial information theory: A theoretical basis for GIS* (pp. 553–568). Berlin, Germany: Springer-Verlag.

Mark, D. M., & Frank, A. U. (1991). *Cognitive and linguistic aspects of geographic space.* Dordrecht, Netherlands: Kluwer Academic.

Mark, D. M., Freksa, C., Hirtle, S. C., Lloyd, R., & Tversky, B. (1999). Cognitive models of geographical space. *International Journal of*

Geographical Information Science, 13, 747–774. doi:10.1080/136588199241003

Mark, D. M., & Freundschuh, S. M. (1995). Spatial concepts and cognitive models for geographic information use. In T. L. Nyerges, D. M. Mark, R. Laurini, & M. J. Egenhofer (Eds.), *Cognitive aspects of human–computer interaction for geographic information systems* (pp. 21–28). Dordrecht, Netherlands: Kluwer Academic.

Montello, D. R. (1993). Scale and multiple psychologies of space. In A. U. Frank & I. Campari (Eds.), *Spatial information theory: A theoretical basis for GIS* (pp. 312–321). Berlin, Germany: Springer-Verlag. doi:10.1007/3-540-57207-4_21

Montello, D. R. (2002). Cognitive map-design research in the twentieth century: Theoretical and empirical approaches. *Cartography and Geographic Information Science, 29*, 283–304. doi:10.1559/152304002782008503

Montello, D. R. (2007). The contribution of space syntax to a comprehensive theory of environmental psychology. In A. S. Kubat, Ö. Ertekin, Y. I. Güney, & E. Eyüboglu (Eds.), *6th International Space Syntax Symposium proceedings* (pp. iv-1–iv-12). Istanbul, Turkey: ITÜ Faculty of Architecture.

Moratz, R., Fischer, K., & Tenbrink, T. (2001). Cognitive modeling of spatial reference for human–robot interaction. *International Journal of Artificial Intelligence Tools, 10*, 589–611. doi:10.1142/S0218213001000672

Moratz, R., Tenbrink, T., Bateman, J., & Fischer, K. (2003). Spatial knowledge representation for human–robot interaction. In C. Freksa, W. Brauer, C. Habel, & K. Wender (Eds.), *Spatial cognition III: Routes and navigation, human memory and learning, spatial representation and spatial learning* (pp. 263–286). Berlin, Germany: Springer-Verlag.

Penn, A. (2003). Space syntax and spatial cognition: Or why the axial line? *Environment and Behavior, 35*, 30–65. doi:10.1177/0013916502238864

Portugali, J. (1993). *Implicate relations: Society and space in the Israeli–Palestinian conflict*. Dordrecht, Netherlands: Kluwer Academic.

Portugali, J. (Ed.). (1996a). *The construction of cognitive maps*. Dordrecht, Netherlands: Kluwer Academic. doi:10.1007/978-0-585-33485-1

Portugali, J. (1996b). Inter-representation networks and cognitive maps. In J. Portugali (Ed.), *The construction of cognitive maps* (pp. 11–43). Dordrecht, Netherlands: Kluwer Academic. doi:10.1007/978-0-585-33485-1_2

Portugali, J. (2000). *Self-organization and the city*. Berlin, Germany: Springer.

Portugali, J., & Haken, H. (1992). Synergetics and cognitive maps. *Geoforum, 23*, 111–130. doi:10.1016/0016-7185(92)90010-2

Ratti, C. (2004). Urban texture and space syntax: some inconsistencies. *Environment and Planning B: Planning and Design, 31*, 487–499. doi:10.1068/b3019

Sas, C., O'Hare, G. M. P., & Reilly, R. (2003, June). *A connectionist model of spatial knowledge acquisition in a virtual environment*. Paper presented at the Ninth International Conference on User Modeling, Pittsburgh, PA.

Siegel, A. W. (1981). The externalization of cognitive maps by children and adults: In search of ways to ask better questions. In L. S. Liben, A. H. Patterson, & N. Newcombe (Eds.), *Spatial representation and behavior across the life span* (pp. 167–194). New York, NY: Academic Press.

Stevens, A., & Coupe, P. (1978). Distortions in judged spatial relations. *Cognitive Psychology, 13*, 422–437. doi:10.1016/0010-0285(78)90006-3

Tom, A., & Denis, M. (2003). Referring to landmark or street information in route directions: What difference does it make? In W. Kuhn, M. F. Worboys, & S. Timpf (Eds.), *Spatial information theory* (Vol. LNCS 2825, pp. 384–397). Berlin, Germany: Springer.

Tversky, B. (1993). Cognitive maps, cognitive collages, and spatial mental models. In A. U. Frank & I. Campari (Eds.), *Spatial information theory: Theoretical basis for GIS*. Berlin, Germany: Springer-Verlag. doi:10.1007/3-540-57207-4_2

Tversky, B., Lee, P., & Mainwaring, S. (1999). Why do speakers mix perspectives? *Spatial Cognition and Computation, 1*, 399–412. doi:10.1023/A:1010091730257

Worboys, M. F., & Duckham, M. (2004). *GIS: A computing perspective* (2nd ed.). Boca Raton, FL: CRC Press.

Yeap, W. K. (1988). Towards a computational theory of cognitive maps. *Artificial Intelligence, 34*, 297–360. doi:10.1016/0004-3702(88)90064-1

PART IV

INTERPERSONAL DIMENSIONS OF SPATIAL COGNITION

CHAPTER 12

I GO RIGHT, NORTH, AND OVER: PROCESSING SPATIAL LANGUAGE

Holly A. Taylor and Tad T. Brunyé

"Where doggie?" 2-year-old Oliver asks while playing a hiding game from across the kitchen table. "Doggie here!" he squeals with glee, pulling the toy dog from under the table. In this scenario, Oliver, through his two-word utterances and behavior shows rudimentary spatial language use and illustrates a skill critical to spatial language comprehension: *cognitive flexibility*. How one person views the world differs from how someone else does, a fact reflected in how one talks about and interacts in the world. Even at age 2, Oliver knows that his perspective differs from his father's—that he can easily see the toy dog in his lap, whereas his father cannot. Recognizing, remembering, and using information about alternative perspectives requires cognitive flexibility and, as we argue in this chapter, is a hallmark of spatial language comprehension. In the present chapter, we explore how spatial language processing reveals cognitive flexibility through the selection, use, and activation of available reference frames and spatial perspectives. Further, we contextualize this ability within a larger cognitive framework.

Considering alternative perspectives can be critical to spatial language comprehension, as illustrated in the following example (see Color Plate 15): Imagine waiting at a coffee house for a friend. The two coffees you have ordered sit on the table. Your friend arrives, sits across from you, and asks, "Which coffee is mine?" You respond, "It's on the right." Your friend reaches out then hesitates, real-

izing she still does not know which coffee is hers. Realizing the ambiguity in "It's on the right" requires knowing that it can be interpreted from two spatial perspectives, hers and yours. In other words, interpreting spatial terms is not always straightforward, being influenced by available, and sometimes conflicting, perspective-specified spatial relationships. Complexities of spatial language grow when locating more objects, stringing locations together in routes, or describing complex layouts. The present chapter explores the need for cognitive flexibility in spatial language processing, focusing on selection, use, and activation of available reference frames and spatial perspectives. The chapter progresses as follows: First, we introduce the basics of spatial reference frames and perspectives necessary for spatial language interpretation. We follow this by discussing spatial language processing and requirements for cognitive flexibility. We then contextualize mechanisms in spatial language processing from two different literatures: general language use, including acquisition, and emerging findings in embodied or grounded cognition.

CONVEYING SPATIAL INFORMATION THROUGH LANGUAGE

Language conveys spatial information at multiple hierarchical levels, ranging from single words to sentences to lengthy discourse. For single words,

DOI: 10.1037/13936-013
Handbook of Spatial Cognition, D. Waller and L. Nadel (Editors)

the spatial information can be direct, using spatial terms, or indirect, as implied through pronouns. Egocentric spatial terms, such as *above, below, left, right, front,* and *back,* and cardinal direction terms *north, south, east,* and *west,* generally convey spatial locations relative to a known location. Other prepositions (e.g., *across, against, along, among, between, near, through, under*) can also convey spatial relationships (Coventry, Carmichael, & Garrod, 1994). These spatial words are generally embedded in sentences used to convey one object's location (*located object*) with respect to another (*reference object*). For example, the sentence "The shoes are under the bed" situates the located object (shoes) relative to the reference object (bed) using the preposition *under.* Pronouns can imply spatial perspective, such as that interpreted in the difference between "*He* is slicing the tomato" and "*I* am slicing the tomato" (Brunyé, Ditman, Mahoney, Augustyn, & Taylor, 2009). Pronouns can further specify spatial information, for example adding *your* to "Your shoes are under your bed," to specify which shoes and which bed.

At the next hierarchical level, sentences can be combined into complex descriptions, such as a room, route, or spatial layout description. Such descriptions can relate different spatial perspectives (e.g., Perrig & Kintsch, 1985; Taylor & Tversky, 1992b) and sometimes mix perspectives (Taylor & Tversky, 1992a; Tversky, Lee, & Mainwaring, 1999). At each of these levels, how people process the spatial information conveyed through language can reveal cognitive flexibility.

REFERENCE FRAMES AND PERSPECTIVES

Spatial language, like spatial arrays, must be interpreted using a reference frame. Visually interpreting a spatial arrangement invokes reference frames, even in nonlingual animals (e.g., human infants, rats; Li & Gleitman, 2002), and a given situation often has multiple potential reference frames. An interesting point of debate lies in whether reference frames play a critical role specifically with language (Gibson & Kingstone, 2006) or a role that extends more generally to understanding spatial location (Gallistel, 2002). Whether general or specific to language, ref-

erence frames play a critical role in defining spatial structure.

Levinson (1996) proposed three reference frames for describing spatial situations: absolute, relative, and intrinsic. An *absolute frame* (sometimes called *allocentric* or *environment-centered;* Gallistel, 2002; Klatzky, 1998) uses an external or environment-centered coordinate system and the terms associated with it (e.g., *north, south, east, west*). A *relative frame* incorporates the speaker's coordinate system, involves a tertiary spatial relationship (e.g., the spoon is left of the mug from my perspective), and uses projective terms (e.g., *left, right, front, back, above, below*). Other terms for this frame include *egocentric, first-person, viewer-centered,* and *deictic.* An *intrinsic* (or *object-centered*) *frame* uses an object- (or other-person-) centered coordinate system, describes a binary relationship (e.g., the lawnmower is in front of the car), and also uses projective terms (e.g., *left, right, front, back, above, below*). Despite terminology disagreement, researchers largely agree that these three systems capture the range of available reference frames needed to generate and/or interpret spatial descriptions. Which frame predominates varies on the basis of numerous factors, including language or culture (e.g., Abarbanell, Montana, & Li, 2011; Emmorey, Tversky, & Taylor, 2000; Haun, Rapold, Janzen, & Levinson, 2011; Levinson, Kita, Haun, & Rasch, 2002; Li, Abarbanell, Gleitman, & Papafragou, 2011; Li & Gleitman, 2002). Although relevant to spatial language processing, issues of language and culture are beyond the scope of the current chapter.

When locating a particular object, two or more reference frames may be available. For example, in Color Plate 16, the instructions to "look for the car keys above the overturned chair" evoke the absolute (gravity-defined; key position A), relative (viewer-defined; key position B), or intrinsic (object-defined; key position C) frames, with each frame suggesting a different location. Reference frames that use the same terms can lead to ambiguity in communication. However, the realization that ambiguity exists signals cognitive flexibility it shows consideration of alternative reference frames.

If multiple reference frames can be used to describe objects' relative locations, how are they used when understanding descriptions of multiple locations? Spatial perspectives structure extended spatial descriptions. In their classic study, Linde and Labov (1975) had New Yorkers describe their apartments, and found that 95% took a linguistic-based imaginary tour. Termed *route descriptions,* these imaginary tours address listeners as *you* and relate spatial locations using *front, back, left,* and *right* with respect to the listener's current imagined position (Taylor & Tversky, 1992b). On the basis of this study, linguists and psycholinguists assumed that the route perspective, because it reflects our direct experience navigating in an environment and successfully linearizes space to match the language's sequential nature, typically structures complex environment descriptions (e.g., Levelt, 1982, 1989) and is the preferred perspective (Klein, 1982, 1983).

Subsequent research has identified two other perspectives that can structure the linearization of space into language and also reflect ways people experience environments: gaze tours and survey perspectives. *Gaze tours* involve systematic eye movement across locations visible from a single viewpoint (Ehrich & Koster, 1983; Levelt, 1982; Shanon, 1984); *survey perspectives* take an above-environment view (e.g., Taylor & Tversky, 1992b). Ullmer-Ehrich (1982) identified three critical differences between gaze and route tours. First, gaze tours use a relative frame, whereas route tours use an intrinsic one. Second, gaze tours use a fixed origin, whereas route tours' origin varies. Finally, gaze tours relate locations to other locations, whereas route tours relate locations to the current, but changing, imagined location. Yet, both gaze and route tours take a within-environment perspective. Thus, gaze tours have some route perspective properties, but other properties fit the survey perspective (Taylor & Tversky, 1992b). People gain a survey perspective by studying maps or viewing an environment from atop a hill or in an airplane. Survey perspective descriptions convey location information by systematic scanning from a single, above-environment vantage point. Both gaze and survey descriptions relate locations to one another. Unlike gaze tours, survey descriptions use an absolute reference frame and canonical terms.

Research on spatial perspectives in discourse has differed from that on reference frames for spatial terms. Rather than focusing on ambiguity resolution, work on spatial discourse has explored how different spatial perspectives' structural framework affects the development and use of the resultant mental representation. This research focus has arisen because the perspective imparted during learning may not match the intended use (Brunyé & Taylor, 2009; Taylor, Naylor, & Chechile, 1999). For example, one may learn from a description that the pizza parlor is east of the library but may then need to know whether it is on the right or left when approaching it to pick up a pizza. Being able to mentally switch to an unlearned perspective reveals cognitive flexibility. Some studies have supported this type of flexibility (e.g., Taylor & Tversky, 1992b), whereas others have not (e.g., Shelton & McNamara, 2004). The current chapter explores conditions favoring this flexibility, tying these conditions to general language processing mechanisms and/or embodied cognitive processes.

LANGUAGE PROCESSING OF SPATIAL LANGUAGE

What is particularly interesting about spatial language is that a verbal medium conveys inherently nonverbal information (i.e. spatial location). What this means is that spatial language use involves both verbal and spatial processing, a fact confirmed by research (Brunyé & Taylor, 2008b; De Beni, Pazzaglia, Gyselinck, & Meneghetti, 2005; Deyzac, Logie, & Denis, 2006). In this section, we explore how cognitive flexibility in spatial language processing reflects similar flexibility in general language processing. We do so by working up the spatial language hierarchy from words to sentences to discourse.

Spatial Pronouns, Spatial Prepositions, and Spatial Terms

As discussed earlier, single words can convey spatial information either directly or indirectly. We combine these single words with object names to form spatial sentences, locating one object with respect to another. In this section, we discuss how words and sentences convey relative spatial information. Although the spatial focus in these issues is clear, it is important not to lose sight of language processing with spatial language.

Pronouns can indicate spatial perspective. For example, comparing the statement, "*I* can see Mount Cube looking out *my* window" with "*You* can see Mount Cube looking out *your* window" suggests a different view, depending on perspective. Thus, spatial perspective can be integral to processing pronouns. Pronouns can disambiguate spatial location when multiple viewpoints and multiple referent objects exist. Return to the coffeehouse example. Although your response of "It's on the right" to your friend's query about her coffee is ambiguous, the addition of a pronoun, "It's on *your* right" disambiguates its location. The pronoun marks that your friend should interpret the location using her own perspective.

The need for pronominal disambiguation suggests activation of multiple meanings or perspectives. Understanding and taking different perspectives, such as when comprehending pronouns, appears to be a general lexical process, here applied to spatial meaning. E. V. Clark (1997) argued a *many-perspectives account* for explaining children's lexical acquisition. This account proposes that during word acquisition, children consider alternative labels for objects and events, thereby considering many perspectives. For example, a child may understand that Mom uses the term *Goldie* when asking the kids to feed their pet, *fish* when describing the pet to her friend, and *goldfish* when at the pet store buying more food, all three terms refer to the same pet. In other words, the child understands that people have different knowledge and different perspectives when labeling this object. This view contrasts with a *one-perspective* view wherein children constrain word meaning, rejecting multiple terms for the same object (e.g., Markman, 1987).

Pronoun acquisition also appears to have a direct link to spatial perspective understanding. Research indicates that children only use pronouns *I* and *you* without error after they completely understand different viewpoints (e.g., E. V. Clark, 1997; Loveland, 1984; Ricard, Girouard, & Decarie, 1999). Using these pronouns correctly, which often occurs around age two, requires the child to understand that *me* can refer to different people

and depends on who is speaking. Understanding that *me* is situationally defined requires cognitive flexibility to properly assign a referent.

Lexical access also shows multiple meaning activation. We coactivate related concepts when naming pictures (Levelt et al., 1991), we interpret idiomatic expressions (e.g., over the hill) faster with both literal and figurative meanings available (Swinney & Cutler, 1979), and we blend simultaneously activated lexical candidates, leading to speech errors (Fromkin, 1973), such as President George W. Bush's blending of *misunderstood* and *underestimated* into *misunderestimated.*

Beyond pronouns, people use spatial terms to convey relative and absolute location information. Different spatial prepositions exist (relational and projective) that describe one object's location with respect to another, whether topological or directional (Retz-Schmidt, 1988). In many cases, someone describes a spatial location amidst multiple objects, reference frames, and/or conversational participants without disambiguating. This can be seen in our coffeehouse example where the "on the right" description is interpreted amidst two coffees, two people, and perhaps other objects (spoons, sugar bowl, menu, etc.). In other words, in real life it would be rare to have only the target and located objects in a scene. The target object (your friend's coffee) is usually among many objects (your coffee, spoons, sugar), any of which could serve as the reference object and some of which may carry the same label. Such complexity can lead to ambiguity, in response to which people could use two cognitive strategies: They may access a dominant or preferred frame, assess its applicability, and reassess alternatives if this frame does not fit (*single activation hypothesis;* Carlson-Radvansky & Irwin, 1994). Alternatively, they may simultaneously activate multiple candidate reference frames and then select one, perhaps guided by context (*multiple frame activation hypothesis;* Carlson-Radvansky & Irwin, 1994).

These two strategies bear resemblance to serial versus parallel processing debates in general information processing models (Townsend, 1990) and have been applied to different language processing phenomena, including syntactic parsing. The single activation or one-perspective accounts are akin to modular approaches (e.g., minimal attachment theory; Frazier & Fodor, 1978) and the multiple frame activation and many-perspective positions are similar to constraint-based models (e.g., Spivey-Knowlton & Sedivy, 1995). Both serial and parallel activation have pros and cons for the cognitive system. Serial processing has lower cognitive load than parallel processing but is generally slower. Because parallel processing allows simultaneous consideration of alternatives, it would seem to afford greater cognitive flexibility.

Studies assessing spatial term and spatial sentence comprehension have largely supported multiple reference frame activation (Carlson-Radvansky & Irwin, 1994), with subsequent inhibition of the ultimately unused frame or frames (Carlson-Radvansky & Jiang, 1998). Carlson-Radvansky and Irwin (1994), looking at the term *above,* for which absolute and intrinsic frames could apply, suggested simultaneous activation of both frames. Later work (Carlson & van Deman, 2008) extended multiple activation to a range of projective spatial terms (*above, below, front, back, left, right*). Using evidence that situational variables shifted final reference frame interpretation, Taylor and Rapp (2004) similarly supported multiple frame activation.

Consideration of multiple reference frames may, in part, be aided by modality-independent spatial processing. Brain imaging data have suggested that spatial preposition processing in language and spatial location processing in perception engage the same system (Hayward & Tarr, 1995). This research has shown reliable processing of projective prepositions in the left supramarginal gyrus (SMG), regardless of whether the comparison modality for the preposition was language or pictures (Damasio et al., 2001; Noordzij, Neggers, Ramsey, & Postma, 2008). By assessing lesion overlap in individuals showing impaired locative preposition knowledge, Tranel and Kemmerer (2004) revealed the roles of left frontal operculum and left SMG. The role of these brain areas seems limited to spatial preposition and location processing, because these patients, although having severe deficits in spatial preposition use, had intact spatial processing and intact conceptual processing for other categories. Behavioral and neuro-physiological research on general concept processing has suggested identical processing mechanisms for concepts, whether presented in language or through pictures (Holcomb & Anderson, 1993; Nigam, Hoffman, & Simons, 1992). However, not all research has supported this modality-independent processing view (Crawford, Regier, & Huttenlocher, 2000).

If people initially activate multiple reference frames and inhibit less relevant ones, what processes are involved in ultimate interpretation? The fact that people settle on one interpretation suggests differential spatial frame accessibility or use, even with multiple frame activation. Online processing measures, such as event-related potentials (ERPs) and negative priming, have helped to elucidate reference frame activation, selection, and use (Carlson, West, Taylor, & Herndon, 2002; Taylor, Faust, Sitnikova, Holcomb, & Naylor, 2001; Taylor, Naylor, Faust, & Holcomb, 1999). Using ERPs, Carlson et al. (2002) identified separable processes of reference frame use associated with different ERP components. In particular, when people apprehend the term *above,* ERP components appeared to modulate on the basis of reference frame selection (P300 component), reference frame competition to assign directions (frontal slow wave), and spatial relation computation and comparison (parietal slow wave). These latter processes of reference frame competition and comparison imply multiple frame activation. Through these steps the final interpretation is determined and applied.

Some factors contributing to final interpretations involve the nature of the reference frames, the relationship between the objects, and processing goals. In regard to the nature of the reference frame, some have salient features, such as the absolute frame's alignment with gravity for terms *above* and *below.* This alignment predicts greater weighting of the absolute frame for these terms (Garnham, 1989). Carlson-Radvansky and Irwin (1993) found results consistent with this prediction but also showed that the intrinsic frame contributed to *above* interpretations. Specific spatial terms apply to some, but not necessarily all, reference frames. *Above* and *below* can be interpreted using all three reference frames, but their relationship to gravity tends to emphasize the absolute. What this means is that context matters, but the range of possible interactions between spatial terms, reference frames, and context are too numerous to identify.

For spatial location, some contextual factors shown to matter include the presence and nature of distractor objects (Carlson & Logan, 2001), recently invoked reference frame (Carlson-Radvansky & Jiang, 1998), reference object rotation (Kojima & Kusumi, 2008), and spatial scale (Lautenschutz, Davies, Raubal, Schwering, & Pederson, 2007). Together, these contextual factors show that aspects of both the reference and located objects can change reference frame use and spatial term interpretation. Consider a basic case, such as whether the reference object has intrinsic sides (e.g., an animal). If the reference object has intrinsic sides, then an intrinsic reference frame can be used. If the reference object does not have intrinsic sides (e.g., a ball), then only the relative or absolute frame can be invoked. As an example, compare the descriptions "The coffee mug is *to the right of* the rubber ball" and "The coffee mug is *to the right of* the pig." From a given vantage point, the first description clearly describes the coffee mug's location. However, because the pig has intrinsic axes, two possible locations match the latter description, one defined by the speaker's viewpoint and the other by the pig's position. Other contextual factors build on this premise.

The relationship, such as functional ones, between objects also affects spatial term interpretation. Acceptable locations for specific terms and reference frame preferences change when the located and relative objects are functionally related (Carlson & Kenny, 2005; Carlson-Radvansky, Covey, & Lattanzi, 1999). The acceptability of a term differs if objects are versus are not functionally related (Carlson-Radvansky et al., 1999; Coventry, 1999; Coventry, Prat-Sala, & Richards, 2001). Further, function influences the orientation of reference frame axes (Carlson-Radvansky & Tang, 2000).

These factors influencing spatial language interpretation can also be seen in general semantic interpretation. Although semantically related concepts prime one another (e.g., Neely, 1977), people work to semantically integrate unrelated concepts (Brown & Hagoort, 1993; Holcomb, 1993). Evidence supporting this contention comes from ERP studies showing that semantic integration difficulties lead to a greater

amplitude N400. N400 amplitude varies as a function of semantic fit or cloze probability (Kutas & Hillyard, 1984). Research has suggested a role for these semantic integration processes with spatial language. Taylor and colleagues (Taylor et al., 2001; Taylor, Naylor, Faust, et al., 1999) pitted relative and intrinsic frames for interpreting spatial terms *front, back, left,* and *right* and showed a larger N400 when the intrinsic reference frame was not used. Further, election and use of the intrinsic frame appears to happen quite early (Carlson et al., 2002).

Goals or intentions also affect spatial term interpretation. Because language is inherently for communication, making this communication goal apparent may make the ambiguity brought on by different reference frames more salient. Supporting this, Schober (1993) found a tendency to coordinate reference frame use in a collaborative context. In this study, participants described a designated circle's location to a real or imaginary partner who either had the same or a different perspective. Speakers used more partner-centered terms with real, compared with imaginary, partners and maintained this strategy when switching roles. These findings fit with work supporting collaborative processing in conversation. People build common ground or shared knowledge over the course of a conversation, relying on it as the conversation proceeds (Keysar, Barr, Balin, & Brauner, 2000; Schober & Clark, 1989; Wilkes-Gibbs & Clark, 1992). Participants in Schober's (1993) study did this with spatial perspective, conversationally determining how perspective information would be used.

Building common ground involves understanding what a conversational partner does or does not know or that some information (i.e., own perspective) may be easier to process. This process has been referred to as *perspective* in a general rather than specifically spatial sense. Thus, establishing common ground requires considering multiple perspectives. Contrasting positions on establishing common ground parallel single and multiple frame activation hypotheses for spatial frame consideration, focusing on whether one or multiple referents are considered at once. The *restricted search* view suggests that people only search for referents within commonly held or mutually perceptually available knowledge

(H. H. Clark & Marshall, 1981). In contrast, the *unrestricted search* view allows for consideration of multiple possible referents (Keysar et al., 2000; Keysar, Barr, Balin, & Paek, 1998).

In conclusion, spatial term and sentence interpretation reveals cognitive flexibility. When describing location, we consider the available reference frames, select the most relevant to use, and eventually inhibit those less relevant. It is the initial multiple activation that suggests cognitive flexibility. Numerous factors then affect the final interpretation. These factors mirror those affecting general language processing. One can see clear parallels between models considered for spatial language, in particular, and language processes, in general. In the next section, we consider parallels between spatial and general discourse processing.

Spatial Discourse: Scenes, Environments, and Routes

Describing more complex scenes or environments requires stringing together spatial sentences into discourse. With the additional complexity comes the ability to gain further insights into spatial language processing. One such insight comes from comparing how people process different spatial terms within scene descriptions. Such comparisons suggest that some spatial terms can be easier to process than others. Franklin and Tversky (1990) compared pairs of spatial terms *head/feet, front/back,* and *left/right.* Participants learned the spatial locations through descriptions, mentally reoriented, and then identified the object corresponding to a particular direction. For the canonical (upright) case, participants responded fastest to *head/feet,* followed by *front/ back* and finally *right/left.* They described these results as supporting a *spatial framework* defined by the relation of body axes to the world (H. H. Clark, 1973). Other work has supported and extended this spatial framework response pattern (Bryant, Tversky, & Franklin, 1992; de Vega, 1994; Franklin, Tversky, & Coon, 1992).

The spatial framework idea fits general text comprehension models, particularly *situation models.* These models suggest that readers build increasingly integrated memory representations that incorporate specific words described in a text

(*surface level*), then meaning-based idea units (*text-based* or *gist level*), and finally they incorporate what a text describes and how it fits with known information (*situation model;* van Dijk & Kintsch, 1983; Zwaan, Langston, & Graesser, 1995; Zwaan & Radvansky, 1998). With situation models, readers can make inferences and adequately comprehend text (e.g., Graesser, Singer, & Trabasso, 1994). The fact that people can make spatial inferences within and across spatial perspectives suggests that they can build spatial situation models from text (e.g., Brunyé, Rapp, & Taylor, 2008; Taylor & Tversky, 1992b).

One model, the *event-indexing model,* suggests that readers track multiple situation model dimensions, including characters, locations, time, intentions, and causality (Zwaan, Langston, et al., 1995; Zwaan & Radvansky, 1998). Relative to these dimensions, readers initiate a new substructure when narrative shifts occur and connect substructures when narratives provide links (Gernsbacher, 1990). One issue of debate with event-indexing (Zwaan & Radvansky, 1998) is the extent to which comprehenders track spatial information (i.e., Morrow, 1994). Some work has suggested limited tracking of described space during naturalistic language comprehension (e.g., reading narratives; Radvansky & Copeland, 2000; Zwaan, Magliano, & Graesser, 1995), although the majority has demonstrated that readers extract spatial information when it is easy to do, tied to functional relevance, or necessary for local and global coherence (e.g., Brunyé & Taylor, 2008a; de Vega, 1995; Estevez & Calvo, 2000; Levine & Klin, 2001; Linderholm & van den Broek, 2002; Magliano, Miller, & Zwaan, 2001; Rinck, Hähnel, Bower, & Glowalla, 1997).

Whether people track spatial information may be tied to other information available. Taylor and colleagues (Rich & Taylor, 2000; Taylor & Tversky, 1997) suggested a reliance on one dimension for situation model organization, but situational flexibility in which dimension is used. Readers predominantly built situation models around characters but used location-centered models when necessary. Other work shows that with a single character, people build a situation model centered on that character, but with multiple characters, they build a location-based model that incorporates all characters (de Vega, 1994; Franklin et al., 1992).

For spatial descriptions, the functional relevance of location is clearly high, suggesting people will engage cognitive resources to track spatial information. This evidence comes from using selective interference tasks (e.g., Brunyé & Taylor, 2008b; Pazzaglia, De Beni, & Meneghetti, 2007) and spatial inconsistencies and discontinuities (e.g., O'Brien & Albrecht, 1992; Zwaan, Langston, et al., 1995). Taken together, the evidence suggests that context influences whether people track spatial information during language comprehension, and under certain circumstances, spatial information may not be deemed important or functionally relevant. Of course, spatial descriptions provide a functionally relevant context for tracking spatial information.

Spatial descriptions reach maximum complexity when relating information about navigable environments. Language provides a viable means of learning about relatively complex environments, and readers can form accurate mental models from spatial descriptions (Avraamides & Kelly, 2010; Avraamides, Loomis, Klatzky, & Golledge, 2004; Brunyé & Taylor, 2008b; Denis & Zimmer, 1992; Ferguson & Hegarty, 1994; Lee & Tversky, 2005; Noordzij & Postma, 2005; Perrig & Kintsch, 1985; Taylor & Tversky, 1992b). Route and survey perspectives, as discussed earlier, can be used to structure extended spatial descriptions. How does the structure imparted by the perspective affect learning and memory of the environment?

Learning environments through descriptions (as with other means) takes time and effort, and this seems to interact with the spatial perspective used (Brunyé & Taylor, 2008a). Brunyé and colleagues (Brunyé et al., 2008; Brunyé & Taylor, 2008a) have found that participants readily formed mental models from survey descriptions but required additional readings of route descriptions to develop mental representations with equivalent functionality. These findings have been supported by others (Lee & Tversky, 2005; Noordzij & Postma, 2005; Noordzij, Zuidhoek, & Postma, 2006; Shelton & McNamara, 2004) and mirror those comparing learning from maps versus navigation (Thorndyke & Hayes-Roth, 1982). These findings suggest that route descrip-

tions impose a greater cognitive demand during learning. Exploring this idea, Brunyé and Taylor (2008b) found that route descriptions engaged visuospatial and sequence generation processing to a greater extent than did survey descriptions (Pazzaglia, Meneghetti, De Beni, & Gyselinck, 2010). Thus, the linear organization (sequence monitoring) and need to relate spatial information to a moving reference point (implied traveler) seem likely contributors to route descriptions' increased cognitive load.

Not all research has supported the survey perspective advantage. Perrig and Kintsch (1985) found some advantage for route descriptions. Others have found an interaction between spatial perspective and visual experience. Although sighted individuals showed the survey perspective advantage, both early and late blind individuals built from route descriptions spatial models that were more effective (Noordzij et al., 2006; Steyvers & Kooijman, 2009). This interaction with visual ability may be due to superior serial memory developed by blind individuals (Raz, Striem, Pundak, Orlov, & Zohary, 2007).

The survey perspective advantage centers on increased cognitive flexibility to make spatial inferences. Inferencing has also been a focus in text comprehension research in general, resulting in a heated debate about which inference types readers make automatically (e.g., Graesser et al., 1994; McKoon & Ratcliff, 1992). The crux of this debate is whether readers make inferences at only a local level (McKoon & Ratcliff, 1992) or at both local and global levels (e.g., Albrecht & O'Brien, 1993). Successful text comprehension involves connecting ideas at both local (cohesion; Graesser, Millis, & Zwaan, 1997) and global (coherence; D. S. McNamara & Magliano, 2009; Trabasso, Suh, & Payton, 1995) levels. At the global level, linking text ideas to an overall framework aids comprehension and memory. Bransford and Johnson (1972) presented texts that had reasonable cohesion but were difficult to integrate globally. If participants received a title that provided global context before reading, they had improved comprehension and memory. Survey perspective descriptions, because they relate locations to an overall spatial layout, maintain integration at both global and local levels. In contrast, route perspective descriptions, which serially link landmarks, focus integration at a local level. Thus, overall layout information provided by the survey perspective serves as a scaffold on which text details can be organized (Brunyé et al., 2008; Kulhavy, Stock, & Caterino, 1994).

Once learned, the role of perspective in memory remains an interesting and open question. Although a spatial perspective provides necessary structure during learning, people gain functional utility through the ability to mentally switch between perspectives. This perspective flexibility allows one to infer spatial relationships not explicitly described and/or from an alternative perspective (i.e., accurately taking the unlearned perspective). Research examining whether mental models retain perspective-specific qualities or have perspective flexibility has come down on both sides of the debate, as well as in the middle. Some research has found perspective flexibility after learning from both route and survey descriptions (e.g., Brunyé et al., 2008; Brunyé & Taylor, 2008b; Taylor & Tversky, 1992b). However, Brunyé and Taylor (2008a) showed that readers needed more time with route, compared with survey, descriptions to achieve the same level of perspective flexibility (see also Lee & Tversky, 2001). Other research has suggested that people maintain the learned perspective in their mental representations, either completely or partially (Bosco, Filomena, Sardone, Scalisi, & Longoni, 1996; Perrig & Kintsch, 1985). Shelton and McNamara (2004), using scene recognition, showed a perspective switching cost, as well as orientation specificity within the learned perspective.

What might explain the range of findings with respect to perspective flexibility after learning from spatial descriptions? General models of discourse comprehension may provide an explanation. Models such as the *tri-partite theory* (van Dijk & Kintsch, 1983) and the *construction-integration model* (Kintsch, 1988) propose iterative processing during text comprehension. Readers draw ideas from specific words in the text, aiming to integrate this information with previous knowledge to form integrated situation models (van Dijk & Kintsch, 1983; Zwaan, Langston, et al., 1995; Zwaan & Radvansky, 1998). This iterative process takes time and interacts

with reading ability (e.g., D. S. McNamara, Kintsch, Songer, & Kintsch, 1996) and text features, such as coherence (e.g., D. S. McNamara & Kintsch, 1996). With more time, and consequently more iterations, readers form better-integrated situation models. The extent of interaction can explain spatial description findings showing increased perspective flexibility with increased reading time (Brunyé & Taylor, 2008a) and the ability to mix perspectives after learning descriptions well (Taylor & Tversky, 1992a; Tversky et al., 1999). When spatial details have been fully integrated, both with other text ideas and background knowledge, the spatial situation model has more interrelated connections on which to base inferences.

In conclusion, we can build accurate mental representations of even complex spatial environments from descriptions (Avraamides & Kelly, 2010; Brunyé & Taylor, 2008b; Lee & Tversky, 2005; Noordzij & Postma, 2005; Taylor & Tversky, 1992b). In doing so, we engage both verbal and visuospatial working memory processes (e.g., Brunyé & Taylor, 2008b; Deyzac et al., 2006; Pazzaglia et al., 2010). Examining memory from spatial discourse, general models of discourse processing help explain the developing and resultant spatial situation models.

EMBODYING SPATIAL LANGUAGE IN ACTION AND PERCEPTION

Recent research has explored language understanding through internal perceptual and action-based simulations, known as an *embodied* or *grounded cognition*. A few studies have applied this approach to spatial language, which makes sense inasmuch as spatial language is commonly used to convey information that is or will become perceptible and actionable. For instance, by informing your child that her pacifier is under the table, you expect that she will map your words onto a perceived space and potentially act on that space in a goal-directed manner. At a larger scale, asking for directions to the Empire State Building may prompt a description that includes the salient environmental features you might perceive on your way (e.g., parks, statues, stores) and action-related information to help you move in the right direction (e.g., turn left, go straight; Tenbrink & Winter, 2009). Whether in your living room or touring New York City, spatial language is used to guide perception and action. Although work examining embodiment of perception and action in spatial descriptions is in its infancy, increasing support for perception and action simulation in general language processing suggests the need to discuss it in the context of spatial language.

Mentally Simulating Described Space

We have already discussed the fact that people can build accurate spatial representations from language, and a number of studies have attempted to elucidate the nature of these spatial representations. In general, there are two complementary theoretical perspectives that attempt to explain the nature of spatial mental models. First is the view that spatial memory is composed of amodal symbolic representations, such as a vast connectionist network that codes for and reflects spatial relationships (e.g., T. P. McNamara, 1991; T. P. McNamara, Hardy, & Hirtle, 1989; Stevens & Coupe, 1978). The second, more recent view adds a substantial modal, analog, and sometimes image-like, component to earlier theories (Barsalou, 1999; Glenberg, 1997), and language-processing researchers have begun to apply this approach (for a review, see Fischer & Zwaan, 2008). For spatial descriptions, this latter theoretical perspective proposes that the building blocks of spatial memory are products of direct perception and action; that is, the perceptual and motoric experiences that take place over time play an important role in shaping both comprehension and the memory representations derived from spatial language.

Over the past few decades, theorists have proposed that language comprehension involves the activation of perceptual symbols (i.e., Barsalou, 1999, 2005; Kosslyn, 1980; Paivio, 1990; Zwaan, 2004) and motoric representations (Glenberg, 1997; Glenberg & Kaschak, 2002; Lakoff, 1987; McNeill, 1992; Zwaan & Taylor, 2006) while readers or listeners mentally simulate what is being described. In this view, the mental representations that support thinking about spaces and events are supported by the same cognitive (Barsalou, 2005; Zwaan, 2004) and neural (Pulvermüller, 2005; Ruby &

Decety, 2001; Tettamanti et al., 2005) mechanisms that support direct perception and action. These mechanisms are thought to include several modalities, including vision (e.g., Yaxley & Zwaan, 2007; Zwaan, Stanfield, & Yaxley, 2002), motor movement (e.g., Glenberg & Kaschak, 2002), and sound (Brunyé, Ditman, Mahoney, Walters, & Taylor, 2010; Brunyé, Mahoney, & Taylor, 2010; Kaschak, Zwaan, Aveyard, & Yaxley, 2006; Kurby, Magliano, & Rapp, 2009). Proponents of this embodied view have argued that these rich, multimodal mental representations form the basis for successful inferencing (Brunyé & Taylor, 2008b; Fincher-Kiefer, 2001; Zwaan, 1999) and disambiguation (Bergen & Chang, 2005) and prepare comprehenders for subsequent perception and action (Barsalou, 1999). Next, we review evidence that comprehending spatial language may engage perceptual and motoric representations. This evidence comes from research in two primary areas: object spatial relationships and extended naturalistic spatial descriptions.

Mentally Simulating Object Relationships

A critical question explored by many disciplines, including linguistics, cognitive psychology, and cognitive neuroscience, is how people link spatial language to mental representations of objects and their relationships (e.g., Carlson-Radvansky & Logan, 1997; Shallice, 1996; Taylor & Tversky, 1992b). This question has direct implications for the embodied cognition view. Researchers have used projective spatial language describing the relationship between at least two objects, such as "The clock is above the door," to examine whether people incorporate perceptual details when representing spatial relationships (Carlson-Radvansky & Logan, 1997; Hayward & Tarr, 1995; Logan & Sadler, 1996; Regier & Carlson, 2001). Regier and Carlson (2001), for instance, had participants view spatial arrangements that included a single landmark (e.g., a red block) and a strategically placed object (e.g., a square). Then participants rated the acceptability of statements describing the landmark–object relationship that included the terms *above, below, to the left of,* or *to the right of* (e.g., "The square is above the red block"). They found strong evidence that attentional focus and visual perception ground understanding of linguistic spatial relations (see also Landau & Jackendoff, 1993). It is notable that they showed that attentional focus guided visual perception and predicted effects of perceptual variables such as distance (i.e., short distances between the objects limit the attentional field to reference landmarks and thus lead to higher acceptability ratings).

Recent research has expanded on the view that attentional focus affects spatial language comprehension by examining pragmatic knowledge in spatial representations (i.e., Coventry & Garrod, 2005). For instance, in the statement "The bottle is over the glass" (Coventry et al., 2010), the comprehender would not only incorporate the attentional factors between the bottle and the glass that define their geometric relationship but would also use motor simulations reflecting experience with this particular spatial relationship (e.g., pouring milk from a bottle into a glass). As discussed earlier, prior knowledge can include the functional role between objects (e.g., a bottle to contain and pour and a glass to receive and serve as a drinking vessel). What the embodied cognition view brings is also an understanding of possible action-related relationships between the objects (i.e., pouring from the bottle into the glass). A number of studies have supported the use of perceptual, motoric, and pragmatic information when understanding spatial relationships, lending a perception–action foundation to the role function plays when interpreting spatial relations. Consider Carlson-Radvansky, Covey, and Lattanzi's (1999) finding that when participants were asked to place one object above another, functional relationships guided placement in line with action-based relationships. For instance, when asked to place a coin above a piggy bank, participants tended to align the coin with the slot on the pig's back, rather than with the center vertical axis. This finding suggests that fully comprehending and using spatial language involves more than representing geometric relationships between objects; it also incorporates functional, action-based knowledge reflecting real-world interactions with objects (Coventry et al., 2001).

The notion that both perception and action-based functional understanding play an important role in understanding spatial language is also sup-

ported by research examining eye movements during spatial language comprehension. Coventry and colleagues (2010) used eye tracking to determine whether participants attended to a predicted end state of falling liquids (e.g., a bottle pouring into a glass) when determining spatial sentence acceptability (e.g., "The bottle is over the glass") in describing a picture. Results demonstrated that people attend to predicted end state regions of a picture (i.e., to the final resting spot of the pouring substance), even when such behavior is not necessary for performing the task (see also Altmann & Kamide, 2007; Chambers, Tanenhaus, Eberhard, Filip, & Carlson, 2002).

Cognitive neuroscience findings complement these behavioral results. Kourtzi and Kanwisher (2000) demonstrated that viewing static images that imply movement (vs. those that do not) activates brain areas responsible for processing motion. If spatial language activates perceptual and action-based imagery, evidence of such imagery would be expected when processing spatial language that describes the relationship between functionally relevant objects. In fact, Coventry (in press) and colleagues, found activation of motion perception brain areas when participants viewed pictures of two objects (e.g., bottle, glass) after reading an action relation (e.g., pouring) versus a comparative relation (e.g., relative size). Thus, it appears that comprehenders activate brain areas responsible for perceiving visual motion when evaluating the relationship between described and pictured objects. In addition to visual perception, evidence for action-based representations underlying spatial language interpretation comes from studies examining the spontaneous activation of fronto–parietal motor circuits when comprehending action sentences. For instance, Tettamanti and colleagues (2005) asked participants in a magnetic resonance imaging scanner to read sentences describing mouth (e.g., "bite an apple"), hand (e.g., "grasp a knife"), or leg (e.g., "kick the ball") actions. Relative to abstract control sentences, they found that the action-based sentences activated premotor cortex areas responsible for performing the described actions (see also Buccino et al., 2004). Although this work did not expressly evaluate spatial descriptions, the results strongly suggested that comprehenders would activate perceptual and motoric representations when comprehending object–object spatial descriptions.

Taken together, a strong and growing body of evidence has implicated modal perception and action representations in guiding understanding of described spatial relations. This evidence comes from research in cognition, typically using measures such as response time, memory accuracy, and eye movements, and also from cognitive neuroscience, using brain activity measures such as positron emission tomography and function magnetic resonance imaging. Thus, comprehending the sentence "The pacifier is under the table" appears to involve mentally simulating the percept and any implied functionally relevant actions.

Mentally Simulating Extended Naturalistic Discourse

To this point, we have described embodied spatial language comprehension and mental simulation as occurring when comprehenders process language that describes simple spatial relations between objects. Further research has considered how these same mechanisms might underlie extended spatial (route or survey) description processing. Evidence for embodied processes during extended spatial discourse comprehension comes from two primary research areas: first, examinations of how selective secondary working memory tasks interfere with the acquisition and use of spatial information from environmental descriptions; second, examinations of how readers spontaneously activate multimodal representations of space from environmental descriptions.

As discussed earlier, spatial descriptions generally adopt one or more perspectives, the most common being route and survey (Golledge, 1992; Siegel & White, 1975; Taylor & Tversky, 1992a, 1992b). Some recent work has suggested that route descriptions may promote the mental simulation of perceptual and motoric elements described by a text, whereas survey descriptions may only promote visual mental imagery (Brunyé & Taylor, 2008b; Pazzaglia et al., 2007).

The first evidence that readers might differentially embody spatial descriptions as a function of perspective comes from studies examining working memory involvement during spatial description reading. In

general, these studies have participants read a spatial text while performing a secondary task designed to specifically interfere with visuospatial or articulatory working memory. Performance decrements on subsequent memory tasks are interpreted as indicating involvement of the targeted working memory subsystem. One common finding is that route descriptions demand multiple working memory systems, including visuospatial, articulatory, and central executive resources; survey descriptions, in contrast, generally demand articulatory and visuospatial resources (Brunyé & Taylor, 2008b; De Beni et al., 2005; Deyzac et al., 2006; Pazzaglia et al., 2007). Further, the extent of visuospatial working memory involvement tends to be greater with route relative to survey descriptions (Brunyé & Taylor, 2008a). The additional visuospatial and central executive involvement for route descriptions implicates several cognitive processes including sequential updating, temporal sequencing, landmark interrelationship inferencing, and active generation of perceptual and motor simulations during reading (cf. Brunyé & Taylor, 2008b; Brunyé, Taylor, Rapp, & Spiro, 2006; Kuipers, 1983; Lovelace, Hegarty, & Montello, 1999; Miyake et al., 2000; Noordzij et al., 2006; Perrig & Kintsch, 1985; Tversky, 1993). Supporting this notion are anecdotal reports from participants who claim to imagine themselves moving through the environment and using mnemonic imagery strategies (e.g., "I imagined seeing a dog as I walked by the park"). Route description readers may imagine themselves moving through a described environment, seeing described landmarks, and maintaining a sense of presence. Survey descriptions may promote the development of visual mental imagery in the form of a "mental map" that represents the environment from a bird's eye perspective; this mental imagery, however, does not appear to code specifically for perceptual and motor information derived from imagining movement through an environment.

Though the previously discussed studies have provided indirect evidence that participants perform mental simulations during route description reading, one study has directly implicated the involvement of perceptual and motor imagery during extended spatial language comprehension (Brunyé, Mahoney, et al., 2010). In this work, we conducted two experiments examining the extent to which readers integrate motor-related sounds into spatial mental models of survey or route descriptions. In Experiment 1, participants read survey and route descriptions one sentence at a time. During reading, they listened to footstep or metronome sounds that alternated between high and low frequency (i.e., walking vs. running or 1 vs. 3 metronome pulses per second). The first evidence of differential embodiment as a function of spatial perspective came from reading times; high versus low frequency metronome pulses facilitated reading times with both survey and route descriptions, but changing the frequency of footstep sounds only affected route description reading times. We concluded that the inherently sensorimotor characteristics of the footstep sounds guided mental simulations of movement through the environment, thus affecting reading times for route, but not survey, descriptions. The second piece of evidence indicating differential embodiment of route and survey descriptions came from memory task performance. When route descriptions were coupled with footstep sounds, participants showed a reduced ability to accurately and efficiently make inferences from the unlearned survey perspective. That is, readers showed perspective specificity when both the spatial description and the presented sounds enforced a ground-level perspective (see also Brunyé, Mahoney, et al., 2010). No other combination of perspective and sounds produced this extent of perspective specificity. In fact, within-perspective inferencing showed above-chance performance, suggesting that participants who read route descriptions while listening to footsteps were comprehending the descriptions and were able to think about the environment from a ground-level perspective. Only when they were asked to switch perspectives was performance impaired. This finding adds to literature that has demonstrated that mental representations resulting from limited exposure to route descriptions are more bound to the perspective characterizing this experience and that this effect is likely due to increased ground-level mental simulations with route descriptions (Brunyé et al., 2008; Brunyé & Taylor, 2008b; Shelton & McNamara, 2004). Further, these results were the first to demonstrate that

increasing embodiment during route description reading can accentuate perspective specificity by promoting multimodal mental simulations of route traversal.

CONCLUSION

The uniquely interesting aspect of spatial language is the use of a verbal medium to relate spatial information. With this combination, it makes sense that people engage both verbal and spatial cognitive processes when comprehending spatial descriptions. They engage verbal processes when reading and comprehending the description and building spatial mental models representing the information. The coordination of verbal processing with a spatial representation occurs at all levels of the spatial language hierarchy, from words to sentences to discourse. People then use their spatial mental model to notice ambiguities and make inferences that go beyond what they learned directly. The present chapter explored how spatial language processing reveals cognitive flexibility also seen in general language processing. Cognitive flexibility is evident when people note ambiguity based on spatial perspective, when they disambiguate pronouns, and when they make inferences about spatial relationships that are not explicitly described. This cognitive flexibility can be seen more generally in data supporting multiple activation models, whether in lexical acquisition, lexical access, syntactic comprehension, or when establishing conversational common ground. Thus, recurring themes addressed in general language processing research provide a starting point for examining spatial language processing. This chapter takes into account both classic and embodied approaches on top of which the unique aspect of spatial language can be overlaid.

SUGGESTED REFERENCES FOR FURTHER READING

Coventry, K. R., Tenbrink, T., & Bateman, J. (2009). *Spatial language and dialogue: Explorations in language and space*. Oxford, England: Oxford University Press.

This edited volume provides cross-disciplinary perspectives on how people talk about the locations.

Specific focus is placed on spatial language in social contexts (i.e., dialogue rather than monologue).

Munnich, E., & Landau, B. (2003). The effects of spatial language on spatial representation: Setting some boundaries. In D. Gentner, & S. Goldin-Meadow (Eds.), *Language in mind: Advances in the study of language and thought* (pp. 113–155). Cambridge, MA: MIT Press.

This chapter discusses how spatial language may exert an influence on spatial representation, considering issues of linguistic relativity. The chapter provides an overview of an important aspect of spatial language that was outside the scope of the current chapter.

References

Abarbanell, L., Montana, R., & Li, P. (2011). Revisiting plasticity in human spatial cognition. *Spatial Information Theory: Lecture Notes in Computer Science, 6899,* 245–263.

Albrecht, J. E., & O'Brien, E. J. (1993). Updating a mental model: Maintaining both local and global coherence. *Journal of Experimental Psychology. Learning, Memory, and Cognition, 19,* 1061–1070. doi:10.1037/0278-7393.19.5.1061

Altmann, G. T. M., & Kamide, Y. (2007). The real-time mediation of visual attention by language and world knowledge: Linking anticipatory (and other) eye movements to linguistic processing. *Journal of Memory and Language, 57,* 502–518. doi:10.1016/j.jml.2006.12.004

Avraamides, M. N., & Kelly, J. W. (2010). Multiple systems of spatial memory: Evidence from described scenes. *Journal of Experimental Psychology: Learning, Memory, and Cognition, 36,* 635–645. doi:10.1037/a0017040

Avraamides, M. N., Loomis, J. M., Klatzky, R. L., & Golledge, R. G. (2004). Functional equivalence of spatial representations derived from vision and language: Evidence from allocentric judgments. *Journal of Experimental Psychology: Learning, Memory, and Cognition, 30,* 801–814. doi:10.1037/0278-7393.30.4.804

Barsalou, L. W. (1999). Perceptual symbol systems. *Behavioral and Brain Sciences, 22,* 577–609.

Barsalou, L. W. (2005). Situated conceptualization. In H. Cohen & C. Lefebvre (Eds.), *Handbook of categorization in cognitive science* (pp. 619–650). St. Louis, MO: Elsevier. doi:10.1016/B978-008044612-7/50083-4

Bergen, B. K., & Chang, N. (2005). Embodied construction grammar in simulation-based language understanding. In J. O. Ostman & M. Fried (Eds.), *Construction grammars: Cognitive groundings and theoretical extensions* (pp.147–190). Philadelphia, PA: John Benjamins.

Bosco, A., Filomena, S., Sardone, L., Scalisi, T. G., & Longoni, A. M. (1996). Spatial models derived from verbal descriptions of fictitious environments: The influence of study time and the individual differences in visuo–spatial ability. *Psychologische Beiträge, 38,* 451–464.

Bransford, J. D., & Johnson, M. K. (1972). Contextual prerequisites for understanding: Some investigations of comprehension and recall. *Journal of Verbal Learning and Verbal Behavior, 11,* 717–726. doi:10.1016/S0022-5371(72)80006-9

Brown, C., & Hagoort, P. (1993). The processing nature of the N400: Evidence from masked priming. *Journal of Cognitive Neuroscience, 5,* 34–44. doi:10.1162/jocn.1993.5.1.34

Brunyé, T. T., Ditman, T., Mahoney, C. R., Augustyn, J. S., & Taylor, H. A. (2009). When you and I share perspectives: Pronouns modulate perspective taking during narrative comprehension. *Psychological Science, 20,* 27–32. doi:10.1111/j.1467-9280.2008.02249.x

Brunyé, T. T., Ditman, T., Mahoney, C. R., Walters, E. K., & Taylor, H. A. (2010). You heard it here first: Readers mentally simulate described sound. *Acta Psychologica, 135,* 209–215. doi:10.1016/j.actpsy.2010.06.008

Brunyé, T. T., Mahoney, C. R., & Taylor, H. A. (2010). Moving through imagined space: Mentally simulating locomotion during spatial description reading. *Acta Psychologica, 134,* 110–124. doi:10.1016/j.actpsy.2010.01.003

Brunyé, T. T., Rapp, D. N., & Taylor, H. A. (2008). Representational flexibiltiy and specificity following spatial descriptions of real-world environments. *Cognition, 108,* 418–443. doi:10.1016/j.cognition.2008.03.005

Brunyé, T. T., & Taylor, H. A. (2008a). Extended experience benefits spatial mental model development with route, but not survey descriptions. *Acta Psychologica, 127,* 340–354. doi:10.1016/j.actpsy.2007.07.002

Brunyé, T. T., & Taylor, H. A. (2008b). Working memory in developing and applying mental models from spatial descriptions. *Journal of Memory and Language, 58,* 701–729. doi:10.1016/j.jml.2007.08.003

Brunyé, T. T., & Taylor, H. A. (2009). When goals constrain: Eye movements and memory for goal-oriented map study. *Applied Cognitive Psychology, 23,* 772–787.

Brunyé, T. T., Taylor, H. A., Rapp, D. N., & Spiro, A. B. (2006). Learning procedures: The role of working memory in multimedia learning experiences. *Applied Cognitive Psychology, 20,* 917–940. doi:10.1002/acp.1236

Bryant, D. J., Tversky, B., & Franklin, N. (1992). Internal and external spatial frameworks for representing described scenes. *Journal of Memory and Language, 31,* 74–98. doi:10.1016/0749-596X(92)90006-J

Buccino, G., Vogt, S., Ritzl, A., Fink, G. R., Zilles, K., Freund, H. J., & Rizzolatti, G. (2004). Neural circuits underlying imitation learning of hand actions: An event-related fMRI study. *Neuron, 42,* 323–334. doi:10.1016/S0896-6273(04)00181-3

Carlson, L. A., & Kenny, R. (2005). Constraints on spatial language comprehension. In D. Pecher & R. Zwaan (Eds.), *Grounding cognition: The role of perception and action in memory, language, and thinking* (pp. 35–64). Cambridge, England: Cambridge University Press. doi:10.1017/CBO9780511499968.003

Carlson, L. A., & Logan, G. D. (2001). Using spatial terms to select an object. *Memory & Cognition, 29,* 883–892. doi:10.3758/BF03196417

Carlson, L. A., & van Deman, S. R. (2008). Inhibition with a reference frame during the interpretation of spatial language. *Cognition, 106,* 384–407. doi:10.1016/j.cognition.2007.03.009

Carlson, L. A., West, R., Taylor, H. A., & Herndon, R. W. (2002). Neural correlates of spatial term use. *Journal of Experimental Psychology: Human Perception and Performance, 28,* 1391–1407. doi:10.1037/0096-1523.28.6.1391

Carlson-Radvansky, L. A., Covey, E. S., & Lattanzi, K. M. (1999). "What" effects on "where": Functional influences on spatial relations. *Psychological Science, 10,* 516–521. doi:10.1111/1467-9280.00198

Carlson-Radvansky, L. A., & Irwin, D. E. (1993). Frames of reference in vision and language: Where is above? *Cognition, 46,* 223–244. doi:10.1016/0010-0277(93)90011-J

Carlson-Radvansky, L. A., & Irwin, D. E. (1994). Reference frame activation during spatial term assignment. *Journal of Memory and Language, 33,* 646–671. doi:10.1006/jmla.1994.1031

Carlson-Radvansky, L. A., & Jiang, Y. (1998). Inhibition accompanies reference-frame selection. *Psychological Science, 9,* 386–391. doi:10.1111/1467-9280.00072

Carlson-Radvansky, L. A., & Logan, G. D. (1997). The influence of reference frame selection on spatial template construction. *Journal of Memory and Language, 37,* 411–437. doi:10.1006/jmla.1997.2519

Carlson-Radvansky, L. A., & Tang, Z. (2000). Functional influences on orienting a reference frame. *Memory & Cognition, 28,* 812–820. doi:10.3758/BF03198416

Chambers, G. D., Tanenhaus, M. K., Eberhard, K. M., Filip, G. N., & Carlson, G. N. (2002). Circumscribing referential domains during real time language com-prehension. *Journal of Memory and Language, 47,* 30–49. doi:10.1006/jmla.2001.2832

Clark, E. V. (1997). Conceptual perspective and lexical choice in acquisition. *Cognition, 64,* 1–37. doi:10.1016/S0010-0277(97)00010-3

Clark, H. H. (1973). Space, time, semantics, and the child. In T. E. Moore (Ed.), *Cognitive development and the acquisition of language* (pp. 28–64). New York, NY: Academic Press.

Clark, H. H., & Marshall, C. R. (1981). Definite reference and mutual knowledge. In A. K. Joshe, B. Webber, & I. A. Sag (Eds.), *Elements of discourse understanding* (pp. 10–63). Cambridge, England: Cambridge University Press.

Coventry, K. R. (1999). Function, geometry, and spatial prepositions: Three experiments. *Spatial Cognition and Computation, 1,* 145–154. doi:10.1023/A:1010064926058

Coventry, K. R. (in press). On the mapping between spatial language and vision and action. In Y. Coello & A. Bartolo (Eds.), *Language and action in cognitive neuroscience.* London, England: Psychology Press.

Coventry, K. R., Carmichael, R., & Garrod, S. C. (1994). Spatial prepositions, object-specific function, and task requirements. *Journal of Semantics, 11,* 289–309. doi:10.1093/jos/11.4.289

Coventry, K. R., & Garrod, S. C. (2005). Spatial prepositions and the functional geometric framework: Toward a classification of extra-geometric influences. In L. A. Carlson & E. van der Zee (Eds.), *Functional features in language and space: Insights from perception, categorization, and development* (pp. 163–173). Oxford, England: Oxford University Press.

Coventry, K. R., Lynott, D., Cangelosi, A., Monrouxe, L., Joyce, D., & Richardson, D. C. (2010). Spatial language, visual attention, and perceptual simulation. *Brain and Language, 112,* 202–213. doi:10.1016/j.bandl.2009.06.001

Coventry, K. R., Prat-Sala, M., & Richards, L. (2001). The interplay between geometry and function in the comprehension of over, under, above, and below. *Journal of Memory and Language, 44,* 376–398. doi:10.1006/jmla.2000.2742

Crawford, L. E., Regier, T., & Huttenlocher, J. (2000). Linguistic and non-linguistic spatial categorization. *Cognition, 75,* 209–235. doi:10.1016/S0010-0277(00)00064-0

Damasio, H., Grabowski, T. J., Tranel, D., Ponto, L. L. B., Hichwa, R. D., & Damasio, A. R. (2001). Neural correlates of naming actions and naming spatial relations. *NeuroImage, 13,* 1053–1064. doi:10.1006/nimg.2001.0775

De Beni, R., Pazzaglia, F., Gyselinck, V., & Meneghetti, C. (2005). Visuospatial working memory and mental representation of spatial descriptions. *European Journal of Cognitive Psychology, 17,* 77–95. doi:10.1080/09541440340000529

Denis, M., & Zimmer, H. D. (1992). Analog properties of cognitive maps constructed from verbal descriptions. *Psychological Research, 54,* 286–298. doi:10.1007/BF01358266

de Vega, M. (1994). Characters and their perspectives in narratives describing spatial environments. *Psychological Research, 56,* 116–126. doi:10.1007/BF00419719

de Vega, M. (1995). Backward updating of mental models during continuous reading of narratives. *Journal of Experimental Psychology: Learning, Memory, and Cognition, 21,* 373–385. doi:10.1037/0278-7393.21.2.373

Deyzac, E., Logie, R. H., & Denis, M. (2006). Visuospatial working memory and the processing of spatial descriptions. *British Journal of Psychology, 97,* 217–243. doi:10.1348/000712605X67484

Ehrich, V., & Koster, C. (1983). Discourse organization and sentence form: The structure of room descriptions in Dutch. *Discourse Processes, 6,* 169–195. doi:10.1080/01638538309544561

Emmorey, K., Tversky, B., & Taylor, H. A. (2000). Using space to describe space: Perspective in speech, sign, and gesture. *Spatial Cognition and Computation, 2,* 157–180. doi:10.1023/A:1013118114571

Estevez, A., & Calvo, M. G. (2000). Working memory capacity and time course of predictive inferences. *Memory, 8,* 51–61. doi:10.1080/096582100387704

Ferguson, E. L., & Hegarty, M. (1994). Properties of cognitive maps constructed from text. *Memory & Cognition, 22,* 455–473. doi:10.3758/BF03200870

Fincher-Kiefer, R. (2001). Perceptual components of situation models. *Memory & Cognition, 29,* 336–343. doi:10.3758/BF03194928

Fischer, M. H., & Zwaan, R. A. (2008). Embodied language: A review of the role of the motor system in language comprehension. *The Quarterly Journal of Experimental Psychology: Human Experimental Psychology, 61,* 825–850. doi:10.1080/17470210701623605

Franklin, N., & Tversky, B. (1990). Searching imagined environments. *Journal of Experimental Psychology: General, 119,* 63–76. doi:10.1037/0096-3445.119.1.63

Franklin, N., Tversky, B., & Coon, V. (1992). Switching points of view in spatial mental models. *Memory & Cognition, 20,* 507–518. doi:10.3758/BF03199583

Frazier, L., & Fodor, J. (1978). The sausage machine: A new two-stage parsing model. *Cognition, 6,* 291–325. doi:10.1016/0010-0277(78)90002-1

Fromkin, V. A. (1973). The non-anomalous nature of anomalous utterances. In V. A. Fromkin (Ed.), *Speech errors as linguistic evidence* (pp. 215–242). The Hague, Netherlands: Mouton.

Gallistel, C. R. (2002). Language and spatial frames of reference in mind and brain. *Trends in Cognitive Sciences, 6,* 321–322. doi:10.1016/S1364-6613(02)01962-9

Garnham, A. (1989). A unified theory of meaning of some spatial relational terms. *Cognition, 31,* 45–60. doi:10.1016/0010-0277(89)90017-6

Gernsbacher, M. A. (1990). *Language comprehension as structure building.* Hillsdale, NJ: Erlbaum.

Gibson, B. S., & Kingstone, A. (2006). Visual attention and the semantics of space: Beyond central and peripheral cues. *Psychological Science, 17,* 622–627. doi:10.1111/j.1467-9280.2006.01754.x

Glenberg, A. M. (1997). What memory is for. *Behavioral and Brain Sciences, 20,* 1–55.

Glenberg, A. M., & Kaschak, M. P. (2002). Grounding language in action. *Psychonomic Bulletin & Review, 9,* 558–565. doi:10.3758/BF03196313

Golledge, R. G. (1992). Place recognition and wayfinding: Making sense of space. *Geoforum, 23,* 199–214. doi:10.1016/0016-7185(92)90017-X

Graesser, A. C., Millis, K. K., & Zwaan, R. A. (1997). Discourse comprehension. *Annual Review of Psychology, 48,* 163–189. doi:10.1146/annurev.psych.48.1.163

Graesser, A. C., Singer, M., & Trabasso, T. (1994). Constructing inferences during narrative text comprehension. *Psychological Review, 101,* 371–395. doi:10.1037/0033-295X.101.3.371

Haun, D. B. M., Rapold, C. J., Janzen, G., & Levinson, S. C. (2011). Plasticity of human spatial cognition: Spatial language and cognition covary across cultures. *Cognition, 119,* 70–80. doi:10.1016/j.cognition.2010.12.009

Hayward, W. G., & Tarr, M. J. (1995). Spatial language and spatial representation. *Cognition, 55,* 39–84. doi:10.1016/0010-0277(94)00643-Y

Holcomb, P. J. (1993). Semantic priming and stimulus degradation: Implications for the role of the N400 in language processing. *Psychophysiology, 30,* 47–61. doi:10.1111/j.1469-8986.1993.tb03204.x

Holcomb, P. J., & Anderson, J. E. (1993). Cross-modal semantic priming: A time-course analysis using event-related brain potentials. *Language and Cognitive Processes, 8,* 379–411. doi:10.1080/01690969308407583

Kaschak, M. P., Zwaan, R. A., Aveyard, M., & Yaxley, R. H. (2006). Perception of auditory motion affects language processing. *Cognitive Science, 30,* 733–744. doi:10.1207/s15516709cog0000_54

Keysar, B., Barr, D. J., Balin, J. A., & Brauner, J. S. (2000). Taking perspective in conversation: The role of mutual knowledge in comprehension. *Psychological Science, 11,* 32–38. doi:10.1111/1467-9280.00211

Keysar, B., Barr, D. J., Balin, J. A., & Paek, T. S. (1998). Definite reference and mutual knowledge: Process models of common ground in comprehension. *Journal of Memory and Language, 39,* 1–20. doi:10.1006/jmla.1998.2563

Kintsch, W. (1988). The role of knowledge in discourse comprehension: A construction-integration model. *Psychological Review, 95,* 163–182. doi:10.1037/0033-295X.95.2.163

Klatzky, R. L. (1998). Allocentric and egocentric spatial representations: Definitions, distinctions, and interconnections. In C. Freksa, C. Habel, & K. F. Wender (Eds.), *Spatial Cognition—An interdisciplinary approach to representation and processing of spatial knowledge* (Lecture Notes in Artificial Intelligence 1404, Vol. 1404, pp. 1–17). Berlin, Germany: Springer-Verlag.

Klein, W. (1982). Local deixis in route directions. In W. Klein & R. J. Jarvella (Eds.), *Speech, place, and action* (pp. 161–182). New York, NY: Wiley.

Klein, W. (1983). Deixis and spatial orientation in route directions. In H. L. Pick, Jr., & L. P. Acredolo (Eds.), *Spatial orientation: Theory, research, and application* (pp. 283–311). New York, NY: Plenum Press.

Kojima, T., & Kusumi, T. (2008). Spatial term apprehension with a reference object's rotation in three-dimensional space. *Cognitive Processing, 9,* 107–119. doi:10.1007/s10339-007-0181-z

Kosslyn, S. M. (1980). *Image and mind.* Cambridge, MA: Harvard University Press.

Kourtzi, Z., & Kanwisher, N. (2000). Activation in human MT/MST for static images with implied motion. *Journal of Cognitive Neuroscience, 12,* 48–55. doi:10.1162/08989290051137594

Kuipers, B. J. (1983). The cognitive map: Could it have been any other way? In H. L. J. Pick & L. P. Acredolo (Eds.), *Spatial orientation: Theory, research, and application* (pp. 345–359). New York, NY: Plenum Press.

Kulhavy, R. W., Stock, W. A., & Caterino, L. C. (1994). Reference maps as a framework for remembering text. *Advances in Psychology, 108,* 153–162. doi:10.1016/S0166-4115(09)60114-X

Kurby, C. A., Magliano, J. P., & Rapp, D. N. (2009). Those voices in your head: Activation of auditory images during reading. *Cognition, 112,* 457–461. doi:10.1016/j.cognition.2009.05.007

Kutas, M., & Hillyard, S. A. (1984, January 12–18). Brain potentials during reading reflect word expectancy and semantic association. *Nature, 307*(5947), 161–163. doi:10.1038/307161a0

Lakoff, G. (1987). *Women, fire, and dangerous things: What categories reveal about the mind.* Chicago, IL: University of Chicago Press.

Landau, B., & Jackendoff, R. (1993). What and where in spatial language and spatial cognition. *Behavioral and Brain Sciences, 16,* 217–265. doi:10.1017/S0140525X00029733

Lautenschutz, A., Davies, C., Raubal, M., Schwering, A., & Pederson, E. (2007). The influence of scale, context, and spatial preposition in linguistic topology. *Proceedings of the 5th International Conference on Spatial cognition, 4387,* 439–452.

Lee, P. U., & Tversky, B. (2001, August). *Costs of switching perspectives in route and survey description.* Paper presented at the 23rd Annual Conference of the Cognitive Science Society, Edinburgh, Scotland.

Lee, P. U., & Tversky, B. (2005). Interplay between visual and spatial: The effect of landmark descriptions on comprehension of route/survey spatial descriptions. *Spatial Cognition and Computation, 5,* 163–185.

Levelt, W. J. M. (1982). Cognitive styles in the use of spatial direction terms. In R. J. Jarvella & W. Klein (Eds.), *Speech, place, and action* (pp. 251–268). New York, NY: Wiley.

Levelt, W. J. M. (1989). *Speaking: From intention to articulation.* Cambridge, MA: MIT Press.

Levelt, W. J. M., Schriefers, H., Vorberg, D., Meyer, A. S., Pechmann, T., & Havinga, J. (1991). The time course of lexical access in speech production: A study of picture naming. *Psychological Review, 98,* 122–142. doi:10.1037/0033-295X.98.1.122

Levine, W. H., & Klin, C. M. (2001). Tracking of spatial information in narratives. *Memory & Cognition, 29,* 327–335. doi:10.3758/BF03194927

Levinson, S. C. (1996). Frames of reference and Molyneux's question: Crosslinguistic evidence. In P. Bloom, M. A. Peterson, L. Nadel, & M. F. Garrett (Eds.), *Language and space* (pp. 109–169). Cambridge, MA: The MIT Press.

Levinson, S. C., Kita, S., Haun, D. B. M., & Rasch, B. H. (2002). Returning the tables: Language affects spatial reasoning. *Cognition, 84,* 155–188. doi:10.1016/S0010-0277(02)00045-8

Li, P., Abarbanell, L., Gleitman, L. R., & Papafragou, A. (2011). Spatial reasoning in Tenejapan Mayans. *Cognition, 120,* 33–53. doi:10.1016/j.cognition.2011.02.012

Li, P., & Gleitman, L. R. (2002). Turning the tables: Language and spatial reasoning. *Cognition, 83,* 265–294. doi:10.1016/S0010-0277(02)00009-4

Linde, C., & Labov, W. (1975). Spatial structures as a site for the study of language and thought. *Language, 51,* 924–939. doi:10.2307/412701

Linderholm, T., & van den Broek, P. (2002). The effect of reading purpose and working memory capacity on the processing of expository text. *Journal of Educational Psychology, 94,* 778–784. doi:10.1037/0022-0663.94.4.778

Logan, G. D., & Sadler, D. D. (1996). A computational analysis of the apprehension of spatial relations. In P. Bloom, M. A. Peterson, L. Nadel, & M. Garrett (Eds.), *Language and space* (pp. 493–529). Cambridge, MA: MIT Press.

Lovelace, K. L., Hegarty, M., & Montello, D. R. (1999). Elements of good route directions in familiar and unfamiliar environments. In C. Freksa & D. M. Mark (Eds.), *Spatial information theory: Cognitive and computational foundations of geographic information science* (pp. 65–82). Berlin, Germany: Springer. doi:10.1007/3-540-48384-5_5

Loveland, K. A. (1984). Learning about points of view: Spatial perspective and the acquisition of "I/you". *Journal of Child Language, 11,* 535–556. doi:10.1017/S0305000900005948

Magliano, J. P., Miller, J., & Zwaan, R. A. (2001). Indexing space and time in film understanding. *Applied Cognitive Psychology, 15,* 533–545. doi:10.1002/acp.724

Markman, E. M. (1987). How children constrain the possible meanings of words. In U. Neisser (Ed.), *Concepts and conceptual development: Ecological and intellectual factors in categorization* (pp. 255–287). Cambridge, England: Cambridge University Press.

McKoon, G., & Ratcliff, R. (1992). Inferences during reading. *Psychological Review, 99,* 440–466. doi:10.1037/0033-295X.99.3.440

McNamara, D. S., & Kintsch, W. (1996). Learning from texts: Effects of prior knowledge and text coherence. *Discourse Processes, 22,* 247–288. doi:10.1080/01638539609544975

McNamara, D. S., Kintsch, E., Songer, N. B., & Kintsch, W. (1996). Are good texts always better? Interactions of text coherence, background knowledge, levels of understanding in learning from text. *Cognition and Instruction, 14,* 1–43. doi:10.1207/s1532690xci1401_1

McNamara, D. S., & Magliano, J. P. (2009). Toward a comprehensive model of comprehension. In B. Ross (Ed.), *The psychology of learning and motivation* (Vol. 51, pp. 297–384). Burlington, MA: Academic Press. doi:10.1016/S0079-7421(09)51009-2

McNamara, T. P. (1991). Memory's view of space. In G. H. Bower (Ed.), *The psychology of learning and motivation* (pp. 147–186). New York, NY: Academic Press.

McNamara, T. P., Hardy, J. K., & Hirtle, S. C. (1989). Subjective hierarchies in spatial memory. *Journal of Experimental Psychology: Learning, Memory, and Cognition, 15,* 211–227. doi:10.1037/0278-7393.15.2.211

McNeill, D. (1992). *Hand and mind: What gestures reveal about thought.* Chicago, IL: University of Chicago Press.

Miyake, A., Friedman, N. P., Emerson, M. J., Witzki, A. H., Howerter, A., & Wager, T. (2000). The unity and diversity of executive functions and their contributions to complex "frontal lobe" tasks: A latent variable analysis. *Cognitive Psychology, 41,* 49–100. doi:10.1006/cogp.1999.0734

Morrow, D. (1994). Spatial models created from text. *Advances in Discourse Processes, 53,* 57–78.

Neely, J. H. (1977). Semantic priming and retrieval from lexical memory: Roles of inhibitionless spreading activation and limited-capacity attention. *Journal of Experimental Psychology: General, 106,* 226–254. doi:10.1037/0096-3445.106.3.226

Nigam, A., Hoffman, J. E., & Simons, R. F. (1992). N400 to semantically anomalous pictures and words. *Journal of Cognitive Neuroscience, 4,* 15–22. doi:10.1162/jocn.1992.4.1.15

Noordzij, M. L., Neggers, S. F. W., Ramsey, N. F., & Postma, A. (2008). Neural correlates of locative prepositions. *Neuropsychologia, 46,* 1576–1580. doi:10.1016/j.neuropsychologia.2007.12.022

Noordzij, M. L., & Postma, A. (2005). Categorical and metric distance information in mental representations derived from route and survey descriptions. *Psychological Research, 69,* 221–232. doi:10.1007/s00426-004-0172-y

Noordzij, M. L., Zuidhoek, S., & Postma, A. (2006). The influence of visual experience on the ability to form spatial mental models based on route and survey descriptions. *Cognition, 100,* 321–342. doi:10.1016/j.cognition.2005.05.006

O'Brien, E. J., & Albrecht, J. E. (1992). Comprehension strategies in the development of a mental model. *Journal of Experimental Psychology: Learning, Memory, and Cognition, 18,* 777–784. doi:10.1037/0278-7393.18.4.777

Paivio, A. (1990). *Mental representations: Dual coding approach.* Oxford, England: Oxford University Press.

Pazzaglia, F., De Beni, R., & Meneghetti, C. (2007). The effects of vebal and spatial interference in the encoding of spatial and nonspatial texts. *Psychological Research, 71,* 484–494. doi:10.1007/s00426-006-0045-7

Pazzaglia, F., Meneghetti, C., De Beni, R., & Gyselinck, V. (2010). Working memory components in survey and route text processing. *Cognitive Processing, 11,* 359–369. doi:10.1007/s10339-009-0353-0

Perrig, W., & Kintsch, W. (1985). Propositional and situational representations of text. *Journal of Memory and Language, 24,* 503–518. doi:10.1016/0749-596X(85)90042-7

Pulvermüller, F. (2005). Brain mechanisms linking language and action. *Nature Reviews Neuroscience, 6,* 576–582. doi:10.1038/nrn1706

Radvansky, G. A., & Copeland, D. E. (2000). Functionality and spatial relations in memory and language. *Memory & Cognition, 28,* 987–992. doi:10.3758/BF03209346

Raz, N., Striem, E., Pundak, G., Orlov, T., & Zohary, E. (2007). Superior serial memory in the blind: A case of cognitive compensatory adjustment. *Current Biology, 17,* 1129–1133. doi:10.1016/j.cub.2007.05.060

Regier, T., & Carlson, L. A. (2001). Grounding spatial language in perception: An empirical and computational investigation. *Journal of Experimental Psychology: General, 130,* 273–298. doi:10.1037/0096-3445.130.2.273

Retz-Schmidt, G. (1988). Various views on spatial prepositions. *AI Magazine, 9,* 95–105.

Ricard, M., Girouard, P. C., & Decarie, T. G. (1999). Personal pronouns and perspective taking in toddlers. *Journal of Child Language, 26,* 681–697. doi:10.1017/S0305000999003943

Rich, S. S., & Taylor, H. A. (2000). Not all narrative shifts function equally. *Memory & Cognition, 28,* 1257–1266. doi:10.3758/BF03211825

Rinck, M., Hähnel, A., Bower, G. H., & Glowalla, U. (1997). The metrics of spatial situation models. *Journal of Experimental Psychology. Learning, Memory, and Cognition, 23,* 622–637. doi:10.1037/0278-7393.23.3.622

Ruby, P., & Decety, J. (2001). Effect of subjective perspective taking during simulation of action: A PET investigation of agency. *Nature Neuroscience, 4,* 546–550.

Schober, M. F. (1993). Spatial perspective-taking in conversation. *Cognition, 47,* 1–24. doi:10.1016/0010-0277(93)90060-9

Schober, M. F., & Clark, H. H. (1989). Understanding by addressees and overhearers. *Cognitive Psychology, 21,* 211–232. doi:10.1016/0010-0285(89)90008-X

Shallice, T. (1996). The language-to-object perception interface: Evidence from neuropsychology. In P. Bloom, M. A. Peterson, L. Nadel, & M. Garrett (Eds.), *Language and space* (pp. 531–552). Cambridge, MA: MIT Press.

Shanon, B. (1984). Room descriptions. *Discourse Processes, 7,* 225–255. doi:10.1080/01638538409544591

Shelton, A. L., & McNamara, T. P. (2004). Orientation and perspective dependence in route and survey learning. *Journal of Experimental Psychology:*

Learning, Memory, and Cognition, 30, 158–170. doi:10.1037/0278-7393.30.1.158

Siegel, A. W., & White, S. H. (1975). The development of spatial representations of large-scale environments. In H. W. Reese (Ed.), *Advances in child development and behavior* (Vol. 10, pp. 9–55). New York, NY: Academic Press.

Spivey-Knowlton, M., & Sedivy, J. C. (1995). Resolving attachment ambiguities with multiple constraints. *Cognition, 55,* 227–267. doi:10.1016/0010-0277(94)00647-4

Stevens, A., & Coupe, P. (1978). Distortions in judged spatial relations. *Cognitive Psychology, 10,* 422–437. doi:10.1016/0010-0285(78)90006-3

Steyvers, F. J. J. M., & Kooijman, A. C. (2009). Using route and survey information to generate cognitive maps: Differences between normally sighted and visually impaired individuals. *Applied Cognitive Psychology, 23,* 223–235. doi:10.1002/acp.1447

Swinney, D. A., & Cutler, A. (1979). The access and processing of ideiomatic expressions. *Journal of Verbal Learning and Verbal Behavior, 18,* 523–534. doi:10.1016/S0022-5371(79)90284-6

Taylor, H. A., Faust, R. R., Sitnikova, T., Holcomb, P. J., & Naylor, S. J. (2001). Is the donut in front of the car? An electrophysiological study examining spatial reference frame processing. *Canadian Journal of Experimental Psychology/Revue canadienne de psychologie expérimentale, 55,* 175–184. doi:10.1037/h0087364

Taylor, H. A., Naylor, S. J., & Chechile, N. A. (1999). Goal-directed influences on the representation of spatial perspective. *Memory & Cognition, 27,* 309–319. doi:10.3758/BF03211414

Taylor, H. A., Naylor, S. J., Faust, R. R., & Holcomb, P. J. (1999). "Could you hand me those keys on the right?" Disentangling spatial reference frames using different methodologies. *Spatial Cognition and Computation, 1,* 381–397. doi:10.1023/A:1010035613419

Taylor, H. A., & Rapp, D. N. (2004). Where is the donut? Factors influencing reference frame use. *Cognitive Processing, 5,* 175–188. doi:10.1007/s10339-004-0022-2

Taylor, H. A., & Tversky, B. (1992a). Descriptions and depictions of environments. *Memory & Cognition, 20,* 483–496. doi:10.3758/BF03199581

Taylor, H. A., & Tversky, B. (1992b). Spatial mental models derived from survey and route descriptions. *Journal of Memory and Language, 31,* 261–292. doi:10.1016/0749-596X(92)90014-O

Taylor, H. A., & Tversky, B. (1997). Indexing events in memory: Evidence of index dominance. *Memory, 5,* 509–542. doi:10.1080/741941434

Tenbrink, T., & Winter, S. (2009). Variable granularity in route directions. *Spatial Cognition and Computation, 9,* 64–93. doi:10.1080/13875860902718172

Tettamanti, M., Buccino, G., Saccuman, M. C., Gallese, V., Danna, M., Scifo, P., . . . Perani, D. (2005). Listening to action-related sentences activates frontoparietal motor circuits. *Journal of Cognitive Neuroscience, 17,* 273–281. doi:10.1162/0898929053124965

Thorndyke, P. W., & Hayes-Roth, B. (1982). Differences in spatial knowledge acquired from maps and navigation. *Cognitive Psychology, 14,* 560–589. doi:10.1016/0010-0285(82)90019-6

Townsend, J. T. (1990). Serial vs. parallel processing: Sometimes they look like Tweedledum and Tweedledee but they can (and should) be distinguished. *Psychological Science, 1,* 46–54. doi:10.1111/j.1467-9280.1990.tb00067.x

Trabasso, T., Suh, S., & Payton, P. (1995). Explanatory coherence in understanding and talking about events. In M. A. Gernsbacher & T. Givon (Eds.), *Coherence in spontaneous text* (pp. 189–214). Amsterdam, Netherlands: John Benjamins.

Tranel, D., & Kemmerer, D. (2004). Neuoanatomical correlates of locative prepositions. *Cognitive Neuropsychology, 21,* 719–749. doi:10.1080/02643290342000627

Tversky, B. (1993). Cognitive maps, cognitive collages, and spatial mental models. *Spatial Information Theory, A Theoretical Basis for GIS. Lecture Notes in Computer Science, 716,* 14–24. doi:10.1007/3-540-57207-4_2

Tversky, B., Lee, P. U., & Mainwaring, S. (1999). Why do speakers mix perspectives? *Spatial Cognition and Computation, 1,* 399–412. doi:10.1023/A:1010091730257

Ullmer-Ehrich, V. (1982). The structure of living space descriptions. In R. J. Jarvella & W. Klein (Eds.), *Speech, place, and action* (pp. 219–249). New York, NY: Wiley.

van Dijk, T. A., & Kintsch, W. (1983). *Strategies of discourse comprehension.* New York, NY: Academic Press.

Wilkes-Gibbs, D., & Clark, H. H. (1992). Coordinating beliefs in conversation. *Journal of Memory and Language, 31,* 183–194. doi:10.1016/0749-596X(92)90010-U

Yaxley, R. H., & Zwaan, R. A. (2007). Simulating visibility during language comprehension. *Cognition, 105,* 229–236. doi:10.1016/j.cognition.2006.09.003

Zwaan, R. A. (1999). Embodied cognition, perceptual symbols, and situation models. *Discourse Processes, 28,* 81–88. doi:10.1080/01638539909545070

Zwaan, R. A. (2004). The immersed experiencer: Toward an embodied theory of language comprehension. In B. H. Ross (Ed.), *The psychology of learning and motivation* (Vol. 44, pp. 35–62). New York, NY: Academic Press.

Zwaan, R. A., Langston, M. C., & Graesser, A. C. (1995). The construction of situation models in narrative comprehension: An even-indexing model. *Psychological Science, 6,* 292–297. doi:10.1111/j.1467-9280.1995.tb00513.x

Zwaan, R. A., Magliano, J. P., & Graesser, A. C. (1995). Dimensions of situation model construction in narrative comprehension. *Journal of Experimental Psychology: Learning, Memory, and Cognition, 21,* 386–397. doi:10.1037/0278-7393.21.2.386

Zwaan, R. A., & Radvansky, G. A. (1998). Situation models in language comprehension and memory. *Psychological Bulletin, 123,* 162–185. doi:10.1037/0033-2909.123.2.162

Zwaan, R. A., Stanfield, R. A., & Yaxley, R. H. (2002). Language comprehenders mentally represent the shapes of objects. *Psychological Science, 13,* 168–171. doi:10.1111/1467-9280.00430

Zwaan, R. A., & Taylor, L. J. (2006). Seeing, acting, understanding: Motor resonance in language comprehension. *Journal of Experimental Psychology: General, 135,* 1–11. doi:10.1037/0096-3445.135.1.1

FUNCTIONS AND APPLICATIONS
OF SPATIAL COGNITION

Daniel R. Montello and Martin Raubal

In this chapter, we address the question of why it is important to study spatial cognition. Spatial cognition plays a central role in numerous human activities and helps solve numerous human problems. In other words, cognition of and with spatiality is a fundamental component of human experience and is functional and relevant in many situations, both routine and exceptional. In fact, it is difficult to overstate the importance and even ubiquity of spatial cognition in mental and behavioral structures and processes. In this chapter, we discuss research on human spatial cognition, with a focus on its functions in life activities and experiences. Then we discuss how studying spatial cognition can inform applications such as designing and evaluating personnel selection methods; training procedures; built environments; and various information tools and systems, such as mobile geographic information services.

Our goals in writing this chapter led us to consider the essential meaning of *spatial cognition*. After all, it is impossible to say whether some task or activity involves or exemplifies spatial cognition unless we are prepared to offer a view on what is and is not spatial cognition. As most readers will suppose, this is no easy task, but we think the effort proves edifying. We start with the essential meaning of *space and spatiality*—its ontology, in the traditional sense of the philosophical study of metaphysics. Providing a clear, correct, and com-

plete definition of space and spatiality is, of course, notoriously difficult to do, especially if we wish to avoid invoking space itself in the definition. After all, spatiality is pervasive and fundamental to existence and experience, as we suggested earlier. Recognizing these difficulties, we can define *spatiality* as the collection of all "extensional properties" of reality. In the sense we mean here, *extensionality* refers to the property of occupying space or having spatiality, which of course is circular. Spatiality is the property of reality that reflects the fact that everything is not at one location, a definition that is somewhat tongue-in-cheek but at least less circular. Alternatively, we can explicate the meaning of spatiality by listing a collection of spatial properties: location, size, distance, direction, shape, connectivity, overlap, dimensionality, hierarchy, and so on. But, however we define spatiality, we probably do not want simply to classify any cognition involving spatial properties as "spatial cognition." After all, one can make a good case that all cognition occurs in space and involves spatial information, at least implicitly. This includes linguistic, numerical, social, and other domains of cognition that we probably do not want to include as central foci of the study of spatial cognition. Thus, we can restrict spatial cognition to cognition that is primarily about spatiality—that serves primarily to solve problems involving spatial properties as a core component. As a contrasting example, reading requires spatial

DOI: 10.1037/13936-014
Handbook of Spatial Cognition, D. Waller and L. Nadel (Editors)

processing as part of orthography and syntax, but it is primarily about understanding written language, not solving a spatial problem (except when reading route directions, etc.).

A list of spatial properties is large and diverse, although not unlimited. One way to organize our understanding of spatial properties is in terms of their level of geometric complexity or sophistication. Especially since the 19th century, we have come to understand geometry as more than just Euclidean metric geometry (Sklar, 1974; van Fraassen, 1985). Alternatives include both non-Euclidean metric geometries and nonmetric geometries such as affine, projective, and topological geometries. The appropriate geometry one should use to model human spatial cognition has been the subject of behavioral research in recent decades (e.g., Cheng & Newcombe, 2005; Dehaene, Izard, Pica, & Spelke, 2006; Golledge & Hubert, 1982; Hartley, Trinkler, & Burgess, 2004; Montello, 1992; Rinck & Denis, 2004). Clearly, spatial tasks do not necessarily require metric spatial knowledge and, in fact, can often be performed well without it. Evidence indicates that people often have a poor or nonexistent understanding of metric spatial properties, especially they concern larger "environmental" spaces. Conversely, evidence also shows that at least some people do acquire something like metric information of fairly high quality about the layout of environments (Ishikawa & Montello, 2006), even if it does not strictly obey the metric axioms.

In addition to the meaning of spatiality, we also delimit the scope of our discussion by considering what to include as *cognitive*. A broad definition of *cognition* includes both relatively low-level and high-level mental processes, both implicit and explicit processes, and processes that are both bottom-up and top-down. The domain of spatial cognition, as it has been studied in various cognitive disciplines, has tended to focus on relatively high-level tasks, such as those involving reasoning, communication, imagination, symbolic representation and interpretation, and the like—tasks that are thought to incorporate internally represented spatial

knowledge that is potentially accessed explicitly. Work like this has excluded tasks requiring only perception–action coordination from the study of spatial cognition (of course, there are debates about how much "cognitive" processing is required for particular tasks). That is, deciding which door to walk through to get outside is a spatial cognition problem; moving one's body to avoid running into the door jamb as you leave is not, notwithstanding that the latter is nontrivial and certainly involves psychological processing of spatial information. Although this distinction is imperfect, and might at times mislead us, we follow this approach in our chapter and delimit our scope by distinguishing the cognition of space from the perception of space and from behavior in space. We do not consider, except incidentally, spatial problems that are primarily perceptual and motor, such as object recognition or maintaining balance while walking.

Thus, we define spatial cognition as the area of research that studies activities centrally involving explicit mental representations of space (or at least potentially explicit).[1] We recognize that this will still fail to satisfy some readers; we are not completely comfortable ourselves with this restriction. At the same time, we recognize that many activities we would not want to include as spatial cognition have spatial cognitive components; we also see that most (all?) spatial cognitive tasks have nonspatial and noncognitive components or can be carried out in alternative ways that are not spatial (e.g., you can reconstruct and scan a spatial mental model or retrieve a verbal description of a situation) or particularly cognitive (you can reason how to get back to your car or simply ask your companion).

FUNCTIONS OF SPATIAL COGNITION

To discuss the functions of spatial cognition is to discuss what spatial cognition is useful for. What tasks does spatial cognition contribute to in a significant way? We include both everyday tasks, such as choosing the right street to take while driving to the store, and specialized tasks, such as choosing

---

[1]Like the referents of verbs, we do not restrict activities only to situations involving movement of all or part of one's body; they include states of being, such as contemplating or sleeping.

EXHIBIT 13.1

Tasks Involving Substantial and Significant Spatial Cognition in Their Performance

1. Wayfinding as part of navigation
2. Acquiring and using spatial knowledge from direct experience
3. Using spatially iconic symbolic representations
4. Using spatial language
5. Imagining places and reasoning with mental models
6. Location allocation

the right vein area to examine while searching for tumors in a patient's liver. This is a large number of tasks taken individually, although they can be grouped into subsets for which spatial cognition clearly plays a similar role or contributes in similar ways to their successful performance. For example, interviews and observations summarized by Hegarty, Keehner, Cohen, Montello, and Lippa (2007) suggest that, like pedestrians in a neighborhood, surgeons and surgery residents use "landmarks" in the human body to remain oriented.

We consider functions of spatial cognition by listing categories of spatial cognitive tasks that people perform—everyday and specialized tasks that involve spatial cognition to a substantial degree (e.g., Eliot & Czarnolewski, 2007). In Exhibit 13.1, we propose six categories of spatial–cognitive tasks.[2] Although we attempt to be comprehensive with our list, we are fairly confident it overlooks some things; for instance, we considered including reasoning about social space as a type. Furthermore, our attempt to formulate distinct categories notwithstanding, they clearly overlap, and we are skeptical that any fairly comprehensive list of functions could approach mutual exclusivity. Wayfinding sometimes utilizes spatial symbolic representations and spatial language, for example. The list is clearly only a starting point.

Our first category of tasks, *wayfinding*, is coordination to the distal environment, which is not immediately accessible to the sensorimotor systems. This contrasts with locomotion, which we consider

as coordination to the proximal or surrounding environment (Montello, 2005; Strelow, 1985). Wayfinding includes specific tasks such as creating and choosing routes, establishing and maintaining orientation with respect to one's starting location or with respect to external features or places, recognizing how landmarks spatially relate to other landmarks or other aspects of the environment, judging distances, remembering sequences of turns, and remembering the locations of objects and events. Wayfinding includes planning multiple activities that are spatially distributed—that take place at different locations in the environment. Examples include sequencing multiple destinations, scheduling time to take account of travel requirements, and designing routes within complex path networks (e.g., Gärling & Gärling, 1988; Golledge, 1995). The role of spatial cognition in wayfinding differs somewhat as a function of movement modality (e.g., walking, driving, eye movements) and the spatial entity in which it takes place (e.g., a city, one's bedroom, the human body, a complex molecule, or a virtual environment). No matter what scale of space we wayfind in, however, a critical task is to establish and maintain a *sense of orientation* while moving—where are we or where some entity is in the world relative to some other location, such as the location of another entity or our own previous location.

The second category of tasks on our list is acquiring and using *spatial knowledge learned directly,* that is, from perceptual–motor experience in the world. This occurs at figural, vista, and environmental scales of space. At *figural scales,* vision and haptics are the most important sensorimotor systems involved in spatial learning by humans. *Vista-scale learning* depends almost entirely on vision and head and eye movements. Spaces at *environmental scales* require considerable body locomotion for their direct apprehension; thus, visual and proprioceptive senses are of principal importance. At environmental scales, we learn about the locations of prominent features (landmarks), path network structures that connect places, and spatial relationships among places, even those we have not directly traveled

[2]Reg Golledge provided special insight and inspiration in developing the list of spatial tasks. The list has also benefited from discussions we have had with Karl Grossner, Mary Hegarty, and Andrea Nuernberger.

between. At all scales, we learn spatial properties at all levels of geometric sophistication, including connections, containments, sequences, distances, directions, shapes, configurations, and so on. This knowledge is acquired both intentionally, during exploration, and incidentally, while we are otherwise carrying out goal-directed tasks such as travel.

Our third category of spatial tasks is using *spatially iconic symbolic representations*. These are graphical and volumetric symbolic representations that represent spatial and nonspatial information through their own spatial properties (and sometimes their temporal and thematic properties). Spatial cognition can be involved in both producing and interpreting these external representations. By definition, spatial learning at miniscule and gigantic scales occurs only through symbolic representations (we do not learn the relative locations of cities in Africa from direct experience but from examining maps), but of course, all scales of spaces are sometimes learned in this way. Two-dimensional (graphical) symbolic representations include maps, graphs, drawings and diagrams (including blueprints), photographs, movies, and other "pictorial" representations. Three-dimensional (volumetric) symbolic representations include physical models and globes.

The cognition involved in producing and interpreting different symbolic representations can vary quite substantially from one to another. For instance, cartographic maps depict a portion of the earth's surface, diagrams typically depict architectural or object spaces, and graphs usually use space metaphorically to depict nonspatial relationships (e.g., quantitative magnitude; Tversky, 1997). Even within each type, there is a large amount of variation in how these representations depict information, what information they depict, how they are used, and more. For instance, maps may be reference maps or thematic maps, they may be used for navigation or for learning world geography, and they may depict metric information such as distance accurately or distort metric information to focus on relationships such as connectivity and sequence. Recently, multivariate representations of large data sets called *spatializations* have been generated that use landscape depictions to represent nonspatial

information metaphorically (Skupin & Fabrikant, 2008). Research by Fabrikant and her colleagues (e.g., Fabrikant, Montello, Ruocco, & Middleton, 2004) has looked at the spatial reasoning involved in interpreting spatialized displays.

Our fourth category of spatial tasks is using *spatial language*, a noniconic form of spatial symbolic representation system (see Chapter 12, this volume). Natural languages describe or instruct about space and spatiality abstractly; they exploit semantics (i.e., word, phrase, and sentence meanings) to communicate spatial properties of individual entities and relations among entities. Of course, there are substantial differences between the psychology of graphical and volumetric representations and that of natural language representations, although in the case of spatial descriptions, they may contain surprisingly similar spatial information content. For instance, Tversky and Lee (1999) found that routes depicted in sketch maps and described verbally similarly included particular landmark features, segmented the environment, and schematized elements such as curves. The way spatial information is encoded and communicated through language is studied in the context of tasks such as describing scenes and giving verbal route directions (Allen, 1997; Bloom, Peterson, Nadel, & Garrett, 1996; Jarvella & Klein, 1982). Researchers are interested in issues such as the precision or vagueness of spatial language, the absence or inclusion of landmarks in route directions, how *deictic* references convey spatial information, cross-linguistic differences and similarities in spatial language and thought, and more. But several prominent theories of language and thought have come to accord spatial thinking a central role in interpreting linguistic expressions in the first place, whether its semantic content is spatial or not. That is, spatial cognition has come to be recognized as essential to nonspatial thinking and communication with language. For instance, the theory of image schemata (Johnson, 1987) proposes that language is interpreted through the metaphorical extension of a few basic iconic mental representations to capture all semantics. Gentner and her colleagues have discussed the role of spatial thinking in temporal thinking and in the spatial alignment of conceptual structures during analogical reasoning more generally (Gattis,

2001; Gentner & Medina, 1998). The geometric theory of conceptual spaces (Gärdenfors, 2000) proposes that concepts are mentally represented as iconic representations whose geometric properties express relational meaning. Such iconic spatial theories of the psychology of semantics are, in fact, consistent with the effort described earlier to use iconic external representations called *spatializations* to communicate nonspatial information.

Our fifth category involves imagining places and reasoning about them with *mental models,* spatial mental representations constructed in working memory. Mental models are apparently constructed as part of interpreting narratives in language (Johnson-Laird, 1983). But they are also constructed from nonlinguistic sources, such as direct experience with entities at figural, vista, or environmental scales (Hegarty & Just, 1993). They are even constructed out of imagination and can represent spatial entities that a person has never directly experienced in any way. Thus, it is sensible to talk about reasoning with mental models of fictional entities that do not exist.

Our sixth category is *location allocation,* which is finding optimal or adequate locations for facilities such as retail businesses, hospitals, and schools. Locations are identified that minimize or reduce various relative cost functions, including traveled distance, that result from putting facilities in particular locations. This task is often handled noncognitively now, by algorithmic and heuristic computer routines that do not mimic human cognition. However, before location allocation was formalized as a computational task, people attempted informally to locate facilities in an adaptive manner. This intensive cognitive task incorporated a great deal of spatial thinking. For example, in preindustrial times, when siting a house, a person would need to consider factors such as the daily path of the sun, distance from water, distances from relatives, location within agricultural fields, safety from wild animals or other mobile threats, and so on. But even today, decisions such as picking a place of residence, a school, or a job, require spatial thinking that can be quite challenging. One must still consider factors such as the distance from one's job, from one's friends or family, from schools, from public transit,

and so on. Individuals rarely if ever use formal technologies and analytic methods to solve these problems, as cognitively challenging as they are.

APPLICATIONS OF SPATIAL COGNITION

In the first part of our chapter, we provided an overview of various functions of spatial cognition. This overview demonstrates that spatial cognition plays a major role in one's daily experience and activities and that it helps solve various problems one encounters both regularly and occasionally. Clearly, then, understanding spatial cognition should have application in a variety of practical domains (Allen, 2007; Golledge, 2004) involving objects and environments as well as external spatial representations such as maps, graphs, linguistic descriptions, and more. The advent of digital media such as GPS-enabled navigation systems is providing new applications for spatial cognition. In this section, we selectively highlight and describe some important application areas of spatial cognition research (see Exhibit 13.2). This list is definitely not comprehensive. We can see potential applications for spatial cognition research in a variety of other areas, such as forensic psychology, clinical and counseling psychology (disabilities, Alzheimer's and other syndromes), athletic training, aviation psychology, transportation and transit engineering, video gaming and digital communities, and more.

Before turning to specific application areas, a general point is warranted about applying research findings in spatial cognition. The experimental tradition in research manipulates variables to explore ways that varying stimulus materials, task settings, and other external factors influence the mental and behavioral responses of individuals. Of course, no

---

EXHIBIT 13.2

Some Important Application Areas for Spatial Cognition Research

1. Location-based services
2. Geographic and other information systems
3. Information display
4. Architecture and planning
5. Personnel selection
6. Spatial education

two individuals are exactly alike, and that applies to virtually every aspect of spatial cognition (Hegarty & Waller, 2005). Furthermore, although researchers in the comparative tradition often explore these differences in terms of aggregate factors, such as age, sex, and culture, that differentiate people, we can ultimately identify differences at the level of the individual (see Chapter 6, this volume). That is, we can distinguish three levels of user parameters for system design and other purposes: generic, group, and individual (Raubal, 2009). The *generic* level covers the general set of cognitive parameters assumed to be applicable to all people. For example, people in general use landmarks for finding their way and for communicating wayfinding directions to others. *Groups* of users can be defined by common sets of cognitive parameters, such as similar abilities, interests, concerns, goals, beliefs, or behavioral practices. This results in various overlaps between different groups of users. Examples are gender groups, such as all women or all men, and cultural groups defined, for example, by sharing a common language. An important question for the design of cognitively engineered technology is what kinds of differences should be taken into account when forming a group of users within a particular spatio–temporal context. Wayfinding instructions, for example, need to be adapted for specific groups in order to be most useful. On the *individual* level, every single person is ultimately different. Although personalization can potentially go a long way, the more parameters that need to be adapted, the more difficult and complex personalization becomes. For example, location-based services must represent individual user preferences, such as "I want to go from location X to location Y by public transport." So all people share some cognitive parameters, but they also fall into various "user groups" and have their individual preferences. Thus, we strongly advocate the need to consider group and individual variations when applying spatial cognition. It is also critical to explore the domain-generality and consistency of differences; to what tasks or skills does a particular difference apply, and how consistently? An informative discussion of these issues can be found in Appendix C of the report by the Committee on Support for Thinking Spatially (2006).

Location-Based Services

Over the last few decades, developed societies have become mobile information societies with the proliferation of spatial technologies. Such technologies comprise geospatial tools and services that support people in making spatio–temporal decisions. Finding one's way from the airport to a hotel in an unfamiliar city can be a demanding task that requires using different cognitive abilities in the context of space and time. Location-aware technologies and location-based services (LBS) support users during such mobile decision making. They are sensitive to the location of a mobile person, having GPS technology built into them, and relate the person's location to the surrounding environment via a geographic information system database. This in turn allows the system to provide location-based information in the form of written instructions or cartographic maps that facilitate the successful completion of spatio–temporal tasks. The widespread adoption of LBS has resulted in tremendous benefits for their users by providing them with real-time spatio–temporal decision support for purposes ranging from the trivial (e.g., friend-finder services) to the critical (e.g., emergency response).

Highly important for this process of information seeking and decision making is the notion of *geographic relevance,* defined as "a relation between a geographic information need and the spatio–temporal expression of the geographic information objects needed to satisfy it" (Raper, 2007, p. 836). That is, the system works well only when it is capable of organizing and filtering information according to the needs of a user. Achieving geographic relevance requires one to consider cognitive abilities and strategies people bring to the spatial problem-solving process. This is the goal of *spatial cognitive engineering:* to design spatial information systems and services based on principles of human communication and reasoning (Raubal, 2009; Taylor, Brunyé, & Taylor, 2009). It is an interdisciplinary endeavor, involving the disciplines of geographic information science, cognitive science, computer science, and engineering. A special focus is put on human–computer interaction on the basis of the integration and processing of spatial and temporal aspects of phenomena. This includes various conceptualizations of space and time, matching spatial and temporal concepts between users and systems, effective communication of information, and qualitative methods of spatial reasoning and decision making that more closely mimic human thought.

Digital navigation services are the most successful and widely adopted category of LBS to date. They support users in finding optimal routes while driving, biking, or walking; they communicate through maps and verbal turn-by-turn instructions; and their maintenance is low (given that up-to-date street network data are used). Navigation services for pedestrians are generally more difficult to implement because pedestrians are not bound to a street network. These services strongly need personalization. For example, route instructions for people in wheelchairs must not include segments with stairways. These days, more and more of these services integrate landmarks because it has been realized that route instructions that rely mainly on quantitative values, such as "Go straight for 1.5 km, then turn right, go 0.8 km," are difficult to follow while being on the move. Cognitive research has shown that providing landmark-based instructions, such as "Turn right after the 6-story building" or "Go straight until you reach In-N-Out Burger,"[3] facilitates navigation for most users, at least in many situations (Denis, Michon, & Tom, 2007). Consequently, a research focus has developed that investigates methods for the automatic detection of landmarks to be used in wayfinding instructions (Sadeghian & Kantardzic, 2008). Spatial cognition research continues to contribute to developing better navigation services that incorporate landmarks people perceive, find salient, and readily identify.

Navigation services are often a part of *mobile guides,* which are portable and location-sensitive digital guides that provide an abundance of information to travelers and tourists. They have been slowly replacing traditional guidebooks and paper maps. Recently, several innovative LBS applications have emerged, and some of them focus on the integration of small mobile displays and large static paper maps. An illustrative application is *WikEar* (Schöning,

Hecht, & Starosielski, 2008; see Color Plate 17), which integrates different perceptual modes (visual and auditory) and generates customized location-based guided tours by mining data from Wikipedia (http://www.wikipedia.org). These data are automatically organized according to principles from narrative theory (from cognitive science and semiotics) and integrated into an educational audio tour that starts and ends at stationary city maps.

Different media can be used for communicating location-based and navigation information. Maps have been the most prominent medium, but several cognitive research issues arise when using maps on cell phones and PDAs. Mobile displays are limited in size and resolution compared with larger screens, which makes map reading more difficult for the average user (Dillemuth, 2005). (And mobile devices are often used in situations of divided attention!) Maps are traditionally aligned on the display with north facing up. Just as users of traditional analog maps often turn the map as travel direction changes, users of mobile devices typically prefer digital maps to maintain "track-up" alignment (Aretz & Wickens, 1992). Sensor-based information can be used to determine a user's direction of movement and automatically provide track-up oriented maps on mobile devices. Mobile map adaptation based on the user's preferences, task, and location, among other context parameters, can help reduce both user interaction with the device and cognitive load for the user. For example, when the user reaches a decision point during a navigation task, the service can automatically zoom in to local detail (Raubal & Panov, 2009). For several applications—notably, navigation services—maps are often complemented or even substituted by verbal instructions (Streeter, Vitello, & Wonsiewicz 1985). The benefit for car drivers is that they can keep their eyes on the road while listening to and following route instructions. Other graphic and pictorial aids, such as arrow graphics or scene photographs, can facilitate the transfer of wayfinding instructions to a traveler's surrounding environment by directing travelers to pertinent

---

[3]This is a regional chain of fast food restaurants with locations in the western United States. Palm trees planted to form an *X* in front of the restaurants add to the "landmarkness" of the sites.

information and by depicting the environment in a less abstract way (Hirtle & Sorrows, 1998).

Geographic and Other Information Systems

Spatial cognition research is relevant to spatial information technologies besides LBS. Generically, *geographic information systems* (GIS) are computer-based systems for storing, processing, and visualizing geographic information (Longley, Goodchild, Maguire, & Rhind, 2011). Their applications are manifold, including resource management, land-use planning, environmental monitoring, transportation, health, emergency management, and geomarketing. GISs have also been used to simulate human behavior in space, such as modeling lost person behavior and managing the search for lost persons (Heth & Cornell, 2007). By simulating individual wayfinding strategies for particular persons within representations of real-world environments modeled with GIS data, these systems can aid search planners and, through the use of mobile devices, search-and-rescue workers in the field.

Spatial cognition can potentially contribute to improving the effectiveness, efficiency, and usability of GISs in many ways (Hoffman & Markman, 2001; Mark, Freksa, Hirtle, Lloyd, & Tversky, 1999; Montello, 2009), especially with regard to the different ways users and systems interact. The design of a GIS should benefit from considering how individuals understand and represent space (Medyckyj-Scott & Blades, 1992). For example, it has been suggested that spatializing user interfaces consistent with the spatial concepts and experiences of users will facilitate human–computer interaction in GISs (Kuhn, 1996). The metaphor of navigation can also be applied to other domains, including the Internet and other information systems that are not explicitly or directly geographic. For example, topologic and metric relations have been used to represent neighborhoods of related web pages and the distances between them, with web pages serving as information "landmarks." In this way, navigation in electronic spaces can be supported by applying what we know about real environments and human interaction with real environments (Hirtle & Sorrows, 2007).

Information Display

Information displays are patterned graphical representations, usually apprehended visually, that symbolically communicate information about something (Card, MacKinlay, & Schneiderman, 1999). Displays often communicate spatial information iconically, by using their own spatial properties to represent spatial properties of information content. An example would be a typical cartographic map, which represents distances in the world by distances on the map display. Displays also communicate spatial information abstractly by using their own spatial properties to represent nonspatial properties of information content. An example would be a graph, which might use height on the graphic space to represent magnitude in an information set (of course, information displays also use many nonspatial properties to represent information content). Computer technology has allowed the development of interactive displays, which can be modified on the go by users who wish to create more customized views of information. Animations add dynamic properties to the static properties of traditional displays to use changing spatial and nonspatial properties of displays to represent spatial, temporal, and thematic properties of information. The metaphorical representation of nonspatial information through spatial properties of displays can be taken much further by using complex and realistic visuo–spatial structures, such as natural or urban landscapes, to facilitate knowledge discovery in large and complex information sets, relying for instance on principles such as the *distance-similarity metaphor* (Fabrikant, Montello, & Mark, 2010; Fabrikant et al., 2004). This principle states that entities that are more similar should be placed closer together when represented in a display, because users will interpret closer entities as being more similar.

It has been recognized for nearly a century that spatial cognition research might contribute to producing better displays and to training people how to use them (Montello, 2002; Trickett & Trafton, 2006) and that display tools should provide representations that are consistent with and support human cognition (MacEachren, 1995). A cognitive approach to information visualization brings individual perception, understanding, and decision making to the design process—for example, providing a theory that explains why particular symbol shapes work or do not work for users. Modern displays, with their increased multivariate information and interactivity, make this even more true (Slocum et al., 2001).

Architecture and Planning

As with information displays, it has been recognized for some time that architecture and planning are essentially environmental design for people, and understanding human characteristics should help design more effective environments (Carlson, Hölscher, Shipley, & Dalton, 2010; Evans, Fellows, Zorn, & Doty, 1980). Effective environments might be easy to orient in, lead to an appropriate level of privacy or sociability, appear interesting without being too confusing, induce feelings of safety, and so on. Spatial cognition is being applied to all of these issues, either at the time an environment is originally designed and built, or later, when attempts are made to improve the usability of environments already constructed.

Clearly, the visual and structural characteristics of environments make it easier or harder to establish orientation while navigating (Montello & Sas, 2006). Weisman (1981) identified four physical variables of environments that affect orientation: signage, differentiation of appearance, visual access, and layout complexity. All of these variables apply to built environments such as buildings and cities, and the first three apply to natural environments such as wilderness areas as well. These variables influence the perceptibility and salience of features in the environment, the memorability of features and spatial relations among features, the ease of updating as one travels about, and the applicability of different strategies for wayfinding. In fact, their importance is even broader, influencing where people are able or allowed to move, how they respond affectively to places, the ease or difficulty of particular kinds of social interactions, and more.

With respect to *signage*, research shows that signs are more effective when they are well designed and placed at decision points during travel; conversely, poor signage can certainly confuse (e.g., Arthur & Passini, 1992). The disorienting effect of misaligned "you-are-here" maps (which can be considered as a type of signage) is one of the most robust and well-known phenomena in spatial cognition research (Klippel, Hirtle, & Davies, 2010; Levine, 1982). *Differentiation of appearance* is the extent to which different parts of the environment look similar to or different from each other, in terms of size, form, color, architectural style, and so on. Environments that are more differentiated generally make orientation easier, but too much unorganized differentiation can become illegible and confusing. *Visual access* is how far one can see in different directions from different places (auditory access is of some relevance, too). It depends on the environmental shape created by opaque structures, but also on topography and atmospheric conditions when outdoors. It also depends on a viewer's position and other characteristics (height, visual acuity). Environments with more visual access generally make orientation easier. *Isovist analysis* provides a method for spatial cognition researchers to measure visual access in different places (Benedikt & Burnham, 1985). An *isovist* is the collected spatial extent of all views, or "vistas," from a single place within an environment.

For spatial cognition researchers, *layout complexity* is probably the most interesting and subtle of Weisman's four variables. It involves the shapes or patterns of rooms, halls, path networks, clearings, and so on. Environments with less layout complexity generally make orientation easier. However, determining layout complexity is not always straightforward and is an ongoing research issue. Cognitive researchers must be part of this effort because complexity is not simply an objective matter to be analyzed, for example, by information theory (e.g., Attneave, 1959). Of concern to cognitive scientists is what makes a layout complex to a person, not just complex mathematically or logically. A variety of factors probably influence subjective complexity, including the overall size of a layout, the orthogonality or obliqueness of turns and intersections (Werner & Schindler, 2004), and the degree of articulation of subspaces, such as hallways or rooms. Some environmental shapes have better form (as in the gestalt concept of Prägnanz) and are probably easier to comprehend, remember, and verbally describe; in fact, layouts appear to be cognitively distorted toward good form (Tversky, 1992). A promising approach to studying layout complexity and spatial cognition is the theory and method of *space syntax* (Penn, 2003). Space syntax is a formal language for describing and measuring properties of layout, especially network patterns and interconnectivity. It simplifies place layout by identifying "pieces" that can then be related in terms of topology, specifically the sequences of connected nodes linked in abstract graph structures. These pieces can represent convex subspaces or straight-line axes of movement or vistas.

Personnel Selection

Spatial cognition research can help to select people who will more likely succeed at a particular activity or career. Personnel selection has been a primary aim of spatial-test development since its inception in the 19th century (Eliot & Smith, 1983). If an activity requires spatial thinking for its successful completion, then people who think better spatially should be more likely to succeed at it. In fact, tests of spatial thinking have been used to select from applicants to dental and medical school (Hegarty et al., 2007). Of course, general aptitude tests such as the SAT and GRE include spatial-thinking items, although these items are typically aggregated with nonspatial logical and mathematical items when used to make admissions decisions.

Although the validity of using measures of spatial abilities to select personnel would hold to some degree no matter the genesis of ability differences, it would be more useful to do so if the differences are relatively less modifiable by training or other experiences. Although innate abilities are not necessarily immutable, they may be less easily improved than those resulting from experience, especially relatively short-term experience. In fact, as Hegarty et al. (2007) discussed in detail, there is a considerable debate in the medical education field about whether the abilities involved in learning anatomy, performing surgery, and so on, are relatively changeable or not (e.g., Gilligan, Welsh, Watts, & Treasure, 1999; Wanzel et al., 2003). If they are, it would probably be misguided to reject applicants with lower scores on those abilities, because they may

be able to achieve adequate levels of performance on relevant tasks with particular types or amounts of experience. In their review, Hegarty et al. (2007) concluded that "high-spatial" students have an advantage early in medical training but that all students who are otherwise qualified will likely be able to acquire necessary skills involving particular types of spatial ability; the relationship of ability to success at mastering medical skills diminishes with training and practice.

Finally, we note that it is important that researchers and practitioners do not restrict themselves to the notion of a unitary, monolithic "spatial ability." Instead, we should continue to refine our understanding of not only "components" of spatial thinking in the traditional psychometric sense but also of task and situation contexts in which different types of spatial thinking are important. We will best be able to predict how well people perform some spatial task if we develop a detailed understanding of the specific knowledge structures and processes involved in performing the task (e.g., Hegarty & Waller, 2005). An example is the apparent difference between reasoning at figural and environmental scales. As another example, the predictors of success at reaching a destination in a timely manner during travel will be rather different for people who conceive of an environment as a collection of one-dimensional routes than for people who conceive of it as a two-dimensional layout (Devlin, 2001).

Spatial Education

Closely related to using spatial cognition research to help with personnel selection is using it to improve education in spatially intensive disciplines and occupations. Many occupations and avocations involve spatial thinking quite centrally, and research in spatial cognition is being applied to designing and evaluating education programs and procedures in these fields (Hsi, Linn, & Bell, 1997). Although people differ in their spatial cognitive abilities, evidence has shown that such abilities are trainable, at least to some extent (e.g., Lohman & Nichols, 1990; Newcombe & Frick, 2010). In most domains, spatial thinking concerns both the phenomenon of interest and symbolic representations of the phenomenon, such as maps, diagrams, and models. Examples of academic and scientific fields for which spatial education is likely to be useful include geography (Gersmehl & Gersmehl, 2006; Marsh, Golledge, & Battersby, 2007) and earth sciences (Kastens & Ishikawa, 2006; Plumert, 1993), mathematics (Bishop, 1980), and medicine and dentistry (Hegarty et al., 2007). Education in spatial cognition can also apply to many nonacademic endeavors, such as carpentry or taxi driving (Maguire et al., 2000).

Several researchers and educators have pushed for the incorporation of technologies such as GIS and computer-aided design into the classroom at all grade levels, on the grounds that such technologies fundamentally entail spatial thinking and will therefore foster more and better spatial thinking (Albert & Golledge, 1999; Committee on Support for Thinking Spatially, 2006). However, as we discuss in our conclusions, spatial technologies usually work largely by replacing spatial thinking rather than enhancing it. In many cases, for instance, the technology turns a thinking problem into a perception problem—I enter a command and then read the answer off a screen. That reservation aside, we agree with the recent recognition that spatial thinking is fundamentally important in many areas of life and that it is underrecognized and underinstructed in education programs. In addition to the 2006 report of the Committee on Support for Thinking Spatially we have already cited, see the Spatial Intelligence and Learning Center (http://www.spatiallearning.org/), the Center for Spatial Studies (http://spatial.ucsb.edu/), and Spatial Literacy in Teaching (http://www.le.ac.uk/gg/splint/).

SUMMARY AND FUTURE PROSPECTS

In this chapter, we have reviewed conceptual ideas and empirical results that focus on functions and applications of spatial cognition. We hope that our review stimulates further questions and future research directions. In particular, we appreciate that many questions remain about the role of spatial cognition research in the development of spatial technologies and about the appropriate use of spatial technologies and their ultimate implications for human life and experience. By now, as we have briefly discussed, there are several demonstrations

of the successful application of spatial cognition research to a variety of problem areas, including aspects of the design of information systems (whether specifically for navigation, search and rescue, or more generally), the design and redesign of architectural spaces, the use of spatial tests for student selection, and the development of education programs in spatial thinking. Nonetheless, we consider it an ongoing question as to what degree research in spatial cognition can improve the functionality of technology, and if so, how. For members of the spatial cognition community, such as ourselves, belief in the practical usefulness of such research is almost a matter of faith. In fact, there are not that many clear demonstrations of this, and there are some reasons to question it. For instance, should navigation systems present maps and verbal directions that mimic human thinking (e.g., Tversky & Lee, 1999), or do we accept that tools and technologies are useful precisely because they do not mimic the limited memory of humans, limited quantitative precision and accuracy, limited reasoning complexity, and so on?

The great benefits of spatial technologies are evident, such as in emergencies where lives are saved. As spatial technologies become more common in societies around the world, however, it is worth contemplating what negative effects they may have. Will our navigation systems make us spatially witless, antisocial, or otherwise less happy and healthy? We have arguments and evidence that using such systems places higher visual and cognitive demands on the driver (Burnett, Summerskill, & Porter, 2004). In the long run, we think it is likely that the regular use of GPS-enabled navigation systems will diminish people's ability to maintain orientation by using old-fashioned perceptual–motor and cognitive systems. Research is starting to verify this (Ishikawa, Fujiwara, Imai, & Okabe, 2008; Parush, Ahuvia-Pick, & Erev, 2007). This technological "infantilization" is admittedly nothing new. Celebrated feats of pretechnological orientation, such as the navigation systems of the Micronesians (Gladwin, 1970), do not result from some "innate primitive intelligence" but from training, practice, and focusing attention on particular details in the world. Our own navigation technologies and environmental modifications partially replace these psychological skills and tendencies with structure and information that do much of the cognitive work for us. In a similar way, one can wonder if the drive to integrate spatial technologies such as GISs into educational settings will end up replacing thinking rather than enhancing it.

We also note that the widespread use and distribution of LBS has led to concerns about people's trust in the information provided by these services; several accidents have been reported which occurred partly because of gullibility about the accuracy of the systems. The question of what factors influence the credibility of information displays is partially a question for spatial cognition researchers (e.g., Smallman & St. John, 2005).

In sum, we believe that addressing issues about spatial technology and cognition would benefit from more studies of how people actually use navigational technologies in daily situations. We recommend that researchers and developers consider how to adapt technology so users achieve immediate and longer term objectives. Can travelers get to their destinations safely and efficiently and at the same time learn more, not less, about their surroundings? That is, can technologies provide functionality but also enhance spatial cognition by integrating cognition in the head with cognition in the world (Norman, 1988)?

SUGGESTED REFERENCES FOR FURTHER READING

Allen, G. L. (Ed.). (2004). *Human spatial memory: Remembering where*. Mahwah, NJ: Erlbaum.

Recent edited collection that surveys basic and applied topics in human spatial memory, particularly at the spatial scale of rooms and larger.

Allen, G. L. (Ed.). (2007). *Applied spatial cognition: From research to cognitive technology*. Mahwah, NJ: Erlbaum.

Recent edited collection that is the most focused and comprehensive discussion of applications of spatial cognition, including in the areas of wayfinding, visualization, architecture, information system design and training, managing search for lost persons, military training, and medical training.

Committee on Support for Thinking Spatially: The Incorporation of Geographic Information Science Across the K–12 Curriculum, National Research Council. (2006). *Learning to think spatially*. Washington, DC: National Academies Press.

Report by a multidisciplinary committee, organized and supported by the U.S. National Academies, which discusses widely ranging functions and applications of spatial cognition in earth and environmental sciences, social sciences, and other disciplines; its Appendix C on "Individual Differences in Spatial Thinking: The Effects of Age, Development, and Sex" is one of the best concise pieces available on the subject.

Hirtle, S. C. (2011). *Geographical design: Spatial cognition and geographical information science*. San Rafael, CA: Morgan & Claypool Publishers.

Recent overview of applications of spatial cognition in the field of geographical information science that is deeply informed by spatial cognition research and theory across the disciplines of psychology, geography, and computer and information science.

Hutchins, E. (1995). *Cognition in the wild*. Cambridge, MA: The MIT Press.

Thoroughly overviews navigation at a functional and mechanistic level and compares traditional Pacific Island navigation with modern technical navigation, thereby presenting a fascinating perspective on the artifactual and social aspects of cognition in non-laboratory situations.

Newcombe, N. S., & Huttenlocher, J. (2000). *Making space: The development of spatial representation and reasoning*. Cambridge, MA: The MIT Press.

Recent summary of theory and research on spatial cognition, particularly its development in infancy and childhood; includes cognition based on direct environmental experience and cartographic maps.

Passini, R. (1992). *Wayfinding in architecture* (2nd ed.). New York, NY: Van Nostrand Reinhold Company.

The most complete discussion available of spatial cognition in the design and experience of architecture, from the perspective of trained architects.

References

Albert, W. S., & Golledge, R. G. (1999). The use of spatial cognitive abilities in geographical information systems: The map overlay operation. *Transactions in GIS, 3*, 7–21. doi:10.1111/1467-9671.00003

Allen, G. L. (1997). From knowledge to words to wayfinding: Issues in the production and comprehension of route directions. In S. C. Hirtle & A. U. Frank (Eds.), *Spatial information theory: A theoretical basis for GIS* (pp. 363–372). Berlin, Germany: Springer. doi:10.1007/3-540-63623-4_61

Allen, G. L. (Ed.). (2007). *Applied spatial cognition: From research to cognitive technology*. Mahwah, NJ: Erlbaum.

Aretz, A. J., & Wickens, C. D. (1992). The mental rotation of map displays. *Human Performance, 5,* 303–328. doi:10.1207/s15327043hup0504_3

Arthur, P., & Passini, R. (1992). *Wayfinding: People, signs, and architecture.* Toronto, Canada: McGraw-Hill Ryerson.

Attneave, F. (1959). *Applications of information theory to psychology: A summary of basic concepts, methods, and results.* New York, NY: Holt.

Benedikt, M., & Burnham, C. A. (1985). Perceiving architectural space: From optic arrays to isovists. In W. H. Warren & R. E. Shaw (Eds.), *Persistence and change: Proceedings of the First International Conference on Event Perception* (pp. 103–114). Hillsdale, NJ: Erlbaum.

Bishop, A. J. (1980). Spatial abilities and mathematics education—A review. *Educational Studies in Mathematics, 11,* 257–269. doi:10.1007/BF00697739

Bloom, P., Peterson, M. A., Nadel, L., & Garrett, M. F. (Eds.). (1996). *Language and space.* Cambridge, MA: The MIT Press.

Burnett, G., Summerskill, S., & Porter, J. (2004). On-the-move destination entry for vehicle navigation systems: Unsafe by any means? *Behaviour & Information Technology, 23,* 265–272. doi:10.1080/01449290410001669950

Card, S. K., MacKinlay, J. D., & Schneiderman, B. (1999). *Readings in information visualization: Using vision to think.* San Francisco, CA: Morgan Kaufmann.

Carlson, L. A., Hölscher, C., Shipley, T. F., & Dalton, R. C. (2010). Getting lost in buildings. *Current Directions in Psychological Science, 19,* 284–289. doi:10.1177/0963721410383243

Cheng, K., & Newcombe, N. S. (2005). Is there a geometric module for spatial orientation? Squaring theory and evidence. *Psychonomic Bulletin & Review, 12,* 1–23. doi:10.3758/BF03196346

Committee on Support for Thinking Spatially: The Incorporation of Geographic Information Science Across the K–12 Curriculum, Committee on Geography, National Research Council. (2006). *Learning to think spatially.* Washington, DC: National Academies Press.

Dehaene, S., Izard, V., Pica, P., & Spelke, E. (2006, January 20). Core knowledge of geometry in an Amazonian indigene group. *Science, 311,* 381–384. doi:10.1126/science.1121739

Denis, M., Michon, P.-E., & Tom, A. (2007). Assisting pedestrian wayfinding in urban settings: Why references to landmarks are crucial in direction-giving. In G. L. Allen (Ed.), *Applied spatial cognition: From research to cognitive technology* (pp. 25–51). Hillsdale, NJ: Erlbaum.

Devlin, A. S. (2001). *Mind and maze: Spatial cognition and environmental behavior.* Westport, CT: Praeger.

Dillemuth, J. (2005). Map design evaluation for mobile display. *Cartography and Geographic Information Science, 32,* 285–301. doi:10.1559/152304005775194773

Eliot, J., & Czarnolewski, M. Y. (2007). Development of an everyday spatial behavioral questionnaire. *Journal of General Psychology, 134,* 361–381. doi:10.3200/GENP.134.3.361-381

Eliot, J., & Smith, I. M. (1983). *An international directory of spatial tests.* Windsor, England: NFER-Nelson.

Evans, G. W., Fellows, J., Zorn, M., & Doty, K. (1980). Cognitive mapping and architecture. *Journal of Applied Psychology, 65,* 474–478. doi:10.1037/0021-9010.65.4.474

Fabrikant, S. I., Montello, D. R., & Mark, D. M. (2010). The natural landscape metaphor in information visualization: The role of commonsense geomorphology. *Journal of the American Society for Information Science and Technology, 61,* 253–270.

Fabrikant, S. I., Montello, D. R., Ruocco, M., & Middleton, R. S. (2004). The distance-similarity metaphor in network-display spatializations. *Cartography and Geographic Information Science, 31,* 237–252. doi:10.1559/1523040042742402

Gärdenfors, P. (2000). *Conceptual spaces: The geometry of thought.* Cambridge, MA: MIT Press.

Gärling, T., & Gärling, E. (1988). Distance minimization in downtown pedestrian shopping. *Environment & Planning A, 20,* 547–554. doi:10.1068/a200547

Gattis, M. (Ed.). (2001). *Spatial schemas in abstract thought.* Cambridge, MA: MIT Press.

Gentner, D., & Medina, J. (1998). Similarity and the development of rules. *Cognition, 65,* 263–297. doi:10.1016/S0010-0277(98)00002-X

Gersmehl, P. J., & Gersmehl, C. A. (2006). Wanted: A concise list of neurologically defensible and assessable spatial-thinking skills. *Research in Geographic Education, 8,* 5–38.

Gilligan, J. H., Welsh, F. K., Watts, C., & Treasure, T. (1999). Square pegs in round holes: Has psychometric testing a place in choosing a surgical career? A preliminary report of work in progress. *Annals of the Royal College of Surgeons of England, 81,* 73–79.

Gladwin, T. (1970). *East is a big bird.* Cambridge, MA: Harvard University Press.

Golledge, R. G. (1995). Path selection and route preference in human navigation: A progress report. In A. U. Frank & W. Kuhn (Eds.), *Spatial information theory: A theoretical basis for GIS* (pp. 207–222). Berlin, Germany: Springer. doi:10.1007/3-540-60392-1_14

Golledge, R. G. (2004). Spatial cognition. In C. Spielberger (Ed.), *Encyclopedia of applied psychology* (Vol. 3, pp. 443–452). Boston, MA: Elsevier. doi:10.1016/B0-12-657410-3/00657-7

Golledge, R. G., & Hubert, L. J. (1982). Some comments on non-Euclidean mental maps. *Environment & Planning A, 14,* 107–118. doi:10.1068/a140107

Hartley, T., Trinkler, I., & Burgess, N. (2004). Geometric determinants of human spatial memory. *Cognition, 94,* 39–75. doi:10.1016/j.cognition.2003.12.001

Hegarty, M., & Just, M. A. (1993). Constructing mental models of machines from text and diagrams. *Journal of Memory and Language, 32,* 717–742. doi:10.1006/jmla.1993.1036

Hegarty, M., Keehner, M., Cohen, C. A., Montello, D. R., & Lippa, Y. (2007). The role of spatial cognition in medicine: Applications for selecting and training professionals. In G. L. Allen (Ed.), *Applied spatial cognition: From research to cognitive technology* (pp. 285–315). Mahwah, NJ: Erlbaum.

Hegarty, M., & Waller, D. A. (2005). Individual differences in spatial abilities. In P. Shah & A. Miyake (Eds.), *The Cambridge handbook of visuospatial thinking* (pp. 121–169). Cambridge, England: Cambridge University Press.

Heth, D., & Cornell, E. (2007). A geographic information system for managing search for lost persons. In G. Allen (Ed.), *Applied spatial cognition: From research to cognitive technology* (pp. 267–284). Mahwah, NJ: Erlbaum.

Hirtle, S. C., & Sorrows, M. E. (1998). Designing a multi-modal tool for locating buildings on a college campus. *Journal of Environmental Psychology, 18,* 265–276. doi:10.1006/jevp.1998.0096

Hirtle, S., & Sorrows, M. (2007). Navigation in electronic environments. In G. Allen (Ed.), *Applied spatial cognition: From research to cognitive technology* (pp. 103–126). Mahwah, NJ: Erlbaum.

Hoffman, R. R., & Markman, A. B. (Eds.). (2001). *The interpretation of remote sensing imagery: The human factor.* Boca Raton, FL: Lewis. doi:10.1201/9781420032819

Hsi, S., Linn, M. C., & Bell, J. E. (1997, April). The role of spatial reasoning in engineering and the design of spatial instruction. *Journal of Engineering Education,* 151–158.

Ishikawa, T., Fujiwara, H., Imai, O., & Okabe, A. (2008). Wayfinding with a GPS-based mobile navigation system: A comparison with maps and direct experience. *Journal of Environmental Psychology, 28,* 74–82. doi:10.1016/j.jenvp.2007.09.002

Ishikawa, T., & Montello, D. R. (2006). Spatial knowledge acquisition from direct experience in the environment: Individual differences in the development of metric knowledge and the integration of separately learned places. *Cognitive Psychology, 52,* 93–129. doi:10.1016/j.cogpsych.2005.08.003

Jarvella, R. J., & Klein, W. (Eds.). (1982). *Speech, place, and action: Studies in deixis and related topics.* New York, NY: Wiley.

Johnson, M. (1987). *The body in the mind: The bodily basis of meaning, imagination, and reason.* Chicago, IL: The University of Chicago Press.

Johnson-Laird, P. N. (1983). *Mental models: Towards a cognitive science of language, inference, and consciousness.* Cambridge, England: Cambridge University Press.

Kastens, K. A., & Ishikawa, T. (2006). Spatial thinking in the geosciences and cognitive sciences: A cross-disciplinary look at the intersection of the two fields. In C. A. Manduca & D. Mogk (Eds.), *Earth and mind: How geologists think and learn about the Earth* (Special Paper 413; pp. 51–74). Boulder, CO: Geological Society of America.

Klippel, A., Hirtle, S., & Davies, C. (Eds.). (2010). You-are-here maps: Creating spatial awareness through map-like representations [Special issue]. *Spatial Cognition and Computation, 10*(2).

Kuhn, W. (1996). Handling data spatially: Spatializing user interfaces. In M. Kraak & M. Molenaar (Eds.), *SDH '96, Advances in GIS Research II, Proceedings* (Vol. 2, pp. 13B.11–13B.23). Delft, Netherlands: International Geographical Union.

Levine, M. (1982). You-are-here maps: Psychological considerations. *Environment and Behavior, 14,* 221–237. doi:10.1177/0013916584142006

Lohman, D. F., & Nichols, P. D. (1990). Training spatial abilities: Effects of practice on rotation and synthesis tasks. *Learning and Individual Differences, 2,* 67–93. doi:10.1016/1041-6080(90)90017-B

Longley, P. A., Goodchild, M. F., Maguire, D. J., & Rhind, D. W. (2011). *Geographic information systems and science* (3rd ed.). Chichester, England: Wiley.

MacEachren, A. M. (1995). *How maps work: Representation, visualization, and design.* New York, NY: Guilford Press.

Maguire, E. A., Gadian, D. G., Johnsrude, I. S., Good, C. D., Ashburner, J., Frackowiak, R. S. J., & Frith, C. D. (2000). Navigation-related structural change in the hippocampi of taxi drivers. *Proceedings of the National Academy of Sciences of the United States of America, 97,* 4398–4403. doi:10.1073/pnas.070039597

Mark, D., Freksa, C., Hirtle, S., Lloyd, R., & Tversky, B. (1999). Cognitive models of geographical space. *International Journal of Geographical Information Science, 13,* 747–774. doi:10.1080/136588199241003

Marsh, M., Golledge, R. G., & Battersby, S. E. (2007). Geospatial concept understanding and recognition in G6–college students: A preliminary argument for minimal GIS. *Annals of the Association of American Geographers. Association of American Geographers, 97*, 696–712. doi:10.1111/j.1467-8306.2007.00578.x

Medyckyj-Scott, D., & Blades, M. (1992). Human spatial cognition: Its relevance to the design and use of spatial information systems. *Geoforum, 23*, 215–226. doi:10.1016/0016-7185(92)90018-Y

Montello, D. R. (1992). The geometry of environmental knowledge. In A. U. Frank, I. Campari, & U. Formentini (Eds.), *Theories and methods of spatio–temporal reasoning in geographic space* (pp. 136–152). Berlin, Germany: Springer-Verlag. doi:10.1007/3-540-55966-3_8

Montello, D. R. (2002). Cognitive map-design research in the twentieth century: Theoretical and empirical approaches. *Cartography and Geographic Information Science, 29*, 283–304. doi:10.1559/152304002782008503

Montello, D. R. (2005). Navigation. In P. Shah & A. Miyake (Eds.), *The Cambridge handbook of visuospatial thinking* (pp. 257–294). Cambridge, England: Cambridge University Press.

Montello, D. R. (2009). Cognitive research in GIScience: Recent achievements and future prospects. *Geography Compass, 3*, 1824–1840. doi:10.1111/j.1749-8198.2009.00273.x

Montello, D. R., & Sas, C. (2006). Human factors of wayfinding in navigation. In W. Karwowski (Ed.), *International encyclopedia of ergonomics and human factors* (2nd ed., pp. 2003–2008). London, England: CRC Press/Taylor & Francis. doi:10.1201/9780849375477.ch394

Newcombe, N. S., & Frick, A. (2010). Early education for spatial intelligence: Why, what, and how. *Mind, Brain, and Education, 4*, 102–111. doi:10.1111/j.1751-228X.2010.01089.x

Norman, D. A. (1988). *The design of everyday things.* New York, NY: Basic Books.

Parush, A., Ahuvia-Pick, S., & Erev, I. (2007). Degradation in spatial knowledge acquisition when using automatic navigation systems. In S. Winter, M. Duckham, L. Kulik, & B. Kuipers (Eds.), *Lecture notes in computer science: Vol. 4736. Spatial information theory* (pp. 238–254). Berlin, Germany: Springer.

Penn, A. (2003). Space syntax and spatial cognition: Or why the axial line? *Environment and Behavior, 35*, 30–65. doi:10.1177/0013916502238864

Plumert, J. M. (1993). The development of children's spatial knowledge: Implications for geographic education. *Cartographic Perspectives, 16*, 9–18.

Raper, J. (2007). Geographic relevance. *The Journal of Documentation, 63*, 836–852. doi:10.1108/00220410710836385

Raubal, M. (2009). Cognitive engineering for geographic information science. *Geography Compass, 3*, 1087–1104. doi:10.1111/j.1749-8198.2009.00224.x

Raubal, M., & Panov, I. (2009). A formal model for mobile map adaptation. In G. Gartner & K. Rehrl (Eds.), *Location based services and telecartography II: From sensor fusion to context models. Selected papers from the 5th International Symposium on LBS & TeleCartography 2008, Salzburg, Austria.* (pp. 11–34). Berlin, Germany: Springer.

Rinck, M., & Denis, M. (2004). The metrics of spatial distance traversed during mental imagery. *Journal of Experimental Psychology: Learning, Memory, and Cognition, 30*, 1211–1218. doi:10.1037/0278-7393.30.6.1211

Sadeghian, P., & Kantardzic, M. (2008). The new generation of automatic landmark detection systems: Challenges and guidelines. *Spatial Cognition and Computation, 8*, 252–287. doi:10.1080/13875860802039257

Schöning, J., Hecht, B., & Starosielski, N. (2008). *Evaluating automatically generated location-based stories for tourists.* Paper presented at the Conference on Human Factors in Computing Systems (CHI '08), Florence, Italy.

Sklar, L. (1974). *Space, time, and spacetime.* Berkeley, CA: University of California.

Skupin, A., & Fabrikant, S. I. (2008). Spatialization. In J. Wilson & S. Fotheringham (Eds.), *The handbook of geographic information science* (pp. 61–79). Malden, MA: Blackwell.

Slocum, T. A., Blok, C., Jiang, B., Koussoulakou, A., Montello, D. R., Fuhrmann, S., & Hedley, N. R. (2001). Cognitive and usability issues in geovisualization. *Cartography and Geographic Information Science, 28*, 61–75. doi:10.1559/152304001782173998

Smallman, H. S., & St. John, M. (2005). Naïve realism: Misplaced faith in realistic displays. *Ergonomics in Design, 13*, 6–13. doi:10.1177/106480460501300303

Streeter, L. A., Vitello, D., & Wonsiewicz, S. A. (1985). How to tell people where to go: Comparing navigational aids. *International Journal of Man-Machine Studies, 22*, 549–562. doi:10.1016/S0020-7373(85)80017-1

Strelow, E. R. (1985). What is needed for a theory of mobility: Direct perception and cognitive maps-lessons from the blind. *Psychological Review, 92*, 226–248. doi:10.1037/0033-295X.92.2.226

Taylor, H. A., Brunyé, T. T., & Taylor, S. (2009). Wayfinding and navigation: Mental representation and implications for navigational system design. In C. M. Carswell (Ed.), *Reviews of human factors and ergonomics* (Vol. 4, pp. 1–40). Santa Monica, CA: Human Factors and Ergonomics Society.

Trickett, S. B., & Trafton, J. G. (2006). Toward a comprehensive model of graph comprehension: Making the case for spatial cognition. In D. Barker-Plummer, R. Cox, & N. Swoboda (Eds.), *Diagrams 2006, LNAI 4045* (pp. 286–300). Berlin, Germany: Springer-Verlag.

Tversky, B. (1992). Distortions in cognitive maps. *Geoforum, 23,* 131–138. doi:10.1016/0016-7185(92)90011-R

Tversky, B. (1997). Memory for pictures, environments, maps, and graphs. In D. Payne & F. Conrad (Eds.), *Intersections in basic and applied memory research* (pp. 257–277). Mahwah, NJ: Erlbaum.

Tversky, B., & Lee, P. U. (1999). Pictorial and verbal tools for conveying routes. In C. Freksa & D. M. Mark (Eds.), *Spatial information theory: Cognitive and computational foundations of geographic information science* (pp. 51–64). Berlin, Germany: Springer. doi:10.1007/3-540-48384-5_4

van Fraassen, B. C. (1985). *An introduction to the philosophy of time and space* (2nd ed.). New York, NY: Columbia University Press.

Wanzel, K. R., Hamstra, S. J., Caminiti, M. F., Anastakis, D. J., Grober, E. D., & Reznick, R. K. (2003). Visual–spatial ability correlates with efficiency of hand motion and successful surgical performance. *Surgery, 134,* 750–757. doi:10.1016/S0039-6060(03)00248-4

Weisman, J. (1981). Evaluating architectural legibility: Way-finding in the built environment. *Environment and Behavior, 13,* 189–204. doi:10.1177/0013916581132004

Werner, S., & Schindler, L. E. (2004). The role of spatial reference frames in architecture: Misalignment impairs way-finding performance. *Environment and Behavior, 36,* 461–482. doi:10.1177/0013916503254829

CHAPTER 14

WAYFINDING, NAVIGATION, AND ENVIRONMENTAL COGNITION FROM A NATURALIST'S STANCE

Harry Heft

The ecological psychologist Roger Barker, a recipient of the American Psychological Association's Distinguished Scientific Contribution Award, once keenly observed that psychology may be unique among the sciences for having started out as an experimental enterprise. Typically, inquiry in the various scientific disciplines begins with careful observation and detailed description of its subject matter; or at the very least, observation and description run parallel with analytical techniques such as experimentation. Sensitivity to its subject matter honed through careful observation has been both a starting point and a touchstone for scientific inquiry. For the life sciences, this takes the form of a *naturalist's stance*, marked by an appreciation for how organisms "make their living" from day to day. In this regard, psychology has been an outlier. From its formal founding in the late 1870s, psychology has been an experimental science. This circumstance sheds much light on the particular course psychology has plotted over its first 130 years. More to the point of the present chapter, this history bears directly on how environmental cognition has been conceptualized and investigated within psychology over the past 3 decades.

To offer a brief overview of what follows, I propose in the first part of the chapter that theory and research on spatial cognition has been dominated by an *intellectualist orientation* to inquiry, by which I mean an analytical stance toward the topic. In contrast to the naturalist who begins inquiry by trying to adopt an intimate and sympathetic stance with regard to his or her subject matter, the "intellectualist" from the outset stands at a remove from the phenomenon, maintaining a detached, dispassionate, and analytic vantage point. Without question, an analytical stance has been remarkably fruitful since the 17th century in directing our efforts to understand the natural world. And yet, I submit, the costs of adopting such a view to the exclusion of naturalist considerations have been considerable for the science of psychology. With regard to the topic of this chapter, one notable consequence has been insufficient attention to the contexts of environmental cognition. Instead, the chief focus of research to date has been primarily on underlying mental mechanisms for wayfinding and orientation, whereas all too rarely have psychologists considered the ecological circumstances in which processes of environmental cognition develop and function. It turns out, however, that the two—context and process—are inseparable.

In the second part of the chapter, I show that owing to the character of terrestrial environments, patterns of structured information become available to terrestrial organisms as they move around the environment. With these ecological considerations as a starting point, I claim that wayfinding involves skilled actions developed in the course of organisms "making a living" in their habitats. Moreover, when

I would like to thank Kerry Marsh, Susan Saegert, Steven Vogel, and David Waller for the insightful comments on an earlier draft of this chapter. I am also grateful to Nicole Barenbaum, Rand Evans, and Moriana Garcia for help in tracking down some historical sources.

DOI: 10.1037/13936-015
Handbook of Spatial Cognition, D. Waller and L. Nadel (Editors)

it comes to understanding human environmental cognition, we need to recognize that wayfinding skills also develop in the midst of cultural practices and often with the support of navigational tools. I argue, in part three of the chapter, that these skills are extended and, to some extent, transformed in the course of a social group's shared history in the face of particular ecological and sociocultural circumstances.

In light of these considerations, it will be seen that the intellectualist stance adopted on its own has had the double effect of (a) ascribing to nonhuman animals, as well as to the young of our own species, operations that are more likely "projections" of established human practices and (b) inversely, of failing to recognize those distinctive qualities of human environmental cognition that stem from our participation in sociocultural practices. Taking the organism–environment system as our unit of analysis, it will be seen that humans differ from other organisms in that their contexts for development offer far reaching possibilities owing to the emergence of tools and techniques for navigation that extend skilled actions of wayfinding.

PSYCHOLOGY'S SINGULAR STANCE

It is beyond dispute that the major figure in 19th century biological thought is Charles Darwin. In this light, it seems remarkable in retrospect that Darwin hardly appears in the writings of psychology's first generation. Timing certainly was not the issue. *On the Origin of Species* (1859) appeared over 20 years before the formal launch of experimental psychology. Psychology in the hands of Wundt, Ebbinghaus, G. E. Mueller, and others was modeled on the work of laboratory scientists. Helmholtz, not Darwin, was the icon. From the outset, the new discipline was committed to controlled experimental investigations of psychological processes in the laboratory.

Darwin, in contrast, exemplifies a less restricted approach to scientific inquiry. The theory of natural selection is built on his and others' careful, detailed observations of the natural world. Similarly, his more obviously psychological works—the book *The Expressions of Emotion in Man and Animals* (1872) and the essay "A Biographical Sketch of an

Infant" (1877)—are based on detailed observation. But they were soon to fall outside of the disciplinary boundaries of the experimental psychology that appeared shortly after their appearance. Less well known are Darwin's experimental efforts, including his remarkable investigations of the habits of earthworms (Darwin, 1881). What distinguishes him from the younger group of scientists who launched experimental psychology is that Darwin approached his subject matter foremost as a naturalist and with a broader vision of legitimate scientific methods.

Over the second half of the 20th century, Darwin was usually portrayed within psychology primarily as a mechanistic thinker who offered up a picture of the dispassionate gears of natural selection doing their mindless business. However, more recent historical scholarship offers a somewhat different assessment (Richards, 1987). Darwin was foremost a naturalist in the tradition of the German scientific romantics rather than a mechanist. True, natural selection is a blind, undirected process, but "mind" figured prominently in Darwin's thinking. He was not reluctant to write about regulated, goal-directed action in organisms as a property of their evolved relationship with their environment. Indeed, a central theme in his writings about human evolution in *The Descent of Man* (1874) was the importance of "sympathy" toward others as a motive. Our modern selves may wish to write off such claims as woolyheaded, old-fashioned thinking lacking in scientific rigor, but few in the life sciences, much less in the nascent psychology, knew their subject matter as intimately as Darwin.

And yet, when it comes to the late 19th century founding of psychology, observation of natural processes, and the "feel for the organism" that it affords, were set aside almost entirely for experimental investigation. The major exception to this stance was William James. James was caustic in his criticism of Wundt, Ebbinghaus, and other so-called brass instrument psychologists. In *The Principles of Psychology,* James (1890) criticized the experimentalists for engaging in an "assault" on mental life without first understanding its character (see pp. 191–193). Rather than "the experimental method" serving as the starting point for a science of psychology, James unreservedly stated that

"Introspective Observation is what we have to rely on first and foremost and always" (p. 185). To the modern reader, the phrase *introspective observation* might seem to lump James in the same camp with these same experimentalists he criticized, but taken in its historical context, this is clearly a mistaken reading. Observation is the critical operation here, with the adjective *introspective* pointing to what is to be observed—namely, immediate experience. In this respect, he was self-consciously following Darwin's lead. James's approach to psychology is that of a naturalist, and he characteristically begins treatment of nearly every topic in *The Principles* with a careful description of the phenomenon under consideration. Surely, a primary reason that James's *The Principles of Psychology* is perhaps the only psychological work of the 19th century still read today is that his audience continues to recognize their own experiences in James's introspective descriptions.

What, then, was the allure of experimentation for the first generation of psychologists? The usual explanation offered is their desire to make psychology a legitimate science. That is no doubt part of the reason, but it is based on a narrow view of what science involves. If Darwin was not engaging in scientific practice, what was he doing? Instead, I suggest that there is a more fundamental reason, which is best revealed in the broader context of the history of ideas.

Experimental inquiry is one of the great contributions of Renaissance and Enlightenment thought, and it is a piece within an overall orientation referred to earlier as *intellectualism*. By *intellectualism,* I mean a particular form of inquiry that involves adopting an analytical stance toward one's subject matter. In post-Renaissance thought, the prototypes for intellectualism are Bacon and Descartes; much of "modern philosophy" that has followed in their wake from Locke to Kant stems from analytical inquiry. A common and problematic feature of intellectualism, as we will see, is to take the results of analysis as the underlying basis for the phenomena under consideration.

Canonical histories of psychology mostly trace this intellectualist line of thought. However, this founding narrative is changing slowly as historians are belatedly recognizing the contributions of scien-

tists interested in life processes who come out of a naturalist tradition (Richards, 2002). This historical tradition and its influence is a much neglected part of psychology's history (see Reed, 1997).

FOUNDATIONS OF THE STUDY OF SPATIAL COGNITION

We can see the hand of intellectualism, as just defined, at work in the recent efforts to investigate spatial cognition. Although researchers typically couch their investigations of spatial cognition in functional terms, once this justification is offered, most treatments of spatial cognition in psychology do not concern themselves with actions, but instead focus on what are presumed to be the mental structures that underlie those actions. Indeed, much of the research in spatial cognition in psychology takes functional concerns to be a secondary consideration, at best, paying little more than lip service to them.

Most of the psychological research in spatial cognition over the past 30 years can be traced to one of three perspectives: (a) a nativist approach to spatial cognition with its roots in Cartesian and Kantian thought; (b) a tradition stemming from Piaget and Inhelder's (1967) work on the development of spatial cognition; and (c) an information-processing approach, with Tolman's (1948) neobehaviorist paper on cognitive maps being the locus classicus.

Kant (1781) stated the classic position concerning *space* quite clearly:

> Space is not an empirical concept which has been derived from outer experiences. For in order that certain sensations be referred to something outside me . . . and similarly in order that I may be able to represent them as outside and alongside one another, and accordingly as not only different but in different places, *the representation of space must be presupposed* [emphasis added]. (p. 68)

Kant was interested in the grounds for our knowledge (*epistemology*) rather than functional considerations; and likewise, a century and a half later, Piaget was concerned with the development of our knowledge (*genetic epistemology*). In both cases, the individual's experience of space and spatial relations at any particular moment is said to presuppose a mental representation of space that plays a role of structuring sensory experience. Action, and the body more generally—Piaget's sensorimotor period notwithstanding, tend to take a backseat to "disembodied" thought.

In contrast, the behaviorist Tolman would have surely rejected both of these positions because of the empiricist roots of his thinking. Instead, he proposed that organisms acquire "expectations" about where actions will lead in the environment. Still, some of Tolman's contemporaries criticized his approach for its understating the place of action in spatial problem solving. Notably, Guthrie (1935) remarked: "In his concern with what goes on in the rat's mind, Tolman has neglected to predict what the rat will do. So far as the theory is concerned the rat is left buried in thought" (p. 127).

These three approaches all share another notable attribute. They take knowledge of the configuration of the environment to be the most advanced form of spatial knowing. *Configurational knowledge* refers to knowledge of the layout of some area with emphasis on the geometric relations among its features. It is notable that knowledge of environmental layout is considered with reference to a vantage point that is not located anywhere on the ground surface but rather from somewhere above it—from a "bird's eye view." The individual is, in effect, detached from the landscape and disembodied rather than being immersed in it. From this perspective, the individual's relationship to the environment is solely analytical.

It should be apparent that this way of conceptualizing spatial cognition is aligned with the long tradition of intellectualism described earlier. However, the results of taking an analytical stance as the starting point for understanding spatial cognition would be, in James's (1890) terms, a case of committing the "the psychologist's fallacy."

Spatial Cognition and the Psychologist's Fallacy

In *The Principles of Psychology* (1890), William James famously described mental life as a stream of experience, a flow of mental events. He held to this position throughout his career, and it became an essential feature of his mature thought, *radical empiricism* (Heft, 2001). The primary obstacle standing in the way of an individual recognizing the flow of experience, according to James, was the adoption of an analytical stance. In a late essay he wrote: "Experience in its immediacy seems perfectly fluent. . . . When the reflective intellect gets at work, however, it discovers incomprehensibilities in the flowing process" (James, 1912, p. 92).

One of these incomprehensibilities is the assumption that mental experience fundamentally consists of discrete elements and disjointed static patterns. From this starting point, organization would seem to be absent from experience itself, only to be imposed by extrinsic factors. However, James (1890) argued, this emphasis on elements, along with a neglect of the dynamic qualities intrinsic to immediate experience, is a result of adopting an analytical stance with regard to immediate experience. Said in other words, such an account of experience is a product of our reflections about immediate experience, derived from our stepping outside of the immediate flow and adopting an analytic stance with respect to it. James warned repeatedly that taking our reflections about immediate experience as being characteristic of immediate experience as such was the basis for continuing confusion in psychological theorizing. William James referred to this analytical misstep variously as the *psychologist's fallacy*. Tellingly, his prototypical example of this error was the assumption that mental representations underlie experience rather than being derived from experience through reflection (James, 1890, p. 195).

This Jamesian perspective on immediate experience grounds a primary thesis of the present chapter. The process of finding one's way in the environment most fundamentally has continuity over time as an individual locomotes or otherwise travels in relation to features of the environmental layout. *Wayfinding,* I argue, is a continuous, integrated perception–action process controlled by the detection of information over time. Conversely, treatments of spatial cognition that take as their starting point conceptual products of reflecting on immediate experience, detached from on-going perception–action, can create unnecessary conceptual difficulties, while also masking the fundamental nature of wayfinding processes.

Taking as our starting point the flow of experience, mental representations of environmental configuration will be seen as being derived from the individual's engagement with the environment, particularly through the mediation of material artifacts, rather than operating as a priori grounds for this engagement. Environmental cognition takes the forms that it does owing to animate organisms engaging environments possessing structure that can be used for wayfinding. And in the case of human experience, characteristic features of environments include tools and artifacts that stem from a social history of collective wayfinding efforts. In this respect, although the developmental context for human environmental cognition shares much with that of other terrestrial animals, in significant respects, it is quite different. An appreciation for both these commonalities and differences is needed for an adequate understanding of human environmental cognition.

Spatial or Environmental Cognition?

The influence of the intellectualist tradition in experimental psychology may be nowhere more evident than in the promiscuous, and often misleading, use of the term *space,* as in the expression "spatial cognition." In this research area, *space* is often employed as a synonym for *environment.* But these terms are not synonymous in any strict sense.

Formally, space is a conceptual abstraction imposed on immediate experience. The utility of this way of thinking cannot be overstated, it having served as a foundational framework for so many advances in science and technology over the past 400 years. Still, the differences between space formally considered and environment are vast. For this reason, the term *space* may mask some of the essential qualities of environments (Gibson, 1979). I suggest that this has been an ongoing problem in the spatial cognition area, and its consequences for understanding environmental cognition have been considerable.

Let us briefly examine some of the differences between space and environments:

- Cartesian space is empty save the objects (or points in space) being locationally specified. In contrast, environments, except in rare circumstances, are cluttered with innumerable features. For this reason, environments, unlike abstract space, have a great deal of potential perceptual structure.
- Commonly, objects in space are conceptualized in isolation, or at most, among a few other objects. But objects in environments tend to rest on ground surfaces (Gibson, 1950) and are situated in a perceptually rich surround providing possibilities for perceiving relational properties, especially from the standpoint of a moving perceiver. These ecological facts have great significance for wayfinding.
- In a similar vein, objects tend to be thought of as being located "in" space, as if space is container-like. But objects are not "in" environments; rather, they are among the features that constitute environments.
- The dimensions of Cartesian space are, in principle, limitless. This is not so in the case of environments. The vertical dimension normally stops at the ground surface, and environments have a horizon, although an ever-shifting one, as the individual moves.
- Spatial frameworks tend to be static, with the positions of objects in a spatial coordinate system temporally fixed. In contrast, only some features of environments are stationary, and many features are animate. It is important that for our purposes here, the local environment as perceived from the perspective of a moving individual is a shifting array, an *optical flow field* generated by the individual's movements.
- Space has a unitary connotation. In contrast, there is not one environment, but many. At the level of species, for example, evolutionary considerations dictate that we differentiate among econiches. At the level of human groups, we typically need to differentiate among places (Barker, 1968; Heft, 2001, 2011).
- Space is typically considered to exist independently of organisms, a vast "out-thereness"

that is wholly disconnected from organismic processes. In contrast, environments, in the sense of econiches, are the contexts for life processes, and as such, animal–environment relations are central. In this regard, not only do animals adjust to changing environmental conditions operating at different time scales but also these conditions themselves are modified through the actions of organisms (Odling-Smee, Laland, & Feldman, 2003).

With such striking differences between space and environments, why has the language of space, and the conceptual baggage it carries, been so dominant in our thinking? Plainly, it is a legacy of the intellectualist tradition described previously (see additional historical comments that follow). Space has assumed a dominant role in psychological theorizing since the 16th and 17th centuries following the landmark contributions of Descartes, and later Newton and Kant. It is likely that if psychology's historical roots had resided more squarely in 19th century biological thought and Darwin's work on species' evolution rather than in 17th century Newtonian physics, the discipline's treatment of the environment would have been quite different than it is at present. But such was not the case, and a result is that the character of environments within which organisms live was routinely superseded by the assumed primacy of universal abstractions such as the concept of space—a case of committing the psychologist's fallacy.

I am not disputing the view that spatial concepts can play a role in human wayfinding. As I argue next, abstract conceptualizations of environmental layout, drawing on material artifacts and spatial reasoning, are instrumental in much of human wayfinding. But these instances are a consequence of applying conceptual tools developed within a particular sociocultural tradition of wayfinding challenges.

With this notion of space at its metatheoretical core, psychology was bound to be slow in incorporating two ecological facts into the discipline: (a) the interdependence of natural entities and with it, the "situatedness" of all natural processes, including psychological processes; and (b) the earth and its inhabitants undergo continuous change, albeit at different time scales. In the remainder of this chapter, I employ the term *environmental cognition*

when it is appropriate, instead of spatial cognition, to reflect this shift in perspective.

WAYFINDING AS A TIME-DEPENDENT PROCESS

Mobile organisms must have some means of directing and controlling their actions to reach particular resources. And once such locations have been identified, they must have perceptual means for remaining on a course that will lead again to those sites on other occasions, permit them return back to their home base, and keep track of where they are in the environment at any particular time. How do they manage to do all this?

It is necessary to recognize that how we address this question depends on the way visual perception is assumed to operate. A perception–action approach compels us to examine the possibility that perceiving processes in support of wayfinding occur over time (Gibson, 1979). The temporal dimension of wayfinding, however, is typically omitted from standard accounts of visual perception, owing to their assumptions that vision is an image-capturing process. But some information that may be essential for wayfinding has an intrinsic, temporal character that emerges from the actions of animals in terrestrial (structured) environments. We can only briefly identify here three time-dependent wayfinding processes.

Homing

One form of wayfinding over time relies on *homing*, which refers to selecting some target feature (a "beacon") in the landscape and directing actions toward that feature. When engaging in homing, the individual need not be aware of features of the landscape other than the target (as well as the ground surface, in the case of terrestrial animals). Nor is it necessary to keep track of direction or distance of movement. The organism does, however, need to perceive that, in fact, it is moving on a path that will intercept the target. That information is available in the optic flow that is generated by movement through feature-rich environments (Gibson, 1958; Lee, 1976; Lee & Aronson, 1974; Warren, 1998; see also Chapter 3, this volume).

Path Integration

Sailors traveling across open seas are faced with the challenge of keeping track of their position relative to landmasses that may be out of sight for long stretches of time. Terrestrial organisms are faced with the same challenge when they are traveling in unfamiliar regions with few prominent landscape features. Sailors have addressed this difficulty by devising methods of piloting that track and integrating estimates of the direction of heading and distance traveled (see, Hutchins, 1995; Rieser & Pick, 2007). Procedures along these lines, but used in a non-self-conscious manner, have been proposed to explain how a wide variety of species keep track of where they are relative to some fixed features.

At present, there is convincing evidence that sensitivity to direction and distance traveled can be used for this purpose by insects (e.g., Collett, Collett, Bisach, & Wehner, 1998; Müller & Wehner, 1988) and by some mammals (e.g., Mittelstaedt & Mittelstaedt, 1982), including humans (Klatzky et al., 1990; for reviews, see Etienne & Jeffery, 2004; Wehner & Srinivasan, 2003). Whereas researchers were initially sympathetic to the idea that path integration gives rise to a configurational knowledge (e.g., a cognitive map; e.g., Gould, 1986), this claim has been largely discredited (Dyer, 1991; Foo, Warren, Duchon, & Tarr, 2005; Healy, Hodgson, & Braithwaite, 2003; Wehner, Bleuler, & Nievergelt, 1990; Wehner & Menzel, 1990). Although consensus on the precise meaning of the cognitive map concept is notoriously difficult to pin down (Bennett, 1996; Collett & Collett, 2006), at minimum it would seem to result in time-independent awareness of the configuration of some environment, in the manner of a geometric-based mental representation. In contrast, path integration seems to operate as a time-dependent, "online" procedure for guiding locomotion (Foo et al., 2005; Knaden, Lange, & Wehner, 2006; Merkle & Wehner, 2008).

Wayfinding as a Process of Perceiving Information Over Time

Wayfinding has a temporal character arising from the perceptual flow of environmental structure that accompanies the individual's movement through some expanse (layout), such as the interior of a building, a neighborhood, or a town. As individuals move through the environment, a structured flow of potential information is generated, and that temporally structured information can be used in wayfinding. A handful of planners and designers have described in their writings the perceived qualities of environments that become apparent when wayfinding along paths through cities and countryside (Appleyard, Lynch, & Myer, 1964; Cullen, 1971; Lynch, 1960; Thiel, 1970, 1997). For the most part, these qualities have been overlooked by psychologists investigating environmental cognition (for some exceptions, see Gibson, 1979; Heft, 1979, 1983, 1996; Inagami & Ohno, 2010; Ohno, 2000; Ohno, Hata, & Kondo, 1997).

Building on Gibson's (1979) framework, I proposed that the information used in wayfinding over time consists of a succession of vistas connected by transitions (1996). A *vista* is a visual expanse, "a semienclosure, a set of unhidden surfaces. [It] is what can be seen from here" (Gibson, 1979, p. 198), recognizing that "here" is typically a moving point of observation, some duration (*durée*) over time. As the individual travels a path within the expanse that is a vista, a pattern of optical flow is generated. As the individual continues along the path of locomotion, inevitably more substantial and prominent changes occur in the field of view other than these local "within-vista" changes. A new vista, a different expanse succeeding the previous one, gradually comes into view. The portion (*durée*) of the route where a previously occluded vista comes into view constitutes a *transition*. From this perspective, wayfinding is a perception–action process that generates a temporal pattern of visual information specific to a path through the environment. "To go from one place to another involves the opening up of the vista ahead and closing in of the vista behind" (Gibson, 1979, p. 198).

A series of experiments (Heft, 1979, 1983, 1996) showed that individuals traveling a route through the environment (a) are sensitive to the sequence of transitions along the path of locomotion, (b) identify the transitions as meaningful places along the route for finding their way, and (c) use the transitions to the exclusion of vistas as information for wayfinding and that the perceived value of transitions for wayfinding increases with repeated exposures to a route.

It is well to pause and reflect on this conceptualization. The information that is used for wayfinding is generated within the relationship between organism and environment. Its relational character is quite easy to demonstrate. When self-movement ceases, there is no optic flow, and information over time for wayfinding is no longer available. This flow of information over time is referred to as *perspective structure,* and it is to be distinguished from *invariant structure,* which persists across transformations in the information flow (Gibson, 1979). In the context of wayfinding, perceiving invariant structure entails an awareness of the overall layout of the immediate environment, independent of any particular location. This is not to say, however, that awareness of invariant structure through the pickup of information over time is comparable to having a mental image of overall layout configuration (a bird's eye view) or, for that matter, having any mental image at all. It is an awareness of how the environment is laid out, as in the manner that one is aware when looking at an object of its temporarily hidden sides that would come into view if a different vantage point were adopted (see Heft, 1996).

Wayfinding, Skill, and Technique

A perception–action approach, emphasizing the pickup of information through directed, coordinated action, invites us to consider wayfinding as a type of skill learning and skilled action. Viewed as a skill, the time-dependent character of wayfinding becomes an unavoidable quality, as does its thorough, practical goal-oriented character. In addition, approaching wayfinding as a skill establishes conceptual grounds for explaining, if only in a preliminary way at this point, how maplike understanding could emerge from perception–action processes.

The philosopher Gilbert Ryle (1949), among others, drew a distinction between two general types of knowing: *knowing that* and *knowing how. Knowing that* refers to knowledge about some state of affairs, such as knowing that the American Museum of Natural History in Manhattan is on the west side of Central Park or that Perth is on the west coast of Australia. *Knowing how,* in contrast, refers to skill-

ful action that results in some desired outcome, such as tying an intricate knot, riding a bicycle, or—I submit—finding your way from home to work without navigational aids. That instances of *knowing how* are different from *knowing that* is usually demonstrated by pointing out the difficulty of articulating how to carry out a skilled action. *Knowing how* refers to "a knowledge and ability which has come about by habit, i.e., has passed into flesh and blood, and which is directed to a producing" (Schadewalt, 1979, as cited in Hickman, 1990, p. 18). It is intelligent action, or *praxis,* developing from opportunities for engaging repeatedly in some activity to realize some end. It is evident in the actions of the accomplished dancer or musician, the skilled potter or weaver, and in the activities of riding a bicycle or skiing down a hillside. In some philosophical writings, the term *techne* has also been employed to refer to a productive skill (Hickman, 1990).

Skills grow out of action rather than explanation, and typically, the best a teacher of a skill can do is to set up conditions for a learner to engage more or less properly in the action. If all goes well, the learner will discover through practice how to produce some intended result. Conveying information declaratively to a learner makes, at best, a minor contribution to setting up conditions for learning. More valuable is directing the learner's attention to certain aspects of the task so that he or she can discover—in the sense of "get the feel of"—what it takes to engage in the particular skilled action leading to the desired end.

It is notable that, unlike *knowing that,* which involves detaching oneself from action to assume a reflective stance, *knowing how* involves acting that engages features or properties of the environment. It must do so because—and the following claim cannot be overemphasized—environmental structures are integral to the act in question. Learning to ride a bicycle involves learning how to "work with" the mechanisms of a particular bicycle and in relation to the affordances of the immediate environment, such as the road surface. Learning to throw pottery involves action in relation to the properties of the clay at hand and the available equipment. That is, skilled action is not merely action of the body, as it sometimes is characterized to be, but it is a body–

environment process (Ingold, 1995). All directed actions are situated actions. Above all, praxis or techne should not be confused with those forms of action that temporarily disconnect us from ongoing events: acts of cognitive reflection such as thinking and remembering. Praxis involves experiencing the world through action. And, it is important that it also involves a transformation of aspects of the world.

> The world of our experience is a real world, but a world that is in need of transformation in order to render it more coherent and secure . . . giving it form that is more useful for our purposes. But knowing in this sense is not something done apart from the world; *it takes place experimentally inside experienced situations* [emphasis added]. (Hickman, 1990, p. 37)

The preceding discussion should help to clarify how the process of wayfinding differs from understanding environmental layout through reflection. Wayfinding, I submit, is fundamentally one form of praxis among many others. Organisms learn to find their way between places in the environment through perception–action processes. In this respect, to know how to get from one location to another is not to draw on time-independent knowledge, such as Euclidean, geometric knowledge, but rather it is to have developed a temporally structured skill specifically enmeshed within a particular terrestrial extent. Like other forms of praxis, any specific instance of wayfinding is not fully separable from the character of a particular path of travel through the environment as experienced over time. This is why telling someone how to get somewhere can never duplicate the experience of actually doing so.

In this light, it may be no more useful to consider wayfinding skills as drawing on a unitary set of processes, such as configurational understanding, any more than cooking skills do. There are many possible ways to reach the same approximate end. As Biryukova and Bril (2008) showed in an elegant study of the stone-knapping skills of Indian artisans, two visibly identical artifacts can be produced by different individuals who use slightly different

patterns of motor movements. Still, pragmatically speaking, there are better and worse ways to proceed. Skill learning involves finding ways to act such that a desired outcome results, whether that is producing a dish with specific taste qualities or finding an efficient way from point A to point B. Such actions cannot take the form of a rote performance (e.g., an algorithm) unless the context for action is guaranteed to remain the same from one occasion to the next—which is unlikely considering the variations attending any circumstance. For this reason, all skilled action requires an on-going sensitivity to the developing context for action—which is another way of saying that it is a perception–action process. In an on-going manner, actions are contingent on the circumstances that arise through prior actions. Just as the act of blending a cake batter involves monitoring its developing consistency as a guide to continuing action or playing a piano piece involves monitoring what is produced as a guide to adjusting the ongoing action, wayfinding likely involves generating a particular perspective flow and adjusting action to maintain or alter the intended flow of perceptual structure. The contingent nature of skilled performance rules out the usefulness of a general, abstract strategy or a "program" for decision making and action.

In short, skilled action requires responsiveness to environmental contingencies as they arise; and these contingencies grow out of the cycle of environment-action processes. For these reasons, the phrase *regulated improvisation* may best capture a distinctive quality of all skilled action (Bourdieu, 1977, p. 8). Such a view may also help us to understand the aesthetic qualities that often accompany skilled action and are lacking in rote performances (Heft, 2010).

To put a finer point on this discussion, it may be unduly limiting to view skilled action as a special type of psychological phenomenon to be distinguished from more obvious processes, such as thinking and reasoning. As I hope to show, we would be well served by following Dewey in viewing action and cognition as means of inquiry rather than knowing. *Inquiry* connotes action, as opposed to the term *knowing*, which conveys detached reflection. The subtle shift in meaning that *inquiry* invites serves to eliminate the traditional, yet artificial, distinction between acts of the body and acts of the mind. In this regard, skills as results of inquiry should be viewed as prototypical of psychological processes (Dewey, 1938; Polanyi, 1967).

TOOLS AND WAYFINDING

Although I have chosen thus far to emphasize time-dependent, perception–action processes such as homing, path integration, and wayfinding, there is no doubt that something like configurational knowledge (time-independent representations) figures in human wayfinding on many occasions. The question is how might configurational knowledge fit conceptually into the account being developed here? Indeed, what is the place of navigational tools, such as cartographic maps, in this perception–action account of wayfinding? We saw that classically the word *techne* was used to designate a productive, skilled action; and *techne* is the root for the word *technology*, as it is used today. The pragmatist philosopher John Dewey saw this etymological connection as offering a unique insight into what a tool is (Hickman, 1990). His analysis in this regard may open up ways of thinking about how time-independent navigational tools can emerge from time-dependent wayfinding processes.

Pragmatism and Inquiry

Dewey put forward a view of humans as active knowing and feeling beings in transaction with the environment. The activity that best illuminates these processes for him was scientific inquiry. Although when formalized, scientific methods appear to be abstract, intellectualist activities, their essential qualities, Dewey pointed out, reveal a great deal about what lies at the heart of the most basic individual–environment transactions.

Scientific inquiry is a process of engaging natural phenomena by systematically probing the workings of nature—that is, trying to gain an understanding of their character through action. Inquiry is a process of ever getting better "in touch with" the environment. Because what is learned through inquiry is partially dependent on the circumstances of inquiry, and because further inquiries hold open the possibility that new findings will be at odds with prior

inquiries, current understanding is always provisional. That is the character of scientific knowledge. However, as Dewey repeatedly pointed out, the two traditional approaches to epistemology, nativism and empiricism, operate differently. They both assume that knowledge preexists before action in some nascent form, either in "internal" mental structures or imposed from without on a passive mind, respectively. They both assume that knowledge is ultimately grounded in fixed foundations, as either certainties about mental processes (Descartes) or certainties about the world (Locke's ideas of primary qualities). This position, known as *foundationalism,* holds "that human activity (and inquiry, the search for knowledge, in particular) takes place within a framework which can be isolated prior to the conclusion of an inquiry—a set of presuppositions discoverable a priori" (Rorty, 1979, pp. 8–9). *Pragmatism,* as advocated by Dewey and others, takes scientific inquiry as it is practiced as a guide to understanding the nature of knowing processes. Because of the dynamic character of inquiry, pragmatism rejects foundationalism. Knowledge, and the grounding assumptions of some body of knowledge, is provisional and revisable. For this reason, Dewey's program has been described as a "radical reconstruction of traditional theories of knowledge [replacing] them with a *theory of inquiry* [emphasis added]" (Hickman, 1990, p. 19).

My reason for raising these philosophical issues in this psychological treatment of environmental cognition is that by chapter's end I will claim that the knowledge reflected in wayfinding activities is likewise provisional and that it does not rest on preestablished certain foundations, such as Euclidean geometry. Accepting then that scientific knowledge is provisional, on what temporary grounds might we say that knowledge, such as knowledge of how to go from place A to place B, has merit? From a pragmatist perspective, what makes something a provisional solution is that "it works" in the circumstances under consideration (James, 1907).

To take an everyday example, I know how hard to step on the brake pedal of my car because I have discovered through past practices that depending on how quickly I need to stop, a particular amount of force is required. However, as conditions change either in the environment (roads become icy) or in the equipment (a loss of brake fluid), the prior "know-how" no longer works, and I must recalibrate to find a new solution. Each provisional solution is fine-tuned and, in extreme instances, even abandoned as new contingencies arise. In this way, what is known is both true and yet possibly revisable. And all of this works without any knowledge of how braking systems operate (foundational belief).

Likewise, in scientific practice I may have discovered that a certain outcome is due to a particular functional relationship between two variables. If I introduce the first of these variables in the presence of the other, the expected outcome should obtain. However, this is only the case, ceteris paribus, if similar testing conditions, relative to the degree of robustness of the effect, are in place. Perhaps within the mindset of a pre-Darwinian worldview—which, after all, was the cultural context for the emergence of intellectualism—one might assume such stability. But amidst the complexities and dynamic flux of the natural world as we have slowly come to understand them, there are no guarantees, no foundational certainties.

Action and the Emergence of Tools

Having previously described wayfinding as skilled action in context, how do tools, such as maps, fit into this account? Here we need to look more closely at Dewey's approach to inquiry. Dewey takes as his starting point for examining individual–environment transactions some on-going activity of an individual functioning unproblematically for the moment in some context (Burke, 1994). In such instances, individual–environment transactions proceed smoothly for a time, at least provisionally. Habits of action previously developed within this context sustain a flow of adaptive, unreflective situated action. Readers should think of any well-practiced action that they carry out as an illustration of this phenomenon.

However, quite commonly, this flow of unreflective, habitual action can hit a snag. Some established sequence of action no longer leads to an outcome that was anticipated within the habitual stream of the action. At those points when the flow of habitual action is disrupted, the individual's engagement

takes on a different character as he or she attempts, in some fashion and typically "on the fly" (Rosch, 1999; Suchman, 1984), to restore the equilibrium or the flow of previous organism–environment transactions. For Dewey, *inquiry,* in a broad sense, is the process of attempting to restore an unproblematic flow of action. What is critical for our discussion here is the following: This effort to restore equilibrium is typically done by "stepping outside" the immediate flow of action to search for an alternative way of reengaging the circumstances. The alternative can be characterized as an effort to formulate a different techne intended to get acting or thinking "back on track." It is an operation arrived at in the course of inquiry (Burke, 1994).

This Deweyan view of techne in the context of inquiry sets the stage for the development of tools. The germ of what eventuates in a material tool, such as a map, may take shape in the efforts (techne) to get action "back on track," such as resuming some interrupted path of travel. It may involve considering the immediate circumstances in a different way—taking a "new slant on things"—to gain leverage for restoring a continuous flow of action (or thought). In this expanded view, a tool ultimately comes about by way of reflective processes that afford a stepping outside of the on-going flow of action when it is disrupted to find a way of restoring that flow. Hickman (1990) put it this way:

> In Dewey's analysis, "reflection" means not only a careful inspection of the traits of the problematic situation with an aim to its resolution, but also an actual *going outside* the immediate situation " . . . to something else to get a leverage for understanding it." There is a search for a *tool* with which to operate on the unsettled situation. The tool becomes part of the active productive skill brought to bear on the situation. The purpose of the tool is to reorganize experience in some way that will overcome its disparity, its incompatibility, or its inconsistency. (p. 21)

Tools are material means devised to address some problem situation. They result eventually—and typically quite incrementally—from operations that arise for the purpose of (re-)establishing an effective flow of individual–environmental transactions. Cartographic maps are tools in this sense (see the section Maps in Western Cultures in this chapter).

Finally, if we bear in mind that individual–environment transactions are ongoing and reciprocal, it can be seen that reflective operations that momentarily made possible a stepping outside of the ongoing flow of action and supported the fashioning of some tool can themselves be altered by the tool they fashioned. This is an iterative process wherein the tool and the reflective processes change in tandem incrementally (and as we will see in the next section, cross generationally). Thus, inquiry in the style of Dewey, prompted by a disruption in the flow of action, may present a slightly different possibility for restoring the action that over time eventuates in the fashioning of a tool. In turn, this tool has the potential to transform iteratively the processes that generated it in the first place.

Arguably, the beginnings of such a process can be seen in some of the results of Foo et al.'s (2005) elegant series of investigations of path integration. The standard path integration task requires participants to walk from one landmark (A) to another (B), and then from A to a different landmark (C)—in effect, walking two legs of a triangle (see Chapter 5, this volume). The accuracy of path integration is then evaluated by having participants identify a shortcut by attempting to walk, or in some cases point, to C from B (or vice versa). Accurately doing so would indicate that path integration processes are operating while walking the first two legs, possibly resulting in metric, Euclidean configurational awareness of the overall layout. Using virtual reality, Foo et al. failed to find support for a claim that accurate configurational knowledge results from path integration. However, some "very coarse and possibly non-Euclidean" (p. 211) awareness did emerge from path integration. Shortcut attempts (walking from C to B) resulted in approximate and variable performance. Awareness of such non-Euclidean relations could be used to formulate crude and at best approximate, though still inaccurate, shortcuts. Although Euclidean configurational knowledge did not result from path integration, this research did suggest the emergence of a bare bones structure that could eventuate into configurational knowledge with further effort. What kind of further effort might be needed? Perhaps it is extrapolating from tools, even very crude and approximate ones, that had been developed through previous experiences. Iteratively, tools developed in the course of experience (i.e., inquiry) might function to bootstrap subsequent reflections—and so on and so on. In this fashion, configurational thinking could gradually emerge from individual–environment transactions. However, there is still something missing from this account.

What's Still Missing?

In the domain of human environmental cognition, the account offered thus far is woefully incomplete. Throughout the preceding discussion, we have skirted around a set of influences that is crucial to an adequate appreciation of human environmental cognition. Dewey's ideas have never fit comfortably into the mainstream of psychological theory because of his insistence that humans are fundamentally social beings developing and living in communities. With psychology's focus on the individual's mind and actions, this fact is often relegated to a minor role (Donald, 2001).

But social considerations are not merely just another influence on the individual among many others. The social is a constitutive factor for being human. Geertz (1973) put the matter this way in his seminal essay, "The Impact of the Concept of Culture on the Concept of Man":

> Undirected by culture patterns . . . man's behavior would be virtually ungovernable, a mere chaos of pointless acts and exploding emotions, his experience virtually shapeless. Culture, the accumulated totality of such patterns, is not just an ornament of human existence but—the principal basis of its specificity—an essential condition of it" (p. 46).

Although mention of culture now seems to be popping up nearly everywhere, it remains in most accounts merely "an ornament of human existence." But there is now abundant paleontological and archeological evidence that culture was not an invention of *Homo sapiens,* as had been long assumed. Our species evolved against a background of protocultural processes that were already in place among our immediate hominid predecessors (Donald, 1991, 2001; Mithen, 1996; Tattersall, 1998). Geertz (1973) was aware of this possibility decades ago, prompting him to conclude: "What this means is that culture, rather than being added on, so to speak, to a finished or virtually finished animal, was ingredient, and centrally ingredient, in the production of that animal itself" (p. 47). The evidence from the unfortunate cases of children who have experienced extreme early and prolonged social isolation or separation from other humans is consistent with this claim (e.g., Lane 1979).

The view of culture as a constitutive factor in the human experience process has yet to be fully assimilated into mainstream psychology. The intellectualist program, which takes the mostly self-sufficient individual at its core, continues to hold sway within cognitive science and, by extension, within investigations of human wayfinding. However, I submit that without recognizing the fundamental role that sociocultural processes play in constituting human cognition during ontogenesis, our account of human wayfinding and navigation will be partial at best and grossly misleading at worst.

For example, as we have seen, investigators typically regard Euclidean configurational knowledge to be the most advanced level of environmental understanding and that the attainment of this level of understanding is an achievement of the individual or, in some instances, an innate birthright. Alternatively, we need to explore the possibility that, along with other forms of environmental cognition, configurational knowledge only develops within sociocultural contexts, embellishing knowledge acquired through individual time-dependent, wayfinding practices. A number of individuals, including Hutchins (1995, 2005), Ingold (1995, 2007), and Widlok (1997), have adopted a similar viewpoint. It is no coincidence that all three of these individuals come to the topic of environmental cognition with a background in cultural anthropology.

Why introduce sociocultural considerations into this account of wayfinding and environmental cognition? I propose that what we often take to be the canonical form of knowledge that supports wayfinding and orientation—configurational knowledge—can be explained by collective efforts over generations to fashion tools, such as maps, and that subsequently those collectively generated tools contribute at the individual level (ontogenetically) to structure thinking about environments. In short, when psychologists think about environments configurationally, they do so because individually each is steeped in developmental contexts that are saturated with maps and map-related discourse. If this is so, we might expect little indication for configurational thinking among individuals developing within sociocultural contexts that lack a map-based tradition.

WAYFINDING CONSIDERED IN A SOCIOCULTURAL CONTEXT

Experimental psychology has long operated as if the patterns of perceiving, thinking, and reasoning that it seeks to illuminate are universal—common, if not to all species, then to all humans. This claim is in keeping with most intellectualist's views that logic, mathematics, and geometry reflect the universal workings of the adult mind. In recent decades, these and other presumed universal patterns of thinking and reasoning have been judged to be evolved characteristics of the species. Here Immanuel Kant meets evolutionary psychology. And here we find the nativist position in new dress. Contemporary universalist claims take the form that in spite of functional differences that might seem to distinguish peoples cross-culturally, such differences are but superficial—with universal patterns of thought operating at a deep level (Atran, 1990; Brown, 1995; Cosmides & Tooby, 1997).

Perhaps, however, the observed functional differences between cultures are more than superficial. Consider the following possibility: Might it be the case that alternative cultural practices in support of wayfinding have developed over time in relation to different local circumstances, and in light of the plasticity of early human development, the character of these cultural practices result ontogenetically in embodied, skillful ways of living (Donald, 2001; Ingold, 1995; Park & Huang, 2010)? It should be noted that this claim differs from most universalist positions in that it is a thorough-going developmental stance. I will return to this point. Local practices that function as a context for development stem from the interweaving of material artifacts and social systems that have emerged over time in relation to the local ecological circumstances of daily life. To the extent that these artifacts and practices "work well enough" in particular circumstances, such local practices would be sustained over time through processes of sociocultural transmission.

One approach to evaluating this position is to examine the wayfinding practices of a variety of cultures. To the extent that wayfinding rests on universal foundations, we should find commonalities across cultures. What commonalities should we look for? Given the claims about the innate character of Euclidean, spatial reasoning, we might expect to find evidence for configurational thinking, and even maplike reasoning, across diverse cultures. We might even expect to find the use of maps as tools. Alternatively, we might find varying systems of wayfinding and navigation stemming from social practices that have developed over generations in the context of the local ecology.

Returning to the naturalist stance mentioned at the outset, all too rarely have psychologists examined the circumstances in which individuals develop. In the case of terrestrial organisms, as described earlier, particular types of structured information should be available to all individuals as they move about owing to the character of terrestrial environments. Here I have extended this argument in the case of humans by hypothesizing that individuals develop wayfinding and navigational skills, as well as acquire knowledge of the environments in which they live, as participants in cultural practices. The basis for these skills stems from the social group's shared history of "making a living" within a particular set of environmental circumstances. In both cases, the claim is that wayfinding is a pattern of skilled action that develops in context.

Let us examine this hypothesis by considering some existing ethnographic data. The data to be considered are from the most detailed examinations of wayfinding practices within specific non-Western cultures that I was able to locate. Although it is not customary for psychologists to rely on reports from a single investigator, as is the case with most ethnographies, psychology has long had proponents of the idiographic approach (see Pandora, 1997). And of course, there is the case of Piaget, who gleaned so much from a small sample. One presumed advantage of this type of approach is the familiarity that the investigator cultivates when working with a single individual or group. It is the dearth of such information, in addition to the lack of data about how individuals make their living from day to day (Barker, 1968), that prompted the naturalist stance of this chapter.

Hai//om of Namibia

The Bushmen of Namibia are touted in southern African hunting circles as having exceptional skills in tracking game. Regional lore has it that these skills are "instinctive" in origin among this ethnic group. Widlok (1997), who has conducted extensive fieldwork among these peoples, has found that there is some merit to the claims about their skill level. He tested a group of men and women in the bush for their accuracy in pointing at distant unseen features, comparing their performance with GPS readings. Their accuracy was remarkably high, although not quite as accurate as legend would have it. There was also more variability than expected and, notably, slightly better performance among women than men. This last point is worth noting because it is the men who do the hunting and tracking in the society. The gender difference seems to reduce the likelihood that such experiences are major factors in explaining the group's exceptional orientation skills. Another finding that appears to rule out the primacy of such experiences is that participants often could point accurately in the direction of places they had never been to.

If individual experience in tracking and hunting did not seem to explain these skills, then what might? Widlok (1997) attributed much of this skill to *topological gossip,* a term coined by Lewis (1976) in his studies of Australian aboriginal societies. As a resident in these communities for a time, Widlok noted that individuals frequently pointed in the direction of places in the course of daily conversation. He wrote: "The ubiquity of pointing and topographical gossip in Hai//om communication suggests that orientation skills . . . are constituted through prolonged social interaction." (p. 321). Moreover, there are "several sets of socially shared and (at times) negotiated categories" (p. 321) that speakers draw on, as well as shared references to particular topological features and the groups that inhabited them. In other words, the layout of the immediate area, and even more distant places, is part of the fabric of social discourse in the community. At the same time, maps are not present in the community. It is striking that when Widlok compared some of these designations with ethnographic data collected over 70 years earlier, they largely remained the same. This stability over time points to the utility of this scheme of designations, as well as their social character.

Perhaps then the Hai//om have developed cognitive maps of the region on the basis of a combination of social discourse and individual experience. Widlok (1997) saw little support for this supposition. The references that are used do not form a complete, interconnected set of locations. In addition, individuals' knowledge of locations does not seem to function independently of goal-directed action. It is notable that "the main activity is that of establishing goals which, *as a side effect* [emphasis added], yield spatial truths that are primarily about life histories, access to resources, or exchange relations" (p. 324). In other words, knowledge of space is, at best, incidental to the daily activities of a group of individuals living in a particular place.

In addition, rather than there being a somewhat well-articulated cognitive map that is shared across individuals, directional references to be used in an encounter appear to be established between individuals at the time and in context of the actions being discussed or planned. That is, it seems that the "spatial network" is generated on an ad hoc basis (their knowledge is situated) while drawing on some socially understood references. This is very remote from anything resembling a cognitive map.

The geographical knowledge of the Hai//om is embedded in the social fabric of life. "In most cases it is a matter, not primarily of getting somewhere geographically but of *getting somewhere socially* [emphasis added], in that one attempts to meet a certain person, to collect a certain fruit, or do a certain job" (Widlok, 1997, p. 324). The place of social practices in cognitive operations of a community's inhabitants has received little if any attention in the cognitive science literature. A notable exception is the recent research by Medin and colleagues comparing categorization practices among North American native people (the Menominee) and North Americans nonnatives (e.g., Medin et al., 2006; Medin, Waxman, Woodring, & Washinawatok, 2010). The central role that sociocultural practices play in human cognition is a recurring theme in the ethnographic literature.

Inuit of the Canadian Artic

The Inuit of the Nunavut region near Baffin Island rely on hunting and fishing to sustain their way of life, and they routinely travel considerable distances over what is snow and ice-covered terrain for much of the year. During their short summer months, the trails used for this essential travel disappear with the snowmelt, and each fall, new trails need to be reestablished. Remarkably, the new trails follow the lines of travel from the previous year, just as they have done with slight modification since at least the early 1800s when visitors first recorded the movements of this region's indigenous people (Aporta, 2004, 2009).

The Inuit of this region travel without maps. On occasion, an "ephemeral map" might be drawn out in the snow or ice, but these instances are exceedingly rare. How then are the networks of trails long traveled by sled, now with snowmobiles, re-created each year? Aporta (2009) showed that the course of the trails is woven into narratives of previous trips that are shared between individuals and across generations. Still, discourse is rarely focused solely on the route itself. Indeed, as we saw with the Hai//om, travel itself is not thought about merely in instrumental terms, as a way of getting from one place to another. Travel is central to the identity of this people. "The network of trails was connected to people's sense of identity, as moving was for the Inuit part of life" (Aporta, 2009, p. 10). For example, the trails are rarely the shortest link between two places.

Rather the trails "usually go through fertile places, across or around lakes, valleys, or open water (on the sea ice) where fish, caribou, and sea mammals can be procured" (Aporta, 2009, p. 10). In addition, because of the seminomadic life that the Inuit have historically led, the trails have served a vital social function. It is along the trails where much social interaction occurs, including the sharing of information about fish and game at other points along the trail networks, about travel conditions, and news concerning life events in the dispersed community, such as births, marriages, and deaths.

The wayfinding information that is woven into retellings of prior trips seems to be related mostly to features that are to be encountered along the way. Judging from Aporta's (2009) data, there does not appear to be much focus on orienting to distant places but instead on the sequence of features that will be experienced, with little indication that these recountings involve survey representations. We have here information for someone in the process of traveling. The trails to be followed are presented as itineraries composed of features to be encountered along the way. Moreover, this is socially mediated navigation in the sense that the trails are sustained through sociocultural processes of communication and teaching. That the same trails are re-created each fall when the snows arrive, and the fact of their recurrence over at least two centuries, testifies to the fact of their social–ecological character.

Visitors to the region are struck by the many place names that are used to identify topographic features. These places names have persisted over long periods, although they may vary between indigenous groups. The names most likely serve to direct travelers' attention to particular landscape features that are valuable in wayfinding. They also help make these features more memorable, which is especially important in terrain where superficial appearances can change over a short time because of falling and drifting snow and seasonally because of melting snow followed by new snowfall.

There still is no formalized training in place for teaching the trail network to new generations of Inuit. Learners travel with knowledgeable elders or hunters, and it is common during travel breaks or overnight camping for them to be asked to point out particular places. It is not surprising, however, that there is a growing reliance on faster means of travel afforded by snowmobiles. Some elders worry that at these higher speeds, travelers will no longer attend primarily to the trail immediately in front of them, as is the case with slower-moving dog sleds. Knowledge of the trails may well be diminished over time because of this change, as might attunement to one's location among landscape features with the introduction of GPS (Aporta & Higgs, 2005). Technological change does not stand apart from human existence as social beings but grows out of it and transforms it.

Micronesian Navigators

The exceptional and distinctive navigation system of the Caroline islanders of Micronesia has been examined in considerable detail by Gladwin (1970), Lewis (1976), and Hutchins (1995, 2005). Some of these analyses are well known to most spatial cognition researchers, and for this reason there is little need for me to reexamine this familiar ground thoroughly. Here I offer only a brief sketch.

What is initially most striking in the case of the Micronesian islanders is their regular trips on outrigger canoes across hundreds of miles of open water during which they are usually out of sight of land. They carry out these lengthy trips without navigational aids such as maps, charts, or compasses. And yet, what to Western eyes is nearly miraculous appears to be quite routine for the Micronesians. How are these voyages possible?

Without minimizing their accomplishments, we should note that the environment that they navigate is certainly far richer in information for them as inhabitants of the area than it would be for someone visiting from afar. Hutchins (1995) provided a partial glimpse into their environment:

> The world of the navigator, however, contains more than a set of tiny islands on an undifferentiated expanse of ocean. Deep below, the presence of submerged reefs changes the apparent color of the water. The surface of the sea undulates with swells born in distant weather systems, and the interac-

tion of the swells with islands produces distinctive swell patterns in the vicinity of lands. Above the sea surface are the winds and weather patterns which govern the fate of sailors. Seabirds abound, especially in the vicinity of land. Finally, at night, there are the stars. (p. 67)

No doubt to an inexperienced eye the seascape would appear lacking in regular structure. For the experienced inhabitant of this region, the environment is sufficiently differentiated in stable ways to provide some structure. As discussed earlier, environments, unlike empty space, are structured, and through processes of perceptual learning, the available structure will become more apparent to the active perceiver.

What is especially noteworthy about the Caroline Islanders is the rather elaborate system of navigation they have developed in relation to one of these environmental regularities, namely, *star paths*. Specific stars rise at the same points on the eastern horizon on successive nights, trace an arc or star path across the dome of the sky, and set at certain points in the west. Collectively, the star paths trace out a reference system that can be used to maintain a course of direction and to keep track of distances traveled (see Hutchins, 1995, for a detailed description).

This celestial navigational system is clearly socially mediated. As in the case of the Inuit, navigation is tied to features of the environment, but those features are selected as being functionally significant in the context of wayfinding. By comparison, the Micronesian system is somewhat more abstract, no doubt because the islanders travel on the water, requiring some means of navigating at night when surface features are less readily perceived. In other words, the celestial system was suited to local circumstances. Owing to its complexity, the system can only be learned over years of practice guided by experienced navigators. And like the knowledge of the Hai//om and the Inuit, the celestial system of the Micronesians is transmitted by means of an oral tradition.

Aboriginals of Western and Central Australia

Like the navigational skills of Micronesian sailors, the wayfinding expertise of Australian aboriginals is

the stuff of legend. Lewis (1976) provided among of the richest of these accounts. As we saw in Widlok's (1997) study of Namibian Bushmen, Lewis found considerable variability in his informants' abilities to point in the direction of places at a distance and out of sight. When he queried his informants as to the basis for their orientation performance, they often attributed it to knowledge they carried around "in their heads." Lewis reported on their ability to update the relative direction to particular sites while traveling. They denied using the sun or, at night, the stars as references, but some mentioned the wind as a basis for orientation. To account for this ability, he invoked the notions of schema or image term *mental map*, but at the same time, he found the sole reliance on this explanation to be wanting.

In this regard, Lewis went to great lengths to emphasize the degree to which functional knowledge and cultural systems of belief are deeply intertwined among the groups he studied. What he was referring to is the belief that the Ancients dreamed the world into existence and that they laid down tracks through the vast terrain of Australia through song. Although for our purposes we may wish to abstract the geographical knowledge possessed by the aboriginals from their cultural system, doing so provides an incomplete understanding of what it is they know. We begin to get a glimpse of what Lewis confronted from the following two passages, the first concerning the long daily drives he and his companions took in "the bush," and the second about conversation in the camp.

> Even so, I failed fully to understand the deep satisfaction elicited in my Aboriginal friends by monotonous driving dawn to dusk day after day, across a landscape that was vivified in sacred myth. Every terrestrial feature, plant or track of an animal was meticulously noted and aroused very lively discussion. Highly coloured subsequent accounts of the country traversed . . . were given to envious friends back at the settlement. (p. 252)

The reasons for these reactions to the landscape and socially sharing of their experiences with others become clearer with Lewis' description of evening camps.

> The Pintupi sang the Dreaming of every rock outcrop, creek bed, or plain, hour after hour, all day as we drove through their "country." The major Dreamings were sung by the campfires until everyone fell asleep, the *Malu Tjukurpa* [a specific path] taking two evenings to sing during which no note-taking, taperecording or photography was permitted. (p. 276)

Three points are worth noting about these passages. First, knowledge for wayfinding is not solely an individual affair, but it is sustained through social discourse and cultural practices. Second, the sacredness of the songs, as evidenced by prohibitions on writing or recording, indicates that this knowledge is viewed by them as being more than merely utilitarian. The songs that mark paths of travel are embedded in an elaborate mythology to which all manner of cultural practices, including art and rituals, are joined. The interweaving of mythology and landscape might well establish an intimacy with a fairly hostile set of circumstances that cannot be achieved through abstract reasoning alone. Third, there is the fact that this knowledge about the environment is shared and sustained in song. In his seminal work on traditional memory practices, Rubin (1997) showed how significant song, and oral traditions more generally, have been for the sociocultural transmission of information across long stretches of time. Song may be especially well suited for wayfinding purposes because of the temporal structure of paths through the environment (Heft, 1996). In short, song functions as a tool, in the full Deweyan sense. Aboriginal song seems to be tied to a stable stream of landscape features that are real and directly confronted in the course of travel. The song provides landscape imagery that within a melodic or rhythmic structure falls into an integrated pattern through the landscape. As such, "songlines" as a tool would have great utility for desert nomads, such as the Aborigine.

Moreover, topographical gossip (Lewis, 1976, p. 274) has great navigational utility. On the basis of Lewis's (1976) report, these practices are impressive:

"All the Aborigines with whom I travelled demonstrated extraordinary acuity of perception of natural signs and ability to interpret them, and almost total recall of every topographical feature of any country they had *ever* crossed" (p. 271). Recall of topographical features at this level of detail goes beyond what we usually characterize as survey knowledge.

The interweaving of paths of locomotion and cultural practices is not unique to this culture. Tuck-Po (2008) reported that among the Batek of Malaysia, paths are more than abstract tracings or configurations of the landscape: "Paths are social phenomena and are remembered in relation to social events" (p. 26). Likewise, Legat (2008) described the trails used by the Dene of the arctic regions of western Canada as being tied to tribal and personal narratives, what she called "walking stories." (p. 35). In these traditional societies, the social and the experience of the landscape are not wholly separable (Ingold, 2007; Ingold & Vergunst, 2008). A question, of course, is whether such social dimensions of wayfinding knowledge occur solely in traditional societies.

Maps in Western Cultures

The navigational or orientation knowledge that exists within any culture is contingent on the environmental character of local conditions and on the sociocultural history of the culture. The confluence of these factors can be seen in all four ethnographic studies considered thus far. Although these factors may endure over long periods, they are subject to change. For example, Hutchins (1995) pointed out that although traditional methods of navigation over long distances were practiced by Polynesians as well, these methods fell into disuse as those islands were colonized. Such changes are on-going in many parts of the world, as can be seen with the increasing use of GPS among the Inuit, not to mention GPS use by automobile drivers in western countries. These instances all support the claim that methods of wayfinding among humans are socially mediated. Surely Hutchins (1995) is correct in stating: "Even the most commonplace aspects of thinking in Western culture, as natural as they seem, are historically contingent" (p. 66).

This perspective should prompt us to reflect on the forms of environmental knowledge that

Westerners—and researchers—often think springs solely from our biological natures. What is it about our own history that contributes to the tendency for taking Euclidean reasoning as canonical? We have already attempted to anchor this way of thinking in an intellectualist tradition. At the same time, this path in the history of ideas is but one thread in a broader fabric of social, economic, and political change, as we will see shortly.

Map use in support of navigation is not unique to Western tradition. As we saw, reports of map use appeared occasionally in the ethnographies of the Inuit and the Australian aborigines summarized earlier. However, these maps were invariably of an ephemeral nature, being drawn superficially in snow or on dirt surfaces on a particular occasion and sketched on the spot to provide directions for another traveler. By some accounts (Ingold, 2007), these maps are drawn in the course of verbally explaining to someone where to go. In this respect, Ingold (2007) suggested that they are more an act of gesturing in support of verbal explanation, than the production of an artifact that will exist outside of social discourse. Like a gesture, they are not intended to last any longer than the individual encounter.

However, in Western tradition, of course, maps secure a much more stable role in individuals' and societies' relationships to landscapes and seascapes. What differs between the cultures considered earlier and the West is a particular sociocultural history. Maps of a freestanding nature in Western intellectual history can be traced at least to the 3rd century BC and to cartography developed over subsequent centuries, as exemplified by Ptolemy's introduction of a grid system to create survey map projections (2nd century AD). However, there is little evidence that such maps at this time were used for navigational purposes (Salway, 2004; Talbert, 2008). Ptolemiac maps of the known world were created solely to depict with some accuracy the layout of the known world and the regions of the Roman Empire on the curved earth's surface. The closest thing to maps used for navigation at this time was *itinerarium,* essentially route maps that enumerated the sequence of sites the traveler would encounter when taking particular routes over land. These depictions were

not intended to provide an accurate survey representation (Talbert, 2004). Instead, they depicted known places and features that would be encountered along various routes. Closer to a route map for navigation were verbal itineraries, "a road map in words," that consisted merely as a list of places and the distances between them (Hunt, 2004, p. 98).

Maps as tools for navigation began to appear in western Europe starting around the 13th century. Their purpose was expressly to support travel on the sea. These early navigational maps, *portolani,* provided rough outlines of coastlines and locations of ports based on prior travels—no doubt, a compilation of experiences among individuals and groups over time. That is to say, they were products of social exchange and collective effort. In addition to providing information about coastlines and ports, portolani also commonly contained markings (compass courses) that would enable the sailor to coordinate compass readings to the maps. These maps were primarily used for navigating within enclosed bodies of water over relatively short distances. For longer distances, they were quite inaccurate because these "geometrically naïve flat pictures" (Crosby, 1997, p. 96) failed to take into account the curvature of the earth.

Map mapping advanced when Ptolemy's *Geographia* was reintroduced to the West in the 14th century. With this, navigational maps began to be produced with an overlay of an abstract, mathematical system of longitude and latitude markings. The 15th and 16th centuries were marked by the expansion of economic and political power through extensive navigation over the seas. European countries were seeking political and strategic influence as well as economic gain through maritime practices that began by the 15th century to span the globe. Distant territories were conquered and divided up into distinguishable European colonies. Boundaries between European nation states were regularly contested and redrawn following conflict and negotiation. The idea of private property rights, and with them individually owned parcels of land, spread perhaps most notably in the founding years of the United States. Skillful map making was an absolute necessity for extending and maintaining positions of power in the new modern era. Maps become extremely valuable in depicting the layout of bodies of water and of landmasses for expanding nations seeking access and control over global resources.

Maps as Tools for Thinking

In the process of developing maps for navigational and surveying purposes, these tools take on a new function beyond that of offering a visual representation of coastlines and other features of the earth's surface. Critically, maps also become a tool for thinking in the face of wayfinding challenges. This shift—from pictorial representation to tool for thinking—is subtle, but momentous. On the one hand, sailors could use the compass courses of the portolani in relation to shoreline profiles to orient a vessel in an intended direction, just as a carpenter might adjust the horizontal position of a board in relation to the air bubble on a level. In such instances, the tool serves as an index for action, and adjustments are made in relation to the index. At this point, the index per se—the map or the level— is not the object of reflection. On the other hand, the tool can also be utilized as a conceptual model for reflecting on what it indexes (Hutchins, 2005). In the example of the level, we may think about it momentarily apart from action, even think about the level when it is not immediately present, as representing one of the orthogonal axes in abstract, three-dimensional space. Likewise, in the case of the map, we can pause in on-going wayfinding processes—that is, "step outside of the flow of on-going actions"—and reflect on the structure of the map itself, even when it is not immediately at hand, and use it as the basis for thinking about wayfinding choices. At this point, the map does more than guide our actions; it also functions to help us think about environmental layout.

This point picks up the thread of our earlier discussion of Dewey's treatment of tools as material artifacts (Hickman, 1990). Material tools that have been designed to assist an individual or group in addressing some concrete problem situation can themselves subsequently transform thinking in similar contexts. Both Dewey and Vygotsky were emphatic that material tools routinely shift from being solely tools "for the hand" to become tools for thinking.

Conceptual confusion ensues, however, when it is forgotten that the mental model is a by-product

of tool use stemming from concrete engagement with the environment rather than arising from psychological processes taken independently of the environment. We saw this type of error earlier when discussing William James's notion of the psychologist's fallacy (James, 1890). In the present case, configurational understanding that grows out of using the map as a means of conceptualizing environmental layout is wrongly taken to be foundational to the use of maps and thinking in configurational maplike terms. In short, the claim being advanced here is that configurational thinking in Euclidean-cartographic fashion stems from the development of maps rather than the other way around. Presupposing the appearance of configurational thinking in any but the most rudimentary form reflects investigators' employment of a cultural tool as a metaphor for "how the mind works," sometimes without appreciating the source of the metaphor (or, in some cases, that even a metaphor is being used).

The history of scientific thought is replete with instances of material artifacts employed metaphorically as tools for thinking. From Kepler's description of the universe as a giant clockwork and Descartes's account of the reflex as a push-and-pull system modeled on 16th century automata, to 20th century information-processing models based on serial processing computers, material artifacts have functioned as a boon for scientific thought but also as a constraint. In fact, the heart of Tolman's (1948) seminal paper on cognitive maps was, in essence, a clash of two different metaphors for rat maze-running: the telephone switch board model that Tolman attributed to Hullians, and the "map control room" model that he proposed.

In sum, ideas or concepts that are often formulated "on the fly" for addressing some problem (Rosch, 1999) can be shaped by the tools at hand. Pragmatically, if those ideas, like the tools that spawned them, prove to "work," then subsequently they can be become part of the conceptual resources we bring to bear on a problem. These influences are not often visible; however, they can show up in the case of errors in thinking, revealing how the influence of underlying "tools for thought" can structure thinking. Consider the well-known findings of Hirtle and Jonides (1985) that participants consistently judge Toronto to be north of Seattle, and Los Angeles to be west of Reno, Nevada. Neither of those judgments is correct, and the bases for these errors become clear once we consult a map of North America. The partitioning of national and state borders that is exhibited on most cartographic maps structures thinking.

An anticipated objection to the claim, stated baldly here, that configurational thinking is a product of map making rather than the grounds for it, is that surely maps could not have been "cut from whole cloth." In other words, there must be some cognitive basis for mapping for it to happen. Indeed, there is evidence for this argument, as the research of Foo et al. (2005; described earlier) has shown. However, this research further showed that this awareness stemming from traveling a path is too imprecise to serve alone as the grounds for wayfinding. It may be best characterized as an unvarnished result of organism–environment processes and the germ of configurational thinking. Efforts to understand the dynamic interplay between the individual and the environment and, in particular, how tools can be utilized to extend thinking are on-going (e.g., Clark, 2008; Donald, 1991). I propose that the extent to which such rudimentary impressions of layout are subsequently sharpened and integrated into wayfinding processes is dependent on sociocultural practices. The ethnographic data considered earlier attest to this possibility, as does the abbreviated history of maps just offered. Mapping and thinking in terms of maps develop out of sociocultural practices that take root in such soil.

"Space" as a Tool for Thinking

In addition to the development of mapping, there is another "tool" that emerges in the course of Western intellectual history and that must be mentioned in this context—namely, the concept of three-dimensional, Cartesian space itself. Here I offer a few historical comments to shed further light on the underpinnings of our current thinking about environmental cognition.

The concept of three-dimensional space developed gradually in the late Middle Ages. The intellectual historian, Lewis Mumford (1934) wrote: "Between the fourteenth and seventeenth century

a revolutionary change in the conception of space takes place in Western Europe. Space as a hierarchy of values was replaced by space as a system of magnitudes" (p. 20). Thinking of space and size as reflecting a hierarchy of values can be seen in many cultural artifacts of the Middle Ages, such as the church spire being the highest object in cities and villages. Similarly, in paintings of this period, height as well as size symbolized the significance of the depicted figure or form. Realistically portraying size or location in the depicted scene was of secondary significance at this time. As art historians, such as Gombrich (1960), and psychologists, such as Hagen (1986) and Kennedy (1974), have pointed out, representing figures and forms in a three-dimensional space—indeed, realism in painting—is a social convention. The appearance of techniques in the Renaissance for representing scenes realistically in Cartesian space levels whatever qualitative differences might have once been attributed to location in medieval space. Differences between locations are not indicative of relative value but are reduced to relative distance and size.

With the expansion of territory and resource acquisition through exploration, space as a conceptual tool for determining distance and direction becomes valued sociopolitically as never before in the West. Widlock (2008) wrote: "The cartographic grid of longitude and latitude is not an abstract and innocent convention but has informed how colonial forces organized space, delimited the land and divided it" (p. 58). The Western conception of three-dimensional space seems to emerge, then, from the confluence of several lines of development, from the artistic and mathematical to the commercial and political. With the appearance in 1787 of Kant's transcendental aesthetic, and its claim that space is an a priori category, three-dimensional space as a container for action ceases to be viewed as a convention and is taken for a human universal.

Conclusion: Sociocultural Processes and Environmental Cognition

By merging these two lines of sociocultural history— map making and conceptions of space—our cultural tradition is provided with a powerful way of thinking about environments for navigational purposes. What results is an abstract framework that, among other things, makes it possible to adopt a point of view that is not normally attainable for a terrestrial organism—namely, a view of the earth's surface as seen from "above," as if it were a cartographic map. This is not the landscape as an embodied, terrestrial organism might perceive it from some location on the ground surface. Rather, it is a disembodied view of the landscape—which in fact, is what configurational knowledge is.

In short, ways of thinking that are sometimes presented as characteristic of species functioning are in fact conceptual abstractions stemming from sociocultural–historical processes. As already discussed, the social and cultural dimensions of experience are more than mere influences ("ornaments") on individual development and thought. Immersion in sociocultural processes is essential for our becoming human, and it is formative from a psychological standpoint (Bruner, 1990; Geertz, 1973). The dimensions of experience that derive from being immersed in culture from the beginning of life structures thinking in fundamental ways (Cole, 1998; Nisbett, 2004; Rogoff, 2003; Uttal, 2000). These patterns of thinking are not Kantian a priori categories, nor are they species' universals from an evolutionary perspective. Material artifacts that we are exposed to in daily life, and the operational skills we need to acquire for using these tools, structure how we think about any number of immediate problems that we confront (Stigler, 1984). These effects are neither universal nor transhistorical. Moreover, we have every reason to expect that these tools for thinking will continue to change over time. But to avoid committing the psychologist's fallacy, it is important to recognize that their origin ultimately resides in sociocultural experiences.

In his landmark book *Cognition in the Wild,* Hutchins (1995) explicitly examined the place of tools and artifacts in the complex thinking processes applied to the task of navigation at sea. He offered compelling evidence for the ways tools structure thinking. Reflecting on this evidence, he wrote, "A way of thinking comes with these techniques and tools. The advances that were made in navigation *were always parts of a surrounding culture* [emphasis added]" (p. 115). He argued that the environ-

ment for the development of thinking and problem solving is an environment of artifacts. Hutchins's point, while alien to much psychological theorizing, is common among cultural anthropologists. The material and ideational tools created through sociocultural processes are the means by which individuals think about the immediate problems facing them, although their role in everyday thinking remain nearly invisible to us.

Still, I maintain that although such tools for thinking do participate in navigation, they need not play a role in wayfinding on any particular occasion. Organisms often find their way without relying on navigational tools or on the cognitive residua of those tools. It was suggested earlier that wayfinding along familiar, previously traveled paths be viewed as a process of skilled performance. As such, wayfinding runs smoothly unless the individual encounters some alteration in the path that habitually has been revealed through perception–action processes. At that point, the individual may momentarily "step outside of the flow" of perception–action, perhaps to use a conceptual aid (cognitive map) or a material artifact (cartographic map) in an effort "to get back on track." These tools are products of the individual's immersion in a sociocultural context where maps and map-related social discourse are present.

CORE KNOWLEDGE AND THE GEOMETRY OF ENVIRONMENTS

The claim just offered clearly runs counter to two sides of the nativist approach to spatial cognition that has developed over the past several decades: that organisms rely on a Euclidean knowledge when engaging environments and that the geometric character of environments are most salient to perceiving organisms (e.g., Gallistel, 1990; Spelke, Lee, & Izard, 2010). A spate of recent studies that focused critically on such nativist claims, however, lead us back to the conclusion that we reached from examining the ethnographic data: that environmental cognition develops, in large part, in the face of local environmental contingencies.

Space limitations here do not permit a thorough review of these bodies of work. In short, though, research with a variety of species indicate that the environmental information many organisms use for reorientation, and in turn for wayfinding, is contingent on the immediate conditions they encounter (see Cheng & Newcombe, 2005; Twyman & Newcombe, 2009). This possibility may be particularly relevant when it comes to children's spatial cognition. A series of studies by Newcombe and her colleagues supported the claim that children are not predisposed to use particular information, such as geometric configuration, but instead, the information they use is highly dependent on the experimental conditions in place as well as on the individual's history (Davies & Uttal, 2007; Learmonth, Nadel, & Newcombe, 2002; Learmonth, Newcombe, & Huttenlocher, 2001; Ratliff & Newcombe, 2008; Smith et al., 2008; Tyman, Friedman, & Spetch, 2007; Twyman & Newcombe, 2010; see also Chapter 10, this volume).

These patterns of findings are reminiscent of a related body of research on spatial cognition from a few decades ago. Of concern were the two related issues of infants' use of egocentric (body-centered) or allocentric (objective) frames of reference and investigations of the A-not-B problem. In each case, the question was whether actions of infants were determined by "internal" developmental constraints or whether they were at least partially contingent on the individual's developmental history and on the environmental conditions at hand. The weight of the evidence favors the latter conclusion (Acredolo, 1978, 1979; Bremner, 1978; Butterworth, Jarrett, & Hicks, 1982; Thelen & Smith, 1994; for a review, see Millar, 1994). Going back a little earlier, a similar lesson emerges from the critiques of the concept of "instinct" offered by Lehrman (1953) and others in the 1960s (e.g., Hailman, 1969) and later by Gottlieb and colleagues (Gottlieb, 1992, 2003; for a review, see Lickliter & Honeycutt, 2003). Psychological functioning is not a matter of processes operating independently of context. This conclusion seems to be a hard-learned lesson.

As for the claim that the geometric character of environments is especially salient to organisms, discernable boundaries of a geometric character seem to be common mostly within designed environments. In those locales not dominated by human-imposed structure, rectilinearity and sharp angles

seem to be far too uncommon for animals to rely on them for orientation purposes. Yet, it is such "natural" (undesigned) circumstances that the postulation of innate geometric modules based on selection pressures requires.

Even if we grant the availability of geometric information in ancestral environments, considering the complexity of most environments, "There is always more than one geometric form that is consistent with the available evidence" (Newcombe & Ratliff, 2007, p. 67). Proposing the operation of a geometric module begs the question of which potential structure is extracted by an individual organism. From a perception–action perspective, structure is revealed in the course of action, and although an individual must select which path to travel, awareness of structure is a consequence of exploration rather than a basis for it.

It is ironic that in the investigation of a topic such as spatial cognition, so obviously tied to functioning in extended environmental layouts, that the conditions under which research is conducted are not more carefully considered. This is all the more surprising in light of the fact that the underlying processes that are posited to determine orientation and wayfinding are claimed to be results of selection operating in ancestral environments.

CONCLUDING COMMENTS

It will be instructive in this concluding section to revisit briefly what is arguably the seminal paper in the study of environmental cognition, Tolman's (1948) "Cognitive Maps in Rats and Man." At stake in Tolman's research program and in the work of its detractors were competing theories of learning. These theories can be represented in the present context by the opposing two questions: Do rats learn about the layout of a maze as a result of response learning, as the mechanistic Hullian tradition would have it; or do rats acquire an "expectation" of the relative location of the reward in the process of learning the maze, as Tolman's place learning account proposes? A flurry of research occurred in the 1950s in an effort to resolve this question.

A watershed in this debate was Restle's (1957) insightful review paper. There he argued convincingly that the debate over "place-versus-response" learning could be accounted for by considering the conditions under which learning and testing occurred. The picture that emerged was not one of an organism following the dictates of an all-encompassing learning theory but instead was one of resourceful organisms using the information available, in relation to their species' capacities, to relocate a reward. Restle (1957) aptly concluded,

> *There is nothing in the nature of a rat* [emphasis added] which makes it a "place" learner, or a "response" learner. A rat in a maze will use all relevant cues, and the importance of any class of cues depends on the amount of relevant stimulation provided as well as the sensory capacities of the animal." (p. 226)

This assertion of Restle's went against the grain of decades' long efforts to identify a grand theory for psychology. In its place, he offered a picture of a pragmatic and opportunistic organism operating within the constraints of its environment.

Instead of a particular mode of psychological functioning dominating actions regardless of circumstances, the bases for action and the strategy adopted on particular occasions appear to a great extent contingent on the circumstances in which organisms find themselves. In this regard, it is striking that the environment often seems to be relegated to a somewhat minor status in considerations of wayfinding and orientation. What has been demonstrated in numerous ways throughout this chapter is that processes of environmental cognition develop and transpire within the context of a particular organism–environment system. This is not to say that all possible strategies are available to all organisms. For one thing, phylogenetic history rules out some possibilities. In addition, the ontogenetic history of the individual organism will favor habitual modes of wayfinding over others. Still, the flexibility of individuals in accommodating to immediate circumstances should given due consideration, as even recent research among invertebrates has shown (e.g., Müller & Wehner, 2007).

Like the quest for a grand learning theory of the 1930s through the 1950s, the last few decades have

seen the emergence of an effort to establish a set of universal foundations as the bases for all manner of human functioning, from cognition to social practices. The grounds for these more recent efforts are located in a particular evolutionary perspective, typically referred to as the *modern synthesis*. This neo-Darwinian approach is based on the convergence of population biology and the genetics that appeared in the mid-20th century. For many psychologists, this approach is taken to be synonymous with the evolutionary perspective, but it is not the only option available (Oyama, 1995). The standard version of the neo-Darwinian perspective holds that selection processes favor individuals who are genetically predisposed to operate in ways that maximize their individual reproductive fitness. This tale is a familiar one in no need of retelling here.

The argument for universal, innate mental operations goes back a long way, preceding evolutionary theory by several centuries. This intellectualist stance is typically companion to the idea of *essentialism,* which is the claim that there are characteristic properties distinguishing one natural kind from another (Dupre, 1993). On these grounds, humans have long been viewed as a special class of natural kinds. Of course, Darwin swept away that latter claim. Perhaps essentialism arguably survives in cognitive science in a different form—namely, in proposals for innate core knowledge modules. However, Darwin not only made an incontestable case for species continuity but his work also undercut essentialism in any form. The primary lesson he drew from his naturalistic inquiries was not the presence of patterns of uniformity in nature but variability writ large.

Intellectualist and essentialist thinking in the area of spatial cognition is in evidence with the claim that spatial reasoning is built on a foundation that approximates Euclidean geometric principles, even as it is later elaborated through experience. As discussed earlier, an assumption of a priori categories that presuppose patterns of thinking is traceable most explicitly to Kant. However, it is well worth noting that in other domains of science, Kantian categories have not fared too well. The philosopher of biology, Sober (1993), wrote:

> In our own century, relativity theory and quantum mechanics stand as admoni-

tions to earlier generations of philosophers who had thought that various principles have the status of *a priori* truths. Kant not only held that space is Euclidean and that determinism is true; he thought that these principles are *necessary for the possibility of experience*. . . . Far from being true and *a priori*, these principles turned out to be empirical and false. It is hard to imagine a more decisive overturning of the Kantian outlook. (p. 145)

Yet in much psychology, and often in the study of spatial cognition, we have yet to abandon our Kantian assumptions.

Classical conceptions of space, time, and causality are pragmatically useful ways of thinking about the world in which are carry out our daily lives. In Deweyian terms, they are splendid techniques for thinking. Much of modern life has been built with their support, and their pervasive influence is evident in everyday discourse, in our cultural tools and artifacts, and in scientific thought. However, we must beware of taking the products of psychological processes, both over ontogenesis and cultural–historical time, as the foundations for thought itself. In this light, is it any coincidence that innate, geometric modes of spatial thinking are proposed within a cultural context that has been profoundly shaped by them?

We can avoid this misstep by maintaining a naturalist perspective, focusing on the manner in which human psychological processes develop in everyday contexts. Particularly useful here will be the adoption of an epigenetic approach to the environmentally contingent character of what was once thought to be innate morphological and behavioral patterns (Blumberg, 2005; Gottlieb & Lickliter, 2007; Lickliter & Honeycutt, 2003) and with it converging revelations into the plasticity of brain development (e.g., Lever, Wills, Cacucci, Burgess, & O'Keefe, 2002; Park & Huang, 2010). From an epigenetic stance, the structural and functional properties of entities, from cells to individuals, cannot be understood apart from their place in their contexts of development. In this regard, humans are a somewhat special case with our lengthy period of relative neurological immaturity and the developmental necessity of a sociocultural context. Children enter a world already filled with the tools of its culture and established ways of living, and human learning is intensely social (Jablonka & Lamb, 2005; Rogoff, 2003; Tomasello, 2001). As a result, ontogenesis and sociocultural practices and artifacts are interwoven over time.

The naturalist perspective offered here calls for attention to human psychological processes that emerge from the interweaving of three historical currents: our species' evolutionary history, the individual's ontogenetic history, and the ever-increasing pace of change in our sociocultural history. Across all three time scales, there is much to be gained from taking the dynamic of organism–environment reciprocity as our focus.

SUGGESTED REFERENCES FOR FURTHER READING

Foo, P. Warren, W. H., Duchon, A., & Tarr, M. J. (2005). Do humans integrate routes into cognitive maps? Map- versus landmark-based navigation of novel shortcuts. *Journal of Experimental Psychology: Human Perception and Performance, 31,* 195–215. doi:10.1037/0278-7393.31.2.195

A series of experiments demonstrating that spatial integration processes can, at best, lead to an approximate understanding of spatial relations, but not to Euclidean, geometric knowledge.

Gibson, J. J. (1979). *The ecological approach to visual perception.* Boston, MA: Houghton Mifflin.

The essential text articulating the ecological approach to psychology, including discussions of many issues pertinent to wayfinding.

Heft, H. (1996). The ecological approach to navigation: A Gibsonian perspective. In J. Portugali (Ed.), *The construction of cognitive maps* (pp. 105–132). Dordrect, Netherlands: Kluwer Academic.

An explication of Gibson's perception–action approach to wayfinding, along with research showing wayfinding as a process of detecting information specific to routes over time.

Hutchins, E. (1995). *Cognition in the wild.* Cambridge, MA: MIT Press.

An examination of the ways that the tools of a culture can structure cognition. A detailed exposition of a non-Western navigation system and a case study of distributed cognition.

Widlok, T. (1997). Orientation in the wild: The shared cognition of Hai‖Om bushpeople. *Journal of the*

Royal Anthropological Institute, 3, 317–332. doi:10.2307/3035022

An ethnographic study of individuals' understanding of the layout of their local environment and the basis for this understanding in individual experience and in social practices.

References

Acredolo, L. P. (1978). Development of spatial orientation in infancy. *Developmental Psychology, 14,* 224–234. doi:10.1037/0012-1649.14.3.224

Acredolo, L. P. (1979). Laboratory versus home: The effect of environment on the 9-month-old infants choice of spatial reference system. *Developmental Psychology, 15,* 666–667. doi:10.1037/0012-1649.15.6.666

Aporta, C. (2004). Routes, trails, and tracks: Trail breaking among the Inuit of Igloolik. *Etudes/Inuit/Studies, 28,* 9–38.

Aporta, C. (2009). The trail as home: Inuit and their pan-Arctic network of routes. *Human Ecology, 37,* 131–146. doi:10.1007/s10745-009-9213-x

Aporta, C., & Higgs, E. (2005). Satellite culture: Global positioning systems, Inuit way-finding, and the need for a new account of technology. *Current Anthropology, 46,* 729–753. doi:10.1086/432651

Appleyard, D., Lynch, K., & Myer, J. R. (1964). *The view from the road.* Cambridge, MA: MIT Press.

Atran, S. (1990). *Cognitive foundations of natural history.* Cambridge, England: Cambridge University Press.

Barker, R. G. (1968). *Ecological psychology.* Palo Alto, CA: Stanford University Press.

Bennett, A. T. D. (1996). Do animals have cognitive maps? *The Journal of Experimental Biology, 199,* 219–224.

Biryukova, E. V., & Bril, B. (2008). Organization of goal-directed action at a high level motor skill: The case of stone knapping in India. *Motor Control, 12,* 181–209.

Blumberg, M. S. (2005). *Basic instinct: The genesis of behavior.* New York, NY: Thunder's Mouth Press.

Bourdieu, P. (1977). *Outline of a theory of practice.* Cambridge, England: University of Cambridge Press.

Bremner, J. G. (1978). Spatial errors made by infants: Inadequate spatial cues or evidence of egocentrism? *British Journal of Psychology, 69,* 77–84. doi:10.1111/j.2044-8295.1978.tb01634.x

Brown, D. (1991). *Human universals.* New York, NY: McGraw-Hill.

Bruner, J. (1990). *Acts of meaning.* Cambridge, MA: Harvard University Press.

Burke, T. (1994). *Dewey's new logic: A reply to Russell.* Chicago, IL: University of Chicago Press.

Butterworth, G., Jarrett, N. L. M., & Hicks, L. (1982). Spatio–temporal identity in infancy: Perceptual competence or conceptual deficit? *Developmental Psychology, 18,* 435–449. doi:10.1037/0012-1649.18.3.435

Cheng, K., & Newcombe, N. (2005). Is there a geometric module for spatial orientation? Squaring theory and evidence. *Psychonomic Bulletin & Review, 12,* 1–23. doi:10.3758/BF03196346

Clark, A. (2008). *Supersizing the mind: Embodiment, action, and cognitive extension.* New York, NY: Oxford University Press.

Cole, M. (1998). *Cultural psychology: A once and future discipline.* Cambridge, MA: Harvard University press.

Collett, M., & Collett, T. S. (2006). Insect navigation: No map at the end of the trail? *Current Biology, 16,* R48–R51. doi:10.1016/j.cub.2006.01.007

Collett, M., Collett, T. S., Bisach, S., & Wehner, R. (1998, July 16). Local and global vectors in desert an navigation. *Nature, 394,* 269–272. doi:10.1038/28378

Cosmides, L., & Tooby, J. (1997). *Evolutionary psychology: A primer.* Retrieved from http://www.psych.ucsb.edu/research/cep/primer.html

Crosby, A. (1997). *The measure of reality: Quantification and Western society 1250–1600.* New York, NY: Cambridge University Press.

Cullen, G. (1971). *The concise townscape.* New York, NY: Van Nostrand Reinhold.

Darwin, C. (1859). *On the origin of species.* New York, NY: Penguin Classics.

Darwin, C. (1872). *The expression of emotions in man and animals.* New York, NY: Penguin Classics. doi:10.1037/10001-000

Darwin, C. (1874). *The descent of man.* New York, NY: Penguin Classics.

Darwin, C. (1877). A biographical sketch of an infant. *Mind, 2,* 285–294. doi:10.1093/mind/os-2.7.285

Davies, C., & Uttal, D. H. (2007). Map use and the development of spatial cognition. In J. Plumert & J. Spencer (Eds.), *The emerging spatial mind* (pp. 219–247). New York, NY: Oxford University Press.

Dewey, J. (1938). *Logic: The theory of inquiry.* New York, NY: Holt.

Donald, M. (1991). *Origins of modern mind.* Cambridge, MA: Harvard University Press.

Donald, M. (2001). *A mind so rare: The evolution of human consciousness.* Cambridge, MA: Harvard University Press.

Dupre, J. (1993). *The disorder of things: Metaphysical foundation of the disunity of science.* Cambridge, MA: Harvard University Press.

Dyer, F. C. (1991). Bees acquire route-based memories but not cognitive maps in a familiar landscape. *Animal Behaviour, 41*, 239–246. doi:10.1016/S0003-3472(05)80475-0

Etienne, A. S., & Jeffery, K. J. (2004). Path integration in mammals. *Hippocampus, 14*, 180–192. doi:10.1002/hipo.10173

Foo, P., Warren, W. H., Duchon, A., & Tarr, M. J. (2005). Do humans integrate routes into cognitive maps? Map- versus landmark-based navigation of novel shortcuts. *Journal of Experimental Psychology: Human Perception and Performance, 31*, 195–215. doi:10.1037/0278-7393.31.2.195

Gallistel, C. R. (1990). *The organization of learning.* Cambridge, MA: MIT Press.

Geertz, C. (1973). *The interpretation of cultures.* New York, NY. Basic Books.

Gibson, J. J. (1950). *The perception of the visual world.* Boston, MA: Houghton Mifflin.

Gibson, J. J. (1958). Visually controlled locomotion and visual orientation in animals. *British Journal of Psychology, 49*, 182–194. doi:10.1111/j.2044-8295.1958.tb00656.x

Gibson, J. J. (1979). *The ecological approach to visual perception.* Boston, MA: Houghton Mifflin.

Gladwin, T. (1970). *East is a big bird: Navigation and logic on Puluwat atoll.* Cambridge, MA: Harvard University Press.

Gombrich, E. H. (1960). *Art and illusion: A study in the psychology of pictorial representation. Bollingen Series XXXV.* Washington, DC: National Gallery of Art.

Gottlieb, G. (1992). *Individual development and evolution: The genesis of novel behavior.* New York, NY: Oxford University Press.

Gottlieb, G. (2003). On making behavioral genetics truly developmental. *Human Development, 46*, 337–355. doi:10.1159/000073306

Gottlieb, G., & Lickliter, R. (2007). Probabilistic epigenesis. *Developmental Science, 10*, 1–11. doi:10.1111/j.1467-7687.2007.00556.x

Gould, J. L. (1986, May 16). The locale of honeybees: Do insects have cognitive maps? *Science, 232*, 861–863. doi:10.1126/science.232.4752.861

Gouteux, S., Thinus-Blanc, C., & Vauclair, J. (2001). Rhesus monkeys use geometric and nongeometric information during a reorientation task. *Journal of Experimental Psychology: General, 130*, 505–519. doi:10.1037/0096-3445.130.3.505

Guthrie, E. R. (1935). *The psychology of learning.* New York, NY: Harper & Brothers.

Hagen, M. A. (1986). *Varieties of realism: Geometries of representational art.* New York, NY: Cambridge University Press.

Hailman, J. P. (1969). How an instinct is learned. *Scientific American, 221*, 98–106.

Healy, S., Hodgson, Z., & Braithwaite, V. (2003). Do animals use maps? In K. J. Jeffery (Ed.), *The neurobiology of spatial behavior* (pp. 104–118). New York, NY: Oxford University Press.

Heft, H. (1979). The role of environmental features in route-learning: Two exploratory studies of wayfinding. *Journal of Nonverbal Behavior, 3*, 172–185. doi:10.1007/BF01142591

Heft, H. (1983). Way-finding as the perception of information over time. *Population & Environment, 6*, 133–150. doi:10.1007/BF01258956

Heft, H. (1996). The ecological approach to navigation: A Gibsonian perspective. In J. Portugali (Ed.), *The construction of cognitive maps* (pp. 105–132). Dordrect, Netherlands: Kluwer Academic.

Heft, H. (2001). *Ecological psychology in context: James Gibson, Roger Barker, and the legacy of William James's radical empiricism.* Mahwah, NJ: Erlbaum.

Heft, H. (2010). Affordances and the perception of landscape: An inquiry into environmental perception and aesthetics. In C. W. Thompson, P. Aspinall, & S. Bell (Eds.), *Innovative approaches to researching landscape and health* (pp. 9–32). London, England: Routledge.

Heft, H. (2011). E. B. Holt's concept of the recession of the stimulus and the emergence of the "situation" in psychology. In E. P. Charles (Ed.), *A new look at new realism: E. B. Holt reconsidered.* Piscataway, NJ. Transactions.

Hickman, L. A. (1990). *John Dewey's pragmatic technology.* Bloomington, IN: Indiana University Press.

Hirtle, S. C., & Jonides, J. (1985). Evidence of hierarchies in cognitive maps. *Memory & Cognition, 13*, 208–217. doi:10.3758/BF03197683

Hunt, D. (2004). Holy land itineraries: Mapping the Bible in late Roman Palestine. In R. Talbert & K. Broderson (Eds.), *Space in the Roman world* (pp. 97–110). New Brunswick, NJ: Transaction.

Hutchins, E. (1995). *Cognition in the wild.* Cambridge, MA: MIT Press.

Hutchins, E. (2005). Material anchors for conceptual blends. *Journal of Pragmatics, 37*, 1555–1577. doi:10.1016/j.pragma.2004.06.008

Inagami, M., & Ohno, R. (2010). Anisotropy of environmental perception caused by spatial changes during locomotion. *Journal of Environmental Psychology, 30*, 258–266. doi:10.1016/j.jenvp.2009.11.008

Ingold, T. (1995). *The perception of the environment.* London, England: Routledge.

Ingold, T. (2007). *Lines: A brief history.* London, England: Routledge.

Ingold, T., & Vergunst, J. L. (Eds.). (2008). *Ways of walking*. Surrey, England: Ashgate.

Jablonka, E., & Lamb, M. J. (2005). *Evolution in four dimensions: Genetic, epigenetic, behavioral, and symbolic variation in the history of life*. Cambridge, MA: MIT Press.

James, W. (1890). *The principles of psychology*. Cambridge, MA: Harvard University Press. doi:10.1037/11059-000

James, W. (1907). *Pragmatism: A new name for some old ways of thinking*. New York, NY: Longmans, Green.

James, W. (1912). *Essays in radical empiricism*. Cambridge, MA: Harvard University Press.

Kant, I. (1781). *Critique of pure reason* (N. K. Smith, Trans.). New York, NY: St. Martin's Press.

Kennedy, J. (1974). *A psychology of picture perception*. San Francisco, CA: Jossey-Bass.

Klatzky, R. L., Loomis, J., Golledge, R., Cincinelli, J. G., Doherty, S., & Pellegrino, J. W. (1990). Acquisition of route and survey knowledge in the absence of vision. *Journal of Motor Behavior, 22*, 19–43.

Knaden, M., Lange, C., & Wehner, R. (2006). Procedural knowledge in path-integrating desert ants. *Current Biology, 16*, 916–917. doi:10.1016/j.cub.2006.09.059

Lane, H. (1979). *The wild boy of Aveyron*. Cambridge, MA: Harvard University Press.

Learmonth, A. E., Nadel, L., & Newcombe, N. (2002). Children's use of landmarks: Implications for modularity theory. *Psychological Science, 13*, 337–341. doi:10.1111/j.0956-7976.2002.00461.x

Learmonth, A. E., Newcombe, N., & Huttenlocher, J. (2001). Toddlers' use of metric information and landmarks to reorient. *Journal of Experimental Child Psychology, 80*, 225–244. doi:10.1006/jecp.2001.2635

Lee, D. N. (1976). A theory of visual control of braking based on information about time-to-collision. *Perception, 5*, 437–459. doi:10.1068/p050437

Lee, D. N., & Aronson, E. (1974). Visual proprioceptive control of standing in human infants. *Perception & Psychophysics, 15*, 529–532. doi:10.3758/BF03199297

Legat, A. (2008). Walking stories: Leaving footprints. In T. Ingold & J. L. Vergunst (Eds.), *Ways of walking* (pp. 22–35). Surrey, England: Ashgate.

Lehrman, D. S. (1953). A critique of Konrad Lorenz's theory of instinctive behavior. *Quarterly Review of Biology, 28*, 337–363. doi:10.1086/399858

Lever, C., Wills, T., Cacucci, F., Burgess, N., & O'Keefe, J. (2002, March 7). Long-term plasticity in hippocampal place-cell representation of environmental geometry. *Nature, 416*, 90–94. doi:10.1038/416090a

Lewis, D. (1976). Observations on route finding and spatial orientation among the Aboriginal peoples of the western desert region of central Australia. *Oceania, 46*, 249–283.

Lickliter, R., & Honeycutt, H. (2003). Developmental dynamics: Toward a biologically plausible evolutionary psychology. *Psychological Bulletin, 129*, 819–835.

Lynch, K. (1960). *The image of the city*. Cambridge, MA: MIT Press.

Medin, D. L., Ross, N. O., Atran, S., Cox, D., Coley, J., Proffitt, J. B., & Blok, S. (2006). Folkbiology of freshwater fish. *Cognition, 99*, 237–273. doi:10.1016/j.cognition.2003.12.005

Medin, D., Waxman, S., Woodring, J., & Washinawatok, K. (2010). Human-centeredness is not a universal feature of young children's reasoning: Culture and experience matter when reasoning about biological entities. *Cognitive Development, 25*, 197–207. doi:10.1016/j.cogdev.2010.02.001

Merkle, T., & Wehner, R. (2008). Landmark guidance and vector navigation in outbound desert ants. *The Journal of Experimental Biology, 211*, 3370–3377. doi:10.1242/jeb.022715

Millar, S. (1994). *Understanding and representing space: Theory and evidence from studies with blind and sighted children*. Oxford, England: Oxford University Press.

Mithen, S. (1996). *The prehistory of mind*. London, England: Thames and Hudson.

Mittelstaedt, H., & Mittelstaedt, M. L. (1982). Homing by path integration. In F. Papi & H. G. Wallgraf (Eds.), *Avian navigation* (pp. 290–297). Berlin, Germany: Springer-Verlag. doi:10.1007/978-3-642-68616-0_29

Müller, M., & Wehner, R. (1988). Path integration in desert ants, *Cataglyphis fortis*. *Proceedings of the National Academy of Sciences of the United States of America, 85*, 5287–5290. doi:10.1073/pnas.85.14.5287

Müller, M., & Wehner, R. (2007). Wind and sky as compass cues in desert ant navigation. *Naturwissenschaften, 94*, 589–594.

Mumford, L. (1934). *Technics and civilization*. New York, NY: Harcourt, Brace.

Newcombe, N. S., & Ratliff, K. R. (2007). Explaining the development of spatial reorientation. In J. Plumert & J. Spencer (Eds.), *The emerging spatial mind* (pp. 53–76). New York, NY: Oxford University Press.

Nisbett, R. (2004). *The geography of thought: How Asians and Westerners think differently and why*. New York, NY: Free Press.

Odling-Smee, F. J., Laland, K. N., & Feldman, M. W. (2003). *Niche construction: The neglected process in evolution*. Princeton, NJ: Princeton University Press.

Ohno, R. (2000). A hypothetical model of environmental perception: Ambient vision and layout of surfaces in the environment. In S. Wapner, J. Demick, T. Yamamoto, & H. Minami (Eds.) *Theoretical perspectives in environment-behavior research: Underlying assumptions, research problems, and methodologies* (pp. 149–156). Dordrecht, Netherlands: Kluwer Academic.

Ohno, R., Hata, T., & Kondo, M. (1997). Experiencing Japanese gardens: Sensory information and behavior. In S. Wapner, J. Demick, T. Yamamoto, & T. Takahashi (Eds.), *Handbook of Japan–United States environment-behavior research* (pp. 163–182). New York, NY: Plenum Press.

Oyama, S. (1995). *The ontogeny of information.* New York, NY: Cambridge University Press.

Pandora, K. (1997). *Rebels within the ranks: Psychologists' critique of scientific authority and democratic realities in New Deal America.* New York, NY: Cambridge University Press. doi:10.1017/CBO9780511572975

Park, D. C., & Huang, C. (2010). Culture wires the brain: A cognitive neuroscience perspective. *Perspectives on Psychological Science, 5,* 391–400. doi:10.1177/1745691610374591

Piaget, J., & Inhelder, B. (1967). *The child's conception of space.* New York, NY: Norton.

Polanyi, M. (1967). *The tacit dimension.* Chicago, IL: The University of Chicago Press.

Ratliff, K. R., & Newcombe, N. (2008). Reorienting when cues conflict: Evidence for an adaptive combination view. *Psychological Science, 19,* 1301–1307. doi:10.1111/j.1467-9280.2008.02239.x

Reed, E. S. (1997). *From soul to mind: The emergence of psychology from Erasmus Darwin to William James.* New Haven, CT: Yale University Press.

Restle, F. (1957). Discrimination of cues in mazes: A resolution of the "place-versus-response" question. *Psychological Review, 64,* 217–228. doi:10.1037/h0040678

Richards, R. J. (1987). *Darwin and the emergence of evolutionary theories of mind and behavior.* Chicago, IL: University of Chicago Press.

Richards, R. J. (2002). *The romantic conception of life: Science and philosophy in the age of Goethe.* Chicago, IL: University of Chicago Press.

Rieser, J. J., & Pick, H. L. (2007). Using locomotion to update spatial orientation: What changes with learning and development? In J. M. Plumert & J. P. Spencer (Eds.), *The emerging spatial mind* (pp. 77–103). New York, NY: Oxford University Press.

Rogoff, B. (2003). *The cultural nature of human development.* New York, NY: Oxford University Press.

Rorty, R. (1979). *Philosophy and the mirror of nature.* Princeton, NJ: Princeton University Press.

Rosch, E. (1999). Reclaiming concepts. *Journal of Consciousness Studies, 6,* 61–77.

Rubin, D. C. (1997). *Memory in oral traditions.* New York, NY: Oxford University Press.

Ryle, G. (1949). *The concept of mind.* Chicago, IL: The University of Chicago Press.

Salway, B. (2004). Sea and river travel in the Roman itinerary literature. In R. Talbert & K. Brodersen (Eds.), *Space in the Roman world* (pp. 43–96). New Brunswick, NJ: Transaction.

Smith, A. D., Gilchrist, I. D., Cater, K., Ikram, N., Mott, K., & Hood, B. M. (2008). Reorientation in the real world: The development of landmark use and integration in a natural environment. *Cognition, 107,* 1102–1111. doi:10.1016/j.cognition.2007.10.008

Sober, E. (1993). *Philosophy of biology.* Boulder, CO: Westview Press.

Spelke, E., Lee, S. A., & Izard, V. (2010). Beyond core knowledge: Natural geometry. *Cognitive Science, 34,* 863–884.

Stigler, J. W. (1984). "Mental abacus": The effect of abacus training on Chinese children's mental calculation. *Cognitive Psychology, 16,* 145–176. doi:10.1016/0010-0285(84)90006-9

Suchman, L. (1984). *Plans and situated action.* New York, NY: Cambridge University Press.

Talbert, R. (2004). Cartography and taste in Peutinger's Roman map. In R. Talbert & K. Brodersen (Eds.), *Space in the Roman world* (pp. 113–144). New Brunswick, NJ: Transaction.

Talbert, R. (2008). Greek and Roman mapping: Twenty-first century perspectives. In R. Talbert & R. Unger (Eds.), *Cartography in antiquity and the middle ages* (pp. 9–27). Boston, MA: Brill.

Tattersall, I. (1998). *Becoming human.* San Diego, CA: Harcourt.

Thelen, E., & Smith, L. B. (1996). *A dynamic systems approach to the development of cognition and action.* Cambridge, MA: MIT Press.

Thiel, P. (1970). Notes on the description, scaling, notation, and scoring of some perceptual and cognitive attributes of the physical environment. In H. M. Proshansky, W. H. Ittelson, & L. G. Rivlin (Eds.), *Environmental psychology: Man and is physical environment* (pp. 593– 619). New York, NY: Holt, Rhinehart & Winston.

Thiel, P. (1997). *People, paths, and purpose: Notations for a participatory envirotecture.* Seattle, WA: University of Washington Press.

Tolman, E. C. (1948). Cognitive maps in rats and men. *Psychological Review, 55,* 189–208. doi:10.1037/h0061626

Tomasello, M. (2001). *The cultural origins of human cognition.* Cambridge, MA: Harvard University Press.

Tuck-Po, L. (2008). Before a step too far: Walking with Batek hunter-gatherers in the forests of Pahang, Malaysia. In T. Ingold & J. L. Vergunst (Eds.), *Ways of walking* (pp. 10–21) Surrey, England: Ashgate.

Twyman, A., Friedman, A., & Spetch, M. L. (2007). Penetrating the geometric module: Catalyzing children's use of landmarks. *Developmental Psychology, 43,* 1523–1530. doi:10.1037/0012-1649.43.6.1523

Twyman, A. D., & Newcombe, N. (2010). Five reasons to doubt the existence of a geometric module. *Cognitive Science, 34,* 1315–1356.

Uttal, D. H. (2000). Seeing the big picture: Map use and the development of spatial cognition. *Developmental Science, 3,* 247–264. doi:10.1111/1467-7687.00119

Warren, W. H. (1998). Visually controlled locomotion: 40 years later. *Ecological Psychology, 10,* 177–219.

Wehner, R., Bleuler, S., Nievergelt, C., & Shah. D. (1990). Bees navigate by using vectors and routes rather than maps. *Naturwissenschaften, 77,* 479–482. doi:10.1007/BF01135926

Wehner, R., & Menzel, R. (1990). Do insects have cognitive maps? *Annual Review of Neuroscience, 13,* 403–414. doi:10.1146/annurev.ne.13.030190.002155

Wehner, R., & Srinivasan, M. V. (2003). Path integration in insects. In K. J. Jeffrey (Ed.), *The neurobiology of spatial behavior* (pp. 9–30). New York, NY: Oxford University Press.

Widlok, T. (1997). Orientation in the wild: The shared cognition of Hai‖Om bushpeople. *The Journal of the Royal Anthropological Institute, 3,* 317–332. doi:10.2307/3035022

Widlok, T. (2008). "The dilemmas of walking: A comparative view." In T. Ingold & J. Vergunst (Eds.), *Ways of walking: Ethnography and practice on foot* (pp. 51–66). Surrey, England: Ashgate.

Index

About the Editors

David Waller, PhD, is an associate professor of psychology at Miami University in Oxford, Ohio. His research seeks to understand all aspects of spatial functioning in people, including the ability to keep track of where things are in one's immediate environment, navigate between places, and remember spatial information. In addition to traditional laboratory experiments and correlational studies, his research has been at the leading edge of using real-time 3-D computer graphics as a tool for investigating environmental cognition. Dr. Waller is cofounder and codirector of the world's largest immersive virtual environment facility (the HIVE) and is an associate editor for *Memory & Cognition,* the *American Journal of Psychology,* and *Presence: Teleoperators and Virtual Environments.* In his personal life, he is an ardent and zealous orienteer as well as a trail runner, pet owner, and gardener.

Lynn Nadel, PhD, is currently Regents Professor of Psychology and director of the Cognition and Neural Systems Program at the University of Arizona. His research, published in over 175 journal articles, chapters, and books, has been supported by grants from the National Institute of Mental Health, National Science Foundation, Eunice Kennedy Schriver National Institute of Child Health and Human Development, National Institute of Neurological Disorders and Stroke, and several private foundations. His work has focused on the functions of the hippocampus in memory and spatial cognition, leading to contributions in the study of stress and memory, sleep and memory, memory reconsolidation, and the mental retardation observed in Down syndrome. He has promulgated, with collaborators, two influential theories in cognitive neuroscience: the cognitive map theory of hippocampal function and the multiple trace theory of memory. Dr. Nadel serves as the editor-in-chief of *WIREs Interdisciplinary Reviews in Cognitive Science* and is on the editorial boards of numerous journals in cognition and neural science. He was the corecipient in 2005 of the Grawemeyer Prize in Psychology, and he received the National Down Syndrome Society's Award for Research (2006). He is a Fellow of the American Psychological Society, the American Association for the Advancement of Science, and the Society of Experimental Psychologists.